THE BUILDINGS OF ENGLAND

JOINT EDITORS: NIKOLAUS PEVSNER
AND JUDY NAIRN

SUFFOLK

NIKOLAUS PEVSNER

REVISED BY ENID RADCLIFFE

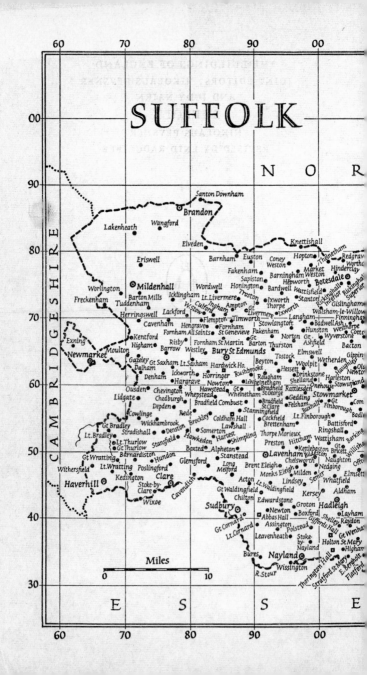

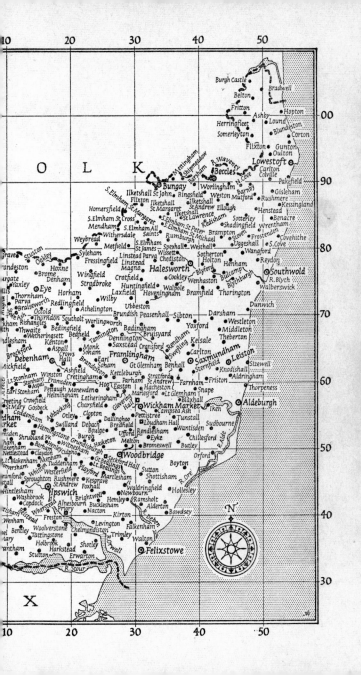

THE BUILDINGS OF ENGLAND

Suffolk

BY

NIKOLAUS PEVSNER

*

REVISED BY

ENID RADCLIFFE

PENGUIN BOOKS

CONTENTS

Map References

The numbers printed in italic type in the margin
against the place names in the gazetteer of the
book indicate the position of the place in question
on the index map (pages 2–3), which is divided
into sections by the 10-kilometre reference lines
of the National Grid. The reference given here
omits the two initial letters (formerly numbers)
which in a full grid reference refer to the 100-
kilometre squares into which the country is divided.
The first two numbers indicate the *western* boundary, and the last two the *southern* boundary, of the
10-kilometre square in which the place in question
is situated. For example, Stanstead (reference
8040) will be found in the 10-kilometre square
bounded by grid lines 80 and 90 on the *west* and 40
and 50 on the *south*; Oakley (reference 1070) in the
square bounded by grid lines 10 and 20 on the *west*
and 70 and 80 on the *south*.

The map contains all those places, whether
towns, villages, or isolated buildings, which are the
subject of separate entries in the text.

FOREWORD TO THE FIRST EDITION (1961)

Work in Suffolk has been a pleasure throughout. The weather was clement, the natives friendly, the scenery and the buildings a delight. Besides, work was easy compared with other counties, thanks to a number of advantages. The lists of buildings of architectural and historical interest which the Ministry of Housing and Local Government (here abbreviated MHLG)* *prepares and once more, generously, put at my disposal, are complete for Suffolk. The late Munro Cautley's* Suffolk Churches, *though brief, is outstanding, and its gazetteer was, as far as it goes, an unfailing guide to me: that is for churches of before the Reformation and on the whole for church furnishings prior to the* C18. *Moreover, Miss Mary Littlemore had done the preparation of all the other material in an exemplary way, and my wife did the driving on A-roads and farm tracks with ever equal and even skill and patience. It is my hope that all these propitious circumstances have helped the book to do its job successfully.*

To achieve this, users must here be warned what not to expect in the following pages. I have listed, described, and often appraised the same type of buildings and furnishings and fittings as have appeared in all the other volumes of The Buildings of England; *all churches except for those of after* c.1830 *(of which a selection is made on grounds of architectural interest), all castles, manor houses, country houses, and town houses which I considered worthy of inclusion, and a number of farmhouses, hardly any moats, all church furnishings except bells, chests, altar tables and chairs, etc., no brasses after the Reformation (with few exceptions), not all church monuments after the Reformation of course, and church plate only in so far as it is dated or datable, of silver or silver gilt, and before 1830. In the descriptions of churches I have not mentioned if they are of flint: that, in Suffolk, goes without saying. As in the preceding volumes, everything described was seen by me personally, with the exception of church plate and such items as I have marked by brackets.*

I have expressed my thanks already to the Ministry of Housing and Local Government, to Miss Littlemore, and to my wife. Mr Terence Miller provided the geological notes, and Mr J. V. S. Megaw the entries on prehistory and Roman antiquities, and I should like also

---

* For the second edition, abbreviated DOE – Department of the Environment.

*to thank them. In addition I mention here with the greatest grati-
tude Mr George McHardy, who visited 392 Suffolk churches with
the typescript for this volume in hand. He found more errors and
omissions than I can count or would care to remember. He spent a
European holiday almost entirely on this, for no other reason but to
increase the usefulness of my book.*

*For assistance in archaeological matters, we would as usual like
to thank the Director General of the Ordnance Survey and the
Staff of the Archaeology Division for help in preparing the gazetteer entries. Once more a particular debt is owed to Mr A. L. F.
Rivet in Iron Age matters; for this volume, however, the greatest
assistance came from Mr R. Rainbird Clarke, who took upon
himself the task of reading through all the first draft of the
archaeological section in the Introduction and offering comments
which can come only from a life-time of knowledge of the county.*

*In library and archive enquiries I was greatly helped by Miss
D. M. White of the Ipswich Central Library, Mr F. Fordham,
Borough Librarian at Bury St Edmunds, and Messrs D. Charman,
M. Statham, and H. C. Wolton, also of Bury St Edmunds. Mr
F. A. Girling put at my disposal his splendid collection of Suffolk
photographs, Mr D. J. King his annotated lists of motte and bailey
castles, Mr E. Croft Murray gave me information on the paintings
at Little Haugh Hall, Mr P. G. M. Dickinson on many problems
connected with the district round Clare and indeed on other districts
as well, Mr W. G. Arnott on similar problems connected with Woodbridge, and Mr C. Ralegh Radford and Mr A. B. Whittingham
on the excavations at Bury St Edmunds; and the Rev. J. A. Burness
of Helmingham, Canon Howard Dobson of Huntingfield, the Rev.
J. A. Humphries of Gazeley, the Rev. C. T. Musgrave-Brown of
Debenham, and Mr F. Walters of Bury St Edmunds answered
specially cumbersome questions referring to their churches. I am most
grateful to all of them and to many more than I can mention, including about a hundred parsons who read and commented on the
galleys of my text referring to their churches. Finally, I shall be
extremely grateful to any users of this volume who will point out to
me omissions or mistakes they may come across.*

FOREWORD TO THE SECOND EDITION (1974)

*For comments, contributions, and corrections used in the preparation
of the second edition by Mrs Radcliffe, special thanks go to Mr
Adrian R. Allan, who gave so much help – in the form both of
corrections and of new material – that his contributions warranted*

the abbreviation ARA; *to Mr Alec Clifton-Taylor for his expansion
of the paragraphs on building materials (pp. 15–18), and for many
corrections; to Mr Nigel Sunter, who brought up to date the entries
on Roman matters; to Mr Charles Green, who excavated for three
years at Burgh Castle and very kindly rewrote that entry, and to Mr
Stanley West, the County Archaeologist, who with equal generosity
supplied an account of his important findings at the Saxon settlement at West Stow; and finally to Mr J. T. Smith, whose contribution is acknowledged at greater length in the final paragraph
of this foreword. Some changes in the county since the first edition
are summed up on pp. 63–5.*

*We are also grateful to the many readers who wrote to us with
information, foremost among them Mr P. R. B. Brooks, Mr D. G.
Claxton, Librarian of the Felixstowe Branch Library, Mr S. E.
Dykes Bower, Mrs Ettlinger, Mr Rupert Gunnis, Mr Thomas
Howlett, Hon. Sec. of the Long Melford Historical and Arch-
aeological Association, Mr W. James of the Lowestoft Central
Library, Mr H. V. Molesworth Roberts, the Rev. J. T. Munday,
Mr D. M. Palliser, Dr Walter Radcliffe, Mr S. E. Rigold, Mr
Norman Smedley, Director of the Abbots Hall Museum of Rural
Life, Stowmarket, Mr G. Spain, Miss Dorothy Stroud, Mrs M. T.
Sugden, Librarian of the Stowmarket Public Library, Mr D.
Sumpster, Mr Paul Thompson, Mr Eugene C. Ulph, Borough
Archivist of Beccles, Miss Dorothy White, Chief Librarian of
the Ipswich Central Library, Mr A. B. Whittingham, Mr W. P.
Wilkins, Miss Susan J. Willsher, Librarian of the Stowmarket
Public Library, and Mr John Wood.*

*A final word. A strenuous effort has been made, with the in-
valuable help of Mr J. T. Smith, to update and amplify the
interpretation of medieval timber roofs. To this end, one of Mr
Smith's many contributions, the note on pp. 65–7, stresses the
structural elements in medieval roof design, and some new terms
(notably 'crown-post') have been added to the glossary together
with new drawings. Many descriptions of individual roofs have been
revised or scrutinized in the light of our expanded roof terminology,
but of course much of this had to be done from photographs or from
existing descriptions. It is pretty inevitable that there will be in-
consistencies and inaccuracies. And so, any readers who discover
crown-posts masquerading as king-posts are cordially invited to
write in, so that we can get it right in the next edition. And this, of
course, applies as always to any serious errors or omissions in
general.*

INTRODUCTION

IN area Suffolk is thirteenth among English counties, in population it is slightly higher up the scale. Its largest town, Ipswich, has only about 123,000 inhabitants, its second town, Lowestoft, no more than 53,000. It is an agricultural county, landowners live on their estates, industries are connected with the soil (agricultural machinery, fertilizers), and tourism is to be reckoned with as a substantial source of income. Tourists go chiefly to the seaside and the broads, but other less visited parts are also worth exploration: the extensive pine plantations on the Norfolk border, round Elveden and Thetford, and the rolling country of the river Stour under its ever-changing skies, the country of East Bergholt, Nayland, Flatford, all places familiar from Constable's landscapes.

Landscape is grounded in geology, but despite the variety of landscape, the GEOLOGICAL STRUCTURE of Suffolk is rather simple. The whole county has a substratum of the familiar English chalk, but only in the NW region, round Mildenhall, Bury, Newmarket, and Brandon, and in some of the SE river-valleys, does it come to the surface. Elsewhere the chalk basement is covered either by a few score of feet of Eocene sands or clays (the 'London Clay' formation, mainly); or by the thin patchy drifts of red and buff shelly sands known locally as 'crag' – Coralline Crag, Red Crag, and Norwich Crag – of Plio-Pleistocene age; or by the indiscriminate spread of glacial sands, gravels, and 'Chalky Boulder Clay', which, in three-quarters of the county, hide the solid rocks below.

As a result of this somewhat unexciting understructure Suffolk is not rich in BUILDING MATERIALS other than flint, and brick, for which suitable clays are almost ubiquitous. Direct quarrying for building stone was possible only in the chalk (but here with the severe limitation that chalk 'clunch' needs protection from wear and the weather); and in the occasional harder varieties of the Coralline Crag, which can be picked out in many of the older buildings of Aldeburgh, Framlingham, and Orford* by the skeletons of fossilized bryozoa (to the Victorian naturalists

* The towers of Chillesford and Wantisden are entirely of Coralline Crag.

'corallines') contained in it. For the rest, stone has either had to
be imported – as in the case of Cretaceous ironstone at Lakenheath – or collected from certain 'host rocks'. Thus what is
perhaps the most characteristic Suffolk building material, flint –
the most usual in the Middle Ages, and already used by the
Anglo-Saxons and the Romans – can either be extracted directly
from its chalk matrix (as from prehistoric times has been done
at Brandon), or got from the seashore storm-beaches, or from
glacial gravel-beds like those at Westleton.

Flint became the normal material for Suffolk churches
throughout the Middle Ages. In its rough undressed state flint
leaves much to be desired aesthetically, and no material makes
uglier ruins. But in the course of time many refinements were
introduced: regular coursing was achieved by selecting stones
(often pebble-flints) of about the same size, which were sometimes inclined to left and right in alternate courses. The introduction of knapped (fractured) flints, which could be squared or
trimmed to more elaborate shapes if desired, marked another
great artistic advance. Sometimes these flints were used in
combination with freestone to produce chequers, bands and the
more elaborate designs characteristic of 'flushwork'. (For this
see p. 33.) But flint was not employed for the humbler type of
house until wood became scarce in the c 17. Similarly, the smooth
grey or brown clay-limestone nodules of the London Clay
('Septaria') were formerly dredged from the foreshores or river-
estuaries and incorporated, usually with other stones, into
42a foundations and walls, as in the keep of Orford Castle. Finally,
the 'erratic blocks' of the glacial deposits, often gathered
together in field-clearance, were used, either as corner-stones,
since some of them were fairly large, or in the main walling, so
that at Wherstead, for example, the church is a kind of geological
museum, with boulders of granite, gneiss, and quartzite, some
very likely brought down by the ice from Scandinavia or Scotland.

'Ordinary' freestone is thus something of an exception in Suf-
16a folk. Examples are Long Melford church, the nave of Lavenham,
the tower of Beccles, the clerestory of St Margaret Ipswich, and the
9 façades of the two main churches of Bury St Edmunds. Timber
must have been used extensively, much more no doubt in the
early centuries than we know now. In churches it is mostly porches
where one finds external timberwork; in houses timber remained
the main structural material to the end of the Middle Ages. The
glory of timber is of course the church roofs, and much will be
said about them later. But domestic half-timbering also attained

an exceptional degree of refinement, with carved angle-posts, barge-boards, delicately moulded door and window frames, and so on: Lavenham has several notable examples. Here and there the original wattle and daub infillings later gave place to brick nogging. Or the wooden framing might be entirely masked by a smart new front of Georgian brick. Frequently in Suffolk timber-framed houses were wholly plastered over. The plaster was more often colourwashed here than in other counties, with a special affection for a shade of pink; and here and there ornamentation was added in the form of pargeting, either incised or in relief, of which Sparrowe's House at Ipswich (p. 301) furnishes a spectacular instance. Weatherboarding, although less common than in Essex, is also in some places a feature of the scenery.

For English brick Suffolk is exceptionally important. The fact is that – curious as it may seem – England lost the art of brick- and tile-making which the Romans had possessed and which the High Middle Ages on the Continent had recovered to such an extent as to make it possible for such gigantic Romanesque churches as Saint-Sernin at Toulouse or the North Italian cathedrals or, somewhat later, the Hanseatic parish churches, to be built exclusively of brick. The Anglo-Saxon builders made ample use of Roman bricks, which they must have trusted more than their own rubble, but apparently did not burn bricks themselves. In the standard literature there is in fact no reference to home-made bricks earlier than those at Little Coggeshall Abbey in Essex of c.1225. But Suffolk possesses at Polstead a church 15a with Norman brick arches inside which are not Roman, and can in all probability be considered of English make. They are 10–11 by 5–7 by 1¾ in.* These bricks are followed by those at Little Wenham Hall of c.1270, etc., and at Herringfleet Priory of 43 c.1300 – still extremely early dates, as far as England is concerned.

Suffolk is one of the best counties in which to enjoy Tudor brickwork. Among the favourite ornamental motifs, nearly always produced with the aid of moulds, were recessed panels with cusped-arched heads, trefoils and quatrefoils set in horizontal bands, finials with various raised designs, and crocketed pinnacles. Some of the moulded brick chimney-stacks of the Tudor period, like the group of four which crowns The 51b Cliftons, a now otherwise unnotable house at Clare (p. 169), must rank among the most exuberant ever made. Unadorned

* Mr Jope, however, kindly informs me of English bricks of pre-Conquest date which have recently come to light at Oxford Castle (see *The Buildings of England: Oxfordshire*, p. 300).

chimney-stacks, rising massively from the centre of the roof-ridge, add dignity, as in Kent, to many other houses of quite modest size. In the C17 Dutch influence was responsible for the appearance of crow-stepped gables and others of curved and scrolled forms.

In addition to red bricks, some parts of Suffolk also produced the 'white' (in fact usually pale yellow or buff) variety. Such bricks can even be seen at Little Wenham Hall, and large numbers were used between 1525 and 1538 at Hengrave Hall, where they blend very well with the richly carved central oriel in King's Cliffe oolite, specially brought from Northampton-shire. But the heyday of 'white' bricks was the C19, when an important centre of production was Woolpit; a great many can be seen in the Ipswich neighbourhood.

At certain places in the north and west of the county the grey Boulder clays were also a source of clay lump. The wet clay, with an admixture of straw, was pressed into large wooden moulds and left to dry out. These outsize but unfired bricks are seldom visible, as they had to be rendered for purposes of preservation, but, next to Norfolk, this is the county in which they were most used.

Suffolk is also believed to keep a higher proportion of thatched roofs than any other county, including nearly twenty church roofs (but Norfolk has many more of these). Reed, usually from Norfolk, is steadily replacing straw as the latter becomes ever more difficult to obtain. But the large majority of Suffolk roofs are now tiled. Both plain tiles and pantiles are used extensively: their reds are delightful.*

But now back to PREHISTORY. At the dawn of prehistory, the whole of East Anglia was in the grip of the fluctuating and gradually retreating ice sheets of the Pleistocene Ice Age. Although the much worn eoliths or 'dawn stones' (dated to about half a million years ago), buried beneath the shelly sandstone marine crag deposits, and flint flakes found in similar beds at Foxhall near Ipswich have been claimed as man-made tools,‡ it is only in the Great Interglacial that we have definite evidence of man's settlement. From Hoxne§ come flint hand-axes in the

* This account of building materials has very kindly been expanded for the second edition by Mr Alec Clifton-Taylor.

‡ A fragment of a human jaw found at Foxhall in 1885 was taken to the United States; its subsequent disappearance eliminates it as a witness.

§ A site first established by John Frere in 1797, who wrote of his finds that they belonged 'to a very remote period indeed and to a people that had not the use of metals'.

typical pear-shaped form of the Acheulian culture. Occasionally, as at High Lodge, Mildenhall, the core hand-axe was replaced by tools made primarily from flakes. Subsequently a cold period of advancing glaciers from the NW led to the retreat southwards of the Acheulian hunters. The general distribution pattern of the period shows a concentration on the gravels of Breckland, the Gipping Valley in the Ipswich region, and the Stour Valley around Sudbury. In the succeeding third interglacial, deposits at Bobbitshole near Ipswich and Brundon near Sudbury show a return to a rich life amongst grassy plains and mixed forests. Alongside the Acheulian hand-axe was introduced a series of flake tools made on prepared cores in the Levallois tradition. From the final glacial period, when only one ice sheet reached as far S as East Anglia, we have no definite proof of human habitation.

The subsequent period is that of the MESOLITHIC (from c. 8000 B.C.), when East Anglia remained linked to the Continent by a series of fens and freshwater lagoons. Just prior to the rise in sea level which was finally to make Britain an island, groups of the Scandinavian Maglemose forest folk made their way to East Anglia, while from further S others with a lighter 'microlithic' Sauveterrian industry settled on the unforested sandy dunes on the edge of the Fens, as at Wangford, where a temporary camp was set up similar to those found in the Colne Valley of Essex, which however also probably belong to the Maglemose culture (see *The Buildings of England: Essex*, 2nd ed., p. 19).

At the beginning of the succeeding Neolithic Age, which introduced semi-pastoral agriculture and pottery-making from the Continent some time in the first half of the third millennium B.C., the original Mesolithic communities seem to have lived on while the new 'Windmill Hill' folk, named after a hilltop 'causewayed camp' or cattle kraal near Avebury, Wiltshire, settled on the Breckland sands and in the Ipswich region. Typical bagshaped pots of Windmill Hill type are common on a group of sites in the Mildenhall region. However, at Hurst Fen, on the N side of the Lark near Mildenhall, there is an absence of deepmined flint, such as was produced by Windmill Hill people in the famous Grime's Graves, Norfolk. This is associated with a second local form of pottery with a marked shoulder. This socalled Mildenhall ware is also found on sites in and around Ipswich which include traces of structures; it may be as early as, if not earlier than, the southward-looking Windmill Hill group

with its close connexions with flint-mining.* We have just noted
what little is known of settlement; funerary monuments are
indicated by the original burial mound at the now destroyed
Swale's Tumulus, Worlington, which, with its original cremation,
is an unusual type of burial only occasionally practised by the
Windmill Hill folk.

In the NW of the county, at Barnham, Honington, and Icklingham, as well as in the Ipswich region, units of the secondary
Neolithic 'Peterborough' culture settled. These peoples, who
had evolved from the aboriginal Mesolithic groups and absorbed
the new techniques and ways of life, used coarse impressed bowls,
and must have dabbled in agriculture, as is proved by sickle flints
found with high gloss indicating their use. Another group using
flat-bottomed geometrically decorated pottery of the so-called
'Rinyo-Clacton' culture (named after sites in the Orkneys and
Essex) is also found in Breckland and the Ipswich zone. At
Honington, where they seem to have arrived somewhat after the
Peterborough group, signs of oval huts with central cooking
hearths have been found. The final Neolithic group to settle in
Anglia were 'Beaker' folk, i.e. the pastoral trading warriors named
after their characteristic S-profile drinking cups. They may have
originated in the Low Countries and along the Middle Rhine,
where they mingled with a North European barrow-burying
warrior group using stone battle-axes, a few members of which
landed in East Anglia just after one of the major sea transgressions
of the Fens (c. 1900 B.C.). Another local amalgam produced the
typically British necked beakers, an East Anglian development of
which was the handled beaker found in large numbers at Wattisfield. Again only slight evidence of settlement has been found,
owing to the nomadic economy of the Beaker folk, but temporary
camps have been noted in the Mildenhall region, where at one
site the scatter of human bones showed a more casual attitude to
the dead than the usual crouched inhumation graves. The one
major site of the period (revealed by air photography) is the
'henge' monument at Stratford St Mary, a circular single-en-
tranced ditched and banked ritual structure of the same type as
can be seen in the first period of Stonehenge.

With the introduction of metal, and the growth of what can be
technically regarded as the BRONZE AGE, one Northern Neolithic
survival was the 'Food Vessel' culture, which appeared in
Breckland c. 1700 B.C. The inhumation burial in a round mound

---

* Finds of comparable pottery were made in the Neolithic barrow at White-
leaf Hill, Bucks (see The Buildings of England: Buckinghamshire, p. 15).

at Mildenhall of a woman found covered by a heap of red deer antler probably predates the cremation rite which, with other finds (e.g. at Icklingham in the NW), seems to represent a local development. The apparently nomadic way of life of these people has resulted in their burial mounds remaining as the only visible record of their settlement, large groups being concentrated E of Ipswich.* This is also the case with the rich warrior traders of the 'Wessex' culture, who about 1500 B.C. infiltrated NE along the Icknield Way. These were the builders of Stonehenge as we see it today. At about this period in the developed second phase of the Wessex culture, a new form of pottery, the 'Cinerary Urn' with its overhanging rim (again showing links with the Neolithic), is found with barrow burials. Many of them form considerable groups, e.g. on Brightwell and Martlesham Heaths E of Ipswich and on the light soils of NW Suffolk. Evidence for settlement is again scanty; on Mildenhall Fen, a small camp showed later occupation by a farming community using cordoned buckets and barrel-shaped urns. At Barton Mere, Pakenham, several bronze spear heads found, associated with a possible hut, probably belong to this period, in which groups settled further S in the Ipswich–Colchester region, cremating their dead and burying them, not in barrow groups, but in flat cemeteries.

The picture which can be offered is no less fragmentary for the last prehistoric phases. The incoming groups of the Hallstatt Early IRON AGE once more made for two distinctive areas: Breckland – where they were with other inhuming groups around the now uninhabitable Fens – and the Ipswich and Lower Thames region. They were simple farmers. Organized corn growing on a large scale is not indicated otherwise than by a group of deep storage pits found at Darmsden, a common feature elsewhere in the period, but otherwise unobserved in Suffolk. The general poverty of material is reflected in the settlements so far discovered, mostly circular huts with rectangular buildings at Rickinghall Inferior belonging to the developed Early Iron Age of the C4 B.C. Beyond our knowledge that both cremation and inhumation were being practised, we have only the mound at Barrow with its two iron copies of Late Bronze Age spearheads to contrast with the more common flat burials of such sites as Creeting St Mary and Lakenheath. The peaceful economy of this period was interrupted by incursions of La Tène warriors from

* In view of the large numbers of barrows visible in the county, both the bell-shaped, usually covering inhumations, and the flat 'disc' barrow associated with female cremations, only the most important groups are noted in the gazetteer.

the Marne region of Northern France. In 1812 the remains of an extended skeleton were found among the sandhills at Mildenhall. With it were a long iron sword, axe, and golden torque of the C2 B.C. and the skeletons of two chariot ponies.* The settlements of the Marnians extended from Cambridgeshire through Breckland to Norfolk, leaving the Ipswich region to continue its simple peasant farming until early in the C1 B.C., when a trans-Rhenish group of Celtic tribes, called the Belgae, displaced by pressure from northern Germanic tribes, landed in the SE of England. They were organized in tribal units with large tribal centres. This new element offered a serious threat to the local groups, who were recorded by Caesar under the name of the Trinovantes of Ipswich and Colchester, while the Iceni of Norfolk and NW Suffolk may be identified with the 'Cenimagni', who submitted to Caesar in 54 B.C. The Trinovantes had their tribal centre at Colchester, while the Iceni may have concentrated round one of the hill forts of the Cambridge region such as Wandlebury (see The Buildings of England: Cambridgeshire, 2nd ed., pp. 262, 459). From the territory of the Trinovantes, finds such as the hoard at Westhall, containing gaily decorated harness mounts and fittings, and others in Breckland show the influence of the Belgic incursion. They date from the C1 A.D., as does a decorated sword scabbard from Lakenheath and a scabbard loop from Icklingham, both with the typical Celtic feel for pattern. The first evidence for the use of coins is late C2 B.C. gold coins of the north French Bellovaci, while the hoard of Atrebatic coins of the C1 B.C. from Haverhill, of a form which was to remain the model for many native-produced examples, also suggests trade, if not direct colonization, by Belgic people.

During the period of Belgic expansion between Caesar's expeditions and the Claudian conquest of A.D. 43, the Catuvellauni, centred on the native town at Wheathampstead near Verulamium (St Albans; see The Buildings of England: Hertfordshire, pp. 13, 276), offered a continual threat. Cremating Belgic groups finally subdued the Trinovantes and spread over SE Suffolk, occupying the so far only scantily populated Stour Valley. The hill fort at Clare, above a tributary of the Stour, the only example of its type in the county, may have been constructed in answer to this threat. The same hostility can be seen between the Belgic groups and the Iceni in Breckland. Belgic penetration here is marked by the cremation burial at Elveden, of the period of

* A similar burial is that from Newnham Croft, Cambridge (see The Buildings of England: Cambridgeshire, 2nd ed., p. 241).

Cunobelin's control of the Trinovantian capital of Camulodunum (Colchester; *see The Buildings of England: Essex*, 2nd ed., pp. 21–2), containing three globular urns and a bronze-plated wooden bucket with decoration similar to that on the bucket from the famous cremation grave at Aylesford, Kent.

Cunobelin leads us to the ROMAN PERIOD, during which the Catuvellauni were engulfed, and the former Trinovantian regions occupied. The Iceni, however, after an abortive resistance in A.D. 47/48, remained nominally independent under the wealthy Prasutagus. Only after the disgraceful behaviour of the Romans towards his widow Boudicca and her two daughters, in A.D. 61, did the Iceni, together with the enthralled Trinovantes, make a last desperate stand for freedom. Retribution rapidly followed their inevitable defeat. The camps and temporary forts found at e.g. Pakenham, Coddenham, and Ixworth give evidence of the ruthless severity of Suetonius, which was to lead to his recall from Britain as well as the removal of the major part of the occupation forces. The succeeding Romanization of the county was indicated by the establishment of a road system. An important route constructed *c*.A.D. 70 to lead from the now Roman *colonia* of Camulodunum to the new cantonal capital of the Iceni at Venta Icenorum (Caistor-by-Norwich, Norfolk) was the Pye Road, which enters the county at Stratford St Mary, where old piles marked the position of a bridge over the Stour. Posting stations were placed at Stoke Ash and Scole, just across the Norfolk border. At Combretovium (Coddenham) was an important cross-roads settlement with a branch road leading NE via Pettaugh to Peasenhall, where it makes an angle with another road to join the high road at Pulham, Norfolk. This road may have led to Dunwich, the possible site of Sitomagus, now submerged, which, like Combretovium, is a candidate for the Trinovantes' administrative centre. E of Combretovium a road ran via a posting station at Long Melford, presumably to join at Wixoe the Via Devana, the route from Camulodunum to Durolipons (Cambridge). N through Long Melford, a road led through Pakenham, where a settlement succeeded the temporary camp, and passed Stanton Chair, the largest villa in the county and perhaps the centre of one of those estates bequeathed by Prasutagus to Nero. At Stanton is the beginning of Peddar's Way running N into Norfolk parallel with the Icknield Way, which was certainly being used as a route at this period; indeed, at its crossing of the Lark, at Icklingham, there is not only the site of a villa but also a group of potteries (at West Stow Heath), which, like the more than two dozen kilns found at Wattisfield, show the growth of local industries. In the southern Trinovantian area settlements are rare, the villa at Whitton, Ipswich, being an exception.

The burial habits of past ages continued in the Roman period – see the line of four barrows at Rougham. Christianity is indicated by the Chi-Rho symbols on a lead tank found near the Icklingham villa and the baptismal spoons of the famous Mildenhall treasure (now in the British Museum). The burial of this great silver hoard, with its imports from the East Mediterranean, must have been made as a result of the threats by the SAXONS, who had, from their first attacks at the end of the C3 A.D., caused the building of the Roman shore forts from the Wash to the Solent. Gariannonum
3b (Burgh Castle) guarded the estuarine entrance to the rivers Yare and Waveney; Walton Castle, near Felixstowe, now submerged, secured the Deben, Stour, Orwell, and Colne estuaries. Despite continued threats, including a major attack in 367 by Saxons, Picts, and Scots, which led to the strengthening of military communications as in the signal station at Corton, near Lowestoft, the Romans held firm for another century. At the end of the C4 A.D. a group of Saxon *foederati* were brought in from north Germany, and may have been responsible for some of the earliest pagan Saxon settlements in East Anglia. These afforded a last line of defence until the final run down of the coastal fortifications *c*. 407/8. The same time saw the end of the fenland farms, owing to gradually increasing flooding.

As for the Saxon period, the confused account of history and archaeology begins with Vortigern's ill-advised invitation for further settlers in Eastern England, against the Picts and Saxons. That Romanized elements remained is clear from coin hoards deposited *c*. 450 at Icklingham and near Ipswich, as well as from some of the pottery deposited in the Lackford cemetery. The remains of the long boat found in 1830 at Ashby in the NE of the county show on the other hand how the newcomers arrived. The sub-Roman population, if not the last of the Romans themselves, may have been responsible for the linear earthworks such as Devil's Dyke, along the edge of Newmarket Heath (*see The Buildings of England: Cambridgeshire*, 2nd ed., pp. 264, 443). Suffolk's only example, the Black Ditches of Cavenham Heath (*see* p. 161), was also possibly intended as an obstacle against the spread of the erstwhile *foederati*, though they may have been constructed as w boundaries for the later Wuffingas kingdom. About 500 a new group of North Jutish settlers, practising

inhumation and using square-headed brooches, arrived in the
Ipswich area, and a second contingent made for Breckland.

This can be seen from the cemeteries at Mildenhall and Lakenheath. This new kingdom, to which Wuffa, son of the founder,
gave his name, had a royal centre at Rendlesham with Sutton
Hoo as its cemetery. The height of the kingdom was under
Raedwald. Following his conversion in 617 his cautious establishment of a Christian altar next to that of the old faith was con-
solidated by his son Sigebert. The new king was also visited by
the Irish Fursey, who, as Bede records and archaeology has recently confirmed (*see* p. 130), established a small *muinntir* within
the Roman fortifications of Burgh Castle. Other monasteries
were situated at Blythburgh and 'Icanhoh' (?Iken), home of the
celebrated Botulf. Of domestic sites of the c6–7 A.D. all we have
are a few scattered hut sites partially dug into the ground, as at
Butley, Mildenhall, and Pakenham. At West Stow remains of
sleeper beams suggest long timber-framed farmhouses similar to
those of the continent. Only the mention of 'Suthbyrig' (Sudbury) in the Anglo-Saxon Chronicle (for 798) suggests a definite
township, though Ipswich in the c7–8 A.D. had become an important trading centre, as can be seen from the kilns found there
which produced wheel-made pottery.

Although the majority of burials were made in urns or flat
cemeteries, some barrow graves are known, such as those on
Brightwell Heath, covering both inhumations and cremations.
At Pakefield, the burial of a local chieftain of the early c7 was
found with his attendant jewellery, while at Snape was the looted
grave of another chieftain interred between 635 and 650 in a 50 ft
long boat. This recollection of Scandinavian practices and the
origins of the Wuffingas dynasty is nowhere so well illustrated as
in the royal cemetery of Sutton Hoo 8 miles s of Snape. The
group of at least eleven barrows overlooking the navigable Deben
estuary included the famous boat-burial cenotaph, with its
echoes of *Beowulf*, discovered in 1939 (*see* p. 456). Here it is
enough to point out the figural decorated visor-helmet, with its
parallels in the rich graves of Swedish Uppland, and the date of
the burial, which can be firmly established by the gold Mero-
vingian *tremises* struck about 650–60 in France. They must
obviously have been introduced at roughly this date into the
barrow.

In the c8 Suffolk formed part of Mercia, then the dominant
power. In the c9–10 the county was the victim of Danish raids,
and in these struggles King Edmund was slain in 869 perhaps at

Hellesdon, near Norwich. In 991 the Danes sacked Ipswich, and in the early C11 Suffolk belonged to Canute's kingdom.

Suffolk is thus poor in ANGLO-SAXON REMAINS, at least in Anglo-Saxon remains *in situ*. Apart from the finds at Sutton Hoo nothing Early Saxon remains, and as for the most conspicuous architectural survival, the round church towers, it is not even certain how many are Saxon. While none of them are datable with certainty, some are evidently Norman, and others may well belong to the familiar and ubiquitous so-called Saxo-Norman overlap of the C11.* There are about forty round towers left in the county, less than in Norfolk, and considerably more than in Essex. That they must be Late Saxon, if they are Saxon at all, there can be no question; for it seems that the earliest round campanili of Italy are not earlier than the C9; *c.* 835 is the date of the two round campanili of the famous parchment plan for St Gall; and the round towers of Ireland are now also regarded as an innovation connected with defence against Norse raiders. The blank arcading on the tower of Thorington makes this a specially likely candidate for Saxon workmanship. The structural reason for the preference for round as against square towers is the absence in Suffolk of good building stone. Without ashlar firm corners are hard to build, and the Saxon technique of long and short work, that is one large cornerstone laid horizontally to bond deep into both walls and then one yet larger cornerstone set up vertically to cover the angle without worth-while bonding, did not make for durability. Long and short work is found at Claydon, Fakenham, Gosbeck, Hemingstone, and Little Livermere, and also in the best piece of Saxon work in Suffolk, the lower parts of the W tower of Debenham. But this is emphatically a piece of 'overlap'.‡ The only complete Saxon church plan is at the Minster at South Elmham St Cross. The ruin is picturesquely sited and enjoyable to explore. It has an interesting W 'porticus' or chamber or narthex as wide as the nave and quite deep. Its date is controversial, but probably not earlier than the C10. Sculptural and decorative fragments (Blaxhall, perhaps Framsden, Halesworth) are minor, with the one exception of the panels at St Nicholas Ipswich (now considered to be early C12) which

* It deserves notice in this context that at Herringfleet a Norman bell-stage was added above the cornice of an older round tower.

‡ Attached to the W of Debenham tower is a GALILEE. This is of C14 date, but the motif as such is an early one, and where it occurs in Suffolk or elsewhere (e.g. at Great Wakering in Essex) a Saxon origin ought at least to be considered. The Suffolk examples are Cavenham (demolished) and Mutford.

occupy a dedication stone, apostles under arcades, and a lintel with St Michael and the dragon similar to C11 work at Southwell and Hoveringham in Notts.

The major monument of Norman architecture in the county was of course the Benedictine monastery of Bury St Edmunds. It was one of the mightiest monastic houses of England, and so this may be the place to record the state of MONASTICISM in Suffolk. In wealth at the time of the Dissolution Bury was inferior only to Westminster, Glastonbury, Canterbury Cathedral, St Albans, and Abingdon, and about equal with Peterborough, Ramsey, Reading, Tewkesbury, Winchester, and St Mary York. Other Benedictine houses were at Edwardstone (very small), Eye, Felixstowe, Hoxne, Rumburgh, Snape, Sudbury, and Wickham Skeith, and Benedictine nunneries at Bungay and Redlingfield. Nearly all of these were founded in the C12. In addition there were three alien cells of the Benedictine house of Bec: Clare, Great Blakenham, and Stoke-by-Clare, the two first established in or about 1090. The Cluniac Benedictines had no more than two priories in Suffolk (Mendham and Wangford, both mid-C12 foundations), and the Cistercians only one (Sibton, founded 1150; a certain amount is preserved). The Augustinian Canons were well represented in Suffolk. Their houses were Alnesbourn near Ipswich, Blythburgh, Butley with its spectacu- 44b lar gatehouse, Chipley, Dodnash, Herringfleet with some minor remains, Holy Trinity Ipswich, St Peter and St Paul Ipswich, Ixworth where some vaulted rooms can still be seen and the plan has been excavated, Kersey, Letheringham, and Woodbridge. In addition there was one alien cell (of Saint-Léonard, near Limoges) at Great Bricett, and of that parts of the church and some extremely interesting monastic remains are extant. Great Bricett was founded c. 1115, Blythburgh c. 1125, and Holy Trinity Ipswich c. 1130–5, all the others between 1170 and c. 1220. Augustinian Canonesses were at Campsea Ash and Flixton. Of the one Premonstratensian house in Suffolk, Leiston, much survives, indeed more than of any other monastic establishment. For completeness' sake the houses of the mendicant friars may also be recorded here, although they are of course all of somewhat later foundation. The earliest in Suffolk was that of the Franciscans (Greyfriars) at Ipswich (before 1236). There were two more in the county: Bury and Dunwich. At Dunwich there was also a Dominican (Blackfriars) house, and others were at Ipswich and Sudbury, all three established between c. 1245 and c. 1265. Ipswich had Carmelites as well, Austin Friars were at

Clare (founded 1248), Orford, and Gorleston,* and Crutched Friars at Little Whelnetham (1274). Finally the Templars had preceptories at Dunwich (later Hospitallers) and Gislingham and the Hospitallers at Battisford.

To return after this digression to NORMAN ARCHITECTURE in Suffolk, the church at Bury St Edmunds was certainly one of the major monuments in East Anglia. It was begun about 1080 and built gradually through the first half of the C12. It was 505 ft long and had an E end with ambulatory and three radiating chapels, N and S transepts with E aisles and a chapel attached to either, a central tower, and a W front probably in its original state more spectacular than any other in England. It had a commanding tower like that of Ely, a W transept like that of Ely, and, as a late C12 addition, octagonal angle towers which gave the front the unparalleled width of 246 ft. Of all this only the scantiest and least elegant fragments stand upright. What does stand, however, four-
41 square and proudly attired, is the Norman gate-tower of c. 1130. As spectacular, before it was allowed to fall into ruin, must have
15b been the chancel of Orford church, which was begun in 1166, with its arcade piers enriched by spiral shafts and vertical shafts in various combinations. It is a technique of decoration rare abroad, but occasionally found in England (Pittington County Durham, Compton Martin North Devon). The only other surviving
15a Norman arcades are at Polstead. They have piers with nook-shafts, the arches with the early English bricks already mentioned, and a Norman clerestory above them, also with brick arches. Otherwise the Norman churches which remain in Suffolk were unaisled. Cruciform plans existed at Orford and Eyke (and perhaps Oulton), but are not preserved, but longitudinally tripartite plans, i.e. with a raised, tower-like central compartment, exist here and there. The most complete example is Ousden. Others are Fritton, probably Lakenheath, Pakenham, and perhaps originally Dallinghoo. At Fritton the chancel compartment is tunnel-vaulted, and there is an apse, at Wissington the central compartment has a tunnel-vault. More elaborate plans are rare and without exception recorded only by excavation. The ambulatory and radiating chapels of Bury have already been mentioned. Eye Priory had the familiar arrangement of staggered apses (en échelon, as the French say), with apses E of the transepts, apsed chancel aisles, and the wider main apse. Great Bricett Priory had only the transept apses and (in all probability) the

* See The Buildings of England, North-East Norfolk and Norwich.

main apse. Orford chancel ended straight, with the sanctuary projecting slightly beyond the ends of the aisles.

In elevation much of Norman work is visible, but again little of it is of more than local interest. Cautley refers to at least 390 Suffolk churches mentioned in the Domesday survey and has counted 174 churches with some Norman features. Yet Suffolk is not a Norman county. That means that either prosperity in the late Middle Ages has swept away what there was before, or that in less prosperous areas nothing Norman and grand ever existed. The bulk of what survives is purely masonry, and not as a rule commented on in the gazetteer, or such minor features as angles with set-in shafts (Badingham, Boyton, Great Thurlow, Moulton, South Elmham All Saints), or towers or chancel arches or doorways. There are more Norman doorways by far than can here be listed. Even confining oneself to such as possess some decoration, the total would be in the neighbourhood of eighty. Specially sumptuous – though by no means comparable to the doorways of e.g. Yorkshire – are those of Braiseworth, Great Bricett, Henstead, Kelsale, Polstead (W), Poslingford, Redisham, Westhall (W doorway with window over), Wissett, and Wissington. Of chancel arches it is enough to note Eyke and Wissington. Round towers have been commented on in connexion with Anglo-Saxon architecture. Cautley counts forty-two in Suffolk. They occur mostly in the NE of the county – nearly half the total.* The most spectacular Norman round tower is at Little Saxham (with 5 blank arcading round the bell-stage). Bramfield has a detached round tower, and at Wortham is the largest in England – with a diameter of nearly 30 ft. Among square towers the only feature of special interest is the spire at Flixton (near Bungay), of a kind typical of the Rhineland and existing in England only once more, at Sompting in Sussex. But the spire is a C19 restoration, and it is not certain whether *Salvin*, the restorer, interpreted correctly what indications he found.

To the square towers may be added the NORMAN KEEPS. Only one square keep remains in a state to be examined and understood, that at Bungay. It dates from *c.* 1160 and had an uncommonly large forebuilding. The hall must have had an arcade or a large arch dividing it into two, on the pattern familiar from Castle Hedingham and Rochester. A little more of a DOMESTIC character is represented by Moyse's Hall at Bury St Edmunds, a private stone house of the C12, or perhaps a dependency of the abbey.

* In the gazetteer the towers will be called Norman, where there is no actual evidence of Saxon origin.

Even more interesting, and rarely taken in by visitors, is the TOWN PLAN of Bury, a grid plan laid out by Abbot Baldwin before 1086.

Almost contemporary with the square keep of Bungay is the 42a irregularly polygonal keep of Orford. This was built for Henry II in 1165–7. The danger for the defender of a square keep was that the enemy might drive a mining gallery underneath one of the angles, thus isolating it, burn the timber props set up during mining, and thus make the whole angle collapse. At Bungay we have indeed the unique survival of such a mining gallery (5 ft tall, 2 ft wide), never used because the castle surrendered in 1174. Orford avoids rectangles, though clearly not as successfully as if the keep had been made circular, as was at that time quite usual in France and soon to be imitated in England (Conisbrough, West Yorkshire, c.1190). The interior of Orford is ingeniously arranged to combine the advantages of defence with those of comfort. From the point of view of the general history of architecture in the county the keep is in addition memorable in that it offers the earliest examples of pointed windows and small pointed vaults. So we are on the threshold of the GOTHIC STYLE.

Of the THIRTEENTH CENTURY very little needs recording, and no consistent picture emerges. Nowhere does work of national interest survive. Plans were aisled or unaisled and some evidence of transepts remains (Pakenham, also of the early C14 Earl Stonham). Arcade piers were circular (Hinderclay, Marlesford, Mendlesham, Sibton, Ufford) or alternatingly circular and octagonal (Bawdsey, Hintlesham, Hollesley – at Peterborough already C12) and in one case quatrefoil (Wetheringsett). For architectural quality, the first place goes to the N chapel and the chancel of Mildenhall, work, it seems, of Ely Cathedral masons; for architectural interest to the surprisingly broad W tower of Rumburgh Priory with its three lancet windows to the W. Beyond that, if the good mid-C13 E wall of Little Blakenham with its deep shafted and trefoiled niches and the good late C13 N transept of Hunston are mentioned, all is said that needs saying. A special minor feature which adds to the attractiveness of chancels is ANGLE PISCINAS, i.e. piscinas placed across the angle of a chancel S window so that the lower part of the jamb and adjoining wall are cut out and the angle of the jamb is caught up by a colonnette. There are plenty of these in the county. They also exist in Norfolk.

If SECULAR ARCHITECTURE is taken into account, the list of *memorabilia* does not become much longer, though there are here at least two buildings of more than regional significance. One of these is Framlingham Castle where in *c.* 1190–1210 the 42b new and improved technique of defence by a curtain wall punctuated by a number of wall towers and a gatehouse was carried through. This technique had been learned by the crusaders from their infidel enemies, and Framlingham is one of its earliest instances in the West. It replaced the defence by keep, whose last and most accomplished forms had only been achieved some ten or twenty years before. It is significant that at Bungay in 1294 the upper part of the keep was taken down and the stones used for erecting a close curtain wall with gatehouses. At Clare in the C13 a large shell-keep was built, but of that there is only a fragment left. To complete the story of the fortress in Suffolk a reference may be added to the big gatehouse and walls at Mettingham of 1342 and at Wingfield, a highly monumental, symmetrical composition of 1384.

The other memorable example of C13 secular building in Suffolk is Little Wenham Hall of *c.* 1270–80. This is memorable for 43 two reasons: first because it is built of home-made brick, as has already been said; and secondly because it is not a keep but a fortified manor house. It is L-shaped, and on its principal floor hall and chapel join and are connected by a very pretty tripartite 44a arrangement of doorway and windows. The same change from fortress to house occurs at the same moment at Stokesay and Acton Burnell in Shropshire, though in different forms. One can say that by 1300 the foundations were laid for the development of the English manor house. If one of the most characteristic features of this is the arrangement of hall, screens passage, and doorways to kitchen, buttery, and pantry, it ought to be noted that the recently uncovered wooden C13 screen at the Augustinian priory of Great Bricett has four such doorways; the fourth probably opened on to a straight stair to the upper chamber.*

With the early C14 and the coming of the DECORATED STYLE architectural events began to gather momentum in Suffolk, as prosperity from the wool and cloth trade began to grow. It becomes less easy to select what ought to figure in a summary such as this. Motifs first, whole buildings second. Window tracery 6b & 7 can be followed in many examples from the Late Geometrical to the flowing Decorated, by such transitional stages as the Y-form, intersection, cusped intersection, intersection broken by a top circle, etc. The most usual Dec form, i.e. a form with ogee curves,

* So Mr J. T. Smith believes.

is that known as reticulated. Flowing forms also occur, but Suffolk cannot here compete with such counties as Lincolnshire. A particularly good example of the pre-ogee stage is the E window of Mildenhall, a particularly good ogee example the E window of Cotton. A typical Suffolk motif is the four-petalled flower or crossing of two figures of eight. The first datable example of this is on the Great Gate at Bury (c. 1330). It occurs in many places and not always in the C14 only. But the most extraordinary window and wall of Suffolk is the E wall of Barsham, where the tracery is carried all over the window and forms a grid of lozenges continued blank over the whole wall. It is not even quite certain whether this bold motif is one of the inventions of that most inventive phase of English medieval decoration or a sign of 'Mannerist' post-Reformation revival. After tracery, towers. Spires are extremely rare. Polstead has one of stone of the C14, Hadleigh and Wickham Market have lead-covered timber spires. Piers are of several forms, the octagonal being the most frequent. A characteristic detail which occurs here and there is one or two blank arch-heads at the top of each side of an octagonal pier. They can be pointed-trefoiled (Lakenheath, Norton, Worlington) or have ogee curves (Bardwell, Walsham-le-Willows). The piers at Burstall have a most unusual, finely detailed section, at Orford they are quatrefoiled with diagonal spurs, at Sproughton filleted main shafts and keeled subsidiary diagonal shafts alternate. Orford is perhaps the best aisled ensemble.

There are plenty of very fine aisleless ensembles, tall naves with tall windows, followed sometimes by tall chancels.

Of the celebrated roofs of Suffolk many must go back to the C14, and some may well be of the C13. But as none of them are securely dated, they will be discussed together with their Perp progeny. On the other hand timber porches can by their detail sometimes be assigned C14 dates with certainty. The simple, robust porch of Somersham may even be of before 1300. Of the early C14 porches the most beautiful is that of Boxford with its flowing tracery, its cusped bargeboarding, and its vault with flying ribs.

Timber-framed houses, it must be reiterated, were the rule in the C13 and C14. But once again there is no safe dating of remains. Nor is there anything of C14 domestic stone architecture to be referred to. Yet the two finest examples of the Decorated style in Suffolk are, if not domestic, both secular – if the gatehouse of a monastery can be regarded as secular. The two are of course the Great Gates of Butley Priory and Bury St Edmunds Abbey, the

former of *c.*1320–5, the latter of *c.*1330–60. At Bury flowing
tracery and ogee arching and gabling appear more sumptuously
than anywhere else in the county, at Butley the same luxuriance
is created by means not of stone carving but of flushwork, and
since datable flushwork does not seem to occur anywhere in England earlier than at Butley, and since moreover flushwork was to
be responsible for many of the finest and most characteristic
effects of Perp architecture in Suffolk, it must here be introduced
in style.

FLUSHWORK is the combination of knapped flint and stone to [10–12]
form patterns in the flat. Flint, used as found, produces an
irregular surface and was originally no doubt meant to be plastered
over. This changed with the introduction of knapping, a technique which could till recently still be studied by watching the
flint knappers of Brandon. The knapper hits a flint with his
hammer so skilfully in strength and direction that the flint breaks
into two halves with a perfectly straight, smooth cleft. Walling is
then done so that these even surfaces form the outside. Flushwork is the flush combination of such knapped flint surfaces
with stone to form chequer patterns or lozenge patterns or blank
arcading or indeed whole blank windows. All these motifs occur
at the Butley gatehouse and form one of the liveliest ensembles
of the date in England. The designers of the C15 and early C16
had little to add to what had been invented, it seems, about 1320.
Cautley does not accept any flushwork as before 1350, and does
not mention Butley.

So we can now get ready for the Golden Age of church building
in Suffolk, the age represented by the PERPENDICULAR STYLE.
That the Perpendicular style starts in the 1330s is familiar. The
first places where it can be found are in London and Gloucester.
When it appeared in Suffolk, it is hard to say. There are no fixed
early dates, and it ought to be remembered that at Wingfield
Castle in or after 1384 flowing tracery was still used.

As so much of the general impression one receives of Suffolk
churches is bound up with the Perp style, a few very general
remarks may first be made. Uncommonly many churches in the
county lie outside the villages, sometimes at least close to the
manor house, sometimes away even from that. That nearly all
Suffolk churches are of flint has already been said. Quite a good
number are thatched. A surprising quantity of churches are in
ruins or marked by the well-known black letter 'remains of' on
the ordnance map. They are an unfailing sign of receding prosperity and depopulation. Among them are some of the grandest

along the coast, especially Covehithe and Walberswick. The
reason here is the decline of sea-borne traffic through these ports.
3a The most moving case of departed greatness, however, is Dunwich, a whole flourishing town which has disappeared, mostly by
the gradual breaking off of the cliff on which it stood.

Yet the Suffolk coast was once a seat of great wealth and pride.
The chain of churches which runs Lowestoft–Kessingland–
10a Covehithe–Southwold–Walberswick–Blythburgh–Aldeburgh is
unforgettable. Here was one centre of the Golden Age Suffolk,
the other was near the Stour and the Essex border, the cause of
prosperity being wool and cloth. It is true that the two largest
parish churches in the county are in neither area but in the shadow
9 of Bury Abbey – St Mary with a length of 213 ft and St James
with 195 ft – but then follow on the one hand Lowestoft with 184,
10a Southwold with 144, Walberswick with 130, and Blythburgh
16a with 128, on the other Lavenham with 156 and Long Melford
with 153. Mildenhall, 168 ft long, is an outlier towards Cambridge.
In the same regions naturally one must look for the most ornate
work. It is due usually to merchants, and they have not infre-
quently seen to it that their names were immortalized on the
buildings or parts for which they had given money. Thus it is
16b with the Cloptons at Long Melford, the Springs and Branches at
27 Lavenham. We are uncommonly well informed on this generosity,
as many wills have been published. Looking at a list of over a
hundred legacies, inscriptions with dates or approximate dates or
without dates, and occasional dates without other inscriptions,
the following can be said. Chronologically very few refer to before
1400, the vast majority – well over 90 per cent – to 1400–1555,
and of these again three-quarters to after 1450. This is of course
partly due to the more probable survival of later documents, but
also to a large extent no doubt to the boom of the cloth trade.
Among the names recorded – and they are, in addition to documents and inscriptions, also recorded in heraldry (see e.g. Framlingham, Hawstead, Lavenham, Metfield, Needham Market) –
the larger number are members of the merchant class, the smaller
of the aristocracy, though the boundaries were of course fluid, and
a niece of Thomas Spring, the richest clothier of Lavenham, could
marry a son of the Earl of Oxford. The son of this Thomas,
another Thomas, left £200 to Lavenham church, an enormous
sum at a time when a legacy of 1s 8d was acceptable (Woolpit).
Money most often went to the building of the tower, a sign of how
towers more than anything else symbolized the pride of a town or
village. More wills refer to towers – about a third of those of

which I know – than to chapels, which, by means of a funeral monument or a chantry altar, one would think, would be more immediately linked to one man's self-glory. The donation to aisles can also often be assumed to have such a personal meaning. Porches in Suffolk to the erection of which money was left, on the other hand, must have had the same general connotations of civic glory as towers. Many legacies also went into pieces of church furnishing and many inscriptions appear on them. To these, however, we must refer somewhat later.

For first the architecture of Perpendicular churches must be summarized, feature by feature, starting with their plans. That most of them have aisles and many chancel aisles goes without saying. That aisles are wide and plans close to the unmitigated parallelogram is also no more than would be expected. A speciality, however, are wide and airy aisleless naves, particularly frequent in the NW. They have tall wide windows, as have the Perp aisles too.

TOWERS are usually to the W, though Cautley counts twenty-one above S porches. The principal area of these is NW to NE of Ipswich. The S tower of Wickham Market, incidentally, is octagonal from its foot. Only one Perp tower is detached from its church, the splendid specimen at Beccles. At Cotton and Wetheringsett the ground floor of the tower is open in a giant arch to the W, with the nave W window appearing at the back of the deep niche thus formed. The Cotton tower is Dec, the Wetheringsett tower Perp.

PORCHES are among the greatest glories of Suffolk church architecture. The most splendid of stone are without doubt those of Woolpit and of Beccles, the latter of the unusual height of 11a 34 ft. Such porches appear with the full orchestration of traceried windows, battlements, niches above the entrance, and carved decoration in the spandrels. Amongst the most usual motifs there are a wild man with a club, said to represent St George, and the symbols of the Trinity and the Passion. The instruments of the Passion are easily recognized, the symbol of the Trinity less so, and as it also occurs frequently on fonts it is here shown on p. 36. Many porches have upper storeys. At Mildenhall (as at Fordham across the Cambridgeshire border) the upper floor is open to the church and serves as a Lady Chapel. The Lady Chapel at Long Melford is of the most unusual shape, an oblong centre surrounded on all sides by an ambulatory.

Regarding the elevations, nothing is more typical, not of Suffolk, but of East Anglia, than the CLERESTORY in major churches

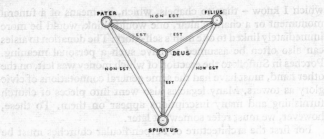

SYMBOL OF THE TRINITY

with closely-set windows to a number twice that of the arcade
bays below. Such it is at Long Melford, where the nave has nine
bays and there are eighteen clerestory windows on either side,
9   such at St Margaret Ipswich and at St Mary Bury, such at Blyth-
10a burgh and Southwold, such at Woolpit and Lavenham. Laven-
&
16a ham displays as a crowning crest lacy openwork BATTLEMENTS,
and the same *tour de force* was accomplished by the carvers of the
Woolpit porch, the N aisle at Bungay, and the clerestory and N
aisle at Hessett. But the supreme skill of the carvers went into the
CHANTRY CHAPELS built by the richest of the merchants – the
16b Clopton Chantry at Long Melford of about 1500, the de la Pole
Chantry at Wingfield of about 1415, and others.

Of individual Perp motifs only a few can be singled out. PIERS
occur in a variety of forms, the most usual remaining the octagon
already equally popular in the C14. It comes as a rule with double-
chamfered arches and stands for the bread and butter of Perp
design. However, many more complex shapes with slender
shafts and thin hollows are to be found, usually developed from
the motif of shafts attached to a lozenge-shaped core of which
often the four sides are hollowed out to a concave shape. A customary refinement (also popular already in the C14) is the with-
drawal of capitals from all shafts except those towards the arch
openings.

Perp TRACERY is not of much interest. It has been investigated
carefully by Miss Ough. A typical motif is transoms crossing the
centre light at a higher level than the side lights and with arches
below them. It is typical of Norfolk too.

As a postscript the two odd ways may be recorded in which
PRIEST'S DOORWAYS occur in the chancels of Suffolk (and other
East Anglian) churches: in a buttress at Bures, Grundisburgh,
and St Stephen Ipswich, and e.g. at Trunch and Warham St

Mary in Norfolk, and behind a flying buttress at Blythburgh, Eye, Framlingham, Spexhall, and Yaxley.

So far no distinction has been made between the various MATERIALS used in Perp churches. From all that has been said before readers must have assumed that FLINT held sway, and indeed that is so; carved stone remained rare and has on the preceding pages been commented on here and there, and flush-work carrying on from Butley went from triumph to triumph. The chief areas are the NE and E and the Stour region. One is hard put to it to decide on preferences. Long Melford must be among them, and Southwold, the porch of Beccles, the tower and porch 10a of Woodbridge, and, without any doubt, that little gem the 12 chapel of Gipping, built as a detached private chapel just before 1500 to serve a mansion of which no stone remains. It appears the most dainty glasshouse inside, and has a most odd N annexe. The motifs of flushwork remain the same as before except that blank Dec tracery becomes blank Perp tracery. What is often added, and gives yet more variety, is initials and monograms, the M of the Virgin Mary, the S with a crown for Sanctus, the IHS for Jesus. BRICK, it will be remembered, had been in use in Suffolk from the C12. But it remained quite rare and only came into its own about 1500. It was used mostly in the rebuilding of towers, and is to be found especially round Ipswich and in the SE towards Essex. Good examples are Charsfield and Ashbocking. Of brick porches 13b perhaps the best are Great Bradley, Ixworth Thorpe, and Great Bealings, and Cautley lists more. Even window frames and tracery were occasionally made of brick, and there is at Barsham even a funeral monument of brick († 1527).

Only one major part of a Suffolk church exists which is made of TIMBER, or rather timber-framing: the chancel of Crowfield. 14a But porches abound. In addition there is that great curiosity the 13a bell-house of East Bergholt, a detached timber cage of c. 1500 14b housing five bells. And there are of course the roofs.

For open TIMBER ROOFS Suffolk stands supreme. There are 18– splendours in other counties as well, especially the other counties 20 of East Anglia and also Somerset. But no county is richer *in toto* or has more varieties of type, and the most ingenious of all English medieval church roofs graces an ugly church right in the middle of the county. The basic division is that between single framing and double framing. In East Anglia the latter developed out of the former. In a single-framed roof all rafters are identical, and each carries its share of the total weight. To strengthen the rafters in their job it is usual to introduce a collar between opposite

rafters fairly high up, and to brace this by diagonal timbers from
the rafters. In addition there are usually verticals on the inner
wall-plate to support the rafters lower down. They are called
ashlar-struts. A roof of this kind such as that at Dennington is in
section similar to seven sides of a dodecagon. An additional and
effective strengthening of roofs can be achieved by tie-beams.
However, as these tie at the foot of the roof, they take away from
the sense of height in a high-pitched roof, even if they are
introduced only between every so many rafters.

But tie-beam roofs are often not single- but double-framed,
as are the finest of them all, those at Mildenhall and Lakenheath. In a double-framed roof a distinction in scantling and
function is made between normal rafters and principal rafters or
principals. It is the principals that carry all the weight. They are
longitudinally connected by the ridge-beam and, at half the
height, by a purlin, or at proportionate heights by more than one
purlin. On this frame rest the other rafters. When clerestories
became usual in the C15 a roof was needed which would not
thrust the walls outwards. The problem was solved by setting the
ridge-piece and purlins on cambered or firred tie-beams, or by
providing short king- or queen-posts, to give a low pitch and
hardly any thrust. And here, if the tie-beam is supported by
arched braces and these have some tracery in the spandrels, and
if there is tracery at the level of the king- or queen-posts, quite a
splendid effect can be obtained.

The simplest and one of the most beautiful forms of double-
framed roofs is that where the principals are supported by
arched braces running uninterruptedly in one long and resilient
curve to just below the ridge, or to a high collar. The result is a
most noble feeling of space. The finest example without a collar
is no doubt Great Glemham; examples with collar are at
Chediston, Cratfield, Ubbeston, and Ufford (chancel). A pretty
variation is to alternate tie-beams and arched braces without
collar, as is done at Wissett and Westhorpe. Another even
prettier variation is the change at Eye between arched braces
springing in the normal way from wall-posts, and arched braces
springing from the apexes of longitudinal arched braces connecting the wall-posts from W to E. Altogether much play can be made
by longitudinal bracing, whether of kingposts to ridge-beam or
of wall-plates.

The next, and the aesthetically as well as structurally most important, innovation was the hammerbeam: that is a beam projecting horizontally into the church and supported by an arched

brace coming forward from a wall-post.* By means of the
hammerbeam the span to be bridged by single braces was
reduced, open roof space was not interfered with, and a much
richer pattern introduced in which the arched braces supporting
the hammerbeam are reiterated by the arched braces surging up
from the hammerbeam to the collar. The effect could be doubled
in richness, even if it was (as Cautley has pointed out) weakened
structurally, by building two tiers of hammerbeams. The
principle of the hammerbeam (according to Mr J. T. Smith) may
have been evolved in large medieval kitchens, such as those at the
Bishop's Palace at Chichester and at Kersey Priory, and was fully
developed by about the middle of the C14 in the Pilgrims' Hall
at Winchester and at Tiptofts and Tendring, both in Essex, but
no major dated example exists earlier than Westminster Hall,
and there the date is *c.* 1395. Indeed the only dated hammerbeam roof in Suffolk (Bardwell) is of 1421. Earl Stonham can
without hesitation be called the most beautiful single-hammer-
beam roof in England. Others are at Badingham, Palgrave,
Rougham, and Westerfield. At Framlingham a charming con-
fusion is playfully created by hiding the hammerbeam and the
braces supporting it by a ribbed coving such as was usual to carry
rood-lofts. The same motif occurs at Laxfield and at the Norfolk
churches of Ringland and St Peter Mancroft, Norwich. Double-
hammerbeam roofs leave us with an *embarras de richesse*. Woolpit 19b
and Grundisburgh are certainly among the finest, although the
latter (as also Wetherden) are structurally false. The others are at
Bacton, Bedingfield, Coddenham, Earl Soham, Framsden, Gislingham, Heveningham, Hitcham, Ipswich St Margaret and St
Mary at Quay, Little Stonham, Market Weston, Rattlesden,
Shotley, Wetherden, and Worlingworth.

There are plenty of variations on the theme of the hammerbeam,
and the fantasy expressed in them is prodigious. One is to alternate between tie-beams and hammerbeams (Badwell Ash, Debenham, Redgrave, Ufford nave, Walsham-le-Willows), another
between normal arched braces and hammerbeams on arched
braces (Bury St Edmunds St Mary, Crowfield, Hawstead, Southwold, Wyverstone) or between normal arched braces and double
hammerbeams on arched braces (Cotton, Tostock). Moreover,
much could be done by sheer ornament or other decoration, such
as the long and incomprehensible story that runs along the wall-

* Much of the above was based on H. M. Cautley's book. Mr J. T. Smith
has pointed out that concerning roofs this is now out of date. On p. 65 is a note
written by Mr Smith and representing up-to-date views.

19a plate at Kersey (and is incidentally carved in stone) or the scenes in the spandrels at Mildenhall, or the pretty conceits in the splendid double-hammerbeam roof of Giffords Hall.

20   One roof finally stands on its own: Needham Market. To understand it, it must be seen and the description on p. 372 read. Perhaps it should primarily be called a hammerbeam roof with vertical posts standing on the hammers and running up to a collar. But the feet of the hammerbeams are longitudinally connected by raking-out boarding similar to the coving at Framlingham, and the rafters do not continue at their regular pitch from the level of the collars upward but are caught by a strong purlin on which a clerestory with ample windows is erected; on this, high above the collars, is a low-pitched tie-beam roof. The space between the posts standing on the hammerbeams and the unusually tall ashlar-struts running from the wall-plate to the rafters is like an aisle suspended in mid air, to which the clerestory is in the right relation, so that the designer continues to its achievement his make-belief of a church floating high above the one in which we stand.

    The halls of the LATE MEDIEVAL HOUSES of Suffolk share the high quality of roofs with the churches. Giffords Hall has
46 already been introduced. It is delightful in every other respect as well. Others, also of timber-framed construction, such as Otley Hall, vie with it in charm and picturesqueness. For houses in
47a towns and villages there is nothing in England to beat Lavenham in numbers or variety. Ipswich has few but interesting ones, especially regarding their plans. There are plenty of others in plenty of other places. To mention just one more, Alston Court, Nayland, is a delight. Of ornamental motifs of these houses the
47b principal are thin buttress-shafts, carved angle-posts with brackets, carved bressumers, carved oriel sills, and carved bargeboards. Abbas Hall has two c 14 wooden arches left inside. Moat Hall Parham is one of the most picturesque, thanks to its moat, but also thanks to the mixture of timber-framing and brickwork.

    Of Early Tudor BRICK HOUSES the first and the only ones with dates are the gateway to Archdeacon Pykenham's mansion at Ipswich, which must date from before 1497 and probably dates
48a from the 70s, and the same lavish prelate's Deanery Tower at Hadleigh built in 1495. In both cases the houses themselves have disappeared. The gatehouse at Ipswich has a stepped gable, the gatehouse at Hadleigh panelled polygonal angle turrets and friezes of little trefoiled arches. All these are current motifs of that moment in England (Faulkbourne Essex, Buckden

Palace Beds, Oxburgh). There are several more Early Tudor gatehouses of brick in Suffolk, the finest no doubt those of Giffords Hall and West Stow Hall, both probably of the 1520s. 48b Gedding Hall, Shelley Hall (before 1533), and Crows Hall are others. They must be looked at in conjunction with the brick mansions and houses of Norfolk and Essex, and, like them, continue straight into the Renaissance, if the introduction of occasional Italian motifs justifies the use of that term. Although modest in size and decoration, a place must also here be found for the gatehouse which is all that survives of Cardinal Wolsey's College at Ipswich. It was built in 1527–9 and has not, unlike the same patron's earlier work at Hampton Court, any indication of the new Humanist fashion. Of the earliest datable pieces of Renaissance decoration more do in fact appear in church furnishings than in houses, and we shall soon have to turn to them.

But first the whole *materia* of earlier CHURCH FURNISHINGS must be reviewed, and there is plenty of it. FONTS first, because there are far more of them than of anything else and because they alone spread over all medieval centuries from the C11 or C12 onwards. From the C12 Cautley lists seventeen in his Introduction and there are more, though none is of more than county interest, except the one which was imported, the square bowl of black Tournai marble at St Peter Ipswich, one of eight existing in England.* Into the late C12 leads the wild font of Great Bricett. A purer E.E. form with gables and stiff-leaf foliage is at Lakenheath. But the most characteristic C13 products are the mass-produced square or octagonal font bowls of Purbeck marble with very shallow blank, round or pointed arches along the sides. There must be a total of over twenty-five of these in Suffolk, the vast majority octagonal with pointed arches. For the C14 the most characteristic designs have arcading, with cusping, crockets, finials, and other decorative motifs. Hemingstone, even if somewhat heavy, is perhaps the best of them. Only one has figurework, that at Kessingland, and, though damaged, it seems to have been of high quality. The date is not later than the end of the C14. Then there is a whole little group of bowls with panels decorated by what might be described as very shallow blank windows with their appropriate tracery. The earliest of these, at

---

* The figure should be ten; for there is a fine fragment at Christchurch 22a Mansion Ipswich and a complete bowl, but with all figure-work chipped off, at Boulge.

Gazeley, need not be later than 1300. The others are at Barningham, Barton Mills, Brightwell, Coney Weston, Icklingham All
Saints, and Rickinghall Inferior.

But the type which Cautley calls East Anglian pure and simple,
and of which indeed, in its various minor modifications, the
county numbers more than 100, is Perp. It is characterized by the
following motifs which need not all be present in all examples: a
stem with four seated lions set against it (this occurs already
c. 1380 at Mutford), or with four lions and four Wild Men (or
woodwoses),* a bowl often supported by angels with spread
wings and occasionally by heads with contemporary head-dresses
23b instead, and an octagonal bowl with on its panels the Signs of the
four Evangelists and four angels or demi-figures of angels holding
shields with armorial bearings, or simply shields, or the emblems
of Christ's Passion or the Trinity (cf. above, p. 36) or flowers, or
any combination of these motifs. There are few in the western
third of the county, i.e. w of say Woolpit. The number is amazing,
and bears out one's impression of Perp England: much lavish dis-
23a play going with much standardization. Sutton is exceptional in
offering an original variation on the standard theme. The most
24 ambitious Perp fonts, however, are those with reliefs of the Seven
Sacraments. They are not confined to Suffolk – Norfolk has more
than Suffolk – but oddly enough Cambridgeshire and Essex have
none. Cautley gives twenty-five to Norfolk and fourteen to Suffolk. As the sacraments could account for only seven out of the
eight panels of the octagonal bowl an eighth scene was necessary,
and this is the Baptism of Christ (four times), the Crucifixion
(four times), or something else. The quality of the figure work
varies, but does not seem to have been very high anywhere. A
number of these ambitious fonts are made yet more ornate and
prominent by being raised on traceried steps. In some cases the
upper step forms a Maltese cross. There are inscriptions on the
steps here and there, and, just as in the case of whole churches or
parts of churches, sometimes one finds an actual date (Tuddenham St Martin 1443, Blythburgh 1449), sometimes an inscription
which helps in dating (Mutford c. 1380, Hessett date of death of
the donor 1510, Snape money for colouring given in 1523), but
more often an inscription without reference to a date (eight
times). Only in one case are we referred to before 1410 (Mutford;

---

* Perhaps one ought to remember that Nicola Pisano's pulpit in the
Baptistery at Pisa has at its foot the lions as well as the Wild Men. It need not
be added that they look very different. The date is c. 1260.

see above); otherwise all is once again the work of piety of the C15 or early C16.*

The mason's work on the font was crowned by the carpenter's work on the FONT COVER, and Suffolk possesses some of the finest and giddiest of England, canopies of great height and intricacy. Ufford need not fear comparison with anything abroad, 25a St Gregory Sudbury is nearly as bold, Worlingworth is high too, and Hepworth of *c.* 1500–20 or later has pretty little men coming seemingly out of pretty little doors. Of the same time probably is Bramford; and Finningham, though much less ambitious, has very curious tracery motifs worth pondering over. A little smaller but charming also is the font cover at Barking. By and large, however, the wood carver's highest achievement was not in font covers but in SCREENS. Again, as in fonts, the C15 and early C16 were more sumptuous than the C14 had been. The earliest wooden screens, at Badley (?), Belton, Brent Eleigh, Burstall, Eriswell, Fritton, Harleston, Lavenham, Lound (partly), Santon Downham, South Elmham St James, and Westhorpe have round shafts with capitals instead of mullions and simple flowing tracery. One fine stone screen of the early C14 also survives, at Bramford, over-restored unfortunately in its upper parts. Of Perp screens there is a glut. The most gorgeous perhaps are those of the Spring 27 Chantry at Lavenham, the chapels at Dennington, the Middleton 26b Chantry at Barham, and the rood screen at Barking. The latter has the coving for its loft preserved, as have also Southwold and Wingfield. Bramfield and Eye have full vaulting, Bramfield to W and E. Dennington has its lovely top parapets, and at Eye rood loft and parapets have been added in the correct style in the C20. In the panels of the dados of Suffolk (and Norfolk) screens there are often painted figures of saints, apostles, and occasionally 26a donors. The aesthetic quality of these paintings is almost without exception low. Stradbroke may be the best. Only once scenes in relief appear instead of the painted figures – at Wyverstone. Nor is the large panel painting of the Wenhaston Doom any better, and WALL PAINTING as a rule is no better either. The Doom of Stanningfield is an example. Churches were extensively painted with figures, scenes, and ornament, and often no doubt all over their interiors. Here again subjects are oddly standardized: St

---

* A similar survey can be made for dates and inscriptions on other pieces of church furnishing: one PULPIT (Stoke-by-Clare): will of 1498; one BENCH (Earl Stonham): inscription, no date; one CROSS outside a church (Thelnetham): will of 1527; three SCREENS (Eye, Walsham-le-Willows, Woodbridge): inscription without date, actual date 1441, will of 1444.

Christopher facing the main door, the Seven Deadly Sins (growing on a tree), the Seven Works of Mercy, the Three Quick and the Three Dead. A so-called Christ of the Trades is at Hessett. Early wall paintings survive at Risby (early C13) and Wissington (mid C13). A specially good series of *c.*1300 is at Little Wenham. But the only painted work in a Suffolk church that bears comparison with the best in England is the retable of Thornham Parva, also of *c.*1300 and probably by the workshop busy in Westminster Abbey at the same time.

31a

STAINED GLASS in Suffolk needs no recording here until we come to the late C15 with the surviving work at Long Melford and to *c.*1525 with the work at Hengrave Hall possibly by the King's Glazier *Galyon Hone.*

32a

Back now to woodwork, and to the job which brought at the end of the Middle Ages results almost as fine and varied as screens: BENCHES. Suffolk benches are many; some churches have whole series. They have poppy-heads and ends decorated excellently or less excellently with tracery patterns. In addition backs and fronts can be traceried, the back rails carved or traceried, and so on. The best of them all are those of Fressingfield and Dennington. On the arms and sometimes the very poppy-heads there can be figures, monsters, animals, human beings, kneeling or seated, and angels. At Tannington and Wilby one can see the Sacraments on the arms, at Finningham and Tannington Vices, at Wilby also the Acts of Mercy, at Ixworth Thorpe the thatcher with his comb, at Withersfield in the poppy-heads St George and the dragon and St Michael weighing souls, at Blythburgh in the poppy-heads Vices, and so on. CHOIR STALLS are of less interest, though here also there are occasionally fine traceried ends (Stowlangtoft) and genre figures on the arms (at Norton a woman whipping a boy, at Earl Stonham a bagpiper), and there are in addition MISERI-CORDS with such scenes as St Martin and the Beggar, the martyrdom of St Thomas (both Fornham St Martin), and the martyrdom of St Edmund and of St Andrew (both Norton). WOODEN DOORS with decoration are something of a speciality. Blank tracery is to be found on over forty, and on fewer doors a border of quatrefoils (e.g. Thorpe Morieux) or a border of foliage trails (e.g. Brettenham) or linenfold panelling (e.g. Lavenham, Nayland), or indeed small figures (Great Bealings, Stoke-by-Nayland). No PULPITS of special beauty or elaboration need notice. One of the best is that at Stoke-by-Clare, commissioned in 1498. The pulpit at Southwold is similar. As a curiosity the graceful PYX CANOPY at Dennington may find a place here. There are only three others in

28a
& b

28b

29

30

the country, and as equal rarities connected with the Blessed Sacrament the Pyx Cloth or SINDON CLOTH of Hessett, the BURSE, or case for the corporal, of Hessett, and the *cuir-bouilli* cylindrical CHALICE CASE at Swefling have to be recorded.

For METALWORK no more than a few lines are required. Some doors have early ironwork, notably that at St Mary at the Elms Ipswich, which seems to be Norman. As for other metals, silver is the material of CHURCH PLATE, of which no more than four pieces of before the Reformation remain (Chalices at Ipswich St Mary-le-Tower and Barnby, Patens at Barsham and Bedingfield), and brass is represented by some stately LECTERNS (Cavendish, Clare, Lowestoft, Woolpit), and of course by funeral monuments.

So the time has come to look at FUNERAL MONUMENTS. We may indeed begin with BRASSES, for Suffolk possesses one of the earliest and finest in England, the Bures brass at Acton of c. 1302.* Other outstanding brasses are the Wingfield at Letheringham of c. 1389, the Felbrigg of c. 1400 at Playford, and the Burgates of c. 1410 at Burgate. There are a large number of others of little aesthetic value, especially in the SW of the county. As for those of the first class, the series ends just before the Renaissance with the large rectangular panel of the Pounders at Ipswich. This is of 1525, and has recently been transferred to Christchurch Mansion. Oaken effigies start a little later than brasses, stone effigies considerably earlier. Of the early C14 is the wooden Knight at Bures, of the late C14 that at Heveningham, of c. 1415 are the de la Poles at Wingfield. Curiously enough there is another couple rendered in wood as late as c. 1587 at Boxted.

At the beginning of the series of stone effigies stands that venerable fragment of a coffin-lid with the lower part of the figure of a Knight at St Stephen's Chapel Bures which comes from Colne Priory and seems to represent Alberic de Vere, who died in 1141. The next de Vere there is of c. 1300. The effigy lies on a tomb-chest, with small fine figures of the early C14, which does not belong to the figure and seems to be part of a former shrine. There is nothing else of importance from the C13 or the early C14 except perhaps a Knight of c. 1290 at Erwarton and a Lady of c. 1310–20 at Newton. Of the late C14 and early C15 the Wingfield at Wingfield who died in 1361 and the de Veres of c. 1370 and c. 1420 at Bures may be mentioned. More of between the mid C15 and the mid C16: the Bardolf † 1441 at Dennington (alabaster), the Sir William Clopton † 1446 at Long Melford, the John Clopton † 1497 at Long Melford, and the Barnardiston † 1503 at Kedington.

Marginal references: P. 70 / PP. 394, 127

* Or c. 1320?

The end of the age seems to be reached with the Sir Edward Eckingham † 1527 at Barsham; for here Early Renaissance decoration occurs. But the Middle Ages died hard. The tomb of Sir John Cornwallis † 1544 at Brome has Corinthian columns, but they are very rough and they carry an ogee arch, and of the three monuments at Lakenheath, Eye, and Mellis commemorating deaths in 1568, 1568, and 1570 the first and third have no Renaissance motif whatever, and the second no more than colonnettes.

At this first meeting with the Renaissance an aside may be excused dealing with things partly before and partly after the moment which we have reached, and having nothing in common but their ODDITY AND CURIOSITY. To this category belong the Key of Framlingham Castle (in the porch of St Michael's church), the Padlock of the door of Parham church, the Sexton's Wheel at Yaxley to determine fast days with, the dozen of tall narrow wall recesses in NE Suffolk churches to keep Processional Banners in, the four Hour Glasses by the pulpit at Earl Stonham, of which three mark quarter hour, half hour, and hour, the Armoury over the porch at Mendlesham with armour from c. 1470 to c. 1610, the Collecting Shoes at Halesworth, Ubbeston, and Worlingworth (the latter dated 1622),* the thirty-three Leather Buckets at Haughley which date from 1725 and 1757, the stoneware Beer Jug of 1724 at Hinderclay (for the bell-ringers) which holds a gallon, and the Fire Engine of 1760 at Worlingworth.

This *pot pourri surprise* has taken us into the C18, and as there is so relatively little of note in C16 to C18 CHURCH ARCHITECTURE AND CHURCH FURNISHINGS the record may as well be made at once and before secular buildings and the mostly secular-looking monuments to their builders are gone into. The RENAISSANCE appears in Suffolk with a number of windows of terracotta made, it seems, by a man who must have been familiar with, or may himself have worked at, Layer Marney in Essex c. 1520–3 and then at Oxburgh, Wymondham, St George Colegate at Norwich, and Bracon Ash, all in Norfolk. These windows are at
50b Shrubland Old Hall and the churches of Barham, Barking, and Henley, all near Shrubland and all about 25 miles from Layer Marney and about 40 miles from the various places in Norfolk. As for the spreading of the Renaissance, this first occurrence is followed by the monument † 1527 at Barsham, mentioned a little higher up and probably made by the same craftsman as the Renaissance windows, and then by Hengrave Hall of c. 1525–38, and more monuments from c. 1545 onwards.

* Cautley counts five collecting shoes in Norfolk.

Of CHURCH FURNISHINGS there is only one dated piece of any sort which is worth a reference, the pulpit at Holy Trinity Bungay which was set up in 1558, a rare date for PULPITS. It has not yet the short stubby blank arches which one connects with Elizabethan and Jacobean woodwork and which are as often Carolean as Jacobean, or more often so. The dates in Suffolk are significant, also for the zest of the Laudian period. Cautley writes that he knows of 117 C17 pulpits. The dated examples are as follows: 1614 Martlesham, 1616 Stonham Aspal, 1617 Cratfield, 1619 Great Ashfield and Redisham (all these have the squat blank arches and the last two are square and not polygonal), 1620 Occold, 1625 Dennington, 1626 Carlton, 1630 Mendlesham, before 1631 Kelsale, 1632 Aldeburgh and Rendham, 1635 Yaxley, the richest of all, finally 1637 Chediston (all these again have blank arches). Apart from blank arches, decoration is by means of panels with arabesques and dolphins or monsters and by raised diamond-cut knobs or the raised motifs which look like exclamation marks. No development can be recognized between 1614 and 1637. After 1640 no memorable pulpits seem to have been commissioned until we come to the two in the Wren–Gibbons style at St Mary-le-Tower and the Unitarian Meeting 17b House at Ipswich. The latter can be dated 1699. Excellent WOODWORK of the same period, actually of c. 1680, is in the church at Euston, furnished by the family of the Hall. Besides the pulpit, it includes a reredos and a screen. Here the contrast against such a 'Jacobean' screen as that of Kedington, dated 1619, is as patent as it is in pulpits, or as it is between such communion rails as those at Chediston of c. 1620–30 and the early C18 ones at Kedington (strongly moulded balusters) or Boxted (twisted balusters). In quite a number of cases (Cautley counts fifteen) communion rails in Suffolk run round three sides of the altar instead of simply across the chancel from N to S. Benches in the C17 continued in the medieval traditions. One can even find C17 poppy-heads (Great Livermere 1601). There are no memorable examples of the later C17. The same is true of font covers. The one at Mendlesham, 25b dated 1630, is the most fanciful. The others are simpler, and that at Syleham with the date 1667 is still decidedly pre-classical.

To Georgian church furnishings Suffolk makes no contribution, unless one is ready to call the ensembles of such churches as Brent Eleigh or Cretingham or Kedington or Little Livermere a contribution. They have their box pews, family pews, three-decker pulpit, etc., uncommonly completely preserved.*

* Two C18 SWORD RESTS of wrought iron are in St Mary-le-Tower Ipswich.

CHURCH BUILDING, as everywhere in England, came to a
standstill with the Reformation and did not recover for a long
time. In Suffolk in fact it never recovered. The Late Middle Ages
had built so much that no new needs arose right into the C19.
What can here be mentioned is almost without exception small
fry, the Perp chancel of 1617–19 at Clare, the hammerbeam roofs
of Jacobean date at Boxted and Wickhambrook, the E window of
1697 at Chevington. The exceptions are the surprising w end of
17a Brightwell, datable c. 1656, where a bell-turret is carried on giant
Tuscan columns, and the church at Euston, built in 1676 on an
elongated central plan of a type undoubtedly derived from
Wren's work in the City of London. The 'Venetian' tracery is
Wrenish too. For the whole C18 no more than two names need be
given, Grundisburgh for its s tower of 1751–2, and Shotley for its
charming, still completely furnished chancel interior of
1745.

On the other hand, the NONCONFORMISTS, who could only
in the C17 begin to build and only in the C18 built freely, contributed a few chapels which ought to find space in any book
dealing with their architecture nationally and not locally. The
earliest is the chapel at Walpole of 1647, enlarged before the end
of the century and well preserved inside and out, the finest the
17b Unitarian Meeting House at Ipswich of 1699. This is an excellent
building by any standards, quiet and dignified, with fine big pediments on carved brackets, and cross-windows, at the time just a
little conservative, and it is nobly fitted up. Like the chapel at
Walpole, only on a larger scale, it has giant columns across the
middle. The Friends built quite a stately meeting house at Woodbridge as early as 1678, and a more modest one at Bury in 1750.
Here the former Presbyterian Chapel dates from 1711–12, at
Framlingham the Unitarian Chapel (still cross-windows) from
1717. The chapels at Long Melford (c. 1724), Rendham (1750),
and Wrentham (1778) need no comment.

The major contributions to the C16–18 in Suffolk are secular
throughout, if one is ready to admit the undeniable fact that the
church monument from Elizabethan times onwards at the latest
had become a secular affair. There is indeed no other job in which
the development of composition as well as decorative motifs can
be studied so readily and so thoroughly. Fireplaces are subsidiary evidence. Moreover, the monuments demonstrate to us
the characters, the ambitions, the social conventions of those who
built the houses. A house cost more than a monument. Often
therefore the house became in the end only an incomplete expres-

sion of its builder's desire for display. For his own monument he was ready to leave enough money – perhaps even troubled by remorse – and so the monument grew to its full size and elaboration.

It will here be attempted to deal with HOUSES and MONUMENTS together, period for period, and first the ELIZABETHAN, or to be accurate the years preparing for the Elizabethan style.

The first signs in the county of the new ornamental fashion which came from Italy and appeared in England between 1510 and 1520 in works done for Henry VIII (monument to Henry VII) and Wolsey (Hampton Court) have already been noted: the terracotta windows of c. 1523–5 made round Shrubland and the 50b Eckingham Monument at Barsham († 1527). It has also been noted that in spite of that, monuments without any indication of Renaissance motifs were still made up to 1570. The situation is the same in houses. Hengrave Hall, built c. 1525–38, is essentially still of the late medieval type, with turreted gatehouse, courtyard, 50a and hall opposite the gatehouse. Its exceedingly pretty oriel window over the doorway is of a design invented it seems about 49b 1500 at Windsor and specially popular for ambitious jobs of c. 1500–20. But the detail of the oriel is Italian, even if not a specially knowledgeably handled Italian. And the cloister-like corridor all round three sides of the courtyard is a remarkably progressive motif. On the other hand the big bay window of the hall with mullions and transoms and arched lights is still entirely Perp. Hengrave is of yellow brick. All other houses and mansions to be noted here over the next hundred years and more will be of red brick. The favourite plan on a large scale becomes that with two far projecting wings (Christchurch Mansion Ipswich 1548–50, Rushbrooke Hall c. 1550 (now alas demolished), Melford Hall 52 complete by 1559 and Kentwell Hall complete before 1563, both at Long Melford, and also formerly Broke House, Nacton – see Kip). In the centre is normally a porch, and attached to the wings in varying positions are two symmetrically placed stair-turrets (Rushbrooke, Melford, Kentwell).

At Christchurch Mansion the lights of the mullioned windows are no longer arched as they had been in the earlier Tudor decades, and since Christchurch Mansion is dated 1548–50 this is remarkable; for Old Somerset House in London of c. 1547–51 has always been regarded as the earliest example of this change. Wenham Place is undated but can also, on account of the arched window lights, be considered of the time of Henry VIII and not

later.* The earliest specific Renaissance motifs after the Hengrave
oriel are in the delightful wooden panelling from Sir Anthony
Wingfield's house at Ipswich (now Christchurch Mansion),
which must be of before 1552. At about the same time the pediment appears above windows, a motif which Lord Protector
Somerset seems to have been the first to take over from France.
53a The earliest occurrences in Suffolk are Freston Tower, a standing,
called 'built within these twelve years' in 1561, where the pediments stand characteristically enough on the hood-mould stops
52 of yore, Melford Hall (one window in the porch) of before 1559,
Thorpe Hall Horham of c. 1560, The Abbey at Woodbridge of
1564, etc. Gables can be straight (Rushbrooke, The Abbey Woodbridge) or stepped (Wantisden Hall 1550, Fleming's Hall Bedingfield c. 1550, Okenhill Hall Badingham 1552, Seckford Hall some
time between 1553 and 1585, etc.), as they had been in East
Anglia for a long time (e.g. Horham Hall Essex and, in Suffolk,
Cockfield Hall Yoxford). Semicircular gables or gablets are a
passing fashion vaguely indicative of the coming of the Renaissance. Their origin is probably Venice and Layer Marney. The
51a two examples in Suffolk are Erwarton Hall gatehouse c. 1549, and
Stutton Hall gatehouse 1553. The latter has another remarkably
progressive motif, coupled pilasters flanking the entrance. This
motif also had only a few years before been introduced to England
(from Italy) at Somerset House. Other porches with columns or
pilasters or superimposed orders are (or were) at Rushbrooke,
Melford Hall, The Abbey Woodbridge 1564, Seckford Hall,
Coldham Hall 1574, etc.

Once these motifs and modes of composition had been made
familiar, they remained in use everywhere for well over fifty
53b years. Stepped gables e.g. are still used in 1593 at Roos Hall
Beccles, in 1607 at Mutford Hall, in 1610 at Bruisyard Hall,
c. 1612 at Newbourn Hall, and even in 1622 at Cottage Farmhouse North Cove, and polygonal angle buttresses or shafts at
Roos Hall and Bruisyard Hall. In plan Smallbridge Hall Bures
(c. 1572) and Hintlesham carry on the type with far-projecting
wings. The E-plan of Seckford Hall was continued e.g. at Playford Hall (1589) and still at Claydon Old Hall (1621). A new
plan typical of parts of Suffolk is of only three by two bays but
53b comparatively great height. The type is best illustrated by Roos
Hall Beccles of 1593. Other examples are Thorpe Hall Horham

* But Thorpe Hall Horham still has arched lights and yet seems to be of
about 1560, and in other counties, e.g. Northamptonshire, arched lights go
on even longer.

of c. 1560, Boundary Farm Framsden, Ash Farmhouse Mutford, and Rushmere. Quite a number of Elizabethan and Jacobean houses are only partly preserved, and that makes it hard to judge their complete original plans (Playford Hall, Weston Hall, Baylham Hall, Parham House).

The only new motif which seems to have been introduced about 1620 is the shaped gable, a gable the sides of which are composed of convex or concave or double-curved parts. They had indeed an Elizabethan pedigree and one precedent of c. 1575 in Suffolk, the pretty strapwork dormers of the Shire Hall at Woodbridge, 55a clearly derived from Netherlandish engravings. Shaped gables with convex quadrant sides and an ogee top are at Claydon Old Hall in 1621 and Hemingstone Hall in 1625, convex-quadrant sides and a semicircular top at Hemingstone as well and at Witnesham and Boundary Farm Framsden.

In TOWN HOUSES also the medieval tradition carried on without a break. Ipswich has fine houses with dates between 1620 and 1640. They are all still timber-framed, and what distinguishes them from their predecessors of c. 1500 is no more than the ornamental motifs on angle posts and bressumers.

For changes more thorough than this Ipswich and the Suffolk countryside had to wait till after 1630 and as a rule after 1670. In INTERIOR DECORATION the change between 1500 and the Elizabethan and Jacobean decades was much more thoroughgoing. The ribbed ceilings at Stutton Hall, and then at Woodbridge (Post Office), Tannington, Troston Hall, Aspall Hall, and in so many other places have no pre-Elizabethan precedent in the county, and Jacobean fireplaces such as those at Moor Farmhouse Middleton and Sotterley Hall are even more novel. The exuberance of such work is only rarely matched in church furnishings.

It was often matched and occasionally surpassed in CHURCH MONUMENTS. Here, after the *incunabula* of Renaissance detail at Barsham and Brome († 1527, † 1544) already referred to, things started more in earnest with the splendid set of Norfolk tombs at Framlingham. They run from c. 1536 to c. 1564. Basically they are still tomb-chests with recumbent effigies, that is in the medieval tradition, but the decoration with first fluted pilasters, then playful balusters, and then columns, and also with shell-niches, tells of a new spirit. The sculpture of the monument to Henry Fitzroy Duke of Richmond † 1536 is still uninfluenced by Italy, but the statuettes in the shell-niches in the monument to the third Duke of Norfolk † 1554 are of a quality that need not fear 34a

comparison with the best work in France or Germany. Yet the
decoration here still has balusters. A few years later, the Codington Monument at Ixworth († 1567) uses decorated pilasters but
combines them with leaf carving of a very pure Italian style.
Also in the sixties the monument to the Countess of Bath at
Hengrave († 1561) has the full accompaniment of a heavy Tuscan
six-column canopy – Elizabethan at its sturdiest and without any
Gothic hangover. But monuments on that scale still remained
rare in Suffolk. The only comparable one before 1600 is the
34b Cordell † 1580 at Long Melford, also with detached columns.
Then the pace quickens, and for the years between 1600 and 1620
at least fifteen monuments ought to be considered here. The
Lewkenor † 1605 at Denham St Mary is a four-poster, the Kitson
† 1608 at Hengrave a six-poster. Judge Clenche †1607 at Holbrook and his wife are represented, not recumbent, but stiffly semi-
reclining on their sides. In a similar pose are Mrs Drury † 1610 at
Hawstead and Sir Robert Gardener † 1619 at Elmswell. The same
pose still remains at Barham in c. 1640, but now more relaxed.

Other big monuments, Jacobean in date or style, may be noted
at Bures († 1613), Stoke-by-Nayland († 1615), Badingham
(† 1616), Little Thurlow († 1619; very good), Milden († 1626;
also very good), and Denham St Mary († 1635). A familiar Eliza-
35 bethan and Jacobean type of monument has kneeling instead of
recumbent effigies (e.g. the Tollemaches at Helmingham of 1615),
the most interesting perhaps being those where, above figures
kneeling in profile, the principal figure is kneeling frontally. Such
it is at Woodbridge († 1627) and such in the d'Ewes Monument
at Stowlangtoft (1624 etc.), the Crane Monument at Chilton
(1626), and the Playters Monument at Sotterley († 1638). Now
the first of these latter three is known to be by *John Johnson*
(contract of 1624 for £16 10s), the second by *Gerard Christmas*
(contract for £50), the third by *Edward Marshall*. So here
monuments cease to be anonymous for us, and individual carvers
appear, even if the individuality of the Johnsons and Christmases
(*J. and M. Christmas* signed a monument, † 1637, at St Stephen
Ipswich, also with kneeling figures) is hardly worth special study.

It is different with *Nicholas Stone*, who was born in 1586 and
died in 1647. We can follow him closely from 1613 onwards, when
he returned to England from Holland where he had studied his
art, and his work always repays attention, partly for reasons of
sculptural quality and partly for reasons of iconography. In Suffolk his accomplishment as a sculptor is patent in all its purity in
the earliest dated work in the county, the Bacon Monument of

1616 at Redgrave, for which he received £200. He deserved it. There is no novel conceit here. The effigy is recumbent, and architecture plays no part. Yet a great nobility is achieved. The same is true of his other monument with a recumbent effigy, that at Bramfield († 1629). Here the most remarkable thing is however the total absence of strapwork, and indeed of almost any ornament. In this Stone had been preceded by the unknown designer of the Cornwallis Monument (†1611) at Oakley, which has neither ornament nor effigy nor other figures and yet much dignity. As for Stone, he did half a dozen more works in Suffolk. Some of them are minor (Redgrave † 1621), but two others are of considerable iconographical interest, as illustrating the most progressive trends in monument design in England. The Whettell Monument (†1628) at Ampton has a frontal bust and the Drury Monument († 1615) at Hawstead a frontal demi-figure in an oval niche. These were forms which are matched or imitated by the two frontal busts praying of the Clenche † 1628 at Great Bealings, the frontal busts in shallow relief placed in oval niches of the Stuteville † 1631 at Dalham, the frontal bust in a circular niche of the Eldred of 1632 at Great Saxham, the two frontal demi-figures in circular niches of the Calthorpes of 1638 at Ampton (by the *Christmas* brothers), the frontal busts in oval niches of the Alston †1641 at Marlesford, and the two demi-figures turning to one another of the Tyrell † 1641 at Stowmarket, the two demi-figures holding hands of the Sayer †1647 at Nettlestead, the three demi-figures of the Gurdon of 1648 at Assington, and the demi-figures of Barnardistons †1653 and † 1669 at Kedington. The list must be extended to 1680; for monuments † 1676 at Sibton and † 1680 at Brome still use the same scheme. But the two most surprising works of the years with which we are concerned are the Timperley † 1629 at Hintlesham, an upright figure engraved with great swagger in a slab of slate, and the Sir Robert Hitcham † 1636 at Framlingham, a 36 black marble slab carried by four white angels. This continues the Dutch type which had appeared in England with Colt's Salisbury Tomb at Hatfield and the Vere Monument in Westminster Abbey. It remained extremely rare, however. The sculptor is *Francis Grigs*, of whom little else is known.

With the 1650s names become more frequent. Nicholas Stone has already been discussed and Edward Marshall mentioned. In addition there are four tablets by *John Stone* (Barrow 1650, Hessett 1653, Belstead both 1656) and a monument with a seated figure at Culford (Bacon, 1654) by *Thomas Stanton*. Seated

figures also were something rare at that time. Stanton received
£300 for it. But more interesting than these are the Essington
monuments at Brightwell, one of 1656 the other of 1660. In
the first is a whole small standing figure, in the second a three-
quarter figure in relief in an oval medallion. The interest is in the
elaborate inscriptions, a pathetic fashion of those years, which
is still exhibited in the Simson Monument († 1697) at Debenham. The figure here is frontal again and three-quarter length.

   With all these monuments a world has opened less stiff, less
artificial and mannered, but also less robust than the Elizabethan
and Early Jacobean. In architecture this new world was ushered
in by Inigo Jones and his truly epoch-making works started in
1616. By the beginning of the Civil War his reform had been
achieved, even if it took another twenty years and more to con-
vince more than a few patrons of it. The impetus was greatest
near the Court, especially after Charles I had ascended the throne.
The provinces hesitated, and Suffolk had now turned very provincial. Little is reflected of the new style in architecture, and
56b what there is, is late. Thus Cupola House at Bury St Edmunds
corresponds with its belvedere on the roof to such houses as
Coleshill of c. 1650 and yet is dated 1693. The most metropolitan
design is perhaps the church at Euston of 1676, mentioned earlier
on as the one example of an echo of Christopher Wren in Suffolk.
Euston Hall, the house to go with the church, was built c. 1666–
70 but does not survive. It was simple and undecorated except
for the somewhat awkward giant pilasters of the porch, a motif
which also occurs at Christchurch Mansion Ipswich c. 1674
and Clopton Hall Rattlesden 1681. The King Charles Gate at
Euston belongs to the provincial mid-C17 Baroque rather than
the Jones–Webb–Wren style. The fragment of Parham House is
undated and mysterious. It is clear that the house had giant
pilasters all along. That is an Inigo Jones motif taken up by John
Webb, but also a motif of that style of the simpler minds which
Sir John Summerson has christened Artisan Mannerism (houses
in Great Queen Street London, c. 1640). The details at Parham
make a date before 1650 more likely than after. The Suffolk
standard motif at that time was still the big shaped gable, and
these went on right down to the C18; at Gateley Hall in Norfolk
it appears as late as 1726. Here are some dates: Whittingham
Hall Fressingfield 1653, stables of Bredfield Hall 1665, Alms-
55b houses Ufford 1690, Reydon Hall 1682, High House Huntingfield 1700. The only occasional change is that from the former
types of shaped gables to that known as Dutch, i.e. crowned

by a pediment. It is a form created in London *c.* 1615–20 and specially popular in 1630–50 (Kew Palace, Swakeleys Middlesex, Raynham Hall Norfolk, etc.). In Suffolk its earliest occurrence is at Stutton Hall, its earliest dated occurrence at Westerfield Hall in 1656. After that it comes at Red House Farmhouse Knodishall 1678, at Darsham House 1679, and with a provincial twist at the Cary Almshouses Halesworth founded in 1686. When Christchurch Mansion Ipswich was partly rebuilt *c.* 1674 after a fire, the gables were given this form. Inside houses the most characteristic motif was now the staircase balusters of dumb-bell shape (Christchurch Mansion after 1675) or twisted (Friends' Meeting House Woodbridge 1678). Plasterwork abandoned ribs and turned to oval wreaths instead. That again was on the pattern of Inigo Jones and Webb, and again it seems to have arrived late in Suffolk. The first example is Sparrowe's House Ipswich, prob- 56a ably of *c.* 1670, where the exterior plasterwork is more important and enjoyable; a lot of motifs, figural and ornamental, presented gaily and naïvely. The oriel windows of Sparrowe's House have a design typical of this date (Hitcham Building Pembroke College Cambridge 1659, Corpus Christi College Cambridge 1667) and characterized by the side lights of a three- or five-light window having a transom and the middle light an arch instead springing from the height of the side transoms. The motif is repeated in other Ipswich houses (24 Fore Street, 30 Tavern Street) and became fashionable once again 200 years later.

Of EIGHTEENTH-CENTURY HOUSES in towns one must not expect much. Ipswich, Newmarket, and Bury were small towns, and they were not specially prosperous. The nicest *ensembles* are at Beccles, Woodbridge, and Southwold, the latter being one of the most delightful small seaside towns in England.

What does now come to the fore, however, is PUBLIC BUILD-INGS, and though the towns of Suffolk were, to say it once more, too small to do anything spectacular, the Butter Cross at Bungay of 1689, the Town Hall at Bury St Edmunds by *Robert Adam* (1774–80), the Angel Hotel in the same town (of 1779), a hotel of the new gentlemanly type, the Athenaeum again at Bury as modified in 1789 and 1804, and the Gaol also at Bury dating from 1803 are all worth notice. The Gaol, of which only the severe entrance wall and gatehouse survive, was once a famous building designed according to the most up-to-date plans. Bury also has pretty Georgian shop windows. At Ipswich nothing comparable exists, at least of before 1820. A Suffolk speciality finally are the HOUSES OF INDUSTRY or Workhouses built from the mid 1760s to the mid 1780s. They are at Bulcamp, Ship-meadow, and Tattingstone (the three earliest, begun in 1765) and then at Barham, Melton, Semer (1780; pulled down), and Stow-market (1777–81); substantial, plain brick buildings of classical composition and without frills. Yet it is said in one case that they resembled gentlemen's residences more than dwellings for paupers. And indeed the typical minor c18 country house of Suffolk does not do much more in the way of enrichment.

Major COUNTRY HOUSES are few and far between. The Eliza-bethans and Jacobeans had built enough, and urgent new demand, that is new wealth, was rare. The first of a pure c18 type is as early as 1693: Bramford House, of seven bays and two storeys with a modillion frieze and a hipped roof. Little Glemham Hall of c. 1720 is large, but in its structure Elizabethan. Little Haugh Hall,
57b Norton, of c. 1730 has inside splendid luxuriant carving and also ceiling paintings. At Hintlesham, again Elizabethan structurally, much was re-done externally and internally from c. 1720 onwards. Sotterley Hall of c. 1744 and Loudham Hall of about the same time are pleasant and complete examples of their date. Browston Hall Belton, unpromising externally, has three sweet Rococo plaster ceilings of c. 1750 inside.

With the Temple or Summer House which *William Kent*, the most imaginative of the earlier Palladians, designed for Euston in 1746, two years before he died, we are once again in the main stream of English developments. It is an exceedingly fine piece. The house at Euston was a few years later remodelled and en-larged by *Matthew Brettingham*, another of the leading Palladians. He also built Benacre Hall (1763–4). Then follow *James Paine* with the centre of the later much altered and enlarged Shrubland Park (1770–2), and *John Johnson*, Surveyor to the County of Essex, with Woolverstone Hall (1776). But the most beautiful, and, if not the grandest, the second grandest Georgian mansion of Suffolk, is Heveningham Hall, built by *Sir Robert Taylor* and fitted up inside by *James Wyatt* (c. 1778–84). The exterior is of great dignity, and with its attic over the whole centre, instead of a pedi-ment, rather more Imperial Roman than Palladian. The interior
59 is exquisite; its stucco-work, its decorative painting, its fireplaces and doors and sconces of a finesse and a unity which show to per-fection Wyatt's felicity and facility. If Heveningham cannot be
60 called the grandest of Georgian houses, that is due to Ickworth, begun in 1795 by *Francis Sandys* to an idea of the owner, that erratic prelate the Earl of Bristol. The centre is a huge domed oval to which quadrant wings and long side pavilions are attached.

The idea is bold, but it has not resulted in much beauty either outside or indeed inside, where the oddest shapes of rooms had to be coped with. The interior was got ready only between 1825 and 1830, and from that time dates the magnificent staircase hall. What *Sandys* could do in the way of good interiors can be seen at Worlingham Hall of *c*. 1800. Also by *Sandys* is Finborough Hall, with the semicircular bow against which stand six detached giant Tuscan columns. The date here is 1795. Finally again of the 1790s Glevering Hall, where however the more interesting work is *Decimus Burton*'s of 1834–5. Due to him is the Orangery with its cast-iron palm-tree columns.

But cast iron is a C19 more than an C18 material, and we are not ready yet for the C19. For C18 architecture two postscripts are desirable, one vernacular, the other sophisticated. The former is the delightful CRINKLE-CRANKLE WALLS of Suffolk, undulating forcing walls of brick, which Mr Norman Scarfe has collected and published. They occur at Long Melford, Heveningham, Easton, Bramfield, Puddingmoor at Beccles, and in many other places.* The other postscript is FOLLIES and, as inhabitable follies, Gothic cottages and houses. Of the latter the prettiest is at Huntingfield, another is Cat House Woolverstone (1793), and St Peter's House at Beccles has a very odd Gothic back. Of follies the most elaborate is at the Old Rectory Claydon. It comprises castellated walls and a grotto, and is said to date from the 1850s; the grotto, however, is more likely to be earlier. An out and out folly is the Tattingstone Wonder, a sham church complete with W tower, built as an eye-catcher, and being in fact three cottages. Yaxley also has an imitation church tower, and the two lodges of the former Rendlesham Hall of *c*. 1790 are flamboyant sham ruins. Not quite a folly is the exceedingly pretty Fishing Lodge, all that remains of Tendring Hall, Stoke-by-Nayland. And not at all follies, though oddities or rarities, are the Ice House at Heveningham and the unique Cyder House at Aspall, with its press brought by a wise emigrant in 1728 from Normandy.

In FUNERAL MONUMENTS, to which we must now return after having left them about 1660, there is no clear break in the decades following 1660, such as we have seen in architecture. The break had been made before. And so a monument might still be made with kneeling figures (Ipswich, St Mary-le-Tower, probably 1694), but the figures are now relaxed. Semi-reclining figures had been the standard for large monuments in the earlier C17; they remain so still, but again with the new relaxation in

* By the end of 1965 Mr Scarfe's count had reached fifty-six.

attitude and the new effusiveness of sentiment. As examples one can quote the white marble figure of Maurice Barrow †1666 at Westhorpe, his hand on his heart, the two figures of the Croftses (he died in 1677) by *Abraham Storey* at Little Saxham, where he lies above and behind her, the Thomas Jermyn † 1692 at Rushbrooke holding a skull in his hand, and then in the C18 *Francis Bird*'s Rev. A. Wingfield in the churchyard of Stonham Aspal, 38b 1715, the Robert Jennens † 1725 at Acton, where for the first time in Suffolk a mourning female figure, his wife, is placed at his feet, the Sir Lionel Tollemache of 1729 at Helmingham with the same new motif and – another innovation for Suffolk – with Roman dress, and the Colman of 1743 at Brent Eleigh which is by *T. Dunn*.

New or relatively new types are rarer. Unique in Suffolk, but occurring twice in London and six times in Norfolk, is a freestanding column as the centre. The monument in question is to Mrs Colman at St Lawrence Ipswich (*c.* 1700). Busts, formerly placed in niches, are now used free-standing – at Somerleyton, at Cockfield († 1723) by *Royce* of Bury St Edmunds, and at Stuston (1727). The standing figure, a great exception before the late C17 (but *see* above for Brightwell † 1656), is now the centre of the un37 commonly excellent later C17 monument to Sir John Poley † 1638 at Boxted. The contrast to the other Poley monument in the same church is revealing. It is of 1725, and much less rhetorical. Altogether, restraint is characteristic of one trend of the twenties and thirties – see e.g. the monuments without any effigy at Rushbrooke († 1722), Benhall († 1732), and Grundisburgh († 1738). The motif of the standing figure of Thomas Maynard († 1742), who leans with one arm on a pedestal, had been made fashionable by Guelfi at Westminster Abbey. The sculptor at Hoxne, where the Maynard Monument is, was *Charles Stanley*. For the seated figure we have had C17 precedent in Suffolk in the monument by Stanton of 1654. The two cases in which it occurs in the C18 are, however, part of a different tradition. They both represent judges, and here the *ex cathedra* 38a posture was customary. The Holt at Redgrave is of 1710 and by *Thomas Green* of Camberwell, the Reynolds † 1738 at Bury St Edmunds Cathedral is unsigned. Seated also are the two 39a Dickinses at Cowlinge. He died in 1747. They have an urn on a pedestal between them and wear Roman dress. The monument is signed by *Scheemakers*.

With him we have reached the great mid-C18 trio. In Suffolk *Roubiliac* has one minor work to his credit (at Framlingham;

without figures), *Rysbrack* none, as his busts made for Little
Haugh Hall can no longer be traced. For the second half of the
c18 memorable sculpture in the county can indeed be listed by
names. There is in any case little to be listed, and one group of
elegant hanging monuments in white, pink, and grey marbles
which belongs to *c.* 1775 (e.g. Finningham † 1781) is, with only
one exception (Worlingworth † 1781, by *Cooper* of Stratford-
le-Bow), unsigned. The first of the named works is *Sir Henry
Cheere*'s, provided it was he who in 1754 made the Justice for the
Bungay Butter Cross. The figure is of lead, a material Cheere
liked. Next in date come the *elder Westmacott*'s monument † 1774
at Shimpling and the *elder John Bacon*'s at Hawstead (1793) and
Finningham (1797), and that is about all. There is a little more after
1800: *John Bacon Junior* at Edwardstone, Hawstead, Nowton,
and Worlingworth († 1808–32), *Flaxman* at Tattingstone († 1814), 39b
Nollekens at Helmingham († 1804 and 1810) and Saxmundham
(† 1812), *Coade* at Worlingworth (1793) and Henstead (1806),
Kendrick with one of his most ambitious works (Thornham 40
Magna † 1821), and so on into the Victorian Age.

The VICTORIAN AGE – we are now ready for it, and it has not
changed Suffolk much. The tourist welcomes that, the omnivor-
ous student is disappointed by it. So some listing to tell him what
he might expect may still be justifiable. Back at the beginning of
the century stand a few pictures by masters not often found in
churches: *Benjamin West*'s altar painting at Sternfield and *Constable*'s at Brantham (1804) and Nayland (1809). Something 32b
equally rare, and this time fully Early Victorian, is the painting
by *Dyce* at Knodishall. The same romantic medievalism inspired 31b
the re-furnishing of Rushbrooke church about 1840. It was done
by Col. Rushbrooke himself, and the arrangement is as if the village were a college. On the other hand *John Thomas*, sculptor and
protégé of Prince Albert, and the king of building contractors, Sir
Morton Peto, made Somerleyton church self-effacingly into a true
Suffolk village church. That was in 1854. At the same time they
were busy converting the half-Elizabethan, half-Queen-Anne
mansion of Somerleyton into a super-Elizabethan wonder, and 62b
Somerleyton village into a second Blaise Hamlet, all oldy-worldy
and thatched and cosy. In the very same years *Sir Charles Barry*
did a country-house job on the same scale and with a similar
profusion of means, the conversion of Paine's Shrubland Park, 64a
already much enlarged by *Gandy-Deering* in 1830–2, into an
Italian super-villa. One may be amused by lodges with their
self-consciously picturesque asymmetry in accordance with what

the pattern-books told the English of Italian villas, and one may
remain unmoved by the house, but the gardens are superb by any
standard, extremely spacious, lavish in their layout, appreciative
of the possibilities of the site, and again adorned by Italian
pavilions. Ipswich meanwhile, where the Assembly Room of
1821 had still been quietly classical and the Temperance Hall of
62a 1840 a Greek Doric temple of sorts, with its Custom House of
1844 by *J. M. Clark* also turned monumental Italianate. The
detail is a little coarse and showy, but the composition unquestion-
ably does justice to the building's prominent position by the
Orwell. Six years later *Fleury* at the Ipswich School went whole-
heartedly if more dignifiedly Elizabethan, like *John Thomas* at
Somerleyton. His patron Peto was as catholic as the Ipswich
patrons. At Lowestoft, which he developed into an up-to-date
seaside resort in the fifties, he went rather gloomily Italianate.
The preceding harbour buildings had been more functional, as are
the warehouses of the forties by the Custom House at Ipswich.*

The VICTORIAN MONUMENTS in churches reflect the same
changes. What was a growing craving for the grand, heavy, and
ornate in architecture is paralleled by the growth of sentimentality
in monuments. Both tendencies illustrate the gradual disappearance of Georgian restraint and discipline. At the beginning we
still see such dignified works as *Sir Richard Westmacott*'s at
Great Finborough († 1833) and Saxmundham († 1838) or *John
Gibson* of Rome's Dudley North of 1833 at Little Glemham, a
monumental figure seated in a monumental chair. The Lady
Rendlesham Monument by *Costoli* of Florence – she died in 1840 –
stands just on the brink of Victorian naturalism and sentimentality, and Lord Rendlesham's monument by *Hopper* – date of
death 1832 – is Gothic. *Thomas Thurlow* of Saxmundham (1819-
99), who had many commissions between 1850 and 1872, can be
Gothic as well as classical. *John Bell*'s Lady Waveney †1871 at
Flixton (near Bungay) with its life-size kneeling figure is definitely
High Victorian.‡

Of HIGH VICTORIAN CHURCHES there are only three or four,
but they represent the two principal trends, the hankering after
correctness and conventionality and the yearning for originality –
both within the bounds of medieval styles. The example of the

---

* And the maltings at Snape (1859 etc.) and the factory at Leiston (1852)
both of an undated but not unimpressive simplicity.

‡ There are also unsigned works; and the Rendlesham Monument † 1814
is far more sentimental and 'Victorian' than anything else before the Lady
Waveney. Unsigned also is the most Grecian monument in Suffolk, the one
of about 1820 at Worlingham.

first is *Scott*'s church at Higham (St Stephen) of 1861 with its handsome vaulted baptistery, the examples of the second a church by *Teulon*, Hopton of 1866, with the weirdest crossing tower, and two churches by that arch-rogue *E. B. Lamb*, at Leiston 21 of 1853 – an almost indescribable riot – and at Braiseworth of 1857. Here Lamb is neo-Norman, one of several architects who took an interest in Norman in the 1840s and 1850s (Nowton 1843, Stoven 1849, Wissington 1853, Flixton (near Bungay) 1856, the latter by *Salvin*).

For HIGH VICTORIAN HOUSES only one can be pointed to in Suffolk, but that one is enough: Elveden, built for the Maharajah 63 Duleep Singh in 1863–70. The architect was *John Norton*, more at home with large Gothic mansions, but here – after special studies in India – quite capable of combining in Indian terms the ideals of correctness and unashamed display. The result is overwhelming. In 1899–1903 *William Young* added much, and in an indifferent Italian by then gone decidedly Baroque. The same architect enlarged equally sweepingly the Georgian house of Culford. The style is feebler.

The LATE VICTORIAN phase is not at its best in monumental buildings. Its patron saints are William Morris and Norman Shaw, and so its favourite scale is intimate. By *Morris & Co.* Suffolk has only some stained glass at Hopton. It is of *c.* 1881 and very fine. Shaw's erstwhile partner *Eden Nesfield* built the lodges of Bradfield House, Bradfield Combust, *E. S. Prior*, a pupil of Shaw and disciple of William Morris's gospel, the eminently characteristic lychgate at Brantham, *Leonard Stokes*, one of the best and most original architects of the end of the century, the small Roman Catholic church at Sudbury (1893), and *Caröe*, a younger follower of the ideals of the Arts and Crafts, the sumptuous church at Elveden (1904–6).

The last paragraph of this introduction must, of course, be dedicated to the TWENTIETH CENTURY. But for the C20 in Suffolk one can almost be silent. The Royal Hospital School at 64b Holbrook of 1925–33 by *Buckland & Haywood* is, it is true, as spaciously planned a major building as any in the neo-Wren-neo-Georgian style. But of originality, of a feeling that a completely new style in architecture was stirring, there is none. To see it in action in this quiet, uneventful, unindustrial county one has to go to buildings – and there are few of them – which belong literally to the last two or three years: the new classrooms at Woolverstone School, built by the Architect's Department of the LCC, the beginnings of Lord Rothschild's new Rushbrooke

Village by *R. Llewelyn-Davies*, small private houses at Oulton by *Tayler & Green* and *J. & S. Reid* and at Nacton by *D. E. Harding*, and the research buildings of Fison's at Levington, which is followed, at the time of writing,* by a tall office building in Princes Street Ipswich, both by *Birkin Haward*. This is, to date, the only large and more prominent example of the C20 style in Suffolk. In fine art the only major work in the C20 style is *Henry Moore*'s beautiful Madonna of 1945–9 in Claydon church.

This ends a survey which has taken up much space and called for much patience. If readers are not tired yet, and if the author's conviction that Suffolk is full of delights and of temptation for study has proved infectious, then these last two pages will fulfil their purpose, pages dedicated to FURTHER READING.

The best general introduction to the county is the new edition of the *Little Guide*, originally written by W. A. Dutt, but largely re-done by P. G. M. Dickinson (here abbreviated L G). This came out in 1957. In addition W. Addison's *Suffolk*, London 1950, makes good reading as regards landscape as well as history. The Suffolk volume by W. A. Dutt of the old *Cambridge County Geography*, Cambridge 1909, is also still useful. So are H. R. Barker's *West Suffolk*, 1907, and *East Suffolk*, 1908–9. The county architectural magazine, the *Proceedings of the Suffolk Institute of Archaeology and Natural History* (*P.S.I.A.*), is of course indispensable.

For the archaeology of the county the first two volumes of the *Victoria County History* are now much out of date, although the section on the Roman period has useful information on early discoveries. However, R. Rainbird Clarke's *East Anglia*, 1960, in the 'Ancient Peoples and Places' series not only offers the most up-to-date summary of early Suffolk down to the later medieval period, but also has an excellent bibliography.

For church architecture H. Munro Cautley: *Suffolk Churches*, 3rd ed., London 1954, already duly praised and characterized (also in its limitations) in the Foreword, has superseded the two volumes by T. H. Bryant in the *County Churches* series (1912). Munro Cautley, who died in 1959 aged eighty-three, was without any doubt the greatest connoisseur of Suffolk, and indeed East Anglian, churches. For Perpendicular churches in particular a London thesis must be mentioned: C. G. Ough: *East Anglian Church Architecture of the fourteenth and fifteenth centuries with special reference to the churches of the Stour Valley*, London University 1939 (in typescript).

* I.e., in 1961. Cf. the 1974 postscript to the introduction (p. 63).

Concerning church furnishings, Suffolk screens and their paintings have been dealt with fully by W. W. Lillie in the *P.S.I.A.*, vols. 20–2, 1928–36, church plate in vols. 8 and 9, 1894–7. On church monuments in general there are of course the books by F. H. Crossley for the Middle Ages and by Mrs Esdaile for the centuries after the Reformation, just as there is for Stuart and Georgian church architecture Mr Whiffen's book. But such general literature cannot be listed here, or else this bibliography would never end.

For Suffolk houses the situation is more difficult. Many have been 'done' by *Country Life*, and for those all is well. For the others one has to search: they may be contained in A. Suckling's admirable *The History and Antiquities of the County of Suffolk*, 2 vols., 1846–8, but that book covers only four Hundreds. Or an illustration may be in H. Davy: *Views of the Seats of Noblemen and Gentlemen in Suffolk*, Southwold 1827.* Or useful references may be in W. A. Coppinger: *The Manors of Suffolk*, 7 vols., 1905–11. The Ipswich library has 6 vols. of cuttings from articles by E. Farrer (*Some Old Houses in Suffolk*). Good essays on various aspects of secular architecture are contained in *Memorials of Old Suffolk* (ed. V. B. Redstone), London 1908, and Basil Oliver's *Old Houses and Village Buildings in East Anglia*, London 1912, will be read with benefit too. On individual places finally I would recommend *Bury St Edmunds* by M. D. Lobel, 1935, *Historic Clare* by P. G. M. Dickinson, 1952, *Ipswich* by L. J. Redstone, 1949, and *Sudbury* by C. G. Grimwood and S. A. Kay, 1952.

POSTSCRIPT TO THE INTRODUCTION (1974)

Since 1961 fortunately few disappearances have called for mention in this second edition. Among them the capital loss is Rushbrooke Hall of *c.* 1550, a rare date for a house of its size. Its demolition (though it was derelict) is a tragedy. Haughley Park of *c.* 1620 (now rebuilt) and the late C18 Hobland Hall, Hopton, have been the victims of fire, and Brome Hall, late C19 Tudor, has been demolished. At Lowestoft C19 and later seaside development losses include the first showpiece, opened in 1849, the Royal Hotel by *John Thomas*, and the Empire Hotel by *Isaacs & Florence*, 1901. The Civic Centre redevelopment at Ipswich (*see* below) did not entail the removal of anything considered

* Davy's notebooks are in the British Museum, MSS. Add. 19081–109. In the British Museum also is manuscript material on Suffolk churches: Add. 32429–29.

worthy of mention in the first edition of this book, but piecemeal demolitions in the town include timber-framed houses, especially in the area near the quay; Gippeswyk Hall, a brick house of *c*. 1600; the Crown Works (originally the Temperance Hall), an ambitious Grecian effort of 1840; and the East Anglian Daily Times building of 1887 in Carr Street, with much scrolly decoration, probably by *T. W. Cotman*. In a bad way at the time of writing but still capable of being saved is the spectacular, orangery-like railway station of 1848 at Newmarket, but already vanished there are some pretty weatherboarded cottages in Market Street.

On the credit side, there have been some imaginative conversions: at Bury, the old town hall and corn exchange now incorporate shops, and the former also an art gallery; at Ipswich, the corn exchange is to be converted (by *Johns, Slater & Haward*, on whom more later) into a multi-purpose entertainment centre; the corn exchange at Sudbury now houses a branch library; and, perhaps the best known and most striking example, the maltings at Snape have been made into a concert hall for the Aldeburgh Festival (the work was done by *Derek Sugden* of *Arup Associates*). Steps have also been taken to conserve the famous Old Wool Hall and the Swan Hotel at Lavenham.

Discoveries since the first edition (many of them due to welcome contributions by readers) include the remains of a circular, possibly Saxon flint building in the churchyard at Little Whelnetham; C14 and C16 wall paintings of high quality at Brent Eleigh church, and wall paintings also at Cadge's House, Long Melford; of medieval halls, one of the late C13 at Purton Green Farm, Stansfield, one of the early C14 at Edgar's Farm, Combs Lane, Stowmarket, and others in the range of domestic buildings of the C14 priests' college at Wingfield and at Campsea Ash. Buildings of later centuries that have been drawn to our attention are Stanstead Hall of *c*. 1620, Wattisham Castle, a large Gothick farmhouse of *c*. 1770, all crenellated, and *George J. Skipper*'s Elizabethan Mancroft Towers, Oulton, of 1898–1900.

Discoveries of a different kind include two significant changes in attribution owing to recent research: at Hengrave Hall most of the decorative masonry from 1536, including the showpiece bay window, is now thought to be by *William Ponyard* and not by *John Sparke*, who seems to have stopped work in 1527; and Great Saxham Hall, previously given to *Adam*, may instead be by an amateur, the owner of the house, *Hutchison Mure*.

Finally new building. The most far-reaching developments

are of course at the Expanding Towns, by the G.L.C., on the largest scale at Haverhill, but also at Mildenhall (planned for 1,400 houses and ancillary buildings), Long Melford (728 houses and 6 factories), and Brandon (576 houses and 12 factories). There are also some interesting buildings of the sixties by *Peter Barefoot* (*see* index), and by *Johns, Slater & Haward*: the striking Sangamo Factory at Felixstowe, 1962–4, and at Ipswich the fire station, additions to the Civic College, the East Anglian Daily Times building, the excellent Fison's offices, and a contribution to the new Civic Centre. The latter, designed by *Vine & Vine*, involved the construction of a completely new dual-carriage road. Immediately to its s is the Greyfriars development, tower blocks and a shopping precinct by *Edward Skipper & Associates*. Other individual good new buildings in the county include the oddly genteel prison at Blundeston, 1962–3 by the *Ministry of Public Works Architect's Department*; old people's houses at Lowestoft by those sensitive architects *Tayler & Green*, 1965; the Forestry Commission Redevelopment at Santon Downham, nicely in keeping with its well-timbered surroundings, by *Kenneth Wood*, 1967; and at Bury St Edmunds the new block of the Shire Hall by *McMorran & Whitby*, 1968 (and also the additions to the cathedral begun in 1960 by *S. E. Dykes Bower*).

A NOTE ON THE DEVELOPMENT OF TIMBER ROOFS

BY J. T. SMITH

Many Suffolk roofs are of rafter- or collar-purlin type, that is to say the weight and thrust of the roof is spread evenly along the side walls rather than being concentrated at a few points. In the oldest houses such roofs are commonly supported by an aisled timber structure, e.g. Edgar's Farm, Stowmarket (*see* p. 446). An early development is to free the floor-space of arcade-posts by, in effect, putting an aisled roof with short posts upon tie-beams and strengthening the latter with arch-braces; Wingfield College (p. 492) is one example, and several more have lately been discovered by Mr David Penrose. The appearance of heaviness created by this arrangement was alleviated by, in effect, cutting away the middle part of the tie-beam between the posts it supported and thereby producing a hammerbeam roof. How far development actually proceeded on these lines and how far the hammerbeam roof arose directly from the desire to clear halls and large kitchens such as that of Kersey Priory of their encumbering posts is difficult to tell, but the aesthetic appeal of the type must always have been as apparent as its usefulness.

By the c15 rafter roofs began to be abandoned in East Anglia in favour of principal rafters and purlins, a system which found favour first in churches where thrust-resistant walls of stone enabled the desire for a lofty, impressive interior to be met more readily than in timber halls. To provide an adequate seating for the foot of the principal rafter a horizontal timber had to be incorporated between it and the wall-plate; extended inwards this timber is called a hammerbeam, and the hammer-posts it carries give a little support to the principal rafter, but in fact the structural significance of these two members has changed and declined; what began as a roof with a middle span flanked by lean-to roofs has become a single unified span; if the walls were strong enough the principal rafters needed no other support. A comparable but different spatial effect was obtained at much the same period by tenoning the horizontal timber into an arch-brace which is itself tenoned top and bottom into the principal rafter and wall-post. Now the need for wall-posts is equally apparent in developed hammerbeam roofs, where they provide a housing for the arch-braces below the hammerbeams, so that in this type two members, arch-brace and hammerbeam, do exactly the same work as one in the arch-braced type of roof. The early development of the hammerbeam roof away from its original structural form and function into something very like an arch-braced roof in essentials makes the old distinction between true and false hammerbeams otiose, for in all such roofs hammer-beams and hammer-posts were provided for aesthetic effect rather than as a unique solution to a structural problem.

It follows that there was no structural difficulty in alternating arch-braced and hammerbeam trusses, and that the reason why hammerbeam and tie-beam trusses were sometimes alternated is probably that the builder feared for the stability of his roof without the latter. Perhaps c15 Suffolk church roofs should be considered primarily in terms of the aesthetic effects their designers strove after, whether the soaring austerity of the arch-braced type or the richer, more complex effects achieved by hammerbeams. And the crown of them all, Needham Market, with its aisled structure suspended high above the floor, shows a remarkable reversion to the principles underlying the first generation of hammerbeam roofs.

For further reading, see R. A. Cordingley, 'British Historical Roof-Types and their Members: A Classification', *Trans.*

Ancient Monuments Soc., N.S. IX (1961), 73–118; J. M. Fletcher and P. S. Spokes, 'The Origin and Development of Crown-post Roofs', *Medieval Archaeology*, VIII (1964), 152–83; F. E. Howard, 'On the Construction of Medieval Roofs', *Archaeol. Journal*, LXXI (1914), 293–352; J. T. Smith, 'Medieval Roofs: A Classification', *Archaeol. Journal*, CXV (1958), 111–49, 'The Reliability of Typological Dating of Medieval English Roofs', in R. Berger (ed.), *Scientific Methods in Medieval Archaeology*, and 'Timber-framed Building in England, its Development and Regional Differences', *Archaeol. Journal*, CXX (1965), 133–58.

SUFFOLK

*

ABBAS HALL

1¾ m. ESE of Sudbury

The exterior Elizabethan; inside, the remains of a possibly late
C13 aisled hall: two massive oak posts with moulded capitals
and straight braces to the roof construction, and two arcades
of the screens passage (DOE).

ABBEY FARMHOUSE *see* HOXNE

ACTON

8040

ALL SAINTS. S aisle and S chapel of *c.* 1300 (Y-tracery). W tower
base of *c.* 1300. The rest of the tower 1913–23. N doorway and
N chapel Dec. Arcades with piers with four polygonal shafts,
those to nave and aisles broader and stronger and without
capitals. Between the chancel and the N chapel big Dec
MONUMENT. Tomb-chest; on top a slab formerly with a
foliated cross; cusped arch, and ogee gable. – COMMUNION
RAIL. Late C17. – BENCH ENDS with poppy-heads, one of
them with a pair of moorhens. – BRASSES. The brass to Sir
Robert de Bures † 1302* is one of the oldest and one of the
finest in England. The figure is 6 ft 6 in. tall. He wears chain-
mail, over his head as well, no helmet, and a long surcoat. His
legs are crossed and the feet are on a lion. His hands are in
prayer. Exquisite engraving. – Alyce de Bryan, *c.* 1435. Under
a triple canopy. The figure is 4 ft 9 in. long. – Henry Bures
† 1528. Knight in armour, 3 ft figure. – MONUMENT. In the
SE chapel the monument to Robert Jennens †1725, adjutant of 38b
the Duke of Marlborough. It was put up, and the chapel built
for it, by Jennens's widow. Standing wall-monument.
Reredos background with fluted pilasters. He lies comfortably
semi-reclining on a mattress. His elbow rests on a pillow and
his head is propped up by his hand. He looks towards his wife,
who is seated by his feet. Minute details of the dress very

* Or 1331, although the brass may have been engraved *c.* 1320 (see J. Page-
Phillips, *Macklin's Monumental Brasses* (1969), p. 25).

ROBERTVS · DE · BVRS

Acton, brass to Sir Robert de Bures, *c.* 1320(?)

competently carved. Emotionally the figures are perhaps less convincing.

ACTON PLACE. Robert Jennens had built himself a very large mansion here. The size can be gauged from the only remaining fragment, a servants' wing, nine bays wide, with a central three-bay pediment. Red brick, two-storeyed, hipped roof. The centre of the house, according to a painting of the C18, 58a was eleven bays wide and four storeys high and had a three-bay pediment and a hipped roof. It was connected with the wings by one-storeyed quadrant arcades. It was pulled down in 1825.

AKENHAM 1040

ST MARY. Unbuttressed s porch tower. Short attached s aisle of early C16 brick. One Norman window in the N wall. – FONT. Octagonal, with pretty cusped tracery patterns on bowl and stem. – PLATE. Cup and Paten 1751.

RISE HALL, near the church. Handsome Late Georgian house of red brick. Two storeys, three bays. Wide doorway with Roman Doric pilasters, a metope frieze, and a straight top.

ALDEBURGH 4050

ST PETER AND ST PAUL. On a hill outside the old town. Quite large, but neither as large nor as impressive as the chain of seaboard churches further N starting with Blythburgh and Walberswick. C14 W tower with a stair-turret reaching higher than the tower. Flushwork-panelled buttresses. The rest of the church is mostly of the C16. Dates of 1525–9 refer to nave, N aisle and N chapel, of 1534–5 to S aisle and S chapel, of 1539 to the S porch, and of 1545 to the chancel. Six-bay aisles and chapels, impressive E end with a five-light chancel window and four-light chapel windows. The aisle S and N windows of three lights. The S buttresses simply panelled. The windows mostly renewed. The church in the early C19, that is at the time of Crabbe's *The Borough*, was in decay, and the windows especially. The distinguishing feature of the church is the S porch, unusually long, with entrances from S, W, and E. Flushwork stars, shields, etc., in the base. In the front much brick. The piers of the arcade have four big shafts and four spurs in the diagonals. The chapels are only one bay long. The details are the same. Spacious interior. Mr Blythe draws attention to the fact that ship auctions were held in the church, and that as late as 1573 the Earl of Leicester's men, that is his troupe of actors, played in it. The roof is a c20 replica of the original roof. – FONT. No original stem. Against the bowl four lions and four angels with shields. – PULPIT. Big and richly carved. Oblong panels with arabesques, above them the familiar blank arches with decorated pilasters, arches, and spandrels. Above them oblong panels with dolphins etc. The pulpit was made by *Charles Warne* in 1632, after the congregation had sent him to Kelsale in 1631 'to see a pulpit'. – READER'S DESK. Probably of the same time but not with exactly the same motifs. – SCREEN. Remains of the dado re-used in the w gallery. This gallery was set up in 1735. – BENCHES. Some with traceried ends, poppy-heads, and formerly animals on the arms (only one left). – PLATE. Elizabethan Cup; Paten on foot of 1727; Cup, Paten, and Flagon 1742. – MONUMENTS. Brass of a Civilian and wife. Only the headless figure of the man remains, 1 ft 7 in. long. The approximate date is 1520. – Several Elizabethan brasses. – Lady Henrietta Vernon † 1786. Large standing monument, unsigned (which is odd). Sarcophagus amply draped. On it over-life-size female figure by an urn. An angel floating above her to the r. Obelisk background. – Crabbe Memorial, N chapel, 1847 by *Thurlow*. – Mrs Louisa Garrett †1903, tablet with allegorical female figures. By *E. M. Rope.* – War Memorial (Dying Soldier) by *Gilbert Bayes*.

PERAMBULATION. Aldeburgh is a town which stretches along the sea as far as it can. It has only 2,700 inhabitants, but the length is nearly a mile. The High Street runs s from Victoria Street, the rising street along which the church and churchyard lie. To its w the cliff rises, and THE TERRACE is the street serving the well-to-do houses up there. To the E of the High Street one more street, on and off, and then the sea front. A perambulation will start at the MARKET CROSS PLACE, where, in the Regency and near-Regency surroundings which are the charm of Aldeburgh, the MOOT HALL stands as incongruously as if it were an exhibit. It must once have been in a little town centre, before the sea pushed its relative position back. It is of *c.* 1520–40, timber-framed, with brick nogging on the upper floor which was inserted in 1654. The original timber arches on the ground floor are a reminder of the fact that the ground floor was an open market. Cambered tie-beam roof upstairs, with clasped purlins (J. T. Smith). At the s end two decorated circular chimneys of typical c16 design.* In now walking along the front, first to the N then to the S, it is hard to single

* REGALIA. Jacobean Mace; Mace of 1648.

out individual houses, for none are very distinguished; but in the sum total they make a pretty picture and seem really unselfconscious. To the W of the Moot Hall a nice three-bay house with a first-floor iron balcony, then to the N the WHITE LION HOTEL with a castellated r. range. After that alas a drab terrace of fourteen bays in yellow and red brick, rather in the style of the Peto efforts at Lowestoft. They belong to the 1870s. The end here is SUNDIAL HOUSE by *Oliver Hill*, *c*. 1925, a bit of an extravaganza, with an odd plan, only one floor, arched windows, high roof. It points with an edge like a ship's prow to the sea. To the S of the Moot Hall one can choose the sea front or the High Street. Along the sea front first some early C20 groups, CRAG HOUSE (1915) and BEACH HOUSE (1910–14) and THE REST (1913), then a variety of cottages, including a tiny one which stands all on its own and is called Fantasia. At the S end view towards the windmill and the Martello Tower. The WINDMILL is another fantasia with the group of houses and the various roofs around it. They are by *R. A. Briggs* and were illustrated in 1903.

MARTELLO TOWER, Slaughden. The Martello Towers were built in 1810–12 by the Royal Engineers as a defence against a Napoleonic invasion. They were designed by *Col. Twiss* and *Capt. Ford*. The name comes from a Torre della Martella in Corsica which impressed the English in the campaign of 1794. The Slaughden Martello Tower is exceptional – larger than the rest of the chain.

The HIGH STREET is pleasant to walk along, although here also no house needs very special mention. One will notice the occasional Georgian doorways (e.g. No. 215 and, the prettiest of them all, No. 229). The principal attraction is the way the street widens at one moment and receives Crabbe Street, which had run parallel between the sea front and High Street. In the centre of this widened space is on the E side the EAST SUF-FOLK HOTEL, with a Tuscan porch carrying a preposterously heavy semicircular hood. Opposite the UNION CHAPEL of 1822 with three arched openings each on two floors. (ELIZA-BETH COURT, old people's housing, is by *Peter Barefoot*, 1964–5.)

The most distinguished houses are on the upper level, that is the top of the cliff. Unfortunately the most promising are almost completely altered. They are THELUSSON LODGE and ADAIR LODGE, the one formerly the Big Casino and in the early C19 a summer residence of the Marquess of Salisbury, the other the Little Casino, built in the C18 and enlarged in 1823. Now they are all heavily romantic Late Victorian brick. Quietly Georgian and decidedly wealthy HALL LODGE, also in The Terrace, CRESPIGNY HOUSE in Hartington Road, whose back still has pilasters in two orders and a pediment, and WYNDHAM HOUSE in Victoria Street, close to the N end of The Terrace.

Further out a number of prosperous and secure looking C20 houses, e.g. SANDHILL in Prior's Hill Road, ¼ m. W of The Terrace, 1925 by *Oliver Hill* (nice symmetrical neo-Georgian with hipped roof), and GORSEHILL, out to the N, neo-Georgian, 1928 by *Horace Field*.

ALDERTON

3040

ST ANDREW. Ruinous W tower. Above the W doorway is a frieze of arched panelling in flushwork. Good N porch in poor condition. Flushwork base with shields, quatrefoils, crowned Ms, etc., flushwork-panelled front. In the spandrels of the entrance a man with a club and a dragon. The nave is Dec, quite big and wide, with tall three-light windows with reticulated tracery.* In the E jamb of the SE window a tall niche with a little vault. Chancel of 1862. – PLATE. Paten 1715; Chalice and Paten 1733.

(ALDERTON HALL. In a farm building remains of C15 stone arches and a buttressed angle. DOE)

THE CEDARS, I m. N. Mid-Georgian, of five bays and two and a half storeys, red brick. Arched doorway with broken pediment. The pilasters fluted only in bands. A fine Venetian window over.

MARTELLO TOWERS. Three, 1½ m. NE, 1¼ m. ENE, and 1¼ m. ESE. Built 1810–12; cf. Aldeburgh, p. 73.

WINDMILL, to the E. A smock-mill, derelict.

ALDHAM

0040

ST MARY. Circular flint tower. Nave and chancel flint. The windows in the style of *c.* 1300. – BENCH ENDS with poppyheads. – LECTERN. Oak, the base original. – (SCULPTURE. Anglo-Saxon fragments with interlace pattern in the jamb of a S window in the nave. LG) – PLATE. Paten 1735; Cup and Cover 1785.

* In an engraving of 1785 the S windows look as if they had no reticulated tracery. But two N windows in the church look reliable.

ALDRINGHAM

4060

St Andrew. Nave and chancel in one; bellcote. Mostly rebuilt after 1842. – FONT. An uncommonly fine example of the East Anglian type. Octagonal. Four lions against the stem. Against the bowl the four Signs of the Evangelists and four angels filling their panels and rising out of crinkly clouds. They hold shields with books and roses.

Baptist Church, on the Common. 1915 by *Cecil Lay*. Neo-Georgian, seven bays wide with giant pilasters, a central entrance, and arched windows.

Barrows. A group behind the village inn, much overgrown, but otherwise in good condition; another one cut into by a golf bunker by the railway N of the road to Thorpeness and another in a copse s of the road. All are presumably of Bronze Age date.

ALL SAINTS SOUTH ELMHAM *see* SOUTH ELMHAM ALL SAINTS

ALNESBOURN PRIORY

1040

2½ m. SE of Ipswich

To the house called Priory Farm belongs a BARN, and the septaria walling of this is supposed to have been part of the Augustinian priory which was founded about 1200.

ALPHETON

8050

St Peter and St Paul. Nave and chancel, and quite a substantial Perp w tower. Pretty s doorway with fleuron decoration; Dec SEDILIA and PISCINA composition damaged by a later window. The piscina is in the angle of the window. Niches l. and r. of the chancel arch, the one to the N re-fixed higher up in the C19. – STALL. The back made up of two misericords. – PULPIT. Jacobean. – SCREEN. Only the dado. – BENCHES. Some ends with poppy-heads. – PAINTING. Late C14 St Christopher, on the N wall; dim.

AMPTON

8070

St Peter. Nave and chancel and w tower. Much restored by *Teulon* about 1848. The only interesting part is the N chantry chapel, built, according to its inscription, as a Capella Perpetue Cantarie Johis Coket. The foundation was granted in 1479. Four-centred arch from the church with cresting over. The arch is panelled inside. Nice boarded chancel roof with painted bosses, etc., re-discovered in 1889. – COMMUNION RAIL. Late C18. – PLATE. Paten 1631; Cup 1637; Flagon 1639; Almsdish 1714. – MONUMENTS. Brasses probably of Cokets: kneeling Civilian and Wife, c. 1480 (18 in.); Lady of c. 1480 (17 in.); Lady c. 1490 (12 in.; palimpsest of portion of a lady of c. 1460); two Sons (only 6 in.) c. 1490. All nave floor, except the Lady of c. 1490. This brass is on the N wall of the nave. – William Whettell † 1628 by *Nicholas Stone*. Rather flatly modelled frontal bust in an arched niche. Good. – Sir Henry Calthorpe, by *John and Matthias Christmas*, 1638. Two frontal demi-figures holding hands; in a circular niche. Small figures of children in the 'predella' below. Two columns support an open segmental pediment. – Dorothy Calthorpe † 1693. Kneeling figure in an arched niche, a conservative motif. – James Calthorpe † 1784. Oval medallion with head in profile, before an obelisk. Attributed to *Bacon* in *Suff. Arch. Soc.* vol. I, but not signed.

AMPTON HALL. Burnt down in 1885 and rebuilt in a restrained Jacobean style by *Balfour & Turner* in 1885–9. To the old Hall belong the fine wrought-iron GATES in the wall towards the street, and also the good rusticated archway with pediment and inscription, probably of c. 1700.

S of the church the SCHOOL of 1705, N of the church the ALMSHOUSES of 1693.

ANGEL HILL *see* EARL STONHAM

ASH ABBEY *see* CAMPSEA ASH

ASHBOCKING

ALL SAINTS. The chancel is of the late C13. The N and S windows are of two lights and have simple plate tracery (a trefoil in a circle), the E window is of three cusped stepped lights and has trefoils, also in plate tracery, in the spandrels. The nave is Dec and has inside a fine big tomb recess with a large cusped ogee arch, the cusps ending in heads. Crocketed top with finials, buttress shafts l. and r. Among the ornamental motifs there is ballflower. Good, solid, broad-chested W tower of early C16 brick with blue brick diapering in its lower part. The brick S porch is probably not original. – FONT. Norman bowl, of cauldron shape with big angle spurs or clasps. – FONT COVER. Simple; Perp. – BENCHES. Some Perp, with poppy-heads, the majority simple C17, straight-topped ends, with thin buttresses up each end. – COMMUNION RAIL. Later C17. – PLATE. Elizabethan Cup; Flagon 1705; Paten c. 1705; Paten 1735. – BRASSES. Edmund Bockinge † 1585 and family.

(ASHBOCKING HALL. C16. Timber-framed. Panelled room with Corinthian pilasters. Part of a panelled plaster ceiling with thin ribs forming curved-sided stars. DOE)

(WALNUT TREE FARMHOUSE. C16. A kingpost truss is preserved. DOE)

Two groups of medieval buildings have been found in the field bordering the road leading to Poplar Farm. One banked enclosure c. 140 by 120 ft contained medieval sherds, another, 200 yds E, contained floors, walls, and traces of timber and plastering from a number of buildings round a central court. Small finds included pottery of early medieval date. Between the two enclosures is a group of buildings occupied from the C1 B.C. native Iron Age into the Roman period; general scatters of Roman sherds occur over the area.

ASHBY 4090

ST MARY. Round tower, below Norman, above probably C16. The upper parts are made octagonal by brick angles. Brick lancet windows and battlements. Nave and chancel thatched, both apparently C13 (lancet windows), probably late (see the PISCINA). – FONT. Square, of Purbeck marble, C12 or C13, the usual flat blank arches almost completely rubbed off. Central support and, unexpectedly, four bulbous wooden supports in addition. – PLATE. Cup of 1568.

ASH FARMHOUSE see MUTFORD

ASHFIELD 2060

ST MARY. 1853. Nave and chancel. Red brick and blue chequer. Weatherboarded bell-turret. – PLATE. Elizabethan Cup; Paten probably Elizabethan.

ST PETER, Thorpe. Round tower, Norman, with later top and a fragment of nave wall. Now fractured and standing at the top of a rock garden.

(CROSS. Mr Dickinson draws attention to a fine cross at Ashfield.)

ASPALL 1060

ST MARY OF GRACE. W tower, nave and chancel. Wooden porch. Of no special interest. – FONT. Octagonal. Four squat lions against the stem; three lions, four flowers, and an angel against the bowl. All re-tooled. – STALLS. In the fronts fragments of the rood screen. – PLATE. Cup and Paten 1634; Almsdish 1794.

ASPALL HALL. A Jacobean house with a Queen Anne front. The front is of red brick chequered with dark blue headers, eleven bays long and two-storeyed, with a pedimented three-bay centre. Doorway with pediment on brackets. A Venetian window above it. Two early C19 porches to replace the former doorway. Inside, the Jacobean past is represented by the position of the hall – the Queen Anne doorway is not in the middle of the hall, but one bay further S – by the former kitchen fireplace, and by one splendid plaster ceiling with frieze, decorated beams, and ribbed panels. Opposite the house the CYDER HOUSE, C16 in structure but converted to its present use in 1728 when C. B. Chevallier brought a cider press over from Normandy to make immigration more tolerable. The original granite and timber presses are still in use.

9030

ASSINGTON

ST EDMUND. Close to the Hall, and once handsome in the contrast of its flint colour to the brick of the Hall. Chancel rebuilt c. 1830. Restored and W tower rebuilt in 1863. What survives of original work is all Perp, including the four-bay arcade. – SOUTH DOOR. A splendid Perp piece with tracery and a border of foliage trails. – PLATE. Set of 1843–4. – MONUMENTS. Brass to a Knight and Lady, c. 1500 (nave floor). – Robert Gurdon † 1577 and wife, and John Gurdon † 1623 and wife. Double monument of c. 1625 with two pairs of the usual kneeling figures facing one another across a prayer-desk. Children in the 'predella'. – Brampton Gurdon, dated 1648. His demi-figure and those of his two wives; represented frontally. He is flanked by columns. Top with a handsome pedimental arrangement. – John Gurdon † 1758 and his wife † 1710. The tablet must be nearer her death than his. Good cartouche and a cherub's head below. – Philip Gurdon † 1817 and wife. Tablet by the younger *Bacon*.

ASSINGTON HALL. Burnt down in 1957. Only ruins of the porch and part of a gable-end remain.

2070

ATHELINGTON

ST PETER. Small; nave and chancel in one. The chancel roof is distinguished inside by fleurons on the wall-plate. Truncated w tower with repaired brick quoins and bell-openings and a pyramid roof. – FONT. Octagonal with tracery patterns in squares, a cusped saltire cross, quatrefoils, a wheel of three mouchettes, etc. – BENCHES. With traceried ends, poppyheads and, to their l. and r., small figures facing the gateway and also small heads. – PLATE. Cup and two Patens 1706; Flagon 1708.

ATHELINGTON HALL. Early C17. The gable-end with two overhangs on decorated beams.

BABERGH HALL see GREAT WALDINGFIELD

BABWELL see BURY ST EDMUNDS, p. 153

BACKS GREEN see ILKETSHALL ST ANDREW

BACTON

0060

ST MARY. Dec w tower. The bell-openings have Y-tracery and also flowing tracery, which is unusual for towers. Early C16 stair-turret of brick. s aisle and s porch Perp. Inscription on the s aisle commemorating Robert Goche and his wife, and James Hobart, his wife, and his parents. Cautley points out that Sir James Hobart was Attorney-General under Henry VII. N aisle also Perp. Clerestory with doubled windows. The arches with intermittent radially placed bricks. The windows are of two lights with panel tracery. A variety of flushwork emblems between them. The arcade is of five bays and has octagonal piers and double-chamfered arches. Nave roof with double hammerbeams, the figures sawn off. Big square flowers on the wall-plates. Fine cresting on the purlins. Colouring over the rood-bays. The aisle roofs also have decorated wall-plates. The chancel roof is cambered and has arched braces. The E bays have coloured stylized symmetrical leaves or palmettes. The roofs were restored in 1860 and 1864 by *Butterfield*. – FONT. Octagonal. Against the stem two tiers of shields and square flowers. Against the bowl angels with shields, a shield, and square flowers. – BENCHES. Two, with carved backs, poppyheads, and on the arms three animals and one kneeling figure. – SCREEN. With one-light divisions, ogee arches, and close panel tracery above them. Two parts under the tower arch. – WALL PAINTING. Dim Doom over the chancel arch. – STAINED GLASS. E window *c.* 1920 by *Morris & Co.*, partly still to the design of *Burne-Jones*. – PLATE. Elizabethan Cup; Paten 1682; Almsdish 1729; Flagon 1756. – MONUMENTS. In the

nave good tablets with cartouches: George Pretyman †1732;
his widow †1738.

MANOR HOUSE FARM. Mr Pretyman's fine brick mansion,
built about 1715–20. Two storeys, red brick with chequer of
dark blue headers. Five-bay centre and two-bay slightly-
projecting wings. Hipped roof. Doorway with open segmental
pediment on carved brackets. Three-bay top pediment with
coat of arms and lively garlands. Staircase with fine twisted
balusters. The staircase rises in the panelled entrance hall,
facing the main doorway. In the house as an overmantel a
painting of Furness Abbey dated 1720, as another a painting of
the house itself dated 1741.

BADINGHAM

ST JOHN BAPTIST. Unbuttressed w tower with Norman windows quite high up (re-used, suggests Cautley). Y-tracery in
the bell-openings. The Norman w angles of the nave show by
their nook-shafts. Norman nook-shafts also flanking the remarkably wide tower arch. Nave C13, see the tall N and S
lancets. Other nave windows Perp, especially the two-light
early C16 brick windows high up, one N, one S, to light the rood.
Chancel of 1879, apparently with one original early C14 N
window. Perp S porch quite ornate. Shields in stone rendered
in flushwork against the base. The whole front flush-panelled.
The porch was built c. 1482 (*Suff. Arch. Soc.* vol. X, pt. 3).
Inside, just E of the doorway, remains, it seems, of a former
arch. In the N wall of the nave a broad, diagonally-set niche for
an image. The mutilated figure of an angel over. Very good
hammerbeam roof. The hammers cant upward, and so do the
collars. The hammerbeams are longitudinally connected by
arched braces along the wall, and the collar beams carry kingposts. Tracery above the hammers and the collars. The angels
against the ends of the hammers are a renewal of 1900, but the
rich decoration of the wall-plate is original. – FONT. Perp,
octagonal. Step with broad tracery. Against the stem demi-
figures of prophets with scrolls. Against the bowl the Seven
Sacraments and the Baptism of Christ. – PULPIT. Probably
mid-C17. A good, very restrained piece, with back panel and
tester. – SCREEN. The dado now forms part of the stalls. –
PLATE. Elizabethan Cup with a Paten dated 1568. – MONU-
MENTS. Very tall, mostly blocked recess in the chancel N wall,
probably a combined monument and Easter Sepulchre.
Tomb-chest with seven panels, four carrying shields. Top

cresting with shields and stone-carved helmets. L. and r. of the whole monument wall-shafts with broad brackets. The date is probably *c.* 1400. – William Cotton † 1616 and his wife † 1621. Large standing monument with painted figures. Recumbent effigies, he behind and a little higher than she. Two kneeling children in profile below. Columns l. and r. All rather rough.

OKENHILL HALL, 1 m. S. With a stepped gable end dated 1552. Two polygonal angle buttresses with polygonal finials. Two windows with pediments, resting however in a characteristically undecided way on hood-mould stops.

BADLEY

0050

ST MARY. A lonely church, and one left happily unnoticed by the Victorian restorers. W tower unbuttressed, with brick top, and with a huge Perp W window put in later than the tower was built. Nave and chancel. In the chancel an early C13 slit lancet. In the nave a S doorway of the same time. Simple pointed arch with one slight chamfer. Rough wooden S porch. The interior is memorable for its untreated, bleached woodwork – a beautifully pale, silvery tone. Crown-post roof with four-way struts. – FONT. Of Purbeck marble, C13, octagonal, with the customary two flat blank pointed arches on each side. – SCREEN. Only the dado. The tracery tops re-used in a family pew. Their tracery makes it likely that the screen was of the C14. – Two-decker PULPIT. – BENCHES. Rough, with poppy-heads and animals on the arms. – COMMUNION RAIL. Of iron, datable 1830 (NMR). – PLATE. Cup and Cover 1630; Paten 1778. – MONUMENTS. Sir Henry Poley † 1707. Inscription flanked by pilasters. Segmental pediment. – Henrietta Robins † 1728. Outside 'the chancel S wall. Elaborate framing of a sarcophagus. – On the floor of the chancel ledger-stone for Dorothy Poley † 1625. The inscription ought to be read.

BADLEY HALL. Two-thirds of the house was pulled down about 1759. The house is timber-framed, of the C16. It still has some buttress-shafts, brackets, and carved beams. The original plan was E-shaped. (Fine C17 DOVECOTE. P. G. M. Dickinson)

BADMONDESFIELD HALL *see* WICKHAMBROOK

BADWELL ASH

9060

ST MARY. The PISCINA in the S aisle is of *c.* 1300, i.e. has no ogee forms yet. The arcade between nave and aisles with tallish octagonal piers and double-chamfered arches. The chancel is Dec too. The tracery in the two-light windows has the motif of the four-petalled flower. The N nave windows are Perp, tall, of two lights. On the s side at that time the clerestory was built or rebuilt with seven windows as against the four bays below. Roof with alternating hammerbeams and tie-beams on short arched braces. Both rest on wall-posts with small figures. Against the hammerbeams bigger figures. The w tower is Perp too. Flushwork emblems on the base, flushwork panelling on the battlements, and an inscription asking for prayers for John Fincham and his wife. Perp finally the s porch. This has a façade with flushwork panelling all over. In the spandrels of the entrance arch St George and the Dragon. Flushwork emblems on the buttresses; for instance a plough and the blacksmith's tools. One niche above the entrance. – FONT. Octagonal, Dec. Shields on the stem. On the bowl ogee arches carried by heads. Embattled top. – PLATE. Elizabethan Cup and Paten.

HIGH HOUSE, I m. E. Fragment of a large Elizabethan brick house. Projections to W and S with polygonal angle buttresses or turrets. Mullioned and transomed windows, mostly C19, some with pediments. Steeply stepped gables.

(THE WURLIE. Kingpost roof inside. DOE)

BALLINGDON HALL see SUDBURY

9070

BARDWELL

ST PETER AND ST PAUL. The biggest church in this neighbourhood. Tall Perp w tower with spike. Fine, tall Perp s porch with the arms of Sir William Berdewell who died in 1434.* Good flushwork decoration, chequerboard and panelling. Entrance with two orders of fleurons. Three niches around it. Side windows with fine tracery. Lofty nave with tall two-light Dec windows. Chancel of 1553. Excellent hammerbeam roof. Thin arched braces. Arched braces also below the ridge. No collar-beams. Of the angel figures which originally held the roof only four remain, one with the date 1421 on the opened pages of a book. Original colouring, including the charming trails on the rafters. – SCREEN. Four panels of a finely traceried dado. – STAINED GLASS. Three kneeling early C15 figures, the largest no doubt Sir William Berdewell. Also some C15 figures, including a German Pietà. – The chancel windows are by

* A will of 1460 leaves 2s. to the repair of the porch (ARA).

O'Connor, with dates in the 1860s. – PLATE. Two Cups and a Paten 1650; two Flagons 1678. – MONUMENT. Thomas Read and wife, dated 1652. Kneeling figures facing each other. In the 'predella' seven children, one lying on its side, two next to it forming a pretty little group.

BARDWELL HALL. Heavily and closely timber-framed with N and S brick ends. Early C16. At the S end big stepped gable and chimneybreast. Projecting to the S a low former brick porch (?) also with stepped gable. To the W the façade with two projecting gables. The hall between them has its outer wall brick-nogged. At the N end of the range also a stepped brick gable. The projections with the gables have Elizabethan brickwork inserted below the formerly oversailing gables. Here five-light windows with transoms and pediments. The back of the house all brick-nogged.*

WINDMILL. A derelict tower mill.

BARHAM

1050

ST MARY. Much restored S porch tower of *c.* 1300 (triple-chamfered entrance with continuous mouldings). Of the same time the nave doorways. Long chancel with Perp windows. Early C16 nave clerestory, although there are no aisles, or at least only a two-bay N chapel (the Middleton Chapel). Attached to this on the E the vestry. This has the most noteworthy feature of the church, a large four-light window of terracotta, made *c.* 1525 by the same workmen who did the windows at Barking, Henley, and at Shrubland Old Hall (*see* p. 46). The details are all in a delicate, completely Italian Early Renaissance. The window is oblong and the lights have straight, not arched, tops. Of the hammerbeam roof inside the nave only the lower parts are original. The collar-beams are placed unusually low. – PULPIT. Panels re-used from the rood screen. – PARCLOSE SCREEN. In the Middleton Chapel, with beautiful Perp tracery, one-light divisions. – COMMUNION RAIL. Italian, it seems, and dated 1700. With putti and dolphins. Another part of the same rail is used in the Middleton Chapel. – BENCHES. With poppy-heads. – PLATE. Cup 1730; Flagon and Paten 1742. – MONUMENTS. Tomb recess in the chancel. Cusped and sub-cusped arch. Ogee top with finial and buttress shafts. – Brass to Robert Southwell † 1514 and wife (chancel floor). The figures are 2 ft

* Mr P. G. M. Dickinson, after a careful examination of the building, told me that he considers most of it a reconstruction with old materials, but that the house incorporates a pre-Reformation stone building.

10 in. long. – Sir Richard Southwell † 1640 and wife. Large, but not spectacular. Two effigies, he recumbent, she behind him on her elbow and contemplating him. Background with coupled columns, a flat arch, obelisks, etc.

GATEWAY and WALL of the former Barham Hall, brick, opposite the church.

BARHAM MANOR, ½ m. E. C16, with stepped end-gables and low mullioned and transomed windows. Octagonal chimneys with star tops. Two rear wings, one rebuilt in the C19.

(WORKHOUSE. Built c. 1770. Partly derelict at the time of writing. Red brick, two-storeyed, on an H-plan, with one-storey offices closing one side of the H. DOE)

ROMAN ROADS. Evidence for two roads just N of the church, one leading to Coddenham church, the second to Baylham. A coin of Domitian (A.D. 81–96) was found on the surface of the first.

BARKING

0050

ST MARY. Late C13 S porch with typical mouldings to the entrance and typical side windows. Of the same time the S doorway, which has one order of shafts and one continuous chamfer. Hood-mould on head-stops. Of the same time also the chancel. The E window is a good example of cusped intersected tracery. Attached to the chancel is a two-storeyed vestry. A little later than the chancel windows, i.e. Dec, the S arcade with octagonal piers and double-hollow-chamfered arches, the N doorway, and the unbuttressed W tower (with polygonal buttresses), which was rebuilt in 1870. Perp N arcade, N windows and S windows, and clerestory. The latest of the windows, one on the N side, goes beyond the Perp style. The tracery is Perp, but the mullions and jambs are in the Early Italian Renaissance, made of terracotta by the same craftsmen who did the windows of Henley and Barham and of Shrubland Old Hall (*see* pp. 83, 265, 418). The same moulds were used throughout. Simple tie-beam roof with arched braces and crown-posts with four-way struts. Much finer N aisle roof. Traceried arched braces, carved purlins. The design alternates in detail. – FONT. Octagonal. Against the stem four Lions and four Wild Men; against the bowl the Signs of the four Evangelists and four Angels. – FONT COVER. Very pretty; late C15. – PULPIT. Incorporating one Flemish late C16 or early C17 relief. – SCREENS. Very fine, complete N and S parclose screens with delicate cresting. The rood screen is

18a

complete too and has three-light divisions and coving. –
DOORS. The W, S, and vestry doors are traceried. In the case of
the W door, the tracery is arranged in panels as on bench ends.
– COMMUNION RAIL. Late C17, with twisted balusters. –
STAINED GLASS. Some in the top of the NE window and the
terracotta window. – HELMET in the S chapel. – PLATE. Set of
1750. – CURIOSUM. Serpent played in the church orchestra
about 1830. – MONUMENT. Crowley family; 1771. Of white,
grey, and pink marble. No figures, but an elegant design.
RECTORY. 1819. Grey brick. Five bays, two storeys. The middle
bay is emphasized rather heavily by giant Tuscan columns *in
antis* and a pediment.
IRON AGE FARM, S of Darmsden Hall, with a series of possible
storage pits indicative of an Early Iron Age date.

BARNARDISTON   7040

ALL SAINTS. Small. The N porch has an exceptionally tall
entrance. Handsome C14 N doorway.* – PULPIT. Simple;
Jacobean. The iron stand for the HOUR GLASS on the wall by
the pulpit. – READER'S DESK. With the same panels as the
pulpit. – SCREEN. One-light divisions, ogee arches with
tracery over. – PANELLING in the chancel, Jacobean. –
COMMUNION RAIL. C17. – SOUTH DOOR. C15, with wicket. –
BENCHES. Simple, with straight tops and some blank tracery.
– PLATE. Paten, early C17; Cup 1663.
Opposite the church some COUNCIL HOUSING by *Sir Albert
Richardson*, a rather formal composition of pairs of neo-
Georgian red brick houses. The corner house is lower and has
a gambrel-pyramid roof.

BARNBY   4080

ST JOHN BAPTIST. Unbuttressed W tower with Dec W window.
Nave and chancel in one, thatched. The chancel seems to be
of *c.* 1300. – FONT. Octagonal, C13, of Purbeck marble, with
two shallow blank arches on each side. – BANNER STAFF
LOCKER. To the W of the S door. Preserved with its original
traceried door. Is this a unique survival? – WALL PAINTINGS.
On the S wall, from E: Crucifixion; Works of Mercy, growing on
a tree; St Christopher. – PLATE. Pre-Reformation Chalice.
(ASH FARM. C16. With a stepped gable and altered windows
whose pediments survive. NMR)

* In the sill of the chancel SW window two incised windmills, one of them
left unfinished. Information kindly given by Mr Philip Dickinson.

8070

BARNHAM

ST GREGORY. Slate roofs. Altogether the church is far too
restored to have an architectural story to tell. The only reason
for the architectural traveller to enter is the PISCINA of the late
C13 with a pointed-trefoiled arch and a pointed trefoil in bar
tracery over it. – PLATE. Elizabethan Cup; Flagon 1755;
Almsdish c. 1756.

ST MARTIN, at the NW end of the village. Only the tower remains, with some adjoining wall. A picturesque object with its
thick clusters of ivy.

YE OLDE HOUSE. C16 house with overhanging upper floor. The
modern inscription recording 1553 could well be the true date.

WINDMILL at the W end of the village, a derelict tower mill.

9070

BARNINGHAM

ST ANDREW. Dec W tower* and chancel. The chancel E window
has flowing tracery. On the S side a low-side window with an
embattled transom. The nave has tall Perp two-light windows.
Inside it should be noticed how the rood-stair ascends in the
window. – FONT. Octagonal, Dec. With tracery patterns,
e.g. a rose of eight radiating arches, and a wheel of three
mouchettes. – SCREEN. Very good and well preserved. One-
light ogee arches with panel tracery; cresting. Of the former
rood beam the cut-off ends remain in the walls. – PULPIT.
The tester looks mid-C17, the body later. – BENCHES. A whole
set. With tracery panels against the ends, carved backs, and
poppy-heads and animals on the arms, also birds, monsters,
one kneeling figure. – PLATE. Elizabethan Cup and Paten;
Flagon 1762. – BRASS. William Goche, rector of Barningham,
† 1499; a 13 in. figure.

7060

BARROW

ALL SAINTS. Much renewed. One Norman window on the N
side. Dec S aisle with four-bay arcade (octagonal piers, double-
chamfered arches, dying into the W and E responds). W window
a lancet, E window Dec. N side all Perp. Chancel renewed
1848, but the E window is correct. Three tall single-chamfered
stepped lancets under one arch. The PISCINA and SEDILIA
clearly belong to the same time, i.e. the mid C13, but are no
longer of value as evidence. – FONT. Perp, octagonal, with

---

* However, Mr Adrian R. Allan has found wills of 1439 and 1440 which
leave money to the fabric of the tower, the latter specifying that it is new
('ad fabric' nov' campanil' ibid' . . .').

eight shields in panels. – STALLS. The fronts perhaps the re-used dado of the screen. The stalls have poppy-heads. – BENCHES. Two with traceried ends and carved backs. – WALL PAINTINGS. In the jambs of the Norman window two small agile figures. – MONUMENTS. Tomb-chest with cusped and decorated lozenges. Niche with lintel on small quadrant arches and cresting. Panelled sides. The whole of Purbeck marble and supposed to belong together with the Elizabethan brasses against the back wall. These commemorate Sir Clement Heigham † 1570 and his two wives. Long poem, worth read-ing, as it describes his life in doggerel. But the monument, with its total absence of Renaissance detail, cannot be so late, even in Suffolk. It is more likely of *c.* 1500. – Sir John Heigham † 1626. By *John Stone*, set up in 1650. Tablet with inscription flanked by heavy volutes supported by square brackets. Open segmental pediment.

(Very varied and interesting HOUSES round the large Green. P. G. M. Dickinson)

BARSHAM

HOLY TRINITY. Round tower with one Norman W window. On top a spike. Norman masonry and one N window in the nave. N additions of 1908. But the great surprise is the E wall and E window. The wall is decorated with one bold trellis of stone lozenges or a diagonal stone grid against the flushwork ground, and the E window is simply made part of it, that is traceried all the way through in this diagonal grid. It is a unique conception, and one is at a loss how to date it. The C14, that is the Dec style, a style never afraid of the unprecedented, has been credited with it, but also the C16 (Cautley, Dickinson, LG) and the C17 (Bryant). The chancel roof was very prettily stuccoed in the Jacobean style in 1906. – Equally pretty the ROOD CANOPY of 1919, gaily painted, rather like Central European folk art. Cut-out painted figures in openwork arches. – FONTS. Norman font, disused, in the chancel. Square, of Purbeck marble, with tapering sides and a large incised zigzag pattern. The Perp font is, as usual, octagonal. Quatrefoil frieze against the bowl. Stem with eight attached shafts and slender blank two-light windows between. – ROOD SCREEN. Partly Jacobean, with nicely decorated posts and pendant arches. – PULPIT. Jacobean and probably contemporary with the screen. Back panel original, tester made up of old parts. – BENCH ENDS. A few with poppy-heads, and on the arms

beasts and birds. – POOR BOX. A simple box on a post, dated
1691. – COMMUNION RAIL (N aisle). 1636, with well shaped
balusters. – SCULPTURE. Majolica plaque in the s aisle.
Florentine Quattrocento(?). – WALL PAINTING. St Christopher: N wall, indistinct. – STAINED GLASS. The whole of
the E window, with about twenty-five single figures, by
Kempe, 1870s. – PLATE. Paten dating from 1450–1540, parcel-
gilt, with a sexfoil depression, spandrels with foliage; Cup
1568; Cup and Paten 1822. – PROCESSIONAL CROSS. Early
C16; said to come from Cadenabbia in North Italy. – MONU-
MENTS. Brass, probably Sir Robert atte Tighe † 1415. Good
figure, 4 ft long. – Sir Edward Eckingham † 1527. Tomb-chest
with remarkably up-to-date and elegantly handled Early
Renaissance decoration. Decorated pilasters, decorated panels.
It is one of seven terracotta tombs recorded in East Anglia,
made *c.* 1530 from a common set of moulds. The product of a
single workshop, they are possibly Flemish, but no continental
examples are known. The decorated panels at Barsham are
identical with those of the tomb at Oxburgh, Norfolk.* –
Thomas Missenden † 1771 (chancel floor). Ledger-stone. The
centre is of coloured marble fragments. Inscriptions on all
four sides, including one in Greek.

RECTORY. Mostly timber-framed, but with a brick shaped gable.

BARSHAM HALL. A medieval flint range, nearly 300 ft long, with
fireplaces, is now a barn of the farm, close to modern farm
buildings. It carries the date 1563.

(GRANGE FARM. With a shaped end-gable. NMR)

7070   BARTON MILLS

ST MARY. Mostly Dec, the w tower perhaps a little earlier. Five-
light E window with a reticulated arrangement in which the top
motif is a pointed oval rather than having ogee top and bottom.
The 'low-side' window on the s side of the chancel has tracery
with a four-petalled flower in the top. Arcade of four bays, with
octagonal piers, double-chamfered arches, and hood-moulds
on heads. The clerestory windows are above the spandrels,
not the apexes of the arcade. – FONT. Octagonal with flat Dec
arch and tracery motifs, almost a mason's pattern-book of such
motifs. – PULPIT. Jacobean. – STAINED GLASS. Original
C14 fragments in the s aisle, also nearly complete (though

---

* See A. P. Baggs, 'Sixteenth Century Terra-cotta Tombs in East Anglia',
Archaeological Journal, CXXV (1968).

headless) figures. – E window by *Clayton & Bell*, c. 1866. –
Chancel N window by *Heaton, Butler & Bayne*, c. 1907, in the
(by then antiquated) Walter Crane style. – SE window by
Ward & Hughes, c. 1867. – PLATE. Paten 1710; Flagon 1746.
– MONUMENT. Civilian and wife, c. 1480. Incised slab, the
effigies mostly effaced.

SW of the church a castellated COTTAGE with a raised centre.
In this a quatrefoil window. The other windows are Gothic.
Probably c. 1800.

By the bridge a charming corner with the BULL HOTEL, a house
opposite, and the lock.

(Another cottage has a tall chimneystack with two elongated
blank arches. It looks Vanbrughian, but had until recently a
date panel 1668. Information from Mr F. A. Girling.)

BRONZE AGE BARROW, on Chalk Hill by the Newmarket road,
1½ m. SW of the village. Completely excavated and reconstructed in 1923. It yielded three inhumations and a central
cremation associated with both Food Vessel and Cinerary Urn
pottery and a bone crescentic necklace perhaps imitating the
form more common in jet. It was originally one of a group of
four in line, and there were two others excavated in 1869
which revealed two inhumations and a cremation. It also
contained Beaker pottery.

BATTISFORD

ST MARY. Nave and chancel and bell-turret with saddle-back
roof. The turret is supported by the oddest brick buttress,
climbing up with seven set-offs. The former W tower has disappeared. Nave and S porches probably of c. 1300. Chancel of
the same time, see the E window. NE vestry and a N attachment
which used to be the squire's pew. Roof with crown-posts with
four-way struts, braced collars, and ashlar-pieces. – FONT.
Bowl with nice cusped tracery; all designs, with the exception
of one, are Dec. – PULPIT. C18; simple. – PLATE. Cup and
Paten Cover 1634. – MONUMENTS. Edward Salter † 1724 and
John Lewis † 1724. Two identical monuments l. and r. of the
altar. No effigies, but a putto on top of the usual obelisk.

There was a house of the Knights Hospitallers at Battisford. It
was founded c. 1154, and nothing remains of it, although ST
JOHN'S MANOR HOUSE has at the base of the principal
chimneystack a terracotta panel with the head of St John
(information from Mr F. A. Girling).

BAWDSEY

St Mary. Very broad w tower of the C14. The top is missing.
w window with cusped intersected tracery. No bell-openings.
The church was largely burnt in 1842 and rebuilt on a reduced
scale. The N and s arcades now in the outer walls were of the
early C13. Alternating octagonal and circular piers with
moulded capitals. – FONT. An C18 baluster font. – PULPIT.
Early C19. Body with slim balusters, open between them. The
book rest on brass brackets. – PLATE. Cup 1773.

Martello Tower, 1 m. ESE. Built 1810–12 (cf. Alderton, and
for more details Aldeburgh, p. 73).

BAYLHAM

St Peter. Unbuttressed w tower of knapped flint. Blocked
Norman N nave doorway. Most other windows Dec, or imitation Dec. The church was heavily restored in 1870, when the
chancel was rebuilt and the transepts were added. In the N
wall of the nave two Perp windows. – FONT. Octagonal, Perp.
With shields on the bowl. – PLATE. Elizabethan Cup; Paten
1715. – MONUMENT. John Acton and family, C17; with
kneeling figures.

Baylham Hall, ¾ m. ENE. Fragment of a C16 brick mansion.
The fragment is of T-shape. The front range has shaped gable-
ends (two convex curves each side). The elevation is irregular
with, in the l. part, angle pilasters in two orders. The windows
are all altered, but the back range has a number of mullioned
and transomed as well as cross-windows of brick, and spiked
dentil friezes. (Fine staircase. LG) Spacious outbuildings,
especially a fine STABLE range, of brick on the ground floor,
with windows with four-centred arches, weatherboarded on
the upper floor.

Rodwell House, just s of the start of the lane to the church.
Georgian, red brick, of five bays and four storeys.

Mill House. Picturesque in its elevation and its position by
the hump-bridge over the Gipping. (The DOE states that the
house has a pre-Reformation core.)

BAYTHORN END see WIXOE
BEALINGS HOUSE see GREAT BEALINGS
BECCLES

St Michael. This is a church not easily forgotten, from a distance because of its commanding position above the river
Waveney, from near by because of its tower standing four-

square and independent, away from the church towards the town. The church and the tower are Perp. A bequest for the s porch was made in 1455, bequests for the tower between 1515 and 1547. But the s doorway to the chancel, though re-done in 1859, looks C13, and on the N side there is evidence of the mid C14 – several windows in the Dec style. So that side with its rood-loft turret now crowned by a pretty ogee cap existed when a renewal of the rest began. It can, in fact, be dated approximately by a legacy of 1369 'ad fabricam novae ecclesiae'. The Perp church is 147 ft long and has no structural division between nave and chancel. The plan is simply a parallelogram. The arcades are eight bays long, with piers of a quatrefoil section and two deep hollows and a shaft in the diagonals. The arches are moulded, and the clerestory has a different rhythm: thirteen windows to the eight arches below. The exterior of the aisles is even too, in spite of certain irregularities in sizes and design of the windows. The principal of these are a four-light window on the N and one opposite, on the s side, both representing bays in which originally arches opened into transepts. The E end has two four-light windows for the aisles and a huge (renewed) seven-light window for the chancel, with tracery of great animation. The grouping of the lights is three-one-three, the heights of the lights alternate and the patterns of the tracery too. Quatrefoil friezes with shields in stone as well as flushwork. The W side has three-, seven-, four-light windows. The middle window here has a composition of three-three-three lights interlocked. w doorway with small shields in barbed quatrefoils along the moulding of jambs and arch. Then the two porches. The s porch is a showpiece indeed: 34 ft high, of two storeys, stone-faced, and with polygonal angle buttresses carrying finials. At the base is a frieze of shields in barbed quatrefoil fields. The parapet is exquisitely detailed and ends with triangular cresting. The same motifs in the NW stair-turret, which rises higher than the porch. Small niches and elaborate traceried panelling l. and r. of the entrance. Above more panelling and three tall niches with canopies. Inside the porch is a tierceron-vault with bosses. The s doorway has an order of jambs and arch completely set out with six niches. The N porch is simpler but also two-storeyed. It has a flushwork-panelled front, and the entrance arch has spandrels with a man wielding a club (St George ?) and a dragon. The tower is 97 ft tall, and its top is so square and unrelieved that it seems likely that money was lacking after 1547 to add parapet, battlements, and pinnacles. The tower is all stone-faced. It has big angle buttresses, their fronts hollowed out in one immensely tall niche with an immensely tall shaft to carry an image. The w side has a doorway with a frieze of lozenge shape over, then three tall niches for images, then a four-light window with blank quatrefoils at the foot between the mullions, and a transom below which the lights are arched. Then follows a two-light window, and then the two two-light bell-openings.

So much for the exterior. What need be said about the interior has already been said. It is in fact rather bald and grey. It was burnt out in 1586. Below the w end of the s aisle is a brick vaulted bone-hole. Beccles church has not much to offer in the way of furnishings. – FONT. Octagonal bowl, C13, of Purbeck marble, with two shallow blank pointed arches on each side – a familiar design. – PLATE. Cup 1567; Cup and Paten 1568; Flagon 1704; Credence Dish 1727; Spoon 1775; Paten 1802. – MONUMENT. Tomb-chest, or rather front of a tomb-chest, with ten niches in which ten little figures of *c.* 1500, worn but not hacked off. The monument is supposed to be that of John Rede, Mayor of Norwich, † 1502. – BRASS. John Denny † 1620 (w wall). No figures. Inscriptions: 'Mors ianua vitae' – 'Mors mihi lucrum' – 'Nascendo morimur' – 'Vita altera morte paratur' – 'Non nos seiungat quos Christus iunxit amore'.

ST BENET (R.C.), St Mary's Road. 1889 by *F. E. Banham* of Beccles. A remarkably ambitious building in the Romanesque style, tunnel-vaulted (i.e. French Romanesque rather than Anglo-Norman), with an unsubdivided gallery and a clerestory inside, with groin-vaulted aisles, transept with a triforium, and an apse intended to have an ambulatory. The church was to be connected with a Benedictine priory.

PERAMBULATION. Four fires between *c.* 1580 and *c.* 1680 destroyed much of the old town. Immediately SE of the church tower the OLD TOWN HALL, a quaintly humble brick building of two storeys in the shape of an elongated octagon. It was built in 1726 and has no ornamental features. From here SALTGATE runs N. The start is marked with restraint, yet not unimpressively, by No. 1, which is of three storeys, brick, whitewashed, with frontages to the churchyard and to Salt-gate. According to the DOE the house is C17 on a probably C16 base structure, refaced in the C18. It was formerly the Grey-hound and Dog Inn. Inside, good panelled rooms, one dated

1790. At the foot of the garden, in the sw corner, is a red-brick
GAZEBO (with hunting, fishing, and boating scenes painted on
the domed ceiling inside). Saltgate then skirts the OLD
MARKET and here, on the Saltgate, i.e. the w, side, is ST
PETER'S HOUSE, a fine c18 brick house of seven bays and two
storeys with a three-bay pediment. It stands on the site of the
pre-Dissolution St Peter's Chapel – a small portion of its
flint fabric remains in a cupboard in the present house.* Its
back, towards the garden, is to one's surprise Gothick, with a
pretty cornice and a pretty though mutilated doorway. This
rear building contains fragments of early stained glass,
possibly from St Peter's Chapel or from St Mary's, demolished
in the late c16 (DOE). (Delightful interior with an elaborate
Gothick fireplace. NMR) By the side of St Peter's Street
PUDDINGMOOR starts its course down to the river. On the
r. the WAVENEY HOUSE HOTEL with a Late Georgian or
later façade, knapped flint with stone trim, and an earlier back
of red brick with giant pilasters. (One of the Suffolk undulating
brick walls or crinkle-crankle walls should be noted.) In the
Old Market on the opposite, i.e. E, side in the N corner RAVENS-
MERE HOUSE, which is dated 1694. It is of five bays and two
storeys, of red and blackish blue chequerwork. Doorway with
Roman Doric pilasters, a metope frieze, and a broad pediment.
A little to the s, facing St Peter's House, No. 5, of three bays
with a doorway with Gibbs surround and pediment.

The N axis then continues down NORTHGATE with several good
c18 houses, first No. 12, which has five bays and two storeys,
the middle three emphasized by heavy giant pilasters and a
heavy attic. Big stone doorway with Tuscan demi-columns, a
metope frieze, and a pediment. The date is probably c. 1720.
Then STAITHE HOUSE, whose façade stands at r. angles to
the street. It has a N gable of c. 1700 with two upright oval
windows and below windows with brick frames and segmental
pediments. (Inside an exceptionally good late c18 fireplace
with a harvest scene. DOE) Opposite is No. 41, THE COT-
TAGE, with a Dutch, i.e. pedimented, gable. Then again on the
E side No. 60, with shaped gables, and No. 62, which is early
c18 and has five bays, brick rusticated quoins, the three-bay
centre also emphasized by such quoins and a three-bay pediment with a blank arch with alternating rustication in it. That
is the end to the N.

s from the church runs Ballygate and here at once we must turn

* Information from Mr Eugene C. Ulph.

off down NEWMARKET. The block on the l. is a curious and
attractive muddle of small properties. This is followed by a
more formal group facing w, first the corner of Market Street
with a shaped gable-end, and then the KING'S HEAD HOTEL,
which is of brick with giant rusticated brick pilasters at the
angles, two and a half storeys high, and has an archway to lead
into an open courtyard. Strange rhythm round the corner,
where one such high bay with the giant pilasters is followed by
a whole lower Georgian house of independent design, after
which the higher part and the giant pilasters repeat, but two
bays wide.*

Back to BALLYGATE STREET, the most attractive street of
Beccles. Nos. 25 and 27 are both good Georgian brick houses,
and both enjoy the view over the meadows and the river
Waveney below. No. 25 has four bays, two and a half storeys,
and a pretty doorway with a decorated frieze. No. 27 has five
bays, two storeys, and a doorway with Roman pilasters, a
metope frieze, and a pediment. THE RECTORY is earlier and
more ambitious with its four giant brick pilasters and pediment
to distinguish the centre. After that, on the w side LEMAN
HOUSE, i.e. the building of the school founded by Sir John
Leman, Alderman of London, in 1631, and beautified in 1762.
The house itself is originally of the c16, but with considerable
later additions (DOE). Straight gable-end with depressed-
arched windows. Front of nine widely spaced bays, bays two
and eight being doorways. The windows look early c19 Tudor,
but some of them may be original, according to the DOE.
(There is one original c16 window frame at the back of the
house, and one c16 attic casement. Also at the back, a small
porch with an ogee brick arched window, over which is a bell-
turret. The alterations of c. 1762 may well have included the
refacing of the front with its present flint with red brick
headers. DOE)

Ballygate Street is continued to the sw by BUNGAY ROAD, and
53b here, in its own grounds, is ROOS HALL, dated 1593. It is of

* The DOE records at No. 23 a geometrically patterned ceiling and a plaster
coat of arms with the date 1589. The latter can now be seen by the staircase
of the Municipal Offices in Blyburgate. The gateway of the former GAOL
or House of Correction, built c. 1806, has been demolished. It was in Gaol
Lane off Newgate Street, in the s wall of MESSRS CLOWES' Printing Works.
Portland stone. Archway with deep eaves over the heavy parapet l. and r.
Plain wall with one sunk panel. The inscription read: ... prohibere quam
punire.

red brick, high and not long. Three-bay front of two and a half
storeys with four-storeyed stepped gable-ends. Polygonal
angle buttresses with circular decorated pinnacles. The
windows are mullioned and transomed of four or five lights
with transom, diminishing to three with transom on the first
floor, and in the gables to three and two without transom. All
the windows are of brick and all the principal ones carry pediments. The doorway still has a four-centred arch with continuous mouldings. Hood-mould on big stops. (Inside, original
panelling and several contemporary stone fireplaces. DOE)

BEDFIELD 2060

ST NICHOLAS. Norman N doorway with one order of colonnettes and zigzag in the arch. The chancel also is at least
partly Norman, see the change in the masonry. Otherwise
mostly Perp. Perp w tower, quite ornate. Base with arched
flushwork panelling, battlements with the same and quatrefoils in addition. w window surrounded by three niches. –
FONT. Octagonal, with cusped tracery patterns, Dec and Perp,
and shields. – FONT COVER. C17, 6 ft 6 in. tall. The lower half
boarded with elongated Tuscan columns. A more usual
curved crown on top. Cautley draws attention to the unusual
way in which the cover opens. Three panels detach completely,
the three opposite hinge upwards and inwards. – SCREEN.
Dado with painted mid-C15 figures. – PULPIT. Simple, of the
second third of the C17. – BENCHES. C17; at the back; plain.
(BEDFIELD HALL. Late C16. With two ornamental plaster
ceilings. DOE)

BEDINGFIELD 1060

ST MARY. Dec w tower with flushwork arcading on the buttresses. Nave and chancel. In the chancel one lancet. The nave
windows Perp. Double-hammerbeam roof with collar-beams. –
FONT. Octagonal, Perp, with simple patterns. – BENCHES.
Dated 1612. With a Jacobean version of poppy-heads. Also in
the same benches re-used Perp ends with poppy-heads and
seated figures. – STAINED GLASS. In the E window, of c. 1853.
Three large figures; coarse but robust. – PLATE. Paten of
1450–1540 with sexfoil depression and head of Christ surrounded by rays; Elizabethan Cup.
FLEMING'S HALL. Built c. 1550. A very fine building. One
long straight front: brick ground floor, timber-framed upper

floor. The gable-ends shaped and carrying groups of four polygonal chimneys. Brick porch of two storeys, not in the middle.
Four-centred entrance arch with pediment, three-light transomed window over. Stepped gable with pinnacles. (Staircase
with a few heavy square moulded balusters on the upper
flight.)

1040

BELSTEAD

ST MARY. Much renewed. With a S porch tower. C16 N chapel of
brick with brick window-frames and door-frame. – FONT.
Perp, octagonal, with four lions against the base, and four
flowers and four demi-figures of angels on the panels of the
bowl. – PULPIT. Jacobean, with the usual blank arches. –
ROOD SCREEN. Dado only, painted with figures of saints,
c. 1500. They are set against a continuous background of landscape. – MONUMENTS. Brass probably to John Goldingham
† 1518. Knight and two wives, 19 in. figures. – Tobias Blosse
and Elizabeth Blosse, both by *John Stone*, and both set up
in 1656. The former is in the form of a hatchment, i.e. a stone
lozenge, with only a little decoration. The other is a tablet with
oval inscription plate, drapery above it, and small figures of
kneeling children below.

(BELSTEAD HALL. Gabled C16 core, C17 and later additions.
One ornamental plaster ceiling with Tudor roses. DOE)

(HOUSE, No. 10, 1 m. NE. Octagonal Gothic lodge. Two-
storey centre, one-storey wings. DOE)

4000

BELTON

ALL SAINTS. Round tower rebuilt in 1849. Dec nave and chancel.
One ought to note the two doorways with ogee arches and
finials, the two-light windows with one reticulation motif and
a smaller one inside it, and the low, ogee-headed recess in the
chancel N wall. The arch rests on two very finely carved heads.
S porch Perp with a little flushwork panelling on the front. –
FONT. Of Purbeck marble, octagonal, with two flat blank
pointed arches to each side; C13. – SCREEN. C14, with shafts
instead of mullions and ogee arches. Circles above them with
wheels of two or three mouchettes. – REREDOS. With carved
groups of the Annunciation, Crucifixion, and Noli me tangere.
1887 by *James Elwell* of Beverley, the setting designed by
Temple Moore. – WALL PAINTINGS. Two impressive large
mid-C14 figures on the N wall: St James and St Christopher.
Partly defaced by a later painting of the familiar story of the

Three Quick and the Three Dead; almost indistinguishable now. – STAINED GLASS. E window by *Kempe*, 1896. – PLATE. Cup 1568.

BELTON OLD HALL. Early Georgian. Red brick, of five bays and two and a half storeys. Giant pilasters of yellow brick at the angles. Doorway with Roman Doric pilasters, a metope frieze, and a pediment. Arched window above it with a surround of yellow brick.

BROWSTON HALL, 1 m. SE. Inside this unassuming house are three startlingly ambitious Rococo stucco ceilings. The staircase (which has three turned balusters to each tread and carved tread-ends) has a large eagle in the centre; another room has a smaller eagle and Rococo ornament, the third a sun face in the centre, medallions with the Four Ages of Woman in the corners and symbols of the seasons close to them, and in the bay window a charming village scene of fishing, swimming, boating, and love-making. There is a cottage in the background and even a church with a round tower. The windows here and in the other room with a plaster ceiling have pretty Chippendale fret surrounds.

BLACK MILL and CALDECOT MILL. Derelict tower-mills built for drainage.

BENACRE

5080

ST MICHAEL. W tower probably early C14. Nave and chancel in one with much C18–19 repair work in brick. The upper N wall probably of 1769. Of the same date probably the pointed chancel windows. Wide C14 S aisle. The arcade has octagonal piers and double-chamfered arches. – FONT. C13. Of Purbeck marble. Octagonal, with the familiar two shallow blank pointed arches on each side. – BOX PEWS. Unusually attractive, with their rounded corners at the back. – Also squire's pew, PULPIT, and a W block of pews including the castellated ORGAN CASE. – PLATE. Paten *c.* 1680; Cup *c.* 1685; Flagon 1767. – MONUMENTS. At least four worth recording. Sir Edward North † 1708. Inscription plate flanked by two standing putti, on the entablature two seated putti. – Sir Thomas Gooch † 1781 and his son Sir Thomas † 1826. By *Behnes*. Heavily Grecian, without figures. – Louisa Anna Maria Gooch † 1838. By *L. Pampaloni*. An angel carrying her and a baby up to heaven. – Sir Thomas Sherlock Gooch † 1851. By *T. Thurlow* of Saxmundham. Remarkably good. Faith, Hope, Charity as three mildly Grecian figures.

BENACRE HALL. Suckling states that the house was built for
Thomas Carthew, who died in 1743, and that the wings were
added by his successor. Davey in his *Seats* says that it was built
by *Brettingham* in 1763–4. The latter date is convincing for
the façade now. Eleven bays, two and a half storeys, grey
brick, quoins, central five-bay pediment. Of *c.* 1830 must be the
deep porte-cochère or portico with six Greek Doric columns.
The interior was gutted by fire in 1926 and has since been
restored.

The STABLES are of red brick with an entrance archway, a
pediment over it, and a crowning bell-turret and cupola. This
front is seven bays wide.

BENHALL

3060

ST MARY. Norman s doorway with one order of colonnettes, and
in the arch zigzag on the front and the inside meeting at r.
angles. Much renewed. The N transept and vestry are C19.
The rest is over-restored. Unbuttressed W tower with flushwork decoration of the battlements. s porch with an entrance
whose arch has fleurons. – PULPIT. Jacobean. – BOX PEWS. –
PLATE. Cup, Paten, and Flagon 1670; Spoon *c.* 1820–30. –
MONUMENT. Sir Edward Duke † 1732. Hanging monument
without effigy. Large inscription plate flanked by columns.
Pediment on which two putti.

BENHALL LODGE, $\frac{1}{2}$ m. s. 1810. Grey brick, six bays, two
storeys. Porch of two pairs of Greek Doric columns. The
stables also have Greek Doric colonnades, and in addition a
central bell-turret.

WALNUT TREE FARM, $\frac{3}{8}$ m. ssw. With a handsome Early
Georgian staircase behind a Venetian window. Twisted
balusters, but still a diagonal string hiding the tread-ends.

OLD SCHOOL, $\frac{1}{2}$ m. SE. Built by the will of Sir Edward Duke in
1736. Much enlarged and altered since. The original building
is of red brick, five bays wide and two storeys high with a
tablet above the entrance.

A cottage at BENHALL GREEN, on the N side of the street, is
dated 1698, and has brown painted or pargetted and painted
geometrical patterns.

BENTLEY

1030

ST MARY. In the chancel N wall one renewed Norman window.
The s doorway into the nave Norman, but completely new.
One original stone with zigzag in the porch. N aisle 1858. Much

restoration then and in 1884. The details mostly renewed or new. Simple hammerbeam roof. – FONTS. A disused C13 bowl of Purbeck marble with the usual shallow blank arches. – The font in use is also octagonal and has three flower, etc., devices, four demi-figures of angels holding shields, and in one panel the seated Virgin. If this is C15, then it must be much re-cut. – BENCH. One with poppy-heads and animals on the arms. – PLATE. Paten and Flagon 1699; Cup 1700.

BENTLEY HALL, N of the church. Partly timber-framed with brick-nogging. A date 1582 on the beam carrying the overhang. Beautiful fifteen-bay BARN, also timber-framed with brick-nogging. Brick ends with dark diapering.

HUBBARD'S HALL FARM. Timber-framed. A date 1591 on a pargetted panel. Mr Alec Clifton-Taylor reports that the house is now (1973) derelict.

BEVILLS see BURES

BEYTON

ALL SAINTS.* Norman round (in fact oval) tower with Perp w window. Simple Norman N doorway. Nave 1854; chancel 1885. – BENCHES. Some original ones with poppy-heads and animals on the arms. The backs of the seats are carved too.

BILDESTON

ST MARY. The church is on a hill outside the village. Dec chancel with inventive five-light E window. Dec N aisle E window with reticulated tracery. Tall Perp w tower. The w doorway big with three niches over. Large Perp aisle windows with segmental arches. Clerestory with twice as many windows as bays of the arcade. S porch with flushwork, entrance with fleuron decoration. The S doorway is excellently decorated with crowns, shields, etc. Hood-mould on seated lions. Spandrels with shields. The arcade of five bays has piers with four filleted shafts and small spurs without capitals in the diagonals. The abaci have rows of small busts or leaf motifs. Many-moulded arches. No chancel arch. Roof with alternating tie-beams and hammerbeams. It is remarkable for a total absence of collar-beams (J. T. Smith). – FONT. Octagonal, Perp. Damaged stem. Bowl with the four Signs of the Evangelists and four demi-angels. – Wooden BALCONY from

* A will of 1461 gives the dedication as St Mary (and leaves money to the fabric of the church), but one proved in 1514 has an All Saints reference (ARA and Peter Northeast).

the upper storey of the porch to the aisle. – COMMUNION
RAIL. Slim turned balusters. – STALLS with simple MISERI-
CORDS, heads, etc., all defaced. – STAINED GLASS. E window
by *Wailes & Strang*, 1874 (TK). Scenes only in the tracery
heads. – One S window by *Kempe*, 1892. Typical of his early
work. – PLATE. Elizabethan Cup; Paten of 1639; Cup of
1780. – BRASS. William Wade † 1599 and wife (wearing a hat).
From the church CHAPEL STREET leads into the village. On the
r. side Nos. 23 etc., a whole group of timber-framed cottages
with oversailing upper storey. Two groups, six and four.
Ground floor with buttress shafts. In the MARKET PLACE the
hideous CLOCK TOWER of 1864. On the N side a stately three-
bay house of the early C19. White brick, Greek Doric porch.
On the E side Georgian red-brick house of seven bays and two
storeys with a broken pediment and a Venetian window below.
In the HIGH STREET N of the Market Place the KING'S HEAD
with a pediment on thickly carved brackets. Then several nice
timber-framed houses. S of the Market Place the CROWN INN,
handsome, timber-framed, and much restored, and at the S
end GARROD'S FARMHOUSE, C15 to C16. The house has
several rare and pretty features, specially the small carved
porch, two small mullioned windows with carved top and sill,
and a doorway with a four-centred arch, a carved lintel, and
carved spandrels.

BIRKFIELD *see* IPSWICH, p. 308

BLACK DITCHES *see* CAVENHAM

BLAXHALL

ST PETER. W tower with pretty doorway. Hood-mould with
fleurons, spandrels with an angel and a monster-head. Quatrefoil frieze in flushwork over. Buttresses with flushwork panelling. The top of the tower repaired in brick. S porch with flushwork decoration including several initials. Nave and chancel,
the windows of *c.* 1300 (especially the E window with cusped
intersected tracery), others Perp (especially one of brick).
Hammerbeam roof in the nave. – FONT. Base with a pretty
tracery design more frequent in the parapets of porches.
Stem with the symbols of the four Evangelists in the diagonals
and close tracery. Bowl with only foils, stars, and shields. –
Diverse works of art and craft by *Ellen Mary Rope* † 1934,
Margaret A. Rope, and *Dorothy Rope* (cf. also Leiston). By the
first the WAR MEMORIAL, the Bates MONUMENT († 1904), and

the STAINED GLASS in the porch, by Margaret A. Rope the STAINED GLASS of the E window, by Dorothy Rope the Wilson Monument († 1934). – SCULPTURE. A piece of Saxon interlace re-set in the w wall. – PLATE. Elizabethan Cup and Cover; Paten 1676.

The BARROW on the heath, ¾ m. E of the village, was reported in 1827 as containing 'Roman urns', though these may in fact have been of the prehistoric period. In 1863 considerable Roman occupation material was found in the vicinity of GROVE FARM.

BLUNDESTON   5090

ST MARY. Norman round w tower with original windows and bell-openings and also the original arch into the nave. The upper storey with its lancets seems to be C13. The tower arch opens into the nave, but not at its centre. The nave was rebuilt in the C14 and made almost double its original width. The resulting lopsidedness did not worry a generation so bent on wide spaces (cf. Fritton). Dec nave windows, tall, of two lights, mostly with a reticulation motif and a smaller one inside it. The chancel was rebuilt in 1851. Altered Norman N doorway and even more altered s doorway. Here two Norman colonnettes have been re-used upside down so that the capitals have become bases. – SCREEN. The dado only with defaced figures. – BENCH ENDS. A number with poppy-heads (against the walls). – PLATE. Cup of 1647; Flagon dated 1721.

BLUNDESTON HOUSE. By Sir John Soane, 1785–6. Very simple, without distinguishing features. Somewhat altered. Alterations and stables by W. Oldham Chambers, c. 1865.

(PRISON. By the Ministry of Public Works Architect's Department, 1962–3. Large, but curiously gentle with its low-pitched roof, doubly curious at a moment in architecture when Brutalism and harsh surfaces and uncompromising cubes were the fashion.)

WINDMILL. A former tower-mill converted into a house.

BLYFORD   4070

ALL SAINTS. Norman N doorway with two orders of colonnettes, one of them spiral-fluted. Several zigzags in the arch. The s doorway is Norman too, but simpler. Nave and chancel in one. The chancel of c. 1300 with a lancet window and windows with Y- and intersected tracery. Angle PISCINA with a pointed trefoiled arch. The nave windows are Perp. So are the s porch and the w tower. The porch has a front of knapped flint with one niche above the entrance and a parapet with stone tracery. The tower has flushwork panelling on base and battlements and a quatrefoil frieze in flushwork above the w doorway. – A tall niche inside, w of the N doorway, served as a BANNER STAFF LOCKER. – PLATE. Elizabethan Cup; Paten 1807.

(SERPENTINE HOUSE, Holton Road, has one of the Suffolk undulating brick walls or crinkle-crankle walls. N. Scarfe)

BLYTHBURGH

4070

HOLY TRINITY. The church of Blythburgh is one of the half dozen grandest Suffolk churches, and with its bare white interior reminiscent of the churches of North Norfolk. It is 128 ft long and has a tower 83 ft high. Until the year 1577 there was a spire on the tower, which must have changed the skyline of the church fundamentally. As it is, the tower of Blythburgh is impressive enough when seen across the creek or from the s. That a water tower was built so near it and to so massive a design remains a barbarism hard to comprehend. The church was built about the middle and through the second half of the C15. A bequest towards the building of the chancel dates from 1442, the N chapel (Hopton Chapel) was founded in 1452, a window in the N aisle was glazed in 1457, one in the chancel in 1462. There is nothing older than the mid C15, except the W tower, which is strangely severe. It has no W doorway, and flushwork decoration only on the battlements. The aisles are eight bays long and the chancel projects yet one more bay. There is no structural division between the two, outside or inside, though a change of tracery marks the division between aisles and chapels. Four-light E and W windows, three-light N and S windows, the chancel E window of five lights. It has a frieze of flushwork initials below and flushwork panelling to the l. and r. There are priest's doorways on both sides, both lying behind a flying buttress. The S aisle is given more prominence than the N aisle by means of a delicious openwork parapet of quatrefoils each with a little ogee hat. Lozenge flushwork runs below. The same motif is continued on the S porch. Its façade is of knapped but undecorated flint. To the r. of the entrance is a pretty stoup with a panelled shaft and angels against the bowl. Inside the porch is a renewed tierceron-vault. It had an inscription recording that the porch was built by John and Katherine Mason. Finally the clerestory, which, with its magnificent rhythm of eighteen closely-set windows separated by flush-panelled shafts, determines more than anything the impression of the church from afar. The arcades inside have quatrefoil piers, or rather square piers with four demi-columns attached. The arches have one hollow chamfer and one wave moulding. The low-pitch roof has firred tie-beams, and from the centres of the tie-beams and their bosses big angels stretch their wings, facing E and W. The rafters are painted with the sign of Jesus and busy little ornamental motifs.

FURNISHINGS. FONT. 1449. On two steps. On the upper an inscription again commemorating John Mason and his wife. Demi-figures of angels against the foot of the stem. All other figures or scenes have been obliterated. – PULPIT. Jacobean. With two tiers of flat carving. Bible-rest along all six sides. – STALLS. The fronts are carved with the figures of the Apostles, an unusual arrangement which makes Cautley think that they were part of the former rood screen. – BENCHES. The benches at Blythburgh are quite different from the common 28b Suffolk type. They have figures in the place of poppy-heads, figures seated or kneeling, facing E or facing the gangways, figures human or heavenly. Among them are the Vices of Slander and Sloth (N side N), Pride, Gluttony, Hypocrisy, and Avarice (S side N), also a man in the stocks and a man with faggots (N side N, the latter meaning December), an angel with the sign of the Trinity, and figures holding flowers, ploughing and threshing (N side S), and sowing, reaping, hay-making, and pig-killing (S side S). – Both the N and S DOORS are original and traceried. – PARCLOSE SCREENS. Tall; not well preserved. With one-light divisions. – LECTERN. Wood, original, with a closely buttressed shaft. – CLOCK JACK. Of 1682 (James). – STAINED GLASS. Figures and fragments in tracery heads of the N and S aisles. – PLATE. Cup and two Patens 1805. – MONUMENTS. Sir John Hopton † 1489, chancel N side. Of Purbeck marble. Tomb-chest with three cusped quatrefoils carrying shields. The brasses on the lid have disappeared. E and W panels with blank arches and tracery carry a canopy with flat four-ribbed ceiling and a big cresting. – Another big tomb-chest in the N aisle.

The WHITE HART INN has a shaped gable with small windows.
THE PRIORY is the name of a house, NE of the church, in whose garden are scanty remains of the Augustinian Priory founded as a cell of St Osyth c. 1125.

BOTESDALE

CHAPEL OF ST BOTOLPH. Botesdale is Botolph's Dale. The
chapel was built *c.* 1500 and later made a chantry by the
generosity of John Sherife, his wife, and Bridget Wykys, as
can be read in the damaged inscription over the door. It is a
simple building without division between nave and chancel.
The windows are Perp. – Inside a rough SCREEN like a hall-
screen separating the entrance bay from the chapel proper.
Undecorated muntins and boards. The chapel later became
the Free School established by Sir Nicholas Bacon in 1576
(*see* Redgrave church), and for the purpose of the school the
house was added which is under one roof with the chapel.

E of the chapel THE PRIORY, red brick of five bays and two
storeys with a Roman Doric doorway with metope frieze. The
windows have Gothick casements. To the w on the N side
HONISTER HOUSE, with a Tudor façade of *c.* 1830, on the s
side OSMOND HOUSE, Georgian, of white brick, three bays
wide, with a nice pedimented doorway. Opposite a house
dated 1637. It has an overhanging upper floor with carved
corner posts and brackets. This is followed by HAMBLYN
HOUSE; C17, with a shaped gable. Then on the s side THE
RIDGE, a Late Georgian five-bay house of grey brick, with a
Roman Doric porch and on the N side a terrace of eight bays,
also grey brick, with three doorways with Roman Doric
pilasters. Finally a good earlier Georgian house of seven bays,
of which the middle three are a little recessed. Blue brick
headers and red brick dressings. Pedimented doorway.

BOULGE

ST MICHAEL. In the grounds of Boulge Hall, which has been
pulled down. Early C16 brick tower. The rest seems all
Victorian. – FONT. A Tournai font (cf. Ipswich, St Peter) with
the figures chipped off. – In the s aisle and s chapel the Fitz
Gerald MONUMENTS. Also in the churchyard a sunk family
mausoleum. The monuments (1837, 1838, 1857) all with
elaborate Gothic frames.

BOUNDARY FARM *see* FRAMSDEN

BOXFORD

ST MARY. The village lies close to the stream (the Box), and the
church is immediately by it. Its most interesting feature is the
13a   timber-built N porch. It may well be the earliest timber porch

in the county. Big Dec two-light windows, and a rib-vault, now a skeleton only but perhaps originally with filled-in cells. There are diagonal ribs, ridge-ribs, and one pair of tiercerons to each side. The s porch is the very opposite, Late Perp, stone-faced, and exceedingly swagger. Money was left for its building at various times between 1441 and 1469.* Four-light windows in two bays, of two different designs, plenty of decoration on the front, the buttresses and parapet, head-stops, gargoyles, etc., all rather wild. C14 w tower, with a pretty lead spirelet, probably early C19. Perp aisles‡ and chancel chapels, Perp clerestory of closely set windows. Perp the pretty door-ways on the w side and the n side. Perp arcades of four bays. Piers with four shafts and four hollows, finely moulded arches. Chancel chapel arcades of two bays, the s details similar to those of the nave arcades, the n side with thinner (later?) elements. At the E end of the s chapel niches in two tiers l. and r. of the window. – FONT. Only the panelled stem of the Perp font. – FONT COVER. C17, cupboard type, with ogee cap. – PULPIT. Nice C18 piece. The staircase with finely twisted balusters, two to the tread. – PANELLING. Some linenfold panelling (s aisle E end). – DOORS. s door with tracery and border with quatrefoils. – n door with only a quatrefoil border. – w door with a border of vine trails. – WEST GALLERY. Handsome, with cusped panels. – PAINTINGS. Above the chancel arch small demi-figure of Christ, and l. and r. large figures of angels with wings spread. A crowned figure on the E wall of the s chapel. – PLATE. Cup and Paten 1565; Flagon 1732. – (Attractive BRASS of a child asleep in his cot – David Birde, 1606. ARA)

In CHURCH STREET, facing the w end of the church, a pretty row of timber-framed houses. The OLD CHEQUERS is much restored, but has a carved bressumer along part of its front. From the n end of Church Street to the w in SWAN STREET lies HENDRICK HOUSE, with an C18 plastered front and a pedimented gable, and a little higher up OLD CASTLE HOUSE with a stuccoed early C19 front, embellished by cas-tellated gables and a castellated porch. It is coarse work. The best spot at Boxford is from the n end of Church Street to the

* The will of 1469 bequeaths 6s. 8d. 'ad novum portic'– presumably this means the s porch. (Discovered by Mr Peter Northeast and conveyed to me by ARA.)

‡ Money was left towards the building of a new aisle in 1468 and 1469 (ARA).

E, at the beginning of BROAD STREET. On the one side the
FLEECE INN with a stately pedimented doorway on Ionic
columns, on the other side RIVERSIDE, a pair of Early Georgian three-bay houses. They have a mansard roof, quoins, and
doorways with Gibbs surrounds and pediments. To their E the
former ENGINE HOUSE, yellow brick, two Gothick arches
side by side. Dated 1828. Further on Broad Street becomes
Ellis Street. At the junction, off to the l. BUTCHER'S LANE,
narrow, with some good timber-framed houses with oversailing upper floors.

BOXTED

8050

HOLY TRINITY. The church lies in the grounds of the house,
an ancient timber-framed mansion made to look too new. The
church is above the house and separated from it by a wide
expanse of grass. Flint and stone. Low arcade with octagonal
piers and double-chamfered arches. Interesting hammerbeam
roof in the chancel, interesting because Jacobean. Attached to
the NE an C18 brick chapel. In it the most interesting feature of
37   the church, the Poley MONUMENTS. There are notably two,
Sir John † 1638 and Dame Abigal, the latter erected in 1725.
Both have standing effigies in arched niches and crowning
pediments with rounded centres. In all else they differ characteristically. Sir John's monument must be of the ending C17
and is certainly the work of an outstanding sculptor. Sir John
stands with one hand on his hip, in a self-assured and a little
mannered attitude, and he has a gold frog in one ear. The
costume is that of his day, not of that of the sculptor. To the
l. and r. standing putti pulling away a big drapery which
seems to hang from the top of the monument. The top of the
niche has a shell pattern. All the decoration is rich and lively –
garlands, foliage borders, etc. Dame Abigal's monument is
demonstratively less demonstrative. It is of alabaster (Mrs
Esdaile says the last English monument in that material),
and has only flanking pilasters; the head of the niche is undecorated. – An earlier Poley monument in the chancel:
William † 1587 and his wife. Two recumbent effigies, a late
example of oak carving for a funeral purpose. – PULPIT. Jacobean, with tester. – POLEY PEW. Jacobean parclose screen
with balusters carrying arches and achievements on top. –
COMMUNION RAIL. Three-sided, with twisted balusters. –
STAINED GLASS. Some original glass in the E window of the

Poley Chapel, e.g. the figure of a king. – PLATE. Almsdish ?1674; Cup, Paten, and Flagon 1708.

BOYTON

3040

ST ANDREW. Short W tower. The nave and chancel mostly of 1869. A Norman nook-shaft at the NW angle of the nave. Nice original S doorway with shields, leopard heads, and fleurons in one moulding of jambs and arch. A Norman doorway re-set in the N transept. It is exceptional in that it has continuous mouldings in three steps, each with zigzag on the face as well as inside. – PLATE. Elizabethan Cup.

ALMSHOUSES. To the W of the church. Three brick ranges of two storeys. The recessed middle range is the original building of 1736. The far-projecting l. wing of 1828, the opposite wing of 1860. Both continue the original style and design without any C19 innovation. There is no crowning or distinguishing central feature.

BOYTON END *see* STOKE-BY-CLARE

BRADFIELD COMBUST

8050

ALL SAINTS. Nave, chancel, S aisle, bellcote. Very mixed and not very interesting. Is the chancel E window with three unenclosed pointed trefoils a true copy of the original? C14 arcade with octagonal piers and double-chamfered arches. – FONT. Square, Norman, with scalloped underside. Later in the Middle Ages the heads at the corners and one quatrefoil panel on the bowl were carved. – SCREEN. Two parts of the dado were re-used for the organ seat. – PAINTINGS. Large, once splendid St George of *c.* 1400; very large St Christopher. – STAINED GLASS. In the S aisle two windows with glass of *c.* 1855 in the C13 style. – Pre-Reformation BELL with the emblems of the four Evangelists. – PLATE. Cup 1570; Paten 1748. – Arthur Young (1741–1820), the agriculturalist and social and political writer, was born at Bradfield. His tomb is in the churchyard, and there is a memorial to him in the S aisle (ARA).

(LODGES to Bradfield House by *Eden Nesfield*.)

BRADFIELD ST CLARE

9050

ST CLARE. Dedication from the St Cleer family? Nave, chancel, and W tower. No architectural interest, except for the roof,

which has arched braces reaching high up to a collar. –
BENCHES. Some simple ones, with poppy-heads. – PLATE.
Cup of 1668.

(HALL, 1 m. E. An ancient moated structure. LG)

9050 BRADFIELD ST GEORGE

ST GEORGE. A Norman window in the nave on the S side. (C13
lancets on the S side of the chancel.) A very charming Dec S
doorway with a much-moulded ogee arch. Perp three-bay
arcade (four shafts and four fine hollows) and diverse Perp
windows. Nave roof of low pitch with arched braces. Their
spandrels have tracery. Perp W tower.* On a W buttress the
name John Bacon is recorded, no doubt as a donor. – FONT.
Octagonal, Perp, simple. – PULPIT. Jacobean, with two tiers
of short blank arches. – BENCH ENDS. With poppy-heads and
traceried backs (N aisle). – STAINED GLASS. Lower half of
the figure of a Knight (chancel S), c. 1500. – PLATE. Cup
1661; Paten 1686; Flagon and Almsdish 1720.

(WEST LODGE. 'A fine mansion of red brick in Neo-Gothic
style.' LG)

WINDMILL. A derelict smock-mill.

5000 BRADWELL

ST NICHOLAS. Norman round tower. The church is Dec.
Arcade of quatrefoil piers with chamfered arches. Dec windows, in the chancel of two lights with a reticulation motif and
a smaller one inside it. Clerestory windows encircled quatrefoils. SEDILIA and PISCINA with cusped arches and embattled
cresting, encircled quatrefoils in the spandrels. At the W end
of the aisles also circular windows. – FONT. Perp, octagonal.
Against the stem four lions. Against the bowl the Signs of the
four Evangelists and four angels, holding shields. – COM-
MUNION RAIL. Late C17, with heavy twisted balusters. –
PLATE. Cup 1668. – MONUMENT. William Vesey † 1644. Two
kneeling wives and he himself appearing ghost-like between
them. In the 'predella' kneeling children and one son lying
stiffly on his side, propped up on his elbow, as they appear so
often in a larger format on Jacobean tombs.

HOBLAND HALL. See Hopton, p. 279.

---

* Mr A. R. Allan tells me of the will of William Cowper of 1496, offering
ten marks towards the 'bylyng of the newe Stepyll'.

BRAISEWORTH

St MARY. 1857 by *E. B. Lamb*. The w side up to his most brutal feats in other places. Three round-arched lancets and an eight-foiled circle over. A bellcote at the top. That sounds harmless enough, but one must see the chamferings and other details to recognize Lamb in all his perversity. The style he chose was neo-Norman, because the original Norman s doorway of the old church (*see* below) was re-used, a sumptuous piece with an inner continuous order of zigzag, then one order of colonnettes with prettily decorated capitals. There are also odd three-dimensional motifs (odd enough to please Lamb) – chain-links with bossy infillings and also a kind of chain of vertebrae in the hood-mould. (The simpler entrance arch into the porch is the N doorway re-used. L G) Inside, Lamb's most surprising motif is the deep rere-arches. – PULPIT. Simple, C17.

OLD CHURCH, ½ m. SE. What remains is the chancel, one Norman N window, one window with Y-tracery to the E, one Perp window to the s.

BRAMFIELD

St ANDREW. The Norman round tower is isolated. E arch of *c.* 1300 into a former nave. The new church of nave and chancel is all Dec. It is now thatched. – SCREEN. Of *c.* 1500. A good piece with one-light divisions and vaulted coving preserved to W and E. Nice ribbing pattern. Much of the ancient colouring survives. Gesso decoration on the horizontal rail above the dado and on the shafts. Of the figures painted on the dado five are left. – The outer bays to the W were clearly used for side altars with painted reredoses over (cf. e.g. Attleborough, Norfolk). – WALL PAINTING. In a large recess in the nave N wall. Very dim now. What is represented is a large cross and four angels in the spaces between the arms. – PLATE. Set of 1707. – MONUMENT. Arthur Coke † 1629 and his wife. By *Nicholas Stone*, and extremely progressive for its date in the sense that no trace of strapwork is left, and indeed all ornament is rejected. Black and white marble. Mrs Coke is represented comfortably recumbent. She is holding a baby. Above, he is shown kneeling in armour; a stern man, it seems.

ALMSHOUSES. Dated 1723, red brick, very modest.

BRAMFIELD HALL. An H-shaped Tudor house with a fine Early Georgian s front (after 1720). The brickwork is clearly Tudor, and in the E wing one fireplace and the moulded beams remain. The new façade is three-storeyed with a recessed five-bay centre and projecting two-bay wings. Later doorway with broken pediment on Tuscan columns. In the garden a surprising number of undulating forcing-walls or crinkle-crankle walls.

HOLLY FARM, ¾ m. NE. Timber-framed with a porch with balustered sides, probably early C17.

WINDMILL. A derelict tower-mill.

BRAMFORD

1040

ST MARY. An impressive and interesting church with a spectacular N façade of Late Perp date. This has much stone decoration to heighten the effect of its flint walls. All parapets of aisle, clerestory, and porch of stone with pretty blank panelling. Short pinnacles with figures of supporters. Tall porch. This porch however was only heightened in the Perp age. Its two-centred entrance arch, with its typical sunk wave mouldings, and its E window are early C14. Niche above the entrance. Two lions as stops of the hood-mould of the entrance arch. The W window of the porch is Perp, of the same design as the aisle windows. In fact much of the church is of the early C14 and late C13. Of the latter date the chancel, see the one S window with its tracery and rere-arch, the plain PISCINA and SEDILIA, and the priest's doorway. However, the chancel arch is only too patently Victorian. Its date is 1864. Of the early C14 most of the rest, namely both arcades (three bays, octagonal piers, double-chamfered arches), though the capitals on the S side were renewed in the Perp style, the N aisle W window (intersected tracery), the S doorway (fine, filleted continuous mouldings), and the W tower (Dec bell-openings and quatrefoil windows in circles below them). The tower has very big angle buttresses,* a NW stair-turret lower than the parapet, and a recessed lead spire. Though the tower is Dec and the arcades are early C14, the former must have been built later than the latter, as its buttressing cuts into their W arches. What remains obscure is why the tall tower arch is not axial with the nave. Perp, apart from the N front already described, are the clerestory, which has six windows against the three arcade arches below and tracery of the same lively type as the aisles below, and the fine roofs of nave, chancel, and S aisle. The former two have

_____

* A niche with a little vault in the W wall, as the Rev. R. G. Christian kindly tells me.

hammerbeams. The vestry was added on the N side in 1896.
It repeats the style of the aisle successfully.– ROOD SCREEN.
Of stone and c. 1300 in date, that is rather part of the architecture than of the furnishing. Three even arches with shafts
carrying capitals left unfinished. The arches have two wave
mouldings. The top parts seem to be a restoration or remodelling of 1864. – FONT. Octagonal, Perp. Against the bowl four
angels and four shields. – FONT COVER. A very fine early C16
piece. Doors folding back. On their panels groups of three
little plinths arranged like the oriel window of Hengrave Hall.
Domed crocketed top. – PULPIT. C16, with linenfold panelling. – STAINED GLASS. E window by *Kempe*, 1905. – PLATE.
Cup and Flagon 1759.

BRAMFORD HOUSE, NW of the church. Of 1693–4, according to
deeds. A very fine façade of red brick in chequer pattern with
dark blue brick. Seven bays and two storeys with pitched roof
on a richly carved modillion frieze. The modillions run
rhythmically in groups of 4–3–3–4–4–3–3–4. The porch is a
later C18 addition. Entrance hall with the staircase placed
inside it. The third of the three flights propped up awkwardly
by two (later) pillars. Handrail and upper gallery rails with
slender twisted balusters.

The house opposite, i.e. between the church and Bramford House,
is timber-framed and has four thin carved pre-Reformation
brackets.

The village has a number of handsome houses.

BRAMPTON

4080

ST PETER. W tower with flushwork panelling on buttresses
and battlements. A niche above the W window. (Parapet with
seated figures at the corners; cf. Haverhill. LG) The S side and
S porch have flushwork decoration on the buttresses. Lancet
windows and Perp windows in nave and chancel. The E window has cusped intersected tracery and is shafted inside. –
FONT. Octagonal, Perp, simple. – SOUTH DOOR. With simple
blank tracery. – STAINED GLASS. One N lancet in the chancel
by *W. Warrington*, 1856. – PLATE. Cup c. 1723; Cup and
Paten 1801; Almsdish 1802.

BRAMPTON HALL. Built in 1796 (Kelly). Red brick, five bays,
two and a half storeys. Porch with Roman Doric columns.

BRANDESTON

2060

ALL SAINTS. An 8 or 9 ft hedge borders the way to the porch.

Chancel of *c.* 1300 with typical windows, e.g. three stepped separate lancets under one arch. The chancel is, however, much renewed. It was called ruinous in 1602. w tower Dec, in spite of the Perp w window. Niches l., r., and over it. Flushwork decoration on base, buttresses, and battlements. Perp nave canted towards the tower. – FONT. C13, octagonal, of Purbeck marble, with the usual flat pointed arches. – PULPIT. Jacobean. – BENCHES. Ten with traceried ends, poppy-heads, and animals, etc., on the arms. – WEST DOOR traceried. – COMMUNION RAIL. With thin twisted balusters turned in their lower parts. Dated 1711. – STAINED GLASS. Old bits in the SW chancel window. – PLATE. Set of 1710–11. – MONUMENT. John Revett † 1671. Inscription tablet flanked by columns. Putti on the open curly pediment. Garlands at the foot (cf. Easton).

BRANDESTON HALL. Large neo-Tudor of 1864. Red brick, asymmetrical. (Inside a mantelpiece from the White Horse Inn Ipswich.)

Many attractive cottages in the village street.

THE PRIORY, ¾ m. NW. A handsome house dated 1586 on the carved beam of the gable towards the street.

HILL HOUSE, ¼ m. ENE. Early C18 with wooden rustication on the timber framing. Five bays, two storeys.

BRANDON

7080

ST PETER. Early Dec chancel with two pretty E turrets with spirelets. For the dating see the windows and the chancel arch. The E window is of five lights, segment-headed, and has an irregular design with reticulated elements. Of the same time probably the W tower. Its doorway and window however are Perp. Of the same time also the five-bay arcade with unusually slim quatrefoil piers and arches with two small quadrant hollows. Perp N and S sides, Perp S chapel. – FONT. Plain, octagonal, C14. The stem has an octagonal core with eight detached shafts. – SCREEN. With one-light divisions. Rather arid. Only the lower parts original. – STALLS. With traceried fronts and poppy-heads. – BENCHES. Some with poppy-heads. – PLATE. Elizabethan Cup; Paten 1776.

TOWN DEVELOPMENT, at the SE corner of the town. Six unit factories have been built in 1969 by the *G.L.C. Department of Architecture and Civic Design.* 200 out of a planned 576 houses have been built – the first two stages of six.

The church lies in Town Street, ½ m. from the little town which developed along the main road. Hardly any houses need mention; perhaps BRANDON HOUSE, N of the bridge, Georgian, red brick, of five bays and two and a half storeys, with one-bay two-storey wings. Porch with Tuscan columns carrying a broken pediment, and Venetian window above the porch. S of the bridge of similar type CONNAUGHT HOUSE, of white brick and with an Ionic porch, and THE LIMES, with a broken segmental pediment on Roman Doric columns. Facing up the High Street at its S end the SCHOOL, red brick, Gothic, with an asymmetrical façade and clock tower, built in 1878 and not attractive.

Site of substantial ROMAN BUILDINGS at FENHOUSE FARM. *Terra sigillata* of the C1-2 A.D. has been found in this area. Brandon was the centre of the East Anglian craft of flint-knapping.

BRANTHAM 1030

ST MICHAEL. Much rebuilt, especially the chancel and upper parts of the tower. The most reliable-looking windows are Dec. Dec also the angle PISCINA in the S wall of the nave. It is of the type of that in the chapel of Little Wenham Hall. – FONT. From St Mary-at-Quay Ipswich. Octagonal. Four lions against the stem, and angels with shields and the Signs of the Evangelists against the bowl. – PAINTING. Christ and the 32b Children, painted by *John Constable* in 1804. Tall, narrow format, the figures in the tradition of late C18 English portraiture. – STAINED GLASS. Parts of C15 figures in a chancel S window. – PLATE. Almsdish 1701.

LYCHGATE. By *E. S. Prior** and very typical of his capricious style. The E and W walls of pebbles, the fronts to the road coming down in a double curve. The pyramid roof starts on the N and S sides in a segmental curve. Carved timbers in the Arts and Crafts taste.

BRANTHAM COURT. By *P. C. Hardwick*, 1850-2. Brick with stone dressings, in the Elizabethan style.

BREDFIELD 2050

ST ANDREW. W tower, nave and chancel. The tower has flushwork decoration in the form of arched panels on base and buttresses. On the base also initials. The battlements are of brick. Nave roof with hammerbeams. Decorated wall-plate. The bays above the rood have the face of the arched ribs decorated with leaf ornament and the monogram of Christ and

* I received this information from Mr I. Nairn.

initial of the Virgin. – PULPIT. Jacobean. The tester is now the
top of a table in the chancel. – PLATE. Cup 1581; Paten 1706.
VILLAGE PUMP, ½ m. SW. A curiously elaborate C18 crown for
a normal hand-pump. Wrought-iron, like the outlines of a
triangular lodge with a Chinese roof, the three ridges of the
roof enriched with scrollwork. On top a crown (original?).
BREDFIELD HALL. Built in 1665. Demolished c. 1950. The
STABLES remain, with big shaped gables at the ends. Semicircular top carried on a lower part with convex outlines. In the
Hall Edward Fitzgerald was born. Plaque by *Brangwyn*.

BRENT ELEIGH
9040

ST MARY. Not big. Dec nave with Perp N windows. Perp W
tower. – FONT. Octagonal Purbeck bowl, two blank pointed
arches to each side. – FONT COVER. Jacobean, pretty. –
PULPIT. Simple, Jacobean. – BOX PEWS. Some are Jacobean,
the majority C18. – BENCH END with poppy-head. – SCREEN
to the SE chapel. Early C14 with shafts with capitals instead of
mullions, and ogee arches. – SOUTH DOOR. A rare piece,
early C14 with blank reticulated tracery. – REREDOS. Early
Georgian, with fluted pilasters. – COMMUNION RAIL. Three-
sided, with twisted balusters, Early Georgian. – (WALL
PAINTINGS. To the l. of the E window, two censing angels,
probably mid-C14. Under the window a Crucifixion, probably
the original reredos and said to date from c. 1300. The work is
of high quality. To the r. of the window, the remains of a
Harrowing of Hell, probably early C16. The paintings were
discovered in 1960.) – PLATE. Cup and Paten of 1694. –
MONUMENT. Edward Colman. By *Thomas Dunn*, 1743.
Standing wall-monument. Reredos background with broken
pediment. Semi-reclining figure in loose dress gesticulating
towards us. Above a putto with a crown. Two more putti on
the pediment.
In the churchyard the former LIBRARY, rebuilt in 1859. Built
originally c. 1700, it used to stand against the E wall of the
church, which at that time had no window.
BRENT ELEIGH HALL. A puzzling and very attractive house.
Centre and two far-projecting wings, as if basically Elizabethan.
The centre with its pediment is now Early Georgian in character, see the staircase with two twisted balusters to the tread.
Above the staircase a painted oval, with a coat of arms with
putti. The oval has a rich stucco garland round. In the spandrels of the oblong ceiling branches with foliage. This looks

c. 1700 rather than later. The giant Tuscan portico along the centre of the garden side between the wings is clearly of *c.* 1800–10. The canted bays of the wings are said to have been added at the same time. Moreover, *Lutyens* was busy at Brent Eleigh Hall in 1933–4. He enlarged the entrance hall, made the Early Georgian-looking entrance doorway, altered the windows, and made the fireplaces in the hall and the dining room. The dining room was also further altered by Lutyens.*

GATEPIERS dated 1763.

(WELLS HALL, ½ m. SE. Moated house with a good C16 brick gatehouse. P.G.M. Dickinson)

COLMAN'S ALMSHOUSES. 1731. Brick, two-storeyed, with segment-headed windows.

BRETTENHAM
9050

ST MARY. Essentially C14, with a s porch tower. Nave w window with flowing tracery. Dec PISCINA in the chancel with the arms of Stafford and Buckingham. But Perp chancel windows. – FONT. C14, octagonal, with crocketed ogee gables in the panels (cf. Rattlesden). – SCREEN. Bits of tracery from the dado preserved. – LECTERN. A C17 turned baluster. – COMMUNION RAIL. With twisted balusters, *c.* 1700. – SOUTH DOOR. With a foliage-trail border. – STAINED GLASS. One s window by *H. Hughes*, 1866. – MONUMENTS. Three coffin-lids with foliated crosses.

POPLARS FARM, 1½ m. SW. Picturesque timber-framed C15 house. Carved bressumer, one original doorway and some original windows.

WINDMILL. A derelict smock-mill.

BRICKWALL FARMHOUSE *see* WETHERDEN

BRIDGE FARMHOUSE *see* GRUNDISBURGH

BRIGHTWELL
2040

ST JOHN BAPTIST. A small but uncommonly interesting church. Nave and chancel seem to be of *c.* 1300, see particularly the chancel windows and the nave N doorway. This church was 'almost ruined' and 'repaired by Thomas Essington' (*Gent. Mag.* 1829 from a later C17 MS), whose house was Brightwell Hall. The date of the remodelling is most probably *c.* 1656 (date of the new plate, *see* below). Due to Thomas Essington

* Information kindly given by Messrs R. Lofts & Son, Decorators.

the W turret of brick with its battlements and obelisk pinnacles and the brick obelisks on the W and E corners and the E gable. The turret has clasping buttresses, and it rests inside on

17a what is the architectural surprise of the church, two white giant Tuscan columns quite out of scale with the rest and carrying the arch on which the E wall of the turret stands. The effect is strikingly like a Hawksmoor effect at first sight, but such work of c. 1660 as the Charles Church at Plymouth ought also to be remembered. Thomas Essington also put up in his church two pathetic MONUMENTS to two of his children, Thomas who died in 1656 aged five and Anna who died in 1660 aged seventeen. The boy's memorial shows him standing in long clothes holding on to a hand which appears from the r. Tree behind the two hands. He stands against spread-out drapery. Above is a medallion which says: 'O Grave where is thy victory.' On the drapery at the top it says: 'O death where is thy sting.' But on the l. on the drapery is written in stone: 'His *owne words* Christ will rais mee.' – His sister's memorial is more elegant, a larger upright oval medallion with her portrait, a three-quarter figure, holding in one hand a scroll and a palm-branch and in the other a skull. On the scroll it says: 'Her dieing words. My mortall shell put on imortality.' The medallion is a garland, and in this are more inscriptions. On top a seated cherub, the inscription below. At the top of the medallion our attention is drawn to 1 Cor. 15:52, at the foot to Eccl. 7:1. – Arthur Barnardiston † 1737. Inscription tablet with pediment and above this obelisk with a profile portrait in an oval medallion.* – FONT. Octagonal, with a shafted stem, and on the bowl a number of cusped tracery patterns, such as an eight-spiked wheel, a reticulation grid, four wheels of three mouchettes each, four quatrefoils, etc. – FONT COVER. Probably of c. 1656. Scrolls meeting a central baluster. – HELMETS etc. of the Barnardiston family. – PLATE. Cup and Paten 1656.

On the heath s of Martlesham airfield is a group of at least sixteen BARROWS. The three on the Foxhall–Martlesham–Kesgrave parish boundary are in the middle of a mixed Saxon cemetery; the rest of the group, including one known locally as the Devil's Ring, was of Bronze Age date. The Devil's Ring and five other barrows in the same group were excavated, and

* Mr Rupert Gunnis told me that *The Gentleman's Magazine* for 1829, part II, p. 209, quotes from a MS. 'of the time of Charles II' that 'In the chancel are two small monuments of alabaster, exceedingly comely and faire, which were the work of a German, whose ancestors were Italians'.

later demolished, in 1952–3.* *See also* Foxhall (p. 216),
Martlesham (p. 358), Waldringfield (p. 473).

BROCKFORD
3 m. NW of Debenham

1060

(A cottage at Brockford Street has circular chimneyshafts with
Tudor patterns. F. A. Girling)

BROCKLEY

8050

ST ANDREW. W tower with diagonal buttresses carrying flushwork panelling. On the base of the S wall of the tower an inscription commemorating Ricardus Coppyng, who no doubt
gave the money for the building of the tower. Nave of *c.* 1300,
chancel Dec and originally much shorter than at present
(Norman?) – see the string course and the change in construction.‡ – In the S wall inside a big ogee-headed recess. –
SOUTH DOOR. With interesting knocker and lock, probably
also early C14. – PLATE. Elizabethan Cup; Flagon 1771;
Almsdish 1817.

BROKE HOUSE *see* NACTON

BROME

1070

ST MARY. Norman round tower with a top of 1875. The rest
mostly of 1863. – STAINED GLASS. Much of the 1860s. –
PLATE. Cup, Norwich-made, 1568–9; Paten *c.* 1600. – MONU-
MENTS. Sir John Cornwallis † 1544. Two recumbent effigies on
a big tomb-chest with shields separated by rough demi-
columns. Back wall at the feet of the effigies with rough Corinthian demi-columns and a top starting with scrolls, but ending
in an ogee arch – a typical example of the unconvinced accept-
ance of the Renaissance. – Sir Thomas Cornwallis † 1604 and
wife. The same type, especially the same tomb-chest. The back
wall now has strapwork decoration. – Henry Cornwallis
† 1598, kneeling figure between heavy piers carrying a curved
top. – Elizabeth Lady Cornwallis † 1680. Bust in oval medallion
above a tablet with a garland at the foot. Two putti open
drapery. Good quality.

* Information from Mr Norman Smedley.
‡ I am grateful to Mr C. R. Paine for drawing my attention to this.
Concerning the tower, Mr D. N. J. MacCulloch informs me that in his will,
dated 16 October 1521, Richard Copping of Brockley leaves money 'that ye
plancher of the Ruffe of the steple of brokley be fullie finished' (Bury R.O.,
Liber Brydon, f. 206). The inscription on the base course probably refers to
his earlier operations.

BROME HALL, demolished in 1963, was mostly late C19 Tudor, with big polygonal tower, mullioned and transomed windows, and bay windows. Extensive topiary gardens.

(BROME GRANGE has one of the undulating or crinkle-crankle walls. N. Scarfe)

GATES, 100 yds SE of the Swan Inn. Wrought-iron; C18.

3050
BROMESWELL

ST EDMUND. Norman S doorway. Three zigzags in flat relief and a hood-mould with billet ornament. A blocked Norman N window (now obscured by the War Memorial). W tower with arched flushwork panelling on base, buttresses, and battlements. S porch of early C16 brick. The entrance, windows, etc., in stone. Victorian brick chancel. In the nave a simple hammerbeam roof. – FONT. Octagonal. Against the stem four tall seated lions. Against the bowl the Signs of the Evangelists and four angels. – PULPIT. Jacobean. – BENCHES. The ends with poppy-heads, but without tracery. Only four of the figures on the arms are left. – COMMUNION RAIL. With turned balusters, mid C17. – PLATE. Elizabethan Cup.*

BROOK FARM see STRATFORD ST MARY

BROOM HILLS see RICKINGHALL INFERIOR

BROWSTON HALL see BELTON

3060
BRUISYARD

ST PETER. Norman round tower. Nave and chancel. Early C16 brick windows in nave and S chapel. – FONT. Octagonal, Perp, with four lions against the stem and eight shields against the bowl. – PULPIT. Plain C18, with tester. – SCREEN to the family chapel. Early C17, plain, with vertically symmetrical balusters above closed panelling. – COMMUNION RAIL. Early C17, with vertically symmetrical balusters. – ENGRAVING. A large hand-coloured engraving of 1794 with the Ten Commandments, Moses, Aaron, and Joshua. – PLATE. Elizabethan Cup; Paten 1568.

BRUISYARD HALL. A chantry college was transferred to Bruisyard from Campsea Ash in 1354 and soon changed to a nunnery of Poor Clares. Of this remains walling and an arch in the W wall of the house. Also less distinct walling in front of the

* A church BELL, made in Malines, and with religious reliefs. It is dated 1530.

s façade and a room in the w range with a heavily beamed
ceiling. The house in its present form dates from 1610. Red
brick, three-storeyed, with a central three-storeyed porch.
This is flanked by slender polygonal buttresses and has a
stepped gable with finials.

BRUNDISH

2060

St Lawrence. Norman square w tower, unbuttressed. Dec
bell-openings. The Norman arch into the nave is blocked.
Dec angle piscina in the chancel. Crocketed ogee arch and
buttresses. Perp nave and chancel. The e window of five lights.
Perp s porch with flushwork front. Entrance with niche over.
Wide interior, the roof ceiled. Tomb recess in the n wall and
in it brass to Sir Edmund de Burnedissh, c. 1360, a priest.
The figure is 2 ft 3 in. long. – screen. Only the dado remains. –
pulpit. Back panel and tester attached uncomfortably to the
n doorway. – bench ends. With poppy-heads and remains of
small figures. – box pews. – plate. Pre-Reformation Paten,
altered; Paten 1678; two-handled Cup 1700.
(Manor House, Brundish Street. Of c. 1500. Two buildings
meeting L-wise at a corner. Thatched. Many original mullioned windows. doe)

BRUNDON see SUDBURY

BUCKLESHAM

2040

St Mary. Mostly of 1878. Nave and chancel in one. Wooden
bell-turret with shingled broach-spire. – font. Octagonal,
with four lions against the stem, the four Signs of the Evangelists and four angels against the bowl.

BUCK'S FARMHOUSE see COOKLEY

BULCAMP

4070

1 m. ese of Blyford

Hospital. Built as a House of Industry, that is a workhouse,
in 1765–6. Partly destroyed in a riot of 1766 and rebuilt. The
first of the interesting series of c18 workhouses in Suffolk.
The plans were drawn by *Thomas Fulcher*, who received 15 gns.
for them and his journeys and attendances. Red brick, of two
storeys, and remarkably extensive. H-shaped plan with wings
projecting a little on one side, very far on the other. On that
side in one wing is the chapel. This has pointed windows with

Y-casements. The other windows are small and segment-headed.* The centre of the recessed part has a three-bay pediment and a lantern. There were lower wings connecting the ends of the projecting wings, one with cells for casuals, but they may not be part of the original scheme. There is also a low office range in front of the other front, and that also may be an addition.

BUNGAY

3080

ST MARY. This church, now the principal parish church of the town, was originally the church of the Benedictine nunnery founded at Bungay by Gundreda, the wife of Roger de Glanville, *c.* 1160. The present church is probably the parochial nave‡ to which a nuns' choir belonged, represented now by ruins E of the church. The fire of 1688 destroyed most of the priory buildings together with the nuns' choir. Conspicuous among the ruins are the remains of the arch of a former chapel to the S and a large window to the N. Immediately attached to the chancel but not quite in line with it runs a wall with a doorway with delicate detail of *c.* 1300 and shafted windows quite probably of the same date. Three of these can be seen. A second doorway cuts into one of them and cannot be *in situ.* This wall must have been connected with a lengthening of the nuns' choir. Of the priory precinct flint walling remains in St Mary's Street as well as Trinity Street. The church itself, in the state which the later Middle Ages gave it, had an entirely parochial character.§

Spectacular parochial S W tower, begun *c.* 1470, 90 ft high. Octagonal buttresses with octagonal turret pinnacles carrying little spires. Very tall three-light bell-openings with transom. Flushwork decoration on the lower parts of the buttresses only.

---

* The DOE points out that they are a transition from cross-casements to sashes. The upper pair of lights slides over the lower operated by an arm from inside.

‡ The walls abutting upon this end of the church are 25 ft 6 in. wide and 20 ft deep. Both Dr J. J. Raven and the architect of the restoration of the church in 1862 considered that they never formed part of the chancel, but were the remains of the nuns' chapel of St Mary, mentioned in 1370. The outlines of a doorway can be seen at the present time which led into the church, immediately behind the high altar. In the Churchwarden's Book in 1540 is the following entry: 'Pd. to ye mason for stoppyn up the door next the Abbey, ijs. iiijd.' (W. M. Lummis, *The Churches of Bungay*, 1965).

§ Mr Hugh Braun has pointed out that the only remains of the original convent church are the walls of the N transept, the angles of which show the clumsy quoining of the period.

On the lower parts of the wall flint and stone chequer pattern. The parapet and battlements are stone-faced and decorated. They were rebuilt in 1702. At the base of the tower a close frieze of quatrefoils and shields. The s aisle was evidently built at about the same time. Knapped flintwork; tall, transomed three-light windows. The nave and N aisle are earlier. The w doorway and the N doorway are both Dec and similar to the priory doorway described above. The w doorway has a hood-mould with fleurons. The nave NW buttress with its niche belongs to the same phase. The N aisle buttresses are also peculiar. They have very unusual set-offs and niches. Charming N aisle parapet with a frieze of quatrefoils and open-work cresting (for the strange bottle-shapes cf. Blythburgh). The N aisle windows are all Perp, but with their two-centred arches earlier than those of the s aisle. The nave received a new w window in the C15, a very large seven-bay window of lively design. The N porch is two-storeyed. Entrance with fleurons in one arch moulding. Spandrels with unusual representations: on the l., seated on a lion he has slain, a knight in armour, bearing on his shield the crowned letter M; on the r., a lion playing with its cub, watched by the head of a man with a halo and a flowing moustache.* Inside the porch, original vaulting shafts, a C19 tierceron-vault, and one original boss.

Inside the church the arcades belong to the early C14. Six bays. Quatrefoil piers with fillets and thin hollows in the diagonals. Two wave mouldings in the arch. PISCINA in the s aisle with two animals in cusped roundels above the arch. The Perp clerestory is not in axis with the arcades. The tower was originally open to the N and E. The blank lancets and circular traceried windows in the later infilling of these arches are C19. – FONT. A fluted pillar and a bowl with rustically carved cherubs' heads and flowers. Ordered no doubt after the fire of 1688. – BREAD (?) CUPBOARD. With carved figures and the date 1675. – PLATE. Cup 1722; Paten 1727; Flagon 1728; Cover 1729; Cup 1822. – MONUMENT. Robert Scales † 1728. Scheemakers, when visiting Bungay (writes Canon Lummis), called the angel on this monument 'very well executed'.

HOLY TRINITY. Holy Trinity lies immediately SE of St Mary's churchyard and the former Priory. Its E end still faces the open country. It has an C11 round tower with herringbone masonry and traces of windows with triangular heads. In the nave a Norman N window. The church consists of nave and chancel

* W. M. Lummis, *The Churches of Bungay*, 1965.

and a wide s aisle. This has at its s w angle a flushwork-panelled
turret. The same decoration in the s porch. The aisle and porch
are Dec; see the w window and the arcade of three bays.
Quatrefoil piers, wave-moulded arches. The fourth bay leads
into the s chapel. It has fine continuous mouldings and is Perp.
Most of the chancel was in ruins from 1558 till 1754, when it
was first restored. The present chancel is of 1926 and by *F. E.
Howard*. – FONT. Fluted pillar and bowl with carving done or
re-done in the C19. The font is probably of *c.* 1700 (cf. St
Mary). – PULPIT. An extremely fine piece, set up in 1558. Two
tiers of simple panelling with square centre and four L-shaped
panels surrounding it. Arabesque ornament on the pilasters
and below the top border. – COMMUNION RAIL. Strongly
swelling turned balusters, *c.* 1660. – AUMBRY. Bronze, l. of the
altar in the s chapel, 1922. Whom by? – PLATE. Cup and
Paten inscribed 1561; Flagon 1762; Almsdish 1766. – MONU-
MENT. Thomas Wilson † 1774, standing putto mourning by
an urn. By *Thomas Scheemakers*.

ST EDMUND (R.C.), St Mary's Street, immediately s of the
churchyard of St Mary. 1892 by *Bernard Smith*. Red brick
with stone dressings. No tower, but a polygonal baptistery
with pyramid roof on the N side, which was added in 1901. It is
rib-vaulted inside and treated in the style of 1300. The church
has a rather over-decorated façade with stone sculpture,
figures as well as reliefs. Much sculpture inside too.

CASTLE. Just w of the yard of the King's Head Hotel. Built by
Roger Bigod, probably at the time of Stephen. Large keep,
70 ft square, with flat buttresses at the angles and in the middle
of each face. The walls stand only to the height of the entrance
floor, i.e. foundations and basement. In the foundations, at the
s w angle that unique survival, a mining gallery, nearly ready
to bring the tower to collapse. The gallery is 5 ft high and 2 ft
wide and runs across from the w wall into the prison at the foot
of the forebuilding. A new gallery was begun but not completed. Its purpose was to isolate the s w angle entirely. The
gallery would remain carefully shored up with timbers until
the moment of the attack had come. The timbers would then
be set on fire and the angle of the keep would come down (as
happened e.g. at Corfe). The galleries belong to the siege of
1174; the castle surrendered. The interior of the keep is
divided by a cross-wall into two chambers. The staircase runs
up in the middle of the N wall at the place of the cross-wall. The
hall was on an upper floor and, according to a scalloped capital

found, had either an arcade or one large arch instead of the cross-wall (cf. Hedingham). In the N W corner at a level between basement and entrance a garderobe. The stones of the upper levels were used as early as the time of the new works of 1294. On the s side remains of what the excavator, Hugh Braun, calls one of the largest and strongest forebuildings in England. In the late C13 the keep was closely surrounded by an irregularly polygonal curtain wall. On the w side a strong gatehouse was built with two semicircular towers faced with ashlar. (During excavations the pit was discovered in which the drawbridge was swivelled. L G)

PERAMBULATION. The pivot of the little town is undoubtedly the BUTTER CROSS in the MARKET PLACE, an open octagonal structure with Tuscan columns and arches, with a dome crowned by a remarkably handsome figure of Justice. The cross was erected after the fire of 1688, in 1689. The statue is of lead and was added in 1754. It could well be by *Cheere*. In the L-shaped Market Place a few worth-while houses, especially the house in the angle of the L which is of *c*. 1700 and has six bays, and whose front round the corner to the l. has late C18 giant pilasters and a bow-shaped oriel, and the two HOTELS, flanking the entrance into EARSHAM STREET. They are both C18 in their present appearance, plastered white and, though of no special interest, very fitting for their position. In Earsham Street, which runs N, Nos. 4–8 are of *c*. 1700, No. 12 (Urban District Council) is Georgian of five bays and two storeys with a hipped roof, No. 15 opposite is similar and dated 1807. At the end to the r. ST MARY'S SCHOOL, again red brick, Georgian, and of five bays, but with only three attic windows (cf. Mettingham). It has a doorcase with Roman Doric pilasters. On the corner opposite and facing the river WAVENEY HOUSE with a Greek Doric porch.

From the Butter Cross to the E runs BRIDGE STREET, where No. 34 is dated 1776. Red brick again, the façade at r. angles to the street. Doorway with pediment on Roman Doric columns. Back to the Butter Cross and to the SE, along TRINITY STREET. The houses here and towards and along the church-yard are mostly enjoyable. No. 7 has a shopfront of *c*. 1830 with Greek Doric angle columns. Then an C18 house, recessed, at the end of a little *place*. It has a fine doorway with Ionic columns. Nos. 11–13 has Dutch gables of the late C17 and a later doorway with Roman Doric columns. The end is TRIN-ITY HALL, facing SE, a fine house of *c*. 1700, of red and rubbed brick with seven bays, two storeys, and a hipped roof. The Doric porch is obviously later; for above it, on the first floor, is that typical late C17 or early C18 motif, a pair of brick pilasters flanking the middle window.

Now from the Butter Cross due s. ST MARY'S STREET starts with the most ambitious Georgian house of Bungay, No. 6, again red brick, again of five bays, but with two and a half storeys. Wide doorway with Tuscan columns and an open pediment. Venetian window over. Top pediment set against the half-storey. Nos. 14–18 also has a pedimented Georgian doorway, but it is a house of c. 1500, and has three oriel windows with original sills. They illustrate the Slaughter of the Philistines by Samson, Samson and Delilah, a man (Hercules?) wrestling with two dragons, three shields supported by putti, and mermaids.

St Mary's Street continues in UPPER OLLAND STREET. Nos. 1–3 are a Georgian pair with identical doorways. Further on the CONGREGATIONAL CHURCH, grey brick of 1818, but the façade clearly altered c. 1840–50. At the end ROSE HALL, dated 1739. This is of red brick with a parapet and hipped roof. Doorway with Roman Doric pilasters on the s side, an upper Venetian window on the E. Behind it is the original staircase with strong turned balusters.

BURES

ST MARY. A stately church. Late C13 to early C14 tower with Dec bell-openings. Tomb recess in the outer N wall. Also C14 the tower arch towards the nave with three chamfers dying into the imposts. Inside the tower springers of a projected vault with fine faces and grotesques. The tower originally carried a spire. C14 N porch of big timbers. C14 arcades of three bays (octagonal piers, double-chamfered arches). Perp aisles and clerestory. Ornate Perp s chapel (Waldegrave Chapel), founded in 1514. Brick, with flushwork battlements to the E. Big windows, two to the s. In the buttress between them small priest's doorway. The piers of the arcade towards the chancel are square with four half-columns with fillets. Of about the same time the big founder's MONUMENT in the chancel and the elegantly decorated doorway next to it. The doorway has fleurons, the tomb a chest with shields in cusped foils. On the lid indents of brasses. Arch above and big angel corbels l. and r. Early C16 s porch of brick, the side windows with brick tracery. The inner doorway, however, belongs to the C14 work. – FONT. Octagonal, Perp. Stem with four tracery panels and at the angles the four Signs of the Evangelists. Bowl with panels with demi-figures of angels. On the shields the arms of England, de Vere, Fitzralph, Mortimer, de Cornard, Waldegrave, de Bures, and Mortimer de Clare. – STOUP. Inside the S porch. On two male demi-figures, one a bishop. – SOUTH DOOR. With tracery and a trail border. – PLATE. Almsdish 1734; Cup and Paten 1740. – MONUMENTS. For the chancel N side see above. – In a N window on the sill beautiful oaken effigy of a Knight, cross-legged, early C14. – In the S chapel tomb-chest with shields on lozenges in square panels. The top rises like a lectern towards the window sill. Indents of brasses on it. – Also in the S chapel small tomb-chest with shields in cusped foils, and free-standing monument to Sir William Waldegrave † 1613 and his wife † 1581. Big square base and recessed square top with coupled columns and pediments. The only figures are the row of small kneeling children on the N side.

ST STEPHEN'S CHAPEL, I m. NE. Dedicated in 1218. Lancet windows and three stepped lancets at the E end, shafted inside. Timber-framed W attachment. Thatched roof. In the chapel three MONUMENTS from Colne Priory, Earls Colne, Essex, the church where the de Veres, Earls of Oxford, were buried. Knight with crossed legs, c. 1300. The tomb-chest does not belong. With its deep kneeling niches it appears more likely for a shrine than a monument. The niches have crocketed ogee arches and are separated by narrow niches with crocketed gables for small, extremely well carved figures, unfortunately headless. Early C14. – A de Vere, c. 1370, alabaster. The stars of the de Veres carved on the jupon. Against the walls of the tomb-chest pairs of mourners under broad depressed nodding ogee arches. The tomb-chest was originally broader and accommodated two effigies. – Knight and Lady of c. 1420. Alabaster. The lady wears a horned head-dress. Pet dogs playing at her feet. Against the tomb-chest alternating, rather flat frontal figures of angels holding shields, and tracery strips in two tiers. – Also the lower half of a mid-C12 coffin lid with the parallel, flatly carved legs of a figure and a flatly ornamented border. Probably Alberic, first de Vere, Great Chamberlain, † 1141. – (STAINED GLASS. Various fragments, perhaps also from Earls Colne Priory.)

On the way from the church to the chapel (in the street called

THE STREET) on the r. THE MALTINGS, fine timber-framed building with a boldly carved bressumer: crown and Tudor rose, big leaves, animals, a figure (the butcher at his block? the smith at the anvil? a carver?).

Off the road to Sudbury, ½ m. out, BEVILLS, a spectacular house of c. 1500, made more spectacular by restorations and additions of c. 1910–20. The brick ends of the long w front belong to these, as do the timber-framed gables and the porch. The old building is timber-framed too and has brick-nogging. Oriel windows, buttress shafts, and carved bressumers. On the roof of this original centre some original decorated brick chimneys.

Off the road to Nayland, 1½ m. SE, SMALLBRIDGE HALL, brick, built before or c. 1572 (date in the armorial glass) by the Waldegrave family. Largely rebuilt in 1874. Restored in 1932. Surrounded by a moat. s front with four small gables or dormers. Hall behind this. To the N two far-projecting wings with only a narrow space between them. Large chimneybreast in the E wall, probably the chimney of the former kitchen. Mullioned and transomed brick windows. The interior mostly altered, but several good panelled rooms, especially on the first floor. Queen Elizabeth I visited the house in 1561 and 1579.

BURGATE

0070

ST MARY. Dec w tower with small upper circular windows with quatrefoils and small quatrefoil windows above the bell-openings. Dec chancel with pretty PISCINA. The fine large E and side windows however seem to belong to the C19 restoration; for in 1851 the Suff. Arch. Soc. reported that the E window was insignificant and had wooden mullions and that the side windows had lost their tracery. Nave N windows Dec, s windows Perp. The interior disastrously altered. No division at all between nave and chancel. – FONT. Octagonal, Perp. Against the stem four lions. The figures against the bowl have been hacked off. On the two-step base inscription referring to Sir William Burgate. – PULPIT. Square, Jacobean. – COMMUNION RAIL. With sturdy balusters, mid-C17. – STAINED GLASS. Bits in a N window. – MONUMENT. Sir William Burgate † 1409 and wife. The best brasses of their date in Suffolk and placed on a fine tomb-chest. The figures are 4 ft 7 in. long and placed under ogee canopies. The engraving is uncommonly bold and economical. The tomb-chest has on its long sides eleven ogee-headed niches with crockets and little but-

Burgate, brass to Sir William Burgate † 1409 and wife

tresses. In five of them on one side hearts with wings, on the other shields.

IRON AGE HUTS. Some signs of Iron Age occupation near Hill House. Also a site surrounded by earthen banks with a track through the wood just s of the church, within which are a group of Saxon sherds.

2050   BURGH

ST BOTOLPH. Nave, chancel, and s porch tower. The tower is Dec, unbuttressed, with battlements decorated by arched panels in flushwork and with small quatrefoil windows below the bell-openings. Nave and chancel all Perp, except for the earlier doorways. – FONT. On the bowl the four Signs of the Evangelists, two angels, and the two figures of the Annunciation. Much recut. – PULPIT. Jacobean. – STAINED GLASS. By *Kempe* the E (1903) and W and chancel s windows (1906). – DOOR HANDLE. Cautley calls it the best feature of the church and dates it C13. – PLATE. Cup and Paten 1637. – At the churchyard entrance a laburnum tree, its trunk and two shoots completely plaited.

OLD RECTORY, ¼ m. NE of Grundisburgh church. Georgian, of red brick. Five bays, two storeys, hipped roof, the centre window on the first floor arched.

THISTLETON HALL. Demolished c. 1955.

CASTLE FIELD. Just N of the church a ROMAN BUILDING lay within a ditch and bank measuring 225 by 220 yds. Examination in 1901 revealed much building material, nails, painted plaster, and *terra sigillata* of the period of Domitian. The coinage dated from Tiberius (14–37) to Valentinian (364–75). Despite the banked enclosure, it does not seem to have been a military site. By 1973* the remains of the villa had disappeared. It overlaid an important Belgic Iron Age site, from which much fine pottery has been obtained.

4000   BURGH CASTLE

ST PETER AND ST PAUL. Norman‡ round tower with brick top. One lancet window in the nave. The N aisle is of 1847. – FONT. Octagonal, Perp. Against the stem four lions, against the bowl four lions and four angels with shields presenting the symbols

* So Mr Norman Smedley told me.

‡ Mr Charles Green, on the evidence of the condition of the wall and other features revealed by excavation, suggests that the tower is possibly Saxon.

of the Trinity (three tiaras) and the Passion. – BENCHES. Some with poppy-heads.

BURGH CASTLE.* Roman fort on the W side of the village above 3b the marshy ground where the Waveney joins Breydon Water. The fort is placed on the 30 ft contour overlooking the Roman commercial harbour of Caister-by-Yarmouth and to the N of a small creek (now Belton Fen) where it is thought lay a naval dockyard, which the fort defended. It covers *c.* 6 acres. It is roughly quadrangular, with standing walls on three sides only, in length 640 ft (E), 300 ft (N), and 325 ft (S). The shorter walls terminate at their W ends on the edge of the high ground above the marsh; at the NE and SE corners the walls sweep round with a 25¼ ft radius at the outer face, and have an average height of 15 ft, the inner face with a smooth slope from *c.* 11 ft thick (on the E side) at the base to about 5 ft at the top. The construction is of alternating courses of bricks and flints, The former being in triple bands every four or five courses; the bricks do not pass right through the wall's thickness, but are of one unit's width from each face. The facing flints and many brick courses have been largely robbed, mainly on the inner sides. The E wall on the landward side has a deep foundation of mortared flint rubble, but the N and S walls are tapered in thickness towards the cliff edge to a 7 ft base at the former W end. They stand on light foundations of clay and puddled chalk and the formerly reported timbering here was apparently no more than level-gauges to guide the builders; they occur rather irregularly at about 10–12 ft intervals. Traces of the W wall foundations of this type were found in 1961 in the higher ground of the cliff edge near the NW angle, and the fallen NW bastion now lies buried on the valley bottom where it fell, below the silt now forming the marsh-pasture. The internal width of the fort was 328 ft. There are six visible pear-shaped bastions, two at the corners, one in the middle of each of the shorter sides, and two set symmetrically on the E wall, in the middle of which is the main gate. All the bastions are basically cylindrical, tangential to the wall, but thickened for attachment on that side, so giving the pear shape. Each is approximately 14½ ft (or 15 Roman ft) in diameter, and they are bonded into the walls in the upper parts only. That they were a later addition to the original design made during the

* The whole description of Burgh Castle has been revised and expanded by Mr Charles Green, who carried out excavations between 1958 and 1962 for the Ministry of Works.

progress of the building is confirmed by the discovery of the foundations of an internal angle-turret in the NE corner, suited to the rounded angle. This was demolished at the time, doubtless, when the bastions were substituted, as a Roman barrack-building rested on part of these foundations. These external bastions were early ones of the type and appear to be 'experimental', for the ballista-mountings of the angle-bastions lay within the intersections of the lines of the fort's faces. The walls in consequence could not be fully enfiladed. There is no sign of an outer ditch.

Within the walls, much grey, colour-coated and a little Romano-Saxon ware, chiefly of the C3–4 A.D., has been found. Many, if not most, of the coins published in the past came, not from the fort, but from the site of a civilian settlement to the S, later associated with the dockyard, and so cannot be used to date the fort. Over 1,200 were found during the excavations. One was an illegible C1, four were C3, beginning with Gallienus (253–61), and the remainder were of C4 types, though the large majority were late copies of those of the first half of the century. As most of them were in large or small hoards of the last days of the Roman occupation, they point to an evacuation date c. 407–8.

The identification of the site as the Saxon Shore fort of Gariannonum mentioned in the C4 list of garrisons, the *Notitia Dignitatum*,* dates from 1774. The 'Cnobheresburg' mentioned by Bede as the place where Sigebert, c. A.D. 635, established the Irish missionary St Fursey has since Camden's day been associated with Burgh Castle, an identification substantially confirmed by the last excavations. At the N end of the enclosure were the remains of oval huts, apparently monks' cells, and what was probably a tiny church. At the S end, below the later Norman motte, was the monastic cemetery in which converts were buried, and adjoining this a floor and other small remains of what was probably the 'mother church', though no walling was left standing. The Middle Saxon pottery, coins, and the sequence of renewed cells point to the establishment's survival until 869, when the Danish host destroyed the East Anglian religious houses. It appears not to have been revived. E of the fort the Roman(?) cemetery included a few Saxon graves containing pottery and brooches of an earlier day, probably from the settlement of Cnobhere's followers in the vicinity.

* See Ives, *Gariannonum of the Romans*.

Until its complete removal in 1839, the sw corner of the fort contained a large ditched mound covering the detached w half of the s wall. This was a Norman motte of the immediate post-Conquest period. The break in the s wall was made by the ditch-diggers, and the vertical holes still visible in this walling were of Norman date, made to hold heavy timbers which laced the mound and supported the timber super-structure. Bases for posts in the central area of the mound had disturbed the burials and showed by their plan that they probably directly underlay the central tower. When this Norman castle was begun, the w wall of the fort had already collapsed. Its place was then taken by a high earthen bank, probably crowned with a timber stockade. The bank thrown up outside the w half of the n wall was also Norman work of this time; it was put there to reinforce the slowly sinking stone wall. This small castle probably served as an outpost of the larger one at Norwich and guarded the entrance from the sea. It was probably built by *Ralph* the Engineer, mentioned in Domesday. During the Middle Ages much of the w wall seems to have been robbed for building material. Roman bricks and tiles are to be seen in the walls of the churches at Burgh Castle, Burgh St Peter, and Reedham. Buildings, probably of Roman date, lie just n of the fort.

OLD HALL FARMHOUSE, 1¼ m. SE. Mid-C17 or a little later, with a centrally placed Dutch gable. The doorway with Gibbs surround and pediment must of course be Georgian.

BURSTALL

ST MARY. Essentially of the early C14 with a most uncommon N arcade of four bays. Very finely moulded piers, their front mouldings running continuously into the arches, their mould-ings towards the arch openings interrupted by capital bands with fleurons. Steep arches. N windows with finely moulded rere-arches. Finely moulded s doorway (continuous mouldings). Early C14 also the lower chancel and the w tower. The bell-openings are cusped lancets, and below them are quatrefoil windows in circles. Perp s porch of timber with cusped side openings and decorated bargeboards. Perp hammerbeam roof in the nave. The chancel roof is single-framed and may be of the same date as the chancel. – SCREENS. Of the Perp rood screen only the dado survives. More interesting is the N par-close screen. This belongs to the C14. It has shafts instead of mullions and several simple patterns of flowing tracery.

8060

BURY ST EDMUNDS

THE ABBEY

INTRODUCTION

St Edmundsbury was one of the four or five most powerful and wealthy Benedictine monasteries in England. What remains of it now is two mighty gates into the precinct, and inside it no more than fragments, which tell their tale only to the student. The precinct, however, is not built over, and so the size of the area can at least be visualized without effort. It is about 1,500 ft from N to S and about 1,000 from W to E. The W boundary is at Angel Hill, the N boundary at Mustow Street, the S boundary by Honey Hill, and the E boundary along the original course of the river Linnet (not the Lark).

A few dates will first be given, and then a description of the whole of the buildings as they were in the Middle Ages. This ought to be read side by side with the maps on pp. 134–5. Then the gates and the fragmentary remains will be described, and they ought also to be compared with the maps.*

A small monastery was apparently founded c. 633. King Edmund was martyred by the Danes in 869. In the C10 the community was of secular priests. King Canute in 1020 replaced these by twenty Benedictine monks. William the Conqueror in 1081 confirmed and increased its privileges and the number of monks was raised to 80. The church was rebuilt then, it seems, and anyway under Abbot Baldwin who ruled from 1065 to 1097. The relics of St Edmund were translated to the new presbytery in 1095. In the next twenty years the parts round the cloister were built. The nave followed, and the W front seems to have been in hand c. 1140 at the latest. More dates will be given as the description demands them. The only general one still to be referred to here is the Riots of 1327, after the death of Edward II, during which the monastery was sacked and much was burnt.

* The crypt and transepts have now been excavated.

THE PLAN

The Norman Gate led straight towards the church. To its N, close to it, is St James's Parish Church, to its S, a good deal further away, St Mary's Parish Church. The ABBEY CHURCH was 505 ft long, i.e. 50 ft longer than Norwich Cathedral and nearly 100 more than Norman St Albans. It had a W front stretching out 246 ft, a width unmatched by any other English medieval church (Ely *c.* 160, Lincoln *c.* 175). The centre of the front, corresponding to nave and aisles, had three deep giant niches, a motif peculiar to England, even if developed from Carolingian and Ottonian German precedent, and to be found at Lincoln and Peterborough.* There were in addition an apsed chapel N and S of this centre, and these were repeated on the upper floor. The W doors were made before 1148, the upper N chapel was consecrated in 1142. The mighty tower over the centre, a feature corresponding to Norman Winchester (begun in 1079) and to Ely, as does the whole feature of a W transept, was built by the famous Samson, first as sub-sacrist, then as abbot, towards the end of the C12. The octagonal N corner tower was probably built at the same time, due E of the present choir of St James's, and after its completion a corresponding S tower.‡ By this work the façade assumed its full width. The W tower fell in 1430–1.§ In 1465 a fire damaged the whole church severely.

The nave was twelve bays long (St Albans 13, Ely 13, Norwich 14). It had an arcade 26 ft in height, and groin-vaulted aisles. There were a gallery, probably unsubdivided in its openings and 19 ft high, and a clerestory. The nave was not vaulted. The transepts projected far N and S. They had an E aisle, and each two apsed chapels to the E. The inner N chapel was replaced by a more spacious, straight-ended Lady Chapel in 1275; E of the inner S chapel a further chapel was added by

---

* There were possibly two smaller subsidiary niches or arches, one into each side chapel. They are shown on an early C19 print (J. Kendall), but there is not now sufficient confirmatory detail visible to show exactly what they were.

‡ Excavations conducted by Mr C. A. Ralegh Radford indicated that the prime purpose of the tower at the N of the W transept was to serve as a stair to the upper chapel – the porticus of St Faith – dedicated in 1142. Both foundations and surviving masonry suggest one build as high as the upper chapel. The same is probably true of the S side.

§ Wills of 1457/8, 1460, and 1465 leave money towards the fabric of the new tower (ARA and Mr Peter Northeast).

BURY ST EDMUNDS ABBEY

(Reproduced by courtesy of Mr A. B. Whittingham and the Archaeological Journal)

1 Cowshed
2 Brewery
3 Bakery
4 Mill
5 Granary
6 Abbot's Stable
7 Abbot's Bakery and Brewery
8 Chamber (?)
9 Watermill at East Gate & Granary(?) next to Pond
10 Kitchen
11 Dovecot
12 Buttery
13 Abbot's Hall over Cellar
14 Queen's Chamber over Larder and Wardrobe
15 Chambery
16 Chambers
17 Procession-way to South Gate
18 Chapel
19 Former Dovecot
20 Dorter over
21 Reredorter
22 Stables
23 Squires (?)
24 Gate
25 Bath
26 Lecture Court
27 Chapel
28 Garden
29 St Benedict's Basilica
30 St Michael's Chapel
31 Chapter House
32 Vestry
33 New Hall
34 Old Hall
35 Spanne
36 St Andrew's Chapel
37 Bridge
38 Sacrist's Camera
39 Sacrist's StaffHouse, Brewery, Bakery, Granary & Stable
40 Sextry Yard
41 Sub Sacrist's Workshops and Mint
42 Gate of Vineyard
43 Line of Norman Wall
44 School (see p. 137n)
45 Song School
46 St John at Hill
47 Feretrar's House
48 Inner Parlour
49 Parlour
50 Treasury
51 Great Hall over Cellar
52 Parlour Court
53 Black Hostry
54 Warming House
55 Pitancery
56 Larder
57 Kitchen
58 Cellarer
59 Porch
60 Bay
61 Hall of Pleas
62 Pentice
63 Culvert
64 Almonry
65 Dyke
66 Gate-porter
67 Master of the Horse
68 Buttressed Wall c. 1150, heightened after 1327
69 Common Stable
70 Trail
71 Charnel
72 Great Cemetery
73 St Mary's Church
74 Norman Gate
75 St James's Church (Cathedral)
76 Great Gate
77 Abbot's Bridge
78 King's Hall
79 Abbot's Palace
80 Prior's House
81 Infirmary
82 Bradfield Hall
83 Refectory
84 Cloister

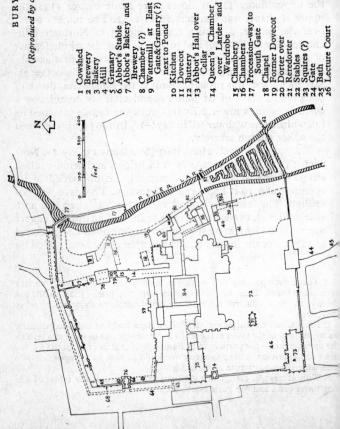

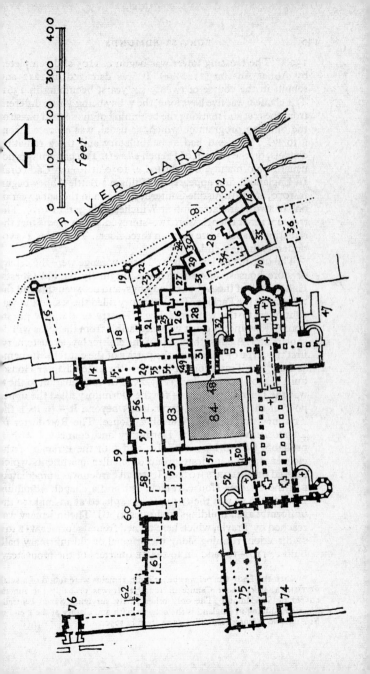

1300.* The crossing tower was begun c. 1105 and complete
by Abbot Anselm (1120–48). It was damaged in 1210 an
rebuilt in the course of twenty-six years, beginning in 1361
The chancel was five bays long, the w bay being a little differen
from the rest and marking the beginning of the second phase o
the building programme which, as usual, was executed fron
E to w. The E end had an ambulatory and three radiating
chapels, on the pattern of French *chevets*. The pattern was no
usual in Normandy, but existed c. 1030 at Rouen Cathedral
In England it first appeared in William's Battle Abbey begun
in 1070, at St Augustine Canterbury begun in the same year o
one or two years later, and at Winchester begun in 1079. The
transept inner chapels were two-storeyed, and it seems that th
radiating chapels were even on three floors. There was a cryp
underneath the E end.

The CLOISTER lay to the N. In the w range were the cellar
or store houses, above which was originally the old Guests
Hall, or hall of the Abbot's Lodgings, and between this and th
church lay the Parlour. The Refectory filled the N side and wa
continued to the w by the Black Hostry or the new guest
house. This and its court were accessible from the w, as will b
shown later. Against the E side of the cloister lay, as customary
first the slype or passage to the parts E of the church – its nam
at Bury was Trayledore or Trayle – then the Chapter House
built c. 1105 but rebuilt c. 1215–25. The continuation to the
was the Dormitory Stairs – for the Dormitory filled the uppe
floor of the E range and extended N beyond it – to its E th
Treasury, to its N the Warming House. The Reredorter o
Lavatories were E of the Dormitory and connected with i
probably by a bridge. S of this and E of the E range of th
cloister was the intricate group of smaller apartments whicl
formed the PRIOR'S HOUSE. Its small garden was immediatel
E of the Chapter House. It had a hall and a chapel. Adjoinin;
these to the SE was the INFIRMARY, placed at an angle to th
uniformly axial buildings so far described. The infirmary wa
reached by Trayle, which here turned from its former W–E to
SE direction, running along the original or old infirmary hall
built c. 1107–10, and on to the SE quarters of the monastery

* When the Lady Chapel was being built, remains were found of a sma
ROTUNDA, built under Canute in 1021–32. It was probably the funera
chapel of St Edmund. The only other partly surviving Saxon central
planned building in England is the octagon with ambulatory at the E end o
St Augustine Canterbury. This dates from c. 1050.

E of the old hall was a garden. Against the N side of this was a Saxon building of great interest, identified by Mr Whittingham with ST BENEDICT'S BASILICA, dedicated c. 1050. It had a clerestoried centre 14 by 20 ft in size, and a tunnel-vaulted passage of 8 ft width and 12 ft height along its four sides. To the E of this was St Michael's Chapel.

S of the Infirmary were two more buildings, according to Mr Whittingham, Bradfield Hall, to which Edward II retired on visits to Bury, and Bradfield Spanne, a kind of convalescent home for monks after blood-letting. The latter was built c. 1260. S of these and again reached by Trayle were the Sacrist's Quarters. Yet somewhat further S was the S wall, continuing E the S side of St Mary's. The SONG SCHOOL was just E of St Mary's (and the GRAMMAR SCHOOL on the present site of the Shire Hall).* The whole area between the church and the W and S walls was the CEMETERY. In the middle of this the CHARNEL HOUSE was built by John of Northwold (1279–1301). This had a triangular E end.

The W wall of the precinct ran due N from St Mary's past the Norman Gate and St James's, until Great Gate was reached. This was the business access to the monastery. It led into GREAT COURT. Against the W wall of this were stables (N) and the Almonry (S). Against the N wall were Brewery, Bakery, Granary, etc. From the NE corner of Great Court the outer precinct wall ran on to the E, then turned S, and then ran across Abbot's Bridge and S to the E of the river Lark towards the large abbey vineyard.

The E side of Great Court was given over to the Abbot's House with (from N to S) its own Stables, Bakery and Brewery, Great Hall, Kitchen, and then a second hall called the Queen's Chamber. E of these by the river Linnet is the Abbot's DOVE-COTE. The N–S line of the abbot's buildings continued direct into the N–S line of Dormitory, Chapter House, etc. Great Court meanwhile had its S side occupied by the monks' kitchen, etc. (which lie N of the Refectory), and W of these the Cellarer's quarters. Here the S range was interrupted by the Cellarer's Gate, through which was access to a Court E of which lay the Black Hostry and the Cloister. W of the Cellarer's Gate the wall of Great Court ran on, apparently with the Hall of Pleas attached to it on the S side, i.e. facing the N side of St James, and ultimately joined up with the W wall.

* And not as shown in the plan on p. 134. This information is from Mr M. P. Statham, County Archivist, quoting B. M. Harley 58, f. 21.

SURVIVING BUILDINGS

41 NORMAN GATE. Built under Abbot Anselm, i.e. between 1120
and 1148, as a gate to the church. It later served as a campanile for St James's Church. A splendid piece of proudly decorated architecture of its date. The face to the town (w) is more
ornate than the others. Big gateway, not vaulted inside. Heavy
block capitals of the columns. The inner order on the w
side has sculpture. Big roll mouldings. The arch projects like
a porch and has a gable with fish-scale decoration. To the l. and
r. are niches with billet decoration. Above these are short
buttresses with intersected arches and pyramid roofs. On the
first floor are two small two-light windows in much taller
blank arches. The blank fields are decorated with a kind of
vertical folding motif. The second and third stages are taken
together by giant shafts with arches. Under these are three
times two-light blank arches and above them three windows.
On the fourth stage there are again giant shafts and arches.
But this time the lower motif is roundels (cf. Norwich Cathedral) and the upper motif windows. Apart from the rich
decoration on the lower stages of the w side, all four sides are
essentially the same. Up to the C19 the gate had its original
battlements. It must thus have been one of the earliest embattled buildings in England.*

45   GREAT GATE. Begun after the riots of 1327 and before 1346.
Completed after 1353. Strong, and yet as exquisitely decorated
as only that moment in medieval English architecture could do.
A very broad, embattled structure. Broad segmental arch
leading from the town into a first part of the passage. There is
then an inner gate and a longer second chamber. The side walls
of these two passages have blank arches on a large scale with the
boldest flowing tracery. Both parts were vaulted with ribs and
tiercerons. The transverse arches did not differ in section or
gauge from the ribs.

Now back to the façade. Above the segmental arch are three
niches and the whole is crowned by a big ogee gable with
foiled circles l. and r. Big buttresses flank this centre. They
have ogee-headed and steeply gabled niches in three tiers, two
for the ground floor so far described, the third corresponding
to a centre composition of five tall blank niches of which the
centre one is wider and taller and has a crocketed gable. It is
again flanked by circles, but inscribed into them are six-

* Mr Wolton's observation.

pointed stars. To the abbey side the ground floor has a shafted doorway, the shafts with leaf capitals, the arch with a double quadrant moulding; the first floor has a large transomed three-light window with at the top a figure of a four-petalled flower. This upper room has a fireplace.

Both gates are set in the abbey precinct wall, mostly built by Abbot Anselm, *c.* 1130, the greater part of which still survives.

ABBEY CHURCH.* The W front is buried perhaps to a depth of 8–10 ft, and has dwelling houses built into that part which remains above ground. Nevertheless it is still possible to appreciate its great scale. The length of the church is more difficult to appreciate. The W end of the nave is still largely buried in gardens. The visible and excavated remains at the E end are the great crypt,‡ which has now been completely cleared, the crossing, part of which stands to full height, the transepts and the E bays of the nave. Ashlar remains only at base level: the rest is flint core work.

CLOISTER. Of the buildings around the cloister something can be recognized of the Parlour at the S end of the W range (one fragment of wall), the Refectory along the N side (where three bare walls stand to sill height), and the Chapter House, etc., on the E side, N of the N transept. N of the Chapter House and night stairs remains of a concave apsidal entrance to the Treasury, whose N wall is bent S to give access to the Warming Room. In the apse, bases of four small columns, two each side, on continuous plinths.

REMAINS EAST AND SOUTH of church or cloister. The buildings E of the E range are inarticulate. S of them and S of the church there is little to discover. A gable in a garden seems to have belonged to the Sacrist's Quarters. A wall here runs N–S (through a private garden) towards the precinct S wall (see below). E of the S turn of Schoolhall Street there is a stretch of the Norman precinct wall of *c.* 1130, continued by a short bit of C13 walling. This ends at the river Linnet, but is continued E of the river Lark by the S wall of the big abbey vineyard (C14 gateway at its W end). S of the W front of the abbey

---

* Trial excavations in 1958 revealed the W wall of the BASILICA OF ST DENIS built *c.* 1080 and demolished *c.* 1140 to make way for the W front. The basilica was replaced by the parish church of St James (now the cathedral).

‡ According to Mr A. D. Saunders some of the decorated wall plaster in the N crypt entrance has been found. It consisted of a diamond pattern in yellow outlined in black, with alternating horizontal rows of white quatrefoils on a red ground, and red on white.

church, in the great cemetery, is the CHARNEL HOUSE, originally a two-storey building of flint and re-used ashlar, with a triangular E end. It now has an C18 pedimented W front, its walls carry C18 and C19 monuments, and it is surrounded by very fine C18 railings.

REMAINS NORTH of church and cloister. N of the Refectory the SE angle of GREAT COURT. N of the angle remains of the QUEEN'S CHAMBER with angle stair-turret. SE of this, in a detached position, one wall of the ABBOT'S CHAPEL, and to the S the REREDORTER with a N wall with detached buttresses. W of the SE angle of Great Court referred to is a fragment of the N wall of the LARDER. Further W, buried under a bank, are foundations which include a fireplace and W of it a porch. Further W what was probably the Sub-Cellarer's Gate, which had a chapel above it. Then the buttressed S wall of Great Court, against which on the S, towards St James, stood the Hall of Pleas. Here a keeled string-course and flat buttresses of c. 1200 and added buttresses of after 1327. S and N of Great Gate stretches of WALL, that to the N of the C12, heightened after the riot of 1327. Remains also of the buttressed N wall, S of Mustow Street. The surviving lancets (now blocked) date the walls to the early C13. From the NE angle of Great Court the Abbot's House ran N–S, and a C14 part of its buttressed W wall remains. A fine buttressed outer wall starts by clasping buttresses of the late C12 and carries on to the E and to the Abbot's Bridge across which it continues S towards the abbey vineyard (see above). Between that stretch of wall and the Abbot's House a polygonal DOVECOTE. To the W of the dovecote fragments of a wing of rooms flanking the garden. The ABBOT'S BRIDGE consists of the bridge proper (visible from the W but best seen from the E), which dates from the late C12, and the wall carried across it with two added C14 breakwaters, chamfered ribs in the arches, and exterior buttresses and flying buttresses.*

THE TOWN

The town was laid out by Abbot Baldwin. By 1086 342 houses had been built. The plan is a grid pattern, still readily recognizable in the area between the abbey and St Andrew's Street. The blocks are rather elongated parallelograms. The whole pattern is strikingly similar to the contemporary one at Ludlow.

* It is a *pont à trous*, i.e. with portcullis or penstocks formerly to each arch (Mr S. E. Rigold).

CHURCHES

ST JAMES, since 1914 the CATHEDRAL. 195 ft long and without a tower, as the Norman tower stands immediately s of the church. The church is essentially Perp. It was built chiefly in c. 1510–30, but completed only under Edward VI, who gave £200 towards it. The designer may well have been *John Wastell*, who designed the vaults and upper parts of King's College Chapel at Cambridge, lived at Bury, and died in 1515. The chancel of St James's was rebuilt by *Scott* in 1865–9.[*] The Perp church was nine bays long in one even composition. For the purposes of a cathedral it was however not big enough, and enlargements were made during the ten years 1960–70 to plans by *S. E. Dykes Bower* (*see* below). The original w front is stone-faced with embattled aisles and a new gable by *Scott*. Original transomed seven-light window below, original transomed five-light aisle w windows. Decorated base, decorated buttresses, tall niches l. and r. of the doorway. The sides all have three-light transomed windows, and the clerestory windows are double in number. The s side is stone-faced. Very tall arcades inside, the piers of lozenge shape with four thin shafts and four broad hollows in the diagonals. The shafts towards the nave rise right up to the roof, a roof unfortunately by *Scott*, and not original.[‡] Only the shafts to the arch openings have capitals.

The work carried out after 1960[§] began with the erection of a new porch at the NW corner of the nave with a room over it to house the cathedral library. Eight (out of a future twelve) bays of the cloisters were then built along the N side of the nave, where the lower level of the ground enabled this to be kept below the sill level of the aisle windows. The new choir, with its flanking chapels, started from the E end and was finished in 1967, after which the crossing and transepts were undertaken to join the choir with the nave.

For reasons of cost it has not as yet been possible to raise the tower above the ridge line of the roofs, or, internally, to face in stone, above the four arches of the crossing, the walls of what will eventually be the lantern. In the N transept too the three arches that will open into a gallery remain temporarily blocked

---

[*] The excavations conducted by Mr Ralegh Radford revealed remains of the earlier chancel of c. 1390–1402.

[‡] Mr Dickinson praises the recent recolouring of the roof.

[§] For the following account of this work we are most grateful to Mr Dykes Bower.

up until the three bays of the cloister that will pass below it (cf. the muniment room at Westminster Abbey over part of the E cloister) can be built. The brick wall of the N aisle of the new choir is also temporary, until an arcade of four arches can be built to open into an outer N aisle giving entrance to a future sacristy and chair store, beyond which will be vestries etc. at ground level and, at first-floor level, a Lady Chapel, chapter house, and song school. The Lady Chapel as planned will be identical in size with the former chancel, designed by Scott, so that its oak roof, stalls, and E window, with fine *Hardman* glass, can be re-used there.

The ultimate scheme comprises, within the space bounded on the N side by the high medieval wall of the monastic bowling green, a complete four-sided cloister connecting under cover all the buildings that a modern cathedral needs. With Angel Hill on the W, the abbey gardens on the N and E, and a spacious and potentially beautiful cathedral close on the S, the cathedral has thus a rare opportunity to create an integrated whole.

Internally much remains to be done to complete the furnishings. The earlier furnishings are as follows.

FURNISHINGS. (FONT. Designed by *Scott* in 1870. The canopy is C20. ARA) – PULPIT. Designed by *Scott* and made by *Kett*. – MOSAIC in the chancel, made for Scott by *Salviati*. – PAINTINGS. In the S chapel a German 'Selbdritt' of *c.* 1500, with two small demi-figures in the predella. – STAINED GLASS. S aisle, first window from the W. Good Flemish early C16 glass, e.g. Story of Susanna, Tree of Jesse. – Most of the C19 glass is by *Clayton & Bell*. – Chancel side windows by *Kempe*, very early: SE 1867, SW 1874. – S aisle W by *Clayton & Bell*, 1898. – E and W windows by *Hardman* (E *c.* 1869). – S chapel E, *c.* 1852 by *Wailes*. – S chapel S, *c.* 1847 by *Warrington*. – PLATE. Two Flagons and Almsdish 1685; Cup and two Patens 1686; Cup 1729; Almsdish 1807. – MONUMENTS. Against the W wall, S of the doorway, James Reynolds, Chief Justice of the Exchequer, † 1738. White and black marble. Seated frontally in robe and wig. Two putti l. and r. No columns. Pediment on brackets. – Against the W wall N of the doorway Mrs Reynolds † 1736. No figure. Sarcophagus with obelisk background and l. and r. two urns on pedestals.

9 ST MARY. 213 ft long. The tower stands on the N side, a little E of the W front. It is broad and sturdy, C14 in its lower part (bequest 'if it shall be built' 1393). Earlier C14 the simple N

doorway of the church, and Dec the chancel, see the chancel arch. The church itself was begun in 1424 (bequests 1425, 1430, 1432, for the rood-loft 1436, for the battlements 1442–5, for the porches 1437), and the chancel chapels were added by Jankyn Smith who died in 1481. The façade is similar to that of St James: stone-facing, embattled aisles, gabled nave. The windows are also transomed though only of four and five lights, and there are niches l. and r. of the doorway. Impressive s side with all windows identical from W to E: all of three lights with transom and under two-centred arches. The former s porch was pulled down in 1831.* The clerestory has twice as many windows as the aisles. At its E end rise two rood-stair turrets with little crocketed spires and finials. The s aisle is stone-faced, the s chapel is not. On the N side the rhythm is less uniform. Here only the chancel chapel has windows with two-centred arches, the aisle windows have four-centred heads. Also there is an early C14 doorway, finely moulded, and there is the porch bequeathed by the will of John Nottyngham in 1437 and commemorating him and his wife. It is placed unusually far E, connected with the position of the church in the abbey precinct. The porch is stone-faced, has pinnacles, a gable with crockets, and three niches above the entrance. Inside it has a charming stone ceiling panelled with a wheel of blank arches the hub of which is an openwork pendant. The chancel projects one bay beyond the chapels. It has a late and bold E window.

The interior is very impressive. Ten bays to the chancel arch. The piers have shafts to the nave, thin triple shafts with capitals to the arch openings, and broad hollows in the diagonals. The nave shafts rise to the roof, but branch off into roll hood-moulds over the arches. Also a shaft rises to the roof from the apex of each arch. The roof is rightly famous. Essentially a roof with principal rafters and tenoned purlins, the principals are strengthened with hammerbeams with large angel figures against them, alternating with moulded arch braces. The latter have 'embryo hammerbeams, not projecting beyond the braces but clamping them and disguised as carved grotesques' (Cautley). The spandrels of the braces are carved with dragons, unicorns, birds, fishes, etc. The collar-beams carry dainty arches with tracery. The wall-plate has demi-figures of angels. The wall-posts stand on corbels with angels, saints, martyrs, prophets, and kings. At the E end of the nave is a window

* A stone arch in the grounds of Nowton Court (*see* p. 381) is said to be the s porch from St Mary (ARA).

above the chancel arch. This was inserted as part of *Cottingham*'s restoration of 1840. The chancel chapels are of three bays. Their piers are slenderer and simpler, but of the same type as in the nave. The chancel roof* is a single-framed, straight-braced rafter roof, panelled. The panels are cusped and have bosses. Amongst the scenes on the bosses a fox preaching to chickens, a dog carrying two water-bottles, two dogs fighting.

FURNISHINGS. FONT. Octagonal, Perp, the base with four seated lions and four small standing figures. The bowl seems altered. – STALLS. On the s side. Poppy-heads, animals on the arms, traceried backs. – STAINED GLASS. W window by *Heaton & Butler*, 1859; s aisle E window by *Gerente*, 1856, the rest of the s aisle windows by *Heaton, Butler & Bayne*, 1880–1 (ARA); N aisle E window by *Heaton & Butler*, 1857; window over the chancel arch by *Willement*, c. 1845; window above the s doorway by *Clutterbuck*, 1854; N aisle w by *Ward & Hughes*, 1868; first from w by *H. Hughes*, 1869; N aisle Transfiguration by *Ward & Hughes*, 1884. – PLATE. Cups 1661 and 1674; Flagon 1683; Flagon 1716; Paten 1745; two Almsdishes 1777. – MONUMENTS. Sir William Carew † 1501. Big tomb-chest with shields in richly cusped quatrefoils. Two recumbent effigies (chancel N). – Sir Robert Drury † 1536 (chancel s), almost a copy of the previous. – Jankyn Smith † 1481 who built the chancel aisles and is supposed to have given the town the Guildhall. Brass, two kneeling figures, 2 ft long (s chancel chapel). – John Baret † 1467 (s aisle E end). Tomb-chest with small shields in lozenge and quatrefoil fields. On it cadaver with this inscription:

> He that wil sadly beholde one with his ie
> May se hys owyn merowr and lerne for to die.

Other inscriptions about the tomb. Especially noteworthy the one on the pedestal (copied here from Tymms):

> Wrappid in a selure as a ful rewli wrecche
> No mor of al myn good to me ward wil strecche
> From erthe I kam and on to erthe i am browht
> This js my natur, for of erthe I was wrowht;
>
> Thus erthe on to erthe to gedir now is knet
> So endeth each creature Q'd John Baret
> Qwerfor ze pepil in weye of charite

* Recently cleaned and restored, together with the ceiling above the Baret tomb (ARA).

Wt zo^r good p^{a}yeris I prey zu help me
For lych as I am right so schal ze all be
Now God on my sowle have m'cy & pite. Amen.

Above the monument, which must have stood in a large
chantry area, the aisle roof is panelled and has his motto 'Grace
me governe' and the Lancastrian SS painted on. – Mary Tudor
† 1533 (chancel N side), the sister of Henry VIII, married to
King Louis XII of France, and after his death (first secretly)
to Charles Brandon Duke of Suffolk. – Brass to Archdeacon
John Fyners † 1509 (N chapel).

ST EDMUND (R.C.), Westgate Street. 1837 by *Charles Day*.
Grecian. Stone-faced façade. Three bays with projecting
centre. Two tall fluted Ionic columns *in antis*. The interior
remodelled 1877. Coved ceiling, the coving partly glazed.
Sanctuary short behind a screen of two Ionic columns. Concealed skylight. The two grand altar surrounds are doorcases
recently taken over from Rushbrooke Hall. Their date is *c.*
1735. The surround to the main entrance was once a marble
fireplace, also from Rushbrooke Hall.* It may be a composite
piece: the supports Dutch mid C17, the frieze probably
slightly earlier, Tuscan(?), with emblems of the Farnese and
della Rovere families. The doors enclosed by it belong to the
altar surrounds. – (SCULPTURE. God the Father, polychrome,
attributed to *Ignaz Günther*.) – PAINTING. Martyrdom of St
Edmund. By *Delafosse*.

ST JOHN, St John's Street. Consecrated 1841. By *Ranger* of
London. Yellow brick, with a W tower and an ignorant spire.
Gaunt recessed porch, under the spire. The style of the church
is E.E. Clerestory with three stepped lancets per bay. Timber
rib-vault. The W end is canted towards the tower. The E end
re-done by *J. Drayton Wyatt* in 1875.‡ – STAINED GLASS.
The E window original, but renovated (i.e. new glass surrounds
to the three scenes) in 1960 (ARA). – PLATE. Set of 1841.

ST PETER, Hospital Road. 1860 by *J. H. Hakewill*.

PRESBYTERIAN CHAPEL (now Pentecostal Church), Churchgate Street. 1711–12. A stately chapel surpassed in Suffolk
only by that at Ipswich. Red brick with rubbed red brick

* I owe this information, and the following comments, to Father B.
Houghton.

‡ An account of Wyatt's alterations, which probably illustrate a tendency
towards ritualism, can be found in *The Bury and Norwich Post* for 20 July
1875, and 27 October 1875 (raising the chancel floor, etc.). Further alterations
are described on 27 October 1891. Wyatt appears to have been inspector of
churches for the archdeaconry of Sudbury (ARA).

trimmings. The bonding of the brickwork is still English. Three-bay façade with big arched windows. Doorway with pilasters carrying a big segmental pediment. The top parapet is raised over the centre. Three galleries inside. The pulpit faces the entrance.

FRIENDS' MEETING HOUSE, St John's Street. 1750. Grey brick face added in 1870, three bays wide, with hipped roof. Central Venetian window.

PUBLIC BUILDINGS

TOWN HALL (now renamed 'Market Cross'), Cornhill. 1774–80 by *Robert Adam*. Built as a market hall and theatre. The finest post-medieval building at Bury. Oblong cruciform plan. Grey brick, the ground floor with stone rustication. Each of the four projections has two giant columns with typical Adam capitals and a pediment. Between them on the upper floor a delicately decorated Venetian window. To the N and S in the recessed angle bays trophy panels on the ground floor, urns in niches on the upper floor. In 1970–1 the archways on the W and N sides were opened up to make arcades, and a new shop front for the Woolwich Building Society built within the W arcade (architect: *Mark A. Pawling*). The upper floor of the building has become an art gallery.

BOROUGH OFFICES, Angel Hill. 1936 by *Basil Oliver*. Neo-Georgian, red brick, nine bays, two storeys, with three-bay pediment. Tactful and completely uneventful. – REGALIA. Two silver-gilt Maces, upper parts early C17, stems 1729. – Mayor's Chain, presented 1705; the oval medal has a bust of William IV. – Sword of State, presented 1684; silver-gilt handle with Justice and Law in relief. – Punch Bowl of 1710. – Two Tankards of 1681. – Two Beadles' Staves, presented 1710. – Two Tickets of 1800 to allow aldermen free entry to the theatre.

SHIRE HALL, St James's Churchyard. 1906–7 by *A. Aynsworth Hunt*. Red brick and yellow stone dressings. Mildly classical; without architectural merit. The new block is by *McMorran & Whitby*, 1968. On the S side of the 1907 block, the court buildings of 1841–2 by *William McIntosh Brooks*. For St Margaret's House, *see* below, p. 150.

CORN EXCHANGE, Abbeygate Street. Built in 1861–2 by *Ellis & Woodard*. Yellow brick, one-storeyed, with a six-column giant portico to Abbeygate Street, arched windows and giant pilasters to the other sides. In 1969–70 the building was converted into ground-floor shops with a hall above. Of the Shambles (now a shop) which adjoin the N end, the columns which divide up the window space were part of the late C18 Shambles which stood near by (ARA).

(POST OFFICE, Cornhill. 1895 by *H. Tanner* of H.M. Office of Works. A pleasant red-brick building with the royal coat of arms on the top gable. ARA)

PUBLIC LIBRARY AND ART GALLERY (former SCHOOL OF ART, built as the Corn Exchange), Cornhill. 1836 and 1848. Two-storeyed S front on the falling ground, the other sides one-storeyed. Yellow brick. Attached Tuscan porticoes to E and W.

KING EDWARD VI GRAMMAR SCHOOL, off Eastgate Street. 1883 by *Sir Arthur Blomfield*, but according to its style rather by his nephew, the future Sir Reginald Blomfield: with brick gables and tile-hung gables, clearly under the influence of Norman Shaw.

WORKHOUSE (former, and stores), Hospital Road. Red brick, cross-shaped, Late Classical. Built in 1836.

NORTHGATE STATION. 1847, from the design of *Sancton Wood*.* Red brick with Dutch gables and two 'Free-Renaissance' towers. The E front is treated symmetrically N and S of the line.

(WATER TOWER, West Road. 1952. Said to be better in design than most.)

PERAMBULATIONS

(*a*) Inner Bury St Edmunds, (*b*) Outer Bury St Edmunds

(*a*) INNER BURY ST EDMUNDS

Bounded by the Abbey Precinct, Brentgovel Street, St Andrew's Street, and Westgate Street.

For the layout of the centre, see above, p. 140. The architectural character of Bury is predominantly Georgian, pleasant and quiet, perhaps a little sleepy, but most attractive. There is no spectacular older timber-framed architecture left, nor any spectacular Tudor brickwork.

The walk starts in ANGEL HILL, the delightful large open 2b space W of the abbey gatehouse, St James, and the Norman

* See the *Bury and Norwich Post*, 24 November 1847 (ARA).

tower. Here on the s side the ATHENAEUM. The façade is
Queen Anne, modified in 1789 and 1804 (top storey renewed).*
Seven wide bays, parapet raised over the centre, and low
dome behind. At the back, facing with five arched windows
into Crown Street, the BALLROOM, assigned to *Robert Adam*
(redecorated 1950). It has an elegant segmental tunnel-vault
with fine stucco decoration, and in the middle of the side
opposite the windows a segmental recess behind a screen of
two columns. On the E side of the square proper, ABBEY
HOUSE, No. 30, seven bays, drably cemented, with an Ionic
porch. The back of the house, inside the Precinct, is older.
The NE bend of Angel Hill is marked by a taller white brick
house, and the corner is sensitively rounded. The houses here,
towards Mustow Street (an extension of Angel Hill), are
mainly older, low two-storeyed cottages, timber-framed and
plastered, backing on to the Abbey walls. Across the road, the
N side of Angel Hill makes a nice group, several houses with
attached Roman Doric columns, or Roman Doric pilasters.
The w side of Angel Hill is all quiet brick fronts. Only the
ANGEL HOTEL rises higher. But its façade is equally quiet.
The original part of 1779 is three-storeyed and of seven bays.
Three-bay pediment. Porch with Adamish columns.‡ The
Council Offices fit adequately into the NW corner. Next door,
ANGEL CORNER, a red-brick house with a rainwater head
dated 1702. Four bays, two storeys, hipped roof.

We turn first w for a short loop, along Abbeygate Street and
back by Churchgate Street, the two main medieval E–W
streets. At the SE corner of ABBEYGATE STREET a handsome
Late Georgian shop, LEESON'S, with unfluted Ionic columns
carrying rather ponderous capitals. Another equally attractive
shop-front follows almost at once, RIDLEY'S, with small
glazing panes. The building in which this shop is is a substantial red brick house of *c.* 1700. Close to the corner of
LOWER BAXTER STREET one of the few timber-framed
houses, with upper overhang. Another such house at the corner
of HIGH BAXTER STREET. On the N side of Abbeygate
Street another good Georgian shop, OLIVER'S, with six
arched Gothick shop windows. Towards the w end and the
Corn Exchange the buildings get more townish, BARCLAYS

* Information from Mr M. P. Statham. The *Bury and Norwich Post* for
9 September 1789 contains a description of the newly completed Assembly
Room. The architect is not named (ARA).
‡ Medieval vaulting can be seen in the basement (ARA).

BANK, three-storeyed in a quiet Renaissance style,* the
ALLIANCE ASSURANCE (1891 by *J. S. Corder*), red with
Dutch gables, and the NATIONAL PROVINCIAL BANK (1868
by *John Gibson*), again quiet Renaissance. Between Barclays
Bank and the Alliance Assurance are Nos. 56 and 58. Both are
timber-framed and have carved angle-posts, No. 56 now inside
the corner shop, No. 58 at its back. Off to the N first in the
BUTTER MARKET the SUFFOLK HOTEL, early C19, stuccoed,
eight windows wide, the ground floor converted *c.* 1873 by
polished pink granite columns with Romanesquoid capitals.‡
Then also off N, in SKINNER STREET, a picturesque timber-
framed house with overhang. Finally, again up N, in THE
TRAVERSE the best C17 house of Bury, CUPOLA HOUSE, 56b
built for the wealthy apothecary Thomas Macro in 1693 and
described by Celia Fiennes in 1698. It is three-storeyed, of
five bays, plastered and with quoins. Pitched roof and on it the
cupola or belvedere, a fashionable feature in the second half
of the C17 (cf. Coleshill, Ashdown, Belton). Inside the cupola
a seat round as in a gazebo.§ Celia Fiennes praised the
'pleasing prospect' to be had from it. In the roof three dormers
with alternating steep triangular and semicircular pediments,
again a typical later C17 feature. The carved brackets carrying
the second-floor balcony are typical too. Tall back in Skinner
Street with two gables. Pretty staircase inside with strong
twisted balusters.

Back to CHURCHGATE STREET. (The part of Guildhall Street
through which we go will be described later.) There is not
much here. Up in HATTER STREET several nice Georgian
doorways, and on the E side No. 8, a three-storeyed, five-bay
house with two bays at the l. and r. end pedimented. Centre
with an oval recessed Tuscan porch and a Venetian window
over. Near the E end of Churchgate Street No. 35 (Y.M.C.A.),
Georgian, of five bays, red brick, nice yellow brick quoins and
plat-band, and a Gibbs lintel to the doorway, and No. 38 of *c.*
1700, with an apsed door-hood on carved brackets. The house

* The E half of the Barclays block was probably built in 1856 (evidence
from Rate Books), and was designed by *H. F. Bacon* of Bury. The W half
(the present bank) was built in the same style in 1880–1 by *J. B. Pearce* of
Norwich (ARA).

‡ There is an account of the conversion in the *Bury and Norwich Post* for
27 January 1874, and an earlier photograph at the Bury Record Office
(ARA).

In No. 25 is a thin-ribbed plaster ceiling (NMR).

§ Information given by Mr I. Nairn.

adjoins Chequer Square, and from there to return to the s end
of Angel Hill is a matter of a few steps.

The tour now continues from Angel Hill E into the former
Precinct.* Here, facing the churchyard of St James, first, on the
N side, the PROVOST'S HOUSE, built c. 1744 as the CLOPTON
ASYLUM. Long, two-storeyed front with two-bay projecting
wings, ten bays deep, and a recessed seven-bay centre. Red
brick and quoins. Parapet and three-bay pediment with coat of
arms. Opposite, on the s side, facing N, is the Shire Hall, and
attached to it ST MARGARET'S HOUSE, Early Georgian, of
seven bays, red brick with rubbed-brick trim, two and a half
storeys. Giant angle pilasters, and giant angle pilasters to mark
the pedimented centre bay. Staircase with three slender
balusters to the step and carved tread ends. Remains of the
C12 Chapel of St Margaret may be seen to the E, in the
exterior s wall, and also in part of the interior (ARA). Then, to
the r. of the Shire Hall, the view opens into HONEY HILL and
to MANOR HOUSE, Early Georgian, of red brick with quoins.
Nine bays wide, two-storeyed, with three-bay pediment.
Doorway with segmental pediment on brackets. (Good
interiors.) The house was built as the Bury residence of the
first Earl of Bristol. It was designed by *Sir James Burrough*.‡

From Honey Hill s for a moment, down Sparhawk Street, to see
ST MARY'S SQUARE, a perfect little square, secluded and
lovable, only alas now crossed by an A-road. On the s side a
plastered house of c. 1700, five bays with quoins, and then the
garden wall and garden of the Square House Hotel, Late
Georgian, seven bays, red brick with an Ionic porch; on the E
side the southernmost house of the late C18, red brick, three
bays, with tripartite windows and Tuscan porch, the northernmost house a nine-bay terrace of two and a half storeys, grey
brick laced with red and yellow. On the N side the easternmost
house is a disused Methodist Chapel of 1811, with arched
windows. A pity the doorway is spoilt.

Now CROWN STREET, i.e. the street which leads s from Angel
Hill and the Athenaeum. It starts with the former PENNY
BANK, a rather unfortunate effort in the Victorian Tudor
Gothic, irregular, red, diapered, turreted. Built in 1846 and
added to. Then comes CHEQUER SQUARE on the W side and
the two corner houses of Churchgate Street. In the square an
C18 OBELISK. Also CHEQUER HOUSE, early C19, grey brick,

of three storeys, with on the first floor an iron balcony, and
windows set in blank arches. Then more pretty Georgian in
Crown Street, e.g. No. 49, No. 45 (where two adjoining doorways have three columns and one pediment together), No. 44
(whose seeming late C17 windows are recent), and also on the
E side No. 10 with a big doorway with Gibbs surround and
finally, again on the w side, the DOG AND PARTRIDGE INN,
timber-framed with a gable at the N end and a long carved
bressumer along the rest of the façade; C17 brackets.

From the S end of Crown Street turn W along WESTGATE
STREET. Opposite the end of Crown Street stands the
THEATRE ROYAL, built in 1819 to designs by *William
Wilkins*, the architect of the National Gallery and Downing
College and a son of William Wilkins, the lessee of this and
other East Anglian theatres. Heavy Tuscan porch with metope
frieze. Off to the N in COLLEGE STREET the former BARN-
ABY ALMSHOUSES of 1826, grey brick, two-storeyed, of
eight bays with hood-moulds over the windows. In Westgate
Street itself a few nice Georgian doorways and not much else.

So turn up GUILDHALL STREET. Here Nos. 66–67 has an oversailing upper floor on scrolly C17 brackets and a Georgian shop-
front. No. 70 is of five bays, red brick, the windows laced
with yellow. No. 74 is early C18 with a Tuscan Doric doorway.
All these are on the w side. Now on the E the former GUILD-
HALL, given, it is said, by Jankyn Smith († 1481). Centre with
angle turrets. Flint and stone, on the upper floor also brick
bands. Embattled parapet with quatrefoils. Inside a C13 doorway with three orders of colonnettes and much dog-tooth
ornament. It has a good late C15 kingpost roof over its whole
length, so the fabric is probably of that date, with the C13
doorway reset (J. T. Smith). The wings were rebuilt in 1807
and are of yellow brick and three bays wide each. Opposite is
Nos. 81–83, Georgian, of two storeys, five-bay centre of the
early C18. The wings were added in 1789 by *Soane*.* They
have pediments, and on the ground floor broad tripartite
windows.

Beyond Abbeygate Street Guildhall Street is continued as
CORNHILL. Cornhill runs N and then turns E and widens into
the market place of Bury. Here the WAR MEMORIAL with a
bronze statue of a wounded soldier by *A. G. Walker*, 1904. The
principal buildings are the Corn Exchange, the Public Library,
and the Town Hall. We are here concerned first with the W

* This information was kindly passed to me by Miss Dorothy Stroud.

side and afterwards with the N side. The hood over the doorway of EVERARD'S HOTEL, facing Abbeygate Street, is not
original. Then follow the premises of Messrs BOOTS, a riotous
and glorious Victorian fantasy, utterly unconcerned with the
spirit of Bury, with lots of timber-framing, gables, and stucco
ornamentation and with niches containing statues of kings.*
On the N side at the E end MOYSE'S HALL, the oldest domestic
building of Bury, Norman, of two storeys, with a C19 E wall.
Flint and stone, and said to have been built by a rich Jew (cf.
the Jew's House and the Jew's Court, both at Lincoln), but
probably connected with the abbey. Broad, flat buttresses,
typically Norman. Interior of two rooms, E and W, on each of
two floors. The hall and solar were on the upper floor. On the
ground floor the W part is vaulted in six bays. Circular piers
with simple capitals made, it seems, for cruciform piers. Broad
N–S arches, single-chamfered E–W arches, groin-vaults. The
arch to the E room is Perp. On the first floor towards Cornhill
two original windows. They are rectangular with a roll moulding and stand under arches, resting on colonnettes with crocket
capitals. The date seems to be c. 1180. The drastic restoration
responsible for several obvious solecisms took place in 1858.

(b) OUTER BURY ST EDMUNDS

Three sallies are suggested, to the NE, to the N, and to the S. To
the NE from the N end of Angel Hill along MUSTOW STREET.
Here on the l. MUSTOW HOUSE, Late Georgian, red brick, of
nine bays and three storeys, and then No. 17, one of the best
timber-framed houses of Bury. Traceried angle-post and
tracery panels along the level of the ground-floor windows.
After that on the r. the Abbot's Bridge (see p. 140). Then in
EASTGATE STREET No. 33 with some exposed buttress posts
on the ground floor, some carving of the bressumers, and two
symmetrical gables with upper overhang to the street. At the
fork of HOLLOW ROAD and Bacton Road an unusually
picturesque sight – picturesque in the original English C18
sense: a church window with its tracery against the blue sky
and a big cedar tree overshadowing it. The window is said to
have come from the former Leper Hospital of St Petronilla and

* Mr Adrian R. Allan writes: 'In a printed diary of 1918 I have seen
illustrations of other Boots shops with exterior decorations very similar to
Bury's. These were (perhaps still are) at Peterborough in particular, and to
a lesser extent at Newcastle, Edinburgh, Kingston-on-Thames, and Shrews-
bury. Evidently a type of architecture peculiarly Boots'.'

belongs now to a house on the site of the former Hospital of
St Nicholas. There were five hospitals at Bury (for the Hospital
of the Saviour *see* below). The window is Dec, of three lights.
Of the Hospital of St Nicholas there remains to the N of the
window and the tree the buttressed end of a building with the
outline of a big W window. To its N a Tudor chimney of a house
which continues with brick-nogging. The chimney is clearly
of the time of Henry VIII. From the corner of the window to
the SE up MOUNT ROAD one gets to MORETON HALL
(formerly St Edmund's Hall), by *Robert Adam, 1773.* Grey
brick, only three bays wide, but three-storeyed and with a
pediment towards the N on giant pilasters. Porch with Ionic
columns. To the S also a pediment, and on the ground floor
Venetian windows to the l. and r. Bow window on the W front,
and behind it a fine room with screens of two columns over the
N and S ends. Plaster ceiling.*

To the N, also from the N end of Angel Hill, up NORTHGATE
STREET. Nos. 1–3 have nice Ionic pilasters at the doors. No. 7
has recently been renovated, when it was discovered to be
basically two early C16 timber-framed houses (ARA). No. 8
is of red brick with quoins, seven bays wide, of which four
belong to the projecting wings. The recessed centre bay has a
pediment; there is a Venetian window below this, and on the
ground floor an odd porch with clustered pilasters behind
which the doorway appears whose entablature, rising to a
point in the centre, dates the façade as Early Georgian. However it too appears to have been originally two timber-framed
houses: the S section perhaps early C16, the N C17. Some C17
panelling in a ground-floor room (ARA). Nos. 9–11 has an early
C19 façade of white brick with a pedimented gable, but behind
this its original hall. The staircase and gallery in the hall have
flat, tapered Jacobean balusters. Then on the opposite side
No. 110 with a Tuscan doorway, and so to the remains of
ST SAVIOUR'S HOSPITAL, just beyond the railway station.
This was founded in 1184/5. What remains is the so-called
gatehouse, which is, however, not a gatehouse, but the W
end of a range 100 ft long. Two-centred entrance arch, looking
early C14. Of the large window above only the lower half of
the frame survives.

Yet further out, at the S end of MILDENHALL ROAD are the
remains of BABWELL FRIARY, the Franciscan house of
Bury. The order had arrived in 1257, but was forced by the

* S. H. A. H[ervey], *Horringer Parish Registers . . .* (1900).

envious abbey in 1262 to pull down its buildings. The abbey
then gave the site at Babwell. Of the Franciscan buildings
nothing stands above ground, though the position and shape
of the church (a plain aisleless oblong) are known. The house
now on the site is C16 to C17. The end to the street has a curved
gable with chimneys and two small Elizabethan or Jacobean
windows. But the E gable end of the corner range is timber-
framed and has a carved bressumer, a lion's head in the gable
and under it a blocked three-light window which seems again
Elizabethan or Jacobean. Georgianized S front of five bays
with Tuscan porch. Much of the boundary walls of the friary
remains.

The S sally is short. From St Mary's Square down SOUTHGATE
STREET past several pleasant Georgian houses (Linnet House,
Nos. 42–48) and a good timber-framed one with a carved
bressumer (Nos. 78–80) and so to SICKLESMERE ROAD and
THE FORT. This lies back from the road and is screened from
it by the spectacular façade of the former GAOL, built in 1803.
The corner is raised and contains the entrance. It is given
vermiculated rustication, and the arch and jambs slope
inwards. This centre is crowned by a pediment. To the l. and
r. forbidding rusticated wings with broad semicircular windows, a motif familiar from the French style of 1760–1800, but
also from George Dance's Newgate Prison. The gaol itself
was built 'after the plan of the celebrated Mr Howard' (Gill-
ingwater, 1804), i.e. with ranges radiating from a centre. This
centre remains. It is a square of red brick, set lozenge-wise and
with bevelled corners. It was the house of the governor, *John
Orridge*, who designed the gaol (which was built by the architect *George Byfield*) and in 1819 designed another, for the
Russian Czar.

(HOUSING, Oliver Road. By *John Whitehead*. White brick and
pantiles. Subtle, but completely without affectation.)

3050

BUTLEY

ST JOHN BAPTIST. Norman nave with one S window, three N
windows, the S doorway (one order of colonnettes, arch with
zigzag on the front and the inside meeting at r. angles along a
roll moulding), and the altered N doorway. Above the S porch
entrance, re-used, parts of a former C13 hood-mould with
stiff-leaf crockets. Chancel of c. 1300 (cusped lancets). Unbuttressed Dec W tower with some flushwork decoration in the
battlements. – FONT. Octagonal, with four lions against the

stem and four lions and four angels against the bowl. – SCREEN. Simple, with one-light divisions and ogee arches. – PLATE. Elizabethan Cup; Paten 1716.

BUTLEY PRIORY. Butley Priory was founded as a house for Augustinian Canons in 1171 by the same Ranulph de Glanville, Justiciar of Henry II, who founded Leiston Abbey. Nothing remains of the church except an arch of *c.* 1300 with two continuous chamfers. This led out of the s transept.

The plan of the church is known from excavations of 1930. The church had a Norman crossing and transepts with square E chapels and a chancel with chancel chapels. The nave and aisles, of nine bays, were of the C13, and the E end was rebuilt straight-ended in the C14. Of the claustral buildings – also C13 in date – parts of the refectory and the reredorter can still be traced in farm buildings. The stone came from the valley of the Yonne in France and was brought by boat to a wharf only 600 ft away. Wharf and canal have also been excavated.

What remains complete, or nearly complete, is only the 44b GATEHOUSE, and this is one of the most ambitious and interesting buildings of the C14 in Suffolk. Its historical importance lies in the fact that the heraldry which is so lavishly displayed on it proves a date about 1320–5 and that it is thus the earliest datable building with flushwork decoration. Nor is the decoration used in any way hesitatingly. On the contrary, stimulated by the general trend of these years, which was all for the greatest luxuriance and elaboration (cf. e.g. Ely Lady Chapel), the designer of the Butley gatehouse got at once as much decorative vivacity out of it as any of his successors ever after. The shape of the gatehouse is different to the inside and the outside. To the outside there is the gateway divided into a pedestrian entrance with a finely and continuously moulded two-centred arch and a carriage entrance with an almost straight-sided depressed arch dying into the imposts, and then to the l. and r. two projecting bays no doubt meant to carry towers. They are square, except that the sides towards the gateway are canted forward towards it and have here two flying buttresses carrying the upper wall. These bases of the towers connect at their backs with a square room each which lies l. and r. of the gateway. To the inside of the priory the plan is simpler. The gateway projects in front of the two square rooms and has a wide single arch of the same kind as the carriage arch to the outside. The arch mouldings are of the typical two-waves variety. Inside the gateway the space, now converted into a living room,

is vaulted in two bays with ribs on wall-shafts with moulded
capitals, with the exception of one which carries handsome
foliage. The vault makes two tierceron stars, and the ribs are
slimmer than the transverse arches. Both have fillets. Exceedingly good leaf-bosses. In the E wall is one two-light window
and a doorway (with a sunk quadrant moulding). Both led to
the porter's room. In the wall towards the Priory the squint
next to the archway has not yet been convincingly explained.
The porter's room and the room corresponding to it on the
other side are both also rib-vaulted, though much more simply
(single-chamfered ribs, quadripartite vault). The cells of the
vault are constructed of brick in a very interesting technique.
They rise in curved courses to an odd crown in the form of a
pointed oval or a *mandorla*. The effect is dome-like in each cell.
The technique is paralleled in Bishop Salmon's porch in the
garden of the Bishop's Palace at Norwich, and Bishop Salmon
died in 1325. In the W room a beautiful large piscina with
cusped ogee arch, crocketed gable, and finials. This was found
in the excavations and no doubt comes from the church. The
precinct wall started from the middles of the sides of the gatehouse. The plan can still be seen on the W side, and here there
is on the upper floor an unexplained large opening with a two-
centred arch towards the wall, too large to be connected with
access to the wall walk for purposes of defence. Nor is it likely
that it can have something to do with the Tudor house which
stood on this side of the gatehouse and was demolished in 1737.
In the same W wall there is also a small quatrefoil window which
belonged to a garderobe. The shoot comes out at the foot of
the wall.

But what demands the closest study at Butley is the decoration of the S and N fronts. On the N front there is flushwork
decoration with a cinquefoil and big mouchettes above the
pedestrian entrance and pointed trefoils in the spandrels of the
carriage entrance. On the buttresses to the l. and r. are niches.
The N fronts of the projecting bays or tower-bases have each a
large sham two-light window with flowing tracery in two different patterns. This is the most attractive decorative motif at
Butley and occurs, as will be seen, in several other places as
well. The sham windows reach up as high as the niches in the
buttresses, and higher than the entrance arches. Above these
follows a large panel with thirty-five shields in five rows. Such
a heraldic display on the gatehouse of a monastery had already
been done in the late C13 at Kirkham in Yorkshire. The

heraldry at Butley has been learnedly expounded by Sir James
Mann. The top row reads as follows: Holy Roman Empire –
France – St Edmund's Bury – Christ's Passion – England –
León and Castile – and, very oddly, Hurtshelve (three axes).
Perhaps it was a Hurtshelve who gave the money for building
the gatehouse. In the row below appear the de Veres, Bohuns,
Beauchamps, Warennes, and Clares. Below that more English
baronial families, e.g. Mortimer. The last two rows are East
Anglian gentry. Above the sham windows are straight-headed
three-light windows with ogee-headed lights to the s. On the
inner sides, i.e. towards the archway, the upper windows have
shouldered lights, and below them is a gay chequerboard of
flushwork on the l., the same motif in diapers on the r. In the
middle, above the heraldry panel, there is one tall two-light
window with renewed tracery and two sham windows of the
same type to its l. and r. These have flowing tracery with a
wheel of five mouchettes. In the gable is a fine group of three
niches, the l. and r. ones with straight-sided climbing arches,
the middle one with a beautiful projecting canopy. All arches
are cusped and sub-cusped.

The s front has above the archway a row of shouldered ogee-
headed blank arches in flushwork, and above these a tall two-
light window corresponding to the northern one. Its tracery is
also renewed. The blank windows to its l. and r. have specially
fanciful tracery: three lights with ogee heads, and above the
middle one a pointed quatrefoil. In the gable a flushwork
wheel of ten spokes with trefoils along the rim.

Later work in the gatehouse is confined to Elizabethan
panelling in one room, including two fluted pilasters, and the
simple but handsome staircase of c. 1737 with slender turned
balusters.

About 1800 two SUMMER HOUSES were built to the l. and r.
of the gatehouse at some little distance. One of them remains.

In MOUNT FIELD, 250 yds E of Neutral Farm, a late Neolithic
'Beaker' settlement. Finds include two hoards of Bronze Age
socketed axes, much Iron Age and Roman occupation material,
and a Saxon rectangular hut floor.

BUTTRUM'S MILL see WOODBRIDGE

BUXHALL

oojo

ST MARY. Nave and chancel and W tower. All Dec except for the
Perp tower, for which money was left in 1392.* Wide nave and

* Information from Mr Peter Northeast.

chancel. Tall two-light windows. Only the E window is bigger – a good piece of five lights with flowing tracery. Double PISCINA with ogee arches and steep gable. The SEDILIA which were set against the window are mostly broken off. Dec N porch with two-light windows. Niche over the entrance. Battlements with flushwork chequerboard decoration. – FONT. Octagonal. Early C14. Simple arches under gables, much use made of the encircled quatrefoil. Embattled top. No ogees. – BENCHES. A few in the chancel. – STAINED GLASS. Fragments in several window-heads. – PLATE. Cup 1624; Paten c. 1710; Almsdish 1765.

MAYPOLE FARMHOUSE, close to the church. C16. Timber-framed, but with a stepped brick gable to the street.

BUXHALL VALE, Fen Street. Early C18, plastered, seven bays wide with a porch with Roman Doric columns.

WINDMILL. A former tower-mill, put to another use.

BUXLOW see KNODISHALL

³⁰⁵⁰

CAMPSEA ASH

ST JOHN BAPTIST. Slender Dec W tower. The battlements decorated with blank arches and initials in flushwork. Flushwork on base and buttresses. Doorway with shields and fleurons in an arch order and a frieze of flushwork above. Nice early C14 S doorway. Nave and chancel very re-done after having been partly rebuilt in 1792. – FONT. Dec, octagonal, with quatrefoils, blank arches etc. – STAINED GLASS. One S window with Faith and Hope, c. 1882, in the style of Crane. – PLATE. Elizabethan Cup; Cover inscribed 1569; Paten and Flagon 1641. – BRASS. Alexander Inglisshe, rector, † 1504 (nave floor), a 2 ft 3 in. figure.

ASH HIGH HOUSE, by Salvin, has been demolished.

ASH ABBEY. Of St Mary's Priory for Augustinian Canonesses, founded c. 1195, a part of the W range survives in the barn. Inside the house itself, the remains of a splendid timber building with raised-aisle type roof (cf. Wingfield College, p. 493) which formerly housed the small college of canons attached to the nuns.

⁰⁰³⁰

CAPEL ST MARY

ST MARY. Dec chancel, the windows on the S side with spurs between the foils or cusps of the tracery. Pretty Dec chancel doorway with foliage decoration. Perp E window. Perp also the S aisle and S porch (outer doorway with fleuron decoration).

Sturdy W tower formerly with a spire. Plain arcade with octagonal piers and double-chamfered arches. Hammerbeam roof, without hammer-posts. The arched braces rest directly on the hammerbeams. There are no collars either. – PULPIT. C18, with tester. Painted in imitation of inlay.

Some timber-framed COTTAGES close to the churchyard.

WINDMILL HILL. A ROMAN BUILDING was discovered in 1928 on a council estate; the site overlooks the valley above Lattingford Bridge, which is on the line of the Roman road to Venta Icenorum (Caistor-by-Norwich, Norfolk). Further excavation in 1946–7 resulted in finds of window glass, painted plaster fragments, C1/2 A.D. pottery, a large number of glass cubes perhaps belonging to a mosaicist, and two bronze lion mounts, whose discovery led to the original investigations. In 1963 further tesserae of glass and Samian ware were found associated with kiln debris, and during bulldozing in 1967, about 60 yds E of the 1928 discovery, a cobbled yard was found which was partly overlaid by the *opus signinum* floor of an outbuilding.

CARLTON

3060

ST PETER. W tower of brick, early C16. Traces of dark blue diapering. Nave and chancel with Norman masonry and fenestration of *c.* 1300. Double-chamfered recess in the chancel S wall. – PULPIT. With two tiers of the usual squat blank arches and oblong ornamented panels above them. Dated 1626. – BENCH ENDS. Some with tracery and poppy-heads. – COMMUNION TABLE. With bulbous legs. Dated 1630. – PLATE. Cup 1701; Paten inscribed '1588 Carlton 1715'. – BRASSES. Civilian of *c.* 1480; 2 ft 2 in. long. – Civilian of *c.* 1490; 18 in. long.

WINDMILL. A tower-mill used as a water tower.

CARLTON COLVILLE

5090

ST PETER. The W tower has an E.E. ground floor (W lancet) and a Dec top with flushwork battlements. In the nave, on the N side, one renewed Norman window. Nave and chancel are all over-restored, but seem to have been Dec. The reticulated tracery of the E window was gone in 1883. – FONT. Octagonal, Perp. Two steps; the upper with quatrefoil decoration. Against the stem four lions, against the bowl four angels and four lions. – STAINED GLASS. In the chancel a two-light window by

Powell, 1863. – PLATE. Elizabethan Cup; Paten of 1567. – (MONUMENT. In the vestry effigy of a priest. LG)
(RECTORY. In the garden one of the Suffolk crinkle-crankle, i.e. undulating forcing, walls. N. Scarfe)

CASTLE HILL *see* GREAT ASHFIELD

CAVENDISH

8040

ST MARY. On the N side of the green, a wide expanse with pretty houses around. Early C14 W tower, the ground floor vaulted with heavy single-chamfered ribs. Low tower arch. The upper floor has a fireplace. The SE stair-turret rises higher than the tower top and carries a triangular bellcote. The S porch is early C14, an unusually early date for such a porch. The side windows are flanked by shafts with moulded capitals. Later, and fully Dec, the S aisle windows. In their tracery the motif of the four-petalled flower. The modest doorway proves the N aisle also to be structurally Dec. The PISCINA inside the chancel looks Dec too, though the chancel was built by the will of Sir John Cavendish who died in 1381. It is in a very original idiom. Priest's doorway with the type of arch which the French call *anse de panier*. The tracery of the side windows specially pretty. The E window was ordinary, but very large (seven lights). Fine Late Perp five-bay arcades with slim piers with single shafts to nave and aisle, triple shafts to the arch openings, and dainty mouldings in the diagonals (money for the S aisle was left in 1471). Clerestory with three-light windows and a good cambered roof. The walls are panelled with flushwork outside. It was erected by the Smyth family. Late Perp also most of the aisle windows. – FONT. Octagonal, Perp. Panelled stem, bowl with Signs of the Evangelists and quatrefoils. – LECTERNS. One big, of brass with eagle, the same type as Woolpit and also Upwell Norfolk, Croft Lincolnshire, Chipping Campden and Corpus Christi College Oxford. – The other of wood, C16. – SCULPTURE. chapel altar. Flemish C16 relief of the Crucifixion. (To the r of the altar statue of St Michael, said to be Florentine C15 work.) Both pieces came from the private chapel of Athelstan Riley's house in London (cf. Little Petherick Cornwall). – STAINED GLASS. Original bits in several windows. – MONUMENT. Sir George Colt † 1570. Tomb-chest with shields in cartouches. Canopied niche above with, on its bracket, two angels carrying the soul of the deceased. Is the niche earlier than the monument?

CHURCH COTTAGES, to the SW. Picturesque as a foil to the church approach.

OLD RECTORY, near the pond. C16. Two-storeyed, timber-framed, with cross wings. Oversailing upper floor.

MANOR COTTAGES. C16. Two-storeyed, timber-framed, with three gables along the front and an overhang. Oriel windows with mullions and transoms. A panelled room inside.

NETHER HALL FARMHOUSE, N of the church. C16. Two-storeyed, timber-framed. Oversailing upper floor. Two-storeyed porch. The windows were originally mullioned. Well restored.

THE MILL, near the station. Picturesque group, mainly C18.

CAVENDISH HALL, 1 m. w. Early C19. White brick. Three bays wide, two storeys high. Porch with a pediment on four Ionic columns.

CAVENHAM

7060

ST ANDREW. Small. Unbuttressed w tower formerly with a two-storey erection in front (cf. Ely, Debenham). C13 chancel, but with a good Dec PISCINA in the angle of the SE window. Angle shafts and crocketed gable. The nave windows minor Dec. – SCREEN. Humble, with one-light divisions, the entrance arch repaired c. 1600. – (PAINTING, subject unknown, discovered on the N wall in 1967. C. R. Paine) – PLATE. Cup of 1830.

BLACK DITCHES. A boundary (?) ditch and bank now visible in two sections. Firstly the s section, traceable for 1½ m. across Risby Poor's Heath to the s and extending over the parish boundary.* It is lost in the arable land SE of the common, though an old hedgerow continues the line of the dyke nearly to Barrow Bottom. Secondly, the N section, 1100 yds in length, lies on Cavenham Heath and extends from just s of Oak Plantation to the river Lark. As with all the East Anglian dykes, the date and purpose of the Black Ditches are unknown, but they are in all likelihood of post-Roman date (see Introduction, p. 24). The s section covers the Icknield Way to the N and its crossing of the Lark at Lackford.

CHADACRE HALL see HARTEST

CHALK HILL see BARTON MILLS

* The section along the edge of Long Plantation takes advantage of the slope above Cavenham Brook.

CHAPEL HILL FARM *see* LITTLE WHELNETHAM

CHARSFIELD*

2050

ST PETER. An exceptionally stately brick tower. Diagonal
buttresses. Along the base a flushwork frieze of unusual
symbols and inscriptions, e.g. the chalice and wafer in a
lozenge with four times the initial of the Virgin in the corners.
The battlements also have flushwork arcading. Nave and
chancel in one. In the nave a Norman N window and part of a
Norman S window. In the chancel one C13 lancet window and
a three-light E window with intersected tracery, probably
reliable. Early C16 brick S porch with polygonal buttresses.
Against the base lively flushwork frieze of quatrefoils, stars,
etc. Entrance with one order of fleurons in the responds and
one on jambs and arch. – FONT. Octagonal; badly preserved.
Eight figures against the stem. The Signs of the Evangelists
and four angels with scrolls against the bowl. – SCREEN. Only
part of the dado remains. – PLATE. Flagon of 1576; Cup probably Elizabethan; Paten 1679.

CHATTISHAM

0040

ALL SAINTS AND ST MARGARET. Nave and chancel and short
W tower. The tower was much repaired and received its
battlements in 1772. The church appears to be early C14 but
was over-restored in 1869. – POOR BOX. Cylindrical, 8 in
high, made of a solid piece of wood. – PLATE. Elizabethan Cup.
(OLD RECTORY. Porch, incorporating pretty frilled bargeboarding, probably from a former church porch. NMR)
WINDMILL. A smock-mill, derelict.

CHEDBURGH

7050

ALL SAINTS. Nave and chancel of septaria and flint, and grey
brick N tower of 1842 with spire. The chancel is also of 1842, but
the E window with reticulated tracery is surely original. Nave
of c. 1300 with renewed lancet and Y-tracery windows.
Original the shafting of one S window. Pretty quatrefoil nave
W window. No furnishings of interest. – STAINED GLASS. Some
old fragments in the E window.

* The village of Charsfield is the one on which Ronald Blythe chiefly based
his book *Akenfield, Portrait of an English Village* (Allen Lane, The Penguin
Press, 1969).

CHEDISTON

3070

ST MARY. The deep reveal of one Norman N window in the
chancel. Otherwise the chancel Dec. The W tower seems C13
below. Later upper part, the battlements panelled in flushwork. The rest of the church is plastered outside. The nave
windows are Perp, but the S doorway is a very graceful piece of
c. 1300, with very thin shafts carrying small leaf capitals and a
finely moulded arch. (The S porch entrance perhaps of the
same date.) Simple N doorway also of *c.*1300. C18 brick
family pew on the N side. The nave roof has arched braces up
to the collar-beams and a decorated wall-plate. Kingposts on
the collar-beams. – FONT. Four Lions and four Wild Men
against the stem; the Signs of the Evangelists and four demi-
figures of angels against the bowl. – PULPIT. From Cookley
church. Dated 1637. Not with the usual arches, but with arches
studded with diamonds and knobs. Panels with arabesque
ornament. – COMMUNION RAIL. Jacobean. Turned balusters
spaced widely and between each two an obelisk and a pendant
not quite meeting (cf. Isleham Cambridgeshire). – BENCHES.
Four ends with poppy-heads. – PAINTING. Large head of
St Christopher; N wall. – PLATE. Cup of 1724; Paten of 1725.
ASH FARMHOUSE. Early C17, timber-framed with a stepped
brick gable at the end. In it remains of six windows. DOE)
Wall footings of a ROMANO-BRITISH BUILDING were found
during trial trenching at Hernehill, and at Chediston Grange
roofing tiles and sherds indicate Romano-British occupation.

CHELMONDISTON

2030

ST ANDREW. Destroyed in the Second World War and rebuilt.
Completion 1957. Not an inkling of any development of
architecture since the turn of the century.

CHELSWORTH

9040

ALL SAINTS. Not a big church. The outstanding feature is the
early C14 tomb recess in the N aisle. It projects to the outside,
and has here a flat flint wall with diagonal buttresses. Top
frieze of ballflower and two circular pinnacles. Inside the
recess has a depressed two-centred arch under a normal two- 33
centred arch under a gable. The arches are carried on short
shafts, still with naturalistic foliage. Between the two arches is
a big, somewhat depressed trefoil, between the upper arch and
the gable a slimmer pointed trefoil. The spandrel surfaces are

diapered. L. and r. buttresses, diapered also in their lower
parts, and ending in finials. The main gable is crocketed and
carries a finial too. The interior of the niche has a rib-vault
with finely moulded ribs. The style is that of the Royal Court
just before the introduction of ogee forms. The buttresses
prevent the adjoining small lancet windows from having
evenly splayed jambs on the l. and the r. Otherwise the church
has an early C14 W tower, a Dec chancel (one s window), and
two early C14 S aisle windows. Of the Perp features the best are
the s porch and s doorway. The porch is tall and has Perp side
windows. Handsome ceiling. The doorway is uncommonly
ambitious. Hood-mould on angel-busts. Fleurons in jambs and
arch. Ogee gable and two niches l. and r. Arcade of three bays.
Tall piers with four attached shafts and moulded arches. –
FONT. C14, with cusped, crocketed little arches. – SOUTH
DOOR with tracery and a border of quatrefoils. – (SCULPTURE.
Two original statues in niches in the s porch. P. G. M. Dickinson) – WALL PAINTING. Doom over the chancel arch, badly
restored in 1849. – (STAINED GLASS, in the s porch. Said to
be of pre-Reformation date.) – PLATE. Cup and Cover 1663;
Paten and Almsdish 1735.

THE GRANGE. By the church. With divers gables, and in the
porch gable a cartouche with the date 1694.

Very pretty village street with houses almost entirely on the N
side facing the trees and the river Brett. Especially attractive
some of the houses opposite the bridge, e.g. one timber
framed and thatched, then the RECTORY, with a stuccoed C18
front and two projecting wings. The BRIDGE is really two
short hump bridges of brick. One is dated 1754 by Jervoise.

7050   CHEVINGTON

ALL SAINTS. Of flint and septaria. Transitional nave, see the s
doorway, which has a round arch, one order of shafts with
thick crocket capitals, and an outer arch order of dog-tooth
repeated in the outer order of the jambs. One small Norman N
window also preserved, and the plain single-chamfered N
doorway. E.E. chancel with windows. The E window is of
1697, still 'Gothic' in so far as the five lights of the straight-
headed windows are arched. The chancel arch is very original
and successful. Tall rather narrow arch on moulded corbels
and two completely plain side arches no doubt to put altars in.
The nave has one C13 window with plate tracery on the s side,
another with slightly later tracery on the N side, and Perp

windows otherwise. The nave roof has carved tie-beams dated 1590 and 1638. The W tower is Perp. Money was left for its building in 1444. Base with flushwork panelling. The prominent pinnacles are a restoration done by the Earl of Bristol, Bishop of Derry, i.e. *c.* 1800.* – FONT. Perp, octagonal. – BENCHES. Broad with blank tracery and poppy-heads, some of them figures with musical instruments. – CHEST. Dec with tracery and large leaves. On the l. upright affronted animals. – PLATE. Cup 1595.

METHODIST CHAPEL, Tan Office Green, ¾ m. SSW. Three bays, of flint with red brick dressings. Arched windows, thatched roof.

CHICKERING HALL FARMHOUSE *see* HOXNE

CHILLESFORD

3050

ST PETER. Unbuttressed W tower of coralline crag, not of flint. Nave and chancel flint. The window tracery points to the early C14. The chancel arch is flanked by two cusped niches, or rather openings into the chancel. – FONT. Octagonal, C13, of Purbeck marble, with two shallow blank arches on each side. – STAINED GLASS. E window 1865 by *C. A. Gibbs*, terrible. – MONUMENT. Inscription tablet to Agnes Claxton † 1624 and her daughter † 1633. The inscription ends:

MATER 🖘　　　　　🖙 FILIA

CHILTON

8040

ST MARY. On no road, about ¼ m. from Chilton Hall. There is no village near either. Flint, but with a C16 W tower of brick. The Crane Chapel at the NE end also of brick. Moreover, a Tudor brick window of two lights in the nave N wall next to a very tall transomed straight-headed stone window also of two lights. The S windows are equally tall and transomed, but of three lights and arched. – FONT. Perp, octagonal, simple. – SCREEN. Only the dado survives. – STAINED GLASS. In the tracery of the E window of the Crane Chapel two original figures. – MONUMENTS. Alabaster effigy probably of George Crane † 1491. – Alabaster effigies of Robert Crane † 1500 and his wife. – Sir Robert Crane † 1643 with his two wives. This

* A reader has pointed out that the top stage of the tower (below the pinnacles) is certainly post-medieval, but looks earlier than 1800. Is it C17 Gothic?

monument was prepared in 1626. The sculptor was *Gerard Christmas*, and the price in the contract is £50. Tripartite composition of the shape of the so-called Venetian window. Columns of touch. Three niches. In the middle one Sir Robert kneeling frontally, in the other two the two wives in profile.

CHILTON HALL. Substantial fragment of an Early Tudor brick mansion surrounded by a well-preserved moat. A brick bridge leads to it. Of the house the most interesting part is the SE corner, with a polygonal angle-turret and a polygonal angle-buttress. There seems to have been a big window originally between them on each floor.

CHIPLEY ABBEY *see* POSLINGFORD

CHOPPINS HILL FARMHOUSE *see* CODDENHAM

7040
CLARE

ST PETER AND ST PAUL. The church stands in a spacious treeless churchyard, and one somehow does not consider it as part of the town, although this stretches around it in all directions. C13 W tower with a W doorway with two orders of shafts and a hood-mould with nailhead decoration. Lancet windows higher up. The W window of five lights is of course Perp, as is the frieze with shields and quatrefoils below it. The tower is unfortunately a little short for the church. Large Perp church, but inside it the arcade piers (six bays) are of the C14 and re-used in the remodelling. They are quatrefoiled and keeled. Of the C14 the S porch with its windows with Y-tracery. It is vaulted and has carved bosses. The second bay of vaulting was half cut off when the aisle of the C14 building was widened later. To the E of the porch is a contemporary chapel (cf. St Gregory Sudbury etc.), and the arch of this towards the aisle is again C14. Beneath this chapel and the porch is a vaulted bone-hole. The rest of the church is all Late Perp, and mostly Early Tudor, except for the chancel, which was all but rebuilt in 1617–19, an example of the effortless Perp survival of those years. There are few (if characteristic) differences between the C15 and the C17 work. The motif of the stepped arches of the lights in the three-light window is the same. In the Perp work it appears in S aisle and S chapel as well as N aisle and N chapel and clerestory. At the E end of the nave is the most easily remembered motif of the church, the two rood-stair turrets

with their crocketed spirelets (cf. Lavenham).* The clerestory
windows are not doubled, as in so many East Anglian churches,
but as all the windows of aisles and clerestory are slender and
closely set, the effect has the same erectness as at Long Melford
and Lavenham. The remodelling of the interior made it very
airy. The C14 piers received castellated capitals, the arches
crocketed hood-moulds. Shafts rise from the piers to the roof.
Above the arches a string-course with demi-figures of angels
and fleurons. Chancel arch and chapel arches go with the
nave. – FONT. Simple, octagonal, Perp. – SCREENS. Remains
of the rood screen re-used at the entrance to the S chapel.
Parclose screen at the E end of the S aisle, fine wide one-light
divisions. – STALLS. Jacobean, some with Jacobean poppy-
heads. – GALLERY in the porch chapel. Jacobean with balusters. – COMMUNION RAIL. With twisted balusters, late
C17. – DOORS. N and S doors and N chancel door with tracery [30]
and a border of foliage trail. – LECTERN. Brass, with a big
eagle. The same type as at St Margaret King's Lynn and Red-
enhall Norfolk (Oman's type II). – (STAINED GLASS. Heraldic
glass of 1617 in the E window.) – PLATE. Richly embossed
silver-gilt Cup, probably Flemish; Cup 1562; Paten 1680;
Flagon 1713.

CLARE PRIORY. Founded for Austin Friars in 1248 by Richard
de Clare, the earliest house of the order in England. Of the
buildings most of the features which remain are early C14,
namely one doorway in the former Cellarium, later the Prior's
Lodging and later still the house of the Frende and Barker
families, then a vaulted chamber at the S end of this range with
one two-light window (single-chamfered ribs), the Lavatorium
arches (see below), the doorway to the Refectory (see below),
the Chapter House entrance from the former E walk, built, it is
known, by Elizabeth de Burgh between 1310 and 1314, and the
remains of the church which was indeed consecrated in 1338.
The church was 168 ft long and had a chancel of six bays with
a S chapel and S vestry, a narrow central tower, and a nave of
six bays with N aisle but no S aisle. The last two bays of the N
aisle were a chapel. Of this a doorway from the nave to the
cloister remains, and in addition the S wall, the sedilia with curious cusped blank arches against the back wall, and the blocked
doorway to the S chancel chapel. The monument to Joan of
Acre, daughter of Edward I, who died in 1305 was to the W of

* A will of 1465 leaves £10 to the making of the rood loft, and one of 1466
:n marks to the fabric of the rood loft 'de novo faciend' (ARA).

the sedilia and cut into them. Of the domestic buildings of th
priory the walls of the cloister remain. In the E wall are th
entrances to the Chapter House and the dormitory staircase
The Dormitory – a unique case – lay 12 ft further E, separate
from the cloister range by an irregular quadrangular courtyard
The Dormitory at the S end overlapped the Infirmary. Thi
has closely set upper windows in blank arches. Reredorte
(i.e. lavatories) at the E end of the Infirmary and at r. angles t
it. Of the Refectory in the S range parts of the walls stand up
In the S wall is a projection for the Reader's Pulpit, at the W en
of the N wall the Lavatorium, or friars' hand-washing place
The Cellarium, i.e. W range, was converted into the prior'
residence in Early Tudor days, and of this time are the lov
mullioned windows with arched lights and the ceiling in th
Hall, i.e. the room behind the C14 doorway. Then the Eliza
bethan period inserted a mullioned and transomed window i
the front and a square bay (built of stone, not of flint) at th
back. (Very fine C17 panelling in the upper room.) To the S o
the Cellarium is an irregular little wooden cloister of which th
W and S ranges remain, complete but altered. The N range wa
of stone. The E range was widened to form a kitchen, whic
stood between Cellarium and Refectory. The date is probabl
the C15. Later on, in the C16–17, the cloister became an inne
courtyard, and an entrance and back door were made throug
the S range.

CASTLE. First mentioned in 1090. Gradually enlarged until i
had, apart from the keep on its mound, two baileys, both
of the keep. The S (inner) bailey is now occupied by th
railway station, the N bailey comprised the priory founded i
1090 by Gilbert de Clare as a cell of Bec in Normandy an
moved to Stoke-by-Clare in 1124. On the mound stands a
impressive fragment of the C13 shell-keep, with three buttresse

PERAMBULATION. At the SW corner of the churchyard lie
THE ANCIENT HOUSE, dated 1473 in the later pargetting
It was the priest's house and has an overhanging gabled en
with brackets and shafts, a window with carved arms and sup
porters, an original doorway, and much bold later pargetting
The house belongs to the High Street which runs S and N from
here. To the N the continuation of this line and the axis of th
church is CALLIS STREET (Calais Street!), with, on the r
THE GROVE, a C15 house with a row of five gables. It has a
oriel bracket with huntsmen and hounds and an early C19 door
way with Greek Doric columns. About ½ m. out on the Chilto

Road is CHAPEL COTTAGE (WENTFORD CHAPEL), a chapel of the late C12 with an original doorway. One order of (missing) shafts with capitals with curly decoration and a round arch. This must have had a tympanum, but the tympanum was in the C13 or early C14 opened into a pointed chamfered arch. Remains of Norman windows in the E gable.

In the HIGH STREETS of the church several good timber-framed houses on the W side. The best single motif is the bracket of the former oriel of the SWAN INN with a big swan and foliage motif, like a magnified misericord. From the S end of the High Street to the E and round the corner into MARKET HILL, where the most interesting house is on the W side. It is now a baker's shop, and has below the shop a vaulted C14 cellar with a central octagonal pier. To the W from Market Hill into NETHERGATE STREET, a wide street with grass l. and r., where on the S side first CLARENCE HOUSE, grey brick, three bays, with Tuscan porch (early C19), and then the NETHERGATE HOTEL with two identical slightly projecting wings with carved bressumers. Chimneys with star tops. Doorway with late C17 pediment. On the other side the RED HOUSE, Georgian, red brick, five bays. Doorway with broken pediment on Tuscan columns. Next to this a house with a completely pargetted gable (believed to be a modern reproduction; DOE), and further on THE CLIFTONS with richly decorated C16 chimneys. Circular shafts, Tudor patterns, star tops. The 51b continuation of Nethergate Street to the W is STOKE ROAD, with two good houses on the l. STOUR HOUSE has an over-hanging upper floor with carved bressumer. RIVERSIDE has the curious peculiarity of the panels between the posts being plastered so as to appear rusticated with alternating sizes.

IRON AGE HILL-FORT, at the N end of the village, just behind Bridewell Street, on Upper Common, near a tributary of the Stour. Roughly square and with a double ditch and bank enclosing c.7 acres. The N side is the most complete, with inner rampart c.9 ft high and counterscarps 12 and 14 ft high. The S and E are much depleted owing to building and gardens; two entrances, possibly original, lie N and S.

CLAYDON 1040

ST PETER. At the W end Saxon long and short work. Inside the S wall the outline of the former Norman doorway. W tower with flushwork arcading on base and buttresses. On the top of the tower angels and beasts as pinnacles. N porch with stepped gable and rough flint chequering. But what dominates the impression is the transepts (with their high cross roof) and the chancel. They are of 1862, and were built by the then rector and patron of the living, George Drury. Only the vestry on the N side of the chancel is Perp, see its roof. The work of 1862 was done most lavishly, and *Drury* did much of it himself. The foliage of the crossing arches is lavish to excess, and the PULPIT with its lacy openwork tracery is very lavish too. – FONT. Octagonal. Panelled stem. Bowl with four crowns and four angels with big shields, all under flat arches. – SCULPTURE. Virgin and Child, 1945 and 1949, by *Henry Moore*. A noble work, a little less hieratic than his other Virgin in a church, that at St Matthew Northampton. It is the sideways movement of the legs that gives this later figure a more informal, more approachable character. The statue is a War Memorial, and it is due to Sir Jasper Ridley (who lies buried in the church-yard) that it was commissioned. – PAINTING. Pentecost, Milanese or Piedmontese, early C16. – STAINED GLASS. Original glass of *c.* 1862 at the E end. – PLATE. Paten of 1676.

OLD RECTORY. To the E of the church a curious group of two towers and walls, made up, it is said, of parts of the old chancel when this was pulled down. The most enjoyable part of this group is an underground GROTTO which, with its shell-work, looks certainly older than 1850. It is exceedingly pretty, and would be worth careful restoration.

CLAYDON OLD HALL. Built in 1621. Red brick. The puzzling look of the house is due to the fact that the top parts of its centre are missing and have been replaced by the roof being taken down lower than it originally went. Two shaped side gables (one convex part and then an ogee top) and between them, rather crowded together, two canted bay windows and a central porch. The porch has Tuscan brick columns on the ground floor. A transomed three-light window above. Pediments only above the top windows under the gables.

CLOCK HOUSE *see* LITTLE STONHAM

2050

CLOPTON

ST MARY. Strong s tower with Perp bell-openings. Wide nave, its s doorway of *c.* 1300. It has two big continuous chamfers. In the nave hammerbeam roof with arched braces to the collar-beams. Kingposts on these. The chancel rebuilt 1883. – FONT. Octagonal, Perp, simple. On a step edged with quatrefoils. – PLATE. Cup 1639.

(CLOPTON HALL. About 1500, with an early C18 front. Inside some good early panelling and an overmantel dated 1617. DOE)

BRIDGE FARMHOUSE. Eminently picturesque. Timber-framed and thatched.

CLOPTON HALL see RATTLESDEN and WICKHAMBROOK

COCKFIELD

9050

ST PETER. Quite big. Dec W tower with flushwork chequer pattern on the buttresses. Dec N aisle. Early C14 chancel, see the outlines of the windows inside, the buttresses with ogee-headed niches, the PISCINA, and the splendid, if grossly over-restored EASTER SEPULCHRE. Niche with three stepped steep gables with blank quatrefoils. Cusped and sub-cusped arches with crockets. Angle buttresses. Hardly any ogee forms yet (cf. e.g. Edmund Crouchback, Westminster Abbey). Perp S aisle and clerestory. Elaborate S aisle battlements. Fine S aisle roof with carved beams. S porch with a front with flushwork panelling. Three niches round the entrance. Doorway with fleurons and shields. The battlements are different from those of the S aisle.* Tall Perp chancel windows. Arcades of five bays Jacobean. – STALLS. Not much survives, but it includes ends with tracery and poppy-heads and some minor MISERICORDS. – COMMUNION RAIL. With twisted balusters; late C17. – STAINED GLASS. (In the easternmost S aisle window four C14–15 heads.) – E window by *Kempe*, 1889. – PLATE. Two Flagons 1743; Almsdish 1759. – MONUMENT. James Harvey † 1723. By *N. Royce* of Bury St Edmunds. Standing wall-monument. Coupled Corinthian columns against coupled Corinthian pilasters. Pediment. Bust on a short black sarcophagus. The quality is not high.

CHURCH COTTAGE. A handsome C15 cottage along the churchyard. Timber-framed with brick infilling. One original doorway.‡

COCKFIELD HALL see YOXFORD

* A will of 1468 refers to the building of the vestibule – presumably the porch (ARA).

‡ Like the Fox and Goose Inn at Fressingfield (p. 223), this is a former church house, i.e. a forerunner of the village hall, used for parish festivals and holidays, especially after the Act of 1571 forbade the use of the church itself for feasting.

1050

CODDENHAM

ST MARY. A Norman window in the chancel (N). Another chancel window with later C13 plate tracery. The chancel was much restored *c*. 1830. Good Dec nave W window. Dec also the S aisle, see the details of the arcade (different in mouldings from the N aisle arcade), the windows, the doorway, and the PISCINA. The church has a NW tower, also Dec. Its battlements are decorated with flushwork arcading. The openings towards the church are continuous double and triple chamfers. Perp clerestory with flushwork arcading between the windows, rich stone decoration of parapet and battlements, and an *Orate* for John Frenche and his wife. Perp also the N porch, set at an angle to the aisle. Flushwork-panelled front. Shields with the Symbols of the Trinity and the monogram of Jesus in the spandrels. Inscription above the entrance. The exciting fact inside is the double-hammerbeam roof with two sets of angels. Good original N aisle roof too. – PULPIT. Jacobean. – STALLS. With two plain MISERICORDS. – (BENCH ENDS. Two, with poppy-heads and animals on the arms.) – PANELLING. Jacobean, in the aisles; good. – COMMUNION RAIL. Late C17, with twisted balusters. Partly instead of the rood screen, partly in the S aisle. – PAINTING. Christ shown to the Multitude. Large figures, by a Netherlandish follower of Caravaggio. – SCULPTURE. Alabaster panel of the Crucifixion (S aisle altar); C15. – PLATE. Set of 1790. – MONUMENTS. The Rev. Baltazar Gardeman † 1739. Fine restrained piece with a pediment above and a cherub's head below. – Philip Bacon † 1666. Even more restrained. Only the long inscription, flanked by fluted composite columns and surmounted by a pediment.

Charming village street running down the hill and up again to the church. The most attractive house is the present POSTOFFICE, of *c*. 1500, formerly an inn. Timber-framed with overhang on buttress-shafts and brackets. Two original windows. C17 pargetting in big, simple geometrical motifs.

VICARAGE. 1770. Red brick, of five windows and two storeys. Ionic porch. (Fine Adam-style interiors.)

CHOPPINS HILL FARMHOUSE, 1 m. N. Timber-framed with overhang. (A kingpost roof inside. *Suff. Arch. Soc.* 1934–6)

COMBRETOVIUM. The site of a Roman posting station and earlier military fort situated at a ford across the Gipping and at the intersection of four routes. Since 1823, much material has come from the fields on the E side of the river N and S of Baylham Mill, where the plan was uncovered of an extensive building dated to the C I A.D. The camp was located from air photographs in the vicinity of Baylham House Farm, and has produced a number of pits containing Romano-British ware of the end of the Claudian period. A section cut in 1953 across the road W of Mill Lane from Camulodunum (Colchester) to Venta Icenorum (Caistor-by-Norwich) produced coins of c.A.D. 70. Other finds – coins of Nero, a statuette of the Emperor (in the British Museum marked 'Barking'), and medallions, all of the late C I A.D. – indicate a possible imperial shrine.

COLDHAM HALL

8050

1 m. SW of Stanningfield

Built in 1574 by Robert Rookwood. H-shaped, of red brick. The windows are mullioned and transomed and seem to be of brick too (see e.g. on the N side). Many of them have low pediments. The front is to the W and has the two wing fronts not identical, a porch not centrally placed, and the big hall bay window with four transoms. The porch is somewhat barbarically detailed, with two orders of fluted pilasters tapering so strongly that they seem almost obelisks. They carry the pediments, which are thus detached from doorway and window. The porch leads into the hall which has its big original fireplace, see the chimneybreast on the E side. Inside on the ground floor in the N W wing a room with a fireplace and a good plaster ceiling. The beams are exposed, and each panel has a large oblong principal motif. Above the hall all along the house runs a long gallery. Off it the former CHAPEL, with pretty Gothic decoration of the 1770s. A 1779 on a rainwater head, a 1771 on the barn. Extremely pretty tall bell-turret of 1851 at the stables.

COLUMBINE HALL see STOWUPLAND

COMBS

0050

ST MARY. Quite a big church, on its own. Big Dec W tower with N and S archways and no W entrance. The archways have three continuous chamfers. Flushwork only at the base. The bell-openings are Perp. Dec chancel. The E window with plain intersected tracery, but two ogee-arched niches l. and r. of it. The S W and N W windows treated as 'low-sides' with a transom. On the S side also a circular window, not quatrefoiled but with a four-petal motif. SEDILIA and PISCINA are mostly the result of restoration but were clearly Dec. Pretty Dec N doorway with two thin shafts with foliage capitals and hood-mould on head-stops. Perp s aisle windows (except for the w window which is early C14).* Perp N aisle windows, Perp clerestory. A stone string-course connects them horizontally. Later brick s porch. Six-bay arcade with octagonal piers and double-chamfered arches. – FONT. C14 probably. Stem with ogee-arched panels. On the bowl knobbly foliage in fields variously detailed. – ROOD SCREEN. Only the dado.‡ – PARCLOSE SCREENS. To N and s chapels. – PULPIT. Jacobean, with scrolly book-rests. – BENCHES. With traceried ends, poppy-heads, and beasts and birds on the arms. Much restored. – STAINED GLASS. In several s windows a good deal of original C15 glass survives. Parts from a life of St Margaret, also from the Seven Works of Mercy, also from a Tree of Jesse. – PLATE. Almsdish c. 1700; two Flagons early C18, made at Danzig, with engraved subjects.

In the village TANNERY with buildings of various date. According to the DOE the back store with the wide queenpost roof goes back to the early C19. The most attractive house in the village is opposite the Post Office. It is of c. 1600 and has carved beams in its gables and carved bargeboarding.

For EDGAR'S FARM and VALLEY FARM see Stowmarket, p. 446.

CONEY WESTON
9070

ST MARY. Outside the village. Nave and chancel, both Dec, the nave thatched. The w tower fell a long time ago. A two-bay N chancel chapel has been pulled down. The nave s wall and the s porch have knapped flint walls. In the outside chancel s wall a low tomb recess. Inside there are two cusped niches to the l. of the chancel arch, and two not quite so tall ones to its r. Angle PISCINA in the chancel with angle shaft and a gable starting with vertical pieces. To its l. remains of a remarkably large niche which must have been placed in the angle between E window and piscina. – FONT. Octagonal, Dec. With a number of tracery motifs of the date and also a panel with twelve roses and two with big square leaves. – TILES. Some in the NW corner. – PLATE. Elizabethan Cup; Paten 1678.

* A will of 1449 leaves money to the making of an aisle; one of 1452 to the making of a new window above the 'aisle of the Holy Trinity'; and others of 1472 towards the making of the E window of the s aisle, and of rood stairs (ARA).

‡ Money was left towards making a new candle-beam in a will proved in 1468 (ARA).

COOKLEY

3070

ST MICHAEL. Slender, unbuttressed Norman w tower, see the blocked window into the nave. Norman N doorway with one order of shafts, and in the arch zigzag on the front and the underside so that they meet in three-dimensional lozenges. Little else externally in its original state (bad restoration 1894). The chancel seems Dec, the nave Perp. Hammerbeam roof in the nave. The wall-posts stand on timber heads. – FONT. The bowl only; with four angels and four lions. – STALLS. The traceried fronts may come from the screen. – BENCHES. Four with poppy-heads. Former figures on the arms. Very good and varied tracery on the ends. – PLATE. Cup and Cover and Paten of 1813.

(HILL FARMHOUSE, ½ m. E. C17. Timber-framed with brick end with a shaped gable. Blocked oval window in it. DOE)

(BUCK'S FARMHOUSE, E of the former. C17. Timber-framed with a brick end with stepped gable. DOE)

COOKLEY FARM *see* EYE

COPDOCK

1040

ST PETER. Perp. Quite an impressive church with its aisleless nave, its tall three-light Perp windows, its various doorways, their jambs and arches decorated with fleurons, crowns, and shields, its N transept separated from the nave by a tall arch, again decorated with shields, and its w tower with flushwork panelling on the diagonal buttresses. – DOOR. N door with tracery. – SCULPTURE. Some Elizabethan panels with figures and ornament (e.g. Edward VI on horseback) used in the w gallery.

(FELCOURT, former Rectory. By *E. B. Lamb*, 1858. Uncommonly large. Built for a rector who was a member of the de Grey family.)

COPDOCK HALL has a spectacular C16 brick BARN of ten bays. Stepped gables at the end. Diapering with blue headers. The small windows arranged chessboard-wise.

CORTON

5090

ST BARTHOLOMEW. Impressive in its semi-ruined state. A big church, the tall w tower open to the sky, and the tracery of the bell-openings broken out. Flushwork panelling on the battlements. The nave also roofless for two-thirds of its length – a

memento as one enters the parts remaining for services. Tall
and wide Dec chancel with tall two-light windows N and S.
They have one reticulation motif and a smaller one inside it.
Large Perp E window. Fine SEDILIA and PISCINA, much re-
stored. Four crocketed ogee arches standing partly against the
SE window. – (REREDOS. With statues said to be ancient.) –
FONT. Octagonal, Perp. Against the stem four lions, against
the bowl four lions and four angels holding shields with the
symbols of the Trinity (three times) and the Passion. – PLATE.
Elizabethan Cup; Flagon 1719; Paten 1732.

ROMAN SIGNAL STATION. A report in 1814 of a building 25 yds
square, with walls constructed of flint and rubble on a timber
base (cf. Burgh Castle), probably refers to the site of a signal
station added in the C4 A.D. to the shore defences.

COTTAGE FARMHOUSE *see* NORTH COVE

0060

COTTON

ST ANDREW. Almost entirely Dec. Chancel with an original
tracery design. Five lights, above them four spherical triangles,
forming the main ogee arches, and above them one large
reticulation unit. The side windows of the chancel are segment-
headed. To the l. and r. of the E window niches outside. Inside
ogee-arched PISCINA and SEDILIA. Of the sedilia the two
seats and arches broken off which stood against the window.
Aisles with segment-headed two-light windows, either with one
spherical triangle or with reticulation motifs treated again very
originally. The latter type of window also in the S porch. The
five-bay aisle arcades have the typical early C14 piers: quatrefoil
with fine diagonal spurs. The arch is moulded in two waves.
The S porch has a parapet with flushwork decoration. Porch
entrance with leaf capitals. Delightful S doorway with three
orders of shafts all with leaf capitals. In the arch one order
closely carved with leaves. The hood-mould also treated in this
way. It rests on the l. on a big lizard. There is exceptionally
much of the original colour preserved. Equally startling the W
tower. Its W side is opened by a tall arch all the height which is
usually occupied by doorway and window. It forms quite a
spectacular W porch. At its E, however, there is no doorway,
only a fine Dec three-light window. The Perp contribution is
the clerestory and the roof.* The clerestory has doubled

---

* A will of 1471 gives a close called Garlekis for the repair and building of
the new roof – on condition that no man of Cotton unjustly claims or induces
a disturbance in his close called Clarys Close in Cotton (ARA).

windows; they are of two lights with panel tracery. The arches with some brick voussoirs. Flushwork emblems between the windows. The roof has double-hammerbeams with collars alternating with arched braces up to the collars. Angels remain against the upper hammerbeams. The purlins have fine crestings. The E bay is boarded, but nothing of its decoration survives. – FONT. The stem with eight small figures (monks? bedesmen?). The bowl is not original. – PULPIT. Jacobean. – READER'S DESK. Made up of Jacobean parts. – BENCHES. One with poppy-heads, and on one end the carving of an iron-bound door. The others plain and solid, straight-headed. – COMMUNION RAIL. With turned balusters; C17. – DOORS. The S door with tracery of reticulation motifs. – The door to the tower stairs is all iron-faced. – STAINED GLASS. Fragments in the aisles and in the N clerestory. – PLATE. Cup probably c. 1600; Paten c. 1675; Flagon 1727.

HEMPNALL'S HALL, ¾ m. NE. C16. With a stepped brick gable to the w. The rest timber-framed. Brick bridge of one arch across the moat.

A cottage has a handsome oval panel in plaster. It contains flowers and the date 1691.

COVEHITHE

5080

ST ANDREW. A moving sight with its commanding w tower and its tall, long, majestic walls through which the wind blows from the sea. There is no proper village here now, let alone anything of the busy port that Covehithe must have been. No more than a few houses stand by the church, and inside a thatched brick building was put up in 1672 to take up services again which had been discontinued after the great church had been ruined in the Civil War. The w tower is Dec; the nave, aisles and chancel are Perp externally, but the arcade, as can be seen from the w responds, was Dec too. It had quatrefoil piers with fillets and spurs in the diagonals. Seven bays and one short bay of projecting chancel. The chancel windows are very tall, that on the E side very wide too; the one on the N side and the one on the S seem immensely tall because they are narrow. Below the chancel was a vaulted crypt (cf. Beccles). The aisle exterior is enriched by flushwork panelling in chequerboard and arches. – FONT. Perp, octagonal, with four lions against the stem, and the four Signs of the Evangelists and four angels with musical instruments against the bowl. – PLATE. Cup and Cover 1567; Paten 1805.

COWLINGE
7050

ST MARGARET.* Brick tower built by Francis Dickins in 1733. Good classical inscription on the E wall. The medieval church is built of septaria and brick. It dates from the early C14. Arcade of octagonal piers with broadly moulded arches. Aisle windows with nice flowing tracery (motif of four-petalled flowers). Perp N porch, clerestory with quatrefoil windows (at least the first N and S from the W), and crown-post roof. Perp E window. – FONT. Perp, octagonal. – SCREENS. Rood screen Perp. Simple, with one-light divisions. The original gates are preserved. – Parclose screen of crude workmanship. – PAINTING. Weighing of Souls, above the chancel arch. An unusual representation. Large St Michael on the r. with a feathered body, large Virgin on the l. reaching across with a long rod to tip the balance. – PLATE. Elizabethan Cup. – MONUMENT.

39a Francis Dickins † 1747, an unrecorded signed work by *Peter Scheemakers*. Base and reredos background with broken pediment on brackets. Two seated figures in Roman dress l. and r. of an urn on a tall pedestal. White marble and grey-veined white marble. Noble, if cool.

(PARSONAGE FARM, by the entrance to Branches Park. C16, with central hall and cross wings, one with overhang. P. G. M. Dickinson)

WINDMILL. A derelict smock-mill.

COX COMMON *see* WESTHALL

CRANLEY HALL *see* EYE

CRANMER GREEN *see* WALSHAM-LE-WILLOWS

CRANSFORD
3060

ST PETER. W tower, nave and chancel. 'Drastically and dreadfully restored. There is nothing of interest except the C15 BELL' (Cautley). – PLATE. Elizabethan Cup; Paten 1568; Almsdish 1697; Flagon 1718.

CRATFIELD
3070

ST MARY. Originally Dec (two S aisle windows; chancel S doorway) converted and added to Perp. Arcades of five bays. The

* The dedication appears as St Andrew in a will of 1470 (ARA).

s arcade is Dec, the N arcade Perp. One ought to compare the mouldings of the capitals of the octagonal piers and of the arches. Perp clerestory with doubled windows. Perp w tower. The battlements are decorated in stone carving, not in flush-work. w doorway with jambs and arch decorated with crowns and the letter M (for St Mary). In the spandrels, strangely enough, a Wild Man (or can it really be St George?) and a dragon. Attached to the chancel on the N side a vestry. The doorway into it decorated with fleurons, the E window with Dec tracery. Fine chancel roof. Arched braces meeting at the collar-beams. Thrice embattled wall-plate. – FONT. Very tall. 24 On two steps, the upper with blank tracery. The stem has at its foot eight seated figures. Against its side eight small standing figures in niches. The bowl is carried by eight demi-figures of angels and has against its sides the Seven Sacraments and the Crucifixion, and at the angles small standing figures. Cautley calls Cratfield font 'probably the most beautiful in the Kingdom'. – PULPIT. With Jacobean parts. Blank depressed arches with arabesques. £10 were given for it in 1617. – SCREEN. What is left of it stands under the tower arch. – BENCHES. C17, with rather baldly stylized poppy-heads. – (STAINED GLASS. In the chancel SE window a good panel of Continental glass.) – PLATE. Elizabethan Cup and Paten; Paten 1712.

CREETING ST MARY
0050

St MARY. w tower and N aisle of 1884–7. s doorway Norman, with one order of colonnettes, scalloped capitals, and one arch with a band of scallop or lunette forms. s porch with a front panelled with flushwork. A niche above the entrance. – FONT. Octagonal, with four lions against the stem, and four angels and the Signs of the four Evangelists against the bowl. – STAINED GLASS. All by *Kempe* and later *Kempe & Tower*. The E window 1886, s nave *c.* 1893, s chancel *c.* 1899 (with the trademark of the wheatsheaf), etc. – PLATE. Elizabethan Cup; silver-gilt Standing Cup with Cover 1593; Patens 1690 and 1730.

CREETING ST PETER
0050

St PETER. The nave N doorway minimum Norman. Early C14 w tower. The w doorway has two continuous chamfers. Nave and chancel with Dec and Perp windows, completely un-restored, it appears. – FONT. Octagonal. Four lions against the stem. Demi-figures of angels carrying the bowl. Four angels and panels with the Crown of Thorns, square interlace, a flower and a heart against the bowl. – PULPIT. Perp, with two-light ogee-arched panels. – PAINTING. Large St Christopher. A long inscribed scroll and the border are partly preserved. – STAINED GLASS. E window 1847, designed by the curate, named *Rawnsley*. – PLATE. Elizabethan Cup and Paten; Paten *c*. 1779.

CREPPING HALL *see* STUTTON

CRETINGHAM

2060

ST PETER. Dec w tower with flushwork arches and quatrefoils in the battlements. Nave and chancel partly *c*. 1300, partly Perp. Nicely complete and mixed interior. Hammerbeam roof with decorated wall-plate, tracery above the hammers, and short arched braces connecting the wall-posts from w to E. On one of them (w end) Cautley found the scene of St George and the Dragon. – FONT. Octagonal, against the stem four lions, against the bowl elaborate quatrefoils with shields and flowers. – Two-decker PULPIT. Jacobean with tester. – BENCH ENDS. With tracery and poppy-heads. – BOX PEWS. – COMMUNION RAIL. Three-sided; mid-C17. – MONUMENTS. Sir Richard Cornewaleys (date of death indecipherable). The usual kneeling figure. – Lady Cornwalies † 1603. No effigy, but good ornamental detail.

MOAT FARMHOUSE, ¾ m. NE. 1602. Timber-framed. The main gable with carved beam on carved brackets.

IRON AGE (?) SETTLEMENT, *c*. 1 m. s of the village, on the E of the Otley–Cretingham road. Unexcavated earthworks and huts are visible; perhaps an Early Iron Age farmstead.

CROWE HALL *see* STUTTON

CROWFIELD

1050

14a ALL SAINTS. The only church in Suffolk with a timber-framed chancel. The framing is exposed externally as well as internally. The roof is solid and rather barn-like, with heavy tie-beams and rough arched braces. Of timber also the s porch. It has in its roof decorated tie-beams and arched braces. The nave has hammerbeams alternating with arched braces, constructed oddly in two stages, with pendants between the two hanging down from the purlins (cf. Ufford). Decorated wall-plate.

Victorian bell-turret. – COMMUNION RAIL. C18. – PLATE.
Cup and Paten 1790.
WINDMILL. A derelict smock-mill.

CROWS HALL

1060

1¼ m. SE of Debenham

Red brick with blue diaperings. Built in 1508, but incorporating
early C14 parts (LG). Finely placed inside a moat which is
crossed by a four-arched brick bridge. The house was much
larger than it is now. All that remains is part of the gatehouse
and the major part of the N wing. There was a corresponding S
wing, and the centre was the E range in line with the gatehouse.
The front of the remaining wing has polygonal angle buttresses,
a straight gable with three pinnacles, and original transomed
wooden windows. The gatehouse also has polygonal buttresses.
Good and unusual C17 baluster staircase illustrated in *Country
Life* in 1899, and much panelling. (Just outside the SW corner
of the moat outbuildings with some terracotta plaques of the
style of the work of *c.* 1525 at Shrubland Old Hall. *P.S.I.A.*
XX, 98)

CULFORD

8070

ST MARY.* In the grounds of the house. Rebuilt in 1856–65 by
Blomfield. N aisle of 1908. The tower partly medieval. –
MONUMENTS. Jane Bacon, 1654 by *Thomas Stanton,* who was
paid £300 to do it 'alle in whit and black marble without the
addition of any other stone whatsoever'. Grey marble with
white marble figures. A large standing wall-monument. Her
husband lies below on his side and elbow. Above, between
Ionic columns, mother and children. She is seated frontally
and holds a small child in her lap. Five more kneeling frontally
to her l. and r. one behind another: a sincere, not at all aristocratic, rather Dutch group. Open segmental pediment. – Sir
Nathaniel Bacon, the amateur painter, † 1627. Lozenge-
shaped tablet with, in the middle, an oval recess with portrait
bust. Garlands l. and r. and also two palettes. – Second Marquess Cornwallis † 1823. By *E. H. Baily.* White urn before a
black obelisk; nothing special. – Beatrix Jane Craven, Countess
Cadogan, † 1907. By Countess *Feodora Gleichen.*‡ Recumbent
effigy of white marble in a vaulted recess. On the back wall
putti, a cross, and large vine-trails.

* The dedication is given as St Michael in a will of 1535 (ARA).
‡ I am indebted to Earl Cadogan for this information.

CULFORD SCHOOL. The first Culford Hall was built by Sir Nathaniel Bacon. The present house was built by the first Marquess of Cornwallis about 1790. It is attributed to *James Wyatt*. It was enlarged out of all recognition by *William Young* for Earl Cadogan *c.*1900. The house of 1790 was of seven bays and two and a half storeys, yellow brick, with a three-bay pediment and little enrichment. To this front a giant portico of eight columns was added in 1807–8 (ARA). It has since been removed. The gargantuan Cadogan enlargements are of white brick, in a weak Italianate style, with an asymmetrically placed tower and large rooms, rich but rather commonplace in their decorations. Excellent however and also said to be of *c.* 1900 the staircase with an iron railing. It is under a coffered vault with glazed centre.

The grounds were laid out by *Humphry Repton*. They are discussed in his *Sketches* of 1794.

BARROW, on the edge of Dixon's Covert, *c.* 1 m. down the West Stow road from the village. A fine example of the large Bronze Age 'bowl' form. Original diameter 150 ft, height 8 ft. One Bronze Age sherd and one native sherd of the C1 A.D. were found in the ditch.

CULPHO

2040

ST BOTOLPH. Nave and s porch tower of *c.* 1300; chancel of 1884. The upper parts of the tower are missing. It has a triple-chamfered entrance arch dying into the imposts. The nave has a N doorway, and windows with details also characteristic of their date. – FONT. Octagonal, Perp, simple. – PLATE. Cup Elizabethan; Paten 1710.

DALHAM

7060

ST MARY. C14 chancel (see the s doorway – the windows are Perp) and s aisle (see one window and the doorway). C14 arcade with octagonal piers and double-chamfered arches. Perp N aisle and lower part of the W tower (flushwork ornament on the buttresses). But most of the tower was rebuilt by Sir Martin Stuteville in 1627 as is recorded in a huge inscription inside and on the parapet to the N. On the w side it says Deo triuni sacrum, but on the s side Keep my sabbaths. That was for the villagers. The Perp W window must be of 1627, unless it was re-used. The Perp chancel s window was made under a will of 1466.* Of the same date presumably also the N chapel (now open to the sky) with its mullioned windows, and the vestry. – SCREEN. Only the dado, with arabesque paintings. – WALL PAINTINGS. On the nave N wall traces of the Seven Deadly Sins (l.) and the Seven Works of Mercy (r.). Over the chancel arch apparently Scenes from the Passion. – STAINED GLASS. E window apparently by *Kempe*, 1908. – PLATE. Good silver-gilt Set of 1691, presented by Bishop Patrick of Ely; Flagon 1712. – MONUMENTS. Thomas Stutevyle † 1571. Tomb-chest with three shields in strapwork cartouches. Free-standing on it an inscription tablet flanked by two columns. – Sir Martin Stuteville † 1631. Three oval niches, the middle one raised, for Sir Martin and his two wives. Frontal busts in flat relief. Black columns l. and r. and entablature with semicircularly raised centre. The children kneel small in the 'predella'. – In the churchyard obelisk to General Sir James Affleck † 1833.

DALHAM HALL. Built in 1704–5 by Bishop Patrick of Ely. Red brick, seven bays, two and a half storeys, hipped roof. The quoins are painted white. No pediment. The front ground floor altered. Good stables, ten bays, with two three-bay projections, and segment-headed windows. They may be in imitation of the style of the house. Fine large walled front garden; the church looks into it from the E. Long avenues in several directions, and in addition an informal yew avenue leading to the church.

WINDMILL. Smock-mill with sails near the SW end of the village. Of five floors, in good repair. The mill stands about 50 ft high and has a pepper-pot cap with a gallery round it. She had a fan-tail and four patent sails and drove three pairs of stones. She has not been worked for a number of years, but has been preserved as a landmark.

DALLINGHOO

ST MARY. The surprise in approaching the church is that it seems to have an E tower. On looking more closely, one sees at once that it was a central tower and that the chancel has been demolished. Herringbone masonry shows that it is structurally Early Norman. The W and E arches are of *c.* 1300 or a little earlier. S porch with a moulding of jambs and arch decorated with fleurons. In the spandrels shields with the symbols of the Trinity and the Passion. The nave roof has arched braces to the

* Information received from the Rev. J. B. Humphries.

collar-beams, and also arched braces running W–E from wall-post to wall-post. – PULPIT. An exceptionally splendid Jacobean piece. The body has at its angles not pilasters but slender brackets of double-curved profile and with Ionic capitals. The back includes an earlier panel with the arms of Catherine of Aragon. Big tester with steep pediments. – READER'S DESK. Made up of Elizabethan or Jacobean pieces. – REREDOS. Jacobean panelling, not *in situ*. – COMMUNION RAIL. C18. – STAINED GLASS. The E window by *A. L. Moore*; aesthetically bad. – PLATE. Flagon and Paten 1771.

DARMSDEN

0050

1 m. S of Needham Market

ST ANDREW. 1880. In the Dec style. – PLATE. Elizabethan Cup; Almsdish dated 1650.

DARSHAM

4060

ALL SAINTS. Norman N and S doorways, both badly treated by time and remodellings. In the chancel on the N side one small early C13 lancet. On the S side of the church all irregular Perp windows. Slender W tower with flushwork panelling on buttresses and battlements. – FONT. Inscription referring to Galfrid Symond, rector of Bradwell, i.e. the beginning of the C15. Against the stem four lions, against the bowl four lions and four angels. They hold shields with the Signs of the Trinity, the Passion, Edward the Confessor, and East Anglia (three Crowns). – PULPIT. Jacobean. – BENCH ENDS. A set with tracery and poppy-heads. – PLATE. Cup and Cover Elizabethan; Almsdish 1673; Cup and Paten 1683. – MONUMENT. Sir Thomas Bedingfeild, 1662. Alabaster and touch tablet, quite large and lavish, with columns and pediment. Two small figures reclining on this.

DARSHAM HOUSE. Dated 1679. Of that date the Dutch gable, i.e. a shaped gable with a pediment. The house is ten bays wide and two storeys high. Four small dormers with alternating triangular and segmental pediments. Staircase with 'Laudian' balusters, i.e. turned balusters of quite pronounced swelling. The back of the house is Early Georgian. Blue brick with rubbed brick trim, including the vertical lacing of the windows. Segment-headed windows. Neo-1650 addition; neo-Georgian additions.

(STATION. Yellow brick; strictly classical. I. Nairn)

DEBACH
2050

ALL SAINTS. 1853. Nave and chancel in one. – FONT. Also of
c. 1853. Octagonal. Against the stem four lions, against the
bowl the Signs of the four Evangelists and four angels. –
PLATE. Cup of 1586.
(DEBACH HOUSE. With two ornamental plaster ceilings of the
early C17. DOE)
MOAT HOUSE. Nice front of 1813. Grey brick, three bays. The
ground-floor and first-floor windows set together in giant
arches in such a way that the segment-headed upper windows
follow part of the curve of the round giant arches. Greek Doric
portico.

DEBENHAM
1060

ST MARY. The principal interest of the church is the W porch,
tower, and galilee. The lower parts of the tower seem to belong
to the so-called Saxo-Norman Overlap. The quoins are clearly
of the Saxon 'long-and-short' type, but the details of the
imposts of the arch towards the nave are equally clearly Norman, and the S window also looks more Norman than Saxon.
In addition, the flint is laid herringbone-wise. The upper part,
starting at the level of the present aisle roofs, is Dec. There are
no flushwork enrichments. The W galilee was added in the
Dec style too, see the side windows on the lower and the upper
floors and the doorway into the tower. Tall entrance arch.
Two niches in the buttresses to its l. and r., and one above its
apex. Knapped flint walls. Later C13 chancel. Characteristic
lancet windows on the N side and windows with plate tracery
on the S side. One order of shafts in the priest's doorway.
Inside, the N and S windows have rere-arches and hood-
moulds, the PISCINA shafts, a pointed-trefoiled arch, and a
gable. The E window is Victorian. Perp S aisle with buttresses,
decorated with flushwork, battlements, and pinnacles. S doorway with crowns up one moulding of the jambs and arch. The
N doorway is different. Fine Perp four-bay arcade. The piers
have four filleted main shafts and thin diagonal shafts. The
capitals are leaf-bands and angels with spread wings alternately.
Wavy arch mouldings. Clerestory windows in double number.
Also a nave E window at clerestory level. Roof with alternating
hammerbeams and crested tie-beams on arched braces. –
FONT. Badly preserved. With angels and Signs of the Evangelists. – PULPIT. Jacobean. – GATE to the galilee. Handsome,

Jacobean, with two tiers of vertically symmetrical balusters. – SCULPTURE. The N aisle piscina is made up of various stone-carved fragments, including a beautiful bishop's head of *c.* 1300. – PLATE. Elizabethan Cup; Paten 1760. – MONUMENTS. Brass to John Framlingham † 1425 (?) and wife, demi-figures, 1 ft 2 in. long (chancel floor). – Sir Charles Framlingham † 1595. Big tomb-chest. Against it short pilasters and short perspective niches in which originally there were kneeling figures. Two recumbent effigies. Against the back wall inscription and big coat of arms flanked by columns. – HELMET above the monument. – The Rev. John Simson † 1697. Tomb-chest on the floor with a Greek inscription. Above three-quarter figure frontal in an arched niche. He raises his hand. Two putti seated l. and r. On top of the arch an urn, l. and r. of the tomb-chest two more urns. Many inscriptions, as was the fashion at that moment. On the arched top of the urn: 'Sic luceat lux vestra.' On the l. pier of the arch 'FIDES', on the r. 'SPES'. Below the niche on the l. 'Esurivi enim', on the r. 'Nudus eram'. On the l. urn 'Extinguor', on the r. urn 'Resurgam'. On the lid of the tomb-chest:

> We boast not here (kind reader) a descent
> From Brittish, Saxon, or the Norman race;
> Nor have we sought an Herauld to invent
> Some Hierogliphick draughts this Stone to grace:
> The Figure of Christ's Cross we choose to wear,
> The Crown which did his Sacred temples tear,
> Badges that his disciples all may bear.
> No mantlings of rich metals, furs, or dye,
> Th' Escocheon owns, (but plaine) to please the eye;
> Such let this unclaim'd bearings mantle be,
> As best may shew our vests of Charitie.
> No Force, or wreath, the Helmet to adorn
> We claime, we give the Chaplet made of thorn;
> The Scepter reed presented him in Scorn.
> Thus here those instruments of shame and paine,
> Which our Dear Lord for man did not disdaine;
> Of honourable arms we in the room
> Display, true ensigns for a Christians tomb.
> > Such Heraldry as this let none despise,
> > Free from the Censure of the good and wise.

PERAMBULATION. The perambulation is one street from N to s, starting at the N end with a nice group of houses on the E side. The space is wide and then begins to close in. At the same time the street rises gently. At the NE corner a house of *c.* 1500, the former GUILDHALL, with a pretty porch with four-centred door-arch and brick-nogging on the upper floor. Opposite the RED LION HOTEL with a handsome (now alas subdivided) plaster ceiling of *c.* 1600. Then the street widens again, but this time on the other (r.) side. The end of this wider part is marked by the free-standing former HITCHAMS SCHOOL of 1666. Overhanging upper floor with decorated beam. Also a carved oriel sill. (On the upper floor a moulded plaster ceiling. DOE) Behind this, at the corner of Gracechurch Street, a house with overhang and brick-nogging on the first floor. To the High Street brackets on former buttress posts. The street begins to descend again from here. On the E side yet another house with a long first-floor overhang. Plait ornament on the bressumer. Then on the w side again the ORDER OF FORES-TERS, apparently a former Nonconformist Chapel, converted and face-lifted (with coupled columns) in 1905.

CROWS HALL. *See* p. 181.

DENHAM

7060

6½ m. SW of Bury St Edmunds

ST MARY. Almost a C19 building. N doorway plainest Norman. NE chapel a C17 addition. – PLATE. Paten 1728. – MONU-MENTS. Sir Edward Lewkenor †1605. Big four-poster with kneeling family, ten of them, in double file, facing E. Big super-structure with obelisks and strapwork. Not good. – Sir Edward Lewkenor † 1635, by *John* and *Matthias Christmas*. White and black marble. Recumbent effigy in armour, his head on a half-rolled-up straw mat. Tomb-chest with columns and cartouches with shields. Back wall with columns carrying an entablature rising in a semicircle in the middle.

DENHAM CASTLE. *See* Gazeley.

DENHAM

1070

4 m. E of Eye

ST JOHN BAPTIST. The w tower exists no longer. Dec chancel, see the S doorway. Perp nave. Much brick repair. The N chapel of one bay has also been demolished. The arch is still visible. – MISERICORDS. The centres in every case hacked off. – STAINED GLASS. In the w window one angel. – MONU-MENTS. Excellent late C13 effigy of a Lady wearing a wimple. She is holding her heart in her hands. Two angels by her head. – BRASS to A. Bedingfield † 1574. Palimpsest of a Flemish brass

to Jacobus Weggheschede, *c.* 1500. The rest is used for a brass
of *c.* 1580 at Yealmpton, Devon.

THORPE HALL. *See* Horham.

DENNINGTON

ST MARY. Perp with a long Dec chancel. This has reticulated
tracery in all its windows, three lights N and S, five lights E.
They are shafted inside, and the shafts carry delicately carved
foliage capitals. Moreover the windows have inner hood-
moulds with equally delicate head-stops. PISCINA and
SEDILIA are strangely and perversely arched. Above the
niches a straight-sided arch, and above this groups of four
'daggers' arranged so as to fill the space up to the arched gable.
Buttress shafts l. and r. The chancel arch is painfully incorrect.
Perp W tower with brick battlements and a stair-turret higher
than the tower. On the W side above the window three stepped
niches. Perp also the NE sacristy of two storeys, the clerestory,
and the roomy N porch. Flushwork panelling on the lower half
of the front. Niches l. and r. of the entrance, and a niche above
it. Arcades of five bays with octagonal piers and double-chamfered arches, C14 rather than C15. Indeed money was left in
1370 for the building of the S aisle and the repairing of the E
end of the N aisle. Nave roof with two collar-beams. Aisle roofs
with arched braces painted with tracery patterns probably on
original evidence. The Bardolph Chapel (S) is treated extremely
lavishly in its internal stonework. Under the S window is a
seat (or tomb-chest?), with shields against the front. The
jambs and arch of the window have fleurons, crowns, and
shields. The window is flanked by stone shafts with candle-
platforms. Above the window a cusped and subcusped arch,
then a tier of panelling and cresting.

    The FURNISHINGS of Dennington church are exceptionally
rich and varied. One must start with the PARCLOSE SCREENS
of the S and N chapels, two prodigious pieces, miraculously well
preserved. They are like rich rood screens of the usual type,
with one-light divisions, crocketed ogee arches, and panel
tracery above with a top cresting. But above that the whole of
the loft is preserved with daintily traceried openwork balustrading to the outside as well as the inside. Of the ROOD
SCREEN only the dado remains. – FONT. Perp, octagonal,
simple. Complete with cover. – PULPIT. Made in 1625 and
converted in 1628 into a three-decker. The tester is not preserved. The ornament has much of diamond or acorn-shaped

applied knobs and some strapwork. – BENCHES. A splendid
set, with intricate tracery on the ends, poppy-heads, and, on
the arms, beasts, birds, a sciapode, a mermaid, and an angel.
Finely carved seat-backs. – BOX PEWS. One group in the N
chapel is dated 1630. Very restrained. The only decoration is
the framing of the panels and the elongated knobs on the top.
The others dated 1765 by Cautley, but according to the *Suff.
Arch. Soc.* 1928–30 those near the pulpit (with the hat hooks)
were placed in 1805. – Traceried DOORS to the rood-loft
stairs in the N and S aisles. – COMMUNION RAIL. Late C17. –
PYX CANOPY. A great rarity. A tall slender canopy made of one
piece of wood, probably *c.* 1500. It is suspended above the
altar. Cautley refers to others at Wells, Milton Abbas, and
Tewkesbury. – STAINED GLASS. Much good canopy work of
the earlier C14 in the chancel N and S windows. – PLATE.
Elizabethan Cup: Paten 1756; Cup 1763; Flagon 1813. –
CURIOSUM. An iron-bound SAFE in a niche in the S chapel. –
MONUMENTS. Lord Bardolph † 1441. Alabaster tomb-chest
with flat niches now without figures. Two pendant ogee arches.
Two flat panels separate the niches. Recumbent effigies;
rather poor. – Sir Thomas Rous † 1603 and wife. The usual
kneeling figures facing one another across a prayer desk.

RECTORY, S of the church. Of 1780,* red brick, two storeys,
five bays, hipped roof, broad low segment-headed windows.

DENNINGTON PLACE, 1 m. w. Timber-framed, C16, with some
brick-nogging.

DENSTON

ST NICHOLAS. Short w tower, probably of the late C14. Excellent
church, all Late Perp and of a piece. The building no doubt
connected with the founding of a college by Sir John Howard
and John Broughton in 1475. Nave, aisles, chapels, and clerestory have three-light windows, only those of the clerestory
without transoms. The windows are tall and fairly close to
each other. S porch with fan-vault inside and a pretty crocketed
and vaulted niche and castellated stoup outside. The N rood-
stair turret and all the buttresses are of stone, not of flint with
stone trim. Arcade of seven bays running without a break from
w to E. Piers of lozenge section with concave-sided polygonal
shafts without capitals towards the nave, i.e. running right up to
the roof. They are crossed by a string-course below the clerestory windows. Good cambered nave roof and lean-to aisle

* Mr Clifton-Taylor believes.

roofs. In the nave alternate tie-beams are unbraced. Wall-plate with affronted lions, hounds, hares, and harts. The arched braces of the nave have carving too. – FONT. On the bowl the Seven Sacraments and the Crucifixion in small figures against a rayed background. The figures are defaced. – PULPIT. Elizabethan; very simple. – SCREENS. The dado only of the rood screen; much restored. – Parclose screens to the chapels. – Above the rood screen the ROOD BEAM, a moulded embattled beam, remains; a rare survival. – STALLS and BENCHES with animal poppy-heads and animals on the arm-rests. The stalls have traceried fronts. Four MISERICORDS are preserved. One of them has a fine figure of a crane. – C18 BOX PEWS in the S aisle. – SOUTH DOOR with tracery, C15. – COMMUNION RAIL. With slender twisted balusters; C18. – STAINED GLASS. The whole E window consists of bits of old glass. – PLATE. Elizabethan Cup; Paten 1640. – MONUMENTS. Unknown couple of Early Tudor date, both represented dead, and both shrouded. Death is shown more frighteningly in him than in her. Good quality. – Brasses to Henry Everard † 1524 and wife (26 in. figures; chancel floor) and to a Lady of c. 1530 (18 in. figure; nave floor). – ARMOUR suspended in the S chapel. The GATES to this chapel are of wood made to look like iron.

DENSTON HALL. Early C18 house of red brick; nine-bay centre and wings. Staircase with twisted balusters of that date. One large stone fireplace perhaps also not later. The circular entrance hall and the rooms to its l. and r. of c. 1770. The room on the l. corresponds by a screen of two columns with the staircase. A 'Wedgwood' frieze above it. Behind the house is a long range of Tudor brick with a number of brick windows with hood-moulds. Its back overlooks the moat. A room with a ceiling with moulded beams and much C15–16 woodwork does not belong to the original house. This range is part of a large house of the early C16 of which we know from old illustrations the tall gatehouse with brick wings, wall, and angle turrets. – On the lawn in front of the house stone MONUMENT to a horse, brought c. 1960 from Dullingham House Cambridgeshire.

DEPDEN

7050

ST MARY. No road leads to the church. Footpath from the N, off the main road. The church is of septaria and flint. Norman S doorway with one order of single-scalloped capitals and one zigzag in the arch. Beautiful late C13 PISCINA in the chancel, of two lights, cusped, with a quatrefoiled circle. The tracery of nave and chancel, if it represents the original, is of the same date. E window Dec (reticulated tracery). Perp W tower.* N porch timber, C 17, with side balusters, badly treated. – FONT. Octagonal, early C 18, with shields in cartouches. – BENCHES. With poppy-heads and blank panels of good tracery; a whole set. – STAINED GLASS. In the E window original canopies, chiefly dark yellow and green. Beneath this later scenes and bits; foreign. – PLATE. A whole Set, silver-gilt, given by Bishop Sparrow of Norwich, who was born at Depden. The Cup is dated 1680. – Paten 1719. – MONUMENT. Lady Anne Jermyn and her husbands, 1572. Kneeling brass figures in a stone frame with two arches.

DOVEDEN HALL see WHEPSTEAD

DRINKSTONE

9060

ALL SAINTS. Dec chancel, the E window new and the former (of three lights with flowing tracery) re-used, it seems, on the S side. Dec N aisle E and W windows with segmental heads. Dec arcades, N and S, with octagonal piers and double-chamfered arches. Perp aisle windows. Brick tower of c. 1694 (see inscription), the brickwork in chequer pattern of red and blue. – FONT. Octagonal, C 13, of Purbeck marble, with the usual pair of flat blank arches on each side. – SCREEN. Tall, one-light divisions, with ogee arches. Close panel-tracery above them. Original cresting. – BENCHES. Some with simple poppy-heads. Parts of a traceried front re-set in the back of the sedilia. – PANELLING. In the sanctuary; C 17. – STAINED GLASS. Fragments in chancel and aisles, notably, though much restored, a seated Virgin (chancel N), and several whole figures (chancel S). – TILES. Some S of the pulpit. – PLATE. Paten 1564; Cup 1567. – MONUMENT. The pulpit stands on a base which seems a very low tomb-chest or part of an Easter Sepulchre. The front is decorated with circles with two, three, or four mouchettes; early or mid C 14 probably.

RECTORY, N of the church. Built c. 1760. Red brick, two storeys, five bays. Quoins of brick. Doorway with segmental pediment on brackets, a Venetian window above.

TICEHURST. See Tostock, p. 467.

WINDMILL, NE of the village. Dated 1689. A typical West Suffolk post-mill. She has been in the Clover family since c. 1756. She drove two pairs of stones situated in the head and

* A will of 1451 leaves money to the tower (ARA).

tail of the mill, and the 'buck', as the body is called in Suffolk, has an unusual framing which alone would date her as C17. The buck has been at some time turned end for end, the former breast being now the tail. There is a lean-to porch to the buck, a flint and brick tiled round-house, two 'common sails' (cloth spread), and two 'spring sails' (shuttered). Originally turned to face the wind by means of a tail-pole, a second-hand fan-tail and gear was fitted and not long afterwards the mill was 'tail-winded'.

There is also a power-driven SMOCK-MILL outside Drinkstone.

DUNWICH

4070

'Dunwich is so enveloped in the halo of traditionary splendour, that he who ventures to elucidate its history by pursuing the path of topographical enquiry must exercise unusual caution, lest he be misled by imaginary light. For unlike those ruined cities whose fragments attest their former grandeur, Dunwich is wasted, desolate, and void. Its palaces and temples are no more, and its very curious present an aspect lonely, stern and wild.'

Thus the Rev. Alfred Suckling in 1848. There is not much one
3a   can add to it. Fields high above the sea, fragrant in the spring and summer, wind-swept in the autumn and winter, some straggling houses, and the ruins of the FRANCISCAN FRIARY, built on this site after 1290. The N wall has buttresses and windows with four-centred heads in two tiers, the S wall is fragmentary. The structure stood along the S side of the cloister, and its ground floor was indeed the S cloister walk. The upper floor probably contained the refectory. The church has utterly disappeared. Of the gatehouse the archway and a smaller doorway can still be seen. Both arches are four-centred. The moulding of the larger has one chamfer and two hollow chamfers. Above the smaller is some flushwork panelling.

The friary had been founded before 1277, but had to be moved further inland in 1289, following the necessities of the site of Dunwich, a site which reduced a Saxon cathedral city and one of the most prosperous ports of Suffolk to its present solitude. Dunwich became a see under St Felix of Burgundy in 632.*

* The association of St Felix's see of Dommoc with Dunwich cannot certainly be traced before the C15. For an alternative siting at Felixstowe (probably in Walton Castle, *see* p. 474), which accords both with early records and archaeological probability, see S. E. Rigold, *Journal of the British Archaeological Association*, 3rd series, XXIV (1961), 55–9.

The town had three churches in the Domesday survey and
later six, a Preceptory of the Templars, a house of the Dominicans, a hospital of St James, and several chapels. They were
destroyed one by one by the onslaughts of the sea, the most
disastrous being those of the C14. The last church to remain
was All Saints, and this began to disappear down the cliff in
1904. The tower went over in 1919. Of the hospital chapel,
however, at least a portion survives (see below).*

ST JAMES. Built in the classical style in 1830 (by *Robert Appleton*),
but with a chancel of 1881, and windows renewed at the same
time. – MONUMENT to Michael Barne † 1837 by *Behnes*.
Sarcophagus with profile head in relief (chancel N wall). – In
the churchyard to the SE of the church the Norman apse of the
HOSPITAL CHAPEL. It has blank arcading and shafted
windows. The arcading also extended into the chancel, as can
be recognized in the SE corner. In the middle of the apse the
large BARNE MAUSOLEUM.

EARL SOHAM

ST MARY. Early C14 chancel. The chancel arch has concave-
sided polygonal responds. They are more probably Perp.
Perp W tower (c. 1475; LG); a fine piece. Arched flushwork
panelling on base, buttresses, and battlements. W doorway with
three niches. On the buttresses inscriptions commemorating
Thomas Edward, builder, and Ranulph Colnett, his assistant.
Perp nave and S porch. The porch has rough flushwork
chequering and a small original figure at the apex of the gable.
In the S doorway the spandrels are decorated with large leaves
and shields with the Symbols of the Trinity and the Passion on
them. One order of the jambs and arch and also the hood-
mould with fleuron decoration. In the nave double-hammerbeam roof. Figures under nodding ogee arches on the wall-
posts. – FONT. Inscription to Robert Kinge, the donor.
Octagonal. Against the stem four lions. Against the bowl four
lions and four angels. – BENCHES. Much restored. Traceried
ends, flanked by two buttresses. Poppy-heads, and on the
buttresses grotesques, animals, figures, sitting and kneeling,
and heads. – PULPIT. Jacobean, with tester. – COMMUNION
RAIL. Mid-C17. – PLATE. Two Patens 1808; Cup 1814. –
MONUMENT. J. C. Hindes † 1824, Margaret Hindes † 1829,

* At the MUSEUM the INSIGNIA of Dunwich are kept: Mace, c. 1600,
I in. long; Badge, late C16.

and Deborah Hindes † 1840. By *Gaffin*. Urn with weeping willow on top of the tablet.

An attractive village with most of the houses along one stree facing s and into the open.

RED HOUSE. Georgian. Red brick, five bays, two storeys. Door way with pediment on brackets.

THE WILLOWS. Early C18, timber-framed and plastered. Three wide bays, doorway with pediment. Windows with wooder cross-casements. Hipped roof.

EARL SOHAM LODGE. Mostly C18, but traces of C16 cantee bays of brick overlooking the moat (cf. Moat Hall, Parham).

(STREET FARMHOUSE, s of the village green. With remains of C18 wall paintings of classical subjects. DOE)

1050

EARL STONHAM

ST MARY. The splendour of the church is its nave roof. But there are signs of an older history first to be inspected. One lancet in the chancel N wall. Dec the present arrangement of crossing and transepts; for Earl Stonham is a cruciform church, al- though it has no crossing tower. The crossing arches look early C14. Those to the N and S have fleuron decoration. Above the S transept arch a tiny quatrefoil window to throw light on to the rood. Dec transept windows. Handsome inner hood-mould to the N transept E window, which had reticulated tracery. Dec also the E half of the chancel. Fine gabled PISCINA, yet with- out ogee arch. The SEDILIA is a window seat. The arm is of stone with a pet dog lying on it. Dec also the w window in the tower, obviously the re-used w window, before the tower existed. Dec finally the s porch with its strong, simple entrance mouldings. The exterior of the lower parts of the church is unfortunately cemented. Above this commonplace zone rises the clerestory and the tower. The clerestory – a significant addition in a church without aisles (all the glory to the roof) – has flushwork arcading between the closely set windows. As for the tower, it has flushwork on the base and the buttresses and culminates in a parapet with flushwork quatrefoils and battlements with tall blank flushwork arcading. w doorway with two orders of fleurons, shields, crowns, etc., and three- light bell-openings.

And now we can enter the nave and look at the roof, one of the richest in a county rich in rich roofs. It is a hammerbeam roof in which trusses with pendant hammer-posts (i.e. the ends of the hammerbeams are tenoned into them) alternate with trusses in which the hammer-post stands on a hammer-beam carved in the form of a prone angel. Arched braces to the collar-beams. From their middles hang pendants, and on their middles stand kingposts. All spandrels are carved. The wall-posts have figures, the wall-plates much decoration (three tiers, the first and the third of angels with spread-out wings). Arched braces rise and fall in a w-e direction from wall-post to wall-post. Embattled collar-beams, embattled ribs, and embattled purlins. Even the common rafters are moulded. The chancel roof is lower and a little simpler. It has fine tracery above the hammerbeams. The transept roofs are largely Victorian, but also contain original timbers. – FONT. Octagonal. The figures against the stem have disappeared. Against the bowl four angels and a flower, the Crown of Thorns, etc. – PULPIT. Jacobean. – Four HOUR GLASSES by the pulpit, three together (for a quarter, a half, and one hour) and one separate in its iron holder. – BENCHES. With poppy-heads and a few figures in relief against the fronts of ends, e.g. a bagpipe player, a pelican, a man with an axe. One poppy-head is a *signum triciput*. On one arm-rest the inscription 'Orate pro anima Necolai Houk'. – WEST DOOR with tracery. – CHEST. Of *c.* 1300, with chip-carved rosettes. – PAINTINGS. The wall paintings of Earl Stonham as they were recorded in 1874 were interesting and instructive. Now very little remains of them. There is a Doom above the chancel arch, and there were a Martyrdom of St Thomas Becket (converted under Henry VIII into a Martyrdom of St Catherine) in the s transept, a St George also in the s transept (w wall), and a Journey of the Magi and Adoration of the Magi in the N transept. – PLATE. Paten 1732; Cup 1789.

WAYLANDS COTTAGES, Wicks's Green, 1 m. NW. C15. Timber-framed with carved bressumer and carved arched braces.

THE LODGE, on the A140, at Angel Hill, ½ m. E. Early C19, three bays, grey brick, with giant Ionic pilasters and a Greek Doric porch.

DEERBOLT HALL. A Queen Anne front of red and blue chequered brick, nine bays, two storeys, with a three-bay pediment, which has partly collapsed.

EAST BERGHOLT

0030

ST MARY. Eminently picturesque, with its incomplete w tower and the brick gable to its E, crowned by an C18 cupola. The church is entirely Late Perp, partly flint and partly brick. The

w tower was begun in 1525 on a sumptuous plan, with a ston
base with quatrefoil frieze and a passage through (cf. Dedham
Essex). Broad N and S entrances. The room inside the towe
was intended to be vaulted. S aisle of coursed flint, tall three
light windows with tracery, battlements decorated with many
shields. The same battlements on the S chancel chapel. Two
storeyed S porch, its entrance again decorated with shields
Polygonal turret in the W angle between porch and aisle. The
N aisle is mainly brick and has a pretty polygonal turret at it
E end. Simpler four-light windows. Battlements as on the
aisle. Ornate N doorway with canopied niches and again with
shields as decoration. When they were still all coloured they
must have made a proud and ostentatious display of heraldry
Interior with five-bay arcades. Piers of four-shafts-and-four
hollows section with capitals only to the shafts. Two-centred
arches. A new aisle is mentioned in a document of 1442–3
Clerestory of ten windows to the five arches below. – ROOI
SCREEN, REREDOS, and STALLS. By Sir T. G. Jackson. –
(WEST and NORTH DOORS. Both have linenfold panelling and
a central Renaissance baluster.) – EASTER SEPULCHRE
Against the back wall C15 WALL PAINTING of the Resurrec
tion, surrounded by large leaf decoration. – STAINED GLASS
In a S window John Constable Memorial window by Constable
of Cambridge, 1897 (TK); bad. – PLATE. Set 1767; Almsdish
1771. – MONUMENT. Edward Lambe † 1617. Kneeling figure
Two well-carved angels l. and r. pull away a curtain.

14b BELL HOUSE. In the churchyard; a unique piece, built probably
when the plan for the W tower had been given up. One
storeyed with steep pyramid roof with louvred top. Heavy
timbers to support the bells inside. The outside walls are a
grille of timbers above a dado. The horizontal timbers woven
through the vertical ones.

Plenty of houses worth examining. Only a few can be recorded
S of the church the ABBEY, mostly white and red brick
of 1857. LITTLE COURT, N of the church, is seven-bay
Georgian. STOUR COTTAGE (close to Stour Court, formerly
West Lodge, a big house) is three bays wide and Gothic
¼ m. E of the church CLAY COTTS, timber-framed, of c. 1500
with good close carving on angle post, angle bracket, and
bressumer. ¼ m. N of the church THE GABLES, excellent
timber-framed C16 house with octagonal chimneys and some
original windows.

(SECONDARY MODERN SCHOOL. 1956–7, by the County

Architect's Department; County Architect *E. J. Symcox*. A nice group, two-storeyed, brick, glass, and timber-cladding.)

EAST END MANOR *see* STONHAM ASPAL

EASTON

2050

ALL SAINTS. W tower, square and unbuttressed below, octagonal with flushwork battlements higher up. Nave; no separate chancel. Dec and Perp windows. Good simple SEDILIA and PISCINA of *c*. 1300. Abutting against the tower an undulating forcing wall belonging to Easton Park. The house has been pulled down. – FONT. Octagonal, heavily moulded. – FAMILY PEWS. L. and r. of the altar. They are identical and very odd. Ionic colonnettes carrying straight lintels on little quadrant arches. Frieze with wreaths and cherub's wings. Is the date *c*. 1690? – BOX PEWS. 1816. – COMMUNION RAIL. Late C17. – STAINED GLASS. Some of the C14 in the tops of the nave and chancel windows. – PLATE. Cup and Paten 1678; Credence 1726. – MONUMENTS. Brass to John Brook † 1426. The figure 2 ft 2 in. long. – Mary Wingfield † 1675. Fine tablet with two columns, a curly pediment, and garlands at the foot (cf. Brandeston near by). – G. R. Savage Nassau † 1823. By *W. Pistell*. Kneeling woman praying by an urn. Against the usual obelisk. – Fifth Earl of Rochford, Seigneur de Zeylesteyn, Leesum, Ginkel, Wayesteyn, etc., † 1830. He was the brother of the former. Unsigned. Exactly the same composition, only against an oblong ground.

DOVECOTE in the grounds of Easton Park. Now put to another use. Octagonal, but circular inside, with a circular cupola. *Suff. Arch. Soc.* 1934–6. Also in the grounds an undulating forcing wall or crinkle-crankle wall. N. Scarfe)

EDWARDSTONE

9040

ST MARY. In the grounds of Edwardstone Hall, a house which has been largely pulled down.* W tower, nave and N aisle (of 1460), no clerestory, tiled roofs. The chancel windows, if reliably restored, point to *c*. 1300. The piers of the arcade Perp: quatrefoil with fillets. The same type between chancel and N chapel. (*Bodley*‡ furnished and beautified the church with painted roof and wall decorations, an organ case, and

* The brick gatehouse of the Hall remains (P. G. M. Dickinson).
‡ I am grateful to Mr S. E. Dykes Bower for letting me have the following otes on Bodley's contribution to the church.

much else. It is a tragedy that in the chancel his diapered walls were obliterated some years ago. However there is much of interest – *Burlison & Grylls* STAINED GLASS, excellent wrought-iron LIGHT FITTINGS (by *Bainbridge Reynolds*?), PEWS, and WALL PANELLING still in first-class condition. – The ORGAN is reputedly a work by *Father Smith*.) – PULPIT. Jacobean, good and big, with back panel and tester. – MONUMENTS. Benjamin Brand † 1636 and wife and children. Brasses in the medieval tradition. The inscription tells us that they were by 'Providence after 35 years conjunction divided (by) Death, after 12 days Divorcement reunited', and that she had twelve children 'all nursed with her unborrowed milk'. – Thomas Dawson, by *John Bacon Jun.*, 1808, with an elegant white urn in front of a grey obelisk.

ELLOUGH

4080

ALL SAINTS. Rather bleak, with its unbuttressed w tower of *c.* 1300 and the almost invisible roofs of nave and chancel, without parapet or battlements. The windows Perp. The nave roof good, re-done in 1882 (Kelly)* but believed by Cautley to be correct. Low pitch, cambered tie-beams, wind-braces. – FONT. Octagonal, Perp, simple. With four shields and four flowers. – BRASSES. Lady of *c.* 1520, the figure 13½ in. long. – Margaret Chewt † 1607. With huge headgear.

ELMSETT

0040

ST PETER. w tower of the C13. Nave and chancel Dec. E window with flowing tracery of a standard pattern. – FONT. Square Norman, of Purbeck marble and originally with the usual flat blank round arches. – PULPIT. Jacobean; from St Mary-at-Quay Ipswich. – PANELLING. Some Jacobean panelling perhaps from former pews. – COMMUNION RAIL. Three-sided; later C17. – PLATE. Elizabethan Cup; C17 Paten Almsdish 1803. – MONUMENT. Edward Sherland † 1609. The usual kneeling figure; alabaster.

ELMSWELL

9060

ST JOHN BAPTIST. w tower with 'probably the finest flint and stone devices' of Suffolk (Cautley). They include two chalices and a lily in a vase. Many emblems and initials in the battlements and also panelling. s aisle (much renewed) and s porch also with flushwork emblems; N aisle of 1872; chancel of 1864

* According to Mr Paul Thompson, the church was restored by *Butterfield* in 1880.

Perp five-bay arcade. The clerestory not with double the number of windows. Inside below the windows a fleuron frieze. On
this wall-shafts for the former roof. – FONT. Base with Ox,
two Eagles, Pelican. Bowl with shields in foiled shapes. On
the shields the letters of the name I. Hedge. Retooled. –
PARCLOSE SCREEN. Good, with two-light divisions. – BENCH
ENDS. Some, with poppy-heads and blank tracery. – MONU-
MENT. Sir Robert Gardener † 1619. Standing monument with
stiff semi-reclining figure. By his feet a rhinoceros, his crest.
To the l. his son, kneeling. At the foot of the monument lie
Sir Robert's robes and part of his armour. Two columns carry
a large coffered arch. – (CHURCHYARD CROSS. The base is old
and has good carvings. LG)

ALMSHOUSES. Founded by Sir Robert Gardener. Dated 1614.
Red brick, one-storeyed, with a steep central gable. Five doorways, four groups of chimneys. The windows are of two lights
with an architrave over.

A ROMANO–BRITISH KILN containing pottery of the C3–4
was discovered during the cutting of a sewer trench in 1964.

ELVEDEN

ELVEDEN HALL was a Georgian building of moderate size. The
Maharaja Duleep Singh enlarged it in 1863–70 into an Oriental
extravaganza unparalleled in England. His architect was *John
Norton*. How can the inveterate Gothicist have felt about it?
The Maharaja's palace has a central domed hall with a glass 63
lantern, with the walls, pillars, and arches covered with the
closest Indian ornamental detail, all made of white Carrara
marble and carved *in situ* by Italian craftsmen. There are plenty
of other Indian rooms, now all white, but some apparently
originally in strong colours, e.g. the cast-iron staircase balustrade. The doors of the Maharaja's pleasure dome are covered
with panels of beaten copper. Then, in 1899–1903 the first
Lord Iveagh enlarged the Maharaja's palace into a yet larger
palace. His architect was *William Young*, whose *magnum opus*
stands in Whitehall. With his help the house has now a front
of three storeys and twenty-five bays, with a centre with a big
porte-cochère and a dome. All this is of brick with stone
dressings. The Maharaja's palace was externally, it seems,
quite harmlessly Italianate; Lord Iveagh's is also Italian, but
more Baroque. The rooms of 1899–1903 are lavishly equipped
too.

Large Italianate water-tower to the W. The STABLES, ALMS-
HOUSES, and ESTATE HOUSES around are more peaceful, red
brick with timber-framed gables.

ST ANDREW AND ST PATRICK. Lord Iveagh behaved as
lavishly to the church as to the Hall. There was an old church N
of the Hall. It had a Norman nave, see one S window, a W tower
of c. 1300, with flushwork panelling at the foot, a Dec S
chapel (four-light E window with flowing tracery, shafted
inside), and a Late Perp S aisle. This was enlarged by Duleep
Singh in 1869. Then, in 1904-6, Lord Iveagh employed Caröe
to raise this to the standard of the Hall. Caröe added a new N
nave and chancel, and in 1922 a new S tower connected with
the old church by a long cloister-walk. All his detail is of the
most ornate Gothic, that version of c. 1900 which can be called
Art Nouveau Gothic. It is full of unexpected and unauthorized
turns. The new front e.g. has a small NW turret to balance on
the S the projecting tower of the old church. The piers between
the end and the old nave defeat description. The roof is of the
double-hammerbeam type, but the chancel is so low that the
effect is completely different from that in medieval predecessors. The new S tower is more correct, though again sumptuously decorated with flushwork. – STAINED GLASS. E window
of the old church by Kempe, 1894; W window of the new
church by Sir Frank Brangwyn, 1937. – PLATE. Elizabethan
Cup; Paten 1724; Set of 1863-5.

WAR MEMORIAL, 2½ m. SW, on the A11 road. Tall composite
column with urn. Erected in 1921 to the design of Clyde
Young.

ROMAN FINDS. In 1953 sherds, quern stones, and other occupation material were found on a Romano-British settlement
site, together with a spouted flask covered by a small dish. The
latter contained 1146 silver coins, ranging from those of
Antoninus Pius to Philip II; the majority are of the early
C3 A.D.

7070

ERISWELL

ST LAURENCE. Late C13 S aisle and S chapel. The rest Dec.
The S chapel has on the S side two lancet windows, and a
PISCINA with stiff-leaf as decoration. Pier towards the chancel
with deeply hollowed-out quatrefoil section and double
chamfered arches. The S aisle has uncusped intersected tracery.
One window deserves special notice. It is small and square, and
its tracery is a centre with four diagonally radiating cusped

arches. Inside below it a seat (or credence table ?) and a piscina. Low gabled outer tomb recess in the s aisle. Dec chancel, with an E window where two intersected ogee arches carry a pointed oval. The nave and chancel side windows are of two lights and of the same date. Arcade with octagonal piers and arches with a moulding of two sunk quadrants. The same in the chancel arch, including the responds. – FONT. Octagonal, with quatrefoil decoration but on an octagonal middle support and eight attached shafts with moulded capitals. They are clearly early C14; so this type of decoration of the font bowl goes back as far as that. – SCREEN. Much restored, but apparently Dec. Shafts and mullions, Dec tracery. – BENCH ENDS. Simple with small poppy-heads. – CORNER FITMENT. A strange stone fitment with two openings across the chancel NE corner. It looks like a double aumbry, but the bottom is considerably deeper than the foot of the doors.* – STAINED GLASS. Bits of original glass in the chancel N windows (and the square s aisle window). – PLATE. Elizabethan Cup bowl.

METHODIST CHAPEL. Grey brick. Built in 1839. Inscription over the door: Wesley's Doctrine. This comes from another chapel.

OLD CHURCH OF ST PETER, Eriswell Hall Farm. Now a farm building. Parts of the N and s walls, flint. In the N wall most of a Perp window and outlines of two C13 lancets.

Cottages around here are mainly of flint with red or yellow brick trim.

ERWARTON

2030

ST MARY. Away from the village and set against trees. Nicely neglected. Built mostly of septaria. Perp W tower with big W doorway and W window. Parapet renewed in brick. Lively Perp clerestory with large windows. Perp also the aisles. The arcades have piers with shafts and capitals only to the arch openings. The chancel seems to have been Dec, but was shortened in the C18 and over-restored in the C19. – FONT. Octagonal, Perp, with lions against the base and on the bowl two panels with lions, two with demi-figures of angels, and four with flowers. – BENCHES. A set with poppy-heads. – PLATE. Cup of 1825; Paten probably 1825. – HELMS connected with the monuments. – MONUMENTS. In the s aisle cross-legged

* The Rev. J. T. Munday suggests that this was originally the site of a statue, and that the stonework is more modern and of re-used material.

Knight of the late C13 on later tomb-chest with quatrefoils. – Also in the S aisle Knight and Lady of c. 1400. Under a canopy. – In the N aisle Lady wearing a wimple, c. 1300. The canopy belongs to the same time. – At the E end of the S aisle fragment of the monument to Sir Philip Calthorpe † 1549. Front with fluted colonnettes. – In the N aisle Sir Philip Parker, 1736. Standing monument with large inscription tablet and no figures.

ALMSHOUSES. 1740. Red brick, humble, one-storeyed, NW of the church.

ERWARTON HALL. The house has been much altered, but the façade remains in a clearly recognizable Elizabethan form, brick, laid in English bond, with mullioned and transomed windows, symmetrical with the five-light bay window corresponding to the porch with three-light windows over. The other windows also of three lights. A date 1575 occurs on the glass of a window pane. The interior is completely changed. The best pieces now a magnificent plaster ceiling with pendant bosses, c. 1575, and a late C17 staircase with strongly turned balusters. The handrail curves boldly round, where the intermediate landing is. There is also one original overmantel with three tiers of the typical short blank arcading. It seems not in situ. But far more spectacular than this is the GATEHOUSE which can be dated for heraldic reasons c. 1549. It lies in line with the entrance of the house. It is also of brick. Round angle buttresses with round pinnacles. Four semicircular gables. Intermediate pinnacles on the sides and through the side gables. The gateway is tunnel-vaulted. The design is similar to that of Beckingham Hall at Tolleshunt Major, Essex, which can be dated c. 1545 with certainty.

51a

8070

EUSTON

EUSTON HALL. Euston Hall as it appears today is in a fragmentary state. The house was originally built for Lord Arlington c. 1666–70. It occupied three sides of a courtyard and had domed angle erections 'after the French', as John Evelyn observed. This house was altered and enlarged by *Matthew Brettingham* in 1750–6. He removed the domes and gave the angle erections low pyramid roofs, so that they looked like those at Holkham and in other country houses of the strict Palladian observance. Two of these erections are still there. Brettingham also thickened the N side of the N range and gave it a new front. This exists, and is now the principal approach

To reach it one crosses under the STABLES, which are of Arlington's time. They are of red brick and have projecting wings and a central cupola. Inside two staircases remain, with plain turned balusters. Brettingham's N front is exceedingly restrained. Nine bays, two storeys, excellent brickwork, simple porch, top balustrade and nothing else. The S range has completely disappeared, and of the connecting W range which contained the centre of the C17 as well as the C18 house only a stump remains at the N end. The C17 centre was a tall porch with giant angle pilasters, the C18 centre a three-bay pediment. The rest of the W range, together with the S range, was burnt in 1902, rebuilt, and demolished in 1950. Of the interior no more need be referred to than the main staircase with its vertically symmetrical balusters.

The GROUNDS to the E, W, and S of the house were laid out by *Kent*. Two drawings have recently been discovered which show his plan. He wanted to re-site and rebuild the house. That was not accepted. But the planting of clumps of trees follows his plan. He also designed the archway to the W and the Temple or Banqueting House, but the latter again for a different site.

ARCHWAY to the W on a hill and in line with the former centre of the house. Simple, of grey brick, with one-storey lodges and a pediment over the arch.

KING CHARLES'S GATE. Its two gatepiers connect the garden of the house to the E with the grounds. It is not in line with the former centre. The date may be the 1670s, though the design is of an earlier style, the mid-C17 Baroque. The piers are pierced by elongated arches and carry little segmental pediments and above these elongated vases. The design is small and busy.

TEMPLE. The temple lies SE of the King Charles Gate and the house, and is a fine mature design of *Kent*'s, dated inside 1746. Octagonal centre with two short lower one-bay extensions. These have Palladian half- or lean-to pediments. The centre is domed. The most noteworthy feature of the temple is the rustication of quoins and principal accents by pieces of white or light grey flint. Kent must have loved putting a local material to this Serlian and Palladian use. The centre has a pedimented principal window to front and back, and this is placed in a niche also surrounded by this flint rustication. Two open staircases lead up to the main room. It has arched openings to the side parts (now converted into doorways) and a finely carved cornice. The dome itself had to be reconstructed after a fire, and the decoration up the eight former ribs was left out. Below this room is a lower one with four free-standing Tuscan columns.

In addition there is, nearer the house, to the NW, a good wrought-iron GATE into the present Victoria Garden. On the N is the GARDENER'S HOUSE, of eight bays and two storeys, flint with red brick dressings and a hipped roof. It could well be of the late C17. On the W is a MILL, red brick, in the form of a church with an embattled tower, no doubt Georgian.

ST GENEVIEVE. The church is in its outer walls and tower still medieval. The rest was rebuilt in 1676. The village near it has completely disappeared. It was probably shifted at that very time. The church is an important document of its date, designed by an unrecorded architect in full knowledge of Wren's City churches and finished with the help of craftsmen as good as his. The plan is a nave of two oblong groin-vaulted bays with aisles, a chancel of two oblong groin-vaulted bays, and between them a bay of identical shape but with square groin-vaulted transepts l. and r. The nave has circular clerestory windows. The second bay of the S aisle is the family pew and has some stucco decoration in the ceiling and at the back an inscription commemorating Lord Arlington. Arched windows, also in the old W tower. In the parts of 1676 they have simple posthumously-Gothic tracery: two lights with round arches and a circle over (what one calls Venetian tracery). – PULPIT. Exquisitely carved in the style of Gibbons and the City churches. – SCREEN. With openwork carving. – REREDOS. Equally beautifully carved. – STAINED GLASS. N transept, c. 1865. – PLATE. Set in copper-gilt, late C17; Set 1820–32. – BRASSES. Civilian and Lady c. 1480; Lady c. 1520 (17 in. figure); half-Civilian and headless Lady c. 1520; half-Civilian and Lady c. 1530 (22 in. figures). – (MONUMENT to Lord Arlington †1685, in the vault.) – Various coffin-plates taken from the coffins in the vault.

EXNING

ST MARTIN. Much renewed. E.E. chancel with lancet windows on the N and S sides. The E window cannot be trusted. W tower late C13 to early C14. Triple-chamfered tower arch with continuous mouldings. W window with reticulated tracery. S transept Dec. The four-light S window also reticulated. The N transept has the same forms, but they seem all new. C14 arcade of four bays with octagonal piers and double-chamfered arches. – PULPIT. C18 with tester; simple. – STALL. With traceried front and poppy-heads. – BENCH ENDS. Straight-headed, with linenfold panelling. – COMMUNION RAIL. C18, with slender turned balusters. – PLATE. Elizabethan Cup; Paten 1637; Paten 1825; Flagon 1830.

EXNING HOUSE (GLANELY REST), Windmill Road. By *Andrews Jelfe* for Mr Shepherd, 1734. Two and a half storeys. Seven bays, red brick, with three-bay pediment and quoins to the angles and also to the angles of the centre. Porch with segmental pediment on well-carved Corinthian columns. Large extension of 1896 on the l.

Since the first edition of this book appeared, several more interesting buildings at Exning have been reported to me. They are:

ROSE HALL, North End Road. Late C18, red brick, two storeys. Four large projecting sash-windows reach to ground level, with four smaller ones above, all with cast-iron hoods decorated with rosettes. Good outbuildings.

LORD ROSEBERY'S HOUSE, Old Station Road. Early to mid C19. Two storeys. Rendered front with four pilasters and a thin cornice. Four-columned Ionic entrance, portico with a decorative railing above. Panelled and partly pierced roof parapet. Large central panel with pediment and flanking scrolls (DOE).

Also five good BARNS: at Exeter Stud Farm, at the s end of the village, originally thatched, now with traditional Suffolk pantiles, whitewashed clunch walls, and a good timber roof structure, about 200 years old; at Exning Stud, at the SE approach to the village, part of a large stableyard complex, with clunch walls and a slate roof, c. 1825–30; at Orchard Farm, at the N end of the village, as above, but lower; across the road from it, Rose Hall barn, of 1870–90, flint, with Burwell-white quoins and string courses; and finally at North-end Farm, perhaps 250 years old, with framed oak walls, ship lap boarding, and a thatched roof.*

LANDWADE. A large Roman building, 1½ m. NW of Exning and

---

* All these barns are discussed by I. J. Richards, *Architectural Review*, CXXXVI (December 1964), from the viewpoint of the contribution to vernacular architecture made by the local craftsman; e.g. the first four of these barns have half-hipped gable-ends, giving maximum storage space as well as reducing the area of roof exposed to wind pressure.

¾ m. sw of Landwade church, on the E side of the former railway, was excavated in 1904–6 and 1957–8. It was of tripartite plan with flanking corridors and a N block containing a hypocaust and bath. Four phases were represented. There was a C1 A.D. ditch, a C2 A.D. building, 100 ft long and constructed on a timber frame, which was rebuilt of flint and mortar in the late C2–3 A.D., and a chambered hypocaust added later. A group of inhumations with associated pottery and glass beads was also found, as well as two wells containing pottery of C1–3 A.D. date; the majority was of the end of the period, and some had been imported from the Nene Valley potteries.

1070   EYE

10b ST PETER AND ST PAUL. The W tower of Eye church is one of the wonders of Suffolk, 101 ft tall and panelled in flushwork from foot to parapet. A frieze of shields at the base. A frieze of shields above the W doorway, which is also flanked by niches. A four-light window with transom, then a small two-light window, another above that, and then the bell-openings, two of two lights side by side in each direction. The parapet is of stone, very tall, and panelled also. It carries battlements and pinnacles. Among the shields is that of the de la Poles. The ground floor of the tower is fan-vaulted. The first floor opens with a stone gallery towards the nave (cf. Mildenhall).* Perp S aisle with battlements decorated by flushwork emblems, Perp S chapel with a flying buttress supporting the wall in front of the priest's doorway (cf. Blythburgh, Yaxley). Chancel with buttresses decorated by flushwork. Clerestory with double windows in the chancel, single windows in the nave. In the chancel flushwork panelling between them. Perp S porch of two stages. The sides are panelled all over, and it certainly adds a piquant touch that at some restoration the flint has here been replaced by brick. The front is all stone-faced. Big polygonal buttresses, left incomplete. Above the entrance a frieze of quatrefoils, then one of lozenges, then a two-light window. The interior was vaulted, but only the angle-shafts remain. All this is Perp, but the S doorway is a survival from a preceding building, a good piece of the C13, with one order of shafts

* Wills of 1458, 1463, and 1469, and one proved in 1462, give money to the repair of the tower. A will of 1465 leaves twelve 'cartfull of Calyōn' to the repair of the tower. Calyon would seem to be flint or pebble. Evidently quite a lot of work was going on at this time (ARA).

carrying crocket capitals and a finely moulded arch. The inner
order has a band of dog-tooth. The nave walls inside cant
towards the tower. The arcades are of five bays, with octagonal
piers, finely moulded capitals, and arches of one chamfer and
one hollow chamfer – rather disappointing after the external
display. Chancel chapels of two bays, C14. The N arcade has
quatrefoil piers and arches with two hollow chamfers, the
S arcade piers are quatrefoil with fillets on the lobes and spurs
in the diagonals. The arches have three hollow chamfers. The
capitals also differ a little. In the N aisle is a big recess with
cusped and sub-cusped arch and crocketed ogee gable flanked
by buttresses carrying finials. That also must be c. 1350 at the
latest. So the whole arcades and the walls of S as well as N aisle
are really pre-Perp. Arch-braced nave roof springing from wall-
posts. They alternate with arched braces springing from the
apexes of wide wall arches made of arched braces running
W–E. – SCREEN. The only screen in Suffolk restored with loft
and rood. On the dado fourteen paintings of c. 1500, all bad. 26a
Rich cusped and sub-cusped entrance arch. Carved foliage
trail on the rail above the dado. The rest in a bad state. Ribbed
coving supported in front by traceried pendant arches. Above
this an upper tier of ribbed coving. A cresting on top. Inscription commemorating John Gold. – Interesting C17 stone
SHELF for charity loaves (S porch). – MONUMENTS. In the
N aisle to Nicholas Cutler, 1568. Tomb-chest with three
shields in lozenges. On this two poor columns and a flat Perp
arch with straight top. Quatrefoil frieze and cresting above this.
The columns are the only indication of the Renaissance. –
William Honyng, 1569, in the S chapel. A copy of the former. –
John Brown † 1732. Unsigned. At the foot an excellent relief
of the Good Samaritan.

PERAMBULATION. Immediately N of the church the GUILD-
HALL, early C16, two-storeyed, timber-framed, and with
upper oriels. Their sills are carved with foliage and a scene
with a stag; but all this is thoroughly re-cut. Angle-post with
the Archangel Gabriel. Next to the Guildhall to the W TUDOR
HOUSE, Georgian of five bays, red brick, but with shaped
gable ends. Now along CASTLE STREET from the SW end of
the churchyard to the W. On the r. on a high overgrown mound
the CASTLE. The cliff of wall which shows comes from a C19
building. The remains of a wing-wall ascend the motte on the
N. The bailey covered two acres below to the SW. Traces of the
ditches are to be seen in BUCKSHORN LANE to the W, where

the scarp is also well preserved. On the s side of Castle Street,
STAYER HOUSE, with a timber-framed back and a Georgian
front provided with a porch of two pairs of unfluted Ionic
columns and an arched centre window; then STANLEY
HOUSE, long and irregular, with a pedimented Georgian
doorway, some timber-framing exposed on the r. (and a
C17 staircase inside: DOE). From the top of Castle Street turn
r. down BROAD STREET. The WHITE LION offers a long,
picturesque and mixed front to the street. (Assembly room
with some late C18 decoration. DOE) To its r. round the corner,
in Church Street, a timber-framed front with overhang and
some original timber arches on the ground floor. Opposite the
horrible TOWN HALL of 1857 with a horrible tower. It is
by *E. B. Lamb*.* Then LAMBSETH STREET with the very
fine LINDEN HOUSE of *c.* 1750 on the r., lying back behind
a row of trees. Seven bays, two storeys, of blue brick with
rubbed red trim. Doorway with pilasters carrying a segmental
pediment. Arched window over. Parapet and hipped roof.
Also in Lambseth Street two cottages which have oriel
windows with animals carved on their sills (cf. Guildhall above).
Towards the n end CHANDOS LODGE with two symmetrical
bow windows. It lies in its gardens, and the brick wall just s of
them towards the street is (like several others in gardens at
Eye) an undulating forcing wall (crinkle-crankle wall).

To see what might be called OUTER EYE, one continues first to
the n to LANGTON GROVE, a house with a stepped brick
gable and two original brick windows. Then out to the E to
THE PRIORY or ABBEY FARM, on the site of a Benedictine
priory founded in the late C11. All that can be seen above
ground is part of the s transept, some masonry of the walls of the
church, and the w wall of the present C18 house (six bays, three
storeys, hipped roof), built of stone and brick in layers, and a
separate oblong building to the NW. This is of brick, assigned
to the early C16, and has windows and a doorway with four-
centred arches. The excavators suggested it may have been the
guest house. They found enough of the church to state that it
had an E end with staggered apses (the plan-type of the second
building at Cluny), i.e. a chancel apse, N and s chapel apses, and
transepts with E apses. Oblong chapter house with apse to the

* REGALIA. Two small Maces C16. – Silver-gilt Mace, 35 in. long, 1670. –
Two silver-gilt Badges, 1673. – Silver Seal, late C17. – Two Punch Bowls
and Punch Ladles, by *Richard Zouch*, 1742. – Two-handled Cup, by *Emes
& Barnard*, 1822. – Alderman's Pall, silk, C19.

N of the transept. So the cloister lay on the N, not the S. ¾ m.
further out E COOKLEY FARM (with a C15 hall with traces of
the screen (DOE) and a remarkable cambered ceiling, early
C16(?), probably of a solar or great chamber (J. T. Smith)).
To the SE EYE PARK, once a house of some consequence. The
red brick LODGES remain, one-storeyed with bow windows
facing one another and a timber colonnade in front of them.
The stables remain too, also red brick, and with pediment and
projecting wings. To the NE of this CRANLEY HALL, a
handsome timber-framed house with some original windows
(and an octagonal summer house with Gothic detail: DOE).
Finally to the SW, ½ m. out, ROOK HALL, with remains of a
C15 to C16 open timber roof.

EYKE

ALL SAINTS. Nave and chancel. No tower. The explanation of
this is that the church had a Norman crossing tower. This
Norman state of the fabric can still be reconstructed. What
survives is the following parts: The W arch and E arch, both
decorated towards the W, the former with one order of colonnettes and one zigzag, the latter with one order of colonnettes
and two zigzags. In addition the completely plain N and S
arches remain and the nook-shafted SW corner of the S transept.
Of the tower windows the eastern one is visible inside the
church, the northern outside. The issue is at first complicated
by the odd decision of the early C14 to rebuild the nave much
wider (cf. Fritton, Oulton) and add a S chapel to that part of the
E end of the nave not continued by the Norman tower space. –
FONT. Octagonal with four lions against the stem and four
flowers and the Signs of the four Evangelists against the bowl. –
COMMUNION RAIL. C18. – PLATE. Elizabethan Cup. – BRASS.
Two headless figures c. 2 ft 2 in. long, supposed to represent
John de Staverton and his wife, c. 1420. – CURIOSUM. A C15
or C16 KEY, the wards of the head forming the letters IKE.

FAKENHAM

ST PETER. The E angles of the nave with long and short work
prove the Saxon origin of this part of the church. Norman one
blocked N and one blocked S window, the latter just W of the
porch gable. In the chancel a pair of C13 lancet windows.
W tower, nave windows, and most chancel windows Dec. –

SCREEN. Much restored; with one-light divisions. – PLATE.
Cup 1629; Paten 1703.

EARTHWORK of doubtful age in Burnthall Plantation, c. ¼ m. s of
the church, on the N bank of the river. There is a circular
ditch and bank with an entrance to the W and an expanded N
end of the rampart; probably an early medieval ring motte.

Also a Roman and earlier SETTLEMENT of more than 200 huts
N of the bridge. The huts are grouped and mainly circular in
plan, though a few are rectangular. There are also indications
of Late Neolithic occupation including a necked beaker and
flint dagger, and late Iron Age and early Anglo-Saxon material.

FALKENHAM

2030

ST ETHELBERT. A rare dedication (cf. Herringswell and Hessett). W tower with some flushwork decoration, especially of the
battlements. W doorway with a moulding of jambs and arch
bases with fleurons. A frieze with three shields above it. Nave
and chancel in one with a minimum apse. All this is of yellow
brick, built in 1806 and Gothicized later in the C19. The
original hammerbeam roof with angels holding shields charged
with the Instruments of the Passion is Perp. – FONT. Octagonal,
with four lions against the stem, and against the bowl the Signs
of the four Evangelists and four angels with shields. On the
shields the Sign of the Trinity, three crowns and an arrow, the
initials of Christ three times repeated, and a Cross. – REREDOS.
This incorporates some fine tracery panels, supposed to come
from a Flemish chest. – PLATE. Cup 1756.

FARNHAM

3060

ST MARY. On a hill facing the church of Stratford St Andrew
across the river Alde. One Norman window in the N wall, one
in the S. The chancel seems all renewed. The W tower is of
brick with a brick W window and battlements. – BOX PEWS. –
(SCREEN. Two traceried panels from the upper part now on the
N side of the nave.) – PLATE. Cup and Paten 1567; Flagon 1636.

FELIXSTOWE

3030

Felixstowe as a seaside resort dates mostly from the end of the
C19 and the early C20. The former CLIFF HOTEL was built
in 1906, the grandly neo-Jacobean FELIX HOTEL (now
Messrs Fison's) with its shaped gables, turrets with ogee caps,
and Hatfieldian lantern turret was built in 1900–3 (to the

designs of the *Hon. Douglas Tollemache* and *T. W. Cotman*). The sea-front developments also seem to belong to those years. Of course building did not stop then, and the CAVENDISH HOTEL near the s end of the sea-front is a characteristic example of the modernistic version of the style of *c.* 1930. Symmetrical front, all block-shapes, all far-projecting eaves and in addition bands of blue glass to streamline the design. 1936–7 by *Stewart & Hendry*.

ST JOHN BAPTIST, Orwell Road, is the church of this new Felixstowe. 1894–5 by *Sir Arthur Blomfield*, large and spacious, of red brick, with a tall s tower crowned by a spire. Lancet windows, clerestory windows in the shape of spherical triangles. Short circular brick piers; straight E end.

Old Felixstowe lies inland and to the NW. Here are the church and a few old houses (e.g. OLD HALL FARM, High Street, of red brick, three bays, doorway with Roman Doric pilasters).

ST PETER AND ST PAUL. Stump of the w tower of septaria with brick buttresses. Septaria also the s porch and the N side of the nave. The N doorway is early C14. The transepts and the apsed chancel date from 1876. But the pulpit stands on what must have been the base of a substantial pier, perhaps the former crossing pier or a pier of the Benedictine Priory of St Felix which was founded late in the C11. It was between the present church and Walton Castle, later moved to near Walton church, where it has been excavated. – FONT. Octagonal, most probably C17. Shields with an angel, a crown of thorns, a ship, the Instruments of the Passion, a cross on steps, a crown. – PULPIT. Jacobean. – BENCHES. With traceried ends, poppy-heads, and animals on the arms. – PLATE. Cup 1728.

The other part of Felixstowe where a few better houses of the pre-Victorian age remain is GRANGE ROAD, sw of Walton Church. Here e.g. the VICARAGE, Late Georgian, four bays wide, of red brick.

In Nos. 9 and 11 FOXGROVE GARDENS Romano–British sherds of the C1 and C2 were found associated with the foundations of two walls at r. angles, an earlier hearth(?), a spread of pink-buff tiles and tegulae, box tile fragments and tile tesserae, painted wall plaster and window glass.

In addition two modern buildings:

ST ANDREW, St Andrew's Road. 1929–31 by *Hilda Mason* and *Raymond Erith*. Nave and aisles and large s porch. The tower forming part of the design has not yet been built. The design is a translation of Suffolk traditions into concrete and glass. This is consistently done, and one can look at the building in either way according to one's mood. The only detail which mars this interesting ambiguity is the four-centred arches, where they occur. (The other modern building is the SANGAMO FACTORY, Langer Road, by *Johns, Slater & Haward*, 1962–4. It is a large, low, oblong block, entirely windowless. No skylights either – an American preference. At one angle a meteorological lantern-turret like the top of an airport control tower.)

Towards the s end of Felixstowe two military oddities:

MARTELLO TOWER, s of Beach Station. Built *c.*1810–12 (cf. Aldeburgh, p. 73). One of several.

LANDGUARD FORT (War Department), near Landguard Point to guard Harwich Harbour. First built in 1540–5. Rebuilt in 1624 etc. as a square with square angle bastions. Again rebuilt in 1717–20 as a low polygon of red brick with angle bastions. In this form the fort remains, though the archway is Victorian, as is the whole interior with its circular building and circular courtyard. That is dated 1875.

WALTON CASTLE. *See* p. 474.

FELSHAM

9050

ST PETER. Dec w tower.* Wide Dec nave with tall two-light windows. On the N side panelled battlements, on the s side a more modest treatment. No aisles. N porch with much flushwork panelling on the buttresses and the battlements. Side windows with tracery. Entrance with three orders of fleurons. Three niches round the entrance.‡ Chancel rebuilt in 1873. – FONT. Octagonal. Really two fonts; for the base is clearly the mutilated bowl of a font. On it animals, human faces, etc., below ogee arches. On the other bowl demi-figures of angels on the underside and tracery patterns on the eight sides. – PLATE. Elizabethan Cup, altered; Paten perhaps C17; Flagon 1717.

MAUSOLEUM. In a field behind Mausoleum House the remains of the square brick mausoleum built *c.* 1755 by a Mr Reynolds for his only child. It is mentioned in Wesley's *Journal*. Later Mr and Mrs Reynolds were also buried in it. Yellow brick with red brick dressings. Blank windows. No other feature survives.

FINBOROUGH HALL *see* GREAT FINBOROUGH

---

* But a will of 1423 refers to the new tower (Mr Peter Northeast).
‡ Wills of 1470 and 1471 give money for glass for windows in the porch (ARA).

FINNINGHAM

ST BARTHOLOMEW. Partly of the early C14, partly Perp. The
w tower is of the earlier date. Bell-openings with Y-tracery,
but that to the E a quatrefoil in a circle. The chancel S doorway
and nave S doorway also of the earlier date. The rest of the S
side Perp. N side all Perp with a simple brick porch. The S
porch is the only ornate piece. It has flushwork panelling,
niches l. and r. of the entrance, and a parapet nicely decorated
with alternating quatrefoils placed upright and diagonally. –
FONT. Octagonal. Simple. The base is of two steps, the upper
in the form of a Maltese Cross. – FONT COVER. Perp, a pinnacle,
but not a high one. The principal decoration is some oblong
panels with squares flanked by little arches. In the squares
interesting combination of squares and circles, e.g. a square
set within a diagonally placed square set within a square. All
three touch. Or a circle set within a square set within a circle
set within a square. All squares and circles touch. It all looks
connected with the masons' mysteries of proportions. – BENCH
ENDS. With tracery and poppy-heads. On the arms figures
seated not towards the E as usual but towards the gangway. –
STAINED GLASS. Some, in the E window. – MONUMENTS.
John Williamson † 1781 by *John Golden* of Holborn. A pretty
tablet of white and pink marble, neo-classical in style. No
figures at all. – Sir John Fenn, editor of the Paston letters,
signed by *John Bacon*, 1797. With a woman kneeling over an
urn.

YEW TREE HOUSE, N of the church. With some late C17 pargetting, perhaps the most handsome in Suffolk.

FLATFORD

The three principal houses are the MANOR HOUSE (VALLEY
FARM), the MILL, and WILLY LOTT'S COTTAGE; all
pleasant to look at, but visited chiefly for their connexions with
John Constable. The mill belonged to his father, and young
John worked for one year in it. Willy Lott's house he painted
more than once. It is said that Willy Lott was born in it and
passed more than eighty years there without ever leaving it for
more than four days. His house and the manor house are timber-
framed and of the C16; the mill is of brick and dates from the
C17. The manor house has the original doorways from the
screens passage to the offices, the mill a pretty C18 outer doorway with a Gibbs surround.

FLEMING'S HALL see BEDINGFIELD

FLEMPTON
8060

ST CATHERINE. Much renewed. w tower rebuilt in 1839. Nave and chancel. The details are late C13 to early C14. The best original feature is the chancel PISCINA with a two-light reticulated head. E window of three lights with minor flowing tracery. One chancel s window has a transom and beneath it a low-side window. – PULPIT. Elizabethan. – DOOR with tracery. – COMMUNION RAIL. With twisted balusters; late C17. – PLATE. Paten 1760.

BARROWS. A pair, 1½ m. SW of the village, on the E side of the track to Lackford (*see also* Risby).

FLIXTON
5090
3 m. N W of Lowestoft

ST ANDREW. The church was ruined by a hurricane in 1730. Only fragments of walls survive, about 10 ft high.

FLIXTON
3080
3 m. SW of Bungay

ST MARY. The w tower looks very neo-Norman. It was built in 1856 by *Salvin* and is said to be an accurate copy of the tower which fell in 1835. The spire with its lozenge-shaped broaches is familiar from the Rhineland and exists just once in England, at Sompting in Sussex. It is said that Salvin found sufficient evidence to conjecture this solution. The nave was rebuilt in 1861, the chancel (in the Norman style) in 1893. Original only the early C14 N arcade of four bays with piers of quatrefoil section, but with spurs in the diagonals. Arches with two wave mouldings. Nice, rib-vaulted NW chapel in the E.E. style to hold the MONUMENT to Theodosia Lady Waveney † 1871. The monument, a kneeling figure, life-size, is one of the major works of *John Bell*. – PULPIT. Jacobean. – BENCHES. Some with poppy-heads. – (PAINTINGS. Two angels, said to be Italian C14 work. Presented by Sir Shafto Adair of Flixton Hall.) – MONUMENT. William Adair † 1783. Tablet with a relief of the Good Samaritan, flanked by curiously Early-Renaissance-looking pilasters.

FLIXTON HALL has been largely demolished, but the DOVECOTE survives; probably Jacobean. It is of red brick and, oddly enough, semicircular in plan. Pretty octagonal cupola. Interesting interior with a revolving ladder and a revolving platform.

PRIORY, ⅜ m. SE. Of the house of Augustinian canonesses founded in 1258 no more survives than part of one wall with an arch.

TEA HOUSE, ¼ m. NW. Small grey brick house of three bays, early C19. The upper windows are ogee-arched. One-bay, one-storey attachments.

FLOWTON   0040

ST MARY. A church with individuality in various details. Of c. 1300, except for the big early C16 S window of brick with panel tracery. Unbuttressed W tower of knapped flint. It has a S, not a W, doorway. W window with Y-tracery flanked by two deep and large cusped niches. Small circular quatrefoiled windows above. Charming E window. It is of three lights with reticulated tracery, but each reticulation unit is filled by the motif of a four-petalled flower. Rough tie-beam roof with kingposts and four-way struts. – FONT. Octagonal, of Purbeck type, C13, with two flat pointed arches to each side. – PLATE. Paten 1697; Cup 1809.

FORNHAM ALL SAINTS   8060

ALL SAINTS. Norman S doorway with one order of shafts. Early C13 W tower, unbuttressed with lancets and a small single-chamfered doorway towards the nave. Nave of c. 1300, see one window with Y-tracery. Tall Dec chancel, the E window reticulated. Perp S aisle attached to the E wall of the S porch. Battlements with initials, shields, etc., in stone and flushwork. The S arcade has two bays, the S chapel one into the chancel. The Perp E window has a niche to its r. in the SE angle. There was also one in the NE angle. – BENCH ENDS. With poppy-heads, and three with animals on the arms. – PLATE. Cup 1566; Paten 1660; Flagon 1762.

FORNHAM ST GENEVIEVE   8060

ST GENEVIEVE. Nothing remains except the W tower.* Un-buttressed, with a lancet on the ground floor and a top parapet.
FORNHAM HALL has been demolished. The stables remain.

FORNHAM ST MARTIN   8060

ST MARTIN. Perp with a S aisle of 1870. The W tower has un-usually tall two-light bell-openings with a transom and battle-ments with flushwork chequerboard decoration. Nave tracery

* A will of 1452 leaves money for its repair (ARA).

with straight-sided arches. N porch of brick with a stepped gable. – FONT. Perp, octagonal, simple. – MISERICORDS. Two, re-used in lectern and reader's desk. They represent St Martin and the Martyrdom of St Thomas Becket. – SCULPTURE. On the altar two small gilded praying putti from some Baroque altar, perhaps in Germany. – COMMUNION RAIL. Mid C17. – PLATE. Cup c. 1566. – (BRASS. To a man in academic dress; c. 1460. LG)

29

FOXBORO HALL *see* MELTON

2040

FOXHALL

1¼ m. NW of Bucklesham

Of the former parish CHURCH one wall forms part of an outbuilding of Foxhall Farm.

BARROWS, Foxhall Heath, N of the Ipswich road. Four 'bowl' barrows, including Pole Hill. These form the W edge of the group which extends on to Brightwell and Martlesham Heaths.

2060

FRAMLINGHAM

ST MICHAEL.* A large and stately church, Perp throughout, of the mid C15 to mid C16, except for the chancel arch, which in all its height must have belonged to a church of the late C12. The capitals are obviously of that date, and the piers then probably marked a crossing. The nave arcades of five bays with their octagonal piers and double-chamfered arches are Perp and not too late. The aisle roofs rest on corbel heads, and there are corbel heads also a little lower to support earlier aisle roofs. In the nave above the arcade stone shafts, built to carry an earlier nave roof. The present roof and a clerestory with its close windows are later. The roof is one of the most beautiful in Suffolk. It is a hammerbeam roof, but the hammerbeams are concealed by an elaborate ribbed coving as of a rood screen, and above it there is a horizontal band which looks exactly like a decorated wall-plate, that is as though the roof proper started only there (cf. St Peter Mancroft Norwich and Ringstead Norfolk). Arched braces to the collar-beams. Externally the clerestory is distinguished by tall arched flushwork panelling. The pretty lead cresting is recent. Flushwork

* Mr Peter Northeast has given me the following from wills: 1387, money left to the work on 'my chancel', John de Harleston, rector of Framlingham; 1464 to the clerestory; 1500 to the making of the steeple, and to the roof; 1520 to new clerestories and to the battlements of the steeple.

panelling also decorates the w tower. This is 96 ft high, and of powerful proportions. It has flushwork stars, wheels, etc., on the base, and a flushwork band below the stars. Battlements with lions instead of pinnacles. w doorway with, in one spandrel, a dragon. Four-light bell-openings. On the base also the shield of Thomas Whiting, who was Auditor to the Accounts of the Castle till 1479. On a buttress the Mowbray arms. The chancel chapels of four bays were added and the chancel lengthened by the third Duke of Norfolk. In 1549 the old work was pulled down and the new not yet built. The purpose of the new building was to house the remains of Henry Fitzroy (*see* below), which had until the time of the Dissolution been at Thetford Priory in Norfolk. The arcade piers are typically Late Perp, with caps only to the shafts towards the arch openings. The window tracery is unusual. The E window is of six lights with a row of shields underneath. The priest's doorway into the s chapel is placed behind a flying buttress (cf. Blythburgh, Eye, Yaxley). In the N wall of the N aisle is a fine image niche, the bracket supported by an angel. The s porch is supposed to date from *c.* 1770.

FURNISHINGS. FONT. Octagonal, of the usual type, and with original cover. Four Lions and four Wild Men against the stem, the Signs of the four Evangelists and four angels with shields against the bowl. The font was given by John Plomer and his wife. – REREDOS. A fine piece of *c.* 1700–10. – BENCHES. Traceried ends re-used in the chancel stalls and reading desks. – ORGAN CASE. By *Tamar* of Peterborough, 1674. Brought from Pembroke College in Cambridge in 1708. – CHANDELIER. Brass. In the chancel. 1742 by *John Giles*. – WALL PAINTING. Trinity (nave N wall). – PLATE. Cup and Cover 1568; Almsdish 1704; Flagon 1742. – HELMET. The Flodden Helmet worn by Thomas Howard, Earl of Surrey, who led the English vanguard at Flodden, hangs above the high altar on the s side. – CURIOSUM. The Key of Framlingham Castle (s porch).

MONUMENTS. One of the best series of mid-C16 Early Renaissance monuments in England, and among them one of a quality almost to match leading work in France. In chronological order: Henry Fitzroy Duke of Richmond † 1536 (natural son of Henry VIII) and his wife Lady Mary Howard † 1557. Large tomb-chest divided by fluted pilasters. In the fields between them shields. Above a frieze of small stories from Genesis separated by tiny termini caryatids, not an Italian, but rather a Flemish motif. No effigies, but four small

angle figures holding shields with the Instruments of the
Passion. Their style is still uninfluenced by Italy. – Thomas
34a Howard, third Duke of Norfolk, † 1554. The tomb-chest here
is divided by balusters, i.e. it is Early not High Renaissance
in derivation. In the fields are niches with shell tops, and in
these the figures of the Apostles carved as beautifully as the
best French work – not of 1550 but of 1520. At the angles
bigger balusters with slender detached balusters set around,
and each with one of the three attached figures left – the one
hardest to damage. Four supporters on these angle balusters.
The effigies are decidedly less accomplished. – The two wives
of the fourth Duke († 1557 and 1564). The tomb-chest is
divided by Corinthian columns and the shields are in egg-and-
dart frames, i.e. High and no longer Early Renaissance.
Plenty more fine Renaissance decoration. Supports at the
corners. The two effigies are again disappointing. The feet of
one wife rest against a stag, of the other against a dragon. Of a
former canopy only the corner bases survive. – Elizabeth,
daughter of the fourth Duke, † c. 1560. Small, almost square
tomb-chest divided by fluted pilasters and with shields in the
fields. No effigy. The crocketed ogee arch above must be re-
used. It stands on fluted pilasters. – Henry Howard, Earl of
Surrey, beheaded in 1547. The monument was made in 1614.
Alabaster, painted. Two recumbent effigies, and on the ground
at the head and the foot of the tomb-chest five kneeling
36   children. – Sir Robert Hitcham † 1636. He bought the castle
and manor from the Howards in 1635 and bequeathed them to
Pembroke College Cambridge. Black marble slab supported
by four kneeling angels and an urn standing in the middle
beneath. Very restrained and classical. Signed by *Francis
Grigs*, 1638. – Richard Porter † 1701, Edward Alpe † 1715,
both with pilasters, pediment, and a cherub's head at the
foot. No effigies (s chapel). – Mrs Kerridge † 1744 and her
daughter † 1747. Two urns draped by curtains. By *Roubiliac*
(s chapel).

CASTLE. The castle belonged to the Bigods in the c 12, until Hugh
Bigod, first Earl of Norfolk, made a nuisance of himself so consistently that Henry II had it dismantled in 1174 by *Alnoth*,
Keeper of the King's Houses. Of the buildings erected by Hugh
about 1150 all that can be seen is traces of the hall and traces of
the chapel. Both are on the E side of the castle, the latter s of
and adjoining the former. The HALL was probably on the
ground floor, as there is here a fine fireplace with shafts. On the

first floor also a fireplace, and in addition arched windows.
Most of the windows here, however, are later. Of the CHAPEL
no more survives than the matrix or mould of its E wall against
the E wall of the present castle. It had the usual broad, flat
buttresses. The arched E window is of *c.* 1190–1210, the time
when the castle was rebuilt by Roger, second Earl of Norfolk,
and received its present shape. This shape is characterized by 42b
the curtain wall and its thirteen towers. The type of fortification represented by this was an innovation in Europe at the
time. It replaced the type with dominant keep which had just
achieved its acme with such keeps as Conisbrough in Yorkshire. The new type was a reflection of what Crusaders had
seen in the Holy Land, and what had been the ancient Roman
type culminating in the unmatched walls of Constantinople of
c. 400. It had been taken over successfully by the Infidels and
made a formidable bulwark against the Crusaders' attacks.
Among the first examples of the new plan and skill is Richard
Cœur de Lion's Château Gaillard in Normandy, built in 1196.
The first examples in England are at Dover and Windsor.
At the Tower of London the same system was probably con-
templated by King John, but not executed till the time of
Henry III. Framlingham is one of the earliest cases of the fortified curtain wall. The main entrance is by an early C16 bridge
and through an early C16 gatehouse, though the inner arches
of this date from the C12. The castle had become Howard
property in the late C15. To the W of the gateway a tower with
garderobes at all levels, and N of this the site of the kitchen
(see the fireplace) and two more garderobes in the curtain wall.
N of the kitchen was the great hall of the castle of *c.* 1200. The
remains of this now form part of the POOR HOUSE, founded by
the will of Sir Robert Hitcham. It is a building of brick and
flint with a recessed nine-bay centre, projecting N and S wings,
and a middle porch. The S wing is of 1636, the centre in its
present form of 1729. Segment-headed ground-floor windows.
Mullion and transom crosses. Of the medieval hall there survive three original W windows, pointed to the outside but with
round rere-arches. One window is of 1729. The gallery in the
hall is late C17 and comes from the church. N of the hall the
former solar. The big chimneybreast and windows are C16.
Opposite this N range, on the E side of the castle, just N of the
mid-C12 hall, a tower with two tunnel-vaulted rooms, one
above the other. S of the hall, between it and the kitchen, the
POSTERN GATE. This continues to the W as a passage between

two walls and has its exit on the s side just before it is blocked
by the PRISON TOWER, also of *c.* 1200. The passage and this
tower form part of the s walls of the LOWER COURT, a bailey w
of the castle. The bigger OUTER BAILEY extended to the s and
se and comprised much of the present town of Framlingham.
Finally, a last glance at the castle must take in the Early Tudor
brick chimneys, which stand somewhat precariously on all the
Plantagenet towers, displaying their crazy and showy decoration.

PERAMBULATION. Of the town not much need be said. From
the exit of the castle CASTLE STREET runs e (to No. 38 of four
bays and two storeys, with a hipped roof and a pretty late c18
doorway which combines compound Gothic shafts with a
metope frieze and a concave-sided pediment) and CHURCH
STREET s. In the latter the most attractive house is No. 7,
opposite the e end of the church, a five-bay Regency house
treated in stucco imitation-rustication and with a central bow
window with first-floor veranda. To the l. and r. of this are two
doorways with broken pediments on Roman Doric columns.
At the se end of the churchyard is No. 2, with a gabled timber-
framed front to the N. At the w end of the churchyard the
RECTORY, of the c16, but with a cemented imitation-Tudor
façade. Off Church Street to the e DOUBLE STREET with a
nice sequence of Georgian cottages, which leads to No. 22, red
brick, *c.* 1820, of five bays with a Greek Doric porch. Still in
Church Street itself No. 5, again a five-bay red brick Georgian
front, and then MARKET HILL, pleasant to look at, if uneventful. The most interesting house, No. 34, is half hidden by trees
and more than half spoiled by alterations. It must once have
had a fine front of *c.* 1660–70. Red brick, nine bays, with three
dormers with the typical semicircular and steeply triangular
pediments of that date. Parapet partly balustraded. Down to the
w along BRIDGE STREET and past the UNITARIAN CHAPEL
of 1717. This is of red and blue brick chequered, and it is three
widely spaced bays wide, two storeys high. It has wooden
cross-windows and a low (altered) hipped roof. Then for a
moment into NEW STREET, across the bridge where the
HITCHAM ALMSHOUSES are, erected in 1654, simple, of
brick, one-storeyed, with a central gable. Back to the bridge
and to the l. along RIVERSIDE to the ANCIENT HOUSE, a
late c17 house of five bays and two storeys with hipped roof,
wooden cross-windows, and some pargetting: two oval
wreaths and swags. Continue along STATION ROAD with, on

the r., the MILLS ALMSHOUSES of 1703, a stately range of twenty bays and two storeys. Red and blue chequered brick, hipped roof. There are eight doors, and they and the windows belonging to the respective dwellings are grouped in four units. After that MILLS HOUSE, C16, timber-framed, with a carved beam on shaped brackets at the foot of the gable. In front of the house is the little MAUSOLEUM of Thomas Mills and his 'faithful servant' William Mayhew. Cemented with Tudor detail. After that, back somewhat, the ROUND HOUSE, a picturesque group round the thatched stump of a smock mill. An oblong wing with Gothic windows. The perambulation ends at the STATION, yellow brick, completely utilitarian, of 1859.

FRAMLINGHAM COLLEGE (formerly Albert Memorial College). 1864 by *Frederick Peck*. Red brick, Gothic. On the terrace bronze STATUE of Prince Albert, 8 ft high, by *Durham*. Chapel of 1866 and 1876. Further additions.

(FRAMLINGHAM HALL, 1½ m. NNW. C16, much altered *c.* 1860. Timber-framed. Two shaped-gabled brick wings at the back, ogee-curved at the apex. Some linenfold panelling in a garden room. DOE)

FRAMSDEN
2050

ST MARY. Substantial contributions of the early C14; namely the nave doorways, the E window of the S aisle (three stepped, cusped lancet lights under one arch), the S aisle PISCINA, the S aisle arcade (five bays, octagonal piers, double-chamfered arches), and the chancel PISCINA. Perp W tower. Flushwork arches on the base, flushwork quatrefoils on the battlements. W doorway with fleurons and crowns up one order of the jambs and arch. In the spandrels shields with three crowns and an arrow and the Instruments of the Passion. Niches l. and r., a frieze of shields over. Late Perp brick windows on the N side of the nave and in the clerestory. S aisle and S porch with flushwork decoration of the battlements. Arched flushwork panelling of the porch front. Three niches around the entrance. In its spandrels a man with a club (St George ?) and a dragon. In the nave a double-hammerbeam roof. The S aisle roof with dates 1620 and 1676. Nice, with queenposts forming arches and with a pendant from their apex. – FONT. Octagonal, with four lions against the stem and four lions and four angels against the bowl. – STALLS and MISERICORDS of the early c 14; damaged. They represent grotesques but also the Annunciation, a demi-figure of a seraph, and a saint or donor with the model of a cruciform church. – BENCHES. Just two, with poppy-heads and traceried ends. – SCULPTURE. Small Saxon (?) figure of a man with one arm akimbo and one raised. Reused in the wall by the chancel NW window. – PLATE. Elizabethan Cup and Cover.

FRAMSDEN HALL. Originally a medieval hall-house. One speretruss and the original canopy remain. The spere-truss has richly moulded posts. The roof is of the kingpost type – rare in medieval buildings s of the Trent – on steeply cambered tiebeams enriched with cresting and cusped panels (J. T. Smith). Fine BARN, 200 ft long. Ground floor late c 17 or c 18 brick, upper floor c 16 timber with brick-nogging.

BOUNDARY FARM, 1 m. NW. An Elizabethan summer house now used as stables. Brick, three-bay front, with the entrance provided with a straight entablature, and the windows l. and r. with pediments. End gables shaped with semicircular tops. Spiked dentil frieze between ground floor and first floor.

WINDMILL, ½ m. w. A fine post-mill, built in 1760.

6070
FRECKENHAM

ST ANDREW. Over-restored or rather rebuilt (by *Street*, 1867). W tower rebuilt 1884. One window with Y-tracery in the vestry, two two-light Perp windows used as a kind of dormer. E window of three stepped lancet lights under one arch, shafted inside, i.e. c. 1300. Arcade with piers of keeled quatrefoil section and arches with one chamfer and one recessed chamfer, i.e. also c. 1300. Nice Perp canted wagon roofs in nave and chancel, with bosses. – BENCH ENDS. With poppy-heads, some in the form of kneeling figures, very pretty. – SCULPTURE. Alabaster relief from a former altar, a scene from the Life of St Eligius, c 15. – PLATE. Elizabethan Cup; Paten 1723.

CASTLE, E of the church. A small motte-and-bailey castle, the bailey now occupied by a garden.

2070
FRESSINGFIELD

ST PETER AND ST PAUL. Dec the W tower, the structure of the chancel (see the shafts inside the Perp E window), and apparently the N chapel (see the continuous double-chamfer of its W arch).* The rest Perp. Both aisles are Perp. So is the clere-

* The LG calls the Sanctus bellcote the best in the county.

story, and so are both porches. The s porch is more ambitious:
two-storeyed, with a small s window flanked by niches. Front
and buttresses with flushwork panelling. Entrance with
fleurons and crowns. The carved spandrels must have been
re-done in the late C17 or C18. Parapet with small frieze of
quatrefoils. Tierceron-vault inside. Three-bay arcade with
octagonal piers and arches with one chamfer and one hollow
chamfer. Hammerbeam roof. Decoration on the wall-plate and
the vertical boarding above it. – SCREEN. The dado only
remains. – BENCHES. One of the best sets in the county
(Cautley says: in the country), with traceried ends of many
patterns, poppy-heads, fragmentary figures on the arms, and
carved seat-backs. – STAINED GLASS. SE window by *Holiday*,
1895, clearly imitated from Morris and Burne-Jones. –
MONUMENTS. (Brass to William Brewes † 1489 and wife. LG) –
Big completely unornamented tomb-chest to Archbishop
Sancroft † 1693, in the churchyard, E of the porch.

Immediately s of the church the former Guild House, now FOX
AND GOOSE INN. Handsome, timber-framed, brick-nogged
front to the churchyard. Corner post with figure of St Margaret.
Like Church Cottage at Cockfield, it is a former church house
(*see* p. 171n). W of the church CHURCH FARM. Its STABLES
are a C15 hall-house. What remains seems to be two bays of a
hall, spanned by an open truss. The roof construction is
interesting: it is essentially an aisled structure raised up on to
tie-beams.*

N of the church the VICARAGE, Georgian, of five bays and two
storeys, and a little to its SE the BAPTIST CHURCH of 1835,
red brick, with a roof of most surprising geometry.

UFFORD HALL, 2 m. SSE. The house where Archbishop Sancroft
lived from 1690 to his death. C17, but must be earlier than 1691,
the date attributed to it. Timber-framed and plastered, with
gables and mullioned and transomed windows.

WHITTINGHAM HALL, 1¼ m. NE. What remains is a fine outbuilding of the former Hall, red brick, wide, two-storeyed,
with two projecting wings ending in shaped gables. A tablet
with the date 1653 over the porch.

FRESTON   *1030*

ST PETER. Flint and stone; standing on its own. Short W tower,
aisleless nave, chancel; over-restored in 1875. – FONT. Perp,

---

* Illustrated in Smith, 'Medieval Roofs', *Archaeological Journal*, CXV,
p. 122.

octagonal, on the sides of the bowl four seated lions and four demi-figures of angels with shields. – PLATE. Cup 1656; Paten perhaps pre-Reformation.

53a FRESTON TOWER. Called in 1561 'built within these twelve years'. Only about 200 yards from the estuary and overlooking it dramatically. A 'standing' or look-out tower, built by one of the Latymer family. Red brick with blue diapering. Six storeys high, 10 by 12 ft in area. Polygonal angle buttresses ending in polygonal pinnacles. To the estuary (N) projecting polygonal stair-turret rising above the pinnacles. Arched openwork top parapet. The windows of three lights, except for the small single-light windows of the staircase turret. On some tiers the latter have pediments. On the other sides the three upper tiers have broad pediments. Only the top windows with transom. The principal room lies behind these.

COTTAGES. The brick cottages close to the tower date back to the same time, as witnessed by the SE gable wall.

(SUMMER HOUSE in the grounds. On the upper floor a loggia of four widely spaced Tuscan columns and a pediment. Seems derelict. NMR)

4060   FRISTON

ST MARY. The surprising W tower can only be the result of the various restorations, especially that of 1899–1900, although Cautley believes its odd C14 motifs to be possibly original. Nave and chancel in one. Nothing of interest except the S doorway which is Transitional with its one order of shafts and its sharply pointed arch with two slight chamfers. – PULPIT. Jacobean. – ROYAL ARMS. Of James I. A spectacular piece of wood-carving. Well re-assembled by Cautley.

WINDMILL. It is not known when she was built, and it is always possible that she stands on the site of an earlier mill. She is a typical East Suffolk post-mill, with a three-storey brick round-house having a boarded roof, a tall buck with an attractive hooded porch, four patent (shuttered) sails (only two of which remain), and a fan-tail to turn her into the wind automatically. She stands over 50 ft high, the height of the buck and the round-house being almost equal. She drives two pairs of stones in the breast, one pair in the tail, a centrifugal flour dresser, a 'jog-scry' (or 'jumper'), and an oat crusher.*

* This paragraph was supplied by Mr Rex Wailes.

FRITTON

4000

ST EDMUND. Norman round tower, thatched nave, low Norman chancel with flat buttresses. The nave is Dec. As one enters, one is struck by the oddest lack of symmetry or, we are inclined to say, propriety. The tower is not in axis with the wide nave but stands against its N half. But while one may not at once notice that, one cannot overlook the fact that the chancel is also attached to the N half of the nave E wall, as if the nave were a former nave and S aisle, which it is not. The fact is that, when in the C14 the Norman nave was rebuilt, wide spaces were so much favoured that the resulting lack of symmetry was not considered an obstacle and the nave was simply widened from 12 to 21 ft without removing the masonry of the old N wall. The chancel of the Norman church remained, and is both interesting and impressive in its lowness and darkness. The chancel itself is tunnel-vaulted, a great rarity in England, and is followed by a vaulted apse with three slit windows (enlarged by colonnettes inside), their arches continued as penetrations into the vault. The tunnel-vault indicates that a tower was built or intended above the chancel bay. – SCREEN. C14 with typical simple circles above the ogee arches. The shafts are C19 but replace original ones. – STALLS. They are indeed a minimum of choir stalls. – PULPIT. C17; very simple, but a complete three-decker. – ORGAN CASE. A pretty Georgian piece with fluted pilasters. – PAINTINGS. St Christopher on the N wall, St Thomas of Canterbury in the E jamb of the SE nave window. – PLATE. Cup and Paten 1627.

(FRITTON OLD HALL. Arch-braced tie-beams inside. DOE)

FRITTON MARSH MILL. A derelict tower mill used originally for drainage.

BARROWS. An isolated group above the Yarmouth road, on Bell Hill and Mill Hill, the latter actually being in Belton parish.

FROSTENDEN

4080

ALL SAINTS. Round tower with later lancet windows. Nave, chancel, and S aisle. In the S aisle two-light Dec windows, renewed. The S porch is the W continuation of the three-bay aisle. It is vaulted with diagonal ribs and ridge ribs. The aisle has an arcade with octagonal piers and double-chamfered arches. Large Perp E window, but the shafting inside and the arch moulding with a kind of half-dog-tooth version of the old zigzag establish a C13 date. The same motif in the shafted

PISCINA and the remains of the E arch of the SEDILIA. –
FONT. Octagonal. The bowl supported by heads. On the bowl
quatrefoils and shields. – BENCHES. Some; also with traceried
ends. – STAINED GLASS. In a s window of the chancel by *A. L.
Moore*, c. 1892; bad. – PLATE. Elizabethan Cup; Cover 1567;
Paten 1685; Flagon 1703.

FROSTENDEN HALL. Mid C17, red brick, with symmetrical
back which has two large shaped gables l. and r. and a straight
gable in the middle. In the gables blocked circular windows.
Small rectangular windows blocked too. The front is C18 and
has a width of five bays and the curious (perhaps not original ?)
feature that the doorway with a pediment on Tuscan columns
is in the fourth bay and is balanced by the same motif surrounding the window in the second bay.

GARDINER'S HALL *see* STOKE ASH

GAVELCROFT *see* HOLTON

GAZELEY

1060

ALL SAINTS. Mostly of the later C13. The chancel is an interesting and individual work. The E window has three lights, the
outer ones a little taller than the middle one. On them stands
not a circle but a spherical triangle with a sexfoil set in, three
foils being pointed and large, the other three round and small.
The whole window is not simply arched, but the outer arches
of the outer lights form part of its outline, which is then continued by the sides of the spherical triangle, forming a normal
arch-head. Inside, the arch has a normal rere-arch, but there
are in addition tall arched panels in the jambs. The side windows
have quatrefoils on pointed-trefoiled lights. PISCINA with
oddly double-cusped arch on shafts. The adjoining SEDILIA
are two stepped seats in the window-sill, separated by a simple
arm with a (defaced) lion *couchant*. On the N side of the chancel
a gabled niche. The westernmost chancel windows are
transomed 'low-side' windows. The arcade of four bays is also
late C13. Quatrefoil piers and boldly moulded capitals. The
chancel roof is a canted wagon roof and has small cusped panels
and many carved bosses. The W tower was rebuilt in 1884, but
its Perp W doorway seems in order. Perp also the aisles and
clerestory. – FONT. Octagonal, of c. 1300 (?). The sides have
plainly represented tracery motifs, all usual about 1300 (e.g.
three stepped lancets under one arch, three-light intersected,

three lancets of the same size, Y-tracery in a round arch, and pointed quatrefoils). – PULPIT. Perp, with simple arched panels. – SCREEN. Much restored; with one-light divisions. – BENCH ENDS. Both with poppy-heads and with straight tops with simple tracery and buttresses. Some backs have tracery and one the name 'Salamon Sayet' instead. Much of the bench ends seems re-used panels from the screen. – PAINTING. Presentation in the Temple. By *Jacques Stella*. From the chapel of Trinity Hall Cambridge, to which it was given in 1729 by the son of Dean Chetwode, who had brought it over about 1700. – PLATE. Elizabethan Cup; Patens 1673 (1662?) and 1696. – MONUMENT. Tomb recess in the s aisle. Tomb-chest with small lozenge-panels. The arch above the recess is nearly a lintel. Top with cresting. The brasses inside are lost.

WINDMILL. A tower-mill, now converted into a house.

DENHAM CASTLE, 2 m. ESE of the village. A motte-and-bailey castle with wet ditches.

BARROWS. There is a group along the Icknield Way extending into Kentford and Higham; two are on the s edge of the New-market road, ½ m. E of Kentford, and one on the edge of Slade Bottom, ½ m. NE.

GEDDING

9050

ST MARY. Nave and chancel, and a W tower finished in brick. In the nave two Norman windows, one N, one S. The rest of the details is Dec. The church has no porches. Its most interesting feature is the chancel arch. It is double-chamfered with continuous mouldings and flanked by one tall cusped lancet-like niche l. and one r. Roof with scissor-bracing below and above the collars. – FONT. Octagonal, Perp, with simple cusped blank arches and shields. – BENCHES. Three; humble. – (There is an old boundary ditch round the churchyard, like a moat.)

GEDDING HALL. The moat and the gatehouse remain, a fine piece of the time of Henry VIII, though in a mutilated state and made part of an extension of 1897 of which the towered r. end with a cupola is indeed very successful. Red brick. The gatehouse has a very tall four-centred archway and two polygonal turrets whose top parts are not preserved. At the height of the springing of the archway they have a frieze of a kind of ballflower. Two-light windows. To the l. a stepped gable-end. To the r. the Tudor walling continues into the work of 1897.

GIFFORDS HALL
2 m. NE of Stoke-by-Nayland

0030

CHAPEL OF ST NICHOLAS. In ruins, opposite the gatehouse to Giffords Hall. The building, of flint, consists of nave and chancel only and has a flat E end. It is supposed to date from the early C13. No more detail survives than the surround of the w window.

GIFFORDS HALL. Built by the Mannocks, who held the manor from 1428 onwards. The house belongs to the time of Henry VII and Henry VIII, but has alterations and additions of the early C18 and late C19, both carried out without doing damage to the impression of the whole. Giffords Hall, as it stands, is one of the loveliest houses of its date in England, neither small nor overwhelmingly grand; warm and varied, happy in scale and in the proportions between its materials. Brick gatehouse no higher than two storeys, with angle turrets. To the outside i.e. the S, four-centred arch, blank tracery in the spandrels, cusped tracery friezes above. One of them occurs identically at Layer Marney in Essex, c. 1520–5. Windows with four-centred heads to the lights. The turrets with angle strips and trefoiled corbel-friezes at the tops of the panels. Three-step battlements and brick pinnacles. Brick pinnacles had been used at Faulkbourne in Essex somewhat earlier, and are to be found c. 1530 at West Stow Hall.* Original doors. The interior of the gatehouse is of flint, not of brick, and probably older. Older also the SE corner, now altered outside, but with kingpost trusses inside. The range w of the gatehouse is flint, of different dates.

46   The courtyard is delightful. The gatehouse faces it with three stepped brick gables. The small pinnacles are set diagonally. Opposite the gatehouse is the hall. It has a brick porch with four-centred entrance and with a timber-framed upper storey. The charming oriel window and bargeboarding are additions of c. 1890. To the w the big chimneybreast with a two-light upper window in it, the flues being conducted to its l. and r. Polygonal chimneys with star tops. The hall bay has been replaced by a brick wall with an C18 Venetian window and a (blank) circular window over. Another Venetian window in the plastered wall E of the hall porch. Beyond the hall to the w and all along the w side of the courtyard timber-framing with gay brick-nogging and much carving. Some of the detail

---

* The CLOCK in the tower is by *Thomas Moore*, early C18.

on the hall side is again Late Victorian. The N side of the S wing also timber-framed. The E range altered in the C18. Irregular exteriors to the N and W. On the W two big chimney-breasts, the chimneys again with star tops.

The hall has a splendid double-hammerbeam roof with nice carving in the three sets of arched braces and tracery in the spandrels. In the spandrels also some pretty carving of little genre scenes: a fish on a plate, a mouse running into a bowl, a mouse running out of a bowl. The hall gallery is late C17 and has twisted balusters. The staircase leading up to it is earlier, probably c. 1630.

GIFFORD'S HALL see WICKHAMBROOK

GIPPING

CHAPEL OF ST NICHOLAS. The private chapel of Sir James Tyrell, who died in 1502. Built probably c. 1483. The chapel was close to a mansion of which not a trace is left. The plastered C19 W tower spoils what would otherwise be a singularly perfect piece of late medieval Suffolk architecture. The building is all of a piece, nave and chancel and a curious N annexe. This has a fireplace in its N wall, and it has been assumed that originally it was the chaplain's dwelling. The wall behind the fireplace is treated as a dummy bay window. It is canted, and the one-light, three-light, one-light rhythm with transoms is all made up of flushwork. W entrance to the room with inscription: 'Pray for Sir Jamys Tirell and dame Ann his wife.' The Tyrell knot appears everywhere in the flushwork decoration, which is generously applied to walls, buttresses, etc. The composition of N and S doorways is identical, and they are charming pieces too. Whereas the other windows are of three lights and transomed, there are here four lights and the lower part of the middle two is taken up by the doorway. The lower parts to its l. and r. are again flushwork dummies, and in the upper parts flushwork also is inserted between the two l. and the two r. lights. E wall with polygonal buttresses. Five-light E window. The interior is as translucent as a glasshouse. What effect the original glass must have had, of which fragments and five small figures remain in the E window, it is hard to guess. – BENCH. One original kneeling-bench; the end is of quite exceptional, very simple shape, and has the Tyrell knot. Twisted-leaf frieze along the back of the seat. – PLATE. Two Patens 1704; Cup 1712.

GIPPING LONE (Old Rectory), N of the church. Early C16. Gable with two overhangs. Carved beams. Stack of four round chimneys with Tudor patterns.

GISLEHAM

5080

HOLY TRINITY. Norman round tower with the original W window and arch to the nave. Simple imposts. The tower top has windows with Y-tracery, i.e. of *c.* 1300, and battlements. The nave and chancel masonry is Norman, but the fenestration Dec. The Norman origin is proved by the scalloped capitals which remain of the original, quite wide, N doorway, the Dec alterations, apart from the window tracery, by the shafting of the chancel s windows and the angle PISCINA in one of them. S porch of flint and stone; shields in the parapet. (Between nave and chancel ROOD BEAM and plaster TYMPANUM. LG) – FONT. Against the stem four lions; against the bowl four shields and four heads. Against the underside instead of angels heads with 'modern' head-dresses (cf. North Cove). – WALL PAINTINGS. In the jambs of two N windows good C15 figures of female Saints, with rays of glory and angels over. – STAINED GLASS. E window by *Kempe, c.* 1896. – BANNER STAFF LOCKER. A tall niche in the tower wall. – PLATE. Elizabethan Cup; Paten 1702.

GISLINGHAM

0070

ST MARY. Chancel Dec with a good four-light E window. Depressed arch, reticulation motifs. Good N porch with an inscription commemorating Robert Chapman and his wife. The entrance arch has little shields in the outer and inner mouldings. The hood-mould rests on seated lions. Perp nave, 21½ ft wide. w tower of 1639, red brick. The interior, without aisles, appears wide and empty. Double-hammerbeam roof. – FONT. Four lions against the stem. The Signs of the four Evangelists and four shields against the bowl. Inscription against the top step of the base also referring to the Chapman family. – PULPIT, a three-decker, and BOX PEWS probably early C19. – SCREEN. Parts under the tower, parts (of the dado) in the church. – COMMUNION RAIL. Jacobean. – STAINED GLASS. Many fragments in N and s windows, e.g. a Coronation of the Virgin, a King, a Crucifixion. – PLATE. Elizabethan Cup?; Almsbowl 1639. – MONUMENT. Anthony Bedingfield † 1652. Large kneeling figure, of indifferent quality. The inscription in Latin with Greek admixtures.

N of the church IVY FARMHOUSE, with carved gable tie-beam. To the W in MILL STREET the OLD GUILDHALL with tie-beams on arched braces and carrying kingposts. Further on, in LITTLE GREEN, MANOR FARMHOUSE, with a corner post with minor decoration and some buttress shafts. At the s end of the village the RECTORY of 1791, red brick, of five bays and two and a half storeys, with simple pedimented doorway. The LITTLE HOUSE next to this has the same roof construction as the Old Guildhall. DOE)

GLEMHAM HOUSE see GREAT GLEMHAM

GLEMSFORD

8040

ST MARY. Dec W tower and Dec nave arcades (octagonal piers, double-chamfered arches, the N side apparently earlier than the s). Perp aisle walls and windows, chancel chapels, clerestory, and porches. The s aisle, s chapel, s porch, and N chapel have flushwork panelling, the N aisle and N porch have not. Large three-light windows, mostly transomed. s doorway with tiny canopied niches in one arch moulding. Money was left for a s window in 1447, a N window in 1454, N clerestory windows in 1474/5 ('according to the design of the first one newly made in that wall'). Good N aisle roof with carved beams. – FONT. Octagonal. Panelled stem with four small figures. Bowl with two Signs of the Evangelists, head with crown, head with mitre, angel with shield, and Virgin of the Annunciation (?). – SOUTH DOOR. With tracery and a scroll along the edge. – (REREDOS in the s aisle C18. LG)

Several houses deserve mention. In EGREMONT STREET to the SW ANGEL HOUSE, timber-framed, of the C15, with a corner-post with two excellent angel figures, one the Archangel Michael. In BROOK STREET, WNW of the church, Nos. 13–17, also timber-framed but later. The W wing has decorated barge-boards, an oriel window on carved brackets, and a (modern) date 1617. A little to the E from here a SILK MILL, early C19, nine bays wide, two storeys high, and of brick. Finally, less than ¼ m. N of the church, a house dated 1614, picturesque and similar to the Brook Street houses.

GLEVERING HALL

3050

1¼ m. SE of Easton

Built in 1792–4 by *John White*. Enlarged by *Decimus Burton* in 1834–5. Stately house of grey brick, two and a half storeys high

and seven by five bays wide; on three sides the centre bay ver
broad and with tripartite windows. The s front has this middl
bay emphasized yet further by coupled giant pilasters startin
above the ground floor and carrying a pediment. Inside,
staircase starting in one arm and returning in two. Simple
pleasant iron balustrade. The house is used as a store at th
time of writing. The fireplaces are gone and the stucco is i
decay. Adjoining are STABLES of grey brick, the front eleve
windows long with three-bay pediments. Adjoining also th
ORANGERY, no doubt by Burton. This has a glass dome in th
centre on cast iron palm-tree columns. The front is seven bay
long with three-bay portico on Adamish columns.

The grounds were originally laid out by *Repton*. They ar
discussed in his *Sketches* of 1794.

GORLESTON

See The Buildings of England: North-East Norfolk and Norwich

1050

GOSBECK

ST MARY. The nave at its E end has quoins in long and shor
work, a sign of Anglo-Saxon construction. On the N side of th
nave one Norman slit window and a Norman doorway com
pletely unmoulded. The w window is Dec, with reticulate
tracery. The chancel, though over-restored, seems to be of c
1300. s porch tower with flushwork arcading on the battle
ments and with eight pinnacles. – PULPIT. Jacobean in parts.
(SCREEN. Parts of the dado with unusual blank tracery.) –
PLATE. Elizabethan Cup in a tooled leather case; Paten 1728

0060

GREAT ASHFIELD

ALL SAINTS. Finely moulded C13 s doorway. One C13 lance
window in the chancel. The chancel on the whole looks al
C19. Original ogee-arched niche to the l. of the E window
Nave and N aisle Perp. The arcade piers have four semi
octagonal shafts. The capitals are treated as one band. Double
chamfered arches. s porch Perp, of brick with flushwor
panelling. w tower of knapped flint with a spike.* Base-frieze o
flushwork panelling. Dec w window. – PULPIT. On shor
bulbous legs. The body square, not polygonal. One tier of th
familiar Elizabethan short blank arches, a tier with simpl
lozenge panels below. Back panel and tester. On the tester th

* A will of 1460 leaves 6s. 8d. 'Panneto de Asshfeld' – presumably th
tower's pinnacle (ARA).

date 1619. – BENCHES. Many, with poppy-heads and animals on the arms. – PANELLING. Behind the altar, in the style of the pulpit. – COMMUNION RAIL. With twisted balusters, *c.* 1700. – PLATE. Elizabethan Cup; Almsdish 1808.

At CASTLE HILL, ½ m. SW of the church, a large motte with a wet ditch. There appear to be no baileys.

GREAT BARTON

8060

HOLY INNOCENTS. W tower Perp,* big, of knapped flint and stone. Flushwork decoration at the top: quatrefoil frieze and panelled battlements. Late C13 chancel with interesting window details, the E window of three lancet lights with three circles at the top, quatrefoiled far back. N and S windows with plate tracery, a lozenge, quatrefoiled far back. At the E angles polygonal buttresses with obelisk roofs. The priest's doorway has an arch on thin shafts, and to its E a big niche with a heavy gable on plain corbels. The chancel arch inside has friezes of leaves on the two capitals. The PISCINA has an ogee gable. The S aisle has an early C14 E window, and the arcade inside also belongs to that style. Four bays, slender octagonal pier and two circular piers, fleurons on the capitals, moulded arches. Perp N arcade of typical details. Perp N aisle of knapped flint. Perp also the other S aisle windows. Perp clerestory windows, double the number of the arcade bays. The hammerbeam roof in the nave is nothing special. – BENCHES. With poppy-heads and seated animals on the arms. Traceried ends. – STAINED GLASS. In the N aisle Perp canopies.

GREAT BEALINGS

2040

ST MARY. W tower with some flushwork decoration on buttresses and battlements. The chancel mostly C19. N porch of brick with polygonal buttresses. On the base flushwork of brick and flint. The inscription above the entrance refers to Thomas Seckford, i.e. *c.* 1520 (cf. Seckford Hall and Woodbridge). – FONT. Octagonal, of Purbeck marble, with two shallow blank pointed arches to each side. – PULPIT. Jacobean, with back panel and tester. – BENCHES. With poppy-heads and animals, birds and human figures both facing E and facing the gangways. – NORTH DOOR. With tracery and three small figures (a rarity).

* A will of 1440 leaves money to the making of the new tower on condition that within a year of the testator's death the parishioners ... prepare the material for this work. Another will of 1449 leaves money to the tower (ARA).

–STAINED GLASS. W window by *H. Hughes*, 1879; one chancel
S window by *Mayer* of Munich, *c.* 1886; one chancel N window
by *Ward & Hughes*, 1882. – PLATE. Elizabethan Cup; Flagon
and two Patens 1799. – MONUMENTS. Sir Thomas Seckford
† 1575 and wife, put up in 1583. No effigies. Coat of arms with
florid surround, flanked by coupled Roman Doric pilasters and
surmounted by a pediment. – John Clenche † 1628. Two
frontal busts, praying. The kneeling children in profile in the
'predella'.

BEALINGS HOUSE, ¾ m. E. Red brick, mid-Georgian. Of seven
bays and two storeys. Parapet and pitched roof. Doorway with
Ionic columns and pediment.

SECKFORD HALL. *See* p. 414.

¹⁰⁵⁰   GREAT BLAKENHAM

ST MARY. Norman probably the unbuttressed W tower in its
lower parts and Norman certainly the nave – see the two remaining S windows, the simple S doorway, and the simple
blocked N doorway. Chancel E.E. with three stepped separated
lancet windows at the E end and one small S window. (Late C12
PISCINA. LG) C14 the upper parts of the tower. C15 the
timber S porch. The single-framed rafter roofs of nave and
chancel are assigned by Cautley to the C13. – FONT. Octagonal,
Perp, with panels decorated by various foiled motifs, framing
emblems of the Passion. – PULPIT. Jacobean, with tester. –
MONUMENT. Richard Swift † 1645. The rhymed inscription
referring to his relations with Russia and Sweden deserves to
be read.

GIPPING WEIR, a little E of the church. Built about 1800. Grey
brick, three widely spaced bays, two storeys, low hipped roof.
Nice doorway.

⁶⁰⁵⁰   GREAT BRADLEY

ST MARY. Late Norman S doorway with spiral-fluted shafts,
decorated capitals, and several zigzags in the arch. The tympanum decoration has disappeared. Is this later than the
simpler N doorway with scalloped capitals to the shafts? Perhaps not necessarily so. Late Norman also the chancel arch with
imposts with a slight notch between the vertical and the
diagonal member. The arch is pointed but has only one slight
chamfer. Chancel in its present form mostly *c.* 1300; shortened in the C18. One bay of fine SEDILIA remains, but the
chancel is over-restored. Perp W tower. On the first set of set-

offs of the buttresses carved animals and arms. Inside a fireplace and an elementary smoke-outlet in the wall with an odd
baffle in front. The SE stair-turret is higher than the tower.
Early Tudor s porch of brick with a stepped gable containing
six niches. Brick porch windows. – FONT. Octagonal, Perp. –
PULPIT. An C18 two-decker. – PLATE. Paten 1684; Cup 1743;
Cup 1809.

(GREAT BRADLEY HALL. C17 and good C19. LG)

GREAT BRICETT

ST MARY AND ST LAURENCE. The church is a fragment of a
church of Augustinian Canons. The priory was founded
c. 1115 by Ralph Fitz-Brian but later became a cell of Saint-
Léonard near Limoges. What remains is a long plain oblong.
But the church had transepts and these had E apses. Their
existence has been proved by excavation, and a main E apse
can be surmised with certainty. That was the plan in the C12.
It is assumed however that in 1110 no transepts were yet envisaged. Towards the end of the C12 the E end was made
straight and second transepts were built to its N and S. Their
responds and arches are still visible in the walls. Of the early
transepts only traces can be detected. The only impressive
Norman piece is the N doorway with one order of shafts,
decorated but defaced, an inner order of jambs and one with
close decoration, zigzag in the arch, and a partly illegible
inscription down the jambs. One blocked Norman slit window
in the N wall, one taller round-arched window in the S wall.
Other windows of c. 1300. The big five-light E window with
flowing tracery is Dec. In fact it is said to date from 1868, but
it is most probably a copy of what was there before. Tie-beam
roof with crown-posts and four-way struts. – FONT. Square,
Norman, with intersected arches on two sides, trefoil arches on
columns on the third, and very oddly pointed-trefoil arches on
the fourth. – PULPIT. A very unusual design; probably Victorian. – STAINED GLASS. Fine figures of the four Evangelists,
early C14; from the tracery of the E window. – PLATE. Elizabethan Cup.

As a token of the domestic quarters of the priory a farmhouse
immediately adjoins the church. It incorporates part of the W
range of the residential buildings, and in it, in 1956, some
structural woodwork of the highest interest was discovered:
a wall with bold cross-bracing and at its foot four ARCHED
DOORWAYS of timber, three of the same size and a smaller

one with dog-tooth ornament on jambs and arch. That alone
dates the work to some time before 1300. The other arches have
shafts, but the arch mouldings have unfortunately been hacked
off. (Cf. Purton Green Farm, Stansfield, p. 436.)

WINDMILL. A smock-mill, now power-driven.

GREAT CORNARD

8040

The village near which Gainsborough painted Cornard Wood
is now more or less a suburb of Sudbury.

ST ANDREW. Flint. C14 W tower. It has diagonally placed niches
l. and r. of the W window and carries a shingled spire. C16
brick stair-turret. The S aisle is of 1887. Low N arcade with
piers of Sudbury type. – FONT. Simple, octagonal, Perp. –
PLATE. Paten 1710.

ABBAS HALL. *See* p. 69.

GREAT FINBOROUGH

0050

ST ANDREW. 1874–7 by *R. M. Phipson*. An expensive building
in the grounds of the Hall. In the style of the district (e.g.
aisleless), except that the W tower is given a tall octagonal upper
part and a needle spire. – PLATE. Paten *c.* 1680; Cup 1733. –
MONUMENTS. Charlton Wollaston † 1729. Over-lifesize
putto unrolling a scroll. – From another monument remain
three big putti hanging a garland round an urn with the profile
head of a lady. – Roger Pettiward † 1833. By *Sir R. Westmacott*.
Large relief of the Good Samaritan.

FINBOROUGH HALL. 1795 by *F. Sandys*. Front with a big bow
window and a colonnade of six Tuscan columns running round
it. Side with four giant Tuscan columns, the middle interstice
being wider than the others. Far-projecting eaves (which is
also a 'Tuscan', i.e. Etruscan, motif). Large staircase hall, the
stairway with a wrought-iron balustrade.

GREAT GLEMHAM

3060

ALL SAINTS. Perp W tower with flushwork panelling on buttresses and battlements. Nave and chancel. The chancel probably of *c.* 1300; see the broad lancets, one N, one S. Priest's
doorway, early C16, of brick. N porch of knapped flint with a
little panelling decoration and a niche over the entrance. The
S aisle looks as if it might be a C19 addition. Extensive repairs
are recorded for 1878. In the N wall of the nave the rood-loft
doorway. It has pretty fleuron decoration with some of the
old colour. Fine roof with arched braces to the ridge. Bosses at

the chief intersections. Pendant bosses along the ridge. Decorated wall-plate. Arched braces also in the w–e direction between the wall-posts. – FONT. Tall step with quatrefoil decoration. Stem with four lilies in vases. Bowl with the Seven Sacraments and the Crucifixion. Rayed backgrounds. A butterfly headdress dates the work as late C15. The carving was originally apparently specially animated. – STAINED GLASS. Fragments in the chancel windows. – PLATE. Elizabethan Cup.

GLEMHAM HOUSE. Built in 1814. Of grey brick, the garden front five bays and two storeys. Tripartite doorway and broad, no doubt originally also tripartite, window over. On the entrance side round the corner one-storeyed Ionic porch with two pillars and two columns. Spacious staircase hall with a fine plaster vault and a circular glazed lantern. Wide staircase with rather heavy wrought iron handrail. (Also other good interiors.) The STABLES and the octagonal DOVECOTE are of red brick. They lie on the w boundary of the grounds. The grounds were originally laid out by *Humphry Repton*. They appear in his *Theory* as early as 1803.

GREAT LIVERMERE

8070

ST PETER. The w tower stands only to roof-height. Above that a weatherboarded top with pyramid roof. The stone parts are Dec, see the w window and the tower arch. Dec also the chancel in its present form, though blocked lancet windows tell of an earlier, C13, state. Dec E window of three lights. Four-centred arch. The tracery consists of arch-heads upon the three arch-heads of the lights and in the two main shapes thus produced two small cusped reticulation motifs one below the other. Inside, niches l. and r. of the window. The nave windows are Dec too, though the simple N doorway seems to be of *c.* 1200. A large niche inside, in the N wall, Perp. Also the outline of a Perp Easter Sepulchre in the chancel N wall. The chancel roof has beautifully carved broad wall-plates with various leaf and tracery patterns. – FONT. Octagonal, Perp, with tracery patterns. – PULPIT. A three-decker of the rare date *c.* 1700; with acanthus foliage. – BENCHES. One end with elaborate tracery. Three later ones with very coarse, under-developed poppy-heads. One of them is dated 1601. – SCREEN. With broad one-light divisions and ogee tops. – COMMUNION RAIL. Three-sided. Very thin, twisted balusters; Georgian. – WALL PAINTING. Two standing C14 figures, perhaps part of the story of the Three Quick and the Three Dead (nave N wall).

Also a Noli me tangere, much faded (nave s wall), and some scroll-work (chancel s wall). – PLATE. Paten c. 1690; Cup 1809; Almsdish 1823.

GREAT SAXHAM

ST ANDREW. Rebuilt in 1798, and gothicized since. The tower and the s porch are medieval, the tower below perhaps pre-Perp, the front Perp.* In addition two humble Norman doorways were preserved, N and s. – FONT. Octagonal, Perp, simple. – PULPIT. Jacobean with two tiers of the usual blank arches. – BENCHES. Some, with poppy-heads. – STAINED GLASS. In the E window some extremely good German early c16 glass, mixed up with much that seems Flemish and Swiss. Swiss glass of minor value in the w window. – MONUMENT. Monument and brass to John Eldred, 1632, a merchant who, as can be read in the inscriptions, had travelled to Syria, Arabia, Egypt, and – as it is called – Babilon. The monument has a frontal bust in a circular niche and no date of death inscribed. The brass is of the traditional medieval composition.

HALL. Begun after a fire in 1779, possibly to designs by the owner, *Hutchison Mure*,‡ but not completed till 1798 (by *Joseph Patience Jun.*). The front probably somewhat altered later. Two-storeyed, rendered. Centre with a portico of four giant columns with Adam-style capitals and a pediment with palm-branches and a coat of arms. To the l. and r. one recessed bay and then a wider angle bay with attached pairs of one pier and one column. Tripartite window on the ground floor between them. The window pediments look all Early Victorian, and that is probably the date of the asymmetrical addition on the l. Fine staircase with classical balustrade of wrought iron; not big. (Three vestibules behind the portico. Dome of the octagonal former Music Room with late c18 paintings.)

(TEMPLE. Moorish Gothic, polygonal, with thin shafts and low ogee arches. Balustrade with obelisks; small dome. – The TEA HOUSE is polygonal and has four Tuscan porches. – Polygonal LODGE with four lower arms and intermittent rocky rustication (NMR). The grounds are said to have been embellished by *Capability Brown*.)

* A will of 1441 gives money for work on the tower (ARA).

‡ Mr Norman Scarfe (*Suffolk Institute of Archaeology, Proceedings*, vol. 26, part 3) has assembled evidence which convincingly suggests that the house is not by *Robert Adam*, as had previously been thought.

GREAT THURLOW

6050

ALL SAINTS. The chancel is structurally Norman; see the nook-shafts at the E end. But the impression of the church is entirely Perp. W tower with higher stair-turret and a pretty lead spire-let. The arcade has lozenge-shaped piers, the arches die into them. – FONT. Square, with pairs of blank arches of curious detail, perhaps C17 imitation Norman. – PULPIT. Jacobean. – SCREENS. The dado of the Perp rood screen now stands against the E wall of the chancel. – Screen to the S chapel; only the top beams remain. Dated 1610. – TOWER SCREEN. Jacobean or mid-C17, with balustrade. – (Nice medieval lattice-frame door with good ring-handle. S. E. Rigold) – PLATE. Cup and Paten, the cup 1567; Paten 1632. – BRASSES. Knight and Lady, c. 1460, 2 ft figures; Knight and Lady and children, c. 1530, 18 in. figures; headless Lady, c. 1460, 1 ft 7 in. figure (in safe).*

HALL. A handsome mid-Georgian building, recently well restored and altered. It is now plastered but originally had its red brick exposed. Original W front of five bays with slightly projecting three-bay centre with giant Ionic pilasters and pediment. The N front is not in its original state. Fine staircase with three turned balusters to each tread and carved tread-ends. Nice late C18 plasterwork.

BRIDGE. With simple but attractive cast-iron balustrade, probably c. 1830.

GREAT WALDINGFIELD

9040

ST LAWRENCE. (Built by John Appleton at the end of the C14. LG) Perp, with some flushwork decoration, chiefly of a chequer-board pattern. W tower with diagonal buttresses of four set-offs. Nave and aisle. Clerestory with single, not double windows. Inscription on the S side in the battlements: 'Pray for the (soul)' – probably of John Appleton. S porch with flushwork. Its entrance and the S doorway have fleurons in the jambs and arches. The N porch is presumably of the restoration of 1827–9. The chancel was rebuilt in 1866–9 by *Butterfield*. Interior with tall arcades. Piers with four shafts and four small hollows. – FONT. Octagonal, Perp, with heavy quatrefoils. – BENCH ENDS. With poppy-heads. – COMMUNION RAIL. From St Michael Cornhill in the City of London. With twisted balusters, and enriched with leaf and garlands. Probably by *William*

* Much mid–C20 refurnishing, so Mr McHardy tells me.

Cleere c. 1670–5. – STAINED GLASS. The E and W windows by *Gibbs*, 1869 and 1877; a N aisle window by *Westlake*, 1877, two in the N aisle by *Lavers*, 1885 and 1887, and one in the S aisle, 1882, by the same. – PLATE. Elizabethan Cup, repaired 1618; Almsdish 1701.

HIGH TREES, close to the church, with a C16 chimneystack with octagonal star-topped chimneys.

Better still the C16 chimneystack at WHITE HALL, 1 m. SW.

(BABERGH HALL, ½ m. NW. 'A fine brick mansion.' LG)

GREAT WELNETHAM *see* GREAT WHELNETHAM

GREAT WENHAM

0030

ST JOHN. Fine Perp W tower with flushwork decoration on base and buttresses. The rest alas plastered. Early C14 chancel with N and S windows which are lancets or have Y-tracery. Three stepped lancets at the E end with pointed trefoiled heads. On the N side a low-side window. – TILES. Many in the chancel, probably of the C15. – HELMET etc. of the East family.

WENHAM PLACE. Interesting remains of a brick mansion of the time of Henry VIII. One projecting wing survives with dark blue diapering, polygonal angle buttresses, gable, and pinnacles. Mullioned and transomed brick windows with arched lights. Part of the walls of the other wing can also be seen, and, in addition, the hall fireplace.

(WENHAM HILL FARM. Timber-framed and plastered. With gables and groups of polygonal chimneys. NMR)

(PRIORY FARM. Timber-framed and plastered. With gables and a plaster ceiling with arabesque scrolls. NMR)

GREAT WHELNETHAM

8050

ST THOMAS A BECKET. Small. Nave and chancel and N aisle. Weatherboarded bell-turret of 1749. The chancel is C13 with N lancets, and finely if simply detailed SEDILIA and PISCINA. The nave perhaps of the same date. Circular, quatrefoiled W window. The N aisle is Dec. Two-bay arcade. Tiny clerestory.* – FONT. Perp, octagonal. – PULPIT. With panels of *c.* 1500. – STAINED GLASS. Plenty of fragments in the chancel SE window. – PLATE. Cup 1658; Almsdish 1691; Flagon 1717.

(HALL. C16; refaced C18. Timber-framed. Five bays wide. DOE. With a complicated system of moats. LG)

* A will proved in 1453 leaves money towards the building of the tower (ARA).

GREAT WRATTING

ST MARY. Septaria and flint. Nave and chancel and w tower, its top of brick. Nice Perp s doorway. Good E.E. chancel with lancet windows. SEDILIA and PISCINA triple-shafted. The corbels under the chancel arch originally supported the rood beam. – PLATE. Cup 1662; Almsdish 1676.

(WEATHERCOCK COTTAGE. A mid-C19 house, built on a cruciform plan for three widows, with a shared kitchen. Dickinson)

GRIMSTONE END see PAKENHAM

GROTON

ST BARTHOLOMEW.* Chancel E window with reticulated tracery; Dec. The w tower contemporary or a little earlier. Otherwise Perp. Nave and clerestory, aisles, s porch. All embattled except for the chancel. Arcade of four bays. Oddly shaped piers with polygonal shafts, those to the nave without capitals, those to the arch openings with capitals. – PLATE. Cup and Cover 1726; Almsdish 1729.

MOTTE. In Groton Park is a motte called Pytches Mount.

GROVE FARMHOUSE see UFFORD

GRUNDISBURGH

ST MARY. S porch tower of 1751–2. Red brick, with angle pilasters, short Doric below, very elongated Doric above. Arched windows; parapet. The chancel is of the late C13, as shown by the PISCINA with dog-tooth decoration and the mouldings of the chancel arch. Dec s aisle, see the arcade (octagonal piers, double-chamfered arches) and the windows. Dec also the N doorway of the nave. The nave windows are Perp, and Perp too is the fine s chapel. Parapet with shields in the battlements and inscription referring to 1527 and Thomas Walle, salter of London, and his wife. Priest's doorway set in the buttress, as at St Stephen Ipswich and at Trunch Norfolk. Perp clerestory of nine closely-set windows. A broad band of flushwork initials, etc., connects them. Perp finally the splendid nave roof, one of the most beautiful in Suffolk. It is a double-hammerbeam roof: the upper hammerbeams end on pendant posts, the lower ones have posts resting on them. Angels against the foot of the arched braces and against the lower hammerbeams. Kingposts, again with small angel figures, on the collars. Short arched braces also connect the

* The dedication is given as St Margaret in a will of 1467 (ARA).

wall-posts in a w–e direction. Richly decorated wall-plate. Good roofs in the s aisle and s chapel too. In the s chapel the arched braces stand on angel corbels of stone. – FONT. On three steps, the upper two with quatrefoil friezes. Against the stem four lions. Against the bowl four lions and four angels, their heads just peeping out behind the shields they hold. – SCREEN. Good rood screen with one-light divisions. The dado of the s chapel screen has the Initials of Christ painted on as a repeat ornament. The upper parts simple. – BENCHES. A few with traceried ends, poppy-heads, and figures. – PAINTING. St Christopher; N wall. Further E on the N wall two C13 figures, discovered recently. – PLATE. Cup perhaps Elizabethan; Cup and Paten 1668; Almsdish 1676. – MONUMENT. Sir Charles Blois † 1738. No effigy. Big inscription tablet with pilasters l. and r. with cherubs' heads instead of, or in front of, the capitals. On top a trumpeting putto.

The church lies in a good position N of the green, but its situation is spoilt by the Victorian school immediately to its w and impaired by the War Memorial, which is a little too grand for the village and the place in front of the church.

BAST'S is a very fine house of c. 1520, a little E of the church, timber-framed but with brick (with dark blue diapering) at two of its corners. Diagonal corner posts and two overhangs. On the NW and SW posts the initials of the Thomas Walle for whom the house was built, and a salt-cellar, because, as has already been said, he was a salter.

GRUNDISBURGH HALL. Of c. 1500, though externally partly early C19 and partly recent neo-Tudor. Only the three gables on the early C19 front betray that something earlier lies behind. (Pre-Reformation hall inside. P.S.I.A., XVIII, 157)

BRIDGE FARMHOUSE, 1 m. SE. With a stepped Tudor gable and a Georgian front.

5090

GUNTON

ST PETER. Norman round tower, ivy-hung at the time of writing. Nave and chancel in one, Norman and renewed early in the C14, it seems. Norman N doorway with two orders of colonnettes with block capitals and scalloped capitals. The arch with one zigzag and one roll moulding. Norman also the s doorway, which has altered jambs and only one incised zigzag in the arch. One Norman N window. – PLATE. Cup 1660; Paten 1670.

HACHESTON

ALL SAINTS. Norman one window in the chancel and the N doorway with one order of colonnettes and some nailhead decoration. W tower with niches on the diagonal buttresses. Nave and chancel with windows of *c.* 1300 and Perp windows. S aisle and attached S porch Late Perp. The S arcade is Perp too. Hammerbeam roof in the nave. In the aisle roof figures on the wall-posts. – FONT. Badly preserved stem. It had four lions and four Wild Men. Against the bowl the Signs of the four Evangelists and four angels. – PULPIT. Jacobean. – BENCHES. Restored set with traceried ends with poppy-heads. The animals on the arms cut off. A strip of twisted leaf ornament on the backs. – SCREEN. Painted dado; now by the font. The figures seem to be of the early C15. – ROOD BEAM. Moulded and embattled. The posts on it presuppose a former tympanum. – SCULPTURE. Fragment of an alabaster panel of the Incredulity of St Thomas. – STAINED GLASS. E window by *Kempe & Tower, c.* 1920. – PLATE. Elizabethan Cup; Almsdish 1808.

In the village street, facing each other, the former QUEEN'S HEAD, with some minor plasterwork of *c.* 1600 in ceilings, and WISTARIA COTTAGE and its neighbour, a specially pretty timber-framed house.

THE GABLES, N of the church, has a late C15 oriel sill with lion and unicorn.

A ROMANO–BRITISH KILN producing indented beakers of plain red ware was found in 1964 on BRIDGE FARM, about 2¼ m. S of Hacheston, and two superimposed double-ended kilns producing cooking pots of C3–4 type were excavated the following year. Evidence for iron- and bronze-working was also found.

HADLEIGH

ST MARY. The church is 163 ft long and has a tower which is crowned by a lead spire, 135 ft high. Externally mostly Perp, except for the tower, which is clearly of the early C14. To the l. and r. of the bell-openings, which have three-light intersected tracery, are circular openings. Of the C14 also a tomb recess in the S aisle (ogee arch cusped); so the S aisle wall is also of that period. There may be more of it (e.g. the chancel walls) but the windows are Perp, large in the aisles, larger still in the E end, where three windows look down Church Street, smaller, in

pairs of two of two lights, in the nave clerestory (renewed). At
the E end to the N a two-storeyed vestry, vaulted below. S
porch of two bays with side windows and three niches above
the entrance. The porch was originally vaulted and had an
upper floor. Arcade of five wide bays. The piers have polygonal
shafts, carrying capitals only towards the arch openings. The
clerestory windows are not above the apexes of the arches, but
above the spandrels. Chancel arch and two-bay arcades of the
chancel chapels of the same type. In the chancel N wall an
EASTER SEPULCHRE, simple, Late Perp, panelled above the
arch. – FONT. Octagonal with finely detailed blank niches, two
to each side, with feigned rib-vaults. – FONT COVER by *Charles
Spooner*, 1925. – SCREENS. Perp, to the N and S chapels. –
BENCH END in the chancel with a representation which has
been interpreted as the wolf finding the head of St Edmund.*
– The SOUTH DOOR has tracery and a border of quatrefoils. –
ORGAN CASE. A fine large piece of the early C18, brought in
1738 from Donyland Hall (Essex). – STAINED GLASS. Odd
bits in the N chapel E window. – S chapel E window (Christ and
the Children) by *Hedgeland*, 1857, very Nazarene. – E window
by *Ward & Hughes*. – PLATE. All silver-gilt: Paten 1685;
Paten 1730; Cup and two Flagons 1745; Paten 1792.‡ –
MONUMENTS. Three brasses of 1593–1637. – Sarah Johnson
† 1793 by *Regnart*. With two putti by an urn. – First World
War Memorial. By *Charles Spooner*. – Dean Carter † 1935.
Tablet by *Eric Gill* (s chapel).

CHURCHYARD. The church lies on a lawn, and to the S and W
sides of this stand the most spectacular buildings of Hadleigh.

48a DEANERY TOWER, W of the church. Of the palace built by
Archdeacon Pykenham in 1495 only the gatehouse survives,
a splendid brick building with polygonal turrets to the entrance
and exit sides, the latter starting on corbels. Four-centred
archway. The middle part is three-storeyed, the higher turrets
have six stages. In the middle on the first floor oriel windows
with a canopy on four trefoiled arches. The same trefoiled
arches in pairs form the top of each of the panels into which the
turrets are divided. Battlements on centre and turrets, on the
centres with pinnacles in the middle. The motifs are similar to
those used in the far more monumental gatehouse of Oxburgh
in Norfolk (1482). The ornate chimneys are of *c.* 1830 and of

* Mr E. J. Carter doubts this, pointing out that the hind feet are cloven.
‡ Hadleigh possesses, exposed on the E side of the tower, the earliest
church BELL in Suffolk, probably of the late C13.

1960. In the first-floor room inside a painting of the church, by a local artist, *Benjamin Coleman*, dated 1629. The room was panelled in 1730. To the l. of the tower first a majestic lime tree and then, in a contemporary wall, two small stone archways, apparently earlier than the tower. These come from a former second s porch further E than the other. To the r. of the tower the DEANERY, also brick, simple imitation Tudor of 1831, enlarged in 1841. Built with the use of some old materials. Mr Carter tells me that to the best of his memory the building was designed by *William Whewell*, Master of Trinity College, Cambridge. It contains two fine C18 chimneypieces and doorways surmounted by classical entablatures. These were transferred from the old house.

GUILDHALL, to the s of the churchyard. Timber-framed. Of two parts, both C15. The centre is of three storeys, with two overhangs. On the ground floor the characteristic thin buttress posts. To the l. of this the Long Room, the former guildhall proper. It is on the first floor. The ground floor was originally almshouses.* To the E of the churchyard CHURCH STREET starts (with good houses on the N side, especially the RED HOUSE) and leads to the main crossroads of Hadleigh.

We must explore in the three other directions, and first to the E down GEORGE STREET. Here the BAPTIST CHAPEL of 1830, red brick, of two storeys, with the windows set in blank giant arches and a doorway with Tuscan pilasters. Then Nos. 22–26, a fine timber-framed group of *c.* 1500, No. 28 with an C18 front but exposed timber-framing at the back, No. 32 with a seven-bay Georgian brick front (two storeys, parapet, porch on columns), and Nos. 44–48, an Elizabethan brick house with two front gables, the l. one with a projecting stair-turret. Under the r. one six-light window. After that opposite, No. 109, three-bay, white brick, with a pretty Late Georgian doorcase. At the end the PYKENHAM ALMSHOUSES of 1807, but with a timber-framed C15 chapel (rebuilt).‡

Back to the main crossing and s along the HIGH STREET. First Nos. 46–48 with some humble pargetting on the front, but inside a good early C17 plaster ceiling and some contemporary wall paintings. Then the WHITE LION, with a widely spaced seven-bay front of white brick. Its neighbour is No. 40, an early C19 house of white brick with a bow window and in front

---

* A deed of 1438 refers to the Markethouse, with almshouses beneath, as being newly built (ARA).

‡ PLATE. Cup of 1756.

of the whole façade a Tuscan six-column colonnade. These two houses face towards the Market Place.

In the MARKET PLACE at the w end a nice early C19 house of white brick, two and a half storeys high, with three widely-spaced windows and a one-bay pediment. To its r. across the square a pair of three-bay houses with two and a half storeys and pedimented doorways. Then a passageway to the w towards the church. After that the CORN EXCHANGE of 1813 (altered 1895) with a broad low portico of Tuscan columns and lantern lighting. Then the former TOWN HALL of 1851, red and yellow brick, round-arched like a Nonconformist chapel, i.e. with a five-bay front, with doorways in the first and the last bays, and windows higher up between. The middle window is Venetian. Opposite the CONGREGATIONAL CHURCH of 1832, brick with upper arched windows and a broad heavy Grecian porch below. Back into the HIGH STREET and on to the s. CONISTON HOUSE, No. 23, is white brick, early C19. Then DUKE STREET with more worth-while houses and at its end TOPPESFIELD BRIDGE, a medieval three-arch bridge of brick with brick parapet. The arches are ribbed. Back again to the HIGH STREET. No. 15 is a good example of the style of c. 1830 (white brick, Tuscan doorway *in antis*), and No. 2 a mid-C18 example (five widely-spaced bays, red brick, doorway with broken pediment).

From the end of the High Street to the E is the STATION, 1847, and a very elementary piece of railway architecture. Red and yellow brick, round-arched windows, including the Venetian type. No platform canopy, only a canopy over the door towards the platform.

The s continuation of the High Street is BENTON STREET. Nos. 31–35 is timber-framed, but has a nice Georgian bay with old casements on the ground floor. No. 43 has a Georgian-Gothic doorcase. Triple shafts with shaft-rings instead of columns. Nos. 69–81 is a good group of timber-framed houses. Then opposite, No. 84, with a Gothic Venetian window. No. 92 has a richly decorated C17 front with oriels on carved brackets, carved eaves brackets, and some decayed pargetting. Nos. 110–118 the RAVEN ALMSHOUSES of c. 1636. Then PRIORY FARM (with an old roof (crown-post?) truss inside).

Finally BENTON END FARMHOUSE, with an C18 front and a timber-framed back wing. At the l. end of the front brick gable on polygonal angle shafts.

Now from the main crossing to the N, again along HIGH STREET.

There is here first the finest house in the street, Nos. 62–66, two-storeyed, with a date 1676 in a window pane. The upper storey has six times repeated the motif of Sparrowe's House, Ipswich, the rectangular window with a Venetian window set in and outlined by casements. Deep carved eaves. The ground floor originally projected. (Good staircase.)

Then a look into QUEEN STREET, which runs to the churchyard, a nice unified composition of *c.* 1838. White brick. The last houses l. and r. before the churchyard are higher and stand more closely together. The narrowing is stressed by rounded corners and rounded windows on the ground floor.

Then on the E side ANGEL STREET, again with several attractive timber-framed houses, especially Nos. 63–79 and Nos. 85–99. At the top a fine red-brick C16 BARN.

From the end of the High Street BRIDGE STREET runs W and continues the other side of the bridge. The best houses are No. 15, timber-framed, with overhang and buttress-posts on the ground floor, No. 21, Early Georgian, of red and blue brick (the blue bricks are all headers) with a nice doorway and a central segment-headed window, and the WHITE HART with an exposed timber wing at the back.

TOWN HOUSE FARM. A ROMANO-BRITISH BUILDING was found in 1954 just N of the railway line. It included a hypocaust dated by remanent magnetism to the late C2–3 A.D.

HALESWORTH

3070

ST MARY. All Perp. A large town church, large partly because of the Victorian additions: outer S aisle and S porch 1868, outer N chapel 1863, chancel arch 1889. W tower, completed *c.* 1430. It replaced a round tower the foundations of which were found inside the present church near the font. W doorway with shields in an arch moulding. Battlements with flushwork panelling and quatrefoils. N porch with flushwork-panelled front, including two quatrefoil friezes. Spandrels of the entrance with shields showing the emblems of the Passion and the Trinity. Inside evidence of the pre-Perp church. The arcades are C14 (e.g. octagonal piers, double-hollow-chamfered arches), and the N arch of a former transeptal chapel is also preserved. Perp S chapel with an ornate arch decorated in several orders with fleurons, in one order towards the chapel also down the jambs. Late Perp doorway from the chancel into the vestry. Two orders with fleurons in jambs and arch, a lion at the apex.

An inscription refers to Thomas Clement and his wife. It dates the doorway c. 1506. The priest's doorway opposite also has shields as decoration of jambs and arch. – FONT. Octagonal, with four lions and four Wild Men against the stem, the four Signs of the Evangelists and four angels with shields against the bowl. Against the step a quatrefoil frieze. – SCULPTURE. Below the chancel piscina some fragments of an Anglo-Saxon frieze fitted together. Hands gripping leaf trails. The suggested date is the later C9. – PLATE. Two Cups and Paten 1567; Paten 1714; Flagon and Almsdishes 1822. – BRASSES. John Everard † 1476, demi-figure, 8 in. long (tower arch). – Lady of c. 1580 and children; head and shoulders only; palimpsest of a Flemish brass of a Civilian of c. 1530 (S aisle E). – MONUMENTS. Two Wedgwood medallions to Sir William and Sir Joseph Hooker, the first directors of Kew Gardens (cf. Kew Church; vestry). – CURIOSUM. A wooden Collecting Shoe with a handle.

There is nothing of special architectural interest at Halesworth. What may be picked out is the following. In the MARKET PLACE, which one reaches through a passage N of the church, the SOCIAL CLUB, formerly an inn, Elizabethan, with two original mullioned and transomed windows, and No. 10, a Georgian house of five wide bays with arched doorway and the window above it set in a blank segment-headed arch. The Market Place has an odd shape and consists really of two separate parts. On the N side, which the two have in common, is No. 27 with a wooden archway on the l. the spandrels of which are carved. Behind the archway two older posts also with carving. Turning W from here in CHEDISTON ROAD No. 124 has a nice bowed Georgian shop-window.

Turning E one is at the real hub of the little town, a triangle from which streets also issue to the N and S. To the S along the churchyard the GOTHIC HOUSE, which has a very odd Jacobean porch, canted, on thick balusters with pendant arches and some ornament. This faces the E end of the church. Facing the S side of the church the CARY ALMSHOUSES, founded in 1686, brick, with gable-ends consisting of a vertical, then a concave quadrant, and then a normal gable. One-storeyed and of no distinction.

From the triangle N leads the street called THOROUGHFARE. In it at once a pair of red Georgian houses, five plus four bays, with parapets. Then the ANGEL HOTEL, of seven bays and with a pedimented doorway with Doric pilasters. No. 6 is timber-framed and has an overhanging upper floor. The bressumer is carved with two big lions and a shield, to their l. Ganymede, to their r. a fox with a basket, a monkey, and a cat (?). The continuation of Thoroughfare is Bridge Street, and from this, past the bridge, QUAY STREET turns off, where, opposite the CONGREGATIONAL CHURCH of 1836, is THE MALTINGS, a very picturesque group of buildings round a courtyard. The little quay at the back still exists under a wide archway. (On a keystone adjoining Creek Side the date 1792. DOE) The manager's pretty house also faces the courtyard. Yet further out in HALTON ROAD is CASTLE HOUSE (built in 1727 and refronted and) dated 1810. No castle airs. Red brick, one-bay three-storeyed centre. Tripartite doorway with segmental arch. The doorway and windows all embraced by a giant blank arch. One-bay, two-storey wings and one-bay, one-storey attachments.

(Miss Nancy Matthews has drawn my attention to THE OLD RECTORY, in Rectory Road, timber-framed, brick-nogged, and plastered. The oldest parts are C16 and C17, with C18 and modern alterations.)

PATRICK STEAD HOSPITAL. By *H. Hall* of London, 1881. In the Elizabethan style.

HARDWICK HOUSE

8060

1½ m. s of Bury St Edmunds

Nothing of the house is left, except an over-lifesize STATUE of Hercules with his club over his shoulder.

HARGRAVE

7060

ST EDMUND. Plain Tudor brick tower with buttresses and a Perp stone window. Nave and chancel. The s doorway Transitional and very simple. The chancel windows E.E. but all C19. Humble N aisle of 1869. – SCREEN. Perp, rather raw; the top parts must have been odd. (On the E face carvings of a dragon, a fox, fishes, a unicorn, etc. Carved rood beam above. LG) – PLATE. Cup 1663.

HARKSTEAD

1030

ST MARY. The church lies all alone, a perfect Constable picture. Flint and septaria, mainly C14, but on the one hand over-restored (chancel and s aisle look all new), and on the other evidence of a much earlier date. In the nave on the N side Norman windows and a simple blocked Norman doorway.

The best piece of the C14 is the Easter Sepulchre, with buttresses, crocketed gable, and finial, probably *c.* 1340. Mid C14 could also be the date of the S arcade, with octagonal piers and double-chamfered arches. Mid C14 too the W tower with its splendid tall three-light W window. Crenellated transom and tracery based on reticulation motifs. At the base of the W tower quatrefoil and tracery panels in stone. The battlements renewed in brick. – (FONT. C15. With emblems of the Apostles. LG) – REREDOS. 1875 by *Powell's*, of tiles and mosaic. – WALL PAINTING in the jamb of one of the Norman windows. C13 figure with outstretched hands. – PLATE. Cup 1731.

HARLESTON

0060

ST AUGUSTINE. Norman nave. Plain Norman S doorway and fragment of the N doorway. C13 chancel with one remaining S lancet. In the nave also a lancet. The W front all of 1860 with its C18-looking fenestration and its very Victorian bell-turret. – SCREEN. An interesting early or mid C14 piece, still with shafts instead of mullions. In the spandrels between the ogee arches circles with three mouchettes. – PLATE. Cup 1754.

HARTEST

8050

ALL SAINTS. Nicely placed in a dip. All Perp, unless the arcades with octagonal piers and double-chamfered arches are earlier. They are certainly earlier than the arches into the chapels. W tower much repaired with brick. N porch of knapped squared flint, over-restored. Three niches over the entrance, and shields with initials l. and r. – PULPIT. Jacobean, good, with two tiers of the usual short blank arches. – PLATE. Cup perhaps Elizabethan; Paten 1710. – MONUMENT. Lt. Harrington, R.N., † 1812. By *Henry Westmacott*. An anchor and, hanging from its top, a ship's sail.

Large green by the church, with a number of nice houses, especially the CROWN INN. (On the E side of the green an attractive Late Georgian CHAPEL, stuccoed, and with round-headed windows.)

(CHADACRE AGRICULTURAL INSTITUTE, 1¼ m. E. The original building was erected as a private house in 1834.)

HASKETON

2050

ST ANDREW. Norman round tower remodelled and provided with an octagonal top *c.* 1300. Parts of a Norman S window in the nave. Nave and chancel were also remodelled *c.* 1300 (s doorway, windows). – FONT. Octagonal. On the bowl four flowers and four angels with the shields of the Brews, Ufford, Shardelow, and Stapleton families. – STAINED GLASS. A nice S window of 1858, with two shields and borders of vine and holly in a strong green. – PLATE. Elizabethan Cup; Paten 1578.

HAUGHLEY

0060

ST MARY. All of c. 1330–40. Nave and chancel, S aisle and S porch tower. Inside the tower good doorway with two orders of slender shafts and a finely moulded arch. The S aisle E window has a very pretty enrichment of the usual reticulation motif. Each unit has a lozenge in the middle held by four bars. The W window has two cusped spherical triangles above the even three lights. The N windows of the nave are segment-headed, again with reticulation motifs. The five-bay arcade which separates the nave from the wide S aisle has octagonal piers and double-hollow-chamfered arches. Beautiful nave roof with alternating tie-beams on arched braces and arched braces meeting at the ridge. Large bosses. S aisle roof on demi-figures of angels. Smaller angels on the wall-plate as well. – FONT. Against the stem four ferocious seated lions and four Wild Men. Against the bowl the Signs of the Evangelists and angels holding shields. – PLATE. Elizabethan Cup; Set of 1758. – CURIOSA. In the porch hang thirty-three leather buckets of 1725 and 1757.

HAUGHLEY PARK, 1¼ m. WSW. The house built c. 1620 for John, the grandson of Sir John Sulyard who died in 1574 (*see* Wetherden), was badly damaged by fire in 1961 and has since been rebuilt. It was of red brick and had an impressive symmetrical E façade on an E-plan. Two angle pieces with tall stepped gables, the porch a smaller stepped gable. All three gables had finials. In the recessed parts two canted bays. The windows were mullioned and transomed, and all the more important ones had pediments. They were of three lights in the angle pieces and the porch, of two lights, i.e. the cross-type, in the bay windows. Doorway in the porch also with pediment. Two circular windows above it. Stepped gables to the back too. Star-topped chimneyshafts. The N front had two bow windows of c. 1820. The windows had Victorian alterations. (Inside a Jacobean staircase and an upper room with Jacobean chimney-piece and panelling.)*

* I am indebted for information on Haughley Park to Mrs Turner Henderson and Mr A. J. Williams.

(CASTLE. Remains of an impressive motte and bailey castle near
the church. It occupies 7 acres and the motte is 210 ft at the
base and 80 ft high. The bailey is rectangular and has a well-
preserved moat. To the W of the bailey another moated enclosure. Built c. 1100 and taken in 1173. LG)

On the GREEN several attractive houses, e.g. DIAL FARMHOUSE
with a carved porch and a ceiling with moulded beams,
HAUGHLEY HOUSE with a surprisingly stately straight door-
hood on carved brackets, and in OLD STREET, S of the Green,
CHILTON HOUSE and its neighbour, a pair of five bays with
two doorways with Gibbs surrounds.

GRAIN DRYER, near the station. By A. Swift of the Ministry of
Works. An excellent, 'anonymous' piece of industrial architecture, and just because it is so at ease it goes perfectly well
with the nature around.

6040   HAVERHILL

ST MARY. A fire in 1665 is recorded. The church looks at present
over-restored in the C19. W tower Dec below (see the arch
towards the nave) and Perp higher up. Stair-turret at the SE
corner rising higher than the tower. Nave and aisles, clerestory,
S chapel, and chancel; all Perp except for a blocked C13 lancet
in the chancel. Pinnacles on the S aisle. N doorway decorated
with fleurons, etc. The arcades inside were rebuilt in 1867;
those in the S chapel are in order (moulding with four shafts
and four hollows, arches with two-wave moulding). – PLATE.
Cup and Paten 1659. – MONUMENT. John Ward, Elizabethan;
no date. Tablet with oddly steep gable with strapwork. The
inscription is framed by mottos such as Watch, Warde,
Lightes here, stares hereafter. The Latin inscription runs as
follows:

> Quo si quis sciuit scitius
> Aut si quis docuit doctius
> At rarus vixit sanctius
> Et nullus tonuit fortius.

The little town has hardly anything to offer to the architectural
tourist. From the church to the E in the HIGH STREET a
former CHAPEL of 1839, red brick with arched windows and
giant pilasters, then BARCLAYS BANK, nice Late Georgian,
five bays, three storeys, grey brick with a porch with Roman
Doric columns, then the TOWN HALL of 1883, by E. Sherman,

pretty terrible Gothic. The continuation is HAMLET ROAD, where first another horror, the CONGREGATIONAL CHURCH by *Charles Bell*, and then the VICARAGE with an endearing early C19 Tudor front, stuccoed, with the trim painted black. Castellated with a castellated veranda. But at the back a Tudor chimney, with star tops. (The building was erected *c.* 1656. LG)

W of the church, in WITHERSFIELD ROAD, two more buildings of little merit, the CORN EXCHANGE of 1889, red brick in what used to be called a free Renaissance style, and the CON-GREGATIONAL CHURCH of 1891 by *Searl & Son* of London, also red, but lighter and Gothic.

(WEAVER'S ROW. Twelve very fine weavers' houses. P. G. M. Dickinson)

(FACTORY of D. Gurteen & Sons. Big and interesting. A range of 1856 flanks the churchyard. A later building is in the French Gothic style. P. G. M. Dickinson)

FACTORY, Duddery Hill. For Messrs Polak & Schwarz. By *E. D. Mills & Partners*, 1956–7. First part of a larger development. 'A clean, effective piece of architecture with simple materials – exposed concrete, infilling panels of well selected brick, and high-level glazing' (Sir Leslie Martin).

TOWN DEVELOPMENT by the G.L.C. and the Haverhill U.D.C., begun in 1958. Architect to the G.L.C., *Sir Hubert Bennett*.

In 1946 the population of Haverhill was about 4,000. A Town Development scheme was proposed in 1955 and has subsequently been amended, until, at the time of writing, it looks as if an ultimate population of 30,000 might be envisaged. Several new factories have been built, and the total number of new houses may increase to 4,500. Of these, the following have been completed:

PARKWAY ESTATE, $\frac{3}{8}$ m. SW of the church, along Camps Road. 1963, by *Sir Hubert Bennett* and his staff of the G.L.C. 540 houses, some semi-detached, and some in terraces, arranged in courts off culs-de-sac. A 3-acre playing field has been designed with houses grouped round it like a village green.

CLEMENTS ESTATE, Camps Road, opposite Parkway Estate. Begun in 1962, by *Sir Hubert Bennett* etc. 997 dwellings with 100 per cent garage provision and complete segregation of pedestrians and traffic.

By the same architect, CHALKSTONE ESTATE, $\frac{1}{4}$ m. NW of the town centre, along the Wratting Road (A143). Begun in 1966.

About 750 houses grouped round open landscaped courts. Again, complete pedestrian/traffic segregation, and 100 per cent garage provision. Flats and a community centre are also being built.

WITHERSFIELD ROAD, ½ m. w of the church. 1964. 80 houses designed by *Harding & Horsman* for Calder: prefabricated timber boxes (two forming the ground floor, two the upper) set on a concrete base. The layout (by G.L.C. architects) is in terraces grouped round a series of linked play areas.

COUPALS ROAD, ½ m. E of the church along A604 (extension of High Street). In 1964 two prototype Anglia houses were erected. These are made from prefabricated concrete units and were designed by the G.L.C. to answer shortages of materials and labour in the expanding towns in East Anglia. Another 85 have been built subsequently on the s side of Clements Estate.

New industrial building includes: the I.F.F. FACTORY, Hollands Road Industrial Estate, by *E. D. Mills & Partners*; HOPKINS & WILLIAMS, Hollands Road Industrial Estate, by *H. Cullerne Pratt*. Designed and built under the direction of the G.L.C. and the Haverhill U.D.C.: the BLOHN FACTORY, Hamlet Green, 1959; the MANSOL FACTORY, Hollands Road Industrial Estate, 1960; CENTAXIAL, Hollands Road Industrial Estate, 1962.

The COUNCIL OFFICES, NW of the church, in High Street, were designed by *Peter Barefoot*, 1964.

7050

HAWKEDON

ST MARY. The church lies in the middle of a wide green surrounded by houses. Its only noteworthy feature is its s porch with a brick top. Pretty trefoil frieze. The porch has an outer stoup. – FONT. Square, Norman, with angle-shafts and big coarse leaf motifs. – PULPIT. Plain, Jacobean. – SCREEN. Dado with fine tracery. The painted figures are almost obliterated. – STALLS. The front of the stalls with tracery survives on the s side. – BENCHES. A whole set, with poppy-heads and unusual seat details. – COMMUNION RAIL. With twisted balusters; C18. – PAINTING. Transfiguration; above the E window, almost unrecognizable. – STAINED GLASS. Considerable fragments in the E window. – PLATE. Silver-gilt Cup and Cover, undated; silver-gilt Flagon 1659. – BRASS. Civilian and Wife, *c.* 1510, 17 in. figures, much rubbed off.

HAWKEDON HALL, S of the church. C18 front, but inside parts of a kingpost roof and a ceiling with moulded beams, i.e. work of the C15. In the garden the stump of the former VILLAGE CROSS.

½ m. NE LANGLEY'S FARMHOUSE, with four round chimneys of the amply decorated type, built about 1520. Tudor patterns; star tops. (One magnificent fireplace; also original screen. Dickinson)

1 m. S two excellent houses, both timber-framed with brick-nogging. SWAN HALL is of the C15 and has one show gable with carved window surrounds, tie-beams, bressumers, etc. THURSTON HALL, though (or because) much restored, is quite a show-piece. Built *c.* 1500 and enlarged in 1607. Large gable on the r. at the end of a projecting wing, gabled hall-bay, gabled porch, gable by the l. end.

HAWSTEAD

8050

ALL SAINTS. Norman doorways, N and S, with one order of shafts and one of zigzag in the arch. Chancel of *c.* 1300 (see the chancel arch and the side windows), but with a Perp E window. Perp W tower, N and S sides, and S porch. The porch has flush-work decoration on the buttresses, the W tower a higher SE stair-turret, flushwork decoration on the battlements, and a base with emblems.* Frieze of shields above the W doorway. The shields refer to Sir Robert Drury (*see* below) and the end of the C15. Very tall tower arch. The nave has windows whose sills form seats. The nave roof must once have been very fine, but it was over-restored in 1858. It is Latest Perp, and money was still given for building it in 1552. Alternating hammerbeams with angel figures against them and arched braces. Wall-plates with shields and small quatrefoils. Pretty Perp chancel roof, canted and panelled with the monogram of Jesus and ara-besques. – (PULPIT. Early C16. LG) – BENCHES. Some with poppy-heads. – FAMILY PEW. Jacobean, with some mar-quetry work. – STALLS. With blank tracery along the fronts and poppy-heads. – (SCREEN, late C15, with the SANCTUS BELL fixed to the top rail. LG) – COMMUNION RAIL. Now in the tower arch. With turned balusters; C17. – LECTERN. With two book-rests, *c.* 1500; minor. – STAINED GLASS. Some C15 and later glass in a nave N window (roundels) and the chancel S W

* Money was left in 1446 towards the building of the tower (ARA).

window. E window by *Heaton & Butler*, 1856. – PLATE. Elizabethan Cup (?); Cup and Paten 1675. – MONUMENTS. Few
churches in Suffolk possess as many as Hawstead. Cross-legged
Knight, fine carving, late C13 (chancel N). The effigy lies on an
early C14 tomb-chest with blank pointed-trefoiled arcading in
an early C14 niche. The niche is richly adorned with thick folia-
tion along the arch moulding and has big buttresses l. and r. and
a top cresting. – Brasses to a boy of *c.* 1500 (10 in.), a girl of *c.*
1530 (8 in.; both S aisle E), and Ursula Allington *c.* 1530 (17 in.
chancel floor). – Tomb-chest for Sir Wilby Drury † 1557.
Lozenges on the tomb-chest; brasses on the lid. – Elizabeth
Drury † 1610. Semi-reclining figure. Alabaster. Under the
back arch a fine cartouche. Good allegorical figure seated
frontally on the arch. – Sir Robert Drury † 1615. By *Nicholas
Stone*. Black and white marble. Big black sarcophagus. Two
columns carrying two arches. Above the spandrel between the
two, high up, demi-figure in oval niche. The oval is held by two
allegorical figures. – Sir Thomas Cullum, signed, according to
Mr Gunnis, by *Jacinthe de Coucy*, 1675. Coloured plaster. Big
and black. Fluted Ionic pillars, strangely voluted top. Sarcophagus in the middle, painted to appear pietra-dura. The surround of the inscription plate is treated in the same way. –
Finally a group of late C18 to early C19 tablets, all variations on
the same theme of the urn with or without mourning allegorical
figures. The earliest is the finest: Lucy Metcalfe. Signed by
Bacon Sen., 1793. Roundel with the relief of Benevolence on
the base of an urn. – Viscountess Carleton † 1810 by *Bacon
Jun.* The female figure lies on the sarcophagus and holds the
inscription scroll. – Christopher Metcalfe † 1794. A woman
mourns over a sarcophagus. Signed *Bacon London and S
Manning* (i.e. Bacon Jun.). – Signed by the same C. B. Metcalfe
† 1801, Philip Metcalfe † 1818, and Frances Jane Metcalfe
† 1830.

METCALFE ALMSHOUSES. 1811. A hungry-looking job of grey
bricks, two storeys high and eleven bays wide, castellated and
with pointed windows. The two middle doorways are taken
together under one ogee arch – the one plum in the cake.

(Round a tree in the village some C15 iron FENCING, once
round the moat of Hawstead Place. LG)

(HAWSTEAD PLACE. Gatepiers of brick, 1675. A stable of *c.* 1400
with a kingpost roof. DOE)

(HAMMOND'S FARMHOUSE, ½ m. W. Two kingpost trusses.
DOE)

HELMINGHAM

ST MARY. Early C14 S doorway; the rest Perp. Flushwork decoration of the S porch façade and the S buttresses. A gabled dormer, oddly domestic-looking, was put in later. A restoration took place c. 1845. Later than the rest is the W tower for which the building contract of 1487/8 exists. However, the date 1543 appears on the SW corner of the parapet. Also in several places the Tollemache arms. The base of the tower is decorated in flushwork with shields, squares, etc., and the inscription:

> Scandit ad ethera
> Virgo puerpera
> Virgula Jesse

Elaborate flushwork decoration of the battlements (blank arches, shields etc.); eight pinnacles. W doorway with niches l. and r. of the entrance and shields in the spandrels. Frieze of shields and sacred initials above. The nave roof is probably of the early C17. Arched braces up to collar-beams. They have pendants, and the centre of each collar-beam has one. Arched braces (or wind-braces) also from W to E to cross-support the purlins. Decorated wall-plate with some sort of beings with large wings. – FONT. Octagonal, with four lions against the stem and four lions and four angels with the Tollemache arms against the bowl. – BENCHES. With poppy-heads. – SOUTH DOOR with tracery. – PLATE. Cup and Cover Elizabethan; Paten and Flagon 1714. – MONUMENTS. Many, of the Tollemache family. The largest is of 1615 and records four Lionels, great-grandfather, grandfather, father, and son,† c. 1550, 1553, 1575, 1605. The monument has a long inscription which deserves to be printed in full:

1. Baptized Lyone Tollemache my Name
   Since Normans Conquest of unsoyled Fame
   Shews my Descent from Ancestors of Worth;
   And that my Life might not belye my Birth,
   Their Virtues Track with heedful steps I trod,
   Rightful to Men, Religious towards God.

   Train'd in the Law, I gain'd the Bar and Bench,
   Not bent to Kindle Strife, but rather Quench;
   Gentle to Clients, in my Counsels Just,
   With Norfolk's Great Duke in no little Trust.
   Sir Joyce his heir was my Fair Faithful Wife;
   Bently my Seat, and Sev'nty Years my Life.

II.   Heir of my Father's Name, Sir Name and Seat,
        Lands, Goods and Goodness towards small & Great.
        By Heav'ns dear Blessing on my best Endeavour,
        In his Fair Footsteps did I well persevere;
        Amongst the Best, above the most admir'd,
        For all the parts my Race and place Requir'd.

        High Sh'riff of Suffolk once, of Norfolk Twice,
        For both approv'd Right, Gentle, Just & Wise;
        Frank House, Frank Heart, Free of my Purse & Port,
        Both Lov'd and Loving towards e'ery Sort.
        Lord Wentworth's Daughter was my Lovely Pheer.
        And Fourscore Sixless liv'd I Pilgrim here.

III.   My Stile and State (least any Question should)
        My Sire, and Grandsire have already told;
        My Fame & Fortune not unlike to Theirs;
        My Life as fair as human Frailty bears;
        My Zeal to God, my Love to e'ery Good,
        My Saviour knows, his Saints have understood.

        My many Virtues, Moral and Divine,
        My Lib'ral Hand, my Loving Heart to mine,
        My Piety, my Pity, Pains and Care,
        My Neighbours, Tenants, Servants, yet declare;
        My Gentle Bride Sr Ambrose Jermyn bred,
        My Years lack Five of half my Grandsire's Thread.

IV.   Here with his Fathers sleeps Sr Lionel,
        Knight, Baronet all Honours worthy well,
        So well the Acts of all his Life expresst,
        His Elders Virtues, and excell'd their best,
        His Prudent Bearing in his Publick Place
        Suffolk's High Sh'riff twice in Sixteen Years Space.

        His Zeal to God & towards Ill Severity,
        His Temperance, his Justice his Sincerity,
        His Native Mildness towards Great & Small,
        His Faith, His Love to Friends, Wife, Children All.
        In Life & Death made him Belov'd & Dear,
        To God & Men, Happy in Heav'n & Here.

        Happy in Soul in Body, Goods and Name
        Happy in Wedlock with a Noble Dame,
        Lord Cromwell's Daughter; Happy in his Heir,
        Whose Spring of Virtues Sprouts so Young so Fair.
        Whose dear Affection to his Founder's Debtor
        Built them this Tomb, but in his Heart a better.

Three kneeling figures in arched recesses, and the fourth
Lionel himself, above, also in an arched recess. Strapwork and

obelisks. All of high quality. It is said that the dormer window was put in to accommodate this monument, but that seems doubtful. – Lionel T. † 1640. Stiffly semi-reclining on his elbow. Three columns by the side and in front carrying two coffered arches. Sculpturally bad. – Lt.-Gen. Thomas T. † 1694. The monument is C18. Free-standing bust in front of an ample trophy. – Sir Lionel T. Unsigned, but dated 1729. A large, important monument. He is represented semi-reclining in Roman costume. At his feet his mourning wife. Background with pilasters and a broken pediment. – Countess of Dysart † 1804. By *Nollekens*. Large relief; she is seated with her elbow on the base of an urn. A weeping putto with a lamb stands on the r. – Lionel R. T. By *Nollekens*, 1810. Convex-sided obelisk and in front trophy. Oval portrait medallion above. – Mrs T. † 1846. By *Bedford*. Inscription and urn with a branch of a weeping willow. – Also by *Bedford* a similar monument to Vice-Admiral J. R. Delap T. † 1837. – Lord Tollemache † 1890. Bust by *Thomas Mayes*.

HELMINGHAM HALL. The impression in approaching Helm- 54 ingham Hall and walking round its four sides is remarkably unified. The house is both grand and lovable, with its wide moat, its drawbridge, and its gabled brick fronts. Yet to the student it reveals a complex history with four periods, *c.* 1500 – the house had come into the Tollemache family by marriage *c.* 1485–8 – then *c.* 1750, 1800 etc., and 1841. Of the earliest period is the plan with four ranges round an inner courtyard, and in addition much of the S range and something in the N range. The finest surviving piece of Tudor building is the main gateway with its gates, original brickwork on the r. wall, original timber-framing with brick-nogging on the l. wall, and above the arch into the courtyard some decorated timber strips (perhaps re-set?) and the foliated corbel of an oriel window. The hall lies in the N range with its porch more or less in line with the gateway. The porch is two-storeyed and has round angle buttresses.

The hall itself is much altered, but to its r., in what is now a cloakroom, some timber-framing was found during the thorough restoration of 1952. Later still, in the present servants hall, E of the cloakroom and forming the original NE corner, a big tripartite fireplace came out, thus establishing that this room, as one might have expected, was the original kitchen.

The rest of the S front is largely the work of *John Nash*, or his Gothic assistant *John Adey Repton*, whose drawings for Helmingham were exhibited at the Royal Academy in 1800 and are partly preserved at the house. Due to him is the pretty cast-iron bridge, the oriel above the gateway, and the gable with its finials above this, also the battlements and the mullions of nearly all the windows. The bay windows at the l. and r. ends however, and the gables above them, are earlier, and may date back to about 1600. Nash is also responsible for the E bridge and the gabled part of the N side (with the kitchen etc. behind). He cemented the façades, incidentally, a characteristic if un-believable step to take. The plaster was renewed again as early as *c.* 1822. The W range was remodelled in 1841 and its N half newly built to replace a gap. The plan at this NW end and also on the N side must originally have been very different from what it is now. Now there are rooms behind the great hall, whereas the other three ranges round the courtyard are only one room deep, as was the Tudor and Elizabethan tradition. However the present kitchen etc. at the present NE corner seems to have been built in a detached position in the later C16 to afford more space than the original kitchen could. The new kitchen was connected with the hall by a passage. In fact, a room above the scullery (i.e. W of the kitchen) has an Elizabethan plaster ceiling.

The finest rooms inside are of *c.* 1750, and the finest of all is the Boudoir, formerly Library, in the SE corner. This is in a rich Venetian style of woodwork, tripartite, with Corinthian columns against the walls to mark the division. Splendidly carved garlands and scrolly pediments. Also of *c.* 1750 is the staircase in the middle of the W range. It has two slim turned and twisted balusters to each step. Again of the same date the Library, originally Drawing Room, in the SW corner. It has a Kentian fireplace and a screen of two Tuscan columns. Above it lies the room in which Queen Elizabeth I is supposed to have lodged on her visit to Helmingham in 1578 or later. She is said to have given to Mrs Tollemache the exquisite lute, kept at the house and made in 1580 by *John Rose* of London. The room has a fireplace to be dated on grounds of heraldry to after 1612 and a coved ceiling probably remodelled by Nash.

In 1841 the Dining Room in the NW corner was built, and the staircase and Drawing Room S of it. Alterations were also made in other parts, notably the hall, where the fireplace and the roof are of that time. The architect of these alterations was probably *Salvin*. He used certain C17 parts brought in from outside, notably the doorcases of *c.* 1640 in the Dining Room which come from Stutton Hall and what original bits are built into the staircase with its square newels and stubby twisted balusters of later C17 style.

STABLES to the E, quite modest in size.

OBELISK of brick to the NW, without an inscription.

HEMINGSTONE 1050

T GREGORY. At the SW angle of the nave Anglo-Saxon long and short work. Nave and chancel in one. Dec and Perp windows. Unbuttressed W tower. Simple brick N porch. – FONT. Dec, octagonal, with five steep crocketed gables and tracery. – SCREEN. Only half the dado remains. – (DOOR. Iron-bound, C14. In the NW corner of the nave. LG) – PLATE. Set 1759. – MONUMENTS. William Cantrell † 1585. Tomb-chest with three shields and termini pilasters. Above an inscription framed by short columns. Top with a semicircular shell pattern and two obelisks. Of rustic quality. – Two identical sarcophagi in arched niches to members of the Brand family. By *J. Smith* of London, 1813, both signed.

EMINGSTONE HALL. 1625. A red brick mansion with two side gables and a gabled porch, nearly but not quite in the middle. The gables are shaped, those on the sides big and consisting of a convex and an ogee part, that of the porch convex and then semicircular. Of the original mullioned and transomed windows not many remain. (Panelled room with twin-arched overmantel. Staircase with turned balusters. NMR)

TONEWALL FARM, ½ m. NE. Handsome timber front of Wealden type. The date may be *c.* 1500. (Inside a kingpost truss. DOE)

HEMLEY 2040

LL SAINTS. W tower of red brick with dark blue diapering. The W window and the bell-openings are of brick too. Nave and chancel mostly of 1889. The blocked N doorway seems in order and of *c.* 1300. – FONT. Square, Norman, on five supports. It is of Purbeck marble cemented and still has traces of the familiar shallow blank arches, four on a side. – REREDOS. Nice boards with the Commandments, Lord's Prayer, and Creed, of *c.* 1840–50. – (DOOR. The S door, with ogee top, is C14; re-used. LG)

HEMPNALL'S HALL see COTTON

HENGRAVE

ST JOHN LATERAN. Small by the side of the grand house. Circular tower, probably Early Norman. Chancel of *c.* 1300 or a little later. The rest of *c.* 1419 and the early C16. Tall Perp windows with transom and segmental heads. N side with a aisle and a clerestory. The arcade has three bays, the clerestory six windows. Arcade piers delicate with four semi-polygonal shafts and spurs in the diagonals. A demi-figure of an angel at the apex of each arch. S porch of knapped flint and a delightful S doorway with dainty fleurons, etc., in the hood-mould. An inscription records that the church was built by Thomas Hengrave (who died in 1419).

The N chapel was built in 1540. Here and in the chancel crowd the MONUMENTS of the Kytsons and their relations. Margaret, Countess of Bath, † 1561, whose second husband was Sir Thomas Kytson † 1552. Six-poster with stubby Tuscan columns. Big superstructure. Two recumbent effigies on slab, and below it a tomb-chest and in front of this another recumbent effigy, her third husband – John Bourchier, Earl of Bath, † 1560. – John Bourchier, Lord Fitzwarren, † 1556. Tomb-chest with shields in roundels. No effigy. – Sir Thomas Kitson † 1608. Six-poster like that of the older Sir Thomas. Very big superstructure with much strapwork. Recumbent effigies of husband and two wives. Poor quality. – Thomas Darcy † 1614, aged twenty-two. Alabaster. Big kneeling figure between columns. On the open segmental pediment two small allegorical figures. – Sir Edmund Gage † 1707. Low tomb-chest with black marble slab. Against the chest cartouches. – Sir Thomas Gage, 1742 by *Benjamin Palmer*. Hanging monument. Bust before grey pyramid.

HENGRAVE HALL. Built by Sir Thomas Kytson, a London merchant. He started *c.* 1525, and the date 1538 over the principal doorway represents no doubt the completion.‡ Many of the original bills exist. They tell us of a 'frame' or model made by an unknown person, of John Eastawe the mason and bricklayer, John Sparke, another mason, Thomas Dyrich

---

* Mr Rigold suggests that the chancel is earlier, and only re-windowed *c.* 1300.

‡ Mr M. R. Airs suggests that the dates of the house are more exactly *c.* 1524–40. He has also discovered that *John Sparke*, who made 'the Bay windowe in the parlar' in 1526, seems to have stopped working for Kytson the following year. Most of the decorative masonry from 1536 onwards was by *William Ponyard*.

the joiner, and Davy the carver. Hengrave Hall is one of the most important and externally one of the most impressive houses of the later years of Henry VIII, in spite of much alteration which tends to confuse the visible history of the building. The original material is yellow brick.* The s side is the spectacular introduction to the house. It is (or was) symmetrical with polygonal angle turrets, a central gatehouse, and a canted bay window in the middle of the distance between this and the angle turret l. as well as r. The r. bay however was removed about 1775, when the r. end of the façade was also stone-faced and embattled (instead of the original gables), the N and E ranges largely rebuilt, and the extensive projecting NE wing with the kitchens demolished. The showpiece of the façade is the bay window above the doorway. It may be the 49b work of *William Ponyard* (*see* footnote p. 262), and is dated 1538. Whereas the doorway has a four-centred arch, Perp mouldings, and Gothic foliage in the spandrels, and whereas the turrets flank the entrance in the way familiar from Hampton Court (1515 etc.), Thornbury (*c.* 1511 etc.), and many others, the bay window includes some significant Renaissance detail. In its curious trefoiled plan it is pre-Renaissance; for that shape goes back to the oriel windows of Henry VII's Tower of *c.* 1500 at Windsor Castle, was repeated on the garden side at Thornbury (*c.* 1511 etc.), and is incidentally also echoed in Henry VII's Chapel at Westminster Abbey begun in 1503. The windows with their arched lights – the shape used throughout the original work at Hengrave – the fantastical, crocketed, scale-covered half-ogee caps of the three parts of the bay, all this is Gothic, but the multiform mouldings at the foot of the bay are certainly meant to be antique, and the little cherubs below who hold the shields with coats of arms are naked and also Italian in origin and intention. Through the archway one enters the square courtyard. This has a corridor round three sides which seems to be original and is certainly a most unusual and progressive feature. The walls of the courtyard are stone-faced. They have a quatrefoil frieze

---

* For more on the building materials, I turn to Mr Alec Clifton-Taylor *The Pattern of English Building*, 1962, p. 232): 'Considerable portions of the façade . . . were faced with ashlar, a fine oolite brought from King's Cliffe in Northamptonshire. For the non-stone parts, a special variety of pale yellow brick was produced, to tone with the stonework. Technically, it is true, this presented no problem, since suitable cretaceous clay was at hand locally, but aesthetically it is noteworthy that even in Tudor times there were already people who did not like the combination of red brick and stone.'

near the ground, mullioned windows on two floors, the upp
one being more prominent and – oriel-wise – slightly pr
jected, and top battlements. The chimneys are of bri
circular in plan and decorated with spirals or raised bri

50a ornament. The N side of the courtyard is different from t
others. It contains the hall, which has the height of the tv
storeys of the other ranges, and a large canted bay window. I
present entrance is of the C19. Against the customary schem
of composition the original entrance to the hall was not in lir
with the gateway. It was actually entered from the corridor,
unique arrangement. The entrance led into the normal scree
passage and from here, again in the normal way, a corridor le
to the kitchen (in the pulled-down NE wing).

The interior of the hall is much remodelled. The hamme
beam roof dates from the C19. Original, however, is the charn
ing fan-vaulting of the bay window and the panelling of t
broad arch between it and the hall. Another surprising ar
prophetic feature is the placing of rooms behind the hall –
double pile, as the C17 called it. Normally the hall of the C
fills completely the depth of the range in which it lies. Oth
notable features of the interior are an Elizabethan stone fir
place in the E range with Ionic pilasters and a painted ove
mantel with strapwork and mermaids etc., and the STAINE
GLASS in the chapel, which lies behind the bay window of t
s front. The glass is of c. 1525 and represents scenes fro
Genesis and the Life of Christ. *Robert Wright* the glazier w
paid £4 in 1527 and considerably more later, and it is n
impossible that he was the maker. *Galyon Hone* the King
Glazier has also been suggested. All the glass is pre-Renaissan
in style except for one piece of quite undated classic
ornament.

After 1897 the house was much tampered with: the NE wir
was rebuilt, the sumptuous Great Gallery on the ground flo
made, etc.

4070

HENHAM

HENHAM HALL was demolished a few years ago. What remai
is the STABLES, of red brick, with a cupola, the DOVECOT
octagonal, also of red brick, with a pretty Gothic lantern, a
the DAIRY etc. to the N of this, which is symmetrical, of thr
ranges, yellow brick, and castellated with a castellated midd
tower. Probably c. 1800. It may be part of *James Wyatt*'s wor

(Long undulating wall in the garden – a crinkle-crankle wall.
NMR)

HENLEY

1050

ST PETER. S doorway with a Norman zigzag arch, re-used and
made pointed. Chancel of c. 1300 with C19 E window. W tower
with inscription to commemorate Thomas Seckford † 1505,
no doubt its donor. Flushwork arcading in the buttresses.
Doorway with a frieze of saltire crosses and inscription and
shield. In the spandrels the crossed keys of St Peter and a
shield. Yet later than the tower, of c. 1525, must be the large
nave S window. This is of terracotta and made by the same
workmen who are found at Barham, Barking, and Old Shrubland Hall (see pp. 83, 84, 418). The window is of three lights and
the lights have cusped heads, the effect of the cusping being
obtained by small and pretty Italian Early Renaissance forms.
The same forms cover the mullions, and the friezes at top and
bottom. – (LECTERN. Said to be of the C13.) – PLATE. Elizabethan Cover; Cup, Plate, and Flagon 1728 (engraved with
Scenes from the Passion).

HENSTEAD

4080

ST MARY. W tower of c. 1470, quite tall. Of knapped flint, the
battlements with flushwork panelling. Nave and chancel in one,
of Norman masonry; now thatched. Ambitious Norman S
doorway with three orders of colonnettes. The middle order has
spiral-fluted shafts. Decorated scalloped capitals. Arch with
billet, zigzag, and pellets. Simple N doorway with one order of
colonnettes and one zigzag. N and S windows Perp and renewed.
The S porch has a front of knapped flint, and panel decoration
at the base. The entrance has a moulding with fleurons. –
BANNER STAFF LOCKER, SW corner of nave. – PLATE. Cup
and Cover 1568; Salver 1750. – MONUMENTS. Two by Coade
& Sealy, both dated 1806: George Mitchell, a sarcophagus
and on it a draped oval medallion with a female figure by an
urn; William Clarke, an inscription tablet and above it a big
weeping cherub seated by a draped urn.

HENSTEAD HALL. Quite a substantial square house of the C18
or early C19, cement-rendered. The front with two canted bay
windows, and between them a Greek Doric portico of two pairs
of columns. The side of the house five bays wide.

9070

HEPWORTH

ST PETER. Burnt down in 1898 and rebuilt by *J. S. Corder* o
Ipswich. The tower arch is completely unmoulded and ma\
well indicate that the lower parts of the tower were early C13
Higher up small Dec windows of quatrefoils in circles. Chance
Dec; nave with tall two-light Perp windows. In the porc\
fragments of the Norman church preceding that which i\
represented by the present building. – FONT COVER. A\
admirable piece and apparently unrestored, i.e. with no missin\
parts replaced. Tall, of pinnacle shape. On the lowest floo\
panelling projecting in five little lobes like the oriel window o
the Hengrave gatehouse or the windows of Henry VII's Chape\
They are meant to represent whole structures; for tiny me\
come out of tiny doors as in the familiar German weather
boxes. – BENCH ENDS. Some; with poppy-heads. – PLATE
Elizabethan Cup; Paten 1817.

4090

HERRINGFLEET

ST MARGARET. Norman round tower with original windows
Above the cornice a Norman top storey with twin bell-opening\
on each side, the two separated originally by a column. Th\
arches are straight-sided, that is triangular, which is a Saxon
not a Norman motif. But the colonnettes flanking the twin ar\
undoubtedly Norman. The tower arch towards the nave is als\
Norman, see the billet moulding around it on the W side, an\
the simple imposts. One Norman window in the chancel on th\
N side. Norman S doorway with saltire crosses in the abacu\
and a zigzag arch. Nave E.E. (one lancet, plain single-chamfere\
N doorway). – SCREEN. The upper, traceried part now used a\
a W gallery. The lower part of the gallery and much Gothi\
furnishing looks *c.* 1830. – STAINED GLASS. In the E windo\
many bits assembled early in the C19. They comprise Englis\
C15 figures and much post-Reformation work, said to com\
from the Franciscan friary at Cologne. Franz Elsholtz in hi\
Wanderungen durch Köln am Rhein und seine Umgebung
Cologne 1820, writes: 'Incidentally, foreigners, and especiall\
Englishmen, who frequently visit here, look for stained glas\
to make a show of it in their collections of art' (cf. e.g. Shrews\
bury St Mary with glass from Altenberg and Herchen). ·
PLATE. Cup 1637; Paten 1703. – MONUMENT. J. Leathe\
†1787. Sarcophagus and urn on it, against a convex-sided gre\
pyramid.

MANOR FARMHOUSE, SE of the church. Dated 1655. With a brick gable, each side of which consists of four convex curves. Adjoining a fine large thatched BARN with walls of brick and flint chequer, one of the largest in Suffolk.

ST OLAVE'S PRIORY, 1½ m. NW. Founded c. 1216 for Augustinian Canons. Above the river Waveney. The lane cuts off the E parts of the buildings, including the crossing and E end of the C13 church. This was originally aisleless but received about 1310 a S aisle of five bays with octagonal piers. The cloister space is visible to the N of the church. This with the square bases of the piers of the S and N walls is also of the C13, as is the remaining W wall. The N range contained the refectory. Its undercroft of c. 1300 survives. In spite of this early date it is of brick, including the rib-vaults which rest on strong octagonal piers of Purbeck marble. The ribs are single-chamfered. The cross-wall belongs to the time after the Dissolution, when the Priory was converted into a house. Of this late date (C16) also the ruins to the N of the range.

WINDMILL. Of c. 1830. A small octagonal smock-mill, with a tower and boat-shaped cap clad in tarred weatherboards, four common (cloth spread) sails, and a tail-pole and winch for winding the cap. She drove a scoop-wheel 16 ft in diameter with floats 11 in. wide at the tip. The mill was used for drainage. The marshman had a couch and a fireplace inside so that the mill could be worked day and night when required. Her work is now done by an oil engine, and she is maintained as a landmark by the Suffolk County Council.

PRIORY MILL. Another windmill, also of the smock type, also for drainage. Small (only 25 ft high) and giraffe-like. Four-sided. Built as late as 1910. Now derelict. She had two patent sails and a fan-tail and an outside ladder for access up to the cap. She drained 100 acres.*

HERRINGSWELL

7060

ST ETHELBERT. Rebuilt by *Blomfield*, 1869–70. The W tower arrangement is odd and rather botched, with two big heavy buttresses sticking out N and S, a buttress reaching up the middle of the W side (with two original single-light windows set in), and inside two octagonal piers to carry the E angles of the

---

* These paragraphs kindly written by Mr Wailes.

tower and a kind of inner flying buttresses to make them safer.* –
STAINED GLASS. All C 20. E window by *Christopher Whall*.
Others by him, by *James Clark* (the landscape windows), and
other artists.

(MEDIEVAL CHURCH. Remains include the responds at the E
end of the nave. They indicate a Norman date. LG)

HESSETT

ST ETHELBERT. All Perp, except for the chancel, which is Dec
and has one E window with flowing tracery. Attached to the
chancel a two-storeyed vestry with barred windows. The lower
room has a small three-light window. The upper room is
reached by an original ladder with solid steps. There is a fireplace too. Along the vestry and part of the N aisle runs a long
inscription reading: John Hoo and his wife 'the qweche hath
mad y chapel aewery deyl heyteynd y westry & batylementyd y
hole'. So with his money he built the N aisle (or N chapel ? *see*
below), heightened the vestry, and embattled the whole.
John Hoo died in 1492. The N aisle indeed has battlements,
which are of very pretty openwork stone-carving. The clerestory has the same, though the pattern differs. Three-light
windows with transoms. The clerestory has not the double
number of windows. The S aisle is similar to the N aisle and has
again openwork battlements. Excellent S porch, partly faced
with stone, partly with knapped flint. Entrance arch with St
George and the Dragon in the spandrels. Three canopied niches.
Base decorated with initials and quatrefoils. The buttresses
have flushwork emblems. Among the initials the K. B. refers
presumably to a member of the Bacon family. John Bacon's
initials appear on the W tower. This has parapet as well as
battlements decorated. The arcades inside are typically Perp.
A slender shaft to the nave without capital, wide diagonal
hollows and shafts to the arch openings with capitals. There are
four bays, and in addition the one-bay chapel to the N to which
reference has already been made. Aisle roofs with arched
braces and a little carving. – FONT. Panelled stem. Bowl with
flowers in cusped quatrefoils and similar decoration. The inscription on the base mentions Robert Hoo who died in 1510. –
SCREEN. Tall, with one-light divisions with broad ogee arches.

* The Rev. J. T. Munday has informed me that an C 18 antiquarian MSS.
notebook at Elvedon Hall describes this arrangement in the tower – so it is
not Blomfield's.

Simple panel tracery over; cresting. – BENCHES. A complete square-headed set in the nave. Also some with poppy-heads, and traceried fronts. One extremely richly carved front of a bench back with birds. – WALL PAINTINGS. On the S wall: St Barbara (E of SE window); St Christopher (over S door). On the N wall: Seven deadly Sins, a tree growing out of the Mouth of Hell. Below Christ of the Trades (note the six of diamonds). – STAINED GLASS. Much preserved in the aisle windows, including an Annunciation, a St Paul with the Sword, and a St Nicholas blessing little boys. One of them holds a golf club. – SINDON CLOTH, i.e. cloth to cover the Pyx. A great rarity. Of linen lace. On loan to the British Museum, as is the BURSE, i.e. case for the corporal, the cloth on which the wafer lies during Mass. Linen, edged with green silk. On the one side Head of Christ in an ogee quatrefoil, on the other Lamb in a similar field. – MONUMENT. Lionel and Anna Bacon, 1653 by *John Stone*. Tablet with inscription in an exuberantly carved cartouche with drapery, two shields, an urn at the top, a pineapple at the foot.

HEVENINGHAM

₃₀₇₀

ST MARGARET. C14 chancel and S arcade of five bays (octagonal piers, double-chamfered arches). W tower with brick battlements. Three-light brick windows in the clerestory. They are early C16 on the S side, but on the N all but one seem to be C17 Gothic. In the E respond of the S arcade a handsome tall Perp niche for an image. Some original paint is preserved. Double-hammerbeam roof. Wall-posts with figures. Tracery above the hammers. – FAMILY PEW. With some original Jacobean parts. – STAINED GLASS. The E and W windows of 1854. – PLATE. Medieval Paten (cf. Barsham); Elizabethan Cup and Cover. – MONUMENTS. Wooden effigy of a Knight, *c.* 1400.

RECTORY, S of the church. Early C19, grey brick, of five bays and two storeys. Greek Doric porch. The window above it set in a blank arch which rises into the pedimental gable.

HEVENINGHAM HALL. Heveningham is without question the grandest Georgian mansion of Suffolk. It was designed about 1778 by *Sir Robert Taylor* for Sir Gerard Vanneck or van Neck, a merchant of Dutch descent. His father and uncle had come over from Holland about 1720 and his father had bought the Heveningham estate in 1752. Sir Robert Taylor completed the exterior of the house but was not asked to design the interior as well. This was entrusted to *James Wyatt*, then in his thirties and established as a brilliant designer of elegant decoration in the style of Robert Adam. He had finished his work by 1784. Exterior and interior are equally outstanding and equally characteristic of their authors. The exterior, of twenty-five bays' width and a height varying from two to two and a half storeys, is built of brick, stuccoed. The composition is in the accepted English Palladian tradition in which Taylor believed, with a seven-bay centre with detached giant Corinthian columns above the blank-arched and rusticated ground floor and three-bay angle pavilions with attached columns. At the angles of the centre the columns are duplicated, at the angles of the pavilions square pillars are set against the columns. But whereas the pavilions carry pediments, as one would expect, the centre has as the chief distinguishing feature of Heveningham a heavy attic decorated with garlands and crowned by two figures with a coat of arms, two vases, and two recumbent lions. This attic establishes a claim to an Imperial Roman descent which is – historically speaking – outside the English c18 adherence to Cinquecento precedent.

59   Wyatt's Hall is one of the most refined rooms of its date in England. Screens of scagliola columns separate the ends – in the Adam way. Pilasters and very restrained panels along the walls. Exquisite tunnel-vault with penetrations. The penetrations are treated fan-vault-wise. Large paterae along the centre of the vault, half-paterae where the penetrations reach the centre. The apple green is the original colour. White stucco and brownish columns. The other principal rooms are to the l. They were damaged by fire in 1949 and have since been carefully restored. Along the front Dining Room and Library. The Dining Room has two shallow apses against its back wall and a third in the wall towards the Hall. Stucco is even more restrained here, and the decoration is chiefly by painted reliefs executed by *Biagio Rebecca*, a distinguished assistant of Adam. The colour scheme is pale blue with the reliefs on a dark red ground. The Library has a screen of columns towards the Dining Room and a tripartite window in its end wall. Colouring greenish-grey and porphyry. Broad-minded oval medallions of Homer, Virgil, Shakespeare, Milton, Dryden, Locke, Pope, Prior, Voltaire, and Rousseau. Towards the back of the house the main apartment is the Ballroom, behind the Dining Room biscuit-coloured with green painting and no stucco. Shallow apsed end walls, shallow segmental vault. Next to this the small Etruscan Room in the Athenian style of red-figure vase painting.

(then called Etruscan), and next to the Etruscan Room the staircase, also accessible from the centre of the back wall of the Hall. Square well and stairs with iron handrail painted blue and white. The rooms to the r. side of the Hall are simpler. The most interesting is the Print Room, a room decorated, according to a fashion, with stuck-on prints.

The back of the house, that is the s side, looks surprisingly unfinished. The angle pavilions only are treated as is the front, but the centre has no decoration at all, and in addition recedes instead of projecting.

The gardens were laid out by *Capability Brown* in 1781–2. Elegant ORANGERY by *Wyatt*, nine bays long, with a semicircular portico on attenuated columns. Simple horseshoe-shaped STABLES of red brick with semicircular windows and a lantern. In the garden an undulating brick forcing wall (crinkle-crankle wall). In the grounds an ICE HOUSE (visible from the main road). It is circular and thatched and has a thatched passage leading into it. (The TEMPLE SE of the house is also probably by *Wyatt*. It is a small classical building with two Ionic columns and two pilasters, with enriched pediment. DOE)

LODGES, to the SSE. Late C18, square, small. Brick, rendered. Pyramid roofs. (Living accommodation was sunk below ground for concealment. DOE) Now derelict.

HIGHAM
1 m. NW of Stratford St Mary

oo3o

ST MARY. Much restored. Simple heavy W tower with small upper windows indicating a C13 date. The tower arch double-chamfered and dying into the imposts may well be *c.* 1300. Otherwise Early Perp and not of great interest. Arcade to the N aisle of four bays. The piers quatrefoil with the foils filleted and the fillets not set off from the foils but running into them in an ogee curve. In the re-entrant angles thin octagonal shafts. The abaci alternatingly with leaf bands and single fleurons. Many-moulded arches, hood-moulds on heads. – FONT. Perp, octagonal, damaged, and disused. – MONUMENT. Robert Hay † 1811. By *Regnart*. Woman kneeling by an urn.

HIGHAM HALL. By the church. Early C19. White brick, five bays, three-bay pediment. Two storeys, the windows tied together by giant segmental arches. Porch.

BARHAMS MANOR HOUSE (Green Farm House), at the main

crossing in the village. Seven-bay C18 front, but inside one
room has Tudor wall painting of interlaced octagons with
fruit motifs, similar to Wolsey's ceiling at Hampton Court.
Near by several timber-framed houses, and especially TUDOR
HOUSE with gabled wings (much restored).

7060
HIGHAM
7 m. w of Bury St Edmunds

ST STEPHEN. By *Sir G. G. Scott*, 1861. In the Geometrical
style. Scott gave himself the pleasure of a round Suffolk tower
with a round spire, and nicely placed the baptistery in it and
vaulted it with a rib-vault. We are grateful for this touch of
fancy. – PLATE. Cup 'bought in Florence, partly C15' (*P.S.I.A.*
IX).
BARROW, on the s edge of the Icknield Way, on the limit of Four
Acre Belt (*see* also Gazeley and Kentford).

HIGH HOUSE *see* BADWELL ASH, HUNTINGFIELD, NETTLESTEAD, *and* OTLEY

HILL FARMHOUSE *see* COOKLEY *and* WITNESHAM

0070
HINDERCLAY

ST MARY. Simple C12 N doorway. Early C13 S arcade of four bays
with short circular piers, round abaci, and double-hollow-
chamfered arches; Dec chancel. Reticulated E window. The
SW window is treated as a low-side window, with a transom.
Angle PISCINA with altered shaft. Perp W tower with tall bell-
openings, the part below the transom blocked and with chequer
flushwork. Battlements with flushwork panelling. Nave and s
aisle Perp. – ROOD BEAM. Remains cut off flush with the N wall.
– BENCH ENDS. With plain, small C17 poppy-heads. – BOX
PEWS in the s aisle. – PLATE. Cup *c.* 1680. – MONUMENT.
George Thompson † 1711. With putti l. and r. and cherubs'
heads at the foot. – CURIOSUM. A pitcher of stoneware to hold
one gallon of beer for the bell-ringers. Inscription with date
1724.
EARLY IRON AGE SETTLEMENT, on the SW edge of Hinderclay
Wood. It is marked by a trackway and a group of hut circles and
a scatter of pottery. Roman kilns were also found (*see* Wattisfield).

HINTLESHAM

0040

ST NICHOLAS. E.E. arcades of four bays. The piers are circular-octagonal-circular on the S side, octagonal-circular-octagonal on the N. Double-chamfered arches. Dec S aisle and chancel, Perp W tower and clerestory. Perp timber porch (renewed ?). The N side is much simpler than the S side. – COMMUNION RAIL. With twisted balusters. – PANELLING. Against the E wall. Perp and crested, which made Cautley suppose that it was originally the rood-loft parapet. – PAINTING. Fragment of a St Christopher in the nave opposite the S entrance. – MONUMENTS. Thomas Tympley † 1593 and his wife and his son's family. The son's date of death is not entered. Two groups of small kneeling figures in the usual arrangement across prayer-desks. – Capt. John Timperley † 1629. A fine, elegant, upright figure, engraved on a large slate plate. The figure has an engraved architectural frame with tympanum and trophies l. and r.

(HINTLESHAM OLD HALL. C16. Timber-framed. Good ceiling with moulded beams. NMR)

HINTLESHAM HALL. Though the façade is Early Georgian the house behind it is – at least in its bones – Elizabethan. The façade then had the customary E-shape with wings projecting quite far. The porch can now no longer be identified, because Richard Powys, who bought Hintlesham in 1720, filled in the space to its l. and r. The façade now is of two storeys with quoins, parapet, and hipped roof. The ground floor of the recessed centre is rusticated in the French banded way and has arched windows. Porch with coupled unfluted Ionic columns. First floor with rather curiously spaced Corinthian pilasters and a central Venetian window. Pediment against the parapet. The wings project by four bays and have a pedimented doorway in the middle. Of the Elizabethan part no more can be seen outside or inside than the big chimneybreasts on the S and E sides. On the W side was a Victorian courtyard, but this was removed in 1938.

Inside, the finest room is the Drawing Room on the first floor. This is not of Powys's time, but of that of Henry Timperley, who held the manor in 1686–91. The plaster ceiling of the 58b room is among the best of the late C17 anywhere in East Anglia. It has a central oval panel and square and oblong panels along the four sides, and the finesse of modelling and boldness of undercutting are prodigious. The work is remarkably similar to that at Melton Constable, Norfolk, and Felbrigg, Norfolk,

both dated 1687. Of after 1720 the long and narrow Entrance
Hall with apsed ends, the two-storeyed Saloon, originally Hall,
with panelling and in its end walls large door-cases with
columns and pediments, and the staircase with slim twisted
balusters and carved tread-ends. A smaller staircase of c. 1690
is in the N wing. This has carved newel-posts with big vases on
top, a carved string, and balusters with the bulb near the foot
decorated with leaves.

Late C17 STABLES of red brick. Two storeys and a square
bell-turret.

HITCHAM

ALL SAINTS. Quite large; at the far S end of the village. Nave
with clerestory and aisles, W tower, S porch, and a chancel
largely rebuilt in 1878. Its forms are Dec, and it probably was
Dec. Vestry to its N, two-storeyed, Dec. N aisle doorway Dec,
aisle windows Dec with segmental heads. Arcades of five
bays with octagonal piers and double-chamfered arches. That
also is probably C14. The clerestory has quatrefoil windows.
Sturdy W tower with stair-turret not going externally to the
top. W doorway with niches l. and r. Perp S porch with flushwork panelling. Entrance with motifs of crowns and lions and
a niche over the arch. Perp S doorway of the same style with
shields and crowns. Hood-mould on seated lions. Fine Perp
lean-to roofs in the aisles with bosses. Fine roof in the nave
alternating between double-hammerbeams and arched braces
masquerading as hammerbeams. Against the lower hammerbeam ends big emblems such as roses, shields, a sun with
crowns over. – SCREEN. Dado with eight painted figures,
c. 1500. – SOUTH DOOR with tracery and a border of foliage
trails. – PLATE. Two Flagons 1637; Cup and Paten 1639;
Paten 1731.

(Former GUILDHALL, c. 1500, adjoining the churchyard gate.
P. G. M. Dickinson)

BRICKHOUSE FARMHOUSE, Hitcham Street. Part of an Early
Tudor brick mansion. At the one end parts of two polygonal
angle turrets, at the other of one. N of the house architectural
fragments of a C15 chapel (?) have been found. Also, a
ROMANO–BRITISH SETTLEMENT is indicated along the
trackway by remains of flint walls, rubbish pits, and scattered
coins and pottery of C2–3 A.D. date.

HOBLAND HALL see HOPTON

HOLBROOK

1030

ALL SAINTS. The best parts are early to mid C14, namely the
SW porch tower with two-light windows on the ground floor
to the E and W and a tierceron-vault, the W window of the nave
and the mouldings etc. inside the W parts of the nave, and the
chancel interior, especially the fine N doorway with its bold
cusped arch, and the SEDILIA and PISCINA. Perp S arcade and
three-light S windows. The piers have shafts with capitals only
towards the arch openings. The shafts have fillets. N aisle of
1863. – MONUMENTS. Brass of Knight in armour, 31 in. long,
late C15. – Judge John Clenche † 1607 and wife, large standing
wall-monument with two effigies reclining stiffly on their sides,
he behind and a little above her. – CURIOSUM. In the chancel
an embalmed head in a jar was found in 1863.

ROYAL HOSPITAL SCHOOL. 1925–33 by *Buckland & Haywood*. 64b
A very large, strictly axial composition of buildings in the neo-
Wren to neo-Georgian style, culminating in a tall stone spire
on the tower which stands at the S end of the central assembly
hall. The main view is from the estuary. Brick with stone
dressings. Long two-storeyed centre with short projecting
wings. Giant portico with the tower referred to. Giant porticoes
also on the sides of the wings. They are here crowned by cupolas.
Behind them lie the dining hall and the gymnasium. Further
to the E the big chapel with Byzantinesque domes (of concrete)
and an apse with mosaics. Big giant portico also in the centre of
the N or entrance side. In axis with this front grouped terrace
housing for the staff, forming a semicircle. More such housing
to the E and W of the main buildings running down to the
estuary, and also along the main road. The whole is certainly
neither imaginative nor inventive, but it is in its scale and
formality undeniably impressive. If the buildings had been
erected at the same time in Central Europe or fifteen years
later in England, they would have looked more lively and more
of our century.

MILL, weatherboarded, by the pond S of the church, a handsome
picture.

HOLBROOK HALL *see* LITTLE WALDINGFIELD

HOLLESLEY

3040

ALL SAINTS. W tower built *c.* 1450 (a legacy is dated 1452).
Flushwork decoration on base, buttresses, and battlements.
Three-light W window with panel tracery. Nave and chancel

much renewed in 1886, when the N aisle was built. However, the arcade was left intact, and this must date from the early C13. Circular and octagonal piers alternating. The arches have one slight chamfer and one slight hollow chamfer. – FONT. Perp, octagonal, simple. The heads which supported the bowl have been hacked off. – PULPIT. Elizabethan. – SCREEN. Only the dado remains. In the blank tracery many small quatrefoils. – BENCHES. Seven, with traceried ends, poppy-heads, and animals on the arms. – PLATE. Paten 1718.

OLD RECTORY. 1845 by *S. S. Teulon.*

HOLLY FARM *see* BRAMFIELD

4070

HOLTON

ST PETER. Norman round tower. The original bell-stage clearly visible. The tower was heightened later. Norman S doorway with one order of colonnettes, one-scallop capitals. The arch has an outer ring of scallops or lunettes. Above the arch a Norman carving of an animal seen from the side. N aisle and N chapel are Victorian. – FONT. Octagonal. The stem with eight attached shafts, the bowl on eight heads and with quatrefoil panels with shields. – PULPIT. Early C16, with linenfold panels. – STAINED GLASS. E window by *Kempe, c.* 1899, showing his hallmark, the wheatsheaf. – PLATE. Paten 1636; Cup 1722.

GAVELCROFT, ¼ m. W. Timber-framed. With brick ends. Shaped gables.

ST MARGARET'S CHAPEL, Mells, ¾ m. S. Norman. The chapel was about 50 ft long and consisted of nave and apsed chancel. The arch between nave and chancel and the gable wall above it are still at once recognizable. What else remains of the walls is too overgrown to be architecturally telling.

WINDMILL. Dated 1752. A post-mill. She ceased work before 1914 but was extensively repaired in 1966–8. She has a white painted timber body, a tarred brick-built round-house, together with a fan-tail, and four cloth spread sails. All the machinery was removed many years ago and a gallery added at the tail. She occupies one of the best mill sites in the county.*

0030

HOLTON ST MARY

ST MARY. Flint and stone. Big incomplete W tower with brick

---

* This paragraph supplied by Mr P. R. B. Brooks.

battlements. C13 chancel (see the piscina). Aisleless C14 nave (see the doorways with their small quadrant mouldings and the big head-stops of the hood-mould). – FONT. Octagonal, Perp.

LATES, ½ m. NW. Timber-framed and plastered. With nice Tudor windows probably of *c.* 1850, and a good six-bay barn, weatherboarded and thatched.

HOLYWELLS *see* IPSWICH, p. 308

HOMERSFIELD

²⁰⁸⁰

ST MARY. Nave and chancel and unbuttressed W tower with bell-openings with Y-tracery. In the nave one Norman S window. – PLATE. Elizabethan Cup; Paten 1567.

BARNFIELD COTTAGES. A group of modern almshouses. By *M. Chesterton c.* 1925–7. Recessed centre and projecting wings. Well in the middle. All thatched and the walls plastered pink.

ROMANO–BRITISH POTTERY KILNS include a C3 kiln excavated in 1959 and a complete kiln containing its last firing which was destroyed by workmen in 1962.

HONINGTON

⁹⁰⁷

ALL SAINTS. Norman S doorway with two orders of shafts. They are decorated with zigzag, and the r. one in addition with three square blocks or bands, also decorated. Hood-moulds on beasts' heads. Norman chancel arch. Imposts with nookshafts, simple, all well preserved. The S side of the nave seems early C14, the N side remodelled Perp. Dec W tower with a stair-turret of brick. Dec chancel. Perp S porch with flushwork panelling; initials etc. Entrance with shields and leaf-motifs. Three niches above the entrance. – FONT. Octagonal, Dec. Panelled stem. On the bowl Dec tracery including three blank rose windows (one High Gothic, one with six mouchettes), and a Crucifixion. – BENCHES. With poppy-heads, and animals in the arms. – WALL PAINTINGS. On the S wall, very faint. Described as Martyrdom of St Thomas Becket and Legend of St Nicholas. – PLATE. Elizabethan Cup; Flagon 1735. – (MONUMENT. Robert Rushbrooke † 1753. Simple, but with exquisite italic lettering.)

HOO

²⁰⁵⁰

ST ANDREW AND ST EUSTACHIUS. W tower of brick, early C16; later parapet. Nave and chancel in one. Dec windows. – FONT. Octagonal. Against the stem four lions, against the bowl one flower and seven figures, including angels with the Instruments of the Passion and the Symbols of the Trinity. – COMMUNION RAIL. Three-sided. – PLATE. Cup probably early C17; Paten 1787.

HOPTON
9070
1½ m. NE of Market Weston

ALL SAINTS. S aisle of the late C13, see the W window with plate tracery (two pointed-trefoiled lights and an enriched quatrefoil). Dec E window. Perp widening. The arcade is pre-Perp, with octagonal piers and double-chamfered arches. Dec W tower with a pretty C18 top. Tall arched bell-openings, and the walls all of flushwork in a chequerboard pattern. The chancel is of c. 1300 or earlier, see the N doorway and the E window (three stepped lancet lights under one arch). Perp N aisle. Late Perp clerestory of brick with two-light windows and a fine roof. Brick shafts help to carry it. Against these small seated figures. The roof is of the hammerbeam type. Against the hammerbeams figures holding a book, a chalice, musical instruments, etc. Carved and coloured wall-plate. – ROOD BEAM. Cut off flush with the walls. – STAINED GLASS. S aisle E window by *Kempe*, 1905. – PLATE. Elizabethan Cup. – (MONUMENT. Thomas Raymond † 1680. LG)

HOPTON
5000
2 m. NNW of Corton

OLD ST MARGARET. In ruins. W tower. The church of the early C14 or Dec. Remains of a three-light reticulated E window in the N aisle, flanked by two niches. Remains of cusped lancets, N and S.

ST MARGARET. By *S. S. Teulon*, 1866. Flint and stone, with low walls and high roofs, lancet windows and windows with plate tracery. Low crossing tower turning octagonal by broaches, a weird idea. Low SE stair-turret with a conical roof. Aisleless nave. W wall with two lancets and a sexfoiled window over. In the nave – another Teulonian oddity – the windows are surmounted by blank arches of red and yellow brick arranged at random, and in addition more elaborate and larger on the N than on the S side. The crossing arches are treated in the same way. – ORGAN CASE. In the heavy Gothic style of Burges or Seddon. – STAINED GLASS. In the chancel, by *Morris* and *Burne-Jones*. About 1881. Beautiful and peaceful after Teulon's architecture. – PLATE. Set 1864.

HOPTON HALL. Of *c.* 1825. With a porch of two pairs of Greek Doric columns.

HOBLAND HALL, 1¼ m. NW. Late C18, of red brick, five bays, two storeys. Doorway with Roman Doric pilasters and a broken pediment. The whole middle bay has a broken top pediment as well (with an arched window below). Entrance hall with a handsome staircase with three turned balusters to the tread and carved tread-ends. One room had an apsed recess in one of its long walls, screened by two Adamish columns. The house was gutted by fire in 1961.

HORHAM

ST MARY. Norman doorways, S with two orders of shafts (scalloped capitals), N with one, S with a roll and a zigzag, N only with a roll. The chancel was rebuilt in 1881. The best piece of the church is the W tower. Flamboyant-panelled base, flushwork panelling on the buttresses. Tall flushwork-panelled battlements. Dec two-light bell-openings. Perp W doorway. – FONT. Against the stem four lions, against the bowl lions and demi-figures of angels. – PULPIT. Jacobean. – READER'S DESK. In the same style, and dated 1631. – BENCHES. A good set with poppy-heads. – TYMPANUM of plaster above the first chancel tie-beam, i.e. the rood-beam. – (PAINTING. Christ carrying the Cross. On the tympanum.) – STAINED GLASS. Bits in the chancel on the S side. – PLATE. Cup and Cover Elizabethan.

THORPE HALL, 1 m. N. An unusual and impressive house, by its style of *c.* 1560, and in its shape almost as if it were a hunting lodge or summer house or standing. Red brick with brick windows. Three bays by two. Two storeys with a three-storeyed gabled centre projection which holds the porch on the N side, and may have held the staircase on the S. End chimneystacks with four circular chimneys with star tops. All the windows are of brick and have mullions and transoms, and still arched lights (cf. Kentwell Hall, Long Melford). Also all the windows have pediments (cf. Old Somerset House London, Melford Hall, Rushbrooke Hall).

HORRINGER

ST LEONARD. Dec chancel with E window of four lights with reticulated tracery. W tower Perp with pretty fleurons in the capitals of the arch towards the nave. The top is of brick, built in 1703. Perp S porch with much flushwork decoration, chequerboard as well as panel designs. A will of 1464 gives money to the new building of the porch and one of 1470 to its repair (ARA). A S chapel is attached to its E wall. The church was restored in 1818.* The N aisle is of 1845. – STAINED GLASS. E window 1946 by *J. E. Nuttgens*. In the mildly Expressionist style of much modern English wood-engraving. – PLATE. Cup 1567–8; Flagon 1664; Paten and Almsdish 1699.

1070

HOXNE

ST PETER AND ST PAUL. One of the grandest of the W towers in this part of Suffolk. Perp. Stair-turret higher than the tower, tall angle pinnacles. Frieze of shields in quatrefoils at the base. Buttresses and battlements with flushwork panelling. W door-way with crowns, mitres, fleurons, and shields in the arch mouldings. Two niches by the W window. Nice, more modest N doorway, but also with shields and fleurons in the arch. Perp also the rest of the church except for the chancel which was rebuilt in 1879. Tall windows. The arcade of six bays seems earlier. Octagonal piers, arches of one chamfer and one hollow chamfer. Perp clerestory on the N side only. – FONT. Octagonal. Against the stem four seated and four standing figures. Against the bowl the Signs of the Evangelists and four angels with shields. – BENCHES. Four with poppy-heads and two seated figures to each end, l. and r. of the poppy-head. – WALL PAINTINGS. Against the N wall, from W to E: St Christopher, the Seven Deadly Sins represented as growing on a tree (two devils are busy sawing it, while at the top of the tree stands an elegant youth), the Seven Works of Mercy with explanatory scrolls. Also the remains of a Last Judgement (?). – PLATE. Set 1790. – MONUMENT. Thomas Maynard † 1742. By *Charles Stanley*. Standing, in the pose made fashionable by Guelfi's Craggs Monument in Westminster Abbey. His elbow leans on an urn standing on a pedestal. Against this a fine relief of a woman and eight children. Obelisk background.

An attractive village centre with a small triangular green and the main street leading up to the church. No house of special interest in the village.

(VICARAGE. Timber-framed with brick-nogging. NMR)

ABBEY FARMHOUSE, ¾ m. S. So called after a Benedictine priory first founded at Hoxne in 950 to commemorate the site of the

* 'Nothing remains of the former edifice, but the plain masonry of the walls', according to the *Bury and Norwich Post* of 14 October 1818 (ARA).

martyrdom of King Edmund. The priory later became a cell
of Norwich. Nothing survives of it. The farmhouse is timber-
framed with brick-nogging, and has one brick gable. An original
arched doorway under an open porch.

CHICKERING HALL FARMHOUSE, 1¾ m. SE. In a room two
excellently carved timber posts of c. 1500, one with a Wild Man,
the other with two huntsmen and a dog.

RED HOUSE, 1½ m. S. C16. Timber-framed with brick-nogging.
The porch has turned balusters l. and r.

HUBBARD'S HALL FARM see BENTLEY

HUNDON   7040

ALL SAINTS. Burnt in 1914 and rebuilt by *Detmar Blow &*
Billerey (GR). W tower with higher SW stair-turret. S porch
with flushwork panelling. S doorway with small shields in one
arch moulding. Two niches l. and r. The S clerestory has pretty
openwork battlements with quatrefoils. Wide nave, low
octagonal piers. – PANELLING in the S chapel, from another
source. – PAINTING. Copy of Titian's earliest dated painting. –
PLATE. Cup and Paten 1749. – MONUMENTS. In the churchyard ambitious monument to Mrs Arethusa Vernon, 1728.
Pyramid on a sarcophagus, carrying a wheatsheaf. – (Also in
the churchyard HEADSTONES by *Thomas Soane* and other
members of his family, C18, probably the earliest in the county.
F. Burgess)

In the village THE THATCHERS, C15, with remains of a kingpost roof and WALL PAINTING above a fireplace. 4 ft medallion with the lamb and flag. Three arched niches between the
fireplace and the paintings.

COUNCIL HOUSING by *Sir Albert Richardson*, neo-Georgian
and very formal and townish. Red-brick, two-storeyed.

HUNSTON   9060

ST MICHAEL. Nave and chancel and W tower. In addition a
remarkable S transept (cf. Pakenham). It is of the later C13 and
has a W doorway with shafts, two lancets to the E, and a renewed
group of three stepped lancets under one arch to the S. Inside,
the entry arch is double-chamfered and rests on two corbels
which turn into the wall like sections of stove-pipes. In the E
wall between the lancets is a niche bordered by huge dog-
tooth, a dog-tooth actually meant to be four petals. Between
the petals is some small playful stiff-leaf. Hood-mould of stiff-
leaf, or at least starting off as stiff-leaf from the l., and after two

motifs turning for the rest into much prettier roses. Angle
PISCINA on three shafts with pointed-trefoiled arches. The
chancel is apparently of the same time. It has an E window
exactly like the transept S window and a very curious semicircular fully trefoiled-cusped window above the priest's doorway. The chancel arch has shafts with two shaft-rings and
primitive capitals with leaves on upright stems. Unbuttressed
W tower of knapped flint.* – BENCHES. Four ends with poppy-
heads and animals on the arms. – SCULPTURE. As evidence of
the predecessor of the present church the decorated head of a
small Norman window survives, built into the wall at the NE
corner. – PLATE. Elizabethan Cup and Cover; Cup, Cover,
and Flagon of 1754.

A thatched house in the village street has a gabled porch with the
date 1619. Decorated bressumer and bargeboards.

MILL HILL, ¼ m. SE of the church. Small motte, rather damaged,
with a wet ditch.

HUNTINGFIELD

3070

ST MARY. The N arcade represents the Norman N wall (see one
upper window) cut through at first roughly to make an aisle.
The arch openings in their present form may be of the C18,
when the Vanneck Pew was built of brick at the NE end. The
church is altogether too renewed to be of much interest. Perp
S aisle with flushwork parapet and SW and SE pinnacles. The
windows seem to have been originally of Tudor brick. S porch
with flushwork panelling. W tower with flushwork decoration
on buttresses and battlements. The most attractive feature of
the church is the roofs, all painted gaily and ornately and in-
tentionally correctly by *Mrs Holland* in 1859–66. She was the
wife of the Rector. She painted not only ornament, but also
large figures of saints and angels. – FONT. Octagonal, with four
lions against the stem and four roses, two lions, and two angels
against the bowl. – FONT COVER. A very tall Gothic canopy
made in memory of Mrs Holland, † 1878. – PLATE. Credence
1729; Flagon 1753; Cup and Paten 1815. – MONUMENT.
Tomb-chest in a recess in the chancel N wall. On it (not *in situ*)
brass inscription to John Paston † 1575. The inscription runs
as follows:

This earthlye coulored marble stone behold with weeping
eyes;

* A will of 1472 leaves money towards the building of a tower, provided
that work starts in that year (ARA).

Under whose cold and massie waight, John Paston buried lyes.
A gentele man by birth and deedes, the second sonne to one
Syr William Paston, worthie knight, deceased long agone.
This gentle esquier in Huntingfield, a widowe tooke to wyfe,
That hight Anne Arrowsmith, with whom he ledde a loving
    lyfe
Eleven yeres space and somewhat more, by whom he also had
One onlye child, a virgine myld, is aged hart to glad.
In youthfull yeres this gentelman a gallant cortier was,
With rarest vertues well adornd, to courtiers all a glasse.
A pencioner to princes foure, Henrye theight, that roye,
To Edward king, to Marye quene, to Elsabethe, our joye.
Which foure he served faythfullie; the court lament his end,
His countrie neybhoures all bewayle the losse of such a frend.
To poore a present remedie, to honest men an ayde,
A father to the fatherles, the widowes playnte he mayde.
Againste the hongrie travailer his doores were never shitt.
Againste the seelie needye soule his purse was never knite.
When he had lyved threeskore yeres and foure, death closd up
    his eyes,
He lyved well, he dyed well, and buryed here he lyes.

Against the back wall C15 PAINTING, Christ and Angels,
indistinct. – MONUMENTS. Many minor tablets.
In the village an extremely pretty Gothic house probably of the
late C18. Was it built as an eye-catcher from Heveningham
Hall? Red brick with a three-bay centre and one-bay slightly
higher wings, treated as angle towers. They as well as the centre
are castellated. Charming doorcase with ogee detail. Pointed
arches to the windows on the ground floor, ogee arches on
the first. The half-floor above has quatrefoil windows.
HIGH HOUSE, 1 m. SW. Dated in large iron letters 1700. The 55b
date is on the two shaped front gables; for in spite of so late a
date the house, a small, compact, red brick house, still has
shaped gables, two to the front, two to the back, and one large
one to each side. Square central chimney with sunk panels.
The porch is recent.

ICKLINGHAM 7070

ALL SAINTS. A thatched church, and not a small one. The nave
is structurally Norman (blocked N windows), the rest is mostly
late C13 to early C14. SW tower with windows belonging to that
date and including a quatrefoil window in a circle. Dec nave,
but with an odd Late Perp W window. Dec S aisle with S
windows with cusped and uncusped intersected tracery, a

pretty frieze of ballflower and other motifs along the top of the walls, and a splendid five-light E window with reticulated tracery, a hood-mould with fleurons to the inside, and, also inside, two ornate niches l. and r., which differ in their details. The r. one has diapered shafts. Dec chancel with a big three-light E window and two low-side windows. Dec arcade with octagonal piers. Perp porch. The interior is impressively bare, with a tiled floor and ancient benches pleasantly left alone. It allows the architecture to speak undisturbedly. Roof with scissor-bracing below and above the collar-beams. – FONT. Early C14, octagonal, with eight different simple motifs of tracery, a veritable mason's pattern-book. – ROOD SCREEN. The dado only is preserved. – PULPIT. Jacobean. – FAMILY PEW. C17. – COMMUNION RAIL. Late C17; with flat twisted balusters. – CHEST. A delightful early C14 piece with close iron scrollwork. – TILES. In the chancel, patterned, and probably C14. – STAINED GLASS. Something of the original glass remains in the chancel and S aisle, including the upper halves of figures and canopies. – PLATE. Elizabethan Cup; Paten 1703.

ST JAMES, ½ m. NW. Chancel of c. 1300, see the E window with cusped intersected tracery and the odd motif of three arches at the foot of the intersecting part. The rest Perp, but with re-used Dec windows. Perp arcades, the piers with polygonal attachments towards the nave and aisles which have no capitals. – FONT. Octagonal, Perp, simple. – (STALLS. They incorporate parts of the rood screen. LG) – PLATE. Elizabethan Cup; Paten probably Elizabethan.

HORSELANDS. There is a Roman VILLA just N of the road on the edge of Weatherhill Farm, ½ m. S of the village. Partial excavation in 1877 revealed part of a hypocaust containing a coin of Carausius (286–93). In the vicinity were found considerable numbers of brooches, pins, and bracelets (now divided between the Ashmolean and British Museums). Ploughing in 1940 uncovered further building material and coins. Also in the vicinity were two lead cisterns. That found in 1939 was decorated with ten panels, one bearing the Christian Alpha and Omega and Chi-Rho monogram.

Roman KILNS were found in 1937 in the adjoining fields. They are similar to those at Wattisfield and are dated to the C3 A.D.

A HOARD of Roman pewter was discovered in 1956 on the S edge of Berners Heath, to the E of Pilgrims Path. It comprised nine vessels, including a pointed oval dish depicting a fish, an iron key, a saw blade, and a sherd of *terra sigillata*. A similar find was made at West Row, Mildenhall, though there the objects were of silver.

Icklingham appears to be the site of CAMBORICUM, mentioned in the Antonine Itinerary as lying between Venta Icenorum and Durolipons (Cambridge).

Slightly S of Berners Heath is a single BARROW, and there are three others in an E–W line ¼ m. NE of Bernersfield Farm. In 1923 a cinerary urn (now destroyed) was reported to have been found in one of these barrows.

ICKWORTH

8060

ST MARY. In the park of the house, a considerable distance from this and anything else. Stuccoed W tower of 1833 in the lancet style. In the porch head of a Norman window with saltire-cross decoration. C13 chancel of knapped flint. On the E side three stepped lancet windows and an oculus over. Double-chamfered reveals. Slit lancets all along the S side. Early C14 N aisle. Three-light intersected windows with cusping. The S aisle is of 1833. – WALL PAINTING. S of the E window. A whole-length figure, probably the angel of the Annunciation. Early C14. – STAINED GLASS. Mostly Flemish roundels. – PLATE. All silver-gilt: Flagon 1697; Almsdish 1758; French Paten C18; Cup 1810.

ICKWORTH. The Herveys have been Lords of the Manor of Ickworth ever since the C15. The manor house stood E of the church. The present house is the work of Frederick, Bishop of Derry in 1768 and fourth Earl of Bristol in 1779, one of England's great eccentrics and not the most attractive of them. He travelled much and was more at home in Rome than in Ireland. Bristol Hotels all over the world owe their name to him. While Bishop of Derry, he began a house for himself at Ballyscullion. It had a circular centre and quadrant wings and was never completed. Ickworth was started in 1795,* and at the time of the Earl's death (in 1803) far from completed. The design is by *Francis Sandys*, but the crazy idea of the oval *corps de logis*, taken over from Ballyscullion, must be the Earl's. It makes for a lumpy appearance from outside and creates very unsatisfactory shapes for most of the rooms inside. The main oval is connected by one-storeyed quadrant wings with two-storeyed nine-bay pavilions. These, of conventional design, with pedimented centres, the pediments resting on attached Ionic

60

* Date supplied by Mr Adrian R. Allan.

columns, were hardly begun at the time when the Earl died.
They were completed only about 1830. The house is 700 ft
long and 100 ft high. It is of brick stuccoed. The pretext for
starting on such a vast mansion was the necessity to house the
collections which the Earl had got together in Italy. However,
they were confiscated by the French in 1798. The Earl had
intended the wings for the collections, the rotunda for himself.
Now the rotunda is open to the public, the wings serve domestic
purposes. The rotunda is covered by a segmental dome. The
walls have attached columns all the way round, unfluted Ionic
below, Corinthian above. A terracotta frieze runs above the
upper columns, a second below the capitals of the lower.
These were copied from *Flaxman*'s designs from Homer by
Casimiro and *Donato Carabelli* of Milan, who worked also for
the façade of Milan Cathedral. The Carabelli brothers left the
friezes unfinished, and they were completed in the 1820s in
Coade stone.* The entrance is marked by a four-column
portico with pediment, rather inorganically attached to the
corners of the rotunda. The entrance hall was remodelled in
1907 by *Sir Reginald Blomfield*. The splendid staircase hall
behind it in the middle of the oval dates from *c.*1825–30. The
stairs themselves are kept behind arcades (and colonnades of
coupled Ionic columns on the second floor) and leave the
centre free. Shallow glass vault. On the floor *Flaxman*'s most
61a   ambitious marble group: 'The Fury of Athamas', commissioned by the Earl in 1790 at a price of 600 gns. It is inspired
by antique sculpture, notably the Laocoon, and hence not as
successful as Flaxman is on a less monumental scale and in a
less exacting context. In the library, which has screens of
two columns at both ends, a fireplace by *Canova*, illustrating
the story of Bacchus and Ariadne. The decoration of the rooms
is nowhere earlier than 1825.

OBELISK erected in 1804 by the inhabitants of Londonderry in
memory of the Earl of Bristol, Bishop of Derry. About 50 ft
tall.

(DOWER HOUSE. C18; good. P. G. M. Dickinson)

IKEN

4050

ST BOTOLPH.‡ By the river Alde, away from any village.
Knapped flint W tower. Money for it was left in 1450. Flush-

---

* This is Mr D. Davidson's interpretation of the accounts as preserved in
the house.
‡ The church is now (1974) burned out.

work decoration on base, buttresses, and battlements. s porch of before 1529 with a front also panelled in flushwork. The top gable renewed in brick. The nave thatched. It is of c. 1300 (see the N side). A Perp niche to the r. of the chancel arch. Chancel of c. 1862. – FONT. Octagonal. With four lions against the stem and the Signs of the four Evangelists and four angels with shields against the bowl. On the shields the Instruments of the Passion (lance, heart, nails, whip). – PLATE. Repoussé Cup 1763.

ILKETSHALL ST ANDREW   3080

ST ANDREW. Norman round tower. The top is octagonal and later. Flushwork-panelled battlements. Norman doorways, on the N plain, on the s with one order of colonnettes and a zig-zag in the arch. One Norman N window. The chancel is of the early C14. Recess in the s wall with a big ogee arch and buttress shafts with finials. Nave windows Perp. s porch Perp, Early Tudor, of brick. The top is all altered. Nave roof with arched braces and carved arched wall-braces running W-E. – FONT. Octagonal, Perp, simple. – (SCREEN. Fragments in the chamber over the porch. Cautley) – BENCH. Late C16 with an inscription referring to John Bonsey (married in 1577). Richly carved back. – PLATE. Altered Cup 1568; Patens 1686 or older, and 1825.
(MANOR HOUSE, at Backs Green, 2 m. s. Timber-framed. Good brick end with polygonal angle buttresses, i.e. C16. DOE)

ILKETSHALL ST JOHN   3080

ST JOHN BAPTIST. Small, with unbuttressed w tower, nave and chancel in one, and all windows renewed. The chancel is C13; see one N lancet. – FONT. Octagonal, Perp. Four lions against the stem, four shields and four flowers against the bowl. – ROOD CANOPY. This is the explanation which Cautley gives of the mostly broken-off frill of wooden ornament in place of the chancel arch. It seems Jacobean. – (BANNER STAFF LOCKER. Tower s pier.) – PLATE. Elizabethan Cup; Paten c. 1680–90.
At MANOR FARM, ½ m. ENE of the church, in a coppice, a well-preserved little motte-and-bailey castle. The moats are still largely wet.

ILKETSHALL ST LAWRENCE   3080

ST LAWRENCE. Small, of nave, chancel, and w tower. – FONT.

Perp, with eight heads carrying the bowl and eight shields on its sides. – PLATE. Elizabethan Cup and Cover; Paten 1705.

3080   ILKETSHALL ST MARGARET

ST MARGARET. Norman round tower with Dec top. Nave and chancel only; small. At the E end a three-light window with intersected tracery. The chancel s doorway has a pretty and rather fantastical arch, C18 Gothic more probably than C14. – FONT. The bowl rests on eight heads. Against its sides four shields, two flowers, and two square leaves. – COMMUNION RAIL. Later C17, with turned balusters. – (WALL PAINTING. Probably St Christopher. LG) – PLATE. Cup and Paten (Norwich-made) 1568; Paten C17.

8070   INGHAM

ST BARTHOLOMEW. Built in 1861 in the local style, with the use of old parts, especially the tower arch on two head corbels. (The old tower was probably begun c. 1455, according to a will of that year. ARA) – STAINED GLASS. Some C15 glass in the s porch.

SCHOOL, N of the church. Gabled. Flint with yellow brick trim and white diamond window panes, a cheerful sight. Built in 1846.

Scenery: Afforestation near Elveden

(a) *Scenery :* Woodbridge, the harbour

(b) *Townscape :* Bury St Edmunds, Angel Hill with the abbey gateway

(a) *Scenery :* Dunwich, coast erosion

(b) *Roman :* Burgh Castle

3

Scenery: Thorpeness, windmill

Church Exteriors: Little Saxham, tower Norman,
south side and porch Perpendicular

(a) *Church Exteriors :* Rickinghall Inferior, tower Norman and early fourteenth century, the rest mainly Decorated

(b) *Decorated Church Exteriors :* Stowmarket, north aisle

Decorated Church Exteriors: Mildenhall, east window, *c.* 1300

(a) *Church Exteriors, Flushwork* : Barsham, east end, fourteenth, sixteenth, or seventeenth century (?)

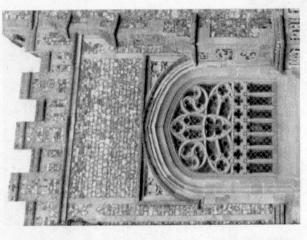

(b) *Perpendicular Church Exteriors* : Stratford St Mary, north porch (window Victorian)

8

Perpendicular Church Exteriors : Bury St Edmunds, St Mary, begun 1424

9

(a) *Perpendicular Church Exteriors, Flushwork:*
Southwold, after c. 1430

(b) *Perpendicular Church Exteriors, Flushwork:*
Eye, west tower

(a) *Perpendicular Church Exteriors*:
Woolpit, south porch, c. 1430–55

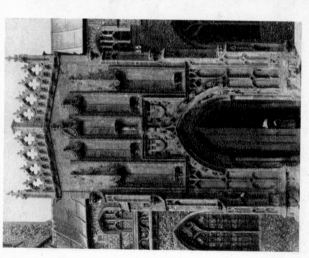

(b) *Perpendicular Church Exteriors, Flushwork*:
Kersey, south porch

Perpendicular Church Exteriors, Flushwork: Woodbridge, c. 1450

(a) *Church Exteriors, Timber : Boxford,*
north porch, Decorated

(b). *Perpendicular Church Exteriors, Brick : Stoke-*
by-Nayland, north porch, early sixteenth century (?)

(a) *Church Exteriors, Timber :* Crowfield, with timber-framed chancel

(b) *Church Buildings, Timber :* East Bergholt, bell house,
sixteenth century

14

(a) *Norman Church Interiors:* Polstead

(b) *Norman Church Interiors:* Orford, chancel, begun 1166

(a) *Perpendicular Church Interiors : Lavenham:*
c. 1500

(b) *Perpendicular Church Interiors : Long Melford,*
Clopton Chantry, *c.* 1500 *(Copyright Country Life)*

(b) *Church Interiors*: Ipswich, Unitarian Meeting
House, by Joseph Clarke, 1699–1700

(a) *Church Interiors*:
Brightwell, west end, c. 1656

17

(b) *Church Roofs: Yaxley*

(a) *Church Roofs: Barking*

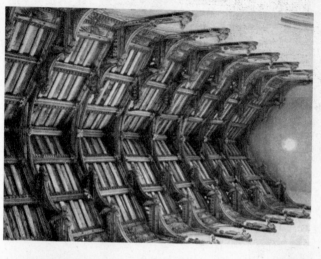

(a) *Perpendicular Church Roofs: Kersey*

(b) *Perpendicular Church Roofs: Woolpit*

19

Perpendicular Church Roofs: Needham Market

Church Interiors: Leiston, by E. B. Lamb, 1853

(a) *Church Furnishings*: Ipswich, Christchurch Mansion, fragment of a Norman font of Tournai marble

(b) *Church Furnishings*: Ipswich, St Peter, Norman font of Tournai marble

(a) *Church Furnishings*: Sutton, font, early fifteenth century (?)

(b) *Church Furnishings*: Pakenham, typical East Anglian font,
Perpendicular

Church Furnishings : Cratfield, font with the Seven Sacraments,
Perpendicular

(a) *Church Furnishings:*
Ufford, font cover,
Perpendicular

(b) *Church Furnishings:*
Mendlesham, font cover,
by John Turner, 1630

(a) *Church Furnishings:* Eye, screen, paintings *c.* 1500

(b) *Church Furnishings:* Dennington, parclose screen, Perpendicular

Church Furnishings : Lavenham, screen to Spring Chantry, after 1523

(a) *Church Furnishings* : Withersfield, bench end

(b) *Church Furnishings* : Blythburgh, bench end

28

Church Furnishings : Fornham St Martin, misericord with St Martin

Church Furnishings : Clare, door in the north porch, Perpendicular

(a) *Painting in Churches*: Thornham Parva, retable, *c.* 1300

(b) *Painting in Churches*: Knodishall, Jacob and Rachel,
by William Dyce, 1851

(a) *Stained Glass:*
Long Melford,
late fifteenth century

(b) *Painting in Churches:*
Brantham, Christ and the Children,
by John Constable, 1804

Church Monuments: Chelsworth, tomb recess,
early fourteenth century

(a) *Church Monuments:* Framlingham, monument to
Thomas Howard, third Duke of Norfolk, †1554

(b) *Church Monuments:* Long Melford, monument to
Sir William Cordell, †1580

Church Monuments : Hengrave, monument to Thomas Darcy, †1614

Church Monuments: Framlingham, monument to Sir Robert Hitcham,
by Francis Grigs, 1638

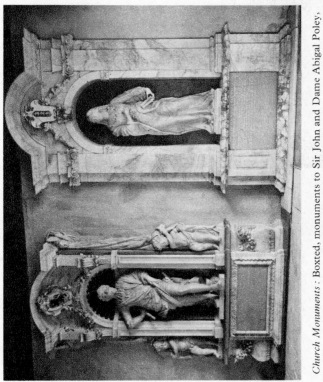

Church Monuments : Boxted, monuments to Sir John and Dame Abigal Poley,
the former *c.* 1675; the latter 1725

(a) *Church Monuments*: Redgrave, monument to Sir John Holt, †1710, by Thomas Green

(b) *Church Monuments*: Acton, monument to Robert Jennens, †1725

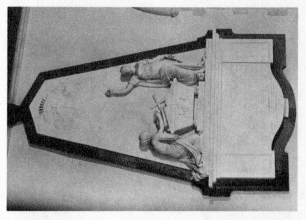

(a) *Church Monuments*: Cowlinge, monument to Francis Dickins, †1747, by Peter Scheemakers

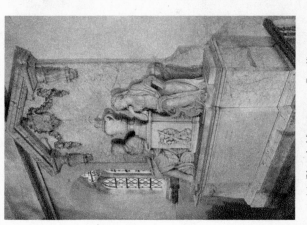

(b) *Church Monuments*: Worlingworth, monument to Elizabeth, Duchess of Chandos, by John Bacon Jun., 1817

Church Monuments: Thornham Magna, monument to
Lord Henniker, †1821, by J. Kendrick

Bury St Edmunds Abbey, Norman Gate, *c.* 1120–48

(a) Orford Castle, keep, 1165–7

(b) Framlingham Castle, c. 1190–1210

Little Wenham Hall, c. 1270–80

43

(a) Little Wenham Hall, chapel, *c.* 1285

(b) Butley Priory, gatehouse, *c.* 1320–5

Bury St Edmunds Abbey, Great Gate, *c.* 1330–40

Giffords Hall after 1428, courtyard (Copyright Country Life)

(b) Ipswich, No. 7 Northgate Street,
c. 1500, angle post

(a) Lavenham, Old Wool Hall, fifteenth
century, from Water Street

(a) Hadleigh, Deanery Tower, 1495

(b) West Stow Hall, gatehouse, c. 1525

(a) Ipswich, Cardinal College of St Mary, begun 1527, gateway

(b) Hengrave Hall, entrance, bay window perhaps by William Ponyard, 1538

(a) Hengrave Hall, begun c. 1525, courtyard

(b) Shrubland Old Hall, terracotta windows, c. 1525

(b) Clare, The Cliftons, chimney,
sixteenth century

(a) Erwarton Hall, gatehouse, c. 1549

51

Long Melford, Melford Hall, after 1545 (*Copyright Country Life*)

(b) Beccles, Roos Hall, 1593

(a) Freston Tower, *c.* 1550

53

Helmingham Hall, c. 1500 and later (*Copyright Country Life*)

54

(a) Woodbridge, Shire Hall, c. 1575 and later

(b) Huntingfield, High House, 1700

55

(a) Ipswich, Sparrowe's House, c. 1670

(b) Bury St Edmunds, Cupola House, 1693

(b) Norton, Little Haugh Hall, landing, c. 1730

(a) Somerleyton Hall, panelling, c. 1730

(a) Acton Place, early eighteenth century

(b) Hintlesham Hall, plaster ceiling, *c.* 1690 (*Copyright Country Life*)

Heveningham Hall, entrance hall, by James Wyatt, before 1784

Ickworth, by Francis Sandys, begun 1795

(a) Ickworth, The Fury of Athamas,
by Flaxman, 1790

(b) Beccles, St Peter's House, Gothick
fireplace, late eighteenth century

(a) Ipswich, Old Custom House, by J. M. Clark, 1844

(b) Somerleyton Hall, by John Thomas, begun 1844, garden front

Elveden Hall, by John Norton, 1863–70, central hall

a) Shrubland Park, by Sir Charles Barry, 1848–52
(*Copyright Country Life*)

(b) Holbrook, Royal Hospital School, by Buckland & Haywood,
1925–33

IPSWICH

INTRODUCTION

Ipswich lies on the estuary of the river Orwell, which in its upper reaches is called the Gipping. Ipswich is Gippeswich. Its position favoured a settlement from the Palaeolithic through the younger prehistoric phases and Roman times* to the Middle Ages and the present day. Ipswich was an important port in the Middle Ages. Already in Domesday it had nine churches, not all of them tallying with those of the later Middle Ages. John Evelyn says it had fourteen or fifteen. More medieval parish churches are preserved at Ipswich than in any other English town of its size. The line of the medieval walls can still be traced from such street names as Tower Ramparts, West-gate Street, and Northgate Street. The Westgate was pulled down only in 1780, the Northgate in 1794. Ipswich had two Augustinian Priories, Holy Trinity founded before 1177 of which now only fragments remain at Christchurch Mansion built on its site, and St Peter and St Paul, founded about the same time. The Franciscans settled about 1236. Friars Road, Grey Friars Road, and an insignificant bit of structure‡ is all that remains of their house. Of that of the Dominicans or Blackfriars, who had come in 1263, only little more survives (in School Street), of that of the Carmelites whose establishment (s of the Buttermarket) dated from c. 1240 nothing at all. The principal late medieval foundation was Wolsey's Cardinal College of St Mary. This was founded in 1527 and endowed by the lands etc. of seven monasteries suppressed for the purpose. It consisted of a Dean, a Sub-Dean, twelve Fellows,

---

* At CASTLE HILL, Whitton, is a Roman VILLA, originally discovered in 1854. It was apparently of corridor type. Finds included a mosaic floor of geometric design (now in the Ipswich Museum) as well as other tesserae, pottery, and coins of the C2–4 A.D., which indicates a long occupation. Partial excavation in 1928–9 and rescue work in 1949–50 revealed in the central part of the building an extensive system of heating channels and furnaces as well as much thick roofing slate probably imported from Wales or Brittany.

‡ Removed to the Greyfriars Concourse.

sixteen Choristers, twelve Bedesmen, a Schoolmaster, two Ushers, and fifty Grammar Children. It extended E of St Peter's and was begun in 1523. It was never completed. Wolsey had been born at Ipswich in 1471, the son of a wealthy butcher and merchant. His age marked the start of the most prosperous era for Ipswich. Evelyn still called it one of the best towns of England, and Defoe also praised it. Yet in Defoe's time its decline had set in. From a town of national importance it was reduced to no more than the centre and port of an agricultural county. Its population was c. 12,000 in 1700, but only 11,000 in 1801. In 1851 it had risen only to 32,000, in 1901 to 60,000. It is now (i.e. in 1971) 122,830.

CHURCHES

ST MARY-LE-TOWER, Tower Street. The principal parish church of Ipswich. Mostly 1860–70, by *Phipson*. Large, with a commanding S porch tower. The recessed spire reaches up 176 ft. Knapped flint with much chequered flushwork. Openwork parapet on the tower. Original Perp work the arcades of five bays and a short sixth bay. In the chancel E wall two niches l. and r. of the window. – FONT. Perp, octagonal. Against the base four lions, against the bowl eight lions. – STALLS. With simple MISERICORDS. – PULPIT. Of c. 1700 with lively carving, similar to that of the Unitarian Meeting House. The tester is preserved. – Two SWORD-RESTS, apparently C18. – PLATE. Pre-Reformation Chalice, remade in 1867; Cup 1631; Credence 1665; two Flagons 1679; Almsdish 1728; Spoon c. 1739. – MONUMENTS. Four brasses in the chancel floor: a Notary of c. 1475 (3 ft 8 in. figure); a Notary of the early C16 with two wives (2 ft 4 in. figures); Alys Baldry † 1506 and two husbands (2 ft 2 in. figures); and Thomas Drayle † 1518 and two wives (2 ft 9 in. figures). – William Smart † 1599, painted panel with inscription in a framing of three-dimensional strapwork, the deceased and his wife kneeling in the bottom corners and a view of Ipswich between (S aisle w). – John Robinson † 1666 and his wife † 1694, kneeling figures facing one another and a group of four figures in the 'predella' below; the figures are all relaxed and no longer retain anything of the Jacobean stiffness of attitude.

ALL SAINTS, Chevallier Street. 1886–7 by *S. Wright*. Red brick with SW porch tower, turning octagonal in its upper part. Small recessed, concave-sided lead spire. Slender brick piers inside. The chancel chapels have half-arches to the W like flying buttresses. The design of the church is conventional but not ordinary.

ST AUGUSTINE, Felixstowe Road. By *H. Munro Cautley*, 1927. Completely conventional exterior. Perp with crossing tower and pebble-dash on the walls. Inside, the aisles are reduced to low narrow passages below the tall windows, an expedient typical of the late C19 and early C20. – FONT. From Linstead Magna. Perp. Octagonal, with four lions against the base and against the bowl four lions and four angels holding shields.

ST BARTHOLOMEW, Newton Road. 1896–1900 by *Charles Spooner*. Red brick; conventional exterior. The NE tower not built. Inside tall polygonal stone piers continued as half-polygons to the timber roof. The arcade arches die into them. At the E end above the altar a rose window with flowing tracery, at the W end a window of seven stepped lights.

ST CLEMENT, St Clement's Church Lane, off Grimwade Street. Still nicely secluded in its churchyard. Perp, but over-restored. Chancel of 1860. Simple slender W tower. Clerestory with twelve closely set windows. Six-bay arcades. Quatrefoil piers with fillets and spurs in the diagonals. – (FONT. Damaged. With four Wild Men and four lions against the stem and four angels and the Signs of the Evangelists against the bowl.) – WEST GALLERY. With Corinthian columns and richly carved cornice. Partly re-erected at the E end of the N aisle. – ROYAL ARMS. 1661. Wood, carved. – PLATE. Set 1683–4.

ST HELEN, St Helen's Street. Mostly C19, i.e. of 1835–7, plus alterations of 1875 (e.g. the W window and a new tower). The tower is at the SW end and rather mean. Original Perp S porch and adjoining S wall with some flushwork decoration. The church in its C19 form is aisleless.

HOLY TRINITY, Fore Hamlet. 1836 by *Harvey* of Ipswich. Grey brick with large arched windows. No aisles. Narrow W tower. The chancel was added in 1895, internally in the kind of Georgian Baroque favoured at that moment. It opens in three arches to the nave.

ST JOHN BAPTIST, Cauldwell Hall Road. 1898–9 by *Sir Arthur Blomfield*. Red brick, big, but with a bellcote only and no tower. The windows are mostly grouped lancets. Wide interior, the brick exposed. Low circular and octagonal piers. Polygonal W baptistery. To the S the modest old church of 1857 still stands.

ST LAWRENCE, Dial Lane. Perp. The W tower was begun with the money of John Bottold, who died in 1431. The chancel was built with the money of John Baldwyn, a draper who died in

1449. The tower was rebuilt sumptuously in 1882 by *F*
Barnes and *H. Gaye*. The height is 97 ft. Much flushwork and
also much decorated stonework, bands of quatrefoils, etc
Large three-light bell-openings. Two-stepped openwork
battlements. The tower was originally open to the N and S. The
simple chamfered arches are now blocked. Tall Perp N and
windows. Buttresses with stone and flint decoration. Doorway
with crowns, shields, and fleurons in jambs and arches. Aisleless interior. – WEST DOOR. Perp with lively blank tracery. –
STAINED GLASS. E window by *Charles Gibbs c.* 1855. In a
romantic version of the C13 style. – PLATE. Paten 1733
Flagon 1745; Cup and Paten 1775; Almsdish 1820. – MONU-
MENT. Mrs Colman, probably *c.* 1700. Hanging monument
without effigy. Coat of arms on a free-standing Ionic column
Little putti l. and r. The column stands against the background
of a short stumpy pilaster. The design much resembles the
Lydcott and Winder monuments at All Hallows Barking in the
City of London, and they are of 1696 and 1699. The same type
of monument also occurs several times in Norfolk.

ST MARGARET, St Margaret's Green. Certainly the most
spectacular church in Ipswich. It is placed so that it presents
itself fully to the approaching traveller, against the background
of the old trees of Christchurch Mansion. It has one of the East
Anglian clerestories with closely set windows, and it has lavish
decoration all over it: the spandrels of the windows, the parapet and the battlements and the pinnacles. The aisle windows
are Dec (intersected tracery on the N side), the W tower has
two tall two-light bell-openings on each side, flushwork
arcading on the top, and (until recently) pinnacles. On the
side a clock of 1737 in a pedimented aedicule surround. S porch
tall with flushwork decoration of the battlements, a flushwork
panelled front, and three niches above the entrance. S transept
with flanking polygonal turrets. Dec arcades of five bays
Octagonal piers and double-hollow-chamfered arches. Low
chancel allowing for three nave E windows, one of them circular. The chancel arch has crowns, fleurons, and shields on
the responds. Splendid double-hammerbeam roof. Figures
against the wall-posts. Decorated wall-plate. Baroque painting
on the panels between the main timbers. – FONT. Damaged
Perp bowl originally with eight angels. One holds a scroll
inscribed 'Sal et Saliva'. – PLATE. Two Elizabethan Cups
Paten 1632; Flagon 1719; Salver 1751. – MONUMENTS. Sir
William Roskin † 1512. Arched recess and coarse panelling

Quatrefoil frieze above the canopy. – Edmund Withipoll, the builder of Christchurch Mansion, † 1574. Slab with fine incised lettering, apparently signed T.L.

т MARY AT THE ELMS, Elm Street. Norman s doorway with one order of colonnettes. Block capitals. A little decoration in the arch. Perp nave and N aisle. Two bays; brick. The third bay represents the Norman N transept. The remains of the former s transept can still be seen outside. N chapel and chancel of 1883. The chancel to the E of the former chancel. Good early Tudor w tower of red brick with black brick diapering. Polygonal clasping buttresses. Bell-openings in pairs of two lights under one joint four-centred arch. Two stepped battlements. – SOUTH DOOR. With ornamented ironwork possibly as early as the s doorway. – PLATE. Set 1758. – MONUMENT. William Acton † 1616. Hanging monument. Kneeling figures facing each other across a prayer desk. Above this a skeleton appears. In the 'predella' stiffly semi-reclining widow.

т MARY AT THE QUAY, Foundation Street (disused). Perp exterior. Money was left in 1448 for the building of the church. The w tower had a pretty c18 lantern (now removed). Frieze of flushwork shields above the w doorway. The nave has a fine hammerbeam roof with figures against the wall-posts. – PLATE. Elizabethan Cup; Almsdish 1721. – MONUMENTS. Henry Tooley † 1551 and family. Brass figures in a stone frame. – Thomas Pounder † 1525 and family. Brass, of excellent quality; Flemish; large, with standing parents and kneeling children; ornamental background. Both these monuments are now at Christchurch Mansion.*

т MARY STOKE, Belstead Road, close to and above the river. A medieval church but so much enlarged and restored that its real date is scarcely noticeable. The old church had an unbuttressed w tower and an aisleless nave with hammerbeam roof. The latter has become the N aisle of the church built in 1870–1 by *Butterfield*. It is not a distinguished example of his gritty style. Flint and stone with some flushwork. Neither the details of this, nor the windows, nor the piers inside are interesting. – STAINED GLASS. E window by *Clayton & Bell*; N aisle E window designed in 1864 by *P. R. Burrell*, later Lord Gwydyr. – PLATE. Cup and Paten 1797.

т MARY, Whitton. Of 1852, with a s aisle and sw tower of 1862. Medieval only the s doorway into the tower. This is a

* The PULPIT of St Mary at the Quay is at Elmsett, the FONT at Branam.

re-set late C13 piece with one order of slim shafts and a deep
moulded arch. – PLATE. Elizabethan Cup.

ST MARY (R.C.), 322 Woodbridge Road. 1826. Enlarged 183
Yellow brick with lancet windows. Small and modest, but th
façade with much going on. – STAINED GLASS. Chancel
and S by *Mayer & Co.* – (The CONVENT of Jesus and Mary
by *George Goldie*, 1867–8. Denis Evinson)

ST MATTHEW, Portman Road. Perp W tower. Battlements wit
some flushwork and openwork. The upper part of the tower wa
rebuilt in 1884. Perp N and S arcades of four bays. The N arcad
has concave-sided octagonal piers, the S arcade norma
octagonal piers with fleurons in the capitals. The S aisle wa
widened in 1845 and refaced in 1884. The S chapel was widene
in 1860. The N aisle was widened and enlarged by *G. G. Sco*
in 1877. The E wall was rebuilt in 1866 and again altered i
1890. – FONT. Octagonal. Base with lions and angels. Bow
supported by demi-figures of angels. Against the bowl tw
foliage panels and small scenes of the Annunciation, the Bap
tism of Christ, the Adoration of the Magi, the Assumption o
the Virgin, the Coronation of the Virgin, and the Virgin *i*
throno. – SCREEN. Six panels of the former rood screen no
used in the N aisle. Four have painted saints, the other two th
unusual motif of groups of kneeling figures of donors: one o
them carries a purse. – STAINED GLASS. S aisle E, designed b
Frank Howard and made by *Hedgeland c.* 1853; S aisle SE 187
S aisle fourth from W 1880, N aisle middle 1882 by *Ward &*
Hughes; SE 1878 by *H. Hughes* alone; S aisle third from W 188
by *W. H. Constable*. – PLATE. Elizabethan Cup. – MONU
MENTS. Two hanging monuments with kneeling coupl
facing one another † 1629 and † 1630.

ST NICHOLAS, Friars Road. Early C14 aisles. Arcades of fo
bays. Quatrefoil piers with fillets. Boldly moulded capital
Arches with two sunk quadrant mouldings. The aisle window
stand so low that their sills are usable as seats. The window
with Y or intersected tracery. The chancel chapels of one wic
bay are C15. Perp W tower rebuilt in 1886. W doorway wit
shields in the spandrels. On the shields the emblems of th
Trinity and the Passion. Three shields with coats of arms abov
the doorway. The tower has flushwork decoration on th
battlements and below them, and also on base and buttresse
Perp dormers on the N and S sides to give light to the rood. The
have original bargeboards. The brick S porch is probably of th
C18. – PULPIT. Mid C17 with tester. The decoration no longe

has the familiar short blank arches. – COMMUNION RAIL.
With twisted balusters; C18. – PANELLING. Aisle walls, C17;
from former box pews. – SCULPTURE. Three panels of the
early C12. One is a dedication stone. It has an inscription: 'In
dedicatione eclesie Omnium Sanctorum' and the relief of a boar.
The second has a St Michael with the Dragon. The inscription
reads: 'Her sanctus Michael feht wid dane dragon.' The style
is similar to that of the lintel at Hoveringham, Notts. On the
other slab are three upright figures of apostles under arches. –
PAINTING. Christ at Emaus, large and now very dark. By *J.
Smart* of Ipswich, 1807 (chancel N wall). – PLATE. Elizabethan
Cup; Flagon 1703; Paten and Almsdish 1766. – BRASSES.
William Style † 1475 and wife (2 ft 2 in. figures). – Civilian,
c. 1500 (s aisle E respond). The figure is 2 ft 7 in. long. – Late
Elizabethan husband and wife.

T PANCRAS (R.C.), Orwell Place. 1860, by *G. Goldie*. Red
brick, with aisles (short circular piers), clerestory, a polygonal
apse, and no tower. The style is C13 with plate tracery.

T PETER, St Peter Street. Close to the site of the Augustinian
priory of St Peter and St Paul founded in the late C12. C14
aisles with Dec windows (note the motif of the four-petalled
flower). Dec arcades of four bays with keeled quatrefoiled
piers. The arches have two hollow chamfers. The N clerestory
windows are sexfoils, also of the C14, the S clerestory, W tower,
s porch, and E end are all Perp. E of the E end traces of continuation, connected probably with Wolsey's College (*see* p. 304).
The arms of Henry VIII outside on a buttress in the chancel E
wall. In Wolsey's time the church served as a chapel to his
college, and the arms are no doubt connected with that. The
aisles were lengthened in 1878 by *Scott*. Of his design also the
E window. The upper part of the tower was rebuilt in 1881. The
tower has flushwork decoration and two niches with big
canopies l. and r. of the W doorway. In the jambs and arches of
the doorway shields and fleurons. – FONT. Large, square, 22b
Romanesque. It is made of black Tournai marble and has a
frieze of monumental lions *passant*. The base is Perp with four
standing figures. – PLATE. Two Patens 1736; Cup 1772;
Flagon 1792; two Cups 1812. – (BRASS to John Knappe and
family, 1604. Said to be very good.*)

T STEPHEN, St Stephen's Lane. Perp, much restored 1866 and
1881. The W tower with much brick repair. Big three-light N
and S windows of nave and S aisle. Traces of a small doorway

* Information from Mr D. M. Palliser and others.

piercing a s aisle buttress. The arcade piers of typical Pe
section are said to be of Purbeck marble. Chancel arch wi
two lancet-shaped side openings l. and r. The nave roof h
tie-beams on braces and king- and queenposts, the chanc
roof hammerbeams. – PLATE. Flagon 1732; Cup and Pat
1775; Knife 1796; Paten 1813. – MONUMENT. Sir Robe
Leman † 1637, Lord Mayor of London. Signed by *J. & N*
Christmas. Kneeling figures facing one another across a pray
desk. Flanking columns and a double-curved open pedimer

BAPTIST CHURCH, London Road. 1875. Red and yellow bri
Centre with coarse pedimented gable. The openings wi
Italianate round arches.

BETHESDA BAPTIST CHURCH, St Margaret's Plain. 1913
F. G. Faunch. The tall four-column portico with its polish
granite columns faces down Northgate Street.

TURRET GREEN BAPTIST CHAPEL (former), Turret Lan
See p. 302n.

CONGREGATIONAL CHURCH, St Nicholas Street. 1829. Gr
brick with lancet windows.

CONGREGATIONAL CHURCH, Dryden Road, Castle Hi
Whitton. By *Johns, Slater & Haward*, 1956–7. In one of t
new housing estates. The church represents that rather 'E
pressionist', jagged, neo-romantic style which, in the m
c20, became an international idiom for ecclesiastical arch
tecture. Big, steeply pitched roof, shallow pitch of the low
adjoining roof, walls of lozenge-pattern, almost entirely glaze
Plain and coloured glass, the colours being dark blue and
deep yellow.

UNITED REFORMED CHURCH, Portman Road. 1870
Frederick Barnes. With asymmetrically placed tower with spi
The walls faced with stone in a crazy-paving fashion.

UNITARIAN MEETING HOUSE, Friars Street. By *Joseph Clar*
a carpenter, 1699–1700.* One of the best of its date in Englar
Front of five bays and two storeys with hipped roof. The fi
and last bays have broad doorways with pediments on we
carved brackets and oval windows over. The other bays
two-storeyed and have wooden cross-windows. The w side
of four bays and two storeys, the E side of five bays with
central doorway decorated like those of the front. Back (s si
of six bays. The four middle ones with tall arched windows a
oval windows over. This fenestration truthfully expresses
internal arrangement. Against the s wall in the middle is t

17b

* The building is timber-framed and plastered.

PULPIT, richly carved and with elegantly curved stairs. The stairs have twisted balusters. The other three sides have a wooden gallery. The stairs up to it also with twisted balusters. In the middle of the room two elongated Tuscan columns of wood helping to carry the flat ceiling. – BOX PEWS. – Fine brass CHANDELIER. – PLATE. Paten 1632; Cups 1691, 1703, 1708; Paten 1764.

PUBLIC BUILDINGS

COUNTY HALL (former Gaol), St Helen's Street. 1836–7, by *W. McIntosh Brooks* of London. Grey brick, two-storeyed with battlements. In the Tudor style. Few windows and a central gatehouse with short turrets. Added to this in 1906 an extension with normal windows and an angle turret, by *J. S. Corder* and *Henry Miller*.

TOWN HALL, Cornhill. 1867–8, by *Bellamy & Hardy* of Lincoln. Italianate, with a French pavilion roof over the raised centre, and quite undistinguished. Only nine bays wide. – INSIGNIA. Two Maces presented by Charles II. – Loving Cup 1734. – Ceremonial Oar 1811.

CIVIC CENTRE. See p. 307.

CORN EXCHANGE (former), King Street. 1878–82, by *Brightwen Binyon* of Ipswich. A tripartite composition in the Italianate style but with French pavilion roof. Also undistinguished. It is being converted (1973) by *Johns, Slater & Haward* into a Multi Purpose Entertainment Centre.

OLD CUSTOM HOUSE, Key Street. 1844, by *J. M. Clark.* 62a Remarkably original. Red and yellow brick. The style is classical and the front towards the river monumental and symmetrical, with a bold raised four-column portico carrying a far-projecting pediment. Large open stairs lead up to it. Behind them on the ground floor a small entrance placed in a deep niche lined with nicely cut ashlar stone and distinguished by a heavy Gibbs surround. The symmetry of this frontage is very self-consciously broken by the tower at the far l. corner (NW).

TELEPHONE EXCHANGE, Portman Road. 1956–7, by *T. F. Winterburn*. Four-storeyed, of yellow brick; up-to-date for its time, and unobtrusive.

IPSWICH MUSEUM, High Street. 1881; won in competition by *Horace Cheston*. In the C17 brick style made fashionable by Norman Shaw. Symmetrical façade, superimposed orders of pilasters. Pedimented gables.

CHRISTCHURCH MANSION AND ART GALLERY. In the large
grounds just N of St Margaret's Church, outside the old town
walls. The mansion stands on the site of the Augustinian
Priory of Holy Trinity, founded c. 1177. Perp fragments of the
priory buildings are exhibited in the mansion. The buildings
were purchased shortly after 1545 by a London merchant-
tailor, Paul Withipoll, and his son Edmund, who built the
house in 1548–50. Dates occur inside the hall (1548), on the
porch (1549), on the E wing (1550), and on the W side of the W
wing (1564). The latter however formed an extension of the
original buildings recognizable by its straight gables. The
original buildings were on the familiar E-plan, with the wings
projecting as far as they do in the contemporary mansions of
Melford Hall and Kentwell Hall, Long Melford, and of Rushbrooke Hall. Red brick, with dark blue brick diapering. Two
storeys. The original windows, as preserved on the ground
floor, were mullioned and transomed. A fire occurred shortly
before 1674, and the upper storey was rebuilt after that. It
occurs in its rebuilt form on Ogilby's map of 1674, and there are
rain-water heads with the date 1675. To this remodelling belong
all the gables. They have curved sides and pediments at the
top, a motif fashionable c. 1630–50, but a little out of date in
1675. Of the same time the cross-windows on the first floor, the
remodelling of the porch, and much interior work. Other
windows were sashed and given pediments probably after 1732,
when the house came into the Fonnereau family. The porch is
oddly awkward, with its elongated giant Ionic columns and its
balcony. Similar columns occur at Clopton Hall, where the
date is 1681. The hall has panelling of c. 1675 including the
large, boldly moulded fireplace surround. On the N wall high
up two mullioned windows of c. 1550 now giving on to a later
corridor. In 1675 also the former hall screen was removed – or
if it had been burnt, not renewed – and instead handsome
blank wooden arcading put up against the W wall. It has pilasters
in two orders. The upper is opened by three arches towards a
gallery. Also of 1675 must be the staircase adjoining the hall
diagonally in the E wing. This has an open well and strong,
sturdy, moulded balusters. In the W wing were the kitchen and
the offices, and the 1564 extension meant an enlargement of
these rooms. In the E wing on the ground floor and upper floor
are two good rooms of c. 1735, the lower with a handsome fireplace, the upper with a richly decorated arch towards the bed
alcove. Both rooms have contemporary flock wallpapers.

As Christchurch Mansion is a museum, the house contains much of interest to the user of this volume. According to the principles of the series, however, it cannot be described in detail.* There are many carved bressumers, corner-posts, etc., of former C16–17 houses of Ipswich. There is also a re-erected timber house of c. 1500 which stood at Major's Corner. It projects to the N of the former N part of the hall. Another extension serves to show the uncommonly rich Early Renaissance panelling of Sir Anthony Wingfield's house in Tacket Street, which later became the Tankard Inn. Wingfield was a Privy Councillor of Henry VIII and one of his executors. He died in 1552.

IPSWICH CIVIC COLLEGE, Rope Walk. By *Johns, Slater & Haward*. The workshop block was completed in 1952; eight-storey block for class-rooms, etc., 1958–60; Assembly Hall, Lecture Theatre, Canteen, Gymnasium, etc., 1961–2. Work is still in progress.

IPSWICH SCHOOL, Henley Road. 1850–2, by *Fleury*. Elizabethan, of red brick, symmetrically composed, with a tower over the entrance. Two-storeyed. On the N a detached Perp chapel of 1852. Further N terraces of houses in the same style and of the same period. They are now the school's preparatory and junior departments. Of the whole group the *Handbook* of Ipswich of 1864 said: 'There is probably no such fine line of modern Elizabethan buildings elsewhere in the Eastern counties.' Many more recent additions.

SPRITES LANE PRIMARY SCHOOL. 1958–60 by *Johns, Slater & Haward*.

SCHOOLS on the Chantry Estate. *See* p. 308.

IPSWICH AND EAST SUFFOLK HOSPITAL, Anglesea Road. The centre is of 1836, yellow brick with giant pilasters and a tight giant portico of unfluted Ionic columns. Above this are attics and a pedimented gable – an awkward composition. The portico is the *point de vue* to which Berners Street leads up (*see* p. 307). The original architect was *John Whiting*. Many more C20 additions, including the water tower and boiler house, Road Wing, by *Peter Barefoot*, 1961–3.

STATION. 1858–60. By *Robert Sinclair*, engineer to the Eastern Counties Railway. Called 'graceful and pretty' in the *Handbook* of 1864. Perhaps it struck people as that when it was new. Yellow and red brick, with round-arched windows, low and

---

* Mention must however be made of the rare C12 FONT of black Tournai 22a marble.

spreading. Centre with two projecting porches and an arcade between.

FIRE STATION, Colchester Road. By *Johns, Slater & Haward*, 1961–2. A large, low, irregular group, partly brick-built, partly brick-faced.

CLIFF QUAY POWER STATION, Sandyhill Lane and Cliff Quay. 1949–50 by *Farmer & Dark*. Light brick, the composition typical of mid-C20 power stations in England, and unlike later work by the same architects. Three chimneys. The main block has tall ground-floor windows and a recessed upper part.

PERAMBULATIONS*

Four are proposed, one to the SE and E, one to the S, one to the N,

* The following is an index of streets, including the sections on churches and public buildings, and the perambulation itself.

and one to the w. All four start from Cornhill or its immediate
vicinity. In addition, a few houses in outer Ipswich will be
mentioned individually.

(A) TO THE SOUTH-EAST AND EAST

CORNHILL is small for a market place, and, with the removal in
1812 of its ornamental market cross, it has lost its chief ornament. The cross was an octagonal structure with Tuscan
columns and a big ogee roof. The public buildings on the s of
Cornhill are no ornament. On the N side the towering brick and
stone building of LLOYDS BANK, mixed Jacobean and Gothic
of 1889 (by *F. G. Cotman*). Its l. half was broken through on
the ground floor in 1930, to open up LLOYDS AVENUE. On the
s side between Town Hall and Post Office starts PRINCES
STREET (*see* below, p. 304).

The first street on the E side is BUTTERMARKET, and here
stands the most spectacular house in Ipswich, SPARROWE'S 56a
HOUSE, also called the Ancient House. It is in fact more ancient
than it looks. The multitude of motifs which the eye is faced
with are clearly of *c.* 1670, but in a room inside the wing extending from the E end of the front range there is, above a carved
plaster ceiling of *c.* 1670, a heavy C15 hammerbeam roof and,
in the room beyond this, early C17 plasterwork. Both these
rooms are on the first floor. On the ground floor of this wing
are panelling and a fireplace of *c.* 1600. The fireplace is dated
1603. The hammerbeam roof no doubt belongs to the solar
wing of a house whose hall was in the front range and was,
internally and externally, converted *c.* 1670. The conversion
consisted of this: Ground floor with closely set heavily carved
posts and brackets. Between them thick garlands. Overhanging
upper floor with four oriel windows to the N and one round the
corner to the w. The wall is plastered and pargetted with
coupled pilasters and reliefs between them: a vase, a big coat of
arms of Charles II, Neptune, a pelican, and around the corner
a shepherd and shepherdess. In the gable on that side is a man
on horseback. To the N the oriel windows also have stucco
reliefs below their sills: they represent Europe with a Gothic
church, Asia with a curiously domed structure, Africa on a
crocodile and under a sunshade, and America with a tobacco
pipe.* Atlas is in the same place on the oriel to the E. The oriels

* On the s side of this N range, to the courtyard, a stucco relief of a tree
heavy with fruit and figures in a chariot with two horses. The court has two
wooden columns to the w carrying the upper floor of the w range.

have convex sides. The arrangement of the glazing bars is
eminently typical of *c.* 1670. The centre light is arched, the
lights in the convex sides are straight. But glazing continues
above the straight top as well as the arched top, so that the
effect is different from that of the so-called Venetian window.
More plaster decoration in the windows to the N. It represents,
it seems, mythological characters. The whole is more ornate
and gayer than any other house of its date in England. Inside
stucco ceiling with oval wreaths also of *c.* 1670 and an C19
frieze with stucco reliefs of Architecture, Music, Painting,
Sculpture, and Geometry. Otherwise, in Buttermarket, No. 11
deserves a glance, built in 1899 in the style of Norman Shaw
with two richly carved oriels.

From the E end of Buttermarket down S through Upper Brook
Street, where nothing calls for notice, into LOWER BROOK
STREET, at the N end of which is the best group of Georgian
houses in Ipswich. None of them is individually startling, but
No. 6 with the lintels of the upper middle windows with a
frilly fringe and Nos. 12 and 14 (with a pretty doorcase) are
pleasant to look at.* Towards the S end of Lower Brook Street
more Georgian doorways and porches, including an early C19
terrace (Nos. 27–35) with Greek Doric columns at the doorways, and on the W side the new EAST ANGLIAN DAILY
TIMES building by *Johns, Slater & Haward*, 1966. The junction with Foundation Street‡ introduces a district which once
had many earlier timber-framed houses. In KEY STREET these
old houses have been replaced by big modern warehouses and
further E, towards the Old Custom House, by Early Victorian
warehouses facing the river along what is called ALBION
WHARF, with colonnades of cast-iron Tuscan columns or
simple iron posts. Their upper parts are weatherboarded,
and they look impressive from the river. The new DOCK had
been built in 1839–42. The engineer was *H. R. Palmer*. It
was at this time the largest in England. Then back and up
FOUNDATION STREET for the TOOLEY ALMSHOUSES,
rebuilt in 1846, a big group of red brick with some fanciful
timberwork, notably the outer staircases in the gable-ends of
the projecting wings. Fanciful, and with timberwork showing

---

* Off to the W along Turret Lane a former BAPTIST CHAPEL, Late
Classical, grey brick, of five bays with a five-bay pediment.
‡ Here stood a house of *c.* 1500, formerly an inn, which has been demolished.
It had a corner post with a carving of the fox preaching to the geese. The
early C19 houses opposite, of grey brick and classical forms, have also gone.

also, the gatehouse of 1861. In SCHOOL STREET remains of
a wall with some arches which was part of the E wall of the refectory of the BLACKFRIARS, who established themselves
at Ipswich in 1263 and whose premises covered much ground.
The refectory measured 120 ft by 24 ft.

From the E end of School Street into FORE STREET, the most
interesting street in Ipswich, as far as private houses are concerned. Several groups of timber-framed structures are preserved. First, near the N end, No. 24 is an excellent example of
the time of Sparrowe's House. It has three oriels and three
gables above them. In the gables, windows of the type of those
in the oriels of Sparrowe's House. The first floor is pargetted
with plain panelling. A little pargetting also on No. 60. The
group from No. 80 to No. 88 is of special interest in what it
reveals of the merchant's life and trade in the C16 and C17.
Dr Hoskins has brought this out very well: 'This type of
house has no direct entrance from the street – or had none
originally. It has a long side-passage off which the doorways
open to give access to the shop and to the kitchen behind. The
passage then emerges into the open at the back into a long
courtyard with long ranges of warehouses or lofts stretching
back along the site until we emerge directly on to the Quay.
On the main street the merchant had his tiny shop and behind
that came the kitchen and the buttery. The other living rooms
were piled up above. At the back door, so to speak, the merchant's ships unloaded straight into his warehouses. At the
front door, he was selling pennyworths of goods to retail
customers. In between, he carried on the wholesale business
that was the mainstay of his livelihood: he covered the whole
range of trading, from importer to retail shopkeeper' (*The
Listener*, 13 June 1957). In the courtyard of No. 82 is a small,
very charming pre-Reformation porch with moulded bressumer. No. 86 was the Neptune Inn. It is dated 1639, and
the external features, especially of the carved oriels, correspond
to that date. But internally there is evidence of earlier date. The
first storey belongs to the C15 and contained the hall, which
went through two floors. It was horizontally subdivided in
1639 (plaster ceiling), but the C15 doorway, and the screens
passage behind it, with two doorways to the E, survived. At the
back a deep W wing, which contained the solar, and a shallow
E wing, both running S. Yet further E, Nos. 132–38, dated
1620, but also basically medieval. Long, even front. Carved
bressumer, carved eaves-board. Off Fore Street, in GRIM-

WADE STREET, Nos. 77–83 are a good group. Nos. 78–83 ar
timber-framed and dated 1631. Windows and doorways ar
much altered. No. 77 has a five-bay brick front of *c.* 1700 wit
parapet.

(B) TO THE SOUTH

Now we leave Cornhill by PRINCES STREET. This street wa
cut through to the SW in the 1850s and 1860s, to connect th
centre with the railway station. At its far end, opposite the
end of Portman Road, FISON HOUSE, excellent offices b
Johns, Slater & Haward, 1959–60. Interesting concrete con
struction, the ground floor mainly left open for car parking
general office space on the first and second floors. The firs
floor is supported on pre-cast V-shaped columns springin
from the foundations; second floor and roof on pre-cast 'H
frames. There is a pretty inner courtyard. In RUSSELL ROAD
opposite, EASTERN ELECTRICITY BOARD ACCOUNTIN
OFFICES, by *Tooley & Foster,* 1964–6; large.

The new ring road, here called FRANCISCAN WAY, crosse
Princes Street just N of the Greyfriars site (*see* p. 307). S from
it leads FRIARS ROAD. The names derive from the house o
the Franciscans or GREYFRIARS which stood here and ha
been founded before 1236. All that remains is a short piece o
wall now at Greyfriars Concourse (*see* p. 308). CUTLE
STREET, running E from the S end of Friars Road, has at th
corner of ST PETER STREET (No. 2) a handsome seven-ba
brick house of *c.* 1700. Quoins, modillion frieze, and a pedi
mented doorway with Ionic columns still on the high pedesta
customary a hundred years before. From this corner first
then N. To the S in St Peter Street, between Nos. 11 and 13
at the back the remains of a good pre-Reformation house
timber-framed. E of the S end of St Peter Street, in COLLEG
STREET, the one remaining fragment of Cardinal Wolsey'
ambitious CARDINAL COLLEGE OF ST MARY. The Cardina
founded this on the site of the Augustinian Priory of St Pete
and St Paul in 1527, but had not enough time to complet
it before he fell. It was meant to be linked with his Cardina
College at Oxford, later Christ Church, in the same way a
Winchester with New College and Eton with King's. Th
49a GATEWAY, immediately E of the churchyard of St Peter'
(which served as the college chapel), cannot have been the mai
gateway. Brick. Coat of arms and four niches over. Polygona
angle buttresses. The former pinnacles have disappeared

The main buildings were to be of Caen stone. They were never
completed, though the school was in full swing in 1529. The
intimate scale is particularly telling in contrast to the towering
mill and warehouses opposite, which cut College Street off
from the river. At its E end College Street is continued by Key
Street; see Perambulation (A).

N of St Peter Street is ST NICHOLAS STREET. Here are several
timber-framed houses, first a group, Nos. 20–10, of no special
value, but then No. 47, continued into SILENT STREET as
Nos. 1–9. This is all uncommonly fine. It dates from the C15
and C16. Big angle post and bracket, both with blank tracery.
Overhang and gables and, on No. 9, two thin buttress shafts.
At the E end of Silent Street Nos. 30 and 32 are two Georgian
five-bay houses. From Silent Street it is only two hundred
yards back to Cornhill.

(C) TO THE NORTH

From Cornhill we must first walk E along TAVERN STREET,*
where Nos. 30–32 is a good, if much restored, example of the
Ipswich timber house of the C17. It has three oriels and three
bargeboarded gables above these. Opposite opens TOWER
STREET with some Georgian houses of red brick, especially
No. 17, which lies back and is detached. It is of five bays and
two storeys and has a Doric porch. The NE end of Tavern
Street has a pair of terrace houses of c. 1815, the date when the
street was widened. They are of grey brick and include the
GREAT WHITE HORSE HOTEL, which inside has remains of
its earlier timber-framed courtyard. In NORTHGATE STREET
this early C19 work carries on. The former *clou* here, opened
as the ASSEMBLY ROOM in 1821, has been obliterated by
conversion into a shop. The giant pilasters remain. Then No. 7,
the corner of OAK LANE, a very fine timber-framed house of
the C15 or early C16. Carved angle post with Renaissance 47b
decoration and a smith at the anvil, carved bracket, carved
bressumers, carved window-sills on the ground floor, thin
buttress shafts. Some original windows, though the most ornate
ones are all new. The house was formerly the Royal Oak Inn.
Behind both Nos. 7 and 9 long wings extend. Georgian houses
in Oak Lane and further along in TOWER CHURCHYARD
(five-bay house with Gibbs doorway). On the E side of Northgate Street further N No. 16, Georgian red brick with rubbed

* (THE WALK, off Tavern Street to the S, is a cosy little bit of half-
timbered pedestrian shopping by *Cautley & Barefoot*, c. 1934.)

brick dressings, of five bays and two storeys with segmental door pediment. Then, again on the w side, the remarkable GATEWAY to Archdeacon Pykenham's former mansion. Pykenham became Archdeacon of Suffolk in 1471, Dean of Stoke Clare College and Rector of Hadleigh in 1472, and died in 1497. For his gateway at Hadleigh *see* p. 244. The Ipswich gateway is of brick and has a four-centred arch and a (rebuilt) stepped gable. The back is timber-framed and the arch and spandrels of the gateway are here of wood too. One of them has a carved pike. A smaller brick gateway a little to the s. (The house behind the gateway has pretty Rococo plasterwork and an elegant staircase with carved tread-ends. NMR)

From the N end of Northgate Street where once the North Gate stood FONNEREAU ROAD runs off and up NW. It is worth a look from the point of view of the Early Victorian variety o styles. It starts with terraces in a style aptly called Debased Classical and continues Italianate as well as Jacobean. E of the s end of Fonnereau Road, at the corner of Soane Street and ST MARGARET'S STREET a good timber-framed house with ground-floor arcading, once open, overhang, buttress shafts, and a corner post which curves forward instead of having a separate bracket. It is decorated with blank tracery. w gable with ornamental bargeboards. Genuine also, though much restored, the corner houses Nos. 35–39, on the other side of the street. In ST MARGARET'S GREEN (which is no longer green) the former MANOR HOUSE; plastered, with two gables (Nos. 10–12). N of it and E of the church in BOLTON LANE is ST MARGARET'S CHURCH HOUSE, dated 1632 on the front. Three gables, carved bressumers on brackets.

Back to Cornhill by way of St Margaret's Street, CARR STREET, and Tavern Street. In Carr Street the building of the EAST ANGLIAN DAILY TIMES* has been demolished to make way for a shopping precinct by *Clifford Culpin & Partners*, 1968–9.

(D) TO THE WEST

First from Cornhill by Lion Street to the ARCADE, an elliptical arch on unfluted Ionic columns. It is not an arcade, but no more than an archway. Then in MUSEUM STREET, at the corner of Elm Street, No. 21, a Jacobean timber-framed house with an oversailing upper floor. The ground floor has

---

* Of 1887, probably by *T. W. Cotman*. Two storeys, red brick, with an angle turret on a bracket. Much scrolly decoration in the window tympana and on the top cornice. For the new building *see* p. 302.

tapering pilasters. Opposite is ELM HOUSE, a three-bay classical Early Victorian villa of grey brick with a Greek Doric porch. S of St Mary-at-the-Elms MRS SMITH'S ALMS-HOUSES of 1760, a simple, dignified brick front with widely spaced windows. N of the church, facing the churchyard, a timber-framed cottage. Now up Museum Street to the N. The most notable building here is the former MUSEUM, built as such (which was then still a rarity) in 1847 by *Christopher Fleury* of Ipswich. It is in a rather rustic version of the scarcely any longer fashionable Grecian style, stuccoed, with crazy giant Tuscan columns recessed in the angles and a Venetian window in the middle of the three-bay front. To its N, and also opposite, nice quiet Early Victorian terraces with classical doorways. Fluted or unfluted Doric or Ionic columns.*

Off to the E in WESTGATE STREET the CROWN AND ANCHOR HOTEL has a simple older l. half and a more ornate later r. half, in the Gothic style with four dormer windows. The older part dates from the 1840s, the younger from 1897. The ground floors are all altered. From here one can continue back to Cornhill.

Parallel with High Street, further W, BERNERS STREET goes up the hill with the portico of the hospital as its *point de vue*. The date of this, 1836, dates Berners Street as well. Terraces along the S half of the street, front gardens in the N half. The best houses are Nos. 31–49. Some of these have big Ionic porches.

The S continuation of Berners Street is CIVIC DRIVE. This and Franciscan Way form an entirely new dual-carriage road between St Matthew's Street and St Nicholas Street, crossing Princes Street (*see* p. 304). A new CIVIC CENTRE designed by *Vine & Vine* occupies a large site on the E of Civic Drive. An UNDERGROUND SPIRAL CAR PARK, also by *Vine & Vine*, was completed in 1967. To the S of this are the LAW COURTS and the POLICE HEADQUARTERS, of 1965–8 and by *Vine & Vine* too. SUFFOLK HOUSE, offices, concrete covered in red tile, is by *Johns, Slater & Haward*, 1966–8. At the junction with Princes Street is an underground concourse formed within the roundabout and connected to the GREYFRIARS site, S of FRANCISCAN WAY. This includes ST FRANCIS TOWER, fifteen storeys, flats and offices, and another tower block,

---

* In HIGH STREET, the northern continuation of Museum Street, was a more ambitious effort in the Grecian idiom, the CROWN WORKS (now demolished), built as the TEMPERANCE HALL in 1840. It had a Greek Doric temple front with attached columns, and seven-bay sides, stuccoed.

ST CLARE HOUSE. All by *Edward Skipper & Associates*,
1964–6. Incorporated into a central feature in the precinct
is a piece of WALL from the Greyfriars site (*see* p. 304) – three
lancet windows with, curiously enough, a transom at the
springing of the arch.

(E) SOME HOUSES OF OUTER IPSWICH*

BIRKFIELD, Belstead Road, ⅝ m. SW. Now St Joseph's College.
The original house dates from *c.* 1830. Nine bays and two
storeys. Low hipped roof. Front veranda. Entrance with
Greek Doric columns on the W side. Several new buildings
for the purposes of the college.

THE CHANTRY, 1 m. ENE. The core is supposed to be the house
built about 1700 by Mr E. Ventris. What can be seen of this
core, however, shows a fine later C18 house of five bays and
two and a half storeys with a three-bay pediment (on rain-
water-heads the date 1772). Inside spacious entrance hall,
and to the r. of it staircase with iron handrail. Good, restrained
stucco decoration of both rooms. To this house, in 1853–4,
wings of one bay, a porte-cochère of two storeys, and a big
bow at the back were added, all in a debased classical or Free
Renaissance style. The bands of vermiculated rustication are
particularly telling. Equally telling the lodge gates.

THE CHANTRY ESTATE is a municipal estate of 3,260 houses
S of Chantry Park. It was begun in 1951 and designed by the
Borough Engineer's Department (*J. B. Storey*). It has a good
SHOPPING CENTRE on three sides of a quadrangle and two
SCHOOLS opposite, both by *Johns, Slater & Haward*. They
have the weird hyperbolic timber roofs then in vogue. A large
amount of private housing in the vicinity forms, with the
council estate, a new residential area of the town.

GIPPESWYK HALL (later called HARVEST HOUSE), Gippeswyk Avenue, has been demolished. It was a three-bay brick
house of *c.* 1600. Diapering with blue bricks. Two-storeyed
with a three-storeyed gabled porch. The entrance had a four-
centred arch and a square hood-mould.

HOLYWELLS, Holywells Park, 1 m. E. The original core of
c. 1820–30 is a grey brick house with a five-bay front with one-
bay pediment. Round the corner a veranda. Early Victorian
irregular additions, including the stables with an asymmetrically placed tower.

* These are all S of the Orwell, and distances are expressed from the railway station.

STOKE PARK, I m. s. A spacious house. Rebuilt in 1935 to the design of *H. R. Hooper* in a style derived from Voysey.

IXWORTH

ST MARY. Dec chancel, almost entirely rebuilt. Dec w windows in the aisles, Dec doorway in the s aisle. All the rest Perp. Big w tower with flushwork frieze at the base and flushwork frieze at the top. Flushwork panelled battlements. On the SE buttress panel with the name of Abbot Schot of Bury St Edmunds, that is of 1470–3; also by the w door a tile with inscription: 'Thome Vyal gaf to the stepil iiij£.' His will is of 1472. Money for the leading of the roof was left in 1533.* – SCREEN. Only the dado remains. – MONUMENT. Richard Codington † 1567 and wife. Tomb-chest with decorated pilasters and three shields. At the back round arch with exceptionally fine Italian leaf carving. Against the back wall brass effigies. The inscription records that Richard Codington was granted the manor of Ixworth after the Dissolution of the Abbey (*see* below) in exchange for Codington in Surrey, then re-named Nonesuch. The grant was indeed made in 1538.

PRIORY. A Priory of Augustinian Canons was founded at Ixworth *c.* 1170. The Norman church was cruciform and about 22 ft long with an aisled chancel. The chancel was extended in the C13 and a N aisle added to the nave in the C14. There was probably a w tower. Foundations of the church and the bases of piers can be seen in the grass N of the house. Part of the w end stands to a height of a few feet.

Parts of the monastic buildings are embedded in the house called IXWORTH ABBEY. The E, dormitory range is fairly complete except for the chapter house which lay at its N end. The undercroft has fine C13 vaulting and is divided into several rooms. At the N end is the slype, rib-vaulted in three bays. It was made into a chapel in the C17–18. Next is a room of four double bays with three octagonal piers and single-chamfered arches. Finally, at the s end, a room of two double bays with much finer rib mouldings. The date of this seems to be *c.* 1230. Above, on the first floor at the s end, a room with fine C16–17 panelling and a C16 fireplace. Of the s, refectory,

---

* The C18 antiquarian Tom Martin noted at the lower part of the s side of the steeple an inscription on a glazed brick to William Dense, Prior of Ixworth from 1467 to *c.* 1484. Wills of 1458 and 1471 give money to the chancel and to the tower, respectively (ARA).

range there survives only some walling at the E end with evidence of the pulpit. E of the dormitory range, and connecting with the S room, is the late C15 timber-framed prior's apartment which apparently replaced an earlier building in the same position. N of this was perhaps the reredorter. There is no trace of the W range. A gatehouse stood across the moat to the N. These buildings were extensively remodelled *c.* 1600, *c.* 1700, and *c.* 1800, and this last remodelling provided the Georgian N and W façades.

In the HIGH STREET and off it several attractive houses, one timber-framed with two gables and some pargetting, and a few with nice Georgian doorways.

WINDMILL, ¾ m. S. *See* Pakenham, p. 389.

STOW LANE. About 1 m. out on the Stowmarket road is a ROMAN BUILDING, first found in 1834. Excavations in 1849 revealed an apsidal building with a pillared hypocaust and a coin of Constantine I (307–37). Further excavations in 1948 showed the massive construction of the building, a furnace house, and a channelled hypocaust. Evidence of destruction and finds of the Saxon period were also recovered; a nearby well contained much Roman debris. A scatter of C1–2 A.D. material seems to indicate an extensive settlement.

IXWORTH THORPE

9070

ALL SAINTS. Outside the village; small and thatched. Weatherboarded bell-turret, nave and chancel. Norman S doorway, very plain. Good brick S porch with stepped gable, and battlements decorated with motifs in flint and brick. Chancel with lancets. In the nave some Dec windows. (The E window has wooden tracery. LG) – PULPIT. Jacobean. – BENCHES. The ends with poppy-heads, the arms with animals and figures, including a mermaid. – COMMUNION RAIL. Three-sided, with late C17 turned balusters. – PLATE. Cup 1676; Paten and Flagon 1678. – MONUMENT. Tablet to John Croft † 1644. The tablet is called in the inscription 'Marmoriolum hoc'.

KEDINGTON

7040

ST PETER AND ST PAUL. *A late C13 nave and chancel (see the uncusped and cusped Y-tracery) and a Dec N aisle (W window) and W tower. Chancel arch also late C13, though the imposts have a simple, Norman-looking moulding. The chancel win-

* The remains of a Roman building are under the pews, and a section of mosaic paving is to be noted in the S outer face of the nave.

dows are shafted inside. The E window is of course a Perp insertion. The PISCINA has the weirdest shape – a steep pointed arch cusped by three steep pointed trefoils. Low arcades between nave and aisles. The piers have a big polygonal shaft without capital to the front, as in many other Suffolk churches, but the polygonal shafts to the aisles have been painted in the C17 or C18 to simulate fluted columns. There is no clerestory. Yet the impression is not of darkness; for a later age has seen fit to put skylights into the false hammerbeam roof. Later ages have done much in other respects too to change the original effect of the interior. Kedington church contains a delightful diversity of furnishings. – FONT. Octagonal, Perp, with quatrefoil decoration. – PULPIT. An uncommonly complete three-decker with tester and hour-glass stand; of Jacobean date. – Of about the same time the ROOD SCREEN. This is actually dated 1619. It is simple and has scrolly ogee tops to the one-light divisions. It folds back like a folding door, which is also highly unusual. – (COMMUNICANTS' STALLS. Late C18; a rarity. LG) – BARNARDISTON PEW. Opposite the pulpit. It is made up of parts of a C15 ROOD SCREEN, with segmental arches and four-plus-four-light tracery over, and of parts of an arched Jacobean screen. – BENCHES. Partly Late Perp, straight-headed with buttresses and linenfold panelling, partly C18. – FAMILY PEWS. C18, in the S aisle and more in the nave. – WEST GALLERY, early C19. Projecting in a semicircle. – CHILDREN'S BENCHES. In rising tiers at the W ends of the two aisles. Opposite them on each side of the block of pews a special boxed-in seat for the schoolmaster and schoolmistress to watch the children. – (POOR BOX. Simple, C15. Hewn out of a tree-trunk. LG) – CHANCEL PANELLING, probably early C18. – WIG STAND. Baluster-shaped. By the pulpit. – COMMUNION RAIL. Three-sided, with strongly moulded turned balusters; given in 1707. – SCULPTURE. Anglo-Saxon Cross with Crucifixion, assigned to c. 900. This is placed above the main altar. – PLATE. Cup and Paten 1663–4; Flagon 1740. – MONUMENTS. Of the Barnardistons. Sir Thomas † 1503 and his wife. Tomb-chest with shields in lozenges and quatrefoils. The effigies badly worn-off. – Sir Thomas and wife. She died in 1520, the date of his death is left blank. Big plain tomb-chest. Two recumbent effigies. Children kneeling small against the chest. Back wall with arms. – Standing wall-monument to Sir Thomas † 1610 and his two wives. He recumbent, they kneeling and facing one another. Big superstructure, not refined. In the base a low segment-headed arch in the middle into which a coffin is just being pushed, as if it were a baking oven. – Grissell † 1609. Adjoining the former and commemorating a daughter of the former. Kneeling figure between columns. The inscription runs like this:

> Loe heere the Image of Lyfe, new inspyr'd
> too wise In choice too olde in youthfull breath:
> too deare to frendes: too much of men desier'd
> therefore bereaft us by untymely death:
> while shee trod Earth shee rais...er mynd farre Higher
> Her actions faire, unstaynd of vice or pride
> truth was her loade stone, heav'ne was her desier:
> Christ was her hope as in his Fayth she dyde.

In the N aisle Sir Nathaniel † 1653 and his wife † 1669. In an oblong recess with garlands l. and r., two frontal demi-figures, both pensively resting their heads on a hand and the elbow on a pillow. – Also N aisle Sir Thomas, 1724. Minor, without effigy, but with two standing putti holding a skull and a torch outside the pilasters which frame the inscription.

The welcoming and parting touch is the COBBLING of the s porch.

RECTORY. Handsome Queen Anne house, ½ m. s of the church. Red brick with segment-headed windows. (Staircase with Rococo ceiling.)

RISBRIDGE HOME, former Workhouse. An ambitious Tudor affair on a symmetrical plan with uncommonly expensive detail. Red brick and stone trim. By *J. F. Clark* of Newmarket, 1859.

3060   KELSALE

ST MARY AND ST PETER. Norman N doorway with two orders of colonnettes. In the arch one order of incised zigzag, one of scallops, one of a kind of elongated merlons, and a hood-mould with billet. Norman s doorway, re-set as priest's doorway in the chancel. Simpler, with one order of colonnettes and two zigzags. Dec sw tower with flushwork panelling on buttresses and battlements. s aisle Dec (rebuilt 1878), see the arcade with its stubby octagonal piers and its double-chamfered arches, and see also one window with reticulated tracery. Perp s chapel (arcade with the often-used pier section of four shafts and four hollows), Perp nave N windows, and nave w window (flushwork panelling beneath it), and Perp also the fine s porch. Front and battlements with flushwork panelling and the unusual motif of crossed keys for St Peter. Entrance with one moulding of shields and one of fleurons, repeated also inside the entrance. Nave roof with scissor-bracing below and above the collar-beams. – FONT. Octagonal, Perp. Four lions against the stem, the Signs of the four Evangelists and angels against the bowl. – PULPIT. A specially elaborate Jacobean piece. It must be of before 1631, when Aldeburgh sent a craftsman to Kelsale to look at the pulpit. – SCREEN. Of iron; 1890. – PLATE. Cup and Paten 1706; Flagon 1788. – MONUMENTS. Thomas Russell † 1730. Sarcophagus and above it trophies coming out to the l. and r. behind a coat of arms. – Samuel Clouting † 1852. Statue by *Thurlow* of Saxmundham. Standing in a niche; otherwise just like a public monument in a market place.

GUILDHALL, 200 yds SW. Of c. 1500. Timber-framed with an oversailing first floor; much restored. (Fine upper open roof with moulded kingpost trusses. DOE)

KELSALE COURT, W of the church. Grey brick, early C19. Of five bays and two and a half storeys. Porch with Roman Doric columns.

(MANOR FARM HOUSE behind the church. Early C16. Timber-framed. Of the corner posts of the originally over-sailing upper floor one can still be seen. DOE)

BARN at Kelsale Lodge, 1¼ m. NW. C16, red brick, with diaper of dark blue brick. Ten bays long. Buttressed at the corners.

KENTFORD 7060

ST MARY. All Dec, except for the brick top of the tower. Much renewed. The most individual motif is the rose window of the tower, with a five-petalled rose in a circle. Dec also the chancel doorway and the E window (reticulated tracery). – BOX PEWS. – WALL PAINTINGS. Late C14, not easily seen. A badly damaged St Christopher, the Seven Deadly Sins, the Seven Works of Mercy (cf. Hoxne for both), and, better preserved and quite impressive with its big figures, the Legend of the three Quick and the three Dead. – PLATE. Cup 1662.

BARROW. On the edge of the workings ½ m. NE of Cock and Bull Farm (*see* also Gazeley and Higham).

KENTON 1060

ALL SAINTS. Transitional S doorway with one order of colonnettes with typical leaf capitals. Round arch with a keeled roll moulding. Simple, single-chamfered round arch in the N doorway too. Dec W tower, with unusual flushwork ornament in the parapet (shields in circles connected by horizontal bands). Perp s aisle with attached s porch. The porch is of flint and has a direct E entrance into the aisle. This is of brick, two bays long, with octagonal brick pier and responds, triple-chamfered arches, and brick windows of two and three lights. The chancel with its over-ornate chancel arch is of 1872. – FONT. Octagonal, of Purbeck marble, C13, with the usual two flat blank arches on each side. – BENCH. One charming Elizabethan bench with open balustrading. It is dated 1595. – PLATE. Elizabethan Cup. – MONUMENT. Brass to John Garneys † 1524 and family. High up on the s aisle wall.

(KENTON HALL. C16. Of two storeys and eight bays, irregularly divided by polygonal buttresses. The lower windows have mullions and transoms and pediments, the upper mullions only. NMR)

KENTWELL HALL see LONG MELFORD

0040

KERSEY

Kersey is the most picturesque village of South Suffolk. The view from the church over the tiled roofs of the houses dipping down to the ford of the river Brett and climbing up the other side is not easily forgotten. The church lies on its own at the s end of the village, which is just one long street with an extension by the stream.

ST MARY. Dates are recorded for the completion of the N aisle (1335) and of the w tower (1481).* Both fit the stylistic evidence. Dec N aisle – see the windows under their almost straight-sided arches and the four-petal motif in the tracery, and the fine, broad, ogee-headed niche between two of them inside. Niches also flank the E window. The chancel windows are Dec too, but the chancel was rebuilt in 1862. Are they correctly renewed? Lying between the two are the SEDILIA and PISCINA of the aisle, one straight-headed composition with four ogee-headed vaulted niches. One of the vaults has miniature ribs. The backs of the three sedilia niches are open in windows to the chancel. Can this motif be original? The N arcade is also of the same period. The piers are octagonal, the arches have one chamfer and one double-wave moulding. Hood-moulds to nave and aisle with pretty fleurons and leaf trails. Finally the aisle roof resting on a uniquely elaborate stone wall-plate, unfortunately ill-preserved. It clearly tells a

* Money was left towards the building of the tower in 1434 and 1445, and to bells in 1446 (ARA).

long story, but what story has not yet been recognized by any student. The roof of the E chapel is ceiled with four big Elizabethan or Jacobean stucco panels. In spite of all these contributions of the early or mid C14, the effect of the church is Perp, thanks to the big W tower, the porches, and most of the windows. The tower has diagonal buttresses with four set-offs. On them long flushwork panels. Battlements with flushwork tracery. Big W doorway. Three-light W window with transom, flanked by flushwork panels. Also niches l. and r. Bell-openings of three lights with transom. S windows Perp. S porch of two 11b bays with flushwork and pinnacles. Inside the S porch ceiling with sixteen very delicately traceried panels. N porch similar but a little simpler. Perp clerestory, the roof with long arched braces meeting at the collar-beam, alternating with hammer- 19a beams.

FURNISHINGS. FONT. A slightly elongated octagon; Perp. Stout stem with quatrefoils. Bowl with four demi-figures of angels. – SCREEN. Dado of the screen to the N chapel, with six painted early C15 figures, not of high quality. – LECTERN. Wooden shaft with thin buttresses and flying buttresses. – WEST DOOR with tracery and a trail border. – SCULPTURE. Fragments of an alabaster altar, e.g. Trinity. Also good bearded heads probably from a reredos (cf. St Cuthbert Wells). From the same perhaps the seated figure of St Anne. – WALL PAINTING. St George and the Dragon, high up on the S wall. – PLATE. Paten 1711; Cup, Paten, and Flagon 1791.

PRIORY. Of the Augustinian priory founded early in the C13 all that remains is one major fragment of the church. Flint. S chancel chapel with two arches to the chancel. Piers with moulded capitals. E wall of transept with lower arch into this chapel and a tall E window now blocked. The chapel was widened later and received big Perp windows to S and E, of which the surrounds survive. The S windows are segment-headed. The church had a N chancel chapel and N transept as well, a crossing tower, and a nave and S aisle. Their W wall forms part of the garden wall. Attached to the house, which has an early C19 front of white brick, the so-called monks' KITCHEN. Its roof is probably of the C13. (The W range of the cloister is the converted hospital of the early C13 which preceded the foundation of the priory. It is now inside the brick-fronted farmhouse. The hall is divided from an aisle by a single pillar, and the roof-truss is of magnificent proportions. P. G. M. Dickinson)

THE VILLAGE. From the church down CHURCH HILL past
WOODBINE COTTAGE, a picturesque timber-framed house of
before the Reformation. Some of the doorways are original.
By the river RIVER HOUSE, timber-framed, with its surprising
Early Elizabethan brick porch. This has angle pilasters with
circular and semicircular panels *à la vénitienne*, a round-headed
doorway with broad pediment, a transomed three-light window over, also with broad pediment, and a semicircular top
with pinnacles l. and r. Then first to the l. for a look into the
street called THE GREEN. Note especially GREENAN COT-
TAGE, a picturesque corner house. Back to the river and over
the bridge. Then THE STREET runs up steeply with many
handsome houses l. and r., e.g. DENBIGH HOUSE at the start
on the l. with two long projecting wings, *c.* 1500 and 1654, the
BELL INN, much restored, and Nos. 5 and 6 with overhang and
traces of chevron pargetting. Unfortunately the continuity of
the old houses is interrupted by bald patches more than once.
The climax is the upper end, with the timber-framed house
opposite the Post Office, the two-gabled house opposite the
White Horse Inn, which has two bay windows on heavy
moulded brick plinths and diaper patterning in the gables, and
the CORNER HOUSE on the other side, with a blocked original
doorway.

KESGRAVE

2040

ALL SAINTS. Surrounded by cedar trees. Nave and chancel and
w tower. The tower was started of flint, like the church, but
continued in red early C16 brick with dark blue diapering. In
the chancel several lancet windows and an interesting E window
of three stepped lancet lights under one arch separated by wall
strips, not by mullions. Above the lights plate tracery, a trefoil
l. and r., above that a quatrefoil l. and r., and at the top a sexfoil.
All this points to a date *c.* 1270 or 1280. (High up in the nave
walls also lancets. Dec porch with ballflower decoration. LG) –
PLATE. Set of 1799.

KESSINGLAND

5080

ST EDMUND. Built *c.* 1450 for the Franciscans of London. The
memorable part is the w tower, no doubt meant as a beacon.
Tall, with diagonal buttresses panelled in flushwork and ending
in a flat brick top probably of the late C17. Flushwork panelling
also at the base. w doorway with two orders of jambs and arch
decorated with fleurons, mitre, crown, shield with the symbol

of the Trinity, anchor, etc. Two angels in the spandrels. Frieze of quatrefoils above the doorway, and in its middle a small seated figure of St Edmund. w window with niches l. and r. The design of the lower parts of the tower has been attributed convincingly to *Richard Russell* of Dunwich, the designer of the Walberswick tower. Nave and chancel, no aisle. There existed a s aisle, however, as is proved by the c14 arcade with octagonal piers visible inside the nave and by the big remaining fragments of its walls now in the churchyard. The nave was damaged and rebuilt in 1694–5. Red brick with blue chequerboard pattern. Windows with wooden crosses and segmental relieving arches. Perp the s doorway with large head-stops. – FONT. A very fine piece, not of the standard of this part of Suffolk. Small standing figures against the stem, seated figures under ogee canopies against the bowl. The date seems to be late c14. The figures are not well preserved, but certainly not mutilated. – STAINED GLASS. E window by *Kempe & Tower*, 1912. – PLATE. Cup, Paten, and Flagon 1750; two Almsdishes 1826.
(GROVE HOUSE has an undulating crinkle-crankle wall in the garden. N. Scarfe)

KETTLEBASTON

9050

ST MARY. Flint and stone. Norman nave, see one blocked N window. Transitional s doorway. The shafts and scalloped capitals are purely Norman, but the arch is decidedly pointed. No zigzag; flat row of small triangles instead. Dec chancel and w tower, see the bell-openings, and in the chancel one s window.* The reticulated E window is of 1902, but may be a correct replacement. Also Dec the PISCINA and SEDILIA. Their forms look in fact rather like *c.* 1300, whereas the preserved window has ogee arches, as has also a tomb recess in the N wall. – FONT. By the same workmen as the s doorway. Square. The decorative motifs are undisciplined: big chevrons not accurately placed, strips of triangles, etc. – PAINTING. In the Norman window three red trails with buds or knobs at the end, as familiar from Norman illumination.

KETTLEBURGH

2060

ST ANDREW. w tower with flushwork at the base, and brick battlements. Nave and chancel with irregular windows, Dec and Perp, including clerestory windows. s porch with flushwork

---

* (Also in the chancel an ogee-headed niche. This is in the SE buttress.)

at the base. A N chapel has been demolished at some time. –
FONT. Octagonal. With four lions and four angels with heraldic
shields. – PULPIT. Incorporating Jacobean panels. – SCREEN.
Very prettily neo-Jacobean; 1891; with some original panels.
– COMMANDMENT BOARDS. Nicely painted; C18 (cf. Saxstead). – BENCHES. A few with poppy-heads and beasts, etc.,
on the arms. – COMMUNION RAIL. Mid-C17. – PLATE. Cup
and Cover 1569.

NEW HALL. C16 (with star-topped chimneys), but with a canted
C17 bay of curious detail. Each side has two tiers of columns
set back in the wall and windows between them, of two lights
in the canted sides and probably originally four in the front.

KIRKLEY see LOWESTOFT, pp. 354, 355

2030   ## KIRTON

ST MARY AND ST MARTIN. For the W tower money was left in
1520. It is of flint and brick at the top, and there is also much
brick repair below. Nave and chancel of no interest. N aisle of
1858. – FONT. Square and, it seems, partly C13. – PLATE. Cup
supposed to be Elizabethan.

9080   ## KNETTISHALL

ALL SAINTS. Disused and decaying. Unbuttressed W tower of
knapped flint, mentioned in wills of 1453 and 1457 (ARA).
Flushwork decoration of the battlements. In the S wall of the
nave a Norman window is still visible.

BARROWS. Two on the heath, about a mile apart, either side of
Norwich Lane.

4060   ## KNODISHALL

ST LAWRENCE. W tower with a little flushwork decoration, including a few symbols high up on the buttresses. The S side
(with one Tudor brick window) propped up with buttresses in
1843. On the N side a simple Norman doorway. The chancel
with windows of c. 1300 much renewed. – FONT. Octagonal,
C13, of Purbeck marble, with the usual two shallow blank
pointed arches on each side. – PULPIT. Jacobean. – SCREEN.
Three parts of the upper ogee arches and tracery re-used in
31b   the tower gallery. – PAINTING. Jacob and Rachel, 1851
by *William Dyce*, three-quarter figures, and an excellent
example of this English 'Nazarene's' art. – PLATE. Elizabethan
Cup and Paten. – BRASS. John Jenney † 1460 and wife. 2 ft
figures.

ST PETER, Buxlow (Knodishall Green), 1¼ m. NW. Of the former
parish church of Buxlow no more survives than two chunks of
walling of the tower, standing about 15 ft up.

RED HOUSE FARMHOUSE, Knodishall Green. Dated 1678.
Still on the Elizabethan E-plan. The two projecting wings have
Dutch gables with segmental pediments at the top. In the
porch on the first floor two blank niches, in the gable a niche
with a statue of St Agnes.

LACKFORD   7070

ST LAWRENCE. Over-restored Dec w tower with C16 brick
battlements. Dec nave (one window shafted inside, simple
doorway); Dec chancel with SEDILIA and a tomb recess
opposite, nicely decorated; Dec N aisle and N chapel. The aisle
arcade is original, with its quatrefoil piers, or rather circular
piers with four broad semicircular attachments, and its double-
chamfered arches. The leaf capitals in the chapel are also
original. But the aisle was later pulled down and rebuilt with
rather minimum windows in the C19. Handsome large shafted
and gabled squint from the aisle in the chancel; it contains a
PISCINA in the aisle. – FONT. Octagonal, late C13, with big
stiff-leaf motifs, but also rose, ivy, etc. – BENCH ENDS. With
poppy-heads; made up into one long seat along the N aisle. –
STAINED GLASS. E window by *Powell* (designed by *Holiday*),
1871.

BARROW, 300 yds w of Cuckoo Hill, ½ m. s of the Manor House.
Originally there was a second, opened in 1869 to reveal a pair
of cremations.

LAKENHEATH   7080

ST MARY. An eminently interesting church, not sufficiently
studied. It has a Norman chancel arch with three orders of
shafts, multi-scalloped capitals, and no other decoration in the
arches than rolls. To the l. is one Norman colonnette with the
beginning of an arch, and this may well indicate blank arcading
of the altar space. The chancel is C13, see the one lancet
window. This C13 work was an extension of the Norman
chancel, the length of which is clear outside, especially on the
s side, where the joint is visible. There was a N chapel, and its
w wall has left traces. The blocked arch from the chancel also
survives. The doorway to the chapel was reset in the blocked
wall. The w tower is in its lower parts of the late C13. It

has a single-chamfered E arch and fine W doorway with four
chamfered continuous mouldings. The latter is not usually
seen, because it is covered by a two-storeyed W attachment
mostly of brick, and of indefinite date.* In it there is a re-used
Perp window. Dec N aisle with charming circular E window
above the altar. Late Perp S aisle windows. The building his
tory is further elucidated by the arcades inside. They have
octagonal piers on both sides, but that is as far as the similarity
goes. On the N side the arcade has three plus two bays, divided
by a piece of solid wall marking, no doubt, the W end of the
Norman building. The three E bays have detail of the early
C14, the two W bays are Dec with a slimmer pier and more
finely moulded capital. These details are the same on the
side, and the N aisle windows, also those of the E bays, go with
them. The later piers have at the top of each side a pointed
trefoiled arch-head. Perp clerestory; also an E window a
clerestory level, unfortunately blocked. Fine roof with alternat
ing tie-beams and hammerbeams and big angels against the
hammerbeams (cf. Mildenhall and also Methwold Norfolk)
queenposts, and tracery above the tie-beams. – FONT. The
finest C13 font in the county. Big, octagonal, with gabled
arches in each panel and much big stiff-leaf decoration
Octagonal stem with eight detached shafts. – PULPIT. Perp
with arched panels and trumpet foot. – BENCHES. A delightfu
set with poppy-heads with all sorts of small animals,
unicorn, a tiger, etc., also a man seated on the ground with hi
knees pulled up. The bench backs have charming lacewor
friezes of different patterns. – LADDER. The ladder in the
tower may well be the original one. – FAMILY PEW. Jacobean
– WALL PAINTINGS. On one of the piers; C14. A seated
figure of St Edmund King and Martyr and above it scene
from the Life of Christ emanating from a tree. Also twice the
Annunciation and the Resurrection. – PLATE. Elizabethan
Cup; Paten 1696. – MONUMENTS. Brass of a Civilian an
wife, c. 1530, 18 in. figures. – Monument to the Stywar
family. Tomb-chest in the S chapel with lozenges with shield
Niche above with panelled ends and a straight top. All this i
purely Perp; but the lettering is Roman, and the date is in fac
as late as 1568. – Joanna Bartney † 1583. Tablet with a tree

* The Rev. J. T. Munday tells me that a post-Reformation document show
it in use as a manor office, and suggests that the structure itself is post
Reformation. For an account of the history of the church as a whole, see hi
booklet, *Lakenheath Church*, 1970.

trunk from which hangs a big shield. A sword at the foot ready presumably to cut the tree.

The cottages are of flint with yellow or red brick trim. Several Nonconformist chapels of the 1830s and 1840s. At the S end of the village a big, orderly Council Estate of red brick cottages built in 1932–7.

There is considerable evidence of Neolithic and Iron Age SETTLEMENT in the area. At MAIDSCROSS HILL, ½ m. E of the village, a group of fields, including one named 'Roman Field', have yielded considerable indications of Neolithic settlement over an area measuring 140 by 120 yds, and much 'necked beaker' pottery. In addition, an early Iron Age FARMSTEAD has been found with a series of pits and hearths and occupation material including an antler weaving comb. A later Romano-British SETTLEMENT is marked by groups of postholes, hearths, and C1–2 A.D. finds, including a bronze hanging bowl and patera, and *terra sigillata*. The site is enclosed by a boundary ditch which appears to be of Saxon date. A second Roman SITE lies to the E in SANDY PLANTATION, where a fine dragonesque brooch (now in the Ashmolean Museum) was found, as well as coins, including one of Theodosius (379–95).

BRAMWELL MEADOW, N of the road to Feltwell, is the site of three Romano-British KILNS, near a deposit of red clay. Two more have been found 1 m. SE.

UNDLEY. Circular EARTHWORK of doubtful date, in a field just NE of Undley Hall Farm, 1¾ m. S W of Lakenheath. It measures c. 132 ft in diameter. The N edge is eroded by ploughing, but there is an entrance to the S. Romano-British ware and C2 A.D. *terra sigillata* have been found in the upper silting of the ditch, together with domestic rubbish.

LANDGUARD FORT *see* FELIXSTOWE

LANDWADE *see* EXNING

LANGHAM   9060

ST MARY. Nave and chancel and Victorian bellcote. Nave rebuilt in 1887. Chancel with four tall windows. The E window is of 1877 but may well represent what was there before: three lights and a large circle enclosing four unencircled quatrefoils. Niches l. and r. of the window inside. The side windows have the familiar four-petalled flower in the tracery heads. – FONT. Dec, octagonal, with shields and lions' heads under ogee arches.

– SCREEN. Very good, with tracery on the dado, one-ligh
divisions, ogee arches, much close panel tracery above them
and the complete loft parapet towards the W. – PLATE. Flago
1712.

LANGHAM HALL. Handsome Georgian house with an Ioni
doorcase (probably re-set further forward), between two cante
bay windows. Red brick, two-storeyed.

LANGLEY'S FARMHOUSE see HAWKEDON

LANGTON GROVE see EYE

LATES see HOLTON ST MARY

LAVENHAM

ST PETER AND ST PAUL. This is, needless to say, one of the mos
famous of the parish churches of Suffolk – rightly so; for it is a
interesting historically as it is rewarding architecturally. I
both respects it is a match for Long Melford. The nave of Mel
ford may be the nobler design, but Lavenham has more unity
To the eye it is a Late Perp church throughout, though the
chancel and the pretty crocketed spirelet for the sanctus bel
are clearly Dec (unknapped flint, Dec window tracery). The
church was built by the efforts of the clothiers of Lavenham
chiefly the Springs, and of the Lord of the Manor, John de
Vere, the thirteenth Earl of Oxford. His arms appear on the
porch, and inscriptions record Thomas Spring on the S chape
and Simon Branch on the N chapel. Wills prove that the towe
was building in c. 1486–95, and its top parts belong to a secon
campaign of c. 1520–5. In 1523 Thomas Spring III left £200, a
large sum, for its completion, and for the building of a chape
for a monument to himself and his wife. Other wills indicat
building in the church itself in 1498 and 1504 (John Rusby
£200). It is worth recording also that a niece of Thoma
Spring II married the second son of the fifteenth Earl of Oxford
Thomas Spring III, when he made his will in 1523, owned
property in 130 places.

Lavenham church makes a perfect picture, away from the
houses of the village on two sides at least. Its W tower is as
mighty as its nave is noble. The only criticism is that the towe
is, perhaps, a little too substantial for the length of the nave
which is shorter than at Long Melford. Height of the tower
141 ft, length of the church 156 ft. Restoration by *Penrose*
1861–7. The tower is of knapped flint. On the plinth the stars
and shields of the de Veres, the merchant marks of the Springs

and the crossed keys of St Peter and crossed swords of St Paul. The buttresses are very unusual, broad and clasping but provided on their two fronts with thinner sub-buttresses which look, of course, as if they were normal set-back buttresses. Five set-offs. On them panelling, and lower down canopied niches. Large W doorway with the arms of the Earl of Oxford and fleuron decoration, ogee gable, and flanking buttress shafts; four-light W window with transom. Three-light bell-openings. Parapet with shields in lozenges. The coat of arms of Thomas Spring III, a very recent acquisition when he died, appears thirty-two times. The pinnacles were never built.

The nave is faced with Casterton stone. Seven bays with large transomed four-light windows. The clerestory has twelve, not fourteen, windows, owing to the interference of the tower buttresses, and the charming irregularity of a rood-turret with spirelet not outside the aisle but between nave and aisle. Aisle buttresses with decoration, aisle battlements with rich open-work decoration, clerestory also with such battlements. A favourite motif is large tripartite leaves set in panels. The N is essentially the same, although the window tracery is a little different, and there is no porch. The S porch is a spectacular piece. The entrance has spandrels with the Oxford boar, above it a niche, a frieze of six shields, again of the de Vere family, and above that openwork battlements. Fan-vault inside. The S (Spring) chapel is dated 1525. The inscription on it reads:

[Orate pro Anim^{us}] Thome Spryng armig et Alicie uxoris ejus qui istam capellam fieri fecerunt anno dni MCCCCC vicesimo quinto.

It is higher than the aisle. It has flushwork-panelled walls, three large transomed four-light windows with tracery different from that of the aisle, and different battlements too. The N (Branch) chapel corresponds to the S chapel but was built earlier, c. 1500. Its inscription is similar:

[Orate pro Anim^{us}] Simonis Branch et Elizabethe uxoris ejus qui istam capellam fieri fecerunt.

Its style is similar too, but the following differences ought to be noted. In the tracery of the Spring Chapel occur ogee arches, in that of the Branch Chapel they do not. The buttresses of the Spring Chapel are more elaborate than those of the Branch Chapel, which are not bonded into the plinth – indicating that the Branch Chapel was probably built on an

older foundation. The battlements of the Spring Chapel are
of stone similar to those of the S aisle, those of the Branch
Chapel have flushwork panelling. From the C14 chancel projects a low E vestry. This is said to date from 1444, was given by
Thomas Spring II, and is of knapped flint with plain battlements. The arcades inside are of six bays. The slender piers
have a complex section with four attached shafts which alone
carry capitals. The capitals have fleuron decoration and battlements. The arch has an outer plain roll moulding, and circular
shafts rise through the spandrels and from the apexes to the
roof. Below the clerestory windows frieze of lozenges with
shields. Cambered roof on small figures of angels. The E bays
above the former rood, are panelled. Fine N aisle roof, lean-to
on angel figures. Carved principals. Wall-posts with niches and
canopies. Along the N aisle wall below the windows frieze of
fleurons, along the S aisle wall of foliage trails. In the N chapel
N wall blank panelling below the windows. Blank panelling
also in the tower N, S, and W walls.

FURNISHINGS. FONT. Perp, octagonal, much decayed. It
had on seven sides two panels with standing figures. – SCREENS.
The rood screen is contemporary with the chancel, i.e. of
c. 1330–40. Screens that early are rare. Simple two-light
divisions with ogee arches and flowing tracery. Original gates.
Cresting. Later are the parclose screens to the N and S chapels.
Parts of several screens, all good, none outstanding. The best
has two-light divisions with a pendant between the two lights
and gables and fine tracery over. – SPRING CHANTRY (N aisle
E end). The screen is a glorious piece of woodwork, as dark as
bronze. Buttresses of openwork mouchettes. Dado with
branches instead of tracery. In the two-light arches the tracery
has also turned organic. Shallow canopies with little imitation
vaults. The chantry was built by the will of Thomas Spring
who died in 1523. – OXFORD CHANTRY (S aisle E end). The
thirteenth Earl died in 1513. The screen round his chantry is
less fantastical, but equally successful. Three-light divisions
with big ogee gables over each six lights. Castellated angle
buttresses and finials. For the monument inside see below. –
DOORS. W door with tracery, S door with linenfold panelling,
no doubt of the date of the porch. Rood stair with a typical
Early Tudor motif (cf. S door Southwold), chancel E end, to
C15 vestry, with tracery. – STALLS. Traceried fronts, poppy-
heads on the ends. – MISERICORDS. E.g. a pelican, a jester, a
man holding a pig (the Oxford boar ?), two figures playing the

lute (?) and the fiddle, etc. – STAINED GLASS. Many small fragments of original glass in the N aisle windows. – E window by *Lavers & Barraud* (*Gent. Mag.* 1861), W window also by *Lavers & Barraud*, designed by *J. M. Allen*, the chancel S window by *Frederick Thompson* 1861. – MONUMENTS. In the Oxford Chantry decayed tomb-chest with pitched roof. – In the chancel monument to Henry Copinger † 1622. Two kneeling figures facing each other, kneeling children in the 'predella'. Columns l. and r. and two angels standing outside them. – BRASSES. Thomas Spryng II † 1486 (E vestry). Kneeling figures. – Allaine Dister † 1534, an Elizabethan plate (N aisle wall). The inscription says of him:

> A Clothier vertuous while he was
> In Lavenham many a yeare
> For as in lyefe he loved best
> The poore to clothe and feede
> So withe the riche and all the rest
> He neighbourlie agreed,
> And did appoynt before he died
> A spïal yearlie rent
> Whiche shoulde be every Whitsontide
> Amonge the poorest spent

– Clopton d'Ewes † 1631, tiny baby (in front of the altar). – Large number of indents.

PERAMBULATION

here is nothing in Suffolk to compete with the timber-framed houses of Lavenham. The church lies at the very end of the village. We start from here and try to see as much as possible without having to retrace our steps. Down CHURCH STREET and first on the l. No. 81, Georgian, red brick, with two canted bay windows, the angles oddly stressed by Tuscan columns set in. Doorway with broken pediment, Venetian window above this, and broken top pediment. On the other side some interesting timber-framed houses (Nos. 13–15 and Nos. 11–12).* Pargetted emblems of the wool trade (mitre, spur-rowel, fleur-de-lys). Then again on the former side timber-framed houses (Nos. 85–87), one with a stucco cartouche. Turn r. into WATER STREET, one of the most rewarding streets. At the corner of LADY STREET the Old Wool Hall, and opposite 'Tudor Shops'. THE OLD WOOL 47a

---

* No. 22 is a reproduction.

HALL is a hall-house of the C15. The hall is open to the roof and has a big six-light transomed window. It is now incorporated into the Swan Hotel (*see* below). TUDOR SHOPS has indeed the three small arches of a former shop, and also a W front with fourteen brackets and shafts with carved capitals. In Water Street opposite these two No. 68 with a bargeboarded gable and remains of bold pargetting. After this the fabulous display of DE VERE HOUSE (No. 60), much restored. The brick herringboning is not old. C15 with oriels on the ground floor, a gable with carved bressumer, soffit, and wall-plate. A second gable round the corner again richly carved. (Also good interiors. DOE) The adjoining Nos. 58 and 55 are also worthwhile (both have flat fronts). Opposite BARN STREET goes up the hill. In it first on the r. THE FACTORY, probably c. 1800 brick, three-storeyed, with segment-headed windows. Then adjoining it, the OLD GRAMMAR SCHOOL, again timber-framed, with traces of buttress posts and carved beams, a most picturesque group. On the other side MULLET HOUSE, only one gable wide, but very good, with original doorway, seven-light ground-floor oriel, oversailing first floor, and carved gable bressumer. From here one can go up to the Market Place. We return to WATER STREET instead and continue to its end. Nos. 23–26 on the l. are picturesque, No. 47 on the r. though much altered, still has many C15 features. Brackets with capitals, good carved bressumers.

From the end of Water Street, SHILLING STREET leads up and into Barn Street. It must be visited because of ARUNDEL HOUSE, with a nice Georgian doorway, and SHILLING OLD GRANGE, a large C15 house, much restored. It has a brick courtyard and good interiors. The porch is not original.

Water Street was a detour. Back to the corner of Church Street and up HIGH STREET. At the corner of Water Street the SWAN HOTEL. Its cellars are said to date back to the C14. Picturesque front, small rear courtyard. Towards Water Street the same pargetted emblems as in Church Street. In 1965 the Swan was extended to incorporate the Old Wool Hall (*see* above), and in 1967–8 No. 101 High Street. The architect was *James Hopwood*. High Street is not eventful. Nos. 6–12 are pretty and date from the C15. After the r. hand turning to the Market Place not much reason to continue. The best houses are Nos. 61–63. They are followed by the dull, stuccoed, Late Classical CONGREGATIONAL CHAPEL of 1827.

So to the MARKET PLACE, which is dominated by the GUILD

HALL of the Guild of Corpus Christi, built shortly after the foundation of the guild in 1529.* It has a splendid porch, varied and diversely decorated. Very ornate, with carved angle-posts, carved spandrels, carved friezes, and an overhang. Oriels on the ground floor, especially fine that towards Lady Street. At the corner of Lady Street carved angle-post with a figure with a lance. The main hall fills the front from the porch to the r. To the l. and projecting at the back two rooms, one behind the other. In LADY STREET a little lower down THE GROVE, timber-framed at the back, but with a Georgian front of grey brick. Doorway with broken pediment, a Venetian window above it.

n the Market Place the MARKET CROSS, probably a former churchyard cross. Of other houses not many need be mentioned. (The ANGEL HOTEL has a C16 plaster ceiling on the first floor and much recently discovered earlier wall-painting. LG) THE GREAT HOUSE in the SE corner, where Barn Street comes up, is Late Georgian with a Doric doorway. THE LITTLE HOUSE is yet another C15 house, much reconstructed. Its side is along PRENTICE STREET, which must in conclusion be visited because of WOOLSTAPLERS (Nos. 23–24), C15, with two different gables with carved C17 brackets. The flat timber-framed front of Nos. 25–26 next door is an excellent foil. (Also in this area, the DOE has recently recorded BAKER'S MILL, a good group of late C19 industrial buildings, to the NE of an enclosed court entered from Prentice Street, with a range of maltings on the SW and SE sides. Red brick with some decorative bands of grey brick; slate roof. The main block of the mill is in a style 'reminiscent of the Italian Romanesque'. On the N, W, and S fronts the ground- and first-floor windows have segmental and the second-floor windows flat brick arches. They are arranged in pairs set in recessed panels topped by a serrated brick dentil course. The frontage to Prentice Street has a gable with shaped brick pendants and a central round-headed window with a moulded brick hood course. The façades are framed by chamfered brick pilasters and a raised plinth. A semicircular brick arched doorway in the N front has an inscribed stone tympanum. At r. angles to the main block, a wing of two and three storeys with a timber loft-hoist. The maltings comprise an L-shaped range of one and two storeys with an oast house drying tower at the SW corner. A C19 red brick and flint wall links the maltings with Little House in the

* Mr W. Godfrey's suggestion.

Market Place (*see* above), and is an integral part of the who group.)

8050 LAWSHALL

ALL SAINTS. A will of 1444 refers to the 'new church' (ARA Quite big. Tall w tower, nave and aisles, clerestory and low chancel, the latter in all its E.E. details Victorian (restoratio by *Butterfield*, 1857*). Arcade of four bays. Piers with fou filleted shafts and in the diagonals a thin shaft between tw hollows. Castellated capitals. Above the arches a string-cour with demi-figures of angels. – FONT. C14, with tracery pane recently rather garishly painted. – MONUMENT. J. B. va Mesdag † 1945. Large inscription plate made up of small tile Designed by the distinguished typographer *Jan van Krimpe* and made at the *Royal Goedewaagen* workshops at Gouda.

LAWSHALL HALL. Some Early Tudor brickwork with bl diapering and two doorways with stone hood-moulds, one head stops, decidedly ecclesiastical-looking.

COLDHAM HALL. *See* p. 173.

2070 LAXFIELD

ALL SAINTS. Dec nave, see the N side, altered Perp. All the re Perp, except for the C19 chancel and vestry. Stone-faced tower, polygonal clasping buttresses with flushwork panellin Flushwork panelling also on the base and flushwork emblen at the top. w doorway with fleurons in the arch. Frieze quatrefoils below the four-light w window, niches to its l. an r. Four-light bell openings. s porch with some flushwo decoration. Two niches on the front buttresses. Entrance ar with shields. Vaulting shafts inside. The porch was intended have an upper storey, but was left incomplete. Four-light windows. The interior is surprising. The roof is accepted original by Cautley; yet it looks as if aisle arcades might hav been taken out at some stage. The nave is 36 ft wide; the ro is of the trussed-rafter type, with long, almost straight brac and scissor bracing at the collar-level. Short hammerbean concealed by coving (cf. Framlingham). – FONT. With th Seven Sacraments and the Baptism of Christ on the bow Alternatingly two- and three-step base with quatrefoils etc. decoration. The third step is in the shape of a Maltese Cross as to form four stools. – PULPIT. Jacobean; and READER DESK made of parts in the same style. – SCREEN. Two-lig

* Information from Mr Paul Thompson.

tracery in the dado. One-light upper divisions with ogee arches and some tracery above them. – BENCHES with traceried ends, poppy-heads, and, on the arms, animals, a seated figure, and also a tower. Carved backs to the benches. (Also a set with Jacobean poppy-heads. G. McHardy) – BOX PEWS, one block of them in rising tiers (NW). In the main block use is made of bench ends and also Early Renaissance panels. – POOR BOX. A thick baluster; dated 1664. – BANNER STAFF LOCKER in the SW corner. – STAINED GLASS. Some fragments in N windows. – PLATE. Elizabethan Cup and Cover dated 1567; late C17 Paten; Flagon 1724.

(BAPTIST CHAPEL. 1808, with excellent fanlights. LG)

GUILDHALL. A pretty timber-framed building with bricknogging, to the S of the church, at the main corner of the village. Six bays wide.

WINDMILL. A smock-mill, now power-driven.

LAYHAM   004⊕

ST ANDREW. Flint, with a brick tower of 1742 (altered c. 1800?). It replaces a tower of c. 1300 of which the tower arch remains. The windows of the church are all of the type of c. 1300, but all renewed. – FONT. Hexagonal, of Purbeck marble, with two arched blank panels on each side. – SCREEN. Fragment of the dado with simple traceried panels. – PLATE. Elizabethan Cup and Cover; Flagon 1774; Paten 1796.

NETHERBURY HALL. By the church. Georgian, red brick, of five bays and two storeys, with parapet and Ionic porch.

(OVERBURY HALL, ½ m. W. Large C16 to C17 house. Ceiling of close-set moulded beams in the dining room. DOE)

LEAVENHEATH   903⊕

ST MATTHEW. 1835 by *G. Russell French*. Chancel, S tower, S aisle, etc., by *Satchell & Edwards*, 1882–3. Rather terrible, so close to Nayland and Stoke-by-Nayland.

LEISTON   406⊕

ST MARGARET. 1853 by *E. B. Lamb*, and as undauntedly and frantically original as this remarkable architect's other churches. The old W tower was preserved, tall and with flushwork in the battlements. The new building is Dec outside, flint with horizontal stone bands. Nothing prepares us for the antics of carpentry inside. The stone walls are as low as possible so as to get as much space as possible for the timber roof. The church has transepts, and the climax of the design is the crossing, marked by four long and strong diagonal beams rising to the apex and four more diagonals rising a little less so as to come to a point a good deal below the apex. They are connected with the higher quadruplet by diagonal struts. Crazily heavy w gallery constructed with arched braces like a bridge on which the road surface (here the gallery floor) is partly suspended. Gargantuan flamboyant tracery. – FONT. Circular, late C13, with a circular stem with eight attached shafts and on the bowl pointed-trefoiled arches. – REREDOS, Children's Corner. Relief by *E. M. Rope* (*see* Blaxhall, p. 100). – PAINTING. Pretty painting of Lamb's time on the jambs of the sanctuary arch: vine and corn ears. – STAINED GLASS. E window by *Kempe* 1898. – N transept N window by *M. E. A. Rope, c.* 1928. – PLATE. Spoon 1763; Cup and Paten 1765; Flagon 1766; Paten 1772. – MONUMENTS. Richard Garrett † 1866. By *Thurlow* of Saxmundham. Frontal bust under an ogee arch. – A. G. M Rope † 1905 as a child. Small panel of beaten silver in the Arts and Crafts taste. By *Dorothy Rope, see* Blaxhall, p. 100. By the same the War Memorial in the churchyard.

THE CUPOLA, s of the church. The front of grey brick looks early C19. It is of two and a half storeys, five windows wide. At the back two one-storey wings of red brick, early C18. The cupola, no doubt also of the early C18, has gone.

LEISTON HALL, W of the church. Symmetrical front of red brick with two projecting wings carrying shaped gables. The date probably the later C17.

LEISTON HOUSE FARM, ¾ m. W. Georgian red-brick façade of three bays. The doorway with Roman Doric pilasters and a metope frieze with prettily decorated metopes.

WORKS HOUSE (Messrs Richard Garrett, Engineering Works). Facing the street the dwelling house of four bays with two adjoining doors separated and framed by three recessed Tuscan columns. This façade is of *c.* 1820–30, though the house itself is older. Behind, among the buildings, the Main Office of *c.* 1830–40 and the Long Shop of 1852. The latter was at the time a model workshop.

LEISTON ABBEY. Founded for Premonstratensian Canons in 1182. The founder was Sir Ranulf Glanville, Lord Chief Justice. Transferred to the present site in 1363 and rebuilt there and after a fire of 1382. Earlier fragments were re-used. The church was 168 ft in length, and had nave and aisles, a square crossing, transepts, a chancel, and chancel aisles pro-

jecting slightly less far E than the chancel. Part of the N wall of
the N aisle is now blocked with brick infillings. The S aisle and
the W end of the nave are part of the house. The N transept
has a very large N window. The imposts of the arch into the N
chancel aisle are of the early C13. They have semicircular
shafts and simply moulded capitals. The E window of the
chancel aisle is Dec and probably of the early C14. Its jambs
were triple-shafted, the middle shaft with a fillet. The windows
of the projecting part of the chancel are also finely shafted. The
E arch of the crossing has late C12 imposts. The S chapel was
simple. Of the monastic ranges the area of the cloister is easily
recognized. To its E was the chapter house, to its S the refectory
above an undercroft. The reader's pulpit and its staircase were
in the S wall. In the SE angle of the cloister ranges the day-
stair to the dormitory went up. The W range contained store-
rooms etc. The vaulting corbels are re-used C13 material. To
this range in the early C16 a brick gatehouse was added. It has
polygonal W turrets.

LETHERINGHAM   2050

LETHERINGHAM ABBEY was a small Augustinian Priory
founded c. 1200 as a cell of St Peter Ipswich. All that remains of
it, except for a part of the church (see below) and odd bits of
stone and tracery in the churchyard wall, is the GATEHOUSE,
C15 brick, with a broad two-centred arch and polygonal angle
buttresses. A blocked three-light window to the S. The gable
is not original.

ST MARY. (The church incorporates the two Norman W bays of
the priory church. LG) Norman S doorway, tall and narrow.
One order of colonnettes with scalloped capitals. Zigzag in the
arch, billet in the hood-mould. The chancel was demolished
c. 1789. Nave with windows of c. 1300, including the good
three-light intersected window at the E end which must come
from the chancel. Dec W tower with flushwork decoration on
buttresses and battlements. Dec W window. (The tower arch
may incorporate re-used Norman work. P. G. M. Dickinson)
S porch of brick with an odd shaped gable (straight sides on
convex lower shanks) dated 1685. – COMMUNION RAIL.
Three-sided. – PULPIT. Simple, Late Georgian. – BOX PEWS.
Some. – PLATE. Elizabethan Cup. – MONUMENTS. Excellent
brass of the late C14, the figure 5 ft long; supposed to be Sir
John Wingfield † 1389. – Another, 3 ft long, to another Sir
John Wingfield, 1481; from the Ashmolean Museum. – Two

kneeling figures from a Jacobean monument now oddly in separate niches.

LETHERINGHAM MILL. A delightfully picturesque group.

LETHERINGHAM HALL, close to the mill. Large ten-bay weatherboarded BARN.

LETHERINGHAM LODGE, 1¼ m. SE. Timber-framed. The original part of the house has four surprisingly massive carved angle-posts and also the remains of a two-light window of the same date (late C15) inside. The DOE suggests that the posts came from the former Shire Hall of Wickham Market, and quotes White's *Directory* of 1835 in support. The house is surrounded by a fine moat.

OLD VICARAGE. Victorian, with many gables, but extensively altered in 1929 by *George Walton* of Glasgow. He added the front in pure Georgian and turned the main direction of the house by 180 degrees.

2030

LEVINGTON

ST PETER. Broad brick tower completed in 1636 by Sir Robert Hitcham. Nave and chancel. Early C16 brick windows. The E window of three lights with panel tracery. (The ROOD BEAM is still *in situ*. It is carved with scrolly leaves.) – FONT. Octagonal, Perp, simple. – PULPIT. Jacobean. – CHANCEL PANELLING. Probably mid-C17. From Brightwell Hall (built in 1663). – (COMMUNION RAIL. Probably of the same time.)

HILL COTTAGE, SE of the church. A minor Gothic effort of *c.* 1800.

ALMSHOUSES, ½ m. N. Founded by Sir Robert Hitcham in 1636. Two small short ranges facing one another. Red brick, one-storeyed.

LEVINGTON RESEARCH STATION (Messrs Fison's), E of the Almshouses. By *Birkin Haward*, 1956–7. A well-designed group of buildings, concrete-framing, light brick, and some weatherboarding. The centre is the Administration and Laboratory Block, four-storeyed, and somewhat square and heavy if seen in isolation. However, it is surrounded by four detached lower buildings, and these all have folded-slab roofs of concrete, in varying shapes, but consistently reminiscent (in C20 terms) of the Suffolk tradition of gabled houses. Their heights and ridge-lines differ, and the whole is stimulating and lively. Inside the main block the transparent entrance and staircase hall. On the l. a tall relief by *John Hutton*, four women symbolizing something agricultural.

Between the Research Station and the Almshouses employees'
housing, designed by the same architect.

BARROWS. A group of seven on Levington Heath, along the
parish boundary, on the N side of the Felixstowe road.

LIDGATE

ST MARY. Norman nave. S doorway of Norman proportions, but
given Perp mouldings. C13 chancel with nobly spaced lancets
on the N side. PISCINA shafted with pointed-trefoiled head. E
window Dec with simple flowing tracery. Arcade Dec. Four
bays, tall octagonal piers, double-chamfered arches. W tower
late C13 or early C14. – PULPIT. Jacobean. – SCREENS. Rood
screen with simple one-light divisions. N parclose screen also
one-light divisions, but prettier tracery. – BENCHES. Straight-
headed, some with linenfold decoration on the ends. – (Brass
CHANDELIER. LG) – PLATE. Silver-gilt Cups said to be
German, C17. – BRASS. A priest, C15, the head renewed. A
20 in. figure said to represent John Lydgate the poet, who was
born at Lidgate in 1375 and died probably in 1451.

CASTLE. Earthworks N of the village represent a motte-and-
bailey castle with a rectangular motte and three baileys. The
church stands in one of the baileys, as do some ivy-clad fragments of walls E of the church. A deep ditch runs N and W of the
churchyard.

SUFFOLK HOUSE, in the village street. Timber-framed, but with
a fine brick end with a stepped gable; early Tudor. The
bressumer in the front of the house partly carved.

LINDSEY

ST PETER. The W tower was removed in 1836 and replaced by a
weatherboarded bell-turret. Early C14 church, see the segment-
headed S aisle and chancel windows. In the nave on the N side
a specially handsome straight-headed two-light window with
intersected top like the famous C13 piscinas of Jesus and St
John's Colleges at Cambridge.* The window has shafts and
niches in the jambs inside, and a second of the same type
further W is blocked. Simple C14 timber S porch. Arcade inside
C14 with octagonal piers and double-chamfered arches. Roof
with tie-beams and kingposts. – FONT. Of c. 1300. Intersected
arches with, in the spandrels, a circle, an encircled trefoil, a
trefoil, etc. – SCREEN. Fragment of the dado with traceried
panels. – BOX PEWS. – BENCH with traceried front and poppy-

* And those of Hardingham and Pulham St Mary in Norfolk.

heads. – COMMUNION RAIL. Three-sided, late C17. – ORGAN
CASE. Pretty and probably early C19. – (WALL PAINTINGS.
On nave and s aisle walls. Recently discovered. LG) – PLATE.
Elizabethan Cup and Cover.

ST JAMES'S CHAPEL. Early C13, with lancet windows. The s
wall is in its original state, with lancet windows and a doorway
with one slight chamfer. PISCINA late C13 (pointed-trefoiled
arch). w doorway Early Tudor brick.

CASTLE. At the Mounts, in the s of the parish, is a motte-and-
bailey castle lying astride a stream, which was probably used
to fill its moats. The motte is low, and the arrangement of the
baileys complicated. The castle was mentioned in the mid C12.

LINSTEAD MAGNA
3070

ST PETER. All that survives is the brick w tower and a fragment
of the SE corner of the nave.

LINSTEAD FARMHOUSE, SW of the church. Timber-framed,
C16, with some original mullioned windows.

LINSTEAD PARVA
3070

ST MARGARET. Nave and chancel and weatherboarded bell-
turret. The chancel of the C13, the nave, at least in its windows
(of brick), of the early C16. If the w front with a lancet flanked
by two niches with pointed-trefoiled heads represents the
original state, this could be C13 too. – FONT. Octagonal, four
seated lions against the stem, the Signs of the Evangelists and
four demi-figures of angels against the bowl. – BENCHES. The
blocks of benches taper off so as to allow enough space for the
font. Two ends with small figures on the arms. – PLATE.
Almsdish 1812. Also at Linstead Parva, but from Linstead
Magna, Paten 1509; Elizabethan Cup; Almsdish 1812.

CHAPEL FARM, w of the church. Handsome timber-framed
front with overhang. Some original mullioned windows.

LITTLE BEALINGS
2040

ALL SAINTS. Unbuttressed s tower. The nave s side of early
C16 brick. The forms of the chancel seem of *c.* 1300; the N
aisle is of 1851. – FONT. Octagonal. Against the stem four lions;
defaced. Against the bowl only one lion and one angel left. –
PULPIT. C17; simple. – PLATE. Elizabethan Cup.

On PLAYFORD HEATH, ¼ m. N of Kesgrave, an Iron Age FARM
SITE is indicated by a group of huts overlying a Late Bronze
Age urnfield and also containing Saxon material.

LITTLE BLAKENHAM

1040

ST MARY. Nave and chancel and unbuttressed W tower. The chancel is E.E. E wall with a window of three stepped lancets under one arch. In the spandrels two pierced trefoils. Inside, l. and r. of the window, deep flat niches with shafts and trefoiled heads. They are probably of the C19. In the N wall one lancet window with deeply splayed reveals. The other windows Dec (one with an elongated sexfoil in the tracery) or Perp. – PAINT-INGS. In the jambs of the E.E. lancet two figures, probably originally C13, but completely re-painted in 1850. L. and r. of the E window Christ carrying the Cross and St John Baptist re-coloured and largely remodelled by *Kashi Dubinski*, in the style of Hans Feibusch. – PLATE. Elizabethan Cup; Paten 1816.
OLD RECTORY, E of the church. The E front has two shaped gables with convex-concave sides and a semicircular top.

LITTLE BRADLEY

6050

ALL SAINTS. The nave and the W part of the chancel in their masonry probably Anglo-Saxon, see the long-and-short work at the NW and SW angles. This was added to a pre-existing, that is doubtless Anglo-Saxon, round tower. Small doorway on simple imposts. The tower top Perp and octagonal.* Early Norman E extension of the chancel with E and N windows. Norman probably also the undecorated S doorway. (The S porch incorporates some C14 woodwork. LG) – PULPIT. With C18 tester. – PLATE. Cup 1789. – MONUMENTS. Three brasses: Civilian and wife, c. 1520 (chancel N wall); headless Knight, 27 in. figure, probably Thomas Knighton, 1530 (chancel S wall); John Daye, the printer, † 1584, and wife (above the Civilian). – Monument to Richard Lehunte † 1540 and his wife † 1558. Kneeling figures. Back wall with short columns l. and r. and above two blank arches.

LITTLE CORNARD

9030

ALL SAINTS. Flint. W tower with little cupola. Nave with brick quoins. S porch with brick windows. Two-storeyed C17 brick vestry. – FONT. Simple, Perp. – STAINED GLASS. E window by *Clutterbuck*, 1857 (TK). – PLATE. Cup 1643; Paten 1707.

LITTLE FINBOROUGH

0050

ST MARY. Nave and chancel and bellcote. Nothing much of

* A will of 1455/6 suggests that alterations were being made to the tower around this date (ARA).

interest. (Plain tympanum between nave and chancel. Cautley)
The nave was rebuilt in 1856.

LITTLE GLEMHAM

3050

ST ANDREW. Norman N doorway with one order of colonnettes
and in the arch one roll moulding and one order of what must
be described as the geometrical substitute for the familiar
beakheads.* Perp W tower with flushwork on base, buttresses,
and battlements. W doorway with fleurons in an arch moulding
and shields in the spandrels. The S doorway is similar. C18
brick chancel, gothicized in the C19. Early C19 family chapel
of the Norths on the N side. In it the MONUMENT of Dudley
North, made in 1833 by *John Gibson* in Rome. White seated
statue in timeless clothes and in a Grecian chair. The surroundings nobly classical too, oblong coffered segmented vault
on four Greek Doric corner columns. Also a number of other
good and quite large North tablets, of the C18, both in the
family chapel and the chancel, e.g. Mrs Catherine † 1715, by
William Holland. – FONT. Octagonal, of Purbeck marble, C13,
with two shallow blank pointed arches on each side. – SCULP-
TURE. Fragment of a panel of the Trinity; SE window. –
STAINED GLASS. A N window of c. 1929 by *M. E. A. Rope*
(cf. Blaxhall and Leiston). – PLATE. Cup 1566; Paten 1567;
Flagon 1636; Paten 1732.

LITTLE GLEMHAM HALL. A large red-brick mansion of c.
1715–25 (rain-water heads 1717, 1722). The entrance side is of
three storeys, with main cornice below the top storey, seven-
bay centre, and two-bay projecting wings. Absolutely flat roof,
and originally no decoration. Tall windows. The only decoration is a porch, which is not original, and two oddly-placed
Tuscan pilasters which seem entirely incongruous if referred
to the present house. However, this was preceded by an Elizabethan house, and the pilasters and the Ionic pilasters whose
traces one can still see above them seem more probable as
Tudor than as Georgian. The old house is still essentially
recognizable on the garden side with its brickwork, its straight
gables, and its mullioned windows (and one mullioned and
transomed cross-window). Inside there is nothing of the old
house. Instead of its great hall, and still in the same asymmetrical (i.e. medieval) position, there is now the Early Georgian

* Or are they, as Mrs Ettlinger suggests, simply beakheads left uncarved ?
Cf. Westhall, where some of the beakheads are finished and some unfinished.

hall, with fine panelling and a beautiful screen of tall Corinthian columns instead of the former screen. Behind the hall and opening from its centre is the staircase, wide and spacious, with twisted balusters and carved tread-ends. It originally had above its very large windows circular windows in addition. In other rooms original panelling too, mostly of *c.* 1725, though in one upper room Elizabethan. Also original fireplaces. Bills exist to show that chimneypieces cost 5*s.* a foot.

STABLES. Red brick, not large, with an unusually pretty bell-turret with lantern over the archway.

LITTLE HAUGH HALL *see* NORTON

LITTLE LIVERMERE
8070

ST PETER AND ST PAUL. In ruins. The w tower was heightened, it is said, to be seen from the Hall, no doubt in the C18. Nave and chancel in one with Y-tracery in brick surrounds, i.e. also C18. The N chapel is an C18 addition with a Gothic plaster vault. The N doorway, however, has a decorated Norman lintel, and the NE corner Saxon long-and-short work. The former BOX PEW arrangement is described by Cautley.

BARROWS. On Seven Hills, on the parish boundary by the Thetford road, is a group much overgrown with fir trees. Three remain.

LITTLE SAXHAM
8060

ST NICHOLAS. The most spectacular Norman round tower in Suffolk. Round the top a rhythmical order of arches on columns. In the four main directions they hold deeply recessed two-light bell-openings, in the diagonals two lower blank arches. Billet frieze along the sill-level. The tower arch into the nave is tall, and s of it is a blank arch on colonnettes with coarse volute capitals. It is the re-used Norman N doorway. All these Norman arches have strong roll mouldings. Norman also the s doorway, also with volute capitals and also with a roll moulding and an outer billet frieze. Dec N aisle with its three-bay arcade (very elementary continuous mouldings) and its clerestory windows over. The s porch belongs to the same time. Finally the Perp contribution: the nave and chancel s sides with uncusped, rather bald tracery, the E window, and the N chapel. – PULPIT. Jacobean. – COMMUNION RAIL. Brought recently from Little Livermere. With C18 balusters. Coming forward in the middle in an elegant double curve. –

SCREEN. Only the dado survives. – STALLS. The fronts have openwork flat tapering balusters, a Jacobean motif. – BENCHES. With reclining animals as poppy-heads. One end has a kneeling and praying figure instead, and one end is traceried. – BIER. A C17 bier in the N aisle; a rare survival. – PLATE. Two Patens 1799. – MONUMENTS. Thomas Fitzlucas † 1531, erected before his death (he was buried in London). Four-centred blank arch with cresting. Inside, the panels with lozenges and quatrefoils with shields which faced the sides of the former tomb-chest. – William, Baron Crofts, † 1677, by *Abraham Storey*, signed by him and with his initials on a badge which the baron holds. Big standing monument of white and black marble. Two semi-reclining effigies, he above and behind her, i.e. a conservative motif in the last quarter of the century. 'Modern' on the other hand the back architecture, with columns carrying a large open scrolly pediment. – Mrs Ann Croftes † 1727. By *W. Palmer*.

LITTLE STONHAM

1050

ST MARY. E window with reticulated tracery. The rest Perp, the stepped gables of nave and chancel supposed to be original and not of 1886. W tower richly decorated with flushwork. Arched panelling at the base, parapet with quatrefoils, battlements with arched panelling and the letter M (for Mary). W doorway with one order of fleurons in the jambs and arch. Frieze of quatrefoils above the doorway and a shield with the Crane arms in the middle. S porch with diagonal buttresses decorated with flushwork. S chapel of one bay added later, to its E. Clerestory with close windows, built at the same time as the fine double-hammerbeam roof. Wall-posts with seated figures in nodding ogee niches; carved spandrels. The chancel roof is Victorian. – FONT. Octagonal. Four lions against the stem. Demi-figures of angels supporting the bowl. Against the bowl three angels, two monograms, the Crown of Thorns, the Crucifixion, and a flower. – WEST DOOR. With tracery. – WEST GALLERY. C18. – PLATE. Cup 1659; Flagon 1737; Paten 1747.

LITTLE STONHAM HALL, W of the church. Georgian. Plastered, five bays, two storeys, with a three-bay pediment.

CLOCK HOUSE, ¾ m. N. A house of the early C14 with the original crown-post truss of the hall. Octagonal post with four-way struts. Early Tudor circular chimneys with fleur-de-lis etc. decoration also survive. The hall was horizontally subdivided *c.* 1600, the time when the good coved plaster ceiling with

geometrical ribbing patterns was put into a first-floor room.
It is, unfortunately, no longer complete.

MAGPIE INN. The inn has a wrought-iron SIGN, probably C18,
suspended from a wooden frame across the main road.

LITTLE THURLOW   6050

ST PETER. Early C14. The W tower has a W window with intersected cusped tracery. The top, with a flushwork chequerboard pattern, is Perp. Both aisles have segment-headed Dec
windows, the S side also two with uncusped Y-tracery. Arcade
with octagonal piers and double-chamfered arches, probably
Dec. The chancel is over-restored; the clerestory N windows
are C17. The N chapel (Soame Chapel) is of brick plastered.
Its date is Jacobean, and it has its original circular windows.
Of the arches to the chancel one has Jacobean plaster decoration. The ceiling is Jacobean also. – FONT. Square, Norman, with angle-shafts and bold foliage motifs, almost like
poppy-heads. – SCREEN. The dado only, with panels with
prettily painted flowers. – FAMILY PEW. Jacobean. – COM-
MUNION RAIL. Three-sided, mid or late C17. – CHANDELIER,
of brass, undated, C17–18. – STAINED GLASS. Early C17 in
the oval W window of the Soame Chapel. – MONUMENTS.
Brass of a Knight and Lady, c. 1520, 18 in. figures. – Sir
Stephen Soame † 1619, Lord Mayor of London, builder of
the chapel in which the monument was erected, and bene-
factor of Little Thurlow. Large and excellent alabaster structure. Two recumbent effigies, he behind and a little above her.
To the l. and r. groups of four columns, two detached, two
attached. The children arranged round and between these
columns and also on the ground, two kneeling frontally l. and r.
of the base, and three in profile in front of the base. The columns
carry little pediments from which springs a well-detailed arch,
e.g. with a frieze of cherubs' heads. On the top, Father Time l.
and an angel r. Original iron grille. – Stephen Soame † 1771 by
J. Walsh of London. Above a big inscription plate strigillated
sarcophagus on which medallion with a relief of a mother and
child. Obelisk background.

(LITTLE THURLOW HALL. Built in 1847. P. G. M. Dickinson)
SCHOOL. At the S end of the village by the main N–S road.
Founded by Sir Stephen Soame in 1614. Red brick, three bays,
the centre bay projecting and gabled. Coat of arms over the
door. – ALMSHOUSES. At the N end of the village by the main
N–S road. For nine poor people. Three ranges facing an oblong

forecourt. Red brick, one-storeyed, except for the gabled
centre. Endowed by Sir Stephen Soame in 1618.

WINDMILL. A smock-mill converted into a house.

LITTLE WALDINGFIELD

ST LAWRENCE. All Perp. The distinguishing feature is the two
rood-stair turrets with their crocketed spirelets. W tower, nave
and aisles and clerestory. The arcades have quatrefoil piers
with embattled capitals and carry arches of one wave and one
hollow with little decorative ogee gables. The same motif over
the aisle windows and also over the doorways. That on the S
side is decorated with crowns, faces, and big square fleurons.
S porch of brick and flint, roughly striped. N porch of brick.*
The front has a stepped gable in front of a steep plain gable. The
latter carries a pinnacle. Niche for an image below this. The
chancel E window looks plain C17 Gothic. The roofs in the
nave, cambered on arched braces, and in the aisles are original.
– FONT. Octagonal, with the Signs of the Evangelists and four
frontal figures of monks with books. – PULPIT. Jacobean; good.
– READING DESK. With panels with similar motifs. – WEST
DOOR. With a band of quatrefoils. – NORTH DOOR. With a
band of foliage trails outside, a band of shields and quatrefoils
inside. – CHEST. Good C15 chest with traceried front. –
BRASSES. John Coleman † 1506, 2 ft 6 in. figure (by the E wall
of the N aisle). – Robert Appleton † 1526 and wife, 20 in.
figures. – John Wyncoll † 1544, 19 in. figure.

THE PRIORY. The brick groin-vaults in the cellar are according
to Mr Dickinson probably the remains of a manor house, not a
monastic establishment. He dates them C14.

HOLBROOK HALL. By *Ewan Christian*, 1883. Brick with stone
dressing. Elizabethan style. Symmetrical front with two stepped
gables.

LITTLE WELNETHAM see
LITTLE WHELNETHAM

LITTLE WENHAM

ALL SAINTS. Built of flint. Nave and chancel, and a W tower
with a brick top probably of the time of Henry VIII. S porch
with timber balusters in the W and E walls, probably Jacobean.
The church is of *c.* 1300, see the fine, slender mullions of the
windows which have Y-tracery on the N and S and three un-

* A will of 1466 leaves money towards the building of new porches
(*hostiorum*) (ARA).

foiled circles in the head of the E window. Also a low-side lancet.
– FONT. Of the same period or a little earlier. Big octagonal
bowl on eight polygonal supports. – PULPIT. C18; simple. –
(SCREEN. Plain rubble wall, 62 in. tall. Cautley) – COM-
MUNION RAIL. Of *c.* 1700, with strong twisted balusters. –
BENCHES. Two, with linenfold panelling. – WALL PAINTINGS.
On the E wall astonishingly good wall paintings contemporary
with the architecture. On the l. Virgin and Child and four
Angels, on the r. St Margaret, St Catherine, and St Mary
Magdalene. Also, on the nave N wall, St Christopher, C15,
more ordinary in quality. – PLATE. Cup and Paten 1791. –
MONUMENTS. Thomas Brewse † 1514, wife and children.
Brasses under handsome double canopy. – Tomb recess, nave
s wall, with big cusped and subcusped arch under ogee gable.
The tomb-chest is decorated with shields in quatrefoils. –
Tomb recess, chancel N wall, latest Perp with simple, some-
what heavy, canopy. – Sir John Brewse † 1585, chancel s wall,
with small kneeling figure in profile. The surround has short
columns l. and r. and a pediment.

LITTLE WENHAM HALL. The house was built *c.* 1270–80, 43
probably for Sir John de Vallibus and his successor Petronilla
of Nerford. It is of great historical importance for two reasons.
The first is that it is built of brick, and represents one of the
earliest uses of home-made brick in England. Flint is used only
for the base of the walls and stone for the much rebuilt buttresses and dressings. The second point of outstanding interest
is that the house is a house and not a keep. It is fortified of
course, but it is in its shape and appointment on the way from
the fortress to the manor house and so ranks with Stokesay and
Acton Burnell of about the same years as one of the *incunabula*
of English domestic architecture. The house is L-shaped with
a spiral staircase in the re-entrant angle. It has always stood on
its own, and the only place where an attachment has existed
and has disappeared is the w half of the s wall. What has disappeared is probably a garderobe. A C16 wing was added at the
s w angle and later pulled down. The entrance is on the first
floor. The ground floor or basement, whatever one chooses to
call it, is rib-vaulted in brick. The arches and ribs have one
hollow chamfer. On the entrance floor lie hall and chapel. The
hall has four windows, all of two lights with plate tracery,
including unencircled trefoils and quatrefoils. From the hall
to the E one enters the chapel. The doorway is flanked, as if it 44a
were that to a miniature chapter house, by two internal two-

light windows with oddly detailed polygonal shafts and quatre-foils in plate tracery. The hall was unvaulted – the present ceiling is assigned to the C16 – but the chapel has a rib-vault with a fine profile to the ribs. The vault rests on corbels, and of these the two earlier ones have stiff-leaf capitals. On the boss St Petronilla is represented, and it has been emphasized in this context that Little Wenham was inherited by Petronilla of Nerford in 1287. So completion was perhaps only after that date. Angle piscina with two pointed trefoiled arches. E window of three lights with bar tracery of trefoiled circles, a form in advance of those of the hall windows. On the N side a low-side window. Above the chapel is the solar (or guard room?). This has two windows with Y-tracery on polygonal shafts. The roofs are embattled, and the different heights of hall range, chapel range, and stair-turret create a picturesque skyline.

LITTLE WENHAM HALL FARM. The house has a handsome C16 BARN, timber-framed with brick-nogging and thatched roof.

8060

LITTLE WHELNETHAM

ST MARY MAGDALEN. Small. Dec W tower and chancel. Nave mostly Perp. Nice Perp brick porch with stepped gable. The nave roof has the unusual rhythm of one pair of principals with hammerbeams and then two simply with arched braces. Figures (mutilated under the Puritans, but largely restored in 1842) against the hammerbeams. In the nave E wall below the roof a sexfoiled circular window. In the nave S wall inside a piece built in that may belong to a former Norman PILLAR PISCINA. (In the chancel low-side window with iron grille. LG) – FONT. Octagonal, Perp, simple. – SCREEN. Only the dado remains. – BENCH ENDS. With poppy-heads and tracery. – In the churchyard, the remains of a circular flint building. It has been suggested that this was originally either a bi-apsidal chapel (as at the Saxon abbey at Winchester) or a Saxon watch tower.*

CHAPEL HILL FARM (CRUTCHED FRIARS), on the main Sud-bury road, 1 m. SW. An interesting and picturesque house. To its E the angle buttress and some flint wall of the house of the Crutched Friars, founded in 1274 and later dependent on the London house. In the E wall of the house more of the flint walling. The rest of the house perhaps built after the Dis-solution. Stepped red-brick gable to the N, another to the S at

* Information conveyed to me by Mr Alec Clifton-Taylor.

the SW end. Pretty ornamental brick panels. Pretty half-enclosed courtyard to the N with arched ground-floor spaces between the posts of the timber-framed structure.

LITTLE WRATTING   6040

HOLY TRINITY. Septaria and flint. Nave and chancel and Victorian bell-turret with short shingled spire. The nave is probably late Anglo-Saxon, see the masonry and the shapes of the S and N doorways. The S doorway has a lintel with a dedication inscription in large letters. It is, unfortunately, incomplete. The E half of the chancel is Dec, the Norman chancel arch is a Victorian introduction. Chancel E window with minor (rather standardized) flowing tracery. Dec also the PISCINA. Perp timberwork at the W end of the nave to support the bell-turret. – BENCHES. Simple, straight-headed, with a little tracery. – One BOX PEW. – SOUTH DOOR. With some Norman ironwork. – PLATE. Cup 1684; Paten 1711. – MONUMENT. One kneeling figure from a Jacobean monument, in a bad state of preservation. The monument stood in a former N chapel (Turnour Chapel) which was pulled down in 1710, but of which the Perp W respond survives.

(WASH FARM. Uncommonly fine C17 central chimneys. Inside the house the basement is pierced longitudinally by a wide passageway between the backs of the two fireplaces. A similar passage upstairs. LG)

LONG MELFORD   8040

HOLY TRINITY. EXTERIOR. Long Melford church is one of the most moving parish churches of England, large, proud, and noble – large certainly with its length inside nave and chancel of 153 ft, proud certainly with the many commemorative inscriptions which distinguish it from all others, and noble also without question with the aristocratic proportions of the exterior of its nave and aisles. The characteristic feature is the two tall transomed three-light windows for each bay, repeated by the tall transomed clerestory windows. So many thin, wiry perpendiculars are rare even in the Perpendicular style. Once this has been said, attention must however be drawn to the many curious impurities which detract from the pleasure one experiences in approaching along the relatively narrow passage from the S. The E chapel of the S aisle (and it is the same on the N side) has different window tracery and a different rhythm, two wider and between them one narrow window above the priest's doorway. Moreover, the projecting chancel has no clerestory and instead an exceedingly tall window to the s (and N), and as this has a two-centred arch, but all the clerestory windows have four-centred ones, the unity is disturbed here. Then there is the strange Lady Chapel – a long, low attachment with three parallel pitched roofs, that make no sense with the very flat pitches of the church roofs and cut painfully into the E window. *Bodley*, who in 1898–1903 replaced the C18 brick tower by one designed by himself, knew more about purity than the builders of the late C15. This tower suits the position and proportions of the nave and aisles better than the late C15 E parts.

The dates of Long Melford can be defined more precisely than that. The church which existed was rebuilt between *c.* 1460 and *c.* 1495. Of the former church no more survives than the C14 piers of the five W bays of the arcade. They have four major and four minor shafts and unmistakable moulded capitals. Externally nothing is older than *c.* 1460. The progress of the building can be followed by the detailed inscriptions. These inscriptions record the names of many who gave money to these buildings, and it is illuminating to see how such a major building enterprise was jointly conducted by the rich men of the prosperous little town, clothiers presumably all of them. The inscriptions run as follows: clerestory N side:

> Pray for ye sowlis of Roberd Spar'we and Marion his wife, and for Thom' Cowper, and Ma'el his wif, of quos goodis Mastr Gilis Dent, John Clopton, Jon Smyth, and Roger Smyth, Wyth ye help of ye weel disposyd me' of this (Town) dede these se'on archis new repare anno domini milesimo cccc (81).

There was in addition an inscription on the same side which was damaged in the fall of the tower and ran as follows:

> Pray for ye sowl of Mastr Giles Dent, late parson of Melford, of whose goodis, John Clopton, Maist; Robt' Coteler and Thomas Elys dede ys arch make and glase, and ye ruf over ye Porch anno domini 14 (81).

Inside, on the N arcade, there was also an inscription, now gone, recording the fact that John Clopton built the first four piers from the E. Outside, on the S clerestory, it says

> Pray for the sowles of Rogere Moryell, Margarete and Kateryn his wyffis, of whose goodis the seyd Kateryn, John Clopton, Mastr Wyllem Qwaytis and John Smyth, ded these VI archis new repare; and ded make the tabill at the hye awtere, anno

domini millesimo quadringentesimo octogesio p'mo. Pray for
ye sowl of Thomas Couper ye wych ye II arche dede repare.
Pray for ye sowl of Law. Martin and Marion hys wif.

Over the N porch the inscription is

Pray for ye sowlis of William Clopton, Margy and Margy his
wifis, and for ye sowle of Alice Clopton and for John Clopto',
and for alle thoo sowlis' yt ye seyd John is bo'nde to prey for.

On the lower windows on the s side from E to W

Pray for ye sowl of Rog: Moriell of whos goods yis arch was
made. Pray for ye sowle of John Keche, and for his Fad' and
Mod' of whose goodis yis arche was made. – Pray for ye sowle
of Thom's Elys and Jone his wife, and for ye good sped of
Jone Elys maks h' of. – Pray for ye sowl of John Pie and Aly his
wife, of whos good yis arch was made and yes twey wy'sdowy'
glasid. Pray for ye soulis of John Distr and Alis, and for ye
good sped of John Distr and X'pian maks h' of.

On the lower windows of the s chapel

Pray for ye soulis of Lawrens Martyn and Marion his wyffe,
Elysabeth Martyn a'd Jone, and for ye good estat of Richard
Martyn and Roger Martyn and ye wyvis and alle ye childri of
whose goodis . . . . made anno Dni millesimi
ccccLxxxIIII.

Finally, round the Lady Chapel

Pray for ye sowle of John Hyll, and for ye sowle of John Clopton Esqwyer, and pray for ye sowle of Rychard Loveday,
boteleyr wyth John Clopton, of whose godys this Chappell ys
imbaytylled by his excewtors. Pray for the soulis of William
Clopto', Esqwyer, Margery and Marg'y his wifis and for all
ther parentis and childri', and for ye sowle of Alice Clopton,
and for John Clopton and for all his childri' and for all ye
soulis that the said John is bonde to p'y for, which ded yis
Chapel new repare anno domo mcccclxxxxvi. Christ' sit
testis hec me no'exhibuisse ut merear laudes, sed ut spiritus
memoretur.

So this gives us 1481 for the clerestory, 1484 for the s chapel,
and 1496 for the Lady Chapel.

We can now turn to a more detailed description. The sides
have eighteen clerestory windows each, corresponding to
twelve lower windows. Flint, with, on the s side – which is of
course the show-front towards the green and the village – much
flushwork decoration. The decoration does not obtrude itself,
which is another proof of the nobility and purity of the designer.

The N side is simpler and has no flushwork. It has no porch
either. S porch, tall, of two bays, with two-light windows. On
the N side at the E end of the aisle a brick rood-stair turret. The
chancel projects one bay, and behind it lies a narrow vestry.
This ends in line with the E end of the Clopton Chantry on the
N side and a low second vestry on the S side. This looks like a
corridor to the Lady Chapel, which is quite an independently
designed, much lower building. It has throughout three-light
windows with depressed arches and no tracery at all. Flushwork
decoration here is less reticent. The E end is curious, because
the 'nave' seems to be represented not by one big E window, but
by two not at all distinguished from the others. There is an
internal reason for this, as we shall see.

INTERIOR. Nine-bay arcades and the chancel bay. The
earlier W bays have already been described. The others are
similar but slimmer and quite characteristically turned Perp.
The upper parts are Perp throughout. Roll mouldings to the
shafts which rise up to the roof principals. The wall below the
clerestory windows is panelled so as to seem a blank continuation of the windows. For the Clopton Chantry *see* below. The
Lady Chapel is internally very strange. It is as though the whole
was a shrine surrounded by a processional way. It seems externally a five-bay building with aisles. In fact it is a three-bay
sanctuary with, instead of aisles, an ambulatory on the W and
E sides as well. So the altar has a solid E wall behind, and the
first bay is separated from the second by a wall with a doorway
(with fleuron decoration) and two two-light windows. Big
frieze with shields in quatrefoils above this group. The
arcade of the 'nave' or shrine is low, but above it there are
blank panelling and niches with canopies. One must think of
all this in its original gay colouring to appreciate it fully.
Exquisite cambered roofs, especially that of the ambulatory,
where the beams rest on corbels with little figures. The
ambulatory character is expressed by the four corner bays
having beams set diagonally.

FURNISHINGS. FONT. Octagonal, Perp, simple, of Purbeck
marble, which is rare in Perp Suffolk. – REREDOS. 1879. –
PULPIT with figure carving of about the same time. – SEAT
(S chapel). Given in 1948. Spanish; from Granada Cathedral.
With the arms of the Reyes Católicos, i.e. of *c.* 1500. – SCULP-
TURE. Fine alabaster relief of the Adoration of the Magi, the
Virgin reclining on a couch. Probably late C14. – STAINED
GLASS. All late C15. A unique collection of kneeling donors in

the W windows of the N wall. In the E window St Andrew, Pietà, and St Edmund, with small kneeling donors at their feet, ₃₂ₐ two more saints with small kneeling donors, and two large kneeling donors. In the E window of the Clopton Chantry a small panel with Lily Crucifixus. Many bits in the N aisle tracery. The glass is probably Norwich-made. Later bits also in the N aisle. One S window signed by *Ward & Hughes*, 1885. – PLATE. Set 1775.

MONUMENTS. The capital monument is the CLOPTON ₁₆ᵦ CHANTRY. It is a whole room E of the N aisle E chapel, which was the Clopton Chapel. From there it is approached by a tiny vestibule or priest's room with a stone fan-vault so flat that it is almost a panelled ceiling. The room has a fireplace. The chantry has a seven-light E window and towards the chancel the monument to John Clopton † 1497. This is a plain sturdy tomb-chest of Purbeck marble with cusped quatrefoils containing shields. No effigy at all. Ogee arch open to the chancel. In the vault beneath this arch and above the tomb-chest paintings, especially a Christ carrying a staff with a cross. Also kneeling figures of John Clopton and his wife. To this arch correspond, as part of the same composition, the SEDILIA and PISCINA. Above this a frieze of shields all along the wall in foiled fields (cf. Lady Chapel), and then a frieze of niches with canopies. Flat ceiling, the cornice painted with a long poem by Lydgate, rope and foliage between the sheets of writing. In the Clopton Chapel proper, that is the N chancel chapel, a series of BRASSES: Lady with long hair, *c.* 1420, 18 in. figure. – Civilian, *c.* 1420, 19 in. – Lady with butterfly head-dress, *c.* 1480, 3 ft. – Another Lady with butterfly head-dress, same date, same size, probably Mrs Harleston, John Clopton's half-sister. – Francis Clopton † 1558, 3 ft. – In the same chapel MONUMENT to Sir William Clopton † 1446, father of John Clopton. Knight on a tomb-chest with quatrefoil decoration. Low arch, almost like a lintel; cresting. In the S chapel (or Martyn Chapel or Chapel of the Jesus Guild) two Martyn brasses of 1615 and 1624 (the Martyns owned Melford Place) and a simple Purbeck tomb-chest with three shields in lozenges. – Finally, in the chancel the grandest monument in the church, to Sir ₃₄ᵦ William Cordell † 1580 who built Melford Hall and was Speaker and Master of the Rolls. Alabaster. Recumbent effigy on a partly rolled-up mat. Front and back and to the l. and r. black columns carrying two coffered arches. Back wall with two figures in niches; walls also between the back and the columns to his head and feet. They are pierced by arches with two more figures. The four represent Prudence, Justice, Temperance, and Fortitude.

PERAMBULATION. Long Melford is long indeed. The whole of this perambulation is the length of the High Street and its continuations s and N. At the risk of irritating faithful users this conducted tour is not to start by the church, but at the far s end of the village. The advantage of this is that only thus can the climax of the church and the Hall be brought out fully. At the s end MELFORD PLACE, externally mostly C18, but comprising the CHAPEL OF ST JAMES with one blocked N window and the shape of the former E window, was destroyed by fire in 1967. The chapel however has been incorporated into the new house.* On the E side of Little St Mary's is CADGE'S HOUSE, basically C15 or earlier and with a carved crown-post in the roof. It is now three cottages, with a later front. Timbered carriage entrance at the s end. Above the centre part (offices of Cadge & Sons) is a room with WALL PAINTINGS, and ceiling beams carved in the same way as those in Melford Place chapel and in the Lady Chapel of the church. N along ST MARY'S, which is part of HALL STREET. In it THE ELMS, a handsome mid-Georgian brick house of four bays and two storeys with a fine doorway (broken pediment) and a Venetian window over. After that grass appears in the street l. and r. and also trees. They do not line the street but appear irregularly in patches. THE LIMES is a Tudor timber-framed house with a Georgian front. On the s side is a complete Queen Anne porch with a head carved under a scalloped canopy. On the w side the UNITED REFORMED CHURCH, c. 1724, red brick with arched doorway and windows and a hipped roof. Its churchyard has one of the welcome undulating or crinkle-crankle walls. Also on the w side THE OLD HOUSE, timber-framed and picturesque (with a horse-chestnut tree in front). Opposite a Late Georgian five-bay house of grey brick. Doorway with Tuscan columns. The house N of the Old House is of the same type and has a doorway with Greek Doric columns. Then on the E side a nice group of timber-framed houses and after that on the w side HANWELL HOUSE, mid-Georgian, red brick, three bays, two storeys and with four Venetian windows. Then nothing noteworthy until the first minor climax comes with the (much restored) timber-framed BULL

* Information from Mr Thomas Howlett, who also kindly provided the notes on Cadge's House and The Limes.

INN on the E side; with BROOKE HOUSE, timber-framed, with brick-nogging, two symmetrical gables, and a gabled porch dated 1610, on the W side; with the bridge and the picturesque MILL HOUSE; and so to the point where the Green starts.

MELFORD GREEN is unforgettable. It is large, forms an elongated triangle, and rises gently to the N. Near its foot, more or less opposite Mill House, is the SCHOOL, built in 1860, a bad moment for an appreciation of the qualities of Melford, one would think. As it is, the architect, *A. H. Parker*, has succeeded in adding to the attractions of the Green. The building is informal, low, and, with its capped little turret, picturesque. The Green itself starts with a group of immense elm trees, giving an unexpected scale to the magnificent buildings along two of its sides and perhaps, one is tempted to think, re-stating the superiority of nature over man. The magnificent buildings are Melford Hall with its turrets, its octagonal summer house, and its gatehouse on the r., and the (alas, over-restored) Hospital and, of course, the church at its upper end. The houses on the l. are modest and unobtrusive; and in a visually quite arbitrary position in the Green stands the brick CONDUIT, square with truncated gables, no doubt once carrying finials like the summer house (*see* below). Of the houses on the l. only one needs special mention: FALKLAND HOUSE with three octagonal star-topped chimneys and an C18 doorway. A little higher up, WESTGATE STREET branches off, and here stands, fortunately out of sight of the centre of the Green so far described, a terrace of early C19 houses, sixteen windows wide, of grey brick, and completely urban. They might stand in any street of Cambridge, for example. Near the Scutcher's Arms in Westgate Street another 'crinkle-crankle' wall.

Finally the TRINITY HOSPITAL, built in 1573 by Sir William Cordell, but much re-done in 1847. It was founded for twelve men and two servants, and is surprisingly big for that number. Red brick, seven bays wide, the first and last projecting as gabled wings. The centre is embattled and has a cupola. Windows of three lights below, two lights above, and with arched lights. A courtyard at the back towards the church and churchyard. For as one approaches the Hospital, the church becomes visible up a not too wide passage on its l. It appears amazingly erect and aristocratic with its cool grey stone and its long slim windows after the robust, sturdy red brick of the Hospital and Melford Hall.

MELFORD HALL. A large and impressive brick mansion, built
at the very beginning of Queen Elizabeth's reign or even a few
years earlier, a time when not much was built, at least in comparison with the vast activity of the later Elizabethan decades.
Before the Dissolution the house belonged to the abbots of
Bury St Edmunds. It was bought after 1545 by Sir William
Cordell, lawyer, and in turn Solicitor-General, Speaker of the
House of Commons, and Master of the Rolls. He is known to
have lived at Melford Hall in 1554. On the bases of the fire-dogs
in the hall the date 1559. The house goes round three sides of a
courtyard, and with its porch and projecting wings faces the
garden.* The back is turned towards the Green. The garden
side is of two storeys, simple with mullioned and transomed
windows. It has as its main accents the porch and four turrets.
The porch has superimposed fluted Doric and Ionic pilasters
and a semicircular shell-top. The entrance arch is round, not
depressed or four-centred, and the upper window has a pediment – both notably pure motifs for use c. 1550–5. The turrets
are placed against the inner sides of the projecting wings, near
their ends but not at their ends. They have ogee tops.‡ Four
more such turrets are placed along the back of the house, and
they also are unexpectedly placed. Two of them front a narrow
centre, which, as it is in line with the porch on the other side,
may represent the gatehouse of the abbots' house. The other
two are in line with the inner sides of the wings if one imagines
them continued to the back of the house. They seem to call for
turrets at the outer corners as well, but there are none there.
Also, to complicate the rhythm yet further, these back ends of
the wings are three-storeyed (and seem to have been so from
the beginning) and the gatehouse is three-storeyed too. Finally
the original building receded between the gatehouse and the
back ends of the wings, but the recession was filled in in 1813.
The majority of the windows on this side as well as the others
were sashed in Georgian times.

Little of Elizabethan work survives inside. The most interesting survival is the Long Gallery on the second floor, alas
deprived of all its fittings. The Hall has a big stone fireplace of
c. 1730, with a heavy overmantel and two Tuscan columns to

* A plan by John Thorpe at the Soane Museum (pp. 249–50) shows the
courtyard closed on the fourth side.
‡ Between them, at the height of the parapet, a record of 1619 proves the
existence of a wooden bridge across the courtyard from which to watch hunting, etc. It may have been a temporary structure.

divide it from the Staircase. This is a grand composition of 1813, ascending with wide steps between solid walls in one straight line with an intermediate landing. On the upper floor it has a gallery l. and r. with slender unfluted Ionic columns carrying a noble coffered segmental tunnel-vault. Another notable room of 1813 is the Library, with apsed ends, the r. apse being behind fragmentary screen walls projecting from l. and r. because this apse fills the area of the former gatehouse. In the Drawing Room a glorious Rococo fireplace. Other C18 decoration was destroyed by a fire during the Second World War (Adam Salon, ceiling of the Cordell Room). During the restoration after that fire a new Staircase was built in the N wing, with graceful C18 parts brought, it is said, from a Cambridge college. Three balusters to the step, two twisted and one fluted. Carved tread-ends.

The GATEWAY from the Green has two polygonal turrets decorated with shell-lunettes like the one over the porch. The lodges are Victorian. Near the gateway stands a SUMMER HOUSE, octagonal, with eight straight gables and simple stumpy pinnacles. Outer staircase from the back to the porch, which has short fluted columns. The windows are sashed.

KENTWELL HALL. Kentwell Hall is out of the village, Melford Hall belongs to it. Kentwell Hall lies N of the church and is approached by an avenue of lime-trees, planted in 1678, and nearly a mile long. The house is mentioned as new in a will of 1563. It is of red brick and consists of a centre and two far-projecting wings. These have a turret each at the inner corners of their fronts. The centre has a buttressed porch in the middle and two large symmetrical bay windows with three transoms. There are also normal symmetrical bay windows in the sides and the fronts of the wings. The interior is not in its original state. There was a fire about 1822, and after that *Hopper* remodelled it. Due to him are the rather heavy-handed decorations of the Hall, which lies behind and to the r. of the porch, and the Dining Room, which has the corresponding tall l. bay window. In the Hall a big stone fireplace of c. 1730, in the Dining Room an even bigger restrainedly Gothic fireplace, completely, i.e. with its high overmantel, done in slate, a surprising and in its sombre way successful effect. Fine open-well staircase of c. 1680 in the E wing with heavy turned balusters. A curiosity of the house is the two brass roundels with holes in the floors of the Hall and another room. They were for central heating and are dated 1827. Originally there was probably a fan rotating behind the brass surface.

Kentwell Hall still has its moat. To the SW of the house a DOVECOTE, said to be the largest in Suffolk. Brick, square, with pyramid roof. Windows in the upper storey.

TOWN DEVELOPMENT, Potkiln Road. 728 houses (of which 166 are Anglias – *see* Haverhill, p. 254), shops, maisonnettes, and six unit factories, by *Sir Hubert Bennett* and his staff of the G.L.C., completed in 1970.

ROMAN SETTLEMENT. Between Liston Lane and the railway finds were made in 1958. They comprised part of a tessellated pavement of white limestone and red tile enclosed in a border of bitumen, limestone, and a moulding of red brick, and also part of a wall, thus indicating a probable bath. Other fragmentary floors contained C1 A.D. Belgic as well as C2 A.D. pottery. There was also a ditch.

Burials and Romano-British occupation material found particularly along the main street include *terra sigillata* and coins of Vespasian (69–79) and Hadrian (117–38).

LOUDHAM HALL

1 m. SE of Wickham Market

3050

Red brick, of the mid C18. The S front is eleven bays wide. Projecting pedimented three-bay centre, then two-bay recessed parts, and then two-bay wings originally projecting by one bay. The centre is curious in so far as it has on the first floor four Ionic brick pilasters, but no Doric ones on the ground floor. There is here only a (later?) doorway with Ionic pilasters and a pediment. Fine entrance hall leading to a screen of two Corinthian columns between which the room forms a kind of alcove with apsed l. and r. ends. From here doors lead to a corridor which crosses the whole length of the house from E to W. The corridor is impressive on the first floor, where all the original panelling and doors remain. The first floor is reached by a very good staircase with three finely twisted balusters to each tread and carved tread-ends. On the ground floor in two rooms good fireplaces.

LOUND

5090

ST JOHN BAPTIST. Norman round tower. Nave and chancel their details all of the restoration. They were, it seems, Dec s porch with a little flushwork panelling. The interior of the

church is made festive by much recent furnishing, and sham-
Gothic pieces, richly gilded. In the SCREEN it is difficult to
recognize the original from the imitation. Original and C14 the
shafts and ogee arches with the pretty mouchette tracery,
imitation, and imitation not of the C14 but the early C16, the
rest. – ROOD and ORGAN CASE by *Comper*, 1914. – FONT.
Octagonal, Perp. Four lions against the stem, four lions and
four angels against the bowl. The angels hold shields, three of
them charged with the symbols of Trinity and Passion. – WALL
PAINTING. St Christopher, also C20, nicely done with refined
rusticity. – STAINED GLASS. Chancel N and S windows by
Holiday, 1893 and 1905.

WINDMILL. A tower-mill, converted into a house in 1962.

LOWE HILL HOUSE *see* STRATFORD ST MARY

LOWER STREET *see* STUTTON *and* UFFORD

LOWESTOFT   *5090*

ST MARGARET. The church, large and quite conscious of being
the parish church of a prosperous town, yet lies a good ½ m.
away from its medieval confines. It is 184 ft long and was
mostly built at the end of the C15. It has a W tower of *c.* 1300
crowned by a recessed spire which brings its height up to over
120 ft. The battlements are flushwork-panelled, and there is
much use of flushwork all over the walls of the church. The
buttresses are panelled, and the base has a chequerboard
panelling of flint and stone. The walls end in low parapets
without battlements or any decoration. At the E end is a tall,
wide, five-light window, very lovely in design by the alteration
in the heights of the transoms and the tracery patterns. The
chancel N and S windows are of three lights and also transomed.
Seven-bay aisles with three-light windows and four lights at
the E and W ends. The N side is a little less ornate. The buttresses
for instance have only panelling in oblongs, not in blank
arches, and there is no N porch. The S porch is large and two-
storeyed. The front is again panelled with flushwork arcading.
Tall entrance, hood-mould on seated lions, decorated with
fleurons. Spandrels with angels holding shields with the
emblems of the Trinity and the Passion. One niche above the
entrance. A tierceron rib-vault inside with bosses. The interior
runs for its seven bays without any structural division between
nave and chancel. Finely moulded piers basically of lozenge
shape, finely moulded arches. Shafts to the roof. The roof was

restored and redecorated by *Bodley* in 1899. It is of low pitch and has short hammerbeams carrying castellated tie-beams. Under the chancel is a crypt, probably of the C14. It is of two bays from W to E, of three from N to S, and has two short octagonal piers carrying heavy single-chamfered ribs and arches. – FONT. Octagonal, Perp, on three steps of which two are decorated with quatrefoil friezes. Stem and bowl are decorated with standing figures, almost entirely hacked off. The niches in which they stand have fleurons up the jambs and round the arches. – LECTERN. (Dated 1504. LG) Of brass, with an eagle to support the back. According to Oman from the same workshop as the lecterns of Holy Trinity Coventry, Newcastle Cathedral, St Gregory Norwich, Oxburgh Norfolk, Southwell Minster, Oundle Northants, St Michael Southampton, the cathedral of Urbino, Wolborough Devon, etc. – BANNER STAFF LOCKER. Just N of the tower arch. The door is a copy of that at Barnby. – STAINED GLASS. In the chancel SE window very rustic parts of the former E window by the local painter *Robert Allen*; 1819. Allen had been employed by the Lowestoft china factory which had started in 1756 and closed down in 1803. The present E window is by *Heaton, Butler & Bayne*, 1891. – BRASSSES (S aisle). Two skeletons in shrouds, *c.* 1500 (27 in. long); Civilian, *c.* 1540 (16 in. long).

ST PETER, St Peter's Street. 1833 by *John Brown* of Norwich. Yellow brick, in the local style, without W tower. A chancel was added by *E. P. Warren* in 1903. It is of red brick and picturesquely varied. Inside it has a wooden tunnel-vault. The church is now closed (1974) and is likely to be demolished.*

ST PETER, Kirkley. 1875–87. Large, in the traditional Suffolk style. – Iron SCREEN 1896. – REREDOS. Triptych by *Anning Bell* and *Dacres Adam*. Carved, painted, 'very arty crafty'.‡ – STAINED GLASS. E window by *Kempe*. – PLATE. Cup 1567.

OUR LADY STAR OF THE SEA (R.C.), Gordon Road. 1900–2 by *G. & R. P. Baines* and *F. W. Richards* (GR). Red brick, big, with a tall and broad W tower and an apse. In the style of 1300. Polished red granite piers inside.

There are a number of Nonconformist chapels of yellow brick in the Italianate style, notably the LONDON ROAD CONGREGATIONAL CHURCH of 1858 and the METHODIST CHURCH

* Information from Mr W. James, who also gave other invaluable help on Lowestoft.

‡ P. F. Anson, *Fashions in Church Furnishing*, 1960.

in the High Street of 1862, which is more 'High Victorian' in that it has thicker decoration on capitals, etc. This is by *J. L. Clemence*. It is now closed (1974). The London Road BAP-TIST CHURCH, demolished in 1974, was depressingly unre-deemed for its late date: 1899. It was still run-of-the-mill Victorian Gothic. Only one year later the CONGREGATIONAL CHURCH, Pakefield Road, Kirkley, 1900–3 by *G. Baines*, showed the much gayer and livelier, and in point of fact remarkably up-to-date, style which characterizes chapels about 1900 and is almost absent from churches. Red brick with many pretty asymmetrically managed motifs or effects derived from Baillie Scott and Stokes. The basic style is Gothic, but treated very freely. On the r. of the façade strongly tapering tower with diagonal buttresses with typically wide top projections like lids (a Voysey motif) and a needle spike. On the l. a small turret with a flat ogee cap. In addi-tion a flèche.

PUBLIC BUILDINGS. *See* Perambulation.

PERAMBULATION. Lowestoft was a fishing town in the Middle Ages; it is a fishing town and a seaside resort now. To get a feel (and a smell) of the fishing town one must climb down one of the SCORES from the High Street and explore the cottages of cobble with brick trim and the curing places below. The best preserved old one, as the DOE has shown, is just behind LANCASTER PLACE, off WHAPLOAD ROAD, with a date-stone 1676; it was badly damaged in the war. Of three storeys, the ground floor with unglazed windows with diagonally placed square mullions. N of these curing places the Gas Works and then the DENES, i.e. turf and a N esplanade built *c*. 1900 etc. to compete with the chief sea front to the S. The Scores run down from the main street of Old Lowestoft, the HIGH STREET, and here a few houses ought to be noted, starting with No. 80 on the E side. This has a date 1586, but is in its façade clearly later. Knapped flint with stone quoins and window surrounds. Then No. 55, the finest house in Lowestoft, mid-Georgian, of red brick, two storeys high with a cornice and a half-storey above the cornice. Doorway with charmingly decorated jambs and frieze, Roman Doric columns, an en-riched metope frieze, and a straight hood. The doorway has a segmental arch, carved spandrels, and a carved head at its apex. Opposite is the CROWN HOTEL, Georgian, it seems, but altered in the Early Victorian years. (Across Compass Street is the Italianate TOWN HALL by *J. L. Clemence*, opened in

1860. In the Council Chamber is some fine Victorian STAINED
GLASS, designed by *John Thomas* and executed by *James
Ballantine* of Edinburgh. It commemorates, presumably
the Treaty of Alliance between England and France of 185
(and was shown at the Paris Exhibition of that year), with
portraits of Victoria and Albert and Napoleon III and
Eugénie. It was presented to Lowestoft by Sir Samuel
Morton Peto.) Then again on the E side No. 49, Late Geor
gian with a pedimented doorcase flanked by Ionic columns
and further N No. 27 of the same type as No. 80. Off to the v
in Melbourne Road the PRINCE ALBERT, by *Tayler & Green*
an uncommonly excellent pub, restrained externally and very
good at catching the atmosphere inside. At the N end of the
High Street stands the HIGH LIGHTHOUSE, completed, i
seems, in 1854. White, of course, and with, behind it and by
its side, the keeper's house, with chalet gables. In a stree
called THE MARINA, to the E, a nightmarish High Victorian
house ought to be sampled, the TOWER HOUSE, dated 1865
yellow brick with an asymmetrically placed tower all canted i
unexpected places. To the W of the High Street also ol
streets with cottages. (At the W end of St Margaret's Road
on CHURCH GREEN opposite the church, OLD PEOPLE'
HOUSING, thirty-six dwellings and a warden's house, b
Tayler & Green, 1965.)

In 1814 *William Cubitt* made a survey for a proposed harbour
of the old town at the mouth of the Waveney. Work was begu
in 1827 and completed in 1831. The CUSTOMS HOUSE i
there, humble, of yellow brick and without adornment, and
of the harbour the HARBOUR HOTEL, white and black, with
two canted bay windows and probably of *c.* 1835. The tw
PIERS were begun in 1846. The railway reached Lowestoft i
1847, and the STATION was built close to the harbour. It i
Italianate, of yellow brick, asymmetrical and 'picturesque'
The conversion of Lowestoft into a seaside resort was due t
Sir Morton Peto (*see* Somerleyton Hall), and the area S of th
harbour ought to be remembered as Peto-Town. Activity
started in 1847. The architect was *John Thomas* (*see* Somerley
ton Hall), or, at least, he is known to have been the architect o
the first show-piece, the ROYAL HOTEL, now demolished
This was opened in 1849. It was four-storeyed and classica
but had Italianate gables and roof. S of it pairs of three
storeyed houses of the same date, with the same gables, bu
much decimated in the Second World War, so that the

meaner houses behind them now face the sea. They are two-and-a-half-storeyed and have no architectural pretensions. Then follows an extensive terrace of yellow and red brick, Italianate, of forty-eight bays with a twelve-bay centre. Then the cliff rises, and the style changes to that of Norman Shaw and Sir Ernest George: typical is the VICTORIA HOTEL, 1897 by *F. W. Skipper.*

MAIDSCROSS HILL *see* LAKENHEATH

MANCROFT TOWERS *see* OULTON

MANSTON HALL *see* WHEPSTEAD

MARKET WESTON

9070

ST MARY. Restored in 1844 by *Cottingham,* who also rebuilt the chancel. The building was Dec, except for the good Perp s porch. Tall two-light windows with panel tracery. Front and battlements with flushwork decoration. The entrance has fleuron decoration, and there are three niches, to the l., to the r., and above the entrance. – PLATE. Elizabethan Cup; Paten 1661; Flagon 1699.

A ROMANO–BRITISH KILN, $2\frac{1}{2}$ ft in diameter, with a circular pedestal, was excavated in 1965 at HILLSIDE FARM, $\frac{1}{2}$ m. SE.

MARLESFORD

3050

ST ANDREW. The s arcade is earlier than the rest of the church. It has a sturdy circular pier of *c.* 1200, even if the capitals are interfered with and the arches are Perp. Perp w tower with flushwork decoration in lozenges on the battlements. s aisle and attached s porch Perp. The porch has a front with flushwork decoration and a stone parapet with wavy tracery. The chancel tracery seems of the transition between Dec and Perp. Good nave and s aisle roofs, the former with arched braces meeting at the collar-beams. – FONT. Octagonal, Perp, with simply arched and cusped panels, almost a latter-day stone version of the C13 Purbeck fonts. – PULPIT. Jacobean, with much arabesque work. – STAINED GLASS. In two N windows by *Ward & Hughes;* bad. – PLATE. Elizabethan Cup and Cover; Paten 1728. – MONUMENT. William Alston † 1641. With two frontal busts in upright oval medallions or wreaths.

MARLESFORD HALL. C18. Of seven bays and two storeys with a big hipped roof, a three-bay pediment, and a small semicircular porch on attenuated columns. NMR)

2040
MARTLESHAM

ST MARY. W tower of knapped flint with sacred initials in flush work at the base and arched flushwork panelling on the battle ments. The nave seems Dec, the chancel was rebuilt in 183 and remodelled in 1905. However, its simple hammerbeam roof is original. – FONT. Octagonal, with two lions and two dogs against the stem, and shields, quatrefoils, etc., against the bowl. – SCREEN. Six divisions of the dado now in the chancel on the s side. – BENCHES. Some with traceried ends, poppy-heads and animals on the arms. – PULPIT. Dated 1614. With plain short blank arches and fluted panels above them. – STAINED GLASS. In the nave a set in the Arts and Crafts style, dated 1903. They are by *Walter J. Pearce*. – WALL PAINTING. S Christopher (N wall). – PLATE. Elizabethan (?) Cup.

RED LION INN. Timber-framed. Below the oversailing gable an oriel window of the type of Sparrowe's House Ipswich, and below that a canted bay window. To the r., startlingly, a Red Lion, which is the figurehead of a Dutch boat captured at the battle of Sole Bay in 1672.

BEACON HILL HOUSE. Early C19. Grey brick of three bays with portico of two pairs of Greek Doric columns.

BARROWS. Two groups on the N edge of the heath, in various states of preservation. Eight lie at the E end of Kesgrave village another three 1 m. E. (*See* also Brightwell, Foxhall, and Waldringfield.)

1070
MELLIS

ST MARY. The tower collapsed in 1730. Dec s porch of two storeys, see the tracery of the side windows. The E end, includ ing the NE vestry, has a flushwork-panelled base, but above all is later repair and restoration. Wide nave with big Perp three-light windows. – FONT. Perp, with four lions against the stem and against the bowl the Signs of the Evangelists and four Tudor roses. – SCREEN. With one-light divisions, ogee arches and some tracery over. Original coving, ribbed in a pretty pattern. – COMMUNION RAIL. C17, re-used as stall fronts. – STAINED GLASS. In a s window. In the tracery heads complete C15 figures. – PLATE. Cup 1682; Paten 1734; Almsdish 1775. – MONUMENT. Richard Yaxley, 1570. Tomb-chest with three lozenges with shields. The brasses on the top are lost. No indication of the Renaissance.

ELM TREE FARM, the first farm NE of the Station. Above the doorway the sill of a former oriel window, early C16. Carved

with an angel holding a shield (cf. Guildhall, Eye). On the
shield the de la Pole arms.

MELLS *see* HOLTON

MELTON   *2050*

ST ANDREW. 1868 by *F. Barnes* (GR). In the Geometrical style,
with a S tower with broach spire. Not at all local. – FONT. On
two steps, the second with tracery. Stem tall, with the Signs of
the four Evangelists and four small figures. Bowl with the
Seven Sacraments and the Martyrdom of St Andrew. –
STAINED GLASS. A S window by *Kempe, c.* 1903.

OLD ST ANDREW. Dec W tower with flushwork decoration on
base, buttresses, and battlements. The W window has reticulated tracery. Nave only, with a small C19 apse. – BRASSES.
Ecclesiastic, Civilian, and Lady, all of *c.* 1430, all *c.* 2 ft 6 in.
figures (NW corner).

FRIARS DENE. A fancy name for the former GAOL. On the main
road S of the Post Office. Plain colour-washed brick, two windows wide. Of interest only historically (e.g. Francis Noone, of
Martlesham Hall, was confined to Melton Gaol in 1558 before
being burnt).

ST AUDRY'S HOSPITAL. Among the buildings is the former
HOUSE OF INDUSTRY, that is, one of the Suffolk workhouses
of the later C18; cf. Introduction, pp. 55–6. Red brick, on an E
plan. DOE)

FOXBORO HALL, ¾ m. NW. Early C19, grey brick with a semicircular portico of giant Ionic columns. The façade rises by a
half storey behind it and ends in a pediment.

MENDHAM   *2080*

ALL SAINTS. Partly Dec, partly Perp. To the earlier style belong
the W tower, the chancel (E window with reticulated tracery, S
doorway), both aisles structurally (the Dec windows are
renewed), and the S arcade inside. Four bays, octagonal piers
with boldly moulded capitals, double-chamfered arches. The
N arcade seems C15. Perp also some aisle windows, the clerestory, and the S porch. This is of squared knapped flint, the
front parapet with flushwork panelling. Three niches round
the entrance. Inside the most unusual feature is the wooden
chancel arch, really a pair of arched braces (cf. Ilketshall St
John). – COMMUNION RAIL. With thin twisted balusters;
late C17. – PAINTING. Presentation in the Temple; probably

Venetian of *c.* 1600. – PLATE. Elizabethan Cup; Paten in
scribed 1666; two Flagons 1710. – MONUMENTS. Members o
the Freston family; after 1692. With pilasters and an odd
sagging inscription tablet. – William Rant † 1754. By *Thoma
Rawlins* of Norwich. – Identical monument to James Ran
† 1743.

(WESTON HOUSE, 1¼ m. E. Dated 1698. With a shaped gable-en
DOE)

MIDDLETON HALL, 1¼ m. NE. Late C17 front of five wide bay
and two storeys. Red brick in English bond. Wooden cross
windows. At the back timber-framed with brick-nogging. I
one room (Dairy) the remains of a fine Jacobean plaster ceilin
with thin ribs forming interlocked quatrefoils and stars. Als
the Gresham coat of arms, the grasshopper; for Cecily Greshar
married into the Hall in 1594. In another room, not *in situ*, tw
oblong plaster panels painted with busts of Roman Emperor
in profile.

MENDLESHAM

ST MARY. An ambitious church at the end of a village street
even with some urban ambitions, as medieval country-tow
scale goes. Much of the C13, but the dominant impressio
Perp. C13 arcade of six bays, the sixth separated from the other
by a little wall and perhaps representing former transepts
Circular piers, circular abaci, double-chamfered arches. Th
E responds of the fifth bay are a fluted corbel on the N side, a
oblong one with dog-tooth on the S side. The sixth-bay arc
stands on short vertical pieces. The same is true of the chance
arch. C13 also the S doorway with three orders of colonnette
and several rolls and hollows in the arch, and the simpler
doorway. Dec S aisle windows. Most of the other window
have two ogee-headed lights under a segmental arch, probabl
also a C14 form. It applies to the clerestory too. Handsom
Perp E window in the N aisle.* The middle light is in its lowe
part blank and contains to the inside a niche. The window
shafted internally. But the showpieces of the church are the
tower (which cuts with its E buttresses into the arcade) and th
porches. The tower has a frieze of flushwork circles etc. at th
base, buttresses flush-decorated in their lower parts, and
parapet with flushwork quatrefoils crowned by battlement
with flushwork arcading. Doorway with shields in the spandrel

* A will of 1463 gives 20*s.* to the 'north syde ledyng'. Could this imply tha
the N aisle was just built ? (ARA)

Two two-light bell-openings on each side. The s porch has a flushwork-panelled front, above the entrance a frieze of quatrefoils in flushwork, and above that sacred initials. Flush-arcaded battlements. The N porch is two-storeyed. It also has a flushwork front. Three niches l., r., and above the entrance. Two two-light upper windows. Flushwork battlements. Big lions and Wild Men serve as pinnacles. – FONT COVER. A beautiful Jacobean piece with a lower tier open between four 25b elongated Tuscan columns and upper tiers with pediments and spiky obelisks. The cover was made in 1630 by *John Turner*, who in the same year made the PULPIT. This is of the familiar type, with the chief panels treated as short sturdy blank arches; below these geometrical panels with a central knob, and above small oblong panels with leaf scrolls and grotesques. – BENCHES. With traceried ends, carved backs, and poppy-heads. The figures on the arms are mostly hacked off. – PLATE. Cup 1588; two Flagons 1664; Paten 1736. – ARMOURY. On the upper floor of the N porch is the most complete armoury of any English parish church. The armour ranges from *c.* 1470 to *c.* 1610. – BRASS. John Knyvet † 1417, in armour, his head on a helmet. The figure is 4 ft 8 in. long (nave floor).

TELEVISION MAST. Built by the Independent Television Authority in 1959. 1,000 ft high.

METFIELD   *2080*

ST JOHN BAPTIST. Money was left in 1385 for the tower. It is tall, with flushwork-panelled battlements. Stone figures instead of pinnacles. Perp windows throughout. Perp s porch, two-storeyed, with a front all panelled in flushwork. Entrance arch decorated with a bishop's head, crowns, and fleurons. Inside the porch a wooden lierne-vault with figured bosses. Nave roof with arched braces meeting at the ridge. The last bay is boarded and has all its original painting, with the initials for Jesus and crowned Ms and pretty ornament around. The chancel roof is also boarded and has carved brackets. – FONT. Against the stem four lions; against the bowl also four lions and four demi-figures of angels. On the shield held by one of them the arms of Sir John Jermy † 1504. – SCREEN. Only the dado remains. – PLATE. Cup 1566; Paten inscribed 1593.

E of the church a pretty, completely urban Regency SHOP. Two windows with the original close glazing bars. Above the central doorway just the name SQUIRE in nice lettering. A tall ash-tree in front of the shop.

3090

METTINGHAM

ALL SAINTS. Round tower. Norman N doorway with one order of colonnettes with scalloped capitals. Two orders of zigzag in the arch. Dec nave and S aisle with an arcade with sturdy octagonal piers and triple-chamfered arches. In the S wall an ogee-arched recess. – FONT. Octagonal, Perp. Against the stem four lions, against the bowl, which is carried by eight heads, four lions and four angels. – BENCH ENDS with poppy-heads. – PLATE. Cup 1568 (made at Norwich); Paten inscribed 1570.

METTINGHAM CASTLE, I m. S. Licence to crenellate was given in 1342. A college was founded at the same time at Raveningham in Norfolk and moved to Mettingham c. 1390. The college took over the castle premises. The chief relic of the castle is the tall GATEHOUSE, with two towers, square to the front but canted towards the adjoining walls. Four-centred archway with two sunk-quadrant mouldings dying into the imposts. The archway was vaulted. Remains of the barbican can still be seen. Of the other buildings only odd fragments of walls survive. The house was built in 1880.

METTINGHAM HALL, ¼ m. SE. Brick, and probably of c. 1700. Five bays with three-bay recessed centre. The wings carry shaped gables. All windows have segmental hood-moulds on dentils. All along the ground floor a frieze of such dentils rising segmentally round the windows. Georgian doorway. Big chimneystack with star-topped chimneys. The cottage next to the hall has the same arch-motif.

METTINGHAM HOUSE, N of the Hall. Red brick, five bays, two and a half storeys, Georgian. The half storey has only three windows (cf. St Mary's School, Earsham Street, Bungay).

1060

MICKFIELD

ST ANDREW. Rather grim from the N. Nave and chancel, the nave roof invisible, no pitch, no battlements, no parapet. Only one chancel and one nave window. S tower with brick parapet. The tower is of the early C14 (entrance with triple-chamfered continuous moulding). So are the nave N and the chancel S doorway. – FONT. Massive, moulded, hard to date. – BENCHES. Five; with traceried ends and poppy-heads. A few mutilated animals. – PLATE. Cup and Cover Paten 1599.

4060

MIDDLETON

HOLY TRINITY. W tower with tall flushwork-panelled battle-

ments. Recessed lead needle-spire. Nave and chancel under one
roof. Norman nook-shaft in the s w corner of the nave. Norman
s doorway with two orders of colonnettes carrying scalloped
capitals and a roll and a zigzag moulding in the arch. The E
window of *c.* 1300, an interesting design of four lights, consisting of two-light parts with Y-tracery. The result is four-light
intersection with two of the top bars left out, a typical idea of
c. 1300. Round the window the voussoirs of a re-used Norman
billet frieze. Similarly some Norman zigzag moulding by a
chancel N window and a Norman voussoir by a chancel s
window. (PISCINA perhaps made up of Norman bits. LG) A
good Perp window in the nave on the N side. – FONT. Octagonal, Perp, with four lions and four Wild Men against the stem
and four angels and the Signs of the four Evangelists against
the bowl. Against the base the inscription: Christ Mote Us
Spede & Helpe Alle at Nede. – BENCHES. Two ends with
poppy-heads made into a lectern. – (ROYAL ARMS. Of George
III. Cast iron. LG) – WALL PAINTING. St Christopher; on
the N wall. – STAINED GLASS. Chancel s w by *Lavers, Barraud
& Westlake, c.* 1877. – PLATE. Cup and Paten 1808. – BRASS.
Civilian and wife, *c.* 1500 (small, nave floor).

MOOR FARMHOUSE, Middleton Moor. C16, with a stepped
brick gable and blocked brick windows. They have architraves
on dentils, and above them is a curious raised brick ornament:
an upright oblong with small circles above and below. This
repeats three times above each window. Fine plaster overmantel
inside, of *c.* 1600. The motifs are those used in contemporary
ceilings and pargetting.

MIDDLETON HALL *see* MENDHAM

MILDEN

9040

St PETER. Nave and chancel. The w tower was demolished as
unsafe in 1827. Norman nave; see one s window and the s
doorway with zigzag arch on plain imposts. The rest has lancet
windows, much renewed and perhaps not reliable. (Good kingpost roof. LG) – PULPIT. Jacobean. – (BENCHES. Dated 1685.
LG) – PLATE. Cup *c.* 1600; Paten 1696; Paten 1783. – MONU-
MENT. James Allington † 1626. Excellent recumbent alabaster
effigy. Handsome frames of the two inscription tablets. The
surround is not in its original state.

MILDEN HALL. Big C18 house with a five-bay centre and one-
bay wings. In their front and the centre of the house Venetian
windows.

MOTTE. Near Milden Hall a motte with what may be the remains
of its bailey. It was the site of a castle in the mid C12.

7070

MILDENHALL

ST MARY AND ST ANDREW. The most ambitious church in this
NW corner of Suffolk, 168 ft long with a tower 120 ft high. The
church stands in the middle of the town, though isolated by its
oblong churchyard. Its E end overlooks the High Street. It is
in this E end that the earliest architecture is to be found: the
chancel and the N chapel, dating back to c. 1240–1300. The N
chapel comes first, work perhaps of an Ely mason. It is of limestone, not of flint, two bays long with an elegant rib-vault inside
in which the transverse arches and the ribs have the same
dimensions and profile. At the E end are three stepped lancets,
and they are shafted inside with detached Purbeck shafts
carrying stiff-leaf capitals. The chancel arch is of the same
date, a beautiful piece, nicely shafted, with keeling to the shafts
and excellent stiff-leaf and crocket capitals. Also small heads.
But the chancel was built slowly. The PISCINA still belongs to
the previous jobs. It has Purbeck shafts and stiff-leaf capitals.
The top of the piscina is not genuine. The SEDILIA are no
more than three stepped window seats, separated by simple
stone arms. But the windows are definitely of c. 1300. The N
and S windows alternate enterprisingly between uncusped
intersected tracery and three stepped lancet lights under one
arch, but with the lower lights connected with the taller middle
one by little token flying buttresses. The E window is a glorious
and quite original design, heralding the later one of Prior
Crauden's Chapel at Ely. Seven lights, the first and last
continued up and around the arch (as in that chapel) by a
border of quatrefoils. The next two on each side are taken together as one and have in the spandrel an irregular cusped
triangle. Over the middle stands a big pointed oval along the
border of which run little quatrefoils again. The centre is an
octofoiled figure.

There is no Dec style at Mildenhall. Perp the W tower first of
all.* Angle buttresses with attached shafts carrying little pinnacles (a Somerset motif). Big renewed doorway, big renewed
six-light W window with a tier of shields at its foot. Inside on the
ground floor the tower has a tunnel-like fan-vault. Above this
the unusual motif of a choir gallery open to the nave, with a
stone balustrade. Perp also are the arcades between nave and

* A will of 1460 leaves money to the repair of the tower.

aisles. They have very thin piers with finely moulded shafts and capitals only towards the arch openings. Shafts rise from these right up to the roof. Perp moreover the renewed clerestory windows and the big aisle windows. The N side is richer than the S. There is a little flushwork decoration here and there on battlements with panel decoration in two tiers and with pinnacles. This is the crowning motif of the N porch too. The porch is long and two-storeyed. Niches in the buttresses, shields above the entrance. Vault inside with ridge-ribs, tiercerons, and bosses. On the upper floor was the Lady Chapel (as at Fordham in Cambridgeshire a few miles away). The S porch is simpler. Excellent nave roof of low pitch, with alternating hammerbeams and cambered tie-beams. The depressed arched braces of the tie-beams are traceried, and there is tracery between the queenposts on the tie-beams. Against the hammerbeams big figures of angels. Angels also against the wall-plate. The aisle roofs have hammerbeams too. In the spandrels of those in the N aisle carved scenes of St George and the Dragon, the Baptism of Christ, the Sacrifice of Isaac, and the Annunciation. Against the wall-posts figures with demi-figures of angels above them serving as canopies. – FONT. Octagonal, Perp, of Purbeck marble with shields in quatrefoils. – NORTH DOOR. With tracery. – PLATE. Cup 1625; Almsdish 1632; Cup and Paten 1642; two enamelled Pewter Dishes given in 1648; Flagon given in 1720. – MONUMENT. Sir Henry North † 1620. Alabaster. Two recumbent effigies. The children kneel below, against the tomb-chest. Background with two black columns, two arches, two small obelisks, and an achievement. – In the churchyard the so-called Read Memorial, in fact the remains of a CHARNEL HOUSE with a chapel of St Michael over. The chapel was endowed in 1387.

The little town of Mildenhall has no house of special interest, but a nice MARKET PLACE with the original (C16?) MARKET CROSS, a hexagonal structure of heavy timbers with a high pole on the roof, and a HIGH STREET with some minor timber-framed (at the corner of Market Place) and Georgian houses.

(MILDENHALL WARREN LODGE. Ruinous and neglected at the time of writing. A strong building originally, like a squat church tower – cf. Warren Lodge, Thetford.*)

TOWN DEVELOPMENT HOUSING AREA, NE of the existing

* See The Buildings of England: North-West and South Norfolk, p. 347. Information from the Rev. J. T. Munday.

town. Work is being carried out by the G.L.C. Architecture Department, under the direction of *Sir Roger Walters*, for Mildenhall R.D.C. Round an open space containing a primary school (1968), shops, and community buildings 1,400 new houses are to be built. They are intended to contribute to an estimated increase in the total population of the parish from 6,580 to 13,500 by 1981. At the time of writing (1974) seven out of eleven stages have been completed. They include for example ST JOHN'S CLOSE, of 1969, 140 houses, designed for families of 2, 4, 5, and 6. Some are terraced, a few detached. There is 100 per cent garage provision, and pedestrian traffic only in the squares beyond the central area. SCOTT AVENUE of 1968 consists of 87 two-storey houses, in traditional brick construction, arranged in six squares. Some are two-bedroom, some four-bedroom houses. There are garages, and partial segregation of pedestrians.

(The LONDON LABEL FACTORY by *John Whitehead* won an award in 1969.)

ST PETER, West Row. Built in 1850, converted into a church and chancel added 1875. – PULPIT. From St Mary, probably mid-C17.

There are several PREHISTORIC SITES (none visible) which yielded evidence of extensive Neolithic and Bronze Age settlement. The Neolithic site mentioned in the Introduction (p. 19) is on HURST FEN, c. ½ m. N of St Helena Farm. An important Late Bronze Age site lies ½ m. due W of Weston Ditch on the S edge of Mildenhall Fen.

THISTLEY GREEN, West Row. In 1932 a Roman two-roomed building was discovered with hypocaust and pottery of C4 A.D. date; huts were visible as well as brickwork and oyster shells. In 1942 ploughing in a field 30 yds away revealed the great hoard of 34 pieces of C4 A.D. Roman silver table-ware (now in the British Museum), the largest object being the great dish, c. 2 ft in diameter, depicting Bacchus's triumph over Hercules. This, together with a pair of platters with rustic scenes of satyrs and maenads, may well have been made in Rome. Also important are two of the spoons engraved with Christian Alpha and Omega and Chi-Rho symbols – baptismal spoons, like those of later date found in the Sutton Hoo ship burial.

MINSMERE LEVEL *see* THEBERTON

MOAT FARMHOUSE *see* CRETINGHAM

MOAT HALL *see* PARHAM

MONEWDEN

2050

ST MARY. In the nave two small Norman windows with later heads. Dec w tower with flushwork decoration on the battlements, arches as well as shields in stars etc. Dec windows in nave and chancel. Early C16 s porch of brick. – FONT. Perp, octagonal, simple. Bowl with suspended shields. – BENCHES. Simple, with poppy-heads. – PLATE. Elizabethan Cup and Cover.

(CHERRY TREE FARMHOUSE. About 1600, timber-framed, with carved tie-beam to gable-end and carved bracket. DOE)

MONEWDEN HALL, ¾ m. NE. Early C18 front of red brick. Seven bays and two and a half storeys. Hipped roof; five dormers in it. Wooden cross-windows.

(RED HOUSE, ¼ m. SW. Dated 1592. Some good plasterwork inside. DOE)

MONKS ELEIGH

9040

ST PETER. A big church. Big Perp w tower with flushwork decoration.* Stair-turret on the s side not at the angle. Set-back buttresses continued near the top in polygonal shafts which end in the pinnacles. w doorway with fleuron decoration and hood-mould on two big heads. Niches l. and r. Nave and aisles and clerestory. N and s porches. The chancel is of 1845. Interior with arcades differing on the N from the s. s arcade with concave-sided octagonal piers (dated C14 by Cautley). N piers normal octagonal. On the s side double-chamfered arches, on the N one chamfer and one sunk quadrant moulding. Ceilure at the E end of the nave roof. – FONT. An odd form, dated C13 by Cautley, and an odd C17-looking cartouche. – PULPIT. With Perp traceried panels. – SOUTH DOOR with tracery. – ALMS BOX. Plain square pillar with the date 1636.

MONKS ELEIGH HALL has the date 1650 on the stack of octagonal chimneys.

A number of attractive houses in the main street, ending at the E end with the weatherboarded MILL (partly C15 ?) and the miller's house (Georgian, of five bays, red brick).

(HIGHLANDS HALL. Hall house with the date 1594 on a beam. F. A. Girling)

At SWINGLETON GREEN is THE FENN, C16 but with an Early Georgian front. Red and blue brick, the blue brick exclusively in headers. Five bays, two storeys, parapet, brick quoins, central

* Money was left towards the building of the steeple in a will of 1434 (ARA).

window segment-headed. To the r. older wing with good central chimneystack.

MONK SOHAM

ST PETER. W tower of *c.* 1300, see the lancets, slits below, larger above, and then with Y-tracery. See also the mouldings of the W doorway. Top with chequerboard flushwork decoration. Of *c.* 1300 also the N doorway of the nave and the fine chancel with its wide five-light window. Intersected cusped tracery. Cusped lancets with pointed trefoils in the top on the N and S sides, connected by a moulding inside which forms a hood-mould over them. Perp nave windows and S porch. The front with flushwork panelling. The entrance with shields, fleurons, etc., up the jambs and round the arch and also round two orders of mouldings inside the entrance. Three niches outside l., r., and above the entrance. Hammerbeam roof in the nave, but the arched braces up to the collar-beams do not start from the end of the hammerbeams, which are therefore structurally wasted. – FONT. Octagonal. Against the bowl the Seven Sacraments. Against the stem the Signs of the four Evangelists and four seated clerics or monks. – (PULPIT. 1604. LG) – SCREEN. Parts of it in the E door of the tower. The rood beam remains *in situ.* – BENCHES. With poppy-heads. – CHEST. C14. Iron-bound, 8 ft long. – PLATE. Elizabethan Cup; two Patens 1808.

(MONK SOHAM HALL contains an ornamented plaster ceiling of the late C16. DOE)

(ABBEY HOUSE, former Rectory. 1846 by *S. S. Teulon.*)

MORETON HALL *see* BURY ST EDMUNDS, p. 153

MOULTON

ST PETER. Norman nook-shafts at the W and E ends of the S side of the nave. (Simpler shafts on the N side too. LG) Late C13 W tower. The tower arch triple-chamfered and dying into the imposts. The rest of the church externally over-restored; Perp. Aisles and transeptal chapels, clerestory. The arcade inside has polygonal shafts with capitals (fleuron and battlement decoration) to the arches, but polygonal attachments without capitals to the nave. The chancel arch corresponds to the former type; so does the W arch of the N transept. The corresponding S arch is lower and heavier. Frieze with fleurons and demi-figures of angels at sill-level of the clerestory.* No furnishings of interest.

* (Remains of an anchorite's cell or ankerhole N of the tower. LG)

BRIDGES. Very impressive C15 bridge of four arches. Further s another narrow bridge, also C15; of flint.

MUTFORD

4080

ST ANDREW. In the nave N wall a re-set Norman zigzag arch, perhaps the former chancel arch. It might, however, also be the entrance arch to the W galilee built to the W of the round tower. This has indeed a round arch, and Suckling in 1846 called it Norman. The tower has C13 lancet windows. Its top is octagonal and has two-light windows with the usual reticulation motif rendered blank in flushwork (cf. Butley Priory). The galilee in its present form and the W doorway into the tower also look Dec. So does the chancel. Large E window with Dec tracery, shafted inside. Equally large blocked N window, also shafted. S aisle also early C14, see the windows with Y-tracery, the ogee-arched PISCINA, and the four-bay arcade with octagonal piers and double-chamfered arches. C18 brick chapel on the S side. – FONT. On two steps. One carries a quatrefoil frieze. On the top inscription referring to Elizabeth de Hengrave, i.e. *c.* 1380. Four lions against the stem, angels' heads against the underside of the bowl (cf. Gisleham), buttresses only against the bowl. Probably representations of the Seven Sacraments have been cleared off completely. – BENCHES. With poppy-heads. – SCREEN. The dado only remains. – STALL FRONTS. Part of these under the tower arch. – WALL PAINTING. St Christopher (N wall). Cautley points out the sea-shells in his river. – PLATE. Cup 1568.

ASH FARMHOUSE, ½ m. NW. Elizabethan, of red brick. Of the same type as Roos Hall, but in a poor state of preservation. Three bays, middle entrance (Georgian), all the main windows pedimented (the pediments remain, the windows are altered). Stepped gable-ends.

(MUTFORD HALL, 1 m. SW. Dated 1607. Brick with four stepped gables, but all the front windows modern reproductions. DOE)

NACTON

2040

ST MARTIN. Short Perp W tower. Three-light W window with panel tracery. Nave and chancel. The church is over-restored and the aisles are of 1907. One original lancet window in the N wall of the chancel. – FONT. Octagonal. Against the stem four lions and four Wild Men, against the bowl the Signs of the four Evangelists and four angels with the Signs of the Passion, the Trinity, and the Initials of Christ. – STAINED GLASS. E window by *Kempe*, 1907. A N window by the same, 1905. – PLATE. Elizabethan Cup.

ORWELL PARK. Built *c.* 1770, and of that time the general shape to the N (red brick, seven bays, two and a half storeys, three-bay pediment), the plasterwork of the entrance hall, and a fireplace to its l. Much was altered and added to in 1854 and again in 1873. Of the latter date the odd observatory tower, of the former, it seems, the SE front towards the river with its weakly Jacobean and Frenchy details, the winter-garden attached to the NW (tiled inside), the separate Italianate NW tower, and perhaps also the clock tower to the SE. Big iron gates.

BROKE HOUSE, ⅝ m. SE. The house was built in the first half of the C16, but it is not easy now to say whether anything goes back to so early a date. The present appearance of the house is early C19 castellated. Symmetrical garden front with slightly recessed centre, where, in the middle, on the first floor, stands a red terracotta statue in a niche. The projecting parts have slender polygonal angle buttresses.

SHOLLOND HILL, NE of the church. Good one-storeyed modern house. 1955 by *D. E. Harding*. A specially nice colour scheme; brick painted grey, the gables purple, the eaves and soffits lime-green. May the colours last.

BARROWS. There are thirteen in the area of Seven Hills, running along the parish boundaries for ¼ m. just N of Orwell Station.

0040

NAUGHTON

ST MARY. Flint. Late C13 to early C14. On the S side a two-light window, still with plate tracery, and a cusped lancet. In the chancel E window intersected tracery. The tower arch triple-chamfered and dying into the imposts. Tie-beam roof with crown-posts and braces springing from wall-posts. – FONT. Norman. It was square and decorated with intersected arches but later made octagonal. – ORGAN. (Dated 1777. LG) – BENCHES. Six C17 ends with poppy-heads. – WALL PAINTINGS. N wall. Discovered in 1953. Upper half of a large St Christopher. Also unidentified scene with two women facing each other. – PLATE. Paten 1711; Cup 1730.

NAUGHTON HALL of the C17 is near the church. Good original brick chimneystack with octagonal shafts. Moat.

NAYLAND

ST JAMES. A surprising sight from Church Street owing to the rich S W porch attached to the W tower and entered from the W. The porch was built of stone by a clothier, William Abell, in 1525, and rebuilt in 1884. It is panelled and castellated and has a (new) vault with many tiercerons but no liernes. There is also a N porch, completed before 1441 according to a will of that year (ARA). The unbuttressed W tower is C14 (but with a brick top of 1834 – a terrible pity), and so are the chancel with its five-light E window displaying flowing tracery, the W window of the N aisle with intersected tracery, and the shape of the former S window. The rest is Perp. Handsome S aisle front with rood-stair turret. This seems the aisle referred to in a will of 1492–3. Arcades of six bays with finely moulded piers. Attached shafts with capitals only towards the arch openings. From shields in the spandrels of the arcade rise shafts which divide the clerestory into pairs of windows. The chancel has a clerestory too. No chancel chapels. – SCREENS. Eight painted panels of *c.* 1500 from the former rood screen are hung up in the S aisle. Indifferent quality. – FONT COVER. By *R. Y. Goodden.* – WEST GALLERY. Simple C18 work. – NORTH DOOR. With linenfold panelling and a border of vine trails. – ALTAR PAINTING. Christ blessing bread and wine. By *John Constable,* 1809 and much less tied to the well-tried-out mannerisms of the late C18 than his picture of 1804 at Brantham. – STAINED GLASS. N aisle W window by *Kempe, c.* 1908. – PLATE. Cup 1562; Paten and Flagon 1825. – BRASSES. Large double canopy (N aisle), *c.* 1440. – Upper half of a Lady with butterfly head-dress under a canopy (Mrs Hacche), *c.* 1485. Original size *c.* 3 ft (nave). – Civilian and wife under double canopy, *c.* 1500 (nave). The figures are 3 ft long. – Civilian and wife with pedimented head-dress, probably Richard Davy † 1514 (N aisle); 18 in. figures.

ALSTON COURT. The hub of the village is Alston Court, a fine and varied house with great surprises. It lies at the S end of the N–S run of Church Street, where this turns E to lead to the church and beyond. The front is plastered and has a W gable, a big doorway of *c.* 1700 with a semicircular deeply apsed hood on big carved brackets, a spectacular early C16 nine-light window with two transoms, and an E gable with timbers showing. The E front has the timbers showing too, and brick-nogging. But the great surprise is the E wing as seen from the courtyard. It also has brick-nogging, and in addition carved bressumers,

several oriel windows, and elegant buttress- and angle-posts.
The hall has a big eight-light window also towards the courtyard. More exposed timber-framing in the other wings. The
dates are not certain, but it is assumed that the E wing dates
from the later C15. The finest rooms inside begin with the hall,
with a tie-beam on arched braces and a kingpost. The braces
have traceried spandrels and rest on wall-shafts. Then N of the
hall the dining room, with heavily moulded and carved beams,
and above this the beautiful solar with a boarded roof of low
pitch supported on generously carved arched braces. They
rest on corbels in the shape of human figures. Much carving
also of the wall-plate.

From Alston Court CHURCH STREET runs E past the S side of the
church and ends by the handsome timber-framed WHITE
HOUSE. It also runs N and here first, on the E side, an obelisk
MILESTONE (56 m. to London, etc.), then on the W side the
QUEEN'S HEAD with exposed timber work to the coaching
yard as well as to the mill stream on the N. To the E the stream
continues between the houses of FENN STREET, a very pretty
sight. From the N end of Church Street to the E BIRCH
STREET with several good timber-framed houses with jutting
upper floors, to the W BEAR STREET with the BUTCHER'S
ARMS (carved bressumer), and opposite a house with a date
1690 in a pargetted cartouche.

EAST ANGLIAN SANATORIUM. The Jane Walker Wing is by
Smith & Brewer and was illustrated in 1910.

NEDGING

9040

ST MARY. Two Transitional (late C13) doorways, round-arched,
with one order of shafts, the capitals thick crockets with applied
decoration or upright leaves. The arches with thick rings round
the main roll moulding. On the S side also a hood-mould of
dog-tooth. Chancel of *c.* 1300, see the windows (E three-light
intersected); nave Dec, W tower also Dec. Nave roof with tie-
beams and kingposts. – BENCHES with poppy-heads. – PLATE.
Cup 1562 (?).

NEEDHAM MARKET

0050

ST JOHN BAPTIST. Its roof is 'the climax of English roof construction' (Crossley), 'the culminating achievement of the
English carpenter' (Cautley). No statements could be truer.
Earl Stonham or Mildenhall may be richer and of a stronger
appeal to the senses, but the intellect must give Needham

20

Market first prize. What the carpenter has achieved here is to build a whole church with nave and aisles and clerestory seemingly in the air. The eye scarcely believes what it sees, and has a hard if worth-while job in working out how this unique effect could be attained. The roof is a hammerbeam roof with hammers coming forward a full 6 ft 6 in. The arched braces supporting them are hidden (as at Framlingham) by a boarded coving with angels with spread-out wings and fleurons. Against the ends of the hammerbeams again angels with alternately swept-upward and spread-out wings (C20). There are also pendants suspended from the hammerbeams. This is done to give the impression that the chief distinguishing structural members of the Needham Market roof – the storey-posts – were not standing on the hammerbeams, but suspended from the top. They are very tall, and carry the cambered tie-beams of the low-pitched roof of the church. But between the hammerbeams and that roof much else is happening. At the point where the arched braces meet the hammerbeams vertical so-called ashlar posts rise, as they do in any canted wagon roof of the single-frame type. And they support, again as in normal canted wagon roofs, the rafters, which reach up like lean-to roofs to the storey-posts. The posts at about one-third of their height are cross-connected, i.e. from W to E, by cambered tie-beams, and at about two-thirds of their height, i.e. just below the place where the lean-to roof reaches them, are transversely connected, i.e. from N to S, by cambered tie-beams on shallow arched braces. Finally, and this is the most astonishing feature, the upper thirds of the storey-posts are cross-connected, i.e. from W to E, by a timber-built clerestory with windows. This feature, as well as the treatment of the ashlar posts and lean-to rafters, creates the impression to which reference was made at the outset, the impression of a whole church in mid-air. The storey-posts are its piers, the rafters on the ashlar posts its aisle roofs. In addition there is plenty of decoration, even if the storey-posts remain a severely structural feature. The tie-beams are all crenellated, and the arched braces carved. Finally, apart from the aesthetic thrill there is the fact that, as Cautley says, 'this would seem to be the only open type of roof which exerts no outward thrust on the walls'.

The roof had to be described in detail to make everybody appreciate what the significance of Needham Market is. For in every other respect the church is a bitter disappointment. Externally it looks like a Nonconformist chapel built in a main street in Victorian times, and with not quite enough money. Internally it is full of C20 imagery. The church was built at the expense of Bishop Grey of Ely (1458–78). His arms appear above the chancel doorway. The exterior is all Perp. The s buttresses have niches with canopies, the NE buttress is pierced for processions to pass. The relation of the large windows below and the small timber-framed clerestory above is far from satisfactory, and there is no tower. This is no doubt due to the fact that the church was a chapel-of-ease till 1907. Indeed, some ignorant and insensible architect in 1883 put up the s porch with its ridiculous and miserly spirelet. – DOORS. Original traceried s and chancel s doors.

PERAMBULATION. W of the church the HIGH STREET starts with No. 123, a big Georgian brick house of two and a half storeys with a porch with broken pediment on Tuscan columns but a surprising ogee-shaped fan-light. Opposite HAWKS-MILL STREET. At the corner of King William Street, almost at once, there is a house with a modern date 1480 and good angle-posts. Then the street runs down and beyond the railway. VALLEY HOUSE is again a Georgian house of five bays. Roman Doric doorway. On in the HIGH STREET, immediately past the church, a good house of c. 1820–30 (No. 92), grey brick, three bays, with a Greek Doric porch. Opposite this (No. 103) a nice shop-front with canted windows and a doorway with Tuscan columns in the middle. After that the BULL HOTEL. It has a corner post with an angel with spread-out wings and some tracery. Close to the Bull in BRIDGE STREET another house with overhanging upper floor, brackets, and two thin buttress-shafts at the angles. On in the HIGH STREET, THE LIMES has a charming wide Georgian doorway with close ornament. The house is again of red brick, five bays, two storeys. On the same side No. 89 with an archway, dated 1772. This leads to the FRIENDS' MEETING HOUSE and GRAVE-YARD. All the tombstones have the same simple design. Further E the ALMSHOUSE of 1836, grey brick, with heavy Tudor details. Inside two Late Gothic wooden figures, prob-ably from the wall-posts of a church roof. The TOWN HALL is a sad building of yellow and red brick with lean round arches. Opposite, the CONGREGATIONAL CHURCH of 1838. Five bays, with a five-bay pediment. Grey brick. The porch or rather loggia dates from c. 1915. At the end of the Perambula-tion No. 1 with a seven-bay plastered C18 façade; opposite the former GRAMMAR SCHOOL, timber-framed, built in 1632 by

Sir Francis Theobald of Barking Hall with materials from the Needham Market Guildhall; and next to this the entrance to STATION ROAD, at whose end the visitor is greeted by the STATION, 'a pleasing structure', as the *Illustrated London News* assured its readers in 1849. It is of brick and Caen stone, by *Frederick Barnes* of Ipswich, in the Elizabethan style, with angle towers and gables, very similar to, and yet different from, the Stowmarket Station.

(Good WATER MILL. P. G. M. Dickinson)

NETTLESTEAD

0040

ST MARY. A Norman window in the N wall. It has the unusual detail of a closely decorated arch: an outer band of intersected arches, a middle one of scrolls, and an inner one of beads. Unbuttressed W tower, nave and chancel. The windows mostly Perp. Dec E window. S porch of brick, C16, with a semicircular gable. – FONT. Against the stem four crowned lions. Against the bowl the uncommon combination of the Signs of the four Evangelists and St Catherine, and in addition the heads of a bishop, a king, and a man putting his tongue out. – PULPIT. Jacobean. – PLATE. Cup and Cover 1601; Paten 1713. – MONUMENTS. Brass of a Knight, *c.* 1500 (nave floor), the figure 1 ft 5 in. long. – Samuel Sayer † 1625 and his wife † 1647. Demi-figures holding hands, a skull between them. The whole architectural setting has disappeared. – In the churchyard a triangular monument in the Gothic style to Stephen Jackson † 1855. Inscription under three big gables. Above a shaft like that of a churchyard cross, ending indeed in a cross. The inscription runs round the three sides line after line.

THE CHACE. Of the Hall of the Wentworth family only an ARCHWAY remains. Round arch, two fluted Doric pilasters on simply decorated bases. Pediment against the attic. The present house is early C19, grey brick, of three bays, with tripartite ground-floor windows and a Tuscan porch. (Large DOVECOTE, attributed to the late C16. *P.S.I.A.*, XVIII, 1922–4)

HIGH HOUSE, ½ m. NW. Red brick, Elizabethan, and clearly only a fragment. The porch is recessed and cannot have had the same relation to the projecting range of two bays as it has now. The porch has two orders of Tuscan pilasters. Its top is missing. The projecting part has mullioned and transomed windows with pediments. (Good overmantel inside with two tiers of blank arches separated by stubby fluted pilasters. NMR)

2040

NEWBOURN

ST MARY. s tower probably Dec, with diagonal buttresses with five set-offs. Flushwork decoration on the double-stepped battlements. Also pinnacles and four (new) angel figures instead of intermediate pinnacles. s aisle of red brick with dark blue diaper; early C16. The s and N doorways are re-used Dec pieces, as is one window. The w wall is dated 1810 and is of brick chequerwork. The chancel doorway is early C16 brick. The E window is shafted inside with what seems two re-used and restored late C12 shafts. – FONT. Against the stem four lions and four Wild Men. Against the bowl the Signs of the four Evangelists and angels with shields illustrating the Trinity and the Passion and the Cross, and M for the Virgin Mary. – (STALLS. Some of the C15. LG) – SCREEN. The simply blank-traceried dado only. – PLATE. Elizabethan Cup; Paten 1570.

NEWBOURN HALL. A timber-framed house of c. 1500 with a ceiling with moulded beams inside, enlarged c. 1612. To the latter date belongs the stepped gable with beneath it three- to five-light transomed windows, the small porch to the old range with brick pilasters, and two ornamented plaster ceilings, that of the former staircase having roses and lilies set between wavy ribs.

NEWBOURN ESTATE. A Government scheme of 1930 to help distressed miners. Now administered by the Land Settlement Board. Each unit consists of a small house of yellow brick, only two windows long, with a high-pitched roof the arch of which is weatherboarded, and two glasshouses and land to grow flowers or vegetables.

6060

NEWMARKET

Newmarket is a coaching town along one of the main roads of South England, and in addition it is the centre of racehorse breeding and one of the centres of horse-racing. As one approaches the town, the scenery at once reveals itself ideal for the exercising of horses and for racing. But architecturally Newmarket has very little to offer. There is the long and wide HIGH STREET running sw from the hideous CLOCK TOWER of 1887, and with some nice minor Georgian and earlier houses. The only ones worth recording* include the RUTLAND

* The DOE also records No. 194: C18, brick and tiled (old Cambridge-shire tiles). Two storeys, attic and basement. Three-storeyed curved bays with old glazing bars, a fanlight, and a modern brick door surround. Good wrought-iron railings and gate.

ARMS HOTEL on the l., now modernized but originally Late Georgian, of brick, with a pediment at an angle to the road and a side along the road, also pedimented (the hotel has an inner courtyard), which has its former stables, one-storeyed with a centre pediment, and ranges on three sides of a courtyard; there is BARCLAYS BANK, of six bays with two doorways with Roman Doric columns; there remains one of the two aesthetic atrocities, the CARLTON, Victorian, much too high and showy in its red brick Renaissance (the other atrocity opposite, the spiky Gothic CONGREGATIONAL CHURCH of 1863 (on the site of Charles II's Palace) has been demolished; the new church is on the first floor of the supermarket building which has taken its place); and there are such pretty C18 houses as No. 119, with giant angle pilasters and a pedimented doorway. The pavement rises where No. 119 stands, and such differences of level are always attractive. Where the High Street runs into the Heath stands the COOPER MEMORIAL FOUNTAIN of 1910, a baldacchino, oval in plan, and with jockeys' caps, saddles, stirrups, etc.

The most interesting building in the High Street is the JOCKEY CLUB. The whole front part is by *Richardson & Gill* (Sir Albert Richardson), built in 1933 and inspired by its Georgian predecessor. Red brick. Recessed centre with a stone-faced arcade, projecting wings with very shallow canted bays. Above the centre a handsome Ionic rotunda of columns carrying a lantern. At the back an earlier much-gabled red brick building of 1882.

Of other buildings EXNING HOSPITAL may be mentioned, the former Workhouse, in plain classical form, of yellow brick, built in 1836, and the former RAILWAY STATION, at the NE end of the town. This was built in 1848 and was the most sumptuously Baroque station of the Early Victorian decades in England. Seven bays, one storey, divided by coupled Ionic giant columns, carrying projecting pieces of entablature and big chunks of decorated attic. Mr Barman has rightly compared it with an orangery. It is now derelict; if it is allowed to disappear, England will have lost one of its most spectacular railway stations.

The STANDS for the Newmarket Races have unfortunately no architectural attractions.

One of the most characteristic features of Newmarket is its rich Victorian and Edwardian houses in their own grounds. On these little information is available. Three can be mentioned:

MURRAY LODGE by *A. N. Prentice*, picturesque, with Dutch
gables, SEFTON LODGE by *W. Young*, and, somewhat later,
WARREN HILL HOUSE, neo-Georgian, 1928 by *Thomas
Tyrwhitt*, an assistant of Aston Webb.

Finally the CHURCHES, which at Newmarket can indeed be
considered last.

ST MARY is the old parish church. It lies close to the old quarter
of MARKET STREET which was demolished in 1969 and is so
restored that practically all is new. The chancel was rebuilt
entirely in 1856. C14 S arcade with keeled quatrefoil piers and
castellated capitals and double-hollow-chamfered arches.
Perp W tower with shingled spire. Perp S doorway with an
angel in the apex of the arch. – PISCINA. C13, with the angle
shaft so often met with in Suffolk. Found at the time of the
restoration. – STAINED GLASS. In the S aisle a window by
Kempe & Tower, 1907. – PAINTINGS. Big Italian or Spanish
C17 painting of the Virgin, with her Mother holding the Child
Christ, and the little St John the Baptist. – Christ entering
Jerusalem, by *J. Wood* (1801–70).

ALL SAINTS. 1876–7. Bad, Geometrical, with a SW tower. –
Inside a CARTOON by *Burne-Jones* of a large angel holding a
bow and sheltering human beings. Inscription from Dante:
'L'amor che muove . . .'. – STAINED GLASS. W window by
Gibbs.

ST AGNES, Bury Road. By *Carpenter*, 1886. Red brick with an
asymmetrically placed spirelet. Inside much decoration with
Spanish TILES. The straight E end is made into one composition
with the large REREDOS by *Boehm*, representing the Assumption of the Virgin (curiously Baroque in the treatment of relief),
and the E.E. arches above it. – PLATE. Cup, Norwegian, 1707;
three Flower Vases 1728.

9040   NEWTON

ALL SAINTS. Norman N doorway. Two shafts with scalloped
capitals. Zigzag in the arch and the hood-mould. Nave of *c.*
1300, see the S doorway and the windows. Chancel Dec with
reticulated E window. Dec also the SEDILIA, simple, but with
a pretty 'two-light' PISCINA. – FONT. Octagonal, Perp,
simple. – PULPIT. Perp, with tracery. Inscription referring to
its being a gift of Richard Modi and his wife Leticie. –
LECTERN. Handsome C17 piece, with mostly consciously used
Gothic motifs. – MONUMENTS. Nave S side. Lady of the

early C14 in low early C14 recess. – Chancel N. Lady of c. 1400. Under an ogee arch with straight cresting.

NEWTON HALL. Timber-framed but externally mostly C18; it has a big weatherboarded BARN with two porches.

ROGERS, ¾ m. NE. Timber-framed, c. 1600, with wall paintings dated 1623 (Life of Samson, Martyrdom of St Stephen).

NEWTON HALL see OLD NEWTON

NORTH COVE   *4080*

ST BOTOLPH. Unbuttressed W tower of flint and brick. Long nave and chancel in one; thatched. Norman S doorway. One order of colonnettes. Two orders of zigzag in the arch. Outer arch with a kind of big nailheads. Nave N doorway and one window E.E. S porch Dec, and chancel perhaps Dec (the windows renewed). – FONT. Early C15, octagonal. The bowl is supported on eight heads with contemporary head-dresses, and has panels with four lions and four angels. – WALL PAINTINGS. In the chancel W of the N window: Scenes from the Passion; W of the S window: Deësis; E of the N window: Resurrection and Harrowing of Hell; E of the S window: Ascension. – PLATE. Cup 1568.

NORTH COVE HALL. Georgian, red brick. Five bays, two storeys, parapet. Porch with Roman Doric pillars, a tripartite window over, and over this a pediment set against the parapet.

(COTTAGE FARMHOUSE, 1 m. S. Dated 1622. Timber-framed, but with a stepped brick gable-end. DOE)

NORTH GREEN FARMHOUSE see STOVEN

NORTON   *9060*

ST ANDREW. Chancel of c. 1300, see e.g. the lancet window above the priest's doorway. The E window however looks transitional between Dec and Perp. The N aisle (see the doorway) must have been built in the early C14, and the tower at least begun. Money was left for its completion in 1442. Of that time or later most of the windows. The S aisle has at its base some flushwork chequerboard patterning. S porch with flushwork decoration and a niche above the entrance. The arcade of three bays has concave-sided octagonal piers, each side provided with a shallow blank ogee arch-head (cf. Lakenheath and other places). Double-hollow-chamfered arches. – FONT. Perp, octagonal, and richly carved. The stem is square and has panels and four figures carrying shields, one of them a Wild Man. On the bowl the four Signs of the Evangelists, and in addition a double eagle, a unicorn, a pelican, and a griffin. – STALLS. Three sections are preserved. They have exceptionally good MISERICORDS, the Martyrdom of St Edmund, the Crucifixion of St Andrew, a Pelican, a Woman warming her feet (January?), a Monk writing, a man whipping a boy's buttocks, a Lion devouring a Wild Man, etc. – BENCHES. In the aisles. The ends with poppy-heads and animals on the arms. – STAINED GLASS. In the chancel on the S side. Whole figures in the tracery. – PLATE. Paten 1722; Almsdish 1761.

RECTORY. Handsome house of c. 1700. Seven bays and two storeys with hipped roof and three dormers with steep triangular pediments.

LITTLE HAUGH HALL. The exterior is very reticent. Long entrance side of grey brick with a two-pillar-two-column porch, evidently early C19. The short S side of the same style. At the back, towards the garden, it becomes clear that the house has a core of c. 1730. Red brick. Doorway with Gibbs surround and a fine Venetian window above it. Two windows l., two windows r. It is only inside that the house reveals itself as the finest of that date in the county. Its magnificence is due to Cox Macro (1683–1757), student of medicine at Cambridge and Leiden, D.D. of Cambridge, chaplain to George II, and a distinguished antiquarian and virtuoso. His father had been a rich grocer at Bury St Edmunds, his grandfather the apothecary Thomas Macro of Cupola House at Bury (*see* p. 149). Splendid staircase behind the Venetian window. Three slender turned balusters to each tread, decorated at the foot. Carved tread-ends, richly carved underside of the upper flight. Equally rich the plaster on the underside of the top landing and the doorcases. On the top landing, that is in a place not usually seen by visitors, the greatest splendour. Façade towards the front room with a niche with pediment over. In the niche originally stood *Rysbrack*'s bust of Tillemans, the painter, who had died at Little Haugh Hall in 1734. Superbly carved loosely bunched garlands l. and r. Doorways l. and r. and round the corners all richly carved. The ceiling coved and with an oval dome. The paintings by *Francis Hayman*, 1743. In the ceiling Galileo, Newton, and Nicholas Saunder surrounded by putti and the instruments or tokens of astronomy, physics (the lever principle), arithmetic, and geometry, architecture, sculpture, etc. In the dome Apollo crowning – whom? (Mr Croft Murray suggests Leonardo da Vinci.) Also

57b

the Nine Muses. Next to the staircase on the ground floor the dining room, on the upper floor a living room, both with plasterwork, especially round the fireplaces, of equally high quality. The woodcarver was *Davis*, the stucco is by *Burrough*, the overdoors by *Tillemans*.

(At LITTLE GREEN, 1¼ m. NE, a brick farmhouse with a big stepped gable and a fine brick BARN. F. A. Girling)

NOWTON

8060

ST PETER. Norman N doorway with one order of shafts and crockety capitals. In the E wall of the N aisle a re-set Norman window. The aisle is painful neo-Norman of 1843. The S doorway is genuinely Norman, but simpler. Chancel of *c.* 1300. Three-light intersected E window, a circle in the top field. Inside two big niches l. and r. Dec W tower. – STAINED GLASS. About seventy-five pieces of foreign glass, C16 to C17, 'from monasteries at Brussels' according to an inscription in the church. – PLATE. Silver-gilt Cup 1643; silver-gilt Cup 1678–9; silver-gilt Almsdish 1824. – MONUMENT. Mrs Oakes † 1811. By *John Bacon Jun.* Praying woman by a sarcophagus set at an angle.

(NOWTON HALL. C16 (a chimney is dated 1595); interesting. LG)

(NOWTON COURT (now a preparatory school). A C19 mansion in the Tudor style. Inside, some fine wooden panelling and a fireplace surround dated 1607. Is it Flemish? In the grounds a stone archway said to be the S porch of St Mary, Bury St Edmunds, and a square font (of the C12?) from Lakenheath. ARA)

OAKLEY

1070

ST NICHOLAS. Dec W tower, the battlements with flushwork panelling. Tower arch with two continuous chamfers. Perp nave and chancel. The windows with two-centred arches in the former, four-centred in the latter. Two-storeyed S porch with flushwork panelling. Entrance with shields in the spandrels and a quatrefoil frieze over. Two small S windows l. and r. of a niche. The rood-loft stair ascends in a N window. In the N wall two ogee-headed image niches side by side. – REREDOS and surround, 1882. Tiled, also with figures and scenes, especially the Last Supper in tiles. Some mosaic-work as well. – STAINED GLASS. Some in the S porch. – PLATE. Cup *c.* 1673; Paten *c.* 1675. – MONUMENT. Large tomb-chest for Sir William Cornwallis † 1611. Alabaster and black marble, very remarkable for the total absence of figures and ornament.

OCCOLD
1070

ST MICHAEL. In the chancel one Norman window (N) and one window with ballflower in the hood-mould (S). One nave S and one N window have fine shafting inside and a pretty niche in the reveal. This is probably Dec. The N and S doorways E.E. The rest Perp. W tower with flushwork panelling on battlements and base. Kelly gives the date 1426 for the tower. The arch of the doorway is decorated with fleurons and crowns. The three-light W window is typical of Suffolk in its tracery. Nave and chancel; NE vestry, two-storeyed. The chancel arch rests on two big head-corbels and may be Dec. – SCREEN. Parts of the dado re-used in the stalls. – PULPIT. 1620. With the familiar short blank arches as the principal motif. The tester is also preserved. – STALLS. One with its MISERICORD: a praying female saint. – STAINED GLASS. Bits in the first window on the S side of the chancel. – PLATE. Elizabethan Cup; Paten *c.* 1675. – BRASSES. William Corbald and wife, *c.* 1490. The figures are 3 ft long (nave floor).

OFFTON
0040

ST MARY. Simple Norman S doorway. Unbuttressed Dec W tower. Flushwork arcading on the battlements. Nave and chancel with Dec and Perp windows. In one Perp S window the soffit is nicely panelled inside. The S porch is of timber; Dec. The tracery of the side openings differs between E and W. Tie-beam roof with crown-posts and four-way struts. (Carved spandrels. LG) – FONT. Octagonal. With four lions against the stem and four angels and four flowers against the bowl. – PULPIT. Jacobean. – SCREEN. Only the dado, made into a bench. – PLATE. Elizabethan Cup.

OKENHILL HALL *see* BADINGHAM

OLD HALL FARMHOUSE *see* BURGH CASTLE

OLD NEWTON
0060

ST MARY. The remaining medieval work is entirely Dec, with good tall two-light windows. The W tower has Y-tracery in the bell-openings and flushwork arcading on the battlements. To the l. and r. of the E window inside two ogee niches. – FONT.

Octagonal. Against the stem four lions and four Wild Men. Against the bowl four lions and four angels. – BENCHES. At the back. Plain, C17, with poppy-heads. – STAINED GLASS. Some in the heads of the nave N windows. – PLATE. Cup *c*. 1680.

NEWTON HALL, ¾ m. SE. Inside a panelled room and an over-mantel with clusters of three colonnettes. Jacobean.

ONEHOUSE

0050

ST JOHN BAPTIST. Norman round tower. Nave and chancel, the chancel Victorian. – FONT. Norman, of cauldron shape, with sharp angles and some decayed ornament.

ONEHOUSE LODGE, ½ m. NE. Early C18, of five bays and two storeys, plastered. Doorway with segmental pediment on pilasters. The shape of the windows and the door-head is unusual.

ORFORD

4040

ST BARTHOLOMEW. The church consists of two parts, today of little connexion with one another: the ruinous Late Norman chancel, begun in 1166, and the Dec nave, aisles, and W tower. The Late Norman church must have been in grandeur a match to the Castle; for the chancel is six bays long, had vaulted five-bay aisles and a straight E end, and was followed to the W by a crossing and transepts with straight-ended E chapels. The piers are circular and were decorated in a bold and varied way, a development from the earlier incised decoration of Durham, Norwich, or Waltham Abbey. At Orford, as at Compton Martin in North Devon and Pittington in County Durham, the decoration is applied in substantial round bands. On the first pair there are four spiral bands or rolls each going once round the whole pier. The second pair had eight vertical shafts, the third four bolder vertical shafts, the fourth eight vertical triple shafts. The capitals are flat, square, and many-scalloped, the arches complex in their mouldings and provided with some zigzag. Of the transept all that survives is the arch from the N chancel aisle into the N transept, the strongly shafted window above it, and remains of the transept windows in two tiers to the N of this. In addition inside the church the shape and shafting of the Norman eastern crossing piers re-mains.

The Dec work culminates in the W tower, the top of which fell in 1830. It is still a monumental piece, with broad diagonal buttresses and a big W doorway. This has two orders of thin shafts and many continuous mouldings. A quatrefoil frieze and a niche above it. Three-light window with standard flowing tracery. The top of the tower had flushwork decoration. The aisle windows are of three lights, and their tracery is either reticulated or consists of three ogee-headed lights and three circles over them with cinquefoils and sexfoils, except for the s aisle w window, which has four lights and a large wheel of six daggers round an octofoil hub. Clerestory with small diagonally placed quatrefoils in circles. Perp s porch with spandrels carrying shields with the emblems of the Passion and the Trinity. In one arch moulding a number of small shields. Finely moulded s doorway. The arcade is typical of the Dec style in Suffolk. Quatrefoil piers with spurs in the diagonals. Arches with two thin filleted rolls and one big sunk quadrant. Tower arch in the same style, but with three sunk quadrants (or waves?).

FURNISHINGS. FONT. On two steps, the upper one with a quatrefoil frieze and an inscription commemorating John Cokerel and his wife. Against the stem four lions and four Wild Men, against the bowl, which is supported on angels' heads, the Signs of the four Evangelists, the Trinity, the Pietà, and angels with the emblems of Trinity and Passion. – SCREENS. Two (re-set) parclose screens (N and S of the high altar) in rough Early Renaissance forms. – Screens of 1712 with fine carving behind the C19 stalls. – PAINTINGS. Holy Family with St John and the donor above the high altar by *Bernardino Luini*, c. 1520 (from Lord Brownlow's collection, *see* A. Ottino della Casa, no. 197). Also Nativity, above the s altar, attributed to *Raffaelino del Colle*. – PLATE. Cup and Flagon 1773. – BRASSES. Eight in the E parts of the church of between c. 1480 and c. 1520. Chancel N: Woman, 14 in., with separate children; Woman, 12 in., with children on the same brass; Civilian, 1 ft 7 in. – Chancel floor: Civilian, 1 ft 4 in. – Chancel s: Civilian and Wife, 1 ft 4 in.; Wife and two husbands, 1 ft 7 in. – s chapel: Praying Civilian, 1 ft 7 in. – In addition several Elizabethan brasses and John Coggishall †1640, a plate with two kneeling figures and their children by a circular praying table on a baluster foot. Several inscriptions on scrolls.

(OLD RECTORY. Largely in the state given it by *Frederick Barnes* in 1878.)

Orford was a town of far greater importance in the Middle Ages than it is now. It had three churches, a house of Austin Friars, and two hospitals. But Defoe, writing in 1722, says that the town is now decayed. The sea daily throws up more land so it is a sea port no longer'. It is now an extremely pleasant brick and timber village, looking delightful from the roof of the castle. Its highlights are the main square and Quay Street leading to the quay and the ferry.

CASTLE. The keep was built for Henry II in 1165–7 by his 42a 'ingeniator' *Alnoth*, Keeper of the King's Houses. It was a revolutionary design; for it seems the first in England to abandon the square or oblong shape in favour of a militarily more advantageous one. At Orford it is an irregular eighteen-sided shape to which was added a square staircase turret and two other square buttresses or turrets, although these really invalidated some of what had been gained by the polygonal centre. The angles of a polygon are less easily mined than the rectangles at the corners of a square keep (cf. Introduction p. 30 and Bungay p. 122) and they are also more easily defended. Chilham in Kent and Odiham in Hampshire are the only other polygonal Norman keeps in England. But Henry II also built or remodelled the polygonal keep of Gisors in Normandy. Conisbrough in the West Riding of Yorkshire, being circular, was an even better solution. This dates from *c*. 1180. By then more radical changes began to appear in defence technique which made even Conisbrough and Orford old-fashioned (cf. Framlingham, p. 218). Grey ashlar and septaria. Recent repairs in mauve cement. Battered ashlar base. Forebuilding to which originally led an outer staircase. The doorway is placed askew. No orders on the l. side, three on the r. Capitals with both straight and trumpet scallops. The three arch orders are unchamfered. The interior on the first floor is circular. It has a fireplace. By a wall passage one reaches the CHAPEL in the forebuilding.* The plan of the chapel is a rectangle with one sloping side. Blank arcading against the walls with shafts carrying scalloped and other capitals. The window surrounds are arched, but the windows themselves straight-headed. The jamb moulding which results has a heavy roll. Gangway to a room in one of the buttress turrets and then to a garderobe. The HALL is on the second and third floors. It is also circular. The landing of the stair from the first to the second floor is rib-vaulted with unmoulded square ribs. The nooks in which the windows are placed have pointed tunnel-vaults. The door-ways are pointed too. Original corbels at half the height of the

* The keep at Newcastle upon Tyne, built for Henry II in 1171 etc., has the chapel also in the forebuilding, but on the ground floor.

hall. Were they to carry a vault? Or simply a wooden galler (LG)? Fireplace with shafts for a former overmantel. The thre turrets rise above the parapet. No other buildings of the castl than the keep are preserved. The buildings were extensive an comprised a curtain wall. A natural gully defends its NE side on the other sides it was protected by double ditches an double banks. On the SW there may have been an outer bailey

ORWELL PARK *see* NACTON

2050

OTLEY

ST MARY. Perp throughout. W tower with former flushwor decoration on the base and brick battlements. A row of shield and foiled shapes above the W doorway. S porch with an entranc decorated by shields up one moulding of jambs and arch. Th same is done in the S doorway. S aisle with typical Perp arcad (four bays). Clerestory. Hammerbeam roof in the nave. Th nave walls as well as the roof cant towards the tower. Interestin roof in the chancel with big curved scrolly pieces of decora tion attached to the principals. The only structural piece otherwise are the collar-beams. There are no real hammer beams. Shields with the symbols of Trinity and Passion an the letters of the word PREPARE. All this is supposed to dat from 1840. – FONT. Octagonal. Four lions against the stem four lions and four angels against the bowl. – Also the grea rarity of an IMMERSION FONT. This is below the floor of th vestry and is 7 by 4 ft in size with curved sides and pointe ends. The theory is that it was used in the mid C17 by Ana baptists. – PULPIT. Jacobean. – WEST DOOR. With tracery an small figures. – BENCH ENDS. With tracery and poppy-heads Also one Jacobean (with heraldry). – SCREEN. The dado i partly original. – PLATE. Elizabethan Cup; a copy of this Cu by *Paul Storr*, who also made a Paten and two identical Chalices His monument is in the chancel S wall (1845).

OTLEY HALL, 1 m. N. One of the most interesting C15 and earl C16 houses in Suffolk. What is preserved of specially remark able features is the four-centred entrance arch with the initial of Robert Gosnold for whom it was built (perhaps not *in situ*) the hall screen with two four-centred arches, the heavil moulded beams and joists of the hall ceiling and its larg eight-light window, and the parlour with its eight-light windov and most beautiful and complete early C16 linenfold panelling In addition a Jacobean wing with a simple staircase, som decoration with painting, and a frieze of pargetting outside

HIGH HOUSE, ½ m. E. A specially attractive timber-framed house of c. 1500. Brick-nogging in parts.

OTLEY BARROW, ¼ m. S of the church. This appears to be misnamed; the mound is in fact a castle motte, and there are traces of its baileys.

OULTON

ST MICHAEL. A Norman church with a central tower. The W and E arches of the central span are preserved, unmoulded arches on the plainest imposts, just one zigzag band facing into the nave. Norman also the S doorway with one zigzag and the yet simpler blocked N doorway. There were transepts too, but their arches are pointed. Dec chancel, Perp N and S windows in the nave. The brick parts at the top of the central tower are probably C18. – FONT. Octagonal, Perp. Four lions against the stem, four flowers, two angels and two lions against the bowl. – WEST GALLERY. 1836. – PLATE. Elizabethan Cup.

(OULTON HIGH HOUSE, Gorleston Road. Two fine elaborate plaster ceilings of the late C16. DOE)

HOUSE, Borrow Road. 1954 by *John & Sylvia Reid.*

HOUSE, Borrow Road and Bret House Lane. 1955–6 by *Tayler & Green.* Inconspicuous, unmannered, and of great charm.

MANCROFT TOWERS, ¼ m. SSW. By *George J. Skipper,* 1898–1900. Large, of brick, in the Elizabethan style, with a massive tower and mullioned and transomed windows, the principal ones with pediments. The hall is 30 by 25 by 18 ft.

OUSDEN

ST PETER. Norman nave. S doorway without shafts. The lintel chip-carved with stars. In the tympanum big lozenges. One S window. The N doorway curious. The l. shaft with a Norman capital, the r. shaft with a moulded C13 capital. Pointed arch with a recurrent ornament in the roll moulding which is like a collar of turned wood. Norman also the central part, provided with a tower. It has arches inside to the W and E with simple shafts and on the capitals scrolls close to the core. To the r. of the E arch of the nave a C13 niche. The chancel itself and the N chapel are C19 brick and Gothic. – FONT. Octagonal, Perp. – COMMUNION RAIL. Later C17; with turned balusters. – PLATE. Cup 1678 or 1736; Paten 1710; Flagon c. 1730; Almsdish c. 1750. – MONUMENT. Laeticia Mosley † 1619. With, at the foot, a gruesome three-quarter skeleton in a shroud.

OUSDEN HALL. Demolished 1955, except for the C18 DOVECOTE and the CLOCK TOWER.

OVERBURY HALL *see* LAYHAM

5090

PAKEFIELD

ST MARGARET AND ALL SAINTS. Really two churches in one. The double dedication represents the fact that there were two parishes and, till 1748, two rectors. (In the C18 the solid wall dividing the two churches was pierced by seven arches. LG) The church was severely damaged in the Second World War and reconsecrated in 1950. But the arcade remained, and, with its octagonal piers and double-chamfered arches (seven bays, no separation of the chancel), it is of the C14. The nuisance of two separate services being held side by side cannot have been regarded as such for so long. The building is two-naved rather than aisled. The tower belongs to the S nave. It is unbuttressed and seems of the same time as the arcade. Both E windows also are Dec. The churchyard still has cottages on three sides and the beach and the sea on the fourth, in spite of the fact that Pakefield is now engulfed in Lowestoft. – FONT. Octagonal, Perp. Against the stem four lions, against the bowl four angels, two white harts (the device of Richard II), and two lions. – SCREEN. A little remains of the dado. – PLATE. Chalice and Paten, inscribed 1769. – BRASSES. John Bowf † 1417 and wife, 2 ft 9 in. figures. – Richard Ffolcard † 1451, a demi-figure, 1 ft 3 in. long.

STOCKS. Outside the N gate to the churchyard.

9060

PAKENHAM

ST MARY. A church with long transepts and crossing tower, something decidedly rare in Suffolk. It is true that only the S transept was built – and re-built in 1849 – and that the N transept was added at that time (by *Teulon*). The transepts and chancel are E.E., late C13 (see the window shapes). The upper part of the tower is C14 and turns octagonal. Several survivals of the preceding Norman church, namely the W and S doorways (one order of shafts, scalloped capitals, heavy roll moulding) and the chancel arch (nook-shafts, saltire crosses in the abacus, moulded arch with one hollow and one half-roll). There was another such arch at the E end of the nave which was altered in 1849. So the Norman church was of the type with nave, central space, and chancel. The nave has two windows with plate

23b tracery. – FONT. Exceptionally good Perp piece. Four seated figures against the stem (somewhat re-cut about 1850?), against the bowl the Signs of the four Evangelists, a dragon with a cross-shaft, a lamb, a unicorn, a pelican. – STALLS. Simple, with poppy-heads. – SCREEN. Simple, and not all original. – COMMUNION RAIL. With twisted balusters, late C17. – PLATE. Cup 1566; Cup and Paten 1817.

NEWE HOUSE. A fine Jacobean brick façade, dated 1622. Completely symmetrical, with three large shaped gables. Windows mullioned and transomed of three and four lights. In the middle a canted bay continuing the round-arched and thinly pedimented doorway and crowned with little lunettes, a rather earlier motif. Square, diagonally placed chimneys.

NETHER HALL. This was the big house at Pakenham, but it seems now entirely Late Victorian (c. 1900, by *Greene & Sons*), except for the four gables on the N side.

WINDMILL. The earliest date in this mill is 1835, but the date of erection is thought to be c. 1820. She has a tarred brick tower of five floors, is about the same height as Friston post-mill, and has four patent sails and a fan-tail. She has a dome-shaped cap with an attractive finial and drives three pairs of stones on the second floor. Lately a gallery has been added to the cap to facilitate painting and repairs. The mill is still in full work and has received a grant for repairs from the Historic Buildings Council.*

MICKLE MERE. A small Roman FORT has been noted from the air between the mill stream and the Grimstone End road.

REDCASTLE FARM. A large Roman VILLA lies to the N of the village on the Great Livermere road; a circular mosaic in a surround of red tesserae (now destroyed) was found in an apse in 1765. Air photographs show possible buildings also on the W side of the road.

GRIMSTONE END, 1¼ m. NE. A brick-floored Roman kiln with a complex system of draught flues and furnaces was found in 1955, and more recently two or possibly three kilns of the common Suffolk 'pedestal' type, and two large floored kilns making coloured-coated wares have been recorded. During quarrying operations in 1960 an unusually small kiln was discovered. Its use as a pottery kiln was confirmed by a pot remaining in the chamber, and its small size may suggest experimental firing. Extensive later excavations‡ have revealed a barrow of the

* This paragraph provided by Mr Wailes.
‡ About which Mr Norman Smedley, of Abbots Hall Museum, Stowmarket, kindly told me.

Early Bronze Age, covering Late Neolithic pottery, and containing eight Roman cremations inserted later. This was overlaid by an Anglo-Saxon site.

A section of Roman BRICKWORK, 9 ft 6 ins thick and constructed on a mortared base, has been reported lying on the parish boundary 200 yds s of the church, on the track leading E from the Thurston Road.

PALGRAVE

1070

St PETER. Along the small green. Dec W tower, unbuttressed. Chancel arch of *c.* 1300, well detailed. The rest of the chancel probably early C19.* N aisle C19. The rest Perp. Ornate s porch. Two-storeyed. Flush-panelled front; flushwork battlements. Entrance with crowns, fleurons, etc., in the arch. Spandrels with St George and the Dragon. Niches l. and r. Nave roof with hammerbeams carrying arched braces which meet at the ridge. The rafters prettily painted with tracery patterns. The roof has no hammer-posts so that the arched braces rest directly on the hammerbeams. – FONT. Late Norman, square, with four big heads at the corners and four crosses in the four fields, a South-Western rather than East Anglian type. Five supports; four with scalloped capitals. – (ARMOUR. Some parish armour above the s doorway. LG) – PLATE. Set 1728. – MONUMENT. In the churchyard tombstone to John Catchpole, wagoner, † 1787. It shows his six-horse team pulling a wagon.

St JOHN'S, 1 m. SW. Early C19, grey brick. Five bays with a semicircular porch on Roman Doric columns. Tripartite window above it, with a segmental arch.

PARHAM

3060

St MARY. Early C14 nave doorways. Dec chancel arch. Dec W tower with a splendid big niche above the W window. The niche was for three images. It has a big cusped arch and a gable with finial and buttress shafts, the latter probably influenced by Butley. (Inside the tower, according to Cautley, the original C14 BELL FRAME.) Finely moulded W doorway. Small quatrefoil windows in the N and S walls of the tower. Perp N porch with flushwork initials etc. at the base, a flushwork-panelled front, and in the spandrels of the entrance a dragon and a man with a club (St George ?). Niche above the entrance.

* Tom Martin the antiquarian (d. 1770) mentions a new chancel in 1729 (ARA).

The nave has six tall Perp two-light windows, the chancel windows are also Perp, also of two lights, but lower. – FONT. With cusped tracery patterns, both Perp and Dec, and three shields. – BENCHES. Four in the chancel, with poppy-heads. – SCREEN. A minimum piece of the Perp style. – COMMUNION RAIL. Mid-C17. – STAINED GLASS. In the E window fragments, also whole small figures. – PLATE. Cup 1785; Paten 1803. – MONUMENTS. Probably from a former monument the heraldic shields in the chancel N wall. – Edmund Warner † 1617 and wife. Incised slab with skeleton. Arms and rising sun in flat relief in sunk ovals. – CURIOSA. In the N door a huge PADLOCK. – HAT BRACKET in the chancel, dated 1716. – STOCKS, preserved in the roofing of the lychgate.

CHURCH FARMHOUSE. On one gable-end C15 buttress shafts and the sill of an oriel with a shield, animals, and a small human figure. By the other gable late C17 re-managements; stuccoed rustication of the window surrounds, and a doorway with a scrolly pediment. (Inside primitively painted C18 panels and a modest plaster ceiling.)

MOAT HALL, ½ m. SE. A wonderful survival. A moated early C16 timber-framed house with substantial brick parts. To the N two canted bays immediately above the moat and traces of a third. They have two- and three-light windows with arched lights, rather low on the ground floor, tall and with transom on the first floor. To the W a fine gable with brick-nogging and a lower brick-faced one. To the S another tall brick window and the traces of the staircase. In addition the GATEWAY with four-centred arch and two niches with Wild Men.

PARHAM HOUSE, I m. NW. Only a fragment, but a most interesting one. What remains is one side of one wing and the beginning of one bay of a recessed centre, all of brick and all with giant pilasters. The date must be c. 1630–50 – an exceedingly early date for giant pilasters in England (cf. Great Queen Street London, Slyfield Manor Surrey, Lees Court Kent, Pocock's School Rye Sussex). On the other hand the pilasters taper so strongly and they have such an odd waistband that dependence on Inigo Jones and the Court Style must be denied. The one remaining corner has curiously bulgy brick rustication. That also would fit in with the 'Artisan Mannerism' of the second third of the C17, to use Sir John Summerson's term. The former centre of the house can be guessed from the position of the gatepiers some distance away.

(ELM TREE FARM. The small doorway has an incongruously big
surround of mid-C17 appearance. It is provided with big pier
which have sunk panels decorated by garlands and a cornice
with foliage scrolls. Might it not be the re-set surround of a
church monument? NMR)

PARK GATE *see* WICKHAMBROOK

PEASENHALL

3060

ST MICHAEL. Perp. w tower with flushwork decoration of
buttresses and battlements. Nave and chancel rebuilt 1860–1
Handsome N porch with flushwork decoration on the front
three niches above the entrance, and in the spandrels of the
entrance a dragon and a Wild Man. – (FONT. Apparently
Norman or Transitional. Octagonal, with interlace pattern and
bulbous corners above the interlace.*) – STAINED GLASS. F
window, a large three-figure Crucifixion, signed by *Thomas
Willement*, 1861.

Behind the church and immediately bordering on the churchyard
the former DRILL MILL, dated 1805 by the DOE. Red brick,
with the typical square, tapering chimney. Front with four
arches.

ANCIENT HOUSE, a little NW of the church, in the village street.
Early C18 front of eight bays. Doorway with Roman Doric
pilasters, a metope frieze, and a pediment. (Inside some C16
linenfold panelling *in situ*. DOE)

(NEW INN, 125 yds NE of the Angel Inn. A small C15 or C16
hall-house with cross-wings, timber-framed and plastered, of
two storeys. The main block has a kingpost roof, still with one
embattled kingpost, and the remains of an original window of
three lights in the rear wall of the upper storey. DOE)

PEASENHALL LODGE, 1 m. NW. Early Georgian, brick, with
five bays and two storeys. Segment-headed windows. Doorway with Roman Doric pilasters and pediment.

(WOODLANDS FARMHOUSE. With a tall shaped brick end-
gable. NMR)

WINDMILL, ½ m. NW. A power-driven smock-mill.

PETTAUGH

1050

ST CATHERINE. Nave and chancel and unbuttressed w tower.
W window Dec. The battlements of the tower with arched
flushwork panelling. S and N doorways into the nave Dec.

---

* Information from D. M. Freeman and others.

Remains of a Norman PILLAR PISCINA. – FONT. Octagonal.
Against the stem four lions, against the bowl four lions and
four angels. – BENCH ENDS. Two, dated 1615, with characteristic poppy-heads. – PLATE. Elizabethan Cup and Paten. –
BRASS. Civilian and wife, c. 1530, the figures 11 in. long
(mounted on a shield!).

PETTISTREE   2050

ST PETER AND ST PAUL. Tall w tower with, at the base and on
the buttresses and the battlements, flushwork decoration in
squares and lozenges. On the s and N sides also such decoration.
Blocked quatrefoil clerestory windows in circles. Chancel
1894. – BENCHES. A few are old. – PLATE. Cup and Cover and
Paten 1704. – (STAINED GLASS. Fragments c 13 and later. LG) –
BRASS. Francis Bacon † 1580 and two wives.
Against the s side of the churchyard the GREYHOUND INN,
formerly perhaps the Church House. Timber-framed. To the
w PETTISTREE LODGE, grey brick with a veranda of four
widely spaced Tuscan columns; probably Late Georgian or a
little later. Further w, belonging to the HOME FARM a square
DOVECOTE on open arches, said to date from c. 1775.
LOUDHAM HALL. See p. 352.

PLAYFORD   2040

ST MARY. s porch tower, nave and chancel. The tower has two
widely separated Perp bell-openings on each side. The entrance
arch is decorated with crowns up one order of jambs and arch
and has an angel at the apex. Shields l. and r., a niche over.
Nicely traceried s window; the same design also in the nave w
window. The nave N doorway seems of c. 1300. The chancel
was rebuilt in 1874. – PLATE. Cup 1619; Paten 1774. – MONU-
MENTS. Good brass (4 ft 9 in. figure) of a Knight, probably Sir
George Felbrigg † 1400. On his jupon a large heraldic lion, no
doubt originally enamelled. – Granite obelisk in the churchyard to Thomas Clarkson, 'the friend of slaves', erected in
1857. – Thomas Clarkson, profile bust in relief in an oval
medallion. By *H. Thornycroft*, 1878. – Sir George Biddell
Airy † 1892. By *F. J. Williamson* of Esher. Frontal bust in
oval medallion. Drapery hangs out over the frame of the
medallion.
PLAYFORD HALL. Fragment of a larger Elizabethan red brick
mansion. What survives is L-shaped. It represents part of the
centre and the w wing projecting to the s. A corresponding E

Playford, brass to Sir George Felbrigg † 1400

wing still existed in the later C18. The front of the wing towards the s is of the early C18, the rest is Elizabethan of 1589
with the windows all re-done. Three mighty chimneybreasts
to the w, facing the moat which surrounds the house.

BARROWS. There is a group of four on the N side of Kesgrave
village. Three are stretched out along the road; the fourth is
some distance to the N.

PLUMPTON HOUSE see WHEPSTEAD

POLSTEAD   9030

ST MARY. Close to Polstead Hall. The age of the church can only
be recognized inside. Originally the church was aisleless and
shorter to the w than it is now. Norman extension by aisles and
a further w bay. Arcade of three bays. Square Norman piers [15a]
with nook-shafts at the angles. These have small capitals.
Rough, single-stepped Norman arches of brick. Clerestory
windows over, also of brick. In addition the w bay remains
separated. It has a brick arch on Norman responds and yet one
more clerestory window. The bricks are most puzzling. They
are in size 10 to 11 in. by 5 to 7 in. by 1¾ in. So they cannot be
Roman: the Roman size is 18 by 12 in. On the other hand the
earliest accepted English bricks, those at Little Coggeshall in
Essex, are 12 by 6 by 1¾ in., and that would go well with Polstead. But Polstead is earlier in all probability, and that would
give it the distinction of having the earliest surviving English
bricks. Norman also are the plain chancel arch and its imposts
and the elaborate w doorway, now leading into the tower and
the window above. The doorway has to the w two orders of
shafts and divers zigzags in the arches. So there was no w tower
originally. The next part in order of time is the w tower of c.
1300 with later spire. It has lancets and Y-tracery. The w arch
of the s arcade may also belong to this period. Of the Dec
style the s doorway, the s aisle E window with reticulated
tracery, and also the N aisle E window with a depressed arch.
Most of the rest is Perp. – FONT. Octagonal, C13, on five supports. – WALL PAINTING. Fragment of a Bishop, nave, N wall.
– COMMUNION RAIL. Three-sided, C18. – STAINED GLASS.
Many fragments, C15 and later, in the chancel. – PLATE. Set
1816. – BRASSES. Priest of the C15, 18 in. figure, chancel N
wall. – Civilian, wife, and children, late C15, 21 in. figure, in
front of the pulpit.

POLSTEAD HALL. Large, simple Georgian house of white brick.
Front with one-storeyed porch *in antis* and two canted bay

windows. Colvin mentions improvements of 1818–19 by *W. Pilkington*. Timber-framed C16 work at the back. (Good interiors.)

At the foot of the rising lane that leads to Hall and church lies the pond, and close to it POND FARMHOUSE. Front of red brick of 1760, back timber-framed and earlier. A square dovecote close by.

POPLARS FARM *see* BRETTENHAM

7040
POSLINGFORD

ST MARY. Very restored. Norman nave with one N window, a fragment of the N doorway, and a good S doorway with one order of shafts with finely decorated scalloped capitals and some geometrical decoration on the abaci. Tympanum with stars, rosettes, and interlace. W tower of the late C13 with triple-chamfered arch towards the nave. Chancel with late C13 windows. Nave with one Dec window with reticulated tracery. Nice Perp S porch of brick with three brick niches above the entrance and brick windows. Nice niche inside a Perp nave window. – SCREEN. Tall, with two-light divisions, segmental arches and tracery over. – PAINTING. C13 scrolls in a chancel window.

(CHIPLEY ABBEY. Farmhouse on the site of Chipley Priory, an Augustinian house founded before 1235. It incorporates a small part of the W range of the claustral buildings. LG)

9050
PRESTON

ST MARY. The W tower was rebuilt in 1868. Dec chancel – see one old S window and the PISCINA in the E jamb of the SE window. Perp aisles and clerestory. The arcade piers have four filleted shafts and squares in the diagonals. Low tomb recess in the N aisle. N porch with rich flushwork panelling. Three-light windows with tracery. Three niches above the entrance. – FONT. Norman, square, with rosettes, stars, intersected arches, a tree of life, and interlace. – ROYAL ARMS and TEN COMMANDMENTS. Painted, of triptych shape, Elizabethan, i.e. exceptionally early, as Commandment Boards go. – STAINED GLASS. About fifty heraldic pieces in the aisle E windows and the clerestory windows. Made, it is said, for Robert Reyce of Preston Hall, † 1638, a noted antiquarian. – In the S aisle a window by *Ward & Hughes*, 1884; terrible. – PLATE. Paten 1624.

PRESTON HALL. Good C16 to C17 house with fine chimneystack. Octagonal chimney-shafts with star tops.

PURTON GREEN see STANSFIELD

RAMSHOLT

3040

ALL SAINTS. Above the Deben estuary. Round, or rather oval, Norman w tower with original archway into the nave. The tower was buttressed later, which gives it an odd outline. Nave and chancel rendered. The nave N and chancel s doorways of *c.* 1300. – FONT. Octagonal, Perp, simple. – PULPIT. An early C19 two-decker. – BOX PEWS. – PLATE. Elizabethan Cup.

RATTLESDEN

9050

ST NICHOLAS. On a slight eminence in the middle of the village. Quite big, with a Dec w tower with clasping polygonal buttresses and a shingled broach-spire. Finely detailed s doorway of *c.* 1300 with a circular window over. In the window a cusped quatrefoil. The s aisle and the clerestory (which has single, not double windows per bay) are given battlements decorated with lozenges and shields. Pretty SE spirelet. The s porch has the same battlements. On the N side the aisle also has them; the clerestory battlements are simple. The s porch has a fine stone-faced façade with a tall entrance. The front is panelled and has one niche above the entrance. (Early C16 chancel chapel with room over. LG) Wide interior. C14 arcades of five bays with octagonal piers, decorated with blank cusped arches at the top, and arches with two hollow chamfers. Good C14 AUMBRY in the chancel N wall. Arched top, crocketed gable, and pinnacles. The tower arch is triple-chamfered. The arch dies into the imposts. The nave roof has double hammer-beams. Unfortunately the angel figures, also those of the arch-braced lean-to roofs in the aisles, are nearly all C19. Below the roof the nave has a large E window. – FONT. C14, octagonal. Panels with thickly decorated ogee arches resting on heads. Castellated top. – SCREEN. Six parts of the dado are preserved under the tower arch. Painted panels, almost unrecognizable, in the back wall of the C19 sedilia. – PULPIT. Jacobean. – BENCHES. Some with poppy-heads. – COMMUNION RAIL. Later C17, re-used in several parts. – STAINED GLASS. Original bits in the w window and the second N window from the E. – E window by *Clayton & Bell*, 1884. – PLATE. Elizabethan Cup; Flagon 1729; Paten 1731.

A timber-framed COTTAGE, SE of the church, by the churchyard, blends happily with the church and the trees.

WINDMILL. A tower-mill, derelict.

CLOPTON HALL. A date 1681 on one of the chimneys. The house is very characteristic of that date. Recessed centre and short projecting wings. Two storeys, timber-framed and plastered, with quoins and hipped roof. The middle bay is given prominence by giant Doric pilasters and a segmental pediment. Unfortunately a porch has been fitted in, which spoils the effect. In it what must have been the big pediment of the doorway.

RAYDON
0030

ST MARY. Mostly late C13 to early C14, see the chancel windows, the nave windows, the N and S doorways, and the priest's doorway (thin shafts and big moulded capitals). On the chancel N side a normal late C13 two-light window with a quatrefoiled circle. The PISCINA inside has the same design – unusual and handsome. The two chancel S windows have in the tracery a circle with a cusped quatrefoil. Low W bell turret with pyramid roof.* Inside the early C14 date is confirmed, apart from the piscina, by a low tomb recess on the N side and by the hoodmoulds of the chancel windows. – BRASS. Lower part of a tiny figure with a butterfly head-dress.

SPIDER HALL (Barrow Hill), Nether Raydon. C16. With a six-bay thatched BARN and a circular early C19 LODGE.

SULLEYS FARM, Nether Raydon. 1704. Seven-bay front of red brick with timber cross-windows. Two weatherboarded BARNS.

REDE
8050

ALL SAINTS. The nave walls are probably Norman – see one window in the NW corner. W tower of c. 1300, see the bell-openings. S porch C15, with pinnacles and a niche crowned by a nodding ogee arch. Chancel 1874. – PULPIT. C17, with scrolls for the bookrest. – BENCHES. Some with poppy-heads. – STAINED GLASS. E window of 1874. It is by Clayton & Bell. – PLATE. Elizabethan Cup; Paten c. 1662.

REDGRAVE
0070

ST MARY THE VIRGIN. All Dec, except for the Perp S aisle

* The LG remarks on the V-shaped buttresses, comparing them to Thorpe Morieux.

windows and the fine clerestory with double windows with panel tracery, and of course except for the w tower of yellow brick, which seems to be of *c*. 1800. The chancel has N and s windows with elongated reticulated tracery and rather common flowing tracery, and a glorious seven-light E window, treated very elaborately and not at all harmoniously. Chancel buttresses with niches and pitched roofs. Very fine s aisle doorway with two orders of delicate shafts with naturalistic leaf capitals. One arch moulding with fleurons etc. Hood-mould on heads. The arcade piers quatrefoil with, in the diagonals, slender shafts with fillets. Arches with wavy mouldings. The chancel arch is of the same design. Perp SEDILIA of beautifully inventive design. Each seat has a canted canopy with a small lierne-vault inside. The canopies are decorated with charming three-light windows. Straight top to the whole sedilia. Perp also the nave roof, with alternating hammerbeams carrying arched braces to the cambered collars and tie-beams carrying queenposts with arched struts. (Vestry roof mid-C16. LG) – FONT. Octagonal, Dec. At the bottom of the bowl eight heads. The panels have gables with many small quatrefoils. – Top of the former REREDOS. Early C18, with PAINTINGS of Moses and Aaron and crazily huge (eight-turn) volutes l. and r. – STAINED GLASS. E window of 1853 by *Thomas Farrow* of Diss. – PLATE. Cup and Cover 1623; two Flagons 1667;* Cup 1668; Paten 1696.

MONUMENTS. An important series, headed by the outstandingly noble monument to Nicholas Bacon and his wife Anne Butts. This is by *Nicholas Stone*, and one of his best works. It was made in 1616, the architectural parts by *Bernard Janssen*, but no doubt to Stone's design. Stone received £200 for the effigies. White and black marble. Restrainedly but tellingly carved effigies. Against the tall tomb-chest inscriptions in cartouches no longer with any memories of strapwork, but in rounded doughy forms characteristic of the mid-C17 future. – Anne Butts † 1609. Brass on the chancel floor, still in the medieval tradition. The figure is 3 ft 3 in. long. At her feet the following inscription:

> The weaker sexes strongest precedent
> Lyes here belowe; seaven fayer yeares she spent
> In wedlock sage; and since that merry age
> Sixty one yeares she lived a widdowe sage

* The Cup is said to be a secular piece and the Cover an adapted Salt cover. The Flagons are deposited at the Fitzwilliam Museum, Cambridge.

Humble as great as full of grace as elde
A second Anna had she beheld
Christ in His flesh whom now she gloeious sees
Belowe that first in time not in degrees.

– By *Nicholas Stone* also the simple tablet to Dorothy Lady
Gawdy † 1621 (chancel s). Oval tablet with thick garlands, segmental pediment at the top, a cherub's head at the foot. – Also
in his style the Bacon tablets of 1660 (Anne Butts) and 1685. –
38a   Sir John Holt, Chief Justice, † 1710. By *Thomas Green* of
Camberwell, his most impressive work. Large tripartite composition. He is seated in the centre between coupled Corinthian
columns. L. and r. stand Justice and Vigilance. On the cornice
putti and putti-groups. The centre is raised and contains a coat
of arms under a segmental top.

REDGRAVE HALL. The house has been demolished. All that
remains are an octagonal domed LODGE of grey brick at the s w
corner of the grounds close to the big lake (doorway with pediment on Tuscan columns), and the STABLES, red brick with
projecting wings and pediment.

In the village street the BARN of Ivyhouse Farmhouse with a
shaped gable and TUDOR LODGE, a five-bay house of the late
C17 with wooden cross-windows.

Bronze or Iron Age SHERDS and occupation material and two
HUTS were found under Beer Lane, N of the church.

RED HOUSE *see* HOXNE *and* MONEWDEN

REDHOUSE FARMHOUSE *see* WITNESHAM

4080   REDISHAM

ST PETER. The w tower fell more than a hundred years ago.
Nave and chancel. Elaborate Norman s doorway with one
order of spiral-fluted colonnettes. The arch has two orders of
zigzag, one of lobed crenellation, and one of raised circles with
cross decoration. A billet frieze runs up the frame of the doorway. The N doorway is simple. One order of colonnettes. One
arch order with zigzag, and in addition lobed crenellation on the
soffit not the front of another order. The chancel E and s
windows are Dec.–FONT. Octagonal, Perp, simple. – BENCHES.
Two in the chancel with poppy-heads and animals on the arms.
– PULPIT. Square; dated 1619. To that date belong some flat
carving and the brackets for the book-rest. – PLATE. Cup
c. 1567.

MOUND, ¾ m. SW of the village. On Mill Mount; a castle mound, presumably later used for the base of a windmill.

REDLINGFIELD

1070

ST ANDREW. The W tower was of red brick with blue diapering. It is only left as a much patched-up stump with a saddle-back roof. Nave and chancel also heavily repaired. But the S doorway and the chancel E window, both Dec, are in order. On the N side a brick window. – FONT. Octagonal, against the stem four lions and four Wild Men, against the bowl four angels and the four Signs of the Evangelists. – PLATE. Cup and Paten *c.* 1620.

NUNNERY. Just S of the church a BARN of flint with buttresses and fragments of windows. This forms part of the buildings of the Benedictine nunnery founded by the Count of Guisnes in 1120.

RENDHAM

3060

ST MICHAEL. W tower with bell-openings with Y-tracery and battlements and buttresses with flushwork panelling. Nave with one lancet, one Dec, and several Perp windows. Chancel E window probably of *c.* 1600. – PULPIT. With back panel and tester. With the familiar short blank arches and attached ornamental piers of the exclamation-mark kind. Dated 1632. – PLATE. Cup and Paten 1567. – BRASS. Chalice and inscription to Thomas Kyng, vicar, † 1523.

CONGREGATIONAL CHURCH and MANSE. Very modest, of red brick. Built in 1750.

RENDLESHAM

3050

ST GREGORY. The W tower has on its base a flushwork chequer-board pattern and on its battlements the same but with lozenges. The tower arch shows the tower to be Dec. Nave and chancel with Perp windows. The E window with its fanciful Dec tracery is of 1783 (*Gent. Mag.*) and made of wood. In the chancel a pretty PISCINA with a frame beset with fleurons. – FONT. Octagonal. Against the stem four lions; against the bowl four lions and four angels. – COMMUNION RAIL. With strong, amphora-like balusters, probably mid-C17, but much renewed. – PLATE. Set of 1812–13. – MONUMENTS. A splendid tomb recess in the chancel, obviously *c.* 1330–40. Thickly crocketed ogee arch; two slender buttress shafts with finials l. and r. Cusped and sub-cusped arch. The figure of a Civilian disappointing. Two semi-reclining angels by his pillow. –

Lady Rendlesham † 1814. Standing monument of white and grey marble. On the base kneel two white figures, one hiding her face, the other looking upward, where, in white relief against a grey obelisk, Lady Rendlesham's body is taken up by an angel. Unsigned. – Lord Rendlesham † 1832. By *H. Hopper*. Gothic monument of triptych shape. L. and r. standing figures. In the middle inscription. – Lady Rendlesham † 1840. By *Aristodemo Costoli*, of Florence, 1842. She rises gently to heaven. The decoration on the watershed between neo-classicism and Victorianism, see e.g. the naturalistic roses.

RECTORY. Whitewashed brick. Early C18, of seven bays with a pedimented three-bay centre.

RENDLESHAM HALL. Exists no longer, but two LODGES survive. And may they long survive; for they are the most memorable follies of Suffolk. The WOODBRIDGE LODGE is a cemented structure, one-storeyed like normal lodges, but surmounted by a curve of three heavy flying buttresses joining to support not a pinnacle but the chimney. The central room is hexagonal. IVY LODGE, 1½ m. SW of Tunstall, is a sham ruin. The big archway has Norman shafts with scalloped capitals but an arch looking *c.* 1300. To its l. is a low ruined turret also with some details meant to look Norman. To the r. is the lodge proper. Its chimney is of flint and indistinct in outline. Both lodges are dated *c.* 1790 by the DOE.

The GROUNDS of Rendlesham Hall were laid out by *Humphry Repton* and are illustrated in his *Theory* of 1803.

At THIRSTLY BELT, about half way between Rendlesham Hall and the Campsea Ash road, is a ring of trees defined by a shallow DITCH, with another shallow ditch dividing it from E to W. This may be connected with the seat of the Saxon Wuffingas dynasty (*see* Introduction, pp. 24–5); there is however no conclusive evidence for its site beyond such clues as the report of the discovery in 1690 of a gold or silver crown, and later evidence for the discovery of a Saxon urn.

REYDON

ST MARGARET. The W tower early C14, and probably basically earlier. Flat stair-turret projection. Battlements with flush-work decoration. The nave and chancel have Perp windows throughout. Inside, most of them have image niches in their E jambs. On the buttresses and the S porch a little flushwork decoration. The foundations of a N chapel were discovered in 1952. – STAINED GLASS. In the E window by *Ward & Hughes*,

1884, in one chancel N window by *A. L. Moore, c.* 1886; both bad. – PLATE. Cup and Cover 1568; Salver 1881. – (Large MONUMENT in the churchyard to Mrs Watts, signed *Paul R. Montford*, 1921. A boldly stepped base and on it three bronze figures: a gentleman in a cloak, a demi-nude man kneeling and weeping, and an angel with up-spread wings. G. McHardy)

REYDON HALL. 1682, much altered and added to in 1860 (Kelly). The date 1682 appears on a big shaped gable whose top is as usual semicircular and whose two side steps are convex-concave again as usual. The original windows are of the cross type, with wooden casements.

RICKINGHALL INFERIOR   *0070*

ST MARY. Norman round tower with arch on plain imposts to 6a the nave. The tower top is of the early C14. It is octagonal and has elaborate flushwork battlements with quatrefoils, shields, etc. Of the early C14 also chancel and chancel arch (one leaf capital) and the S aisle and S porch. The porch is two-storeyed. The sides have two small windows with Y-tracery, and between them, a little higher up, a quatrefoil window. On the upper floor below the window flushwork emblems. Inside heavy two-bay arcading with a semi-octagonal middle shaft. The S aisle is curious. The four-bay arcade with its piers of quatrefoiled section, the lobes with fillets, and spurs in the diagonals, and with its arches of one chamfer and one sunk quadrant moulding, looks early C14. But the S windows are of a type more late C13 than early C14. Two pointed-trefoiled lights with pointed trefoils over and in the head three circles with quatrefoils (cf. Thelnetham). The SE window on the other hand has dainty foliage in the various spandrels, and that is of the knobbly kind of after 1300. The S aisle E window is Perp, the W window of a rather muddled early C14 design, still without any ogees. Inside the E window the shafting of its Dec predecessor and a charming leaf frieze below the sill. The aisle has buttresses with crocketed gables and spirelets. – FONT. Octagonal, early C14, with fine tracery patterns of the various types found in windows. One of them is remarkably similar to the S aisle W window. – (REREDOS. With panels from the rood-loft. LG) – STAINED GLASS. Fragments in the SE window. – PLATE. Elizabethan Cup.

BROOM HILLS, ¾ m. N. Dark brick with rubbed dressings. Late C17 or early C18. Six bays, two storeys, with pedimented doorway and pitched roof. The house was the Dower House of Redgrave Hall.

At Rickinghall Inferior a Romano-British pottery KILN has been found, dating from the late C1 or early C2.

CALKE WOOD. Iron Age site, *see* Wattisfield, p. 477.

RICKINGHALL SUPERIOR

0070

ST MARY, 1 m. SW of the village, ½ m. S of the church of Rickinghall Inferior. W tower Dec with battlements panelled in flushwork and small upper quatrefoil windows. Chancel Dec with a delightful E window. Intersected tracery finely filled in with smaller patterns. Ogee-headed priest's doorway. Perp PISCINA with crenellated top. Nave with rough stone and flint chequer patterns. Very large Perp three-light windows with small and busy tracery under four-centred arches. At the base flushwork frieze with shields. Two-storeyed S porch with flushwork decoration. Initials above the entrance. Tierceron-vault inside. The nave is wide. All along the N and S walls run stone seats. On these stand shafts which carry arches embracing the windows. – FONT. Octagonal, Dec, with elaborately cusped blank tracery patterns. – PLATE. Cup probably Elizabethan; Paten 1710.

RINGSFIELD

4080

ALL SAINTS. Unbuttressed W tower, the top C17 flint and brick panelling. Nave and chancel in one. Much rebuilt by *Butterfield* in 1883, the chancel completely. C16 S porch with stepped gable, probably Elizabethan. – FONT. Octagonal, Perp. Four lions against the stem, lions, angels, flowers against the bowl. – PULPIT. Jacobean, with back panel and tester. – PEWS. Of the same date and style as the pulpit. The ends are straight-topped. The ends towards the middle passage have, alternatingly, nice knobs. – SCREEN. Only side parts, framing a wide entrance. Jacobean, with balusters and obelisks above the dado. – PLATE. Cup Elizabethan; Paten probably Elizabethan. – MONUMENTS. A strange recess in the outer chancel S wall: a brick aedicule with pilasters and pediment and inside it a segmental arch under which an inscription with a pediment. Below that a BRASS to Nicholas Garneys † 1599 and family. Inspired by the Garneys brass at Kenton, which was that of his great-grandparents. The niche looks *c.* 1700. – Robert Shelford † 1701. Very plain, with pediment and sunk panels; nice inscription. The monument was erected during his life-time and may well help to date the outer aedicule as well. – Caroline Murat, grand-daughter of Napoleon's sister. In the churchyard, erected in 1902. Large angel pointing with one hand to heaven and holding a trumpet in the other. A big recumbent cross at his feet. Two kneeling angels as well. Signed by *Sanders* of London, but rather Père Lachaise in style.

RECTORY. Early C19. Five bays, two storeys, red brick. Extended by walls l. and r. with blank arches. Also undulating forcing walls (crinkle-crankle walls).

RINGSHALL

0050

ST KATHERINE. Unbuttressed Norman w tower. An original s window on the ground floor, and an altered N window. Norman windows in the nave, two on the N side (visible only inside), one altered on the s. The tower was completed and remodelled *c.* 1300, see the arch towards the nave with triple chamfering dying into the imposts. Of the same time the simple s doorway, and the chancel s doorway. Dec chancel E window, and also Dec the timber s porch. Very rough nave roof with tie-beams, crown-posts, and two-way struts. The tie-beams are placed uncommonly low and go right through the walls. In the chancel hammerbeam roof with arched braces to collar-beams. Arched braces also connecting the wall-posts from w to E. These braces are carved. – FONT. C13; Purbeck marble, octagonal. With the usual two shallow blank pointed arches on each side. – PLATE. Cup and Cover Elizabethan.

(THE CHESTNUTS. In the garden an undulating brick forcing wall. N. Scarfe)

(HILLHOUSE FARMHOUSE. Early C17, with a good staircase with pierced slat balusters. NMR)

RISBY

7060

ST GILES. Norman round tower. Two tiers of arched openings at the top. Rude arch with one order of shafts into the nave. Norman nave – see the top of one former window visible inside. The windows mostly *c.* 1300; also of that date the doorway. Norman chancel arch, or at least Dec chancel arch in which Norman imposts and abaci and a whole order of Late Norman arch decoration are re-used. To the l. and r. of the wide pointed arch richly Dec niches, two l. and two r., with crocketed ogee gables. The chancel is clearly Dec. The tracery is of the reticulated kind. To the l. and r. of the E window niches with ogee arches. Also ogee-arched PISCINA. Contemporary a small and pretty N doorway with hood-mould on head-stops. – FONT. Octagonal, Perp, with the Signs of the Evangelists and the Annunciation. – PULPIT. Jacobean. – SCREEN. Narrow but uncommonly fine. L. and r. of the entrance one three-light division (three-light divisions are unusual in Suffolk). Crock-eted ogee lights with a trellis of cusped tracery over. – BENCHES. With poppy-heads and decorated seat-backs. – WALL PAINT-INGS. A memorable series, though only dimly recognizable. On the N wall, near the W end, a large Ecclesiastic, c. 1200 or a little later. Of the same time scenes in arcades a little further E: the Nativity Story above (e.g. Massacre of the Innocents, Flight into Egypt), Lives of Saints below. Much scroll-work of the C13. Noli me tangere, W of the W window, late C14. – ALTAR CROSS, designed by *Pugin*. – STAINED GLASS. Chancel SE many C14 fragments. – Nave SE by *Kempe*, c. 1892. – PLATE. Silver-gilt Paten c. 1580; silver-gilt Chalice 1633.

BARROWS, c. ½ m. S of Black Ditches (*see* Cavenham, p. 161), one each side of the road. Both were examined in 1869. One revealed cremations, the other inhumation and cremation burials and a secondary inhumation with a typical Iron Age 'Marnian' pot. A second pair lies about ½ m. NE, and yet another on the parish boundary, on Risby Poor's Heath, to the W of the track to Lackford. (*See* also Flempton, p. 214.)

RISHANGLES

1060

ST MARGARET. S porch tower. Entrance with one order of jambs and arch decorated with fleurons. Battlements decorated with blank flushwork arcading. In the nave Norman windows, one S and one N. Inside, in the N wall, traces of yet another. The others mostly Perp. The S doorway is Transitional. One order of colonnettes with the most elementary moulded capitals. Round arch with one keeled roll moulding. Hood-mould with dog-tooth ornament. – FONT. A curious piece, most probably a self-conscious imitation of Perp East Anglian fonts. The bowl corresponds to what is only too familiar. But against the stem, in niches, standing figures in the costume of 1530. It is said that the font was dated 1599. If that is true, it would be an interestingly early case of medievalism. – BENCHES. With poppy-heads. – STAINED GLASS. Bits in the tracery of the nave S window. – PLATE. Elizabethan Cup; Paten c. 1610.

ROGERS *see* NEWTON

ROOK HALL *see* EYE

ROOS HALL see BECCLES

ROUGHAM   9060

ST MARY.* S aisle and the very special S porch, chancel, and N
aisle all Dec; tower and much remodelling Perp. The S porch
has three-light side openings not with mullions but with strong
shafts. Ogee arches and straight top. Finely moulded entrance
arch. The S and N aisles both have simple Dec E windows. W
lancet in the S aisle. The other S aisle windows Late Perp without tracery. N aisle and clerestory embattled with enriched
lozenges as decoration. Perp N aisle windows. The chancel is
not embattled. It has a large five-light window with reticulated
tracery. The W tower has below the top a lively frieze of tracery
motifs and a parapet with flushwork decoration. On it were
recorded John Tillot and 'Drury', no doubt Sir Roger (see
below), and no doubt both as donors. On a N aisle buttress the
date 1514 and the name of a rector. Dec arcades with piers of
four strong shafts and in the diagonals four thin ones without
capitals. Double-chamfered arches. The chancel arch is of the
same design. Nave roof with hammerbeams with arch-braces
joining moulded principals and cambered collars. Headless
angels against them. Wall-plate decorated with quatrefoil
friezes. – FONT. Octagonal, with simple arches of different
forms. – BENCHES. A whole set, ends with tracery patterns of
great variety. Poppy-heads. The figures on the arms have been
cut off. – STAINED GLASS. Bits in the N aisle E window. –
PLATE. Set 1683. – BRASS. Fine large brass of Sir Roger
Drury (death date blank) and his wife who died in 1405. The
figures 4 ft long.

ROUGHAM HALL. Large picturesque brick mansion of c. 1834,
with battlements and towers. Derelict at the time of writing.

ROMAN BARROW, on EASTLOW HILL, at the intersection of
the Rougham Green road with the old Roman route now taken
by the road from Little Whelnetham; the only survivor of a
group of four, originally forming a line NE–SW, and excavated
in 1843–6. The three now destroyed were c. 50 ft in diameter,
the southernmost being intersected by the modern road. Two
of them contained cist burials, glass ware, and early C2 A.D.
terra sigillata. The larger barrow on Eastlow Hill covered a
brick-gabled burial chamber on a mortared footing. In it was
an unaccompanied extended male skeleton contained in a lead

* Wills of 1460, 1461, 1462, 1464/5, and 1472 give the dedication as St
John. They also leave money to the fabric of the new tower (ARA).

coffin which probably had a wooden inner casing. The absence of finds may point to a Christian burial. About 250 yds E, remains of a Roman building with white stucco flooring were also found in the 1840s.

RUMBURGH

ST MICHAEL AND ST FELIX. The church was built, not as a parish church, but as the church of a small Benedictine Priory founded c. 1065 from Hulme and in the second half of the C12 given to St Mary, York. The plan is oddly Saxon. Broad W tower (instead of a Saxon porch), nave of the same width and chancel of the same width. No aisles, no chapels. The most impressive part is the W tower or W block, wider than it is deep. It stands close to a group of maple trees. It dates in its present form from the mid C13. Small, insignificant doorway with continuous double-chamfer. Above three tall, widely-spaced lancet windows, the middle one slightly taller than the others. Low angle buttresses. Above that a timber storey, weatherboarded, and an odd hipped roof. The tower arch towards the nave has one continuous chamfer and one semi-octagonal respond. The simply chamfered S doorway and N chancel doorway could be of the same date or about fifty years older. (In the N wall of the chancel a grated watching-window from the former dormitory. LG) – SCREEN. With one-light divisions, ogee arches and much cusped tracery over them. – PULPIT. Jacobean, on a sturdy baluster foot. Scrolls help to support the body. – BENCHES. Some with old poppy-heads. – PLATE. Cup and Cover 1569; Paten 1806.
ABBEY FARMHOUSE. Timber-framed with detail of the late C17. It stands on the site of the refectory of the priory.

RUSHBROOKE

ST NICHOLAS. A small church, with a Dec W tower, but otherwise Perp,* and mostly of brick. There is a S but no N aisle. Stepped gables. Very strange interior. The S aisle is of two bays, followed by one which is the family pew, followed by yet one more which is the funeral chapel. Moreover, the nave is treated in its Early Victorian furnishings as a chancel, or as a college chapel, i.e. with STALLS facing each other instead of pews. All this is said to have been the handiwork of Col. Rushbrooke c. 1840. He used a number of bits of medieval woodwork. In addition there is the rare survival of the ROOD BEAM, carved

* The LG suggests the late C16.

and supported by arched braces, standing on small figures which themselves stand on bases beneath which is the top of a further canopy. And finally, above the rood beam is a TYM-PANUM, again a rarity, and displayed on it the carved and painted ROYAL ARMS of Henry VIII, not only rare, but, it is maintained by Cautley, unique. (Excellent roofs: arch-braced in the nave, and with cambered tie-beam in the chancel. A. Clifton-Taylor) – FONT. Of timber, also by *Col. Rushbrooke*. – STAINED GLASS. Fragments in the S and N windows, and especially the E window, where there are two complete figures. – PLATE. Silver-gilt Set of 1661, Parisian. – MONUMENTS. Thomas Jermyn † 1692. White and black standing monument. Reclining figure, one hand resting on a skull. Background with open pediment. – Sir Robert Davers † 1722. No effigy. Grey sarcophagus below broken pediment with well carved garland. – Several minor monuments.

THE HAMLET. From 1955 to 1963 Lord Rothschild rebuilt the hamlet, which lies to the immediate S and W of the church. The hamlet was designed by *Richard Llewelyn-Davies* and *John Weeks*. The principle applied, a principle equally convincing visually and socially, was to group the houses in such a way that they should form a homogeneous entity instead of a mechanical repetition of identical units in pairs or terraces. The plans of the cottages are not identical, but varied from a basic standard plan, and their positions are staggered in a variety of ways. They are connected by high walls so as to emphasize the privacy of the single house from inside and the unity of the whole village from outside. Brick, rendered. Sloping roofs of single or double pitch carried low down. Single-storey, but with a store- or play-room in the roof. The centre of the estate is a Well House which was already in existence. The Club House (or village hall) lies at the end towards the church.

RUSHBROOKE HALL has been demolished – a tragedy.* It must have dated from *c.* 1550, a date rare in major English mansions, and belonged to the same type as Melford Hall and Kentwell Hall. Like Melford and Kentwell it was of red brick and had a recessed centre with two long projecting wings, and like Kentwell it had two polygonal turrets at their end, only here standing at the outer, not the inner angles. Most of the fenestration was C18. The exception was the mullioned and

---

* Doorcases and a fireplace have been re-used at St Edmund (R.C.), Bury St Edmunds (*see* p. 145).

transomed windows in the gable-ends of the wings. The eaves line was broken by some pedimented dormers. The centre was a porch flanked at the angles by Tuscan columns. In the porch a round-headed doorway. On the porch two pilasters crowned by supporters. Between the pilasters coat of arms. The opposite side had been completely georgianized, except for angle turrets. Eleven bays, two storeys, with three-bay pediment. Inside was a spacious entrance hall with gay Rococo stucco decoration, and to its l. side a free-wheeling staircase, i.e. a flying curved staircase with a large open well. Wrought-iron handrail.

9080

RUSHFORD HALL

¼ m. SE of Rushford, Norfolk

(Large, early C18.)

4080

RUSHMERE

ST MICHAEL. Round tower, the bell-openings of c. 1300. Blocked lancet windows below and a pointed tower arch towards the nave. Nave and chancel; both thatched. Their fenestration also looks c. 1300. Pretty PISCINA, small, set in the E jamb of the SE window. Ogee arch and a little blank tracery above it. Tall stone niche W of the S door, probably for use as a BANNER STAFF LOCKER. – FONT. Against the stem four lions. The bowl has four angels and four flowers and square leaves. – PULPIT. With Jacobean panels and back panel. – PLATE. Paten 1712; Cup and Paten 1715.

RUSHMERE HALL. With stepped gable-ends carrying finials. The house is three bays long and has window pediments on the ground floor and the upper floor. The windows themselves are altered. The house is Elizabethan, and so the windows probably originally had mullions and transoms.

2040

RUSHMERE ST ANDREW

ST ANDREW. By *E. C. Hakewill* (GR), 1861, except for the W tower and the S doorway. The tower has arched flushwork decoration on the double-stepped battlements. The Signs of the Evangelists (renewed) instead of pinnacles at the corners, and normal pinnacles on the middle of the sides. Money was bequeathed in 1521 for the tower to be built 'of like fashion, bigness and workmanship with that at Tuddenham'. The S doorway is Norman, with one order of spiral-fluted colonnettes and an arch with much zigzag. – PLATE. Two Almsdishes 1812.

ST JOHN'S *see* PALGRAVE

ST OLAVE'S PRIORY *see* HERRINGFLEET

SANTON DOWNHAM

8080

ST MARY. Small, Norman, with an unbuttressed Perp w tower. At the foot of the tower initials in stone-carved panels and also the names of those who gave money for its erection (John Watt, John Reve, John Dow..., Margret Reve, Patsey Styles, William Toller).* Some flushwork panelling too. Norman s doorway with spiral-fluted shafts and roll-moulded arch, N doorway the same but with altered arch. Above the s doorway an interesting carved panel, a lion in profile, its tail ending in a kind of fleur-de-lis. Norman window splay on the N side converted into a lancet. Priest's doorway into the chancel Norman, but with some dog-tooth in the arch. Not *in situ*. Chancel with C13 N windows and a low tomb recess. One Dec s window. The church had a s chapel. Part of its pointed arch has been uncovered and has C13 WALL PAINTING of thin scrolls. There was also a N chapel. The moulding of the arch looks *c.* 1300. – PULPIT. Jacobean. – SCREEN. Very early C14. Shafts, not mullions. Wide ogee-arched entrance with tracery over. – BENCHES. Two with poppy-heads. – STAINED GLASS. Several windows by *Kempe*, including the w window of *c.* 1880–1. – PLATE. Elizabethan Cup and Cover.

(FORESTRY COMMISSION REDEVELOPMENT. By *Kenneth Wood*, 1967. An excellent group of three elements: administration offices, servicing buildings and fire station, and stores. The development forms a large element in the village group. Rough, over-burnt stock bricks, black stained unwrought timber, chosen to relate to the strong character of local flint and tile vernacular.)

Just sw of High Lodge House, in Downham High Lodge Warren, an Early Iron Age FARMSTEAD was excavated in 1935. It was marked by pits and hearths containing pottery.

SAPISTON

9070

ST ANDREW. Nave, chancel, and w tower; s porch. All *c.* 1300 and a little later. The only older element is the s doorway:

* Cf. West Tofts, near by but in Norfolk.

Norman, with two orders of shafts, single-scalloped capitals, and arch with an unusual ornamental motif.

3060

SAXMUNDHAM

St JOHN BAPTIST. w tower Dec with flushwork decoration of the parapet. N aisle 1851. s aisle Perp. Attached to its w side was formerly a s porch. Attached to its E side the Swann Chapel of two bays built in 1308. This date is well confirmed by the one window with Y-tracery, and also by the arcade with circular pier, circular abacus, and double-chamfered arches. The s aisle arcade has octagonal piers and arches with three slight chamfers, also not a late form. The E respond of the aisle arcade has the demi-figure of an angel as its capital. Clerestory Perp. Beneath the last clerestory window on the N side a pretty castellated frieze with fleurons, connected no doubt with the rood. Beneath the window opposite an inscription (Sanct. Johannes ora pro nobis). Hammerbeam roof. – FONT. Octagonal, Perp, with two lions and two Wild Men against the stem, four lions and four angels against the bowl. Jacobean cover. – REREDOS. Victorian Gothic, by *Thomas Thurlow* of Saxmundham, 1873. – SCREEN. Two bays of the traceried dado are now the front of a table in the chancel. – STAINED GLASS. In the s aisle E window a number of Flemish C16 and C17 panels. In the s chapel one two-light window by *Powell*, 1873, designed by *Wooldridge*, characteristic of progressive work of the seventies, more like Crane than like William Morris. – PLATE. Cup and Paten 1757.* – MONUMENTS. Charles Long † 1778 and wife. In a refined Louis XVI taste, with little ornamentation. – Beeston Long † 1785 and wife. Signed by *W. Tyler*. Similar. – Charles Long † 1812 by *Nollekens*. With a big seated weeping putto on a sarcophagus. – Lord Farnborough † 1838. By *Sir Richard Westmacott*, with a profile head on a circular medallion. – J. C. Crampin † 1869. By *Thurlow*. An elaborate Gothic frame.

The church lies a little outside the town, at its s end, to the E, on the N boundary of the estate of HURTS HALL, a neo-Elizabethan mansion of 1893, replacing one of 1803 by *Samuel Wyatt*. About 200 yds SE of the house the largest DOVECOTE in Suffolk, brick, octagonal, with a high-pitched roof and a glazed lantern.

In the main street of Saxmundham little need be noted. The centre is the BELL HOTEL of 1842. Grey brick, five bays, two

* C15 church BELL with the Signs of the four Evangelists.

and a half storeys, with a Tuscan porch. Immediately adjoining it on the s, and a little recessed as if it were an assembly room, is the former TOWN HALL of 1846, also grey brick, three bays, with three blank arches and a decorated parapet. The motif of the blank arches is carried forward on the end wall of the Bell Hotel and the other house adjoining the Town Hall so as to stress the little *place* in front of the Town Hall. Walking N from here one passes the POST OFFICE and TELEPHONE EX-CHANGE, a clean, perfectly unmannered job, mostly of curtain walling. 1953–4 by *T. F. Winterburn*.

A little further on, past the railway, on the l. a house with a pretty and funny Gothic doorway, on the r. a stately early C18 house, lying slightly back. Red brick, five bays, two storeys, parapet, hipped roof. Doorway with Tuscan pilasters, a metope frieze, and a segmental pediment. Its l. hand neighbour is similar but a little less formal.

SAXSTEAD

ALL SAINTS. Nave and chancel. The tower fell in 1805. s porch with a front panelled in flushwork. Spandrels of the entrance with animals in scrolly foliage. s doorway with fleuron enrich-ment up the jambs and arch. Fine Dec chancel with a large three-light E window with flowing tracery. Also in the chancel angle PISCINA with ogee arches. Hammerbeam roof in the nave with tracery above the hammers and decorated wall-plate. – FONT. Octagonal, Perp, simple. – REREDOS. With parts of the rood screen. – CREED, COMMANDMENTS, and LORD'S PRAYER, painted, C18. – BENCHES. With poppy-heads. – COMMUNION RAIL. Later C17. – PLATE. Elizabethan Cup. – STOCKS. Kept in the porch.

WINDMILL, Saxstead Green. A typical East Suffolk post-mill. She is only a few feet shorter than Friston Mill, with three-storey round-house, white painted buck with a hooded porch, four patent sails, and a fan-tail. There are two pairs of stones in the breast of the buck and two pairs and a centrifugal dressing machine, all engine-driven, in the round-house. It is not known when she was built, but the earliest reference to her is in 1706. She has been altered and raised more than once, and though no longer in work she is in the care of the Department of the Environment.*

* Mr Wailes kindly wrote this paragraph.

2040

SECKFORD HALL

1½ m. E of Great Bealings

Built some time between 1553 and 1585. Red brick. A long, symmetrical N front. Big stepped gables to the l. and r. and beneath them four- to two-light transomed windows with pediments. The gables are followed by smaller ones towards the centre, two l. and two r. In the centre a two-storeyed porch without a gable. This centre and the two gabled wings have polygonal angle shafts with very good finials. It has been suggested that the façade was originally E-shaped and the infilling done shortly after its erection. This would account for the unusual fact that the hall does not fill the depth of the house, but that there are small rooms N of it. The hall has kept its screen with Roman Doric columns. Another screen is clearly of ecclesiastical origin. It is said to come from a church in Somerset. Towards the S two projecting wings of unequal length. The longer one has a doorway with Doric pilasters and a pediment. The same motif repeats in the centre, and here the Doric is followed on the first floor by the Ionic. Many windows are renewed. The house was partly in ruins thirty years ago and is altogether much restored. To the NW a fine BARN with a diapered gable-end. To the NE a SUMMER HOUSE, square, tall, with stepped gables.

9040

SEMER

ALL SAINTS. In the meadow by the stream amid old trees. Much renewed. Chancel 1873, timber S porch 1899. – FONT. Square, plain, C14. – PAINTINGS. Moses and Aaron, C18. – PLATE. Elizabethan Cup and Cover.

4030

SHADINGFIELD

ST JOHN BAPTIST. W tower, and nave and chancel in one. Transitional nave, see one still entirely Norman N window and the two doorways, both with pointed arches, one with dogtooth, the other with slight chamfers. C13 chancel, see one lancet window. The rest of the chancel mostly of 1841. S porch of brick with embattled top and polygonal buttresses, first half of the C16. Corbel heads at the division between nave and chancel inside, probably for the rood beam. – Long, narrow BANNER STAFF LOCKER N of the tower arch. – FONT. On three steps, the third in the shape of a Maltese cross. This fragmentary step has quatrefoil decoration. The bowl is supported by heads and has shields and flowers in various foiled shapes. – ORGAN CASE. Nice, late C18. – ALTAR CLOTH. Linen, edged with lace, presented on Christmas Day 1632. – PLATE. Almsdish 1778; Cup and Paten 1780.

SHADINGFIELD HALL. Built by the then Rector in 1814. Grey brick, five bays, two and half storeys. Porch with Greek Doric columns. The ground-floor windows under blank arches.

(MOAT FARMHOUSE. C16. One room with linenfold panelling. DOE)

SHELLAND
9060

KING CHARLES THE MARTYR. Mainly of 1767. Plastered bell-turret with ogee cap. The windows must have been altered after 1767. The chancel inside, on the other hand, retains a pretty Gothic cornice, and the strong blue colour of the plaster ceiling may also be C18. – FONT. Octagonal, with big, coarse leaf panels and three shields. – BOX PEWS and TWO-DECKER PULPIT.

SHELLEY
0030

ALL SAINTS. An irregular group. E.E. chancel, see the blocked s lancets. The nave projects w beyond the N tower. The latter is early C14; so is the s aisle (see one window with intersected tracery). Low arcade with octagonal piers and double-chamfered arches. Late Perp N window, straight-headed, of four lights. Late Perp brick N chapel with brick windows. The arch from the chancel into the chapel has been replaced by an oblong opening panelled with various ornamental panels. – CHANCEL STALLS with poppy-heads and the Tylney arms. – PULPIT. With linenfold panels. More linenfold panels used in BENCH FRONTS. – MONUMENTS. In the chancel N wall a Late Gothic tomb-chest. Arms under arches. – In the N chapel a fine square panel with the Tylney arms, c. 1540–50. – Dame Margaret Tylney, 1598. Recumbent effigy, stumps of flanking columns.

SHELLEY HALL. Important fragment of Sir Philip Tylney's mansion. Sir Philip died in 1533. Red brick with blue diapering. Gateway, now at the end of the house and blocked, with panelled polygonal buttresses.* More buttresses on front and back, and at the back also two original brick windows.

* Cf. Great Cressingham, Norfolk.

SHIMPLING

8350

St George. Reached along an avenue of lime trees. Mostly Dec,
see the E window with a usual pattern of flowing tracery, the
segment-headed s aisle windows, the N windows, and the
arcade inside of low octagonal piers and arches with one chamfer and one hollow chamfer. The chancel s doorway has a
frieze of dog-tooth inside, a motif usually earlier than the date of
the church. – FONT. Odd, octagonal, probably C14. Stem with
eight attached shafts. Bowl shallow with quatrefoils and
tracery. – MONUMENTS. Elizabeth Plampin † 1774. By *R.
Westmacott Sen.* Woman standing by an urn on a sarcophagus. – Thomas Hallifax † 1850. Unsigned. Niche with two
angels in profile kneeling symmetrically against an altar with
a cross over it.

(SHIMPLING HALL, near the church. It dates from *c.* 1475.
P. G. M. Dickinson)

SHIPMEADOW

3090

St Bartholomew. W tower, early C16, of flint and brick.
Nave and chancel. The windows mostly of *c.* 1300 (Y-tracery),
but one blocked Norman N window. – FONT. Octagonal, Perp.
Four lions against the stem, three shields and five flowers and
square leaves against the bowl. – SCREEN. Only the dado.
Unusual the blank tracery with a mullion reaching up into the
apex of the four-centred arch.

Former WORKHOUSE. A large building of red brick, erected in
1765. E-shaped plan with the front of nineteen bays unbroken
and the wings at the back. Small windows, hipped roof. In 1866
G. E. Street added a CHAPEL. Red brick, apsed, with a flèche
at the E end of the nave. Windows of two lights with plate
tracery.

SHORT'S FARM *see* THORNDON

SHOTLEY

2030

St Mary. A somewhat awkward-looking church. The exterior
mostly treated with pebbledash. W tower no higher than the
nave. In the best parts the flint is exposed, i.e. in the clerestory
and the ornate s porch, which was, however, completed in brick.
Aisle windows with simple Dec tracery, mostly replaced by
Y-tracery of *c.* 1800. In addition the chancel is of 1745, handsome, with arched windows and a big Venetian E window high
up above the reredos. C14 arcades with octagonal piers and

arches with two hollow chamfers. There are slight differences
between N and S. Late Perp double-hammerbeam roof, and, of
the same time, the N aisle roof with decorated wall-plate and
bosses. – The CHANCEL FURNISHINGS of c. 1745 are well
preserved: wood panelling of the chancel arch, plasterwork of
the coved ceiling, black and white floor PAVING, REREDOS
with paintings of Moses and Aaron, COMMUNION TABLE
with elegant cabriole legs, and three-sided COMMUNION
RAIL with vertically symmetrical balusters, probably older. –
PLATE. Big Set 1744.

SHOTLEY HALL, ¼ m. W. One good early C16 gable with overhang. Much addition in the same style in 1885. Weatherboarded
six-bay BARN.

RECTORY, yet further W, on the main road. Dated 1697. Two
storeys and seven (now eight) bays. Hipped roof. Late C18
doorcase.

SHOTTISHAM   3040

ST MARGARET. Perp W tower. Nave and chancel with several
lancets, looking more or less trustworthy. N aisle 1868. – FONT.
Octagonal, of Purbeck marble, C13, with the usual two shallow
blank pointed arches on all sides. – PLATE. Cup 1713.

WATER MILL. A nice group with the weatherboarded mill and
the miller's house.

(WOOD HALL, ¾ m. W. Symmetrical Jacobean house on an E plan.
Two storeys; straight gables. Doorway with four-centred head,
mullioned and transomed windows. A circular window in the
gable of the porch. Polygonal chimneys (NMR). The house
was considerably enlarged in 1903; of that date are the present
mullioned windows, chimneystacks, and gables (D. C.
Pickering).)

SHRUBLAND PARK   1050

Sir Charles Barry's spectacular Italianate fronts conceal the work
of two predecessors: James Paine and J. P. Gandy-Deering.
Paine built a house here for the Rev. John Bacon in 1770–2. It
was his last, and it survives essentially and forms the centre of
Barry's mansion. It has five bays and is of grey brick. The
ground floor was probably rusticated. Above there are slim
Ionic pilasters through two storeys. The whole was crowned
by a pediment. The Grotto Room at the foot remains, with two
oval plaques and columns with bands of rustication. Inside
this centre of the present house the decoration of Paine's time

also survives in the main rooms. Classical plaster ceilings with lively detail, not only on the principal but also on the upper floor. By Paine also the Oval Hall in the basement and the vaulted corridors there. They were, of course, in Paine's time ground floor and not basement.

Gandy-Deering in 1830–2 remodelled Paine's plan. He added the wings, and replaced Paine's w entrance by a new E entrance and Paine's staircase by a new and much grander one with solid side walls and a shallow white segmental vault. He also built the terrace on the w side and the conservatory on the s side with its severe Tuscan pilasters and its iron and glass interior.

64a However, it is *Barry* who dominates the house and its splendid surroundings. His work dates from 1848–52. As at Harewood he heightened the effects contrived by his predecessors, and as at Mount Felix, Walton-on-Thames, he built as his main accent an asymmetrically placed Italianate tower; an effect anticipated by Wyatville's Chatsworth of 1821–32 and more immediately by Prince Albert's Osborne of 1845–9. By Barry also the balustrade, two richly Louis XV rooms, the E entrance with curved wings, and the Entrance Hall or Lower Hall, making ingenious use of the contours of the site. It has Corinthian columns and glass domes. Finally by Barry also the GARDENS. The w garden carried down in terraces on the model of the Villa d'Este at Tivoli works wonders with the little Suffolk landscape offered. The procession starts in front of the house with a richly ornamented transparent TEMPLE or archway, C18 in its sources, and ends at the bottom with a GLORIETTE or loggia in the lightest Cinquecento style. The scale is ample. The details are no longer in their original state. They were simplified by *William Robinson*, creator of the English herbaceous border, in 1888.

In the style of the Barry work are the three LODGES of 1841. The NW one symmetrical with curved walls to lead to it. Grey brick. Tripartite with raised centre carrying an Italianate roof. The other two lodges, the Coddenham and the Ipswich Lodges, are emphatically asymmetrical and also emphatically Italianate. Their particular brand of picturesque villa motifs corresponds to Loudon's suggestions in his *Encyclopaedia*.

In the grounds is the OLD HALL, which has two uncommonly
50b interesting three-light windows. They are of c. 1525, made of terracotta and decorated in the new Italian fashion. The same moulds are used as for church windows at Henley, Barham,

and Barking in the immediate neighbourhood. The workman or workmen came probably from Layer Marney, where the workshop busy on Lord Marney's grand mansion was dispersed about 1523–5. The lights have triangular tops with dolphins instead of cusping and with Catherine wheels in the spandrels. The terracotta workshop responsible for funeral monuments of the same time in Norfolk (Oxburgh, Wymondham, etc.) must also be connected.

SIBTON

3060

ST PETER. The S and N doorways are of c. 1200, that on the N side simple with one order of shafts, that on the S side with two, of which one has shaft-rings. Good moulded arch, still round. N arcade C13 with circular piers and octagonal abaci.* The arches with two slight chamfers. The exterior of nave, N aisle, and chancel all C19. The chancel is of 1872. W tower with flushwork motifs below the battlements which could be C17. Obelisk pinnacles. The tower originally had a spire. In the nave E wall, to the l. and r. of the chancel arch, pretty Perp niches, two on either side. Nave roof with hammerbeams and arched braces up to the collars. Small angels holding shields. Decorated wall-plate. – FONT. Octagonal. Against the stem two lions and two Wild Men; against the bowl the Signs of the Evangelists and four angels with shields. – SCREEN. The very fine tracery and crocketed ogee arches of four bays of the top parts of the screen are used as a dado. – PULPIT. Jacobean or later, very reticently decorated. – PLATE. Elizabethan Cup and Cover; Paten 1572; Paten and Flagon 1713. – MONUMENTS. John Scrivener † 1662. Alabaster tablet with elaborate surround. – Sir Edmond Barker † 1676 and wife. Big hanging monument. The centre two interlocked upright oval niches with frontal busts, excellently characterized. On the ledge below the tiny figures of a baby and a little girl. Segmental top pediment.

SIBTON ABBEY. The only Cistercian abbey in Suffolk. Founded in 1150. Only overgrown walls remain, especially the S wall of the aisle N of the cloister, and, S of the cloister, remains of the refectory. Drawings made in 1892 show clearly the tall S windows of this and the small round-arched N windows above the cloister. (Inside the refectory a large blank Norman arch (LG) and a square FONT with a little decoration, possibly Norman (D. M. Freeman and others).) Facing the cloister a fine SE double lavatorium niche. (W of the refectory the ruins

* The LG suggests that the piers come from the abbey; see below.

of the kitchen. Of the w range of the cloister very little is left.
LG)

SIBTON PARK. Built in 1827. Two-storeyed and cemented.
Entrance with semicircular porch of four unfluted giant Ionic
columns, tall and narrow. Garden front round the corner of
five bays with bays one and five flanked by giant pilasters.
Classical greenhouse with raised centre. (Good interiors.
DOE)

A COTTAGE opposite the lodge to Sibton Park has a pargetted
frieze and some other elementary pargetting motifs (cf. Yoxford and Theberton).

4060   SIZEWELL
                   2 m. N of Thorpeness

(NUCLEAR POWER STATION. By *Sir Frederick Gibberd*,
1961–6, for the C.E.G.B. Clad in aluminium. It is the sixth
commercial nuclear power station in Britain's first nuclear
power programme. A second power station is in 1974 only
at plan stage.)

SLAUGHDEN *see* ALDEBURGH

SMALLBRIDGE HALL *see* BURES

3050   SNAPE

ST JOHN BAPTIST. w tower, nave and chancel. The tower has
brick and stone decoration in the battlements. Nave and
chancel Perp with some traces of *c.* 1300. Pretty s porch with
arched panelling and quatrefoils in flushwork. Stone parapet
with blank tracery, brick gable. In the spandrels of the entrance
shields with the symbols of the Trinity and the Passion.
Finely detailed s doorway. One order of fleurons in jambs and
arch. Dragons in the spandrels. – FONT. On the base a quatrefoil frieze and an inscription referring to Richard Mey and his
family as donors. On the foot of the stem small beasts crawling.
Against the stem the four Signs of the Evangelists set diagonally and kings and bishops placed frontally. Against the bowl
seven figures, all holding one long scroll. In the eighth field the
Trinity with the two donors. Money for colouring the font was
given in 1523. – PLATE. Elizabethan Cup; Paten 1808.

SNAPE PRIORY. Founded as a cell of the Benedictine Priory of
Colchester in *c.* 1155. No remains.

THE MALTINGS. Until 1966 this was an uncommonly impressive group of Early Industrial buildings, built in what the

Architectural Review calls the functional tradition. Red brick, also yellow brick, much white weatherboarding. Four hoists. The oldest part was on the quay-side. The dates recorded on the road front are 1859 and 1884 and 1885, and also 1952. The original buildings were erected for Newson Garrett (1812–93), father of Elizabeth Garrett Anderson and Dame Millicent Garrett Fawcett (cf. Leiston). In 1966–7 *Derek Sugden* of *Arup Associates* converted the maltings into a CONCERT HALL for the Aldeburgh Festival. A fire destroyed much of what had been done, and full restoration was undertaken in 1969–70. The conversion is the ideal solution of the problem and ought to inspire many throughout the country. The character of the maltings was kept. The main external alteration was to make the great roof over the concert hall itself dominate. Internally also the roof dominates. The construction is shown and in no way embellished. The bricks of the walls are also exposed and not dolled up. – Moving MONUMENT of a disk painted with a pattern inspired by Norwegian lakes and fjords and of twenty-five stainless steel mirrors, the whole encased in a rhombicube octahedron space-frame. The artist is *Keith Grant*, the date 1969.

BARROW, on the s side of the Aldeburgh road, at the corner of the road to Rookery Farm. The easternmost and only survivor of a group of at least six which originally lay on both sides of the main road. Three of them were excavated between 1840 and 1863. The famous Saxon SHIP BURIAL was within a few yards of the surviving barrow. Though the burial had been robbed, when opened, remains were found of a clinker-built long boat, 46 to 48 ft long, with a beam of about 10 ft. It had been placed in a 60-ft lay trench dug in the centre of a flat cremation urn-field, and a scraped-up mound had been piled over it. Though there was no sign of a body, some reddish hair was found (perhaps from shaggy cloaks, as also indicated at the contemporary ship burial at Sutton Hoo 8 m. SW), together with an imported Rhenish glass claw beaker and fragments of other vessels. There was also a classical onyx engraved with a figure symbolizing 'Bonus Eventus', set in a Saxon gold ring and dated to *c.* 635–50 A.D. (now British Museum.) This then was probably the burial of a wealthy but not necessarily royal individual.

SOMERLEYTON

4090

SOMERLEYTON HALL was built by *John Thomas* for Sir Morton Peto. It was begun in 1844 and fully described in the *Illus-*

trated London News in 1857. John Thomas (1813–62) was a remarkable man: a sculptor, occasionally turning his hand to architecture. He had been discovered by Barry and was a protégé of Prince Albert. Peto also was a remarkable man, starting as a bricklayer and a builder's apprentice and before he was thirty one of the busiest and most enterprising builder-entrepreneurs. He was builder for the Hungerford Market and Nelson's Column, the Reform and other clubs, the St James's and other theatres, and then for many railways including work in the Argentine, Africa, Australia, Canada, France, Norway, and Russia. He was an M.P. and one of the guarantors for the 1851 Exhibition. In 1855 he was knighted; in 1866 his firm went bankrupt, and the house was bought as it stood by Sir Francis Crossley. The house is more Jacobean than any original Jacobean house. The impression as one approaches it from the E is not easily forgotten. Two projecting wings; a colonnade with a one-storeyed projecting porch between, whose decoration with ornamental columns, with supporters, with a cupola, defeats description; an Italianate, quite un-Jacobean but very Early-Victorian tower asymmetrically placed on the l.; and a stables block on the r. with its own equally asymmetrically placed little tower with strapwork-traceried bell-openings and cupola.

62b The garden (w) front is quieter and less Jacobean, except for the three-storeyed porch with superimposed orders of variously enriched columns. But the heavily arched dormer windows again are purely Victorian. The house is of brick with the amplest stone dressings, and appears purely of its date from wherever one looks at it. Yet it contains a C17 core and Queen Anne additions. The C17 house had shaped gables and one of these is visible near the Italianate tower. The Queen Anne additions had giant pilasters which have disappeared. But what remains

57a of that time and also of *c.* 1730 is the panelling of the present staircase hall, the NW room with very bold and deeply moulded garlands over the fireplace and doorcases, all in the Gibbons style, and doorcases also in the present Dining Room. Otherwise the interior is unabashedly sham-Jacobean and thereby as Victorian as can be. Entrance Hall with a glazed dome with stained glass of ducks and other water fowl of the Fritton–Flixton neighbourhood. In the Hall a very engaging seated portrait figure of a boy with shells in his lap, by *Durham*, 1865. Durham also made the fountain (now no longer in position) in the large Winter Garden adjoining the house on the N. This is now open to the sky, and only its outer walls remain. The one to the E against the stables is nicely decorated with arches. The verdict of the *Illustrated London News* on the house is that the exterior has 'something fairy-like about it' and the interior, especially 'when lighted by its well-managed gas jets, is quite a scene of enchantment'.

ST MARY. By *John Thomas*, 1854. A replica of the local churches of flint and stone with w tower, nave, and chancel, surprisingly self-effacing for the designer of the Hall. – FONT. Octagonal, Perp, with four lions against the stem, four lions and four angels against the bowl. – SCREEN. The dado has sixteen painted figures of early C15 style and indifferent quality (cf. Kersey). Upper parts of one-light divisions with steep crocketed ogee gables, some simple panel tracery over, and a broad crocketed entrance arch. – SCULPTURE. A stone panel above the s door with the Signs of the four Evangelists. What can it have been made for? – PLATE. Cup 1722; Paten 1726. – MONUMENTS. Sir Thomas Gernegan, early C16. Tomb-chest with lozenges containing quatrefoils containing shields. – John Wentworth † 1651. Black and white marble, early C18. Two free-standing busts side by side with black columns l. and r. carrying an open segmental pediment.

THE VILLAGE. Sir Morton Peto built a weird village w of the church, evidently on the pattern of Nash's Blaise Hamlet near Bristol. There is a green here too, though a square one, and the houses are of brick or sham timber-framing, of a great variety of shapes, and thatched. The designer was no doubt *John Thomas* again.

(PARK FARMHOUSE. With a C15 one-storey wing. One room has a stone recess with a trefoil-arched head. Tie-beams on arched braces. DOE)

SOMERSHAM

ST MARY. Unbuttressed w tower of *c.* 1300–40. Nave and chancel of the same time. s porch of timber, perhaps not later. The simple tracery in the side openings differs between w and E. Cautley regards the porch itself (without the side openings) as of the C13. (Sanctus bell bracket attached to the beam in the chancel. Rev. W. A. Martin) – COMMUNION RAIL. Mid-C17. – PAINTINGS. Moses and Aaron, still in their original position, l. and r. of the reredos. The panelling is *in situ* too. The painting is surprisingly good, done with considerable brio. One suspects a painter who knew London, and Sebastiano Ricci in particular. Kelly says that the paintings were given to the church in 1750.

TUDOR GRANGE, w of the inn, across the bridge (actually in Nettlestead parish). Timber-framed, c16, highly picturesque with its (later) brick-nogging.

8050
SOMERTON

ALL SAINTS. Norman nave. Small N doorway with one order of shafts carrying scalloped capitals and an undecorated arch. Early C14 chancel and chancel chapel, surprisingly spacious. The chancel has one cusped lancet w of the chapel. The arcade pier has big filleted shafts and spurs in the diagonals. In the chapel also one cusped lancet. The neighbouring window is segment-headed. The E window is a Perp insertion, but has the early C14 shafting preserved inside. A curious device is the shafted squint which leads into the chancel PISCINA. – FONT. Perp, octagonal, simple. – PULPIT. Jacobean. – COMMUNION RAIL, now in the place of the rood screen. Jacobean or Early Stuart. – PLATE. Cup, Paten, and Almsdish 1761.

(SOMERTON HALL. C18 and C19. LG)

4070
SOTHERTON

ST ANDREW. Mostly of 1854 by B. Ferrey, but old materials were used. They were Dec, and so is the new church. Nave and chancel and stone bellcote. C14 tomb recesses, low, in the nave N and S walls. The roof is also largely original, with arched braces meeting at the collar-beams. – FONT. Octagonal, Perp, simple. – FONT COVER. Jacobean. – SCREEN. Two painted panels from the dado are now used in the vestry door. – (SCULPTURE. Bust of the first Earl of Stradbrooke, magnificent, signed by Nollekens, 1811. – Second Earl, unsigned, and fifth son of the third Earl, signed by C. W. Gilbert of Melbourne, 1925. Information from Mr McHardy. These busts are on loan from the demolished Henham Hall.) – PLATE. Cup with Elizabethan stem and a bowl inscribed 1668. – MONUMENT. A good, more than life-size effigy of a Knight. The date is the later C13, not the C14. The face unfortunately defaced.

(SOTHERTON HALL FARMHOUSE. C16 to C17. Timber-framed with a shaped gable over the end of the dairy wing. DOE)

4080
SOTTERLEY

ST MARGARET. In the park of Sotterley Hall, near the house. Unbuttressed, very markedly tapering w tower. The w window with cusped Y-tracery, the bell-openings with the same uncusped; c. 1300. Nave and chancel with Perp windows except for one with uncusped Y-tracery on the s side, some chancel windows with the same tracery, and a two-light window on the N side which seems re-set in a larger space shafted inside. W of the s doorway a tall BANNER STAFF LOCKER. – FONT. Octagonal, Perp, with the four Signs of the Evangelists and four angels with shields charged with the symbols of the Passion and the Trinity. – SCREEN. On the dado twelve painted figures, much repainted. The tracery above is missing, and when the coving for the loft was taken down the marks were covered with C17 scrolls or brackets. – STALLS. With traceried fronts and poppy-heads. – STAINED GLASS. Some original fragments in the nave. – Two small but good C15 figures in the W window. – E window by *Kempe*, 1900. – PLATE. Cup and Paten 1568. – BRASSES. Knight of c. 1470, an 18 in. figure. – Thomas Playters, 1479, and wife, well engraved figures of 2 ft 5 in. length. – Christopher Playters † 1547, 19 in. figure. – Also two Elizabethan brasses. – MONUMENTS. William Playters † 1512 and wife. Tomb-chest with three lozenges with foiled fields carrying shields. – Sir Thomas Playters † 1638. By *Edward Marshall* (much later Master Mason to the king). White and black marble. Three kneeling figures, very well characterized. He frontal in a niche a little above his two wives, who are in profile. There are, however, three arches above the three figures at the same height, those above the wives being pediments rather than arches. A segmental top pediment carried by two black columns which frame the whole composition. In the 'predella' below kneel twenty-one children and in addition lies one baby. One of the little girls turns round and makes a face at her sister.

SOTTERLEY HALL. Built about 1744. Red brick, of two storeys, on an H-plan, with brick quoins and a top balustrade. The brickwork looks older and may go back to a preceding house. The bonding is still English. The centre of the E façade was pushed forward a little in the C20. This façade has a recessed centre of five bays with a slightly projecting middle part of three bays carrying a pediment with a coat of arms. The projecting wings are two bays wide each. The same is repeated on the opposite (W) side, where c. 1820 long, low, much farther projecting brick wings were added. Here also is a three-bay pediment. The doorway in the façade is sumptuously carved with Corinthian columns and a pediment. The door-frame also has delicate wood-carving. The Ionic doorway on the w side is a little rougher and also pedimented. The N side had the kitchens and was altered in the early C19 or a little later. On the s side a different composition but no less a display was attempted. In the pediment is a tripartite lunette, below it a Venetian window on big brackets, and below that a kind of Venetian doorway with an oddly heavy pediment. Inside there are some exceedingly good fireplaces, notably a heavy and very ornate Jacobean one taken over from the preceding house and given a place of honour in the Entrance Hall. Coupled columns l. and r. and an overmantel with caryatids and much detached strapwork, coarse, lusty, and not without skill. Facing the back of this the most luscious fireplace of *c.* 1745 in what must have been the Saloon of the house. Large face in the middle, and by the sides buxom caryatid maidens in profile. Quite a number of good fireplaces in other rooms as well, also on the upper floor. The most noteworthy one has a big head of Bacchus in the middle. A little plasterwork survives, some of it in a restrained Gothic. Finally the Staircase, with an open well and two slender balusters to a tread, one turned, one twisted. Carved tread-ends.

SOUTH COVE
9080

ST LAWRENCE. On its own, and not a large church. w tower with flushwork decoration on buttresses and battlements. Nave and chancel, thatched. Norman masonry and Norman doorways, on the N plain, on the s with one order of colonnettes and some zigzag in the arch. The windows of nave and chancel of *c.* 1300; renewed. Nave roof with arched braces meeting at the collar-beam. – A tall BANNER STAFF LOCKER at the w end of the N wall. – FONT. Octagonal, Perp. Against the bowl, rather defaced, the Signs of the four Evangelists, three angels, and a shield. – PULPIT. Of the Jacobean type. – SCREEN. Half the dado remains, with some painting of ornamental motifs. – BENCHES. Some good benches with fully traceried ends and poppy-heads. – NORTH DOOR. With blank crocketed ogee arches and some tracery over. – PAINTING. St Michael, C15 on a wooden board, now the door to the rood loft stairs. – PLATE. Elizabethan Cup.

SOUTH ELMHAM ALL SAINTS
3080

ALL SAINTS, situated at St Nicholas South Elmham. Norman round tower heightened and very restored. Norman nave, see the lower part of a nook-shaft in the NW corner and two Norman N windows, but not the S doorway. C14 S arcade with octagonal piers and double-chamfered arches. To this period belong perhaps the small cusped lancets in the N wall. – FONT. Square, of Purbeck marble, with seven flutings or vestiges of shallow blank arches on each side. – TOWER SCREEN. An elaborately carved Jacobean door. – BENCHES. Two in the porch with poppy-heads and grotesques on the arms. The set of benches inside just have poppy-heads. – PLATE. Cup 1716. (CHURCH FARMHOUSE, by the church. Good carved beams over fireplaces. DOE)

SOUTH ELMHAM ST CROSS

3080

ST CROSS. Norman S doorway with one order of shafts carrying one volute and one flower capital. Roll moulding. Simpler, blocked Norman N doorway. Dec W tower, the bell-openings with cusped Y-tracery. Fine tower arch, the capitals of the semi-octagonal responds with small heads. The outer jamb and arch moulding with fleurons. Dec chancel, the E window tall with cusped intersected tracery. To the N one window like the bell-openings of the tower. Again such a window in the nave on the N side. Dec also the S porch, see its entrance. Semicircular responds with fillets. Perp N side with brick windows in the clerestory. Roof with arched braces. – FONT. Against the stem four lions, against the bowl four lions and four angels. – SCREEN. Two panels re-used as part of the reredos, completely repainted. – PLATE. Cup and Paten 1638.

To the parish of St Cross belongs a monument of great national interest and one that should be made more easily accessible.

MINSTER. The church whose impressive ruin should be visited lies in a coppice ½ m. SSW of South Elmham Hall. It was in all probability not a minster or cathedral. The bishopric founded by Felix c. 630 at Dunwich and divided c. 670 between Dunwich and Elmham refers to North Elmham in Norfolk. The South Elmham church is mysterious in purpose and also in date and plan. It has been assigned to the C7, the C10, and the mid or late C11, but excavations now suggest a date not earlier than the C10.* Its plan is curious in that it consists of an apse nearly as wide as the nave (not preserved but excavated), a short, wide nave without aisles, and at its W end a square apartment of the same width as the nave. This may

* Information from Mr Norman Smedley.

have been a porch or a *porticus* or the substructure of a tower, as at North Elmham. It is connected with the nave by a pair of openings, and the sleeper wall between nave and apse makes it likely that there was a tripartite division here, as at Bradwell, Reculver, etc., in the C7. The whole was 101 ft long. The walls of flint stand up to *c.* 15 ft.

SOUTH ELMHAM HALL. A C16 house with a stepped brick gable-end. Inside it several stone arches which were built as doorways at the time when the Bishops of Norwich had a summer house here. The arches are mostly Perp. By the side of the house the ruins of the so-called CHAPEL, a rectangular gabled building with no evidence of religious use.

(HOME FARMHOUSE. Early C17. Timber-framed and plastered. Gable-end of brick with brick mullioned windows. DOE)

3080

SOUTH ELMHAM ST JAMES

ST JAMES. Small. Unbuttressed W tower, probably Norman below. Early C14 bell-openings. Norman the imposts of the N doorway and the pieces of arch with billet decoration re-used to form a pointed arch. Part of a Norman N window visible inside. In the chancel one early C13 lancet window. Divers other windows. S arcade C13 or early C14, see the capitals of the octagonal piers. Double-chamfered arches. The W bay is larger and later. – FONT. Square, Norman, of Purbeck marble, the familiar table type. On each side five flat blank arches with flat tops. Much decayed. – PULPIT. Square, Jacobean. – SCREEN. At the W end of the S aisle remains of a C14 screen; shafts instead of mullions. The pointed-trefoiled arches could also be original. – BRASS. Civilian and wife, *c.* 1520, 18 in. figures (nave floor).

3080

SOUTH ELMHAM ST MARGARET

ST MARGARET. Norman S doorway with one order of shafts. Volute capitals. Small vertical zigzag in the abacus. Roll moulding. One Norman S window. W tower early C14. Flush-work panelling at the base. Higher up to the S a square quatre-foiled window; to the N it contains an eight-spoked wheel. Most of the exterior is Perp. Inside, the N chapel of one bay appears early C14. Responds and arch fit such a date. To its E an Easter Sepulchre, simple, Perp, with an ogee gable and some decoration with quatrefoils etc. The nave roof is attractive. Arched braces to the collar-beams. Decorated wall-plate. – FONT. Octagonal. Against the stem four lions, against the bowl Signs of the four Evangelists and four demi-figures of angels. – SCREEN. Parts of the dado re-used in the sanctuary. A little ornamental painting remains. – HOUR GLASS by the pulpit. – STAINED GLASS. Canopy in the vestry window. – STOCKS. The village stocks are kept in the porch. – PLATE. Chalice and Cover 1567; Paten (Irish) 1705.

SOUTH ELMHAM ST MICHAEL

3080

ST MICHAEL. Small, of nave and chancel, with an unbuttressed W tower, the battlements decorated with flushwork. Norman s doorway. One order of colonnettes, one roll moulding in the arch, and one frieze of lunettes or scallops. Hood-mould with billet. C16 timber porch (S. E. Rigold). – FONT. Octagonal, Perp. Four lions against the stem, four lions and four angels against the bowl. – PULPIT. Simple, C18. – PLATE. Cup and Paten 1567–8; Paten 1722.

(BOUNDARY FARMHOUSE. Partly early C16. Fine ceiling with moulded beams. The mouldings are carried down the wall-posts. On the upper floor a doorway with leaf ornament in the spandrels. DOE)

SOUTH ELMHAM ST NICHOLAS *see* SOUTH ELMHAM ALL SAINTS

SOUTH ELMHAM ST PETER

3080

ST PETER. Small, of nave and chancel, with a W tower decorated with flushwork on the buttresses and battlements. Early Norman s doorway. One order of colonnettes with block capitals. No arch decoration. Plain, blocked Norman N doorway. Handsome C14 chancel arch. Semicircular responds, and also one continuous moulding with fleurons, heads, etc., up the jambs and along the arch. – FONT. Octagonal, Perp, with four lions against the stem and four flowers and four shields against the bowl. – SCREEN. Nicely carved, of 1923. – PLATE. Cup 1567–8. – CHURCHYARD CROSS. The base has tracery. The shaft is no longer on it.

ST PETER'S HALL. A baffling building. It is of stone, not of flint, and has a chimneybreast apparently Early Tudor. On the other hand the three-light Gothic windows of various design are clearly not domestic. It has been suggested that they came from the demolished church of South Elmham St Nicholas or from Flixton Priory. The flushwork emblems and monograms certainly are a familiar motif of Suffolk parish churches. The entrance (N) side has not been much altered since Suckling's day. (Interior: Massive entrance door. One kingpost of the original hall roof. Big fireplace inserted *c.* 1500 to divide the hall into two rooms. The ceilings in these two rooms also of *c.* 1500. *P.S.I.A.*, xx, 1930)

SOUTHOLT
1060

ST MARGARET. Nave and chancel and bellcote. The nave is faced with knapped flint, and the s porch has a front with chequerboard flushwork. The brick chancel is of 1907. – FONT. Octagonal. Against the stem four lions and four Wild Men. Against the bowl the Signs of the four Evangelists and four angels with shields. – COMMUNION RAIL. Mid-C17. – STAINED GLASS. Parts of figures in the tracery of the nave SE window. – PLATE. Paten 1696; two-handled Cup 1802.

SOUTHWOLD
5070

10a ST EDMUND. The epitome of Suffolk flushwork. The church is large,* 144 ft long, and with its tower, 100 ft tall, imposing from near as well as far. From far, especially the estuary on the s side, the skyline used to be perfect, with the lighthouse as a happy contrast. No one can call the water tower a happy contrast. It is a crime not to have erected something more transparent in so important a position. The church was built after a fire of *c.* 1430 had destroyed its predecessor. Legacies allow its progress to be followed to a certain extent. After 1460 they concern the interior.

EXTERIOR. The w tower is in four stages, the base with flushwork arches, the buttresses with arched flushwork panels, the parapet with flushwork in patterned lozenges. There are no battlements or pinnacles, which is again of importance to the distant view. The w doorway is decorated by two orders of fleurons etc. up the jambs and round the arch. In the spandrels two dragons. There is flushwork panelling to its l. and r. Above the doorway runs a cresting with shields. To the l. and r. of the w window are two elaborate niches. Above it is an inscription in flushwork: 'S(an)ct(us) Edmund(us) ora p(ro) nobis.' The letters are crowned. The bell-openings are on each side two tall transomed two-light windows. The aisles are seven bays long and the chancel projects by one more. All windows below are large, culminating in the four-light E

---

* But in 1722 Defoe noted that it had a congregation of only about twenty-seven, though the Dissenters' meeting houses were full.

window. The clerestory has eighteen closely set windows with
stone shafts between. There is a stair-turret at the w end of the
N aisle. Otherwise the s aisle is the one which has received more
distinction. It has battlements, whereas the N aisle has a plain
parapet. The rest tallies. Buttresses with flushwork chequering,
the base with flushwork blank arches. A frieze of heads and
fleurons below the parapet. The E end of the chancel again has
flushwork-panelled buttresses, and in addition a tall frieze of
flushwork arcading below the window. The tracery of the
windows is Victorian. Finally the s porch, a spectacular piece
of two storeys. Close chequerboard flushwork to the E and w.
The parapets with flushwork arcading and quatrefoils. Flushwork initials on the base of the façade. Flushwork panelling
l. and r. of the entrance. A niche above the entrance between
the two two-light windows. Tierceron-vault inside. On the N
side there is no porch, but the doorway has two orders of
fleurons etc. up the jambs and round the arch. About halfway
along the roof, which runs without any break in height or
shape from the tower to the E end, is a pretty flèche. This was
rebuilt in 1867, but, it is said, correctly. This, small as it is,
also tells a great deal in views from a distance. It gives a Dutch
look to the long church.

INTERIOR. The arcades inside have tall piers with four
shafts and four small hollows. The arches have two wave
mouldings. The roofs were re-done in 1867, also, according to
reports, correctly. Alternating hammerbeams with arched
braces to the collars and arched braces meeting at the collars.
In the chancel the roof is boarded and prettily painted. (Above
the former rood also a ceilure.) The chancel windows have
pretty inner fleuron friezes up the jambs and round the arches.
Angel figures with inscriptions or the Instruments of the Passion. The SEDILIA are treated like a tomb-chest with a row of
shields against the front. A little coving of stone acts as their
upper termination.

FURNISHINGS. FONT. Octagonal, Perp. Set on two steps,
the upper in the shape of a Maltese cross. Both of the steps are
decorated with quatrefoils. Stem and bowl have niches, but
the figures and scenes (probably the Seven Sacraments) have
been chopped off. The COVER is of 1935. – ROOD SCREEN.
Tall, and running right across nave and aisles. The dado is
painted with a total of thirty-six figures. They were cleaned in
1930 by Professor *E. W. Tristram*. The upper part has tall
arcading without any tracery but with prettily cusped and

subcusped arches (cf. many screens in Norfolk). Ribbed coving to the E. Much colour preserved. – This and the two AISLE SCREENS are by three different hands. On the S aisle screen is an inscription to the donor, John Bishop. There is also a record of a bequest in 1460 of £20 (then a considerable sum) to the 'Perke', i.e. the screen. – STALLS. Amongst the richest in the county, heavily decorated with tracery. Against the inner ends next to the poppy-heads polygonal posts with knobs. On the arms between the stalls good figures and heads. Also MISERICORDS, but not of special interest. – PULPIT. Perp, closely traceried, on a trumpet stem, recently repainted. – ORGAN CASE. A piece in very elaborate Gothic forms; 1887. – SOUTH DOOR. With heavy panels, Early Tudor. – CHEST. C14. With an uncommonly richly decorated front. Blind tracery and, in the centre, small figure of St George on horseback. – COMMUNION TABLE. Circular (a great rarity), Elizabethan. – STAINED GLASS. E window 1954 by *Sir Ninian Comper*. – CLOCK JACK, N of the tower arch. Said to be of *c.* 1470, and with original colouring. – PLATE. Cup and Cover 1661. – MONUMENT. In the churchyard the Shrine or Mausoleum of William Bardwell † 1853. Hideously picturesque in its decay. Marble, brick, terracotta, and four heavy stone pinnacles.

SACRED HEART OF JESUS (R.C.), Wymering Road. By the Rev. *Benedict Williamson*, 1916.

CONGREGATIONAL CHAPEL. *See* Perambulation, p. 433.

METHODIST CHAPEL (former). *See* Perambulation, p. 433.

PERAMBULATION. Southwold is one of the happiest and most picturesque seaside towns in England; happy, but not cheerful in the cheerio-sense, and picturesque, but not in the quaint sense of Clovelly. It is a live little town, and it has, at least in its S half, hardly a building that is a visual nuisance. The scale of streets and houses is small. Urban three storeys are absent or rare. The inhabitants appreciate the character of the town. They keep the colours fresh, and the gardens trim. The perambulation is brief, as there are no outstanding buildings and the attraction of the many minor ones eludes description.* We start from the church, and note our disappointment at its immediate surroundings, which are rather in the style of council housing. To reach the High Street we choose CHURCH STREET. On the r. a row of one-storeyed cottages, Nos. 3–21, white and very Dutch, on the l. Nos. 24–26, entertaining in their humble pretension. Two storeys, red brick, the two

* Among the Corporation REGALIA two old Maces, one dated 1642 (LG).

doorways together, and above them, instead of the normal windows, a pediment against the wall with one oval window. Now the HIGH STREET, first towards the NE. On the N side the CROWN HOTEL with its Greek Doric porch, on the S side the CONGREGATIONAL CHAPEL of 1837, yellow brick, three bays, two storeys, with giant pilasters and a pediment. Next to this the MANOR HOUSE, the stateliest house in Southwold, five bays, two storeys, parapet, red brick, doorway with rustication of alternating sizes and pediment. (In SUTHERLAND HOUSE, on the other side, are two highly enriched plaster ceilings of the late C16. DOE)

At the other end of the High Street is the MARKET PLACE, a triangle. In the middle the town pump of 1873. On the N side the SWAN HOTEL, three-storeyed, with two symmetrical bay windows crowned by segmental pediments. A pleasantly fitting, mildly neo-Georgian enlargement in yellow brick on the r. (by *J. A. Sherman*, 1938). Opposite No. 17, a fine Early Georgian house of yellow and red brick, two-storeyed, with a cornice and a half-storey above it. Segment-headed windows. Porch with Roman Doric columns carrying a broad segmental pediment. From the Market Place W into MILL LANE to see the tiny former METHODIST CHAPEL, red brick, three by three bays, a cottage really, and distinguished only by the three closely set arches on the ground floor for doorway and two windows. The chapel dates from 1835. Then S from the Market Place down QUEEN STREET, where Nos. 1–3 have a doorway with Gibbs surround. At the end of Queen Street opens SOUTH GREEN, the largest of Southwold's many greens. What houses should be singled out? It is the whole that is remembered. At the NW corner between Lorne Road and Park Lane GREYFRIARS, early C19, yellow brick, with a generous bow window in the front (the top storey is later). Pretty houses also in Lorne Road and Park Lane. Facing South Green follows HILL HOUSE, rather more pretentious owing to its late C19 top floor. Early C19 with Ionic porch and heavy balconies to all windows. On the other side of the green, really in GUN HILL, facing the sea, ERIN VILLA, a Regency villa of three bays, with an added bay on each side with a glazed dummy window. From here we turn N along the cliff and first find the only early attempt of Southwold at a seaside development, CENTRE CLIFF of c. 1820–30. This has a five-bay rendered centre with top balustrade. The windows of the two storeys are set in blank giant arches. Wings of three bays l. and r., of yellow brick exposed, with the same giant blank arches. Adjoining Centre Cliff on the r. a curious villa, Early Victorian probably, with its bow window flanked by little bastions. The end of the tour is at the NE corner of ST JAMES GREEN, where there is a house deserving to be called a cottage orné, though very minor. Behind it and surrounded, it seems, by houses appears the LIGHTHOUSE, white and benevolent. It dates from 1890. N of this the Southwold front becomes the normal drab English seafront. Only big hotels are missing, thanks to bombing in the Second World War.

ST FELIX'S SCHOOL. By *Arnold Mitchell*, c. 1900 (illustrated in 1902). Of brick. In a freely neo-Georgian or neo-William-and-Mary style. Large symmetrical composition with recessed centre, gables, hipped roof. The centre contains the hall, the gymnasium, and classrooms. It has a steep gable and a scrolly lantern. In the wings four 'houses'. Detached to the r. staff houses. Many additions in 1929–38.

THE HARBOUR. The piers flanking the mouth of the river Blyth were built in 1749 and 1752, and lengthened about 1905.

³⁰⁸⁰ SPEXHALL

ST PETER. Round tower of 1910 to replace one which fell in 1720. Norman N doorway with some defaced carving in the arch. Early C14 S doorway. Of the same time the priest's doorway in the chancel, protected by a flying buttress in front. All windows Perp. The E end rebuilt in 1713 in a pretty brick and flint trellis pattern. Rough roof with tie-beams on arched braces and arched braces from the tie-beams to the collar-beams. – FONT. Octagonal, Perp, simple. – PLATE. Elizabethan Cup.

¹⁰⁴⁰ SPROUGHTON

ALL SAINTS. Very renewed. Unbuttressed W tower. The body of the church essentially of the early C14. Excellent three-bay arcades. The piers deeply moulded with four filleted shafts and four keeled shafts in the diagonals. The hollows between are continuous. Deeply moulded capitals and arches. S doorway with two orders of filleted shafts. Chancel arch of two broad continuous chamfers. Chancel N doorway more nicely designed, with two pretty head-stops. The DOUBLE PISCINA opposite has bar tracery and a gable. – STAINED GLASS. E chapel S window by *Ward & Hughes*, 1881; bad. – One N aisle window by *Whall*, 1924. – PLATE. Cup and Cover 1568; Flagon 1757; Paten 1758. – MONUMENTS. Mrs Bull † 1634.

Kneeling figure. Two standing angels pull away a curtain. – Metcalfe Russell of The Chantry † 1785. Good. No effigies. Urn against a black relief obelisk. L. and r. of the inscription excessively elongated poplar trees.

MILL, N of the church. Red brick, Late Georgian. Five bays and four storeys. Set across the mill stream.

RED HOUSE. Red brick, Georgian. Six bays with pedimented doorway. Two storeys, parapet, pitched roof.

THE CHANTRY and CHANTRY ESTATE. *See* Ipswich, p. 308.

STANNINGFIELD
8050

ST NICHOLAS. Norman nave. Preserved one N and one S window and the N doorway. Shafts with decayed capitals, arch with slightly decorated zigzag. The church has an incomplete W tower and an uncommonly interesting chancel of *c.* 1300. The designer certainly liked personal tracery, see the E window with cusped intersections broken by a quatrefoiled circle at the top, the N windows with double-cusped quatrefoils in circles, and particularly the S windows with four pointed trefoils radially in a circle. Squint in the form of a quatrefoil diagonally from the chancel to the outside, that is really a low-side window. Nice, modest contemporary S doorway into the nave, with two orders of closely set fleurons in jambs and arches and a hood-mould with ballflower. – FONT. Octagonal, C14. Panelled stem. Bowl with shields in quatrefoils and panels with blank arches. – SCREEN. Simple, with one-light divisions. – WALL PAINTING. Big C15 Doom over the chancel arch. Dark and not well preserved. – MONUMENT. Good monument to Thomas Rokewode, Late Perp, chancel N wall. Tomb-chest with shields in quatrefoils. Segmental arch and cresting with shields.

COLDHAM HALL. *See* p. 173.

WINDMILL. A post-mill, derelict.

Romano-British tile and pottery wasters indicate the presence of KILNS working in the C3–4.

STANSFIELD
7050

ALL SAINTS. Quite big; not in the village. Nave of *c.* 1300, W tower (with three niches round the W window) Dec. Chancel Dec. The side windows with tracery including the motif of the four-petalled flower. E end with two niches outside to the l. and r. of the window and a PISCINA with ogee arch squeezed into the corner of the SE window. – PULPIT. Jacobean. – SCREEN.

The base only. – CHEST. C14; iron-bound. – STAINED GLASS. Fragments in the chancel. – PLATE. Elizabethan Cup and Cover; Patens 1666 and 1685.

(ELM HALL, to the S. Good, well-restored, timber-framed house of the C15–16 with brick-nogging. On the upper floor some C16 wall paintings. P. G. M. Dickinson)

(PURTON GREEN FARM, ½ m. N. A late C13 aisled hall of two bays, with a third (screens) bay of two storeys. The hall roof has collars and passing-braces. The end wall of the hall to the screens formerly had an arcade of six(?) pointed arches, of which some must have been blind; there were probably four openings (cf. Great Bricett Priory, pp. 31 and 235). The upper bay of the hall was rebuilt, and narrowed, as a parlour, with a chimney, in the mid to late C16. The walls of the lower bay were rebuilt perhaps in the early C16. J. T. Smith)

STANSTEAD

8040

ST JAMES. Small; mostly Perp. Earlier the W tower with small lancets and the N doorway and the chancel doorway: early C14.

(STANSTEAD HALL, a little S of the church. Built c. 1620, brick, with shaped gables and still with square hoodmoulds over the windows. Large hexagonal chimney with moulded caps.)

OAKLANDS, Stanstead Street. An attractive timber-framed house with a carved bressumer.

STANTON

9070

ALL SAINTS. Fine spacious Dec chancel (spoiled by the organ!) with reticulated E window, ogee-headed PISCINA, and SEDILIA, three seats plainly separated by stone arms. Ornate Dec S aisle with segment-headed three-light E window, also with reticulated tracery. S windows straight-headed. Ballflower frieze all along the outside. Four-bay arcade, not high, with octagonal piers and double-chamfered arches. Low clerestory with quatrefoil windows. In the aisle tall damaged tomb recess, cusped and subcusped and crowned by a big crocketed ogee gable. Pretty PISCINA in the window corner, also Dec. The nave is Dec, see the N windows. The S porch tower could, if anything, be a little earlier. Double-chamfered entrance with continuous moulding. Inside originally two-bay blank arcading. The tower top fell in 1906.

ST JOHN. Abandoned. W tower with the rare motif of a passage through from S to N. The mouldings look c. 1300 or a little later. Nave of about the same time. With tall two-light windows. The chancel was rebuilt in 1616.

(RECTORY. Built in 1864 by *Jekyll*.)

WINDMILL. A derelict post-mill.

ROMAN VILLA at STANTON CHAIR FARM, ½ m. NW of the village, on the Bardwell road. Discovered in 1933. Partial excavation of the SW edge of the settlement (now under cultivation) revealed a wing *c*. 300 ft long consisting of a double apsidal building joined to a bath block by a corridor. The interior of what seems to have been a large estate building included painted rooms, window glass, and coins ranging from Nero to Honorius.

STERNFIELD   3060

ST MARY MAGDALENE. Unbuttressed W tower. Nave and chancel, the chancel rebuilt in 1764 and re-gothicized in 1877. In the nave the masonry is old (Norman?). The windows nearly all new. The S porch is very unusual. Its length is exceptional. The side openings have shafts and shouldered lintels. The entrance arch stands on semicircular responds and has a two-wave moulding. The date is probably some time early in the C14. Early C14 also the PISCINA of the N chapel (ballflower). – FONT. Octagonal, Perp, simple. – BENCHES. Some with traceried ends, poppy-heads, and animals on the arms. – PAINTING. Above the altar a picture of moderate size by *Benjamin West*, given by Lord Farnborough. It represents Christ healing the blind man. – PLATE. Cup and Paten 1568.

STOKE see IPSWICH, pp. 293, 309

STOKE ASH   1070

ALL SAINTS. In the chancel one and in the nave two very plain round-arched, slightly chamfered doorways, probably late C12. Dec W tower, see the doorway and the bell-openings. Dec nave window with the motif of the four-petalled flower in the tracery. Simple late C15 brick porch. – PULPIT. Jacobean. – STAINED GLASS. A little in the tracery of the SE window. – PLATE. Paten 1628.

RECTORY. Behind the Rectory a square brick DOVECOTE. It was erected in 1600.

GARDINER'S HALL. Dated 1666 on a gable beam decorated with vine. The brick-nogging is recent.

STOKE-BY-CLARE

ST JOHN BAPTIST. Big Perp church. The tower is Dec. It belonged to an aisleless church with a chancel and a N vestry of two storeys. The ceiling beams of this and an upper doorway still exist in the N wall of the present chancel. When the new church was built in the C15 it was placed somewhat further N, so that the former nave S wall became the S wall of the aisle, and the W respond of the S arcade stood against the middle of the blocked former tower arch. The Perp windows are nearly all of the same design, with straight-sided arches to the individual lights. Nave and aisles and clerestory. Projecting transeptal S chapel, probably part of the other church. The arcade piers quatrefoil with keeled foils; castellated capitals of the same design as at Clare. The piers are probably re-used, also as at Clare. Double-hollow-chamfered arches. The chancel arch of the same design. – PULPIT. Richest Perp, the richest in the county, and very small. Two tiers of tracery panels. Money was left towards its making in 1498. – BENCHES. With traceried fronts and poppy-heads. – WALL PAINTING. Doom, at the E end of the N chapel, assigned to the 1550s by Mr Rouse. – (STAINED GLASS. Fragments of the C15 in the S transept, including a post-mill. LG) – PLATE. Flagon 1674. – BRASS. Unknown Lady, early C16, 18 in. figure.

N of the churchyard a small GREEN with a group of fine, very tall horse-chestnut trees. Along the E side pretty timber-framed and plastered cottages. A little before the railway bridge GREEN FARMHOUSE, early C18, red brick, two storeys, five bays. Against the S side of the green by the church is the entrance to the grounds of the COLLEGE (now Grenville College). The college incorporates minor parts of the Bene-dictine PRIORY founded c. 1090 by Geoffrey of Clare at Clare Castle and transferred to Stoke in 1124. It became a college of secular priests in 1415. At the entrance to the grounds square, early C16 DOVECOTE, with initials and an unusual grille pattern in one place in dark blue headers. Segment-headed archway and small segment-headed window over. The house is early C18, the doorway with carved brackets probably re-set. Nice, quiet seven-bay S front. Good staircase with twisted balusters. Queen Anne panelling in two rooms. Of the priory little remains. It has been investigated by Mr Dickinson (see LG), and consists of the E parts of the Norman nave, made two-storeyed by the college, the transepts used for domestic pur-poses, and the cloister E walk and dormitory. In the cloister walk part of a blocked doorway and a window. The dormitory is now bedrooms. To the w early c18 STABLES, red brick, with projecting wings. *Lutyens* altered the house in 1897 for Lord Loch, his wife's uncle. By him the w court with billiard-room and bachelors' wing. By him also the layout of the garden and the unmistakable garden wall with the Chinese motif of a circular landscape window.

(The LG in addition remarks on carved c16 beams at LAYER COTTAGE and the unaltered condition of the early c17 HILL FARM at Boyton End, 1½ m. NW.)

STOKE-BY-NAYLAND   *9030*

ST MARY. Large Perp church, in its upper parts mostly of brick with a substantial w tower. The church is 168 ft long, the tower 120 ft high. The tower is remarkably ornate. Money was left for its building by local merchants in 1439, 1440, 1441, etc., to 1462. Stone frieze with shields at the base. w doorway with the shields of the Tendring and Howard families. Up the jambs and arch oblong panels with lions' heads and foliage. Ogee gable, buttresses on corbels l. and r. carrying supporters. Big four-light w window. Three two-light windows, and above these three-light bell-openings. The tower has four stages in all. Very big polygonal buttresses with diagonal buttress attachments, the latter decorated with niches with nodding ogee canopies. Decorated battlements and pinnacles. Chancel with transomed five-light (E) and three-light windows. Nave with clerestory and arches; early c14 N chapel, N of the N aisle. Three-light aisle windows, clerestory windows of 1865. Two-storeyed s porch, partly early c14, partly c19. Rib-vaulted with carved bosses. On the N side simpler porch of brick, early 13b c16.* Six-bay arcades inside with thin piers with eight thin attached shafts, the four main ones carrying fillets. Eight individual capitals, many-moulded arches. At the sill-level of the clerestory string-course with angel figures and fleurons. Very tall tower arch. Chancel chapels of two bays with simpler piers: four attached shafts and four thin filleted shafts without capitals in the diagonals. The chancel also has clerestory windows.

FURNISHINGS. FONT. Perp, octagonal. Stem with eight niches with nodding ogee arches. Shields of the Tendring and Howard families against the seats formed by the uppermost of

* A will of 1457 leaves money to the repair of the N porch. Is this the existing porch? (ARA)

the three steps on which the font stands. Bowl with the Signs of the Evangelists and four other figures. Whom do they represent? – REREDOS. 1865. – SCREENS. To the N and S chapels; simple, Perp. – STALLS. With little figures against the ends of the arms; also some MISERICORDS. – DOORS. W door with tracery, S door with tracery and a Tree of Jesse in small figures. – STAINED GLASS. W window by *O'Connor*, 1865; E window by *Capronnier* of Brussels, 1876; S chapel and N chapel E window by *Capronnier*, 1868 and 1869. – PLATE. Cup and two Patens 1774; Cover 1791; Flagon 1819. – MONUMENTS. Brasses in the S chapel, probably of Lady Clopton, later Lady Tendring † 1403 (4 ft figure); Sir William Tendring † 1408 (6 ft figure with a beard); double canopy of Sir John Howard † 1421 (?) and wife; Lady Catherine Molyns, wife of Lord John Howard, † 1465, made *c.* 1535 (3 ft 2 in.). – John, son of Lord Windsor, † 1588. In chrysom robe. Incised slab. – Lady Ann Windesor † 1615, standing wall-monument with recumbent alabaster effigy, children kneeling at her head and feet. Background architecture of no special interest. – Sir Francis Mannock of Giffords Hall † 1634. Recumbent alabaster effigy. Columns of touch l. and r. carrying a semicircular pediment and two small, well carved figures l. and r. On the base thick garland, a sign of the coming of the new, classical Inigo Jones style.

ST EDMUND (R.C.), Withermarsh Green. Early C19 brick.

The best houses at Stoke-by-Nayland are immediately W of the church in SCHOOL STREET, the GUILDHALL and the MALTINGS, both C16 and both timber-framed. The Guildhall has on the ground floor closely set moulded shafts with capitals. The upper floor projects. The Maltings was originally two houses. From the E end of the church CHURCH STREET runs E and at the main crossing meets POLSTEAD STREET from the N, PARK STREET from the S, and SCOTLAND STREET from the E. All these ought to be seen. There are no spectacular individual houses, but there is much of enjoyable timber-framed and plastered cottages and houses. Nothing in Georgian brick, such as there is e.g. at Dedham, across the Essex border. Examples that deserve special notice are the CROWN INN and the WHITE HOUSE in Park Street, and SCOTLAND PLACE at the bottom of Scotland Street, a little further out.

TENDRING HALL by *Sir John Soane*, 1784, has been demolished. All that survives is a small extravaganza by the main road to Nayland, a FISHING LODGE of the mid C18, symmetrical and pretty with a very deep-eaved roof. Centre with very large

upper window set under a deep arch and overlooking the lake.
Wings of one bay with rising roofs as if they were parts of
pediments.

THORINGTON HALL. *See* p. 462.

STONEWALL FARM *see* HEMINGSTONE

STONHAM ASPAL   *1050*

ST MARY AND ST LAMBERT. Dec and Perp. Dec the big s
tower, see the entrance with a triple-chamfered arch dying into
the imposts and also the s doorway into which a smaller doorway has been set. The mouldings towards the nave of this and
also the N doorway are typically early C14. The top of the tower
is of 1743, more curious than beautiful. Weatherboarded bell-
stage, wooden pinnacles. Dec also the N aisle E window with its
reticulated tracery, the nave W window with its intersected
tracery, and the chancel (see the two niches l. and r. of the E
window). But the chancel windows are all renewed. Dec moreover probably the four-bay arcade with octagonal piers and
double-chamfered arches. Perp most of the windows, notably
those of the clerestory. There are eight, and they are separated
by buttresses with decoration. Triple-stepped battlements
with quatrefoils, shields, etc. It is a disappointment that no
open timber roof corresponds to this display. The nave has a
white ceiling. – FONT. Stem with flat blank arcading, bowl with
flat pointed-trefoiled arches; probably *c*. 1300. – PULPIT. With
the usual squat blank arches as the principal motif. The tester
(now used as a table-top in the N aisle) is dated 1616. – SCREEN.
Parts of the dado re-used (with hat-pegs) in the vestry. –
BENCHES. Ten Jacobean benches with poppy-heads at the W
end. – CHEST. C15, iron-bound, 8 ft long, with a bar and twelve
locks. – STAINED GLASS. Bits in the N and s aisle windows and
in the clerestory. – PLATE. Elizabethan Cup; Paten 1676. –
CURIOSA. Handcuffs and Batons of the village constable
(vestry). – MONUMENT. Knight of *c*. 1330 in a Victorian
recess in the chancel N wall. – The Rev. Anthony Wingfield,
1715 by *Francis Bird*. In the churchyard and hence decayed
on its surface. The figure lies on a bulgy sarcophagus with big
volutes. Semi-reclining, one elbow on a pillow, the other hand
holding something. The eyes look upward. The design is so
unlike anything one is used to in churchyards that one feels a
monument in Westminster Abbey may be taking a country
holiday.

(BROUGHTON HALL, near the church. With a moat and two massive chimneys of which one has three niches and an octagonal top. LG)

EAST END MANOR, 1¼ m. E. Of the C15. Timber-framed, with the original crown-post on an arch-braced tie-beam. Also parts of a primitive hall screen.

ROMANO-BRITISH BATH HOUSE. Robbed remains of two rooms each 10 ft long by 8 ft wide were discovered during the cutting of a sewerage trench in 1962. The bath house was erected in the C3, and originally consisted of a cold room with plunge bath attached and an apsidal heated room. In the last phase the functions of the two rooms were reversed, and a plunge bath and water tank were added. The building was apparently half-timbered on stone footings, with a tiled roof, glazed windows, and gaily painted walls.

4080   STOVEN

ST MARGARET. A depressing neo-Norman job of 1849, with a thin w tower and large shafted windows in nave and chancel. The s doorway alone is original, and no doubt responsible for this ignorant progeny. One order of colonnettes, decorated block capitals, some rope ornament of the neck, arch with zigzag. Hood-mould on beasts' heads with billet. – PLATE. Cup and Cover 1562.

(NORTH GREEN FARMHOUSE, 1 m. NW. With good C16 plasterwork inside connected with external plasterwork in the district. DOE)

9060   STOWLANGTOFT

ST GEORGE. A fine Perp building, tall and aisleless, and vigorous in the simplicity of its decorative enrichments. Said to have been built by Robert Davey, who died in 1401. Flushwork chequerboarding on buttresses and parapets. Flushwork panelling on the s porch. E window of five lights with much panel tracery, nave and chancel with very tall two-light windows, also with panel tracery. The s porch has an entrance still entirely C14 in its responds and arch. One niche above the entrance. Cambered roof with tie-beams in the church. (Ceilure above the rood screen.) – FONT. Octagonal, early C14. Bowl with eight figures under crocketed gables. – SCREEN. Only the dado. Tall and traceried. The panels painted red and green. – BENCHES. Fine set with traceried ends, poppy-heads, and animals on the arms, also seated and kneeling figures. – STALLS.

With close tracery on the ends and instead of poppy-heads small standing figures: a preacher in the pulpit, a deacon, a man holding a candlestick, men holding shields, etc. Traceried fronts. Also some MISERICORDS (bird, demi-figure of angel, cockatrice, etc.). – (DOOR. To the upper stages of the tower. Iron-bound in a wickerwork pattern. G. McHardy) – SCULPTURE. L. and r. of the reredos nine Flemish early C16 reliefs. – WALL PAINTING. Huge St Christopher on the N wall. The heron, the lobster, and the fishing hermit ought to be noted. – PLATE. Cup 1562; Salver 1740. – MONUMENTS. Paul d'Ewes. By *John Johnson*, the contract of 1624 preserved (for £16 10s.). Stone, painted. Two kneeling wives facing one another. Between them, kneeling frontally, the husband. Children in the 'predella'. Flat architecture ending in a flat open segmental pediment. – Sir Willoughby d'Ewes † 1685. Handsome, with scrolly Corinthian pillars and an open pediment.

ALMSHOUSES. Mid C18. Red brick, one-storeyed, with four doors and four windows of three lights. Doors as well as windows have pediments. Pitched roof with three dormers.

STOWLANGTOFT HALL. 1859 by *Hakewill* (F. O. Morris). Symmetrical main block of seven bays with projecting wings to entrance and garden. Segment-headed windows, Ionic porch. Big asymmetrically placed Italianate tower between house and offices. Conservatory facing the offices towards the garden. Some C18 furnishings remain, especially the fine fireplace in the Entrance Hall. The Dining Room is Victorian Rococo.

STOWMARKET <small>0050</small>

ST PETER AND ST MARY. Externally all Dec, except for the porches, the tower, and the clerestory. W tower, called 'new' in a will of 1453 (ARA), with flushwork arcading on the battlements and a recessed lead spire of 1712 (LG) with a balcony near its base. Dec the embattled S aisle with, in the windows, reticulated tracery with flowing motifs in the reticulation units, and flowing tracery. Of the same time or begun a little earlier the N aisle. At the W end below the window three 6b odd seven-foiled windows in a row. The chancel windows are also Dec, and the E window is shafted inside. Two-storeyed NE vestry. The N arcade is Dec too, of seven bays, with quatrefoil piers with spurs in the diagonals and arches with wave mouldings. Hood-moulds on leaf crockets. The S arcade was remodelled Perp – see the different details of the piers. The Perp s porch has its front decorated with flushwork arcading below, with flushwork diapering above. Niches l. and r. of and above the entrance. The N porch is similar, but less elaborate. It is called newly built in 1443. – PULPIT. Including bits from the rood screen. – ORGAN. The instrument was made by Father *Schmidt* for Walsall parish church and bought by Stowmarket in 1800, but the case is Victorian Gothic. – DOOR to the vestry. With a leaf border. – WIG STAND. Of iron, 1675. – PLATE. Paten 1651; Flagon 1698; Almsdishes 1732 and 1791; Spoon 1824. – MONUMENTS. In the E bay of the N aisle low tomb-chest with indent of the brass of an abbot (probably of St Osyth). Big ogee arch. A variety of tracery in the spandrels. – Margaret English and Thomas and Mary Tirell and family; 1604. Kneeling figures, the mother facing all the rest of them across a prayer-desk. – William Tyrell † 1641 and wife. Two demi-figures turning to one another. A cushion on the parapet between them. The children below, a little daughter kneeling in the middle, two babies on couches. Pedimented top. – Ann Tyrell † 1638, aged eight. Brass. In her little shroud. The inscription runs:

> Deare Virgine Child Farewell Thy Mothers teares
> Cannot advance thy Memory, wch beares
> A Crowne above the Starres: yet I mvst Movrne,
> And shew the World my Offrings at thine Vrne.
> And, yet, nor meerly, as a Mother, make
> This sad Oblation for a Childs deare sake:
> For (Readers) know, shee was more, then a Child,
> In Infant-Age shee was as grave as Mild,
> All, that, in Children, Dvty call'd Might be,
> In her, was Frendship and trwe Pietie.
> By Reason and Religion Shee at Seaven,
> Prepar'd her selfe & Fovnd her way to Heaven.
> High Heaven thov hast her & didst take her hence
> The Perfect Patterne of Obedience,
> At those Few yeares, as onely lent to show,
> What Dvty yovng ones to their Parents owe,
> And (by her early Gravity, Appearing
> Fvll ripe for God, by serving & by Fearing)
> To teach the Old, to Fixe on Him their Trvst,
> Before their Bodies shall retvrne to Dvst.

OUR LADY OF THE SEVEN DOLOURS (R.C.). 1884 by *Purdie*. With a small octagonal campanile crowned by a spire.
CONGREGATIONAL CHURCH, High Street. 1953–5, by *A. D. Cooke*. Brick with a bold square tower asymmetrically decorated

at the top. Brick front to the r. of this with three canted balconies above the three entrances and a further extension to the
r. In the interior oak in its natural colour dominates. The church
has a recessed chancel with oak slatting up its back wall and
along its ceiling. Pulpit and reading desk at the l. and r. angles
of the chancel.

SECONDARY GRAMMAR SCHOOL, Onehouse Road. 1955–6 by
the County Architect's Department (*E. J. Symcox*).

STOW LODGE HOSPITAL, Onehouse Road. Built as a Workhouse in 1777–81 under the Gilbert Act. Red brick, the façade
seventeen bays wide, with a three-bay pediment. Long wings
at the back. The DOE quotes a remark made in 1810 that the
building has 'more the appearance of a gentleman's seat than
a receptacle for paupers'.

PERAMBULATION. The church lies just behind the Market
Place. Off the Market Place to the N is the main street-crossing
of Stowmarket. STATION ROAD runs along the N side of the
churchyard and ends at the STATION, an elaborate piece of
Elizabethan architecture by *Frederick J. Barnes*, 1849. Red
and yellow brick, symmetrical, with shaped gables and angle
towers. On the way one passes LYNTON HOUSE, the Stowmarket house of the Tyrell family of Gipping. Early Georgian,
of five bays and two and a half storeys, the half storey being
above the cornice. Yellow brick, with red brick dressings and
red vertical lacing of the windows. Pedimented doorway with
Tuscan pilasters.

From the main crossing N runs BURY STREET, winding, with
nice houses here and there, but nothing special. From the
same place W in TAVERN STREET No. 15, C17 but altered in
1770. Five bays, two storeys. Pedimented doorway with
Tuscan pilasters. (Handsome staircase inside with three fluted
balusters per tread. DOE) Off Tavern Street in FINBOROUGH
ROAD the VICARAGE. (Inside an early C18 staircase with two
twisted balusters per tread. DOE)

In the MARKET PLACE the most noteworthy house is No. 14,
Late Georgian, of three bays and three storeys with a middle
pediment, a window below flanked by pilasters, and a handsome shop-front with Roman Doric columns. Off the Market
Place down the short CROW STREET and to ABBOT'S HALL,
which is really outside the town. The house is of the early
C18, red brick, five bays, two storeys, with a hipped roof and
five dormers. Porch with doorway crowned by an open segmental pediment. The house lies in a large garden. It stands in

the place of the Stowmarket grange of the abbots of St Osyth. A Late medieval BARN, formerly 160 ft long, now forms part of the Rural Life Museum. On an island in the lake, perhaps formerly a fishpond, is a square red-brick SUMMER HOUSE.

From the Market Place SE IPSWICH STREET. Here the KING'S HEAD HOTEL, with a Georgian doorway (Roman Doric half-columns) but a sturdy Jacobean staircase and a modest plaster ceiling of the same time, has been demolished and replaced by Lipton's supermarket. At the end of STRICKLANDS ROAD, to the r., and again outside the town THE STRICKLANDS. The continuation of Ipswich Street is IPSWICH ROAD. No. 27 has a plastered five-bay front of 1702, with a later Tuscan porch. Yet further out, on the NEEDHAM ROAD, 1 m. SE of the church, is THE CEDARS. Early C18 front of three widely spaced bays with a jolly doorway. Fluted Corinthian pilasters and an open scrolly pediment.

In COMBS LANE, ¾ m. SW, is VALLEY FARM, a timber-framed Elizabethan house with a porch not placed symmetrically. It has open balustraded sides and a carved bressumer above. (Also in Combs Lane, EDGAR'S FARM. The oldest part is early C14, a timber-framed aisled hall of two bays, originally open to the roof, with a third bay of two storeys at the lower end. Crown-post roof and passing-braces. Good moulded capitals to the arcade posts. J. T. Smith)

0050

STOWUPLAND

HOLY TRINITY. 1843. Yellow brick, in the lancet style, with a short chancel not lengthened by the Victorians and a W tower with broach-spire. W gallery on cast-iron columns. – PULPIT. Very ornate, probably Flemish, later C16, with scenes from the life of Christ and fantastical caryatids. – (ROYAL ARMS. Of George IV; made of cast iron.) – PLATE. Cup 1732.

COLUMBINE HALL, ½ m. NW. Built of flint, with a timber-framed oversailing upper storey. Diagonal angle-post.

2070

STRADBROKE

ALL SAINTS. The churchyard lies along the High Street. The exterior of the church is mostly Perp, the interior has a Dec arcade. Five bays, piers with four shafts with fillets, thin keeled shafts in the diagonals. The arches have one hollow chamfer and one wave. The chancel also seems to be Dec (one S window; shafting inside the E window; doorway altered). The Perp W tower, similar to that at Hoxne, is an ambitious piece.

The stair-turret is higher than the tower. Flushwork panelling on buttresses and battlements. w doorway with decoration of crowns and fleurons in the arch, w window flanked by niches. The s porch is faced with knapped squared flint, and has a parapet with a quatrefoil frieze. Flushwork panelling on the buttresses. Simpler N porch, but also decorated with flushwork. Perp aisle windows and Perp two-light clerestory windows, the latter grouped 1:2:2:2:2:1. The pairs stand above the spandrels of the arcade inside, not the apexes. One-bay Perp chancel chapel. The arch mouldings with big fleurons, crowns, and portcullis. A very ornate tall Perp niche in the chancel N wall with a trellis vault represented inside. Roof with tie-beams on arched braces and arched braces rising from the top of the wall-plate to the principals. Many bosses. – FONT. Against the stem four lions and four Wild Men, against the bowl the Signs of the Evangelists and four angels. Commemorative inscription round the base. – SCREEN. Two painted Kings from the dado, c. 1500, similar to those on the screen at Eye. Of unusually high quality, with angular folds. – PLATE. Cup and Cover Paten c. 1567; Flagon 1696. – MONUMENT. Elizabeth White † 1840, by *Gaffin*. In the Grecian style. Woman standing by a tall altar with acroteria.

(HEPWOOD LODGE FARM, ¾ m. SSW. Pretty Gothic shafts l. and r. of the doorway. NMR)

STRADISHALL

7050

ST MARGARET. Small, but with a clerestory. N aisle (see the E window) and w tower of c. 1300. s aisle and chancel Dec. s porch of raw timber. – FONT. Octagonal, Perp, very closely decorated. – SCREEN. Only the r. part of the dado. – BENCH ENDS, and COMMUNION RAIL. Fragments built into the chancel stalls. Some bench ends also at the w end of the nave. – PAINTING. St Christopher; N wall. – PLATE. Two Almsdishes 1638; Paten 1694; Cup 1799.

RECTORY (former). According to Cautley panels from the screen of the church frame some of the windows.

STRATFORD ST ANDREW

3060

ST ANDREW. Norman nave, see one blocked s window. All other windows in nave and chancel seem to belong to the restoration. w tower with flushwork decoration of the battlements. Brick porch on the N side, much repaired. – FONT. An imitation of the C13 Purbeck type with shallow blank arches on the eight sides. The proportions of the bowl are wrong. – PULPIT. Jacobean. – PLATE. Elizabethan Cup; Paten 1583.

STUD FARM, ¾ m. NW. With a shaped gable-end, the gable crowned by a pediment. Two blocked oval windows below the pediment. Probably mid or late C17.

STRATFORD ST MARY

ST MARY. A large Perp church, immediately along the road. Nave with tall clerestory and aisles, chancel and chancel aisles, W tower. All embattled except for the chancel. The tower is largely rebuilt. NW stair-turret corbelled out and ending in a square turret with its own pinnacles. The stone details of the body of the church also much renewed, the E window e.g. entirely C19. The S aisle windows and those in the N porch (*see* below) date from 1876–9, when the church was restored by *Woodyer*. The show front of the church is to the N. Ornate chancel chapel and N aisle, ornate N porch. Everywhere here flushwork decoration. Below the windows inscriptions referring to the donors of the money. On the walls and buttresses the curious feature of an alphabet. The N porch has to the E and W very broad, low C19 windows (cf. above). A print of 1846 shows the arches completely open.* The Perp building history, as far as is known from bills and inscriptions, is as follows: S aisle C15; N aisle paid for by the clothier Thomas Mors, who in his will of 1500 asked to be buried in the N aisle because he had made it anew. He also left money for the building of the clerestory. His wife, who died in 1510, left money for the building of the porch, but on the porch are the date 1532 and the initials of another merchant, John Smith. The N chancel chapel was given by Thomas Mors's son Edward, who died in 1526. He left money for it to be made to the same form as the S chapel. Interior with four-bay arcade. Thin piers with four thin shafts carrying small capitals. The broad hollows between the shafts are carried into the arches without capitals. The apex of each arch an ogee point. On this rise shafts between each pair of clerestory windows. Shafts also stand on the pier shafts towards the nave, so that all clerestory windows are framed by shafts. Low-pitched roof. Angel figures against the middles of the tie-beams. The chancel chapels have similar piers, but four-centred instead of two-centred arches. – PARCLOSE SCREEN. Original parts preserved. – STAINED GLASS. Some original glass in the N aisle W window. – PLATE.

* Information kindly given by Miss A. Green.

Cup and Paten 1702–3; Almsdish 1823. – BRASSES. Edward
Crane † 1558 and wife. Nothing special.

w of the church, on the s side of the road, PRIEST'S HOUSE,
c. 1500, timber-framed, the window tracery and w porch not
original. Towards the sw exit, i.e. the bridge across the Stour
and into Essex, first CORNER HOUSE with carved bressumer
(a date 1596 on plaster – DOE), then WEAVER'S HOUSE, a
good early C16 house. Nearly opposite this BAY HOUSE,
early C19, with a bay between two porches with Roman Doric
columns.

½ m. NW of the church BROOK FARM (Lowe Hill House), a good
timber-framed farmhouse of c. 1500. Inside some Tudor wall
painting of intricate strapwork.

STUSTON

1070

ALL SAINTS. Norman round tower with Dec octagonal top.
Chancel over-restored. N transept 1878. The chancel interior is
truly terrible, of yellow, red, and blackish blue brick. – PLATE.
Cup inscribed 1582; Flagon 1692–6; Almsdish 1723 (?). –
MONUMENT. Sir John Castleton, 1727. Standing monument.
Two busts standing on a ledge and above them, against the
pedimented back wall, three oval medallions with the portraits
of children.

STUTTON

1030

ST PETER. A Norman window re-set in the E wall of the C19
vestry. Above and below it bits of Norman decoration. The
chancel, the N transept, and the N aisle are of 1875. The nave
W window seems Dec, tall, of two lights. Fine big C15 s tower
serving as porch below. Tall entrance arch. – SOUTH DOOR.
Original, with simple metalwork. – BENCH ENDS. With poppy-
heads. – STAINED GLASS. Pretty glass of c. 1840 in the chancel
windows, only one completely preserved. Another well-
preserved one in the N transept. – MONUMENTS. Two hanging
monuments, of identical composition, to Isaac Jermy and his
wife who died in 1623 and to their son John Jermy † 1662 and
his wife. The couples kneel facing each other across a prayer-
desk. The ornamental detail and costumes characteristically
different in the two pieces. The monument of 1623 has the
inscription ΕΘΗΚΕΝ Ο ΦΙΛΟΣ on the prayer-desk, and the
monument of 1662 a poem written by John Jermy in memory
of his wife a little before his death. It runs as follows:

Martha's checkt for neglect of Christ's pure word
Mary for her love thereto's on record
This my deare Mary had noe less regard
Unto the sacred words of God's Herauld
Another Anna I may truly say
For her fastings & prayers night and day
Ciconia like the longer that she liv'd
The sweeter breath & more spiritu'liz'd
Not spiderlike figuring vanity
But like the silkeworme seekeing verity
This pious Matron stood upon her guard
Resisting him, whome else wold her have marr'd.

In various parts of the scattered parish a number of worth-while houses.

STUTTON HOUSE, opposite the church. Built of brick as the rectory in 1750, and provided with the deceivingly shaped gables in 1832. The centre of the entrance side is a Venetian window. Nice staircase.

STUTTON HALL. Built, it is said, by Sir Edmund Jermy in 1553 (DOE). An extremely interesting house of a date not often to be met. The N side is very spectacular with its walled garden, and the S side with its view across the estuary of the Stour. The house was originally timber-framed, and only its chimneys were of brick, but in the later C19 and early C20 the walls were rebuilt of brick, and on the W side alterations and additions were made. The chimneybreasts are very big and carry delightfully ornamented round chimneys of the familiar Early Tudor patterns. There are three original ones of these, two in the S wall, one in the E wall. The walls of the garden are also of brick. They are punctuated by pinnacles. In the N wall is a pretty gatehouse with semicircular pediment and pinnacles. To the S stuccoed coupled pilasters. The original entry into the house must have been in line with this gatehouse. The Hall presumably lay to the l. (E) of this entrance. The other big chimney in the S wall may then have belonged to the original Kitchen. The third is in what was from the beginning the Parlour Wing. Good plasterwork inside, especially vine etc. friezes. More sumptuous the ceiling of the Great Chamber, which lies above the Hall. This has coved panels with patterns of thin ribs and pendants.

CREPPING HALL, E of Stutton Hall. Georgian, brick, four bays, two storeys, parapet and hipped roof. In the middle of the first floor low Venetian window. The back is timber-framed

and earlier. There is a weatherboarded and thatched C16
BARN.

CROWE HALL, E of Crepping Hall. A three-storeyed mid-C17
part, and much addition of *c.* 1825 (date 1826 in the Drawing
Room). Stuccoed, castellated and pinnacled, picturesquely
irregular. In the C17 part an elaborate plaster ceiling with
figures in high relief comparable to those of Sparrowe's House,
Ipswich. In the Drawing Room also elaborate plasterwork.
This is imitation Perp.

HORSESHOE COTTAGE, LOWER STREET, N of Crowe Hall.
(Formerly a maltings. DOE) One-storeyed, with big vine
pattern pargetted all over the front.

MANOR HOUSE, UPPER STREET. Mid-Georgian, brick, five
bays, two storeys, with three-bay pediment. Doorway with
Tuscan columns attached to a rusticated background, metope
frieze, pediment. Low Venetian window above; fine cedar
tree in front of the façade.

A Romano-British HUT has been located on the golf course N of
the village and S of the river Waveney, near the crossing of the
Roman road.

SUDBOURNE

ALL SAINTS. Blocked Norman S doorway, with two orders of
colonnettes much restored. One Norman S window. S porch
with fleurons in the hood-mould and a square frame above it.
Spandrels with shields exhibiting the symbols of the Passion
and the Trinity. The same decoration in the N porch. W tower
with spike. In the battlements arched panels of stone against
raw flint, not knapped flint. Much renewed and added to
(transepts) in 1878. – FONT. Of *c.* 1200; a big stone cauldron
on four strong shafts with moulded capitals. – PULPIT. Very
pretty, of *c.* 1700 or a little later. – FAMILY PEW. With equally
fine early C18 woodwork. – PLATE. Silver-gilt Cup and two
Patens 1723. – MONUMENT. Sir Michaell Stanhope; Jacobean.
Big standing monument of alabaster. Large kneeling figure,
wife and children kneeling on the floor in front. Four black
columns. At the top inscription tablet and obelisks.

SUDBOURNE HALL, built by *James Wyatt c.* 1784 and much
enlarged for Sir Richard Wallace (of the Wallace Collection),
has been demolished.

CHURCH FARMHOUSE. C17, with shaped gable-ends.

SUDBURY

ST GREGORY. The mother church of Sudbury. By the green at the W end of the town, the third of its medieval parishes. Perp, built of flint. W tower with diagonal buttresses with five set-offs. SE stair-turret. At its foot on the S side MONUMENT. Tomb-chest with shields in lozenges and recessed niche above. Nave and aisles, clerestory, not with doubled windows. S porch with a chapel attached to its E side (cf. Clare Suffolk and St Botolph Cambridge). Tall transomed chancel windows. Brick vestry to the N of the E end, early C16. C14 arcades of four bays. Polygonal attachments to the piers towards nave and aisle without capitals, semicircular shafts with capitals towards the arch openings. The capitals on the S side simpler and earlier, on the N finer. The church is supposed to have been rebuilt by Archbishop Sudbury, who founded a college here in 1375 (*see* below) and was executed in 1381, and to have been remodelled *c.* 1485. Nice cambered nave roof, the E bays ceiled, flat chancel ceiling, painted with a pattern of squares and elongated hexagons, more Renaissance than Gothic in character. The church was restored in 1862 by *Butterfield.* – FONT. Perp, octagonal. Bowl shallow with tracery motifs, probably late C14. – FONT COVER. One of the finest medieval font covers in the country. Tall, with two tiers of panels with ogee arches and gables, the upper tier placed so that its panels stand above the edges of the panels below. – SCREEN. One panel, at the W end of the nave, with a painting of Master John Schorn healing the gout by conjuring a devil out of a boot. – STALLS. Heads on the arms, MISERICORDS with heads etc. More panels of the screen dado used for the stall backs. – SOUTH DOOR. With tracery and a trail border. – MONUMENT. Incised slab with Normano-French inscription to the wife of the Sieur de St Quentin, *c.* 1325. Foreign, according to Mr Greenhill (S chapel floor). – CURIOSUM. The skull of Archbishop Sudbury is preserved in the vestry.

To the SW of the church the GATEWAY to the College founded by Archbishop Sudbury. Stone arch in brick surround.

ST PETER. Perp: although large and convincingly expressing the wealth of a prosperous wool-manufacturing town, this church was built as a chapel of ease. The W tower is of *c.* 1460–85. It had a pretty copper spirelet of 1810 that told much in distant views, but this was taken down in 1968 and is unlikely to be replaced. Nave and aisles, clerestory with a doubling of windows. Chancel and chancel chapels. The aisles embrace the

tower. s porch two-storeyed, three niches in the front. The
ground floor was intended to be vaulted. No N porch. Tall
arcades of five rather narrow bays, the piers with four attached
shafts and four small hollows in the diagonals. The church was
restored in 1859 by *Butterfield*, and again in 1968. The chancel
was redecorated by *Bodley* in 1898, but after the restoration of
1968 only the work on the chancel arch remains. Vestry under
the chancel. – By *Bodley* also the tall REREDOS. – PARCLOSE
SCREENS. Very rich, though with only one-light divisions.
But the arches are broad and there is much cusped tracery. –
DOORS. s and N doors with tracery. – FONT. Octagonal, Perp.
The bowl with cusped pointed quatrefoils. – EMBROIDERY.
Alderman's Pall, C15. Among the embroidered motifs a small
kneeling figure in a shroud, with prayers from the Vulgate. –
Preaching Cloth, i.e. Pulpit Frontal, Jacobean.

ALL SAINTS, Church Street. At the foot of the town, not far
from the bridge. Perp w tower with big angle buttresses and
big SE stair-turret. Nave and aisles, the N aisle *c.* 1459 (bequest
towards its building). Clerestory with doubled windows.
Chancel with family chapels N (Eden family) and s (Felton
family). The former chapel was building in 1465. To the N of
the chancel also a two-storeyed vestry attachment with barred
E windows. The arch into it from the chancel is blocked. Arcades of five bays, the piers of the same design as at St Peter
(above). In an arch moulding small suspended shields and
fleurons. Good cambered roofs in nave and aisles. – FONT.
Octagonal, Perp, simple. – PULPIT. With Perp tracery panels.
– READER'S DESKS. With some Perp tracery panels. – SCREENS
to the N and s chapels. Large, with one-light divisions and much
cusped and crocketed detail (cf. St Peter). – DOORS. N and w
doors with tracery. – PAINTING. Entertaining but deteriorat-
ing family tree of the Eden family in the N chapel; early C17. –
PLATE. Elizabethan Cup and Cover; Flagon 1757; Patens
1761.

OUR LADY (R.C.), The Croft, close to St Gregory. Brick with
stone dressings. E (ritual w) front with a pretty recessed porch
turret on the l., carrying a fancy spirelet, very typical of *c.* 1900,
but designed in 1893 by that excellent architect *Leonard
Stokes*. The interior is of less interest.

PERAMBULATION. The hub of the town is the church of St
Peter. The town extends from there in all directions, but there
is nothing of architectural interest to the NE. To the SW
MARKET HILL slopes gently down. On it bronze STATUE of

Gainsborough, who was born at Sudbury. By *Sir Bertram Mackennel*, 1913. Behind the church, that is by the NE end of the Market Place, the only house which is worth remembering is No. 2 KING STREET, grey brick, five bays, with a Greek Doric porch, probably *c.* 1820–30. Close to it, across the road, is the TOWN HALL, a modest but dignified building of 1828. By *Thomas Ginn* of Sudbury. Grey brick. Three generously spaced bays, the middle one projecting a little and enriched by tall coupled unfluted Ionic columns carrying a pediment.* Below the church an even run of houses. Only a few are memorable. On the NW side the BLACKBOY HOTEL, timber-framed and much re-done, and then, at the corner of Weavers Lane, a house with exposed timber-framing and a jutting upper floor. On the SE side LLOYDS BANK, a handsome Georgian brick house of five bays and three storeys with a broad Ionic porch. Then the WESTMINSTER BANK, a good building of 1903 (by *Cheston & Perkins*), red and blue brick, in an imitation Early Georgian style. The CORN EXCHANGE next door also deserves a glance, if only to meditate on the Early Victorian sense of security, superiority, and prosperity; 1841 by *H. E. Kendall*. Four giant Tuscan columns carry projecting parts of the entablature. A scrolly top line with wheatsheaves instead of urns. The group of resting reapers above the façade is by *F. L. Coates* of Lambeth. Inside, a nave and aisles plan, with tall cast-iron columns supporting a clerestory. In order to house the new Branch Library (1968) a mezzanine floor has been 'floated within the existing volume' in an attempt to emphasize the independence between old and new. The design is by *Jack Digby*, the County Architect, and his department. A little lower the INSTITUTE CLUB, founded in 1834. Narrow Greco-Egyptian front with giant columns *in antis*. Top acroterion. (Interior modernized.)

From the foot of Market Hill two streets proceed, Gainsborough Street and Friars Street. We descend by the former and return by the latter. In GAINSBOROUGH STREET the only memorable house is No. 46, where Gainsborough was born. The family bought the house in 1725, and that must be about the date of the new building. Red brick (only headers) and rubbed brick trim. Five bays, two storeys, parapet. Segment-headed windows. Doorway with Doric pilasters and straight entablature.

* INSIGNIA. Two silver-gilt Maces, partly 1614; Common Seal 1616; Tankard 1675 with scenes of fire and a plague.

The continuation of Gainsborough Street is STOUR STREET. Several attractive timber-framed houses (e.g. ST MARY'S with an C18 doorway) before the climax comes – with The Chantry and Salter's Hall, side by side. THE CHANTRY is of the C15 and has a good corner-post, carved with the figure of an angel, and thin buttress shafts. SALTER'S HALL is yet finer. Built c. 1450, buttress shafts and a pretty oriel on a carved soffit with a man and some animals, windows with delightfully delicate tracery. STOUR HOUSE, opposite, is later and also good.

Stour Street is continued in CROSS STREET with the so-called OLD MOOT HALL (the Moot Hall was in fact in Market Hill). This is another C15 house. Big gable on the l. with oversailing first floor below it. Handsome oriel window. Some original doorways.

Back towards the centre by Church Street. Past All Saints Church and to the r. into FRIARS STREET. Here on the r. some scanty and re-used remains of the BLACKFRIARS, the Dominican Priory founded before 1248. Archway and doorway of timber, probably from the gatehouse. Then several nice timber-framed (e.g. No. 17) and Georgian houses (not the doorways of Nos. 58 and 31). Also down BULLOCK'S LANE to the r. to the RED HOUSE, the stateliest Georgian house in Sudbury: five bays, but a very wide centre with Venetian window (later widened) and pedimented gable. So we return to Market Hill.

A postscript is now necessary on a few outlying buildings. By St Gregory lies the former WORKHOUSE, now a hospital. Red brick, 1836, gabled Tudor style. By *John Brown* of Norwich.

At the SW end beyond the Bridge BALLINGDON HALL, built by Sir Thomas Eden c. 1593. Timber-framed with four canted bay windows on brick plinths. Only three gables.*

In Acton Lane, N of the town, are three new public buildings, a POLICE STATION, a CLINIC, and an AMBULANCE STATION, by the *County Architect's Department*, 1967.

Finally to the NW, off the Melford Road, on the W side BRUNDON HALL (Georgian, red brick, three bays, central Venetian window) with the weatherboarded MILL and adjoining cottages, and to the E the former CHAPEL OF ST BARTHOLO-MEW of a Benedictine Priory founded c. 1115. Perp, flint, nave and chancel in one. One doorway and the window surrounds survive.

* In 1972 the house was moved about 200 yds without being dismantled.

3040

SUTTON

ALL SAINTS. Nave and chancel all renewed. The tower fell in
1642. – FONT. Quite an exceptional piece, probably of the
23a early C15. Eight small standing figures against the stem. In the
panels of the bowl the Signs of the four Evangelists and
Gabriel, the Virgin of the Annunciation, a Prophet (?), and
another angel, voluminous figures with broad, heavy, rounded
draperies and long hair. The style seems directly influenced by
Burgundy. – SCREEN. Tracery panels re-used in the communion rail. – STAINED GLASS. E window by *W. Warrington*
1861. – PLATE. Elizabethan Cup; Paten 1569; Flagon 1637.
BARROW GROUP, ¼ m. S of Sutton Hoo, on the crest of a sandy
heath escarpment 100 ft above the river Deben. Evidence of
the Saxon royal cemetery of Rendlesham is suggested by the
remains of at least eleven barrows. Three were excavated in
1938, the northernmost of the group producing an 18 ft long
boat and a cremation. The SHIP BURIAL uncovered in 1939
was the largest of the group. It was contained in an oval
mound, which had lost its W half owing to robbers who in
the C16–17 sank a shallow pit in the top of the mound in
search of loot. Originally measuring *c.* 100 ft by 12 ft high, it
covered a trench in which was placed a clinker-built sea-going
rowing boat* 86 ft long, with provision for thirty-eight oarsmen
and a gabled cabin 10 ft high amidships. The contents of the
burial (now in the British Museum), which have been
described as 'the richest and most brilliant treasure ever found
on British soil', outstripping other princely Saxon burials such
as at Taplow (*see The Buildings of England: Buckinghamshire*
p. 266), demands a summary description.

Although no sign of a body was discovered, the finds
were numerous and can be divided into three groups: (1)
Domestic equipment and weapons including iron-band wooden
buckets, cauldrons, a pottery bottle probably imported from
Kent, iron spears and javelins, a battle axe, and remains of
drinking cups made of the horns of the extinct aurochs. The
largest of these holds six pints. They and a set of gourds were
fitted with silver mountings. Fragments of a small harp (the
earliest extant in N Europe), originally with six strings, were
found inside a bronze bowl made in Alexandria. Other Mediterranean imports included a great Byzantine silver dish with
the control stamp of Anastasius (491–518), covering a fluted

---

* *See* also Snape.

silver bowl bearing a classical head in relief, a silver ladle
and cup and ten bowls each with a central geometric design,
and two silver baptismal spoons (cf. Mildenhall) with the
Greek for Saul and Paul engraved on the handles. Finally,
the three bronze bowls with ornamented fittings decorated in
Northumbrian style belong to a group of so-called 'hanging
bowls', whose ritual use is supported by the fish on a pedestal
in the centre of one of the Sutton Hoo bowls (? of Christian
use). (2) Personal objects. These were concentrated along the
line of the keel in the centre of the ship and include a sword with
jewelled pommel and scabbard mountings, a shield with bird
and dragon mountings, and a visor-helmet with plates of
repoussé ornament, all three objects being paralleled in the
rich c 7 A.D. graves of Swedish Uppland. There were also
nineteen pieces of gold jewellery (presumably the product of a
local workshop), including a solid gold buckle weighing 14 ozs
and measuring 5·2 ins with an interlace design of beasts, and a
purse lid with polychrome garnet-fitted cloisons. This purse
contained two small gold ingots, three coin blanks, and thirty-
seven gold Frankish *tremises* (⅓ of a *solidus*, the standard imperial Roman coin) dated 650–60 A.D. (3) Emblems of royalty.
An iron 'standard' 6 ft 4 ins high bearing on its top a stag
recalling the 'tufa' which Bede said was born in the presence
of Edwin of Northumbria. Also a whetstone of square section,
c. 2 ft long, tapering at each end, with an openwork cage round
the reddened terminals bearing human masks; a unique object,
perhaps linked with the northern veneration of the master
smith. The question of whom the ship burial commemorates
is a vexed one. Aethelhere, one of the Wuffingas dynasty and
a lapsed Christian, who died in battle in 665 and was buried in
the flood waters at Winwaed, Yorks, is the most reasonable
candidate, and a typical hero in the pagan tradition.

EARTHWORKS or a fortified post, of doubtful date, lie 300 ft
NW of Bussock House, 1 m. NE of Shottisham.

(WOOD HALL. Jacobean. Symmetrical, on an E-plan. Two-
storeyed, with straight gables. Mullioned and transomed
windows. Four-centred doorhead. Porch-gable with circular
window. Polygonal chimneyshafts. NMR)

SWAN HALL see HAWKEDON

SWEFLING 306⊕

ST MARY. Transitional N and S doorways. That on the S side has

one order of shafts. Capitals with upright leaves. Round arch
with roll moulding. The N doorway has a round single-chamfered arch. Chancel of *c.* 1300 with some renewed lancet
windows and a trustworthy E window with uncusped intersected tracery. Dec W tower with flushwork decoration on the
battlements. Nave and chancel only. The N side much repaired
in brick. Good S porch with flushwork front (arched panels,
quatrefoils, sacred initials). In the spandrels of the entrance a
Dragon and a Wild Man. – FONT. C13, octagonal, Purbeck
marble, with two shallow blank arches on each side. – PLATE.
Elizabethan Cup and Paten; Paten 1761. – LEATHER COVER,
probably to hold a chalice. Cylindrical, tooled. On the lid five
shields. Dated C14 by Cautley.

SWILLAND

1050

ST MARY. Norman S doorway. Two orders of colonnettes; arch
with zigzag. The lintel curves upward. W tower of early C16
brick with dark diapering. On it – alas, the most prominent
feature of the church – an extraordinary Victorian contraption
in lieu of a normal tower top and spire. It is French in character
and vaguely of *c.* 1500 in its motifs. Two steep gables to W and E,
two steep dormers to N and S. Open spiky lantern. The feature
was designed by *J. S. Corder* of Ipswich and is not, as one
might think, of *c.* 1865 but of 1897. Simple hammerbeam roof
inside. – PULPIT. Jacobean. – ROYAL ARMS of Queen Anne.
Excellently carved. – PLATE. Elizabethan Cup; Paten 1683.

SWINGLETON GREEN *see* MONKS ELEIGH

SYLEHAM

2070

ST MARY. Traces of Anglo-Saxon long-and-short work at the
NW angle. Norman round tower, the top with cusped lancet
windows and some flushwork chequerboard panelling, i.e.
early C14. Chancel C13 with lancet windows. Nave Perp. Tall
two- and three-light windows. S porch with crowns and
fleurons in the entrance arch and one niche over it. S doorway
with shields in the arch. The roof is Victorian. It has arched
braces meeting at the top. – FONT. The base with big volutes is
Norman. (The FONT COVER is dated 1667. LG) – PULPIT.
Plain, Jacobean. – BENCH ENDS. Some, with poppy-heads. –
(SOUTH DOOR. With C13 ironwork. LG) – PLATE. Elizabethan
Cup; Elizabethan Paten dated 1605.

MANOR HOUSE, ¼ m. E. Georgian, of the usual red brick with the usual five bays and two storeys. What distinguishes the house is the curved walls coming forward towards the street. The sections nearest the house are treated as three blank arches.

MONK'S HALL, ⅛ m. SW. Fine timber-framed house with a projecting wing ending in a stepped brick gable. Near the top, l. and r., circular openings. On the timber-framed part a chimneystack with circular decorated chimneys. C16.

WINDMILL. A small post mill with a two-storey plastered and tarred brick round-house, having a boarded roof. The buck has a very attractive lean-to porch with side wings and there are four patent sails and a fan-tail. She originally drove three pairs of stones, one each in the head and tail of the buck and a third pair in the round-house; engine-driven. There was a flour dresser on the first floor of the buck. In 1946 she was tail-winded in a thunderstorm and lost two sails but she was until recently still at work with the remaining two. The date of erection is unknown.*

TANNINGTON 2060

ST ETHELBERT. N doorway in the Transitional style. One order of colonnettes with characteristic details. The arch with a keeled roll moulding and a chamfer. Chancel of c. 1300. Nave and chancel windows mixed Dec and Perp. S porch with flush-work panelling on the front and the battlements. One niche above the entrance. W tower. The nave roof is a canted wagon roof. The two bays above the rood are ceiled and have bosses. – FONT. C13, octagonal, of Purbeck marble, with the usual two blank pointed arches on each side. – BENCHES. No tracery, but poppy-heads and little figures to their l. and r. On one end a crowned, seated figure. The little figures represent Vices, Mass and Penance (of a series of the Sacraments), and the Mouth of Hell.

(TANNINGTON HALL, ¾ m. NW. With two very fine plaster ceilings. DOE)

TAN OFFICE GREEN see CHEVINGTON

TATTINGSTONE 1030

ST MARY. Flint, much repaired with brick. W tower with E wall renewed in brick. Nave C14, chancel C15. N and S porches.

* Mr Wailes contributed this paragraph.

Double-hammerbeam roof. – FONT. Octagonal, C13, of the familiar Purbeck type, with two blank pointed arches in each panel. – PLATE. Cup 1791. – MONUMENT. Rear Admiral Thomas Western † 1814, by *Flaxman*. White and grey marble. Seated female figure in front of a big dark base. On it flag and anchor.

TATTINGSTONE PLACE. Big, red brick, called a new building in 1764. Externally not specially attractive. In ornamental grounds with a lake.

TATTINGSTONE WONDER. Built as an eye-catcher ¼ m. S of the house. The date is probably 1790 (date cut in a chimney brick). Two older cottages were given a new flint front with church windows, and a third was added in the form of a flint church tower. On the S side the tower has no wall at all, as this is not visible from the house, and the cottages have their normal brick wall.

ST MARY'S HOSPITAL. N of the hall and on the axis of the tower of St Mary. Built as a House of Industry in 1765, enlarged 1819 and 1837. Large and stately, though simple. Red brick, three sides of a quadrangle, open towards the church. The wings lower than the centre. In the centre a low apsed chapel projects which is not part of the original design.

TEA HOUSE *see* FLIXTON

TENDRING HALL *see* STOKE-BY-NAYLAND

THEBERTON

ST PETER. W tower; nave and chancel in one, thatched; S aisle and S porch. Norman chancel, see the corbel-table. The E parts of the chancel are Dec. Norman N side of the nave, see the doorway with two orders of colonnettes and three orders of zigzag in the arch, and see also inside one window with quite an ambitious surround with shafts and roll-moulded arch. The round tower is also in its lower parts Norman. The top turns octagonal and Dec with bell-openings of Y-tracery and blank windows with Y-tracery represented in flushwork. Flushwork decoration also in the battlements. Dec probably the S arcade too. Three bays, octagonal piers and arches with three hollow chamfers. The piers and arches are painted, as is also the Perp lean-to roof. Good Perp S porch. The front is decorated with flushwork and has a parapet with some blank stone tracery. Above the entrance a niche with, in the spandrels, the crossed keys and crossed swords of St Peter and St Paul. The porch is attached to the s aisle (which was rebuilt in 1848). Of the niches to the l. and r. of the E window one is signed by *T. Thurlow*. – FONT. Octagonal, with four lions and four Wild Men against the stem and four lions and four angels against the bowl. – PULPIT. Perp. The tracery at the top of the panels filled with foliage. – (SCREEN. Panels used in the choir stalls. LG) – SOUTH DOOR. With tracery. – PLATE. Elizabethan Chalice. – MONU-MENT. Frederica Doughty † 1843. Gothic, with cusped arch and three figures on the top.

CHAPEL, by the sea. The remains form part of a small stone house. The chapel is supposed to be connected with the original buildings of Leiston Abbey, founded in 1183 and moved to Leiston in the C14.

OLD MANOR HOUSE, w of the church. With some pargetting made with the same moulds as used at Yoxford and Sibton.

THEBERTON HALL. Said to have been built in 1792. Grey brick, five bays, two storeys. Porch with two pillars and two Ionic columns. Several alterations of 1852 are clearly visible. They include the top enrichments and a veranda of coupled Tuscan columns round the bow window on the side.

WINDMILLS. There are two marsh mills E of Theberton, by the estuary of the river Minsmere. One is called East Bridge Mill, the other Sea Wall Mill. They are both tower mills and both derelict.

THELNETHAM

0070

ST NICHOLAS. Outside the village. Much overgrown with ivy, and how handsome that is, and how rarely one sees it in these archaeological times! The creepers even hang down over the E window. The church is all of c. 1300 and a little later. In the w tower Perp w window with a niche above. Above this small circular windows with quatrefoils. In the s aisle the E and w windows intersected-cusped, in the chancel the E window (of five lights) an unusual, clearly Dec, variation of the theme of intersected tracery. The lights have ogee arches to start with, and there are small motifs interpolated in some of the inter-secting fields too. The arcade of four bays has octagonal piers and arches of one chamfer and one sunk quadrant, both dying into the piers. Good angle PISCINA with naturalistic foliage, a pointed-trefoiled arch with dog-tooth enrichment, and a gable with ballflower. – SCULPTURE. Good circular relief of the Flight into Egypt, C18 and probably Italian. – STAINED GLASS.

Small bits in the s aisle e window and a chancel s window. –
PLATE. Set 1744. – MONUMENT. Henry Bokenham † 1648
and his wife † 1654. Two demi-figures in an arched niche, with
books and a skull. Looped-up curtains l. and r. In the 'predella'
son and daughter, small, frontal, in oval niches. The quality of
the monument is poor.

(EVERGREEN OAK INN. In the orchard the base and about a foot
of the shaft of a CROSS erected by John Cole in accordance with
his will of 1527. He left 10s. for it. DOE)

WINDMILL. A derelict tower-mill.

THISTLETON HALL *see* BURGH

4070
THORINGTON

ST PETER. Round tower with the unusual distinction of a band
of tall blank arches at half its height and of twin bell-openings
separated by deeply set-back columns. The tower and the
blank arches may well be late Anglo-Saxon. Early c16 brick
battlements. This fine tower is marred by a shocking, showy
neo-Norman tower arch towards the nave. Nave and chancel;
the chancel all but rebuilt in 1862. In the nave just above the s
porch roof the remaining part of a Norman arch with chip-
carved star patterns. It must have been the surround of a lavish
window. – FONT. Octagonal, of Purbeck marble, c13, of the
familiar pattern with two shallow blank pointed arches to each
side. The stem is Perp, of the equally familiar pattern with
four seated lions. – BENCHES. Some, with poppy-heads. –
PLATE. Cup and Paten 1652; Flagon and Almsdish 1659.
THORINGTON HALL has been demolished. The pretty 'orné'
NE LODGE remains, with thatched roofs.

0030
THORINGTON HALL
1½ m. ESE of Stoke-by-Nayland

A house of the c16 with additions of the early c18. Of the former
period the handsome oriel window at the back with the bressumer over, and also the chimneys with octagonal stacks
carrying star tops; of the latter period the s doorway with its
open curly pediment. (Good interior features, including a
staircase with vertically symmetrical balusters and thickly
decorated newel-posts. NMR)

THORNDON

ALL SAINTS. The earliest detail is the N doorway of *c.* 1200 or a
little later. Then follows the tower – a S porch tower. This is of
c. 1300, see the entrance with its continuous four chamfers and
the (altered) S entry into the church. Perp nave otherwise. Good
W front with flushwork-panelled buttresses and a doorway
with shields and crowns up one order of the jambs and arch.
On a S nave buttress and the tower NW buttress the arms of the
Earls of Ufford. Outside the chancel (S) a low tomb recess. The
interior is wide and without structural division between nave
and chancel. – FONT. Octagonal. Four lions against the stem,
four lions and four angels against the bowl. – PULPIT. Jacobean. – STAINED GLASS. In the chancel NW window fragments
of the original and also of Flemish glass. – PLATE. Elizabethan
Cup.

SHORT'S FARM, 1 m. S. A stepped brick gable on the l. with
polygonal buttresses and transomed windows. The rest of the
front timber-framed with exposed timbers.

THORNHAM MAGNA

ST MARY. Dec W tower. The chancel also originally Dec, see the
S doorway and the angle PISCINA. The rest Perp, especially the
S porch. Front with flushwork panelling. Entrance with shields
in the spandrels and niches l., r., and above. The latter has a
little vault. – STAINED GLASS. A S window by *Morris & Co.,*
c. 1901–2; three large figures. Other windows mainly of
c. 1850 (restoration of the church 1851). – PLATE. Cup *c.* 1630;
Paten 1726; Flagon 1731; Almsdish 1807. – MONUMENT.
Lord Henniker † 1821 and wife. By *J. Kendrick,* one of his 40
major works. Standing monument. Two large allegorical
female figures by an urn on a high pedestal. On the urn the
profiles of Lord and Lady Henniker.

THORNHAM PARVA

ST MARY. Nave and chancel and short unbuttressed W tower.
All thatched. S and N doorways Norman, that on the N completely plain, that on the S with one order of shafts, scalloped
capitals, and one roll moulding. One Norman S window. The
circular W window high up is attributed by Cautley to the
Saxon period, because of its splay.* The chancel seems Dec;
the nave also has one Dec window. – FONT. Octagonal, Dec,
with simple tracery patterns. – (PULPIT. C17. The tester under

* Cf. indeed the many Saxon circular windows in Norfolk.

the tower. LG) – ALTARBACK. Jacobean panelling. – SCREEN.
With simple one-light divisions. Two cut-off ends of the rood-
loft beam remain in the wall. – WALL PAINTINGS. On the N
and S walls, hardly recognizable. – PAINTING. The Thornham
31a Parva Retable, discovered in 1927, is famous enough. It must
date from c. 1300, and seems to be the work of the royal workshops, especially close to the sedilia in Westminster Abbey.
Crucifixion and eight saints, four l. in one row, and four r.
The two outer ones are Dominicans. It is unknown for what
church the retable was made. The figures are slim and swaying.
The drapery folds have deep troughs across the waist and then
fall diagonally. The background is treated in fine gesso patterns. The spandrels have various flowers and leaves in relief,
also painted. – PLATE. Cup probably Elizabethan; Paten
c. 1675; Flagon 1715; Almsdish 1825.

THORPE see ASHFIELD

THORPE HALL see HORHAM

9050
THORPE MORIEUX

ST MARY. All C13 to C14. The chancel PISCINA in the angle of
the SE window with its angle shaft and stiff-leaf foliage must be
C13. The tower looks c. 1300, the nave c. 1320–30. The chancel
windows are renewed and represent a date c. 1300. The nave
buttresses are V-shaped (cf. Raydon; LG). – Fine C14 timber
porch with traceried bargeboards and simply traceried three-
plus-three side openings. – FONT. Plain, square, C13, on five
supports. – DOORS. S and W doors with quatrefoil borders. –
SCULPTURE. An elaborately carved bracket with embattled
cresting. Late Perp. What did it originally belong to? – PLATE.
Paten 1708; Flagon 1751; Cup 1765. – MONUMENT. John
Fiske † 1764. Nice restrained standing wall-monument. No
figures. The centre is a cartouche with a coat of arms.
HALL. With fragments of Tudor brickwork, especially a buttressed porch with a steep concave-sided gable.

4050
THORPENESS

Thorpeness is something extremely rare, a planned seaside
resort. It was built largely in the course of some twenty years
and to the design first of *W. G. Wilson* and later of *F. Forbes
Glennie*. The property remained in the hands of the same
family during that time and has not changed hands since. The
resort is kept relatively small, and the style of architecture is

domestic and undemonstrative, with timber-framing and weatherboarding. Work started in 1910, promisingly and imaginatively, with the making of a lake 65 acres in extent and called The Meare. In 1911 the COUNTRY CLUB and also the houses along THE BENTHILLS towards the sea, THE DUNES, THE HAVEN, and THE WHINLANDS, were started, that is the core of the estate. At the N end of The Whinlands is the Dolphin Inn and the small shopping square. The most prominent building in this whole area is the red-brick WEST BAR WATER TOWER. After the First World War followed the houses N of The Meare in Lakeside Avenue and The Uplands, Westgate, the Golf Club, and the ALMSHOUSES (1928, with brick centre through which the road from The Whinlands leads N). As one goes S towards Aldeburgh the HOUSE IN THE CLOUDS is the most prominent sight, another water tower, treated like a super-dovecote.

Next to this a WINDMILL, moved here from Aldringham. She is a 4 post-mill and was built *c.* 1803. When moved, she was given a square concrete 'round-house' with a pantiled roof and set to work to pump water into the water tower just mentioned, all the corn-grinding machinery being removed. She has an attractive hooded porch, four patent sails, and a fan-tail, but, though preserved, has not been used since the last war.

Additions of 1936–7 were the church, ST MARY, by *Wilson*, round-arched and with a crossing tower, and THE HEADLANDS, a crescent on the seafront.

THRANDESTON

1070

ST MARGARET. The exterior all Perp. W tower of knapped squared flint.* Base and buttresses with flushwork decoration. Three-light bell-openings. Frieze of shields below the W window. Inscription with the name Sulyard (*see* Haughley Park). (The chancel has good C13 detail in the rere-arches of the windows on N and S.) N of the chancel a two-storeyed vestry. Arcades of four bays with octagonal piers and double-chamfered arches. An ogee-headed niche in the N wall. Nave roof with tie-beams on arched braces alternating with hammerbeams. Coving boarded and decorated with shields. – FONT. Octagonal, Perp. Four lions against the stem, the Signs of the Evangelists and four Tudor roses against the bowl. – SCREEN. Dado of a rhythm different from that of the

* The will of Roger Ropkyn asks that 'the window and tower' be made of his goods (ARA).

upper one-light divisions. Ogee-arched lights. – STALLS. Traceried fronts. – BENCHES. With poppy-heads, and two with small figures facing the gangway. – STAINED GLASS. Canopies in a N aisle window. – PLATE. Elizabethan Cup; Paten inscribed 1568 and 1674.

Several attractive timber-framed houses.

GOSWOLD HALL. The house is reached by a brick bridge across the river. – DOVECOTE, C17, rectangular, with shaped gables.

THURSTON

9060

ST PETER. Mostly 1861–2 by *E. C. Hakewill*, after the tower had fallen. The Perp arcade seems correct and the Perp chancel original. Nice SEDILIA and PISCINA reaching evenly to the sill-frieze below the windows. The piscina has two arches and a shelf across. The wall arcading of the aisles which embraces the windows can also hardly have been Hakewill's invention. – FONT. Big leaf panels of different species, probably C14. – STALLS. Traceried fronts, the ends with simple poppy-heads. – BENCHES. With poppy-heads, traceried ends, and the seat backs carved on their backs. – STAINED GLASS. Fragments in aisle and chancel windows. – PLATE. Cup 1675.

THURSTON HOUSE. Early C18. Of seven bays, red brick. The dormer windows with alternatingly triangular and segmental pediments.

THURSTON HALL see HAWKEDON

1060

THWAITE

ST GEORGE. Nave and chancel and C19 bellcote. The w tower fell about 1800. In the chancel one slit lancet, i.e. of *c.* 1200. Early C16 brick S porch. Its roof on big wooden head corbels. The nave roof is called by Cautley a hammerbeam roof, but it is more likely that it has tie-beams which were cut off at a later date. The remaining tie-beam, the apparent hammers, and the collar-beams are embattled. – FONT. Octagonal. With various cusped tracery patterns. – PULPIT. An excellent Perp piece, each side with two ogee-arched panels and quatrefoils below. – READER'S DESK. Made up of Early Renaissance pieces, perhaps domestic. – STAINED GLASS. Some C14 bits in several windows. – The W window typical of its commemoration date, 1846. – PLATE. Elizabethan Cup.

TICEHURST see TOSTOCK

TIMWORTH

8060

ST ANDREW. Though called rebuilt in 1868, much is clearly of the old building, especially the s porch and the early C14 doorway. Dec nave, E.E. chancel. – COMMUNION RAIL. With twisted balusters.

TOSTOCK

9060

ST ANDREW. Chancel of the late C13. The E window has three lights and quatrefoiled circles. The chancel arch is well detailed. Dec w tower with buttresses decorated with flushwork panelling. Dec s porch with very strange side windows, now largely blocked. They are oblong, and have one reticulation motif in the middle, with four mouchettes, two above, two below. Perp N and s aisles. Both have a recess in the exterior of the E wall. The N aisle front has a rough flint and stone chequer effect. The nave roof alternates between arch-braced principals and double hammerbeams. The latter have pendant hammer-posts below, and arch braces spring from the upper hammer-beams. Figures on the pendants. Tracery in the spandrels. – FONT. Octagonal, early C14. Fluted stem, leaf or flower panels on the bowl, the carving crude, but the leaves intended to be true to nature. – BENCHES. A set with poppy-heads and beasts and birds on the arms and carved backs. – COMMUNION RAIL. Of *c.* 1660. – STAINED GLASS. Bits of original glass in the E window. – PLATE. Elizabethan Cup; Paten 1558.

TOSTOCK OLD HALL. The decoration of the overhang and the dormers of *c.* 1600. Of about the same date a mantelpiece and the staircase.

TICEHURST, ½ m. SW. Dated 1599. With two carved bressumers and carved bargeboards.

TRIMLEY

2030

The two churches of Trimley St Martin and Trimley St Mary lie on the boundaries of their respective parishes – so much so that they are in the same churchyard.

ST MARTIN. Mostly C19. Dec s doorway, Perp N doorway. N chapel of brick, early C16, with a low tomb recess inside. – FONT. Square, called Norman, but very doubtful.

ST MARY. Ruinous w tower of *c.* 1430–50, but with a row of shields above the doorway which can by their heraldry be dated late C13. The doorway has one order of fleurons in the arch and shields in the spandrels. s porch entrance also with fleurons up one order of jambs and along the arch. The N and s doorways are of the C14; ogee-headed. The chancel arch is clearly Dec. – CARTOON for a mosaic, 'by an Italian artist', given in 1901. The style is that of the school of image-painters, inspired by such successful artists as Barabino. – PLATE. Cup and Paten 1793.

(OLD RECTORY. By *Barnes*, 1858.)

⁹⁰⁷⁰
TROSTON

ST MARY. E.E. chancel with lancet windows N and S (broad rere-arches inside) and an E window with three stepped lancet lights. W tower of *c.* 1300. Fine, steep tower arch. Dec nave; the two-light windows have in the tracery head the favourite figure of the four-petalled flower. The nave roof has scissor-bracing above as well as below the collar-beams. Perp S porch with flushwork panelling. Entrance with fleurons etc. Three niches above it. Battlements with initials. – PULPIT. Two-decker, made up of various parts. The pulpit itself Jacobean, the reader's desk with parts which may be Italian. – SCREEN. Of one-light divisions, with ogee arches and tracery over.* – ROOD LOFT. The E front re-used behind the altar, a rare sur-vival. – COMMUNION RAIL. Jacobean. – BENCHES. With poppy-heads and animals on the arms. – WALL PAINTINGS. A large C15 St George, a large C15 St Christopher, a smaller St George of *c.* 1250, and a Martyrdom of St Edmund. Fragment of a Doom over the chancel arch. – STAINED GLASS. Canopies etc. in the N windows. – PLATE. Almsdish inscribed 1715; Set 1778.

TROSTON HALL. Timber-framed and mostly incongruously but prettily tile-hung, probably about 1875. Symmetrical front with two projecting gabled wings. Inside three excellent plaster ceilings, one in the middle room above the hall, and two in the wings, one above and one below. In the middle room patterns of curved ribs and a frieze with unicorns, goats, and a man trying to club a lion. In the other upper room the walls have pretty Chippendale panelling. Fine staircase of *c.* 1680 with twisted balusters. Good Elizabethan fireplaces.

¹⁰⁴⁰
TUDDENHAM
3 m. NE of Ipswich

ST MARTIN. W tower modest with flushwork on the buttresses and battlements. Legacies for the building of the tower date

---

* A will proved in 1459/60 leaves 6s. 8d. to the new making of the candle-beam (ARA).

from 1452–60. w doorway with fleurons on one order of jambs and arch. Hood-mould on two lions. Nave and chancel. The N doorway is Norman. Two orders of colonnettes with scalloped capitals. Much zigzag in the arch. Hammerbeam roof in the nave with prone angels, their heads cut off. Moulded wall-plate. – FONT. Dated 1443, but unfortunately completely re-cut. Base with quatrefoils and inscription. Stem with four large and four small figures. Bowl with two angels, the two figures of the Annunciation, and the four Signs of the Evangelists. – PULPIT. Perp. With ogee-arched panels and small figures on shafts against the angle posts. – BENCHES. The ends with tracery, poppy-heads, beasts, and birds.

TUDDENHAM HALL. Mid-C17 with much Late Victorian addition. Two original gables and gabled porch. The latter has a pediment to crown its gable – a typical mid-C17 motif – and a niche beneath with the figure of a Wild Man. One of the two big gables is also pedimented.

(FOUNTAIN INN. C16. With an ornamental plaster ceiling. DOE)

TUDDENHAM
3 m. SE of Mildenhall

7070

ST MARY. Mostly Dec. The w tower has a pretty front with two niches flanking a circular window with a quatrefoil. Dec N nave and (less good) s aisle windows. Interesting E window with reticulation, in which, however, the top reticulation motif is wilfully replaced by a circle enclosing three cusped spherical triangles. Inside, the window is flanked by niches. Tall gabled s porch of the same date (side windows with Y-tracery). The s arcade has the typical C14 octagonal piers and double-chamfered arches. Tomb recess in the N wall. Perp clerestory and hammerbeam roof. – PLATE. Cup and Paten 1626.

TUNSTALL

3050

ST MICHAEL. Tall w tower. Base and buttresses with flushwork decoration. The top repaired in brick. w doorway with a little fleuron enrichment in one arch moulding. s porch with quatrefoils on the base, flushwork panelling, and an entrance with shields in the spandrels charged with the Symbols of the Passion and the Trinity. Nave with tall three-light Perp windows. (In the chancel priest's doorway with ballflower ornament. LG) – FONT. Perp foot and stem, but the bowl Late

Norman, of Purbeck marble, octagonal, with two shallow round-arched panels on each side. – BOX PEWS.

BAPTIST CHAPEL, Tunstall Common. 1805. Of red brick, simple.

THE GABLE. Timber-framed farmhouse s of the church, with one gable and one side picturesquely brick-nogged.

UBBESTON

3070

ST PETER. Norman s doorway with one order of shafts and one zigzag in the arch. Early C16 w tower of red brick with double-stepped battlements. The brick s porch is clearly later. In the nave and chancel two brick windows. Roof with arched braces up to a high collar. – FONT. Octagonal, Perp, simple. – PLATE. Elizabethan Cup and Paten; Paten 1721. – MISCELLANEA. A COLLECTING SHOE dated 1683.

UBBESTON HALL. Early C18. Red brick, three widely spaced bays. Segment-headed windows. Parapet and hipped roof. Nice stables with rusticated quoins and hipped roof.

UFFORD

2050

ST MARY. Norman N walling. Re-used Norman doorway in the chancel. The arcade consists of two parts. The two E bays are of c. 1200, with massive round pier and responds; the four-centred arches are Perp. The w bays are later; octagonal pier and two-centred arches. All the arches are double-chamfered. W tower with a little flushwork decoration, s porch with much: stars with shields, quatrefoils, a wavy tracery band, and arched panelling. Three niches above the entrance. Clerestory of eight windows against the four bays below. Fine roof with alternating hammerbeams and tie-beams supporting moulded principals which rise to the ridge-piece without any collar-beam (J. T. Smith). Chancel roof with collars on long arched braces. The braces are divided in two by pendants coming down from the purlins (cf. Crowfield). The purlins are longitudinally arch-braced, and the wall-plate is richly decorated with battlements and small angels with spread wings. – FONT. The bowl is supported by heads. Against the bowl shields and roses set in quatrefoils and similar fields. – FONT COVER. A prodigious and delightful piece reaching right up to the roof. Munro Cautley calls it 'the most beautiful in the world'. Richly crocketed and beset with finials in six or seven tiers, or three, according to how one counts in this thicket of fine decoration. At the very top a Pelican in her Piety. The lower

25a

panels slide up over part of the upper. – SCREEN. Dado with painted figures, and rood beam. – BENCHES. With much tracery and poppy-heads on the ends, and to the l. and r. of the poppy-heads animals. – (SOUTH DOOR. With C14 ironwork. LG) – BELL. Of c. 1400 (on the floor at the w end). – PROCESSIONAL CROSS. Said to be C17 Flemish. – CANDLESTICKS and CRUCIFIX on the high altar, said to be dated 1707 and Italian. – PLATE. Cup and Paten 1671. – MONUMENTS. Brass to Symon Brooke † 1483 and three wives. 18 in. figures (nave floor). – Sir Henry Wood † 1671. At the w end of the s aisle big sarcophagus and on it a shrine-like black marble shape crowned by a cartouche with a coat of arms. Free-standing on the sarcophagus an urn. – Outside the w wall of the churchyard STOCKS.

ALMSHOUSES. 1690. Red brick with big, simply profiled shaped gables and low segment-headed windows. Two storeys; three doors.

PARK HOUSE, Lower Street. Early C16 wing with ornamented circular chimneys.

In UPPER STREET the RED HOUSE, C18, of two storeys and four bays. The middle window on the first floor is arched. To its N, on the opposite side, CROWN FARM HOUSE with a pretty gable towards the street. Timber-framed with bricknogging. Two overhangs.

GROVE FARMHOUSE, 1¼ m. w of the church. Front with three big identical shaped gables. Probably late C17.

UFFORD HALL see FRESSINGFIELD

UGGESHALL

4080

ST MARY. Norman nave, see the blocked N doorway and the general shape of the s doorway. C14 chancel, much altered and with an C18 E wall of flint and brick chequerwork. Weatherboarded tower stump. Inscription below the w window, asking for prayers for John Jewle and his wife. The nave roof has arched braces meeting at the collar-beams. – FONT. Octagonal, Perp. Against the stem four lions, against the bowl four flowers, two lions, and two angels. – PULPIT. Jacobean. – PLATE. Cup and Cover 1568; Almsdish 1682; Credence 1808.

RECTORY, close to the church. Early Georgian. Red brick, with five windows, two storeys, a pedimented doorway, and a hipped roof.

UNDLEY see LAKENHEATH

UPPER STREET *see* STUTTON *and* UFFORD

WALBERSWICK

Walberswick was once a prosperous little town, and the church which now lies right outside was no doubt nearer. The pretty green must also have looked more urban than it does today.

ST ANDREW. A church as stately as Southwold or Blythburgh, but now three quarters a ruin – and all the more impressive for it. The length is 130 ft, the height of the tower *c.* 85 ft. The agreement for the building of the tower dates from 1426. The masons were *Richard Russell* of Dunwich and *Adam Powle* of Blythburgh. They were supposed to go in their design by features of the towers of Tunstall and Halesworth. Russell was a man of some standing at Dunwich, three times one of the two Bailiffs of the town, and also one of its M.Ps. The church was dedicated in 1493 and the N aisle added *c.* 1507. The superfluous parts were taken down as early as 1695. The tall W tower and part of the S aisle are all that function. The W tower is in four stages and has three-light bell-openings, a parapet with shields and tracery, battlements with flushwork decoration along the base, a niche above the entrance, and a tierceron-vault inside. The aisles were six bays long; only four of the S aisle are in use. The chancel projected by one bay. The windows were tall. The arcade piers were quatrefoil with small spurs in the diagonals. The clerestory had the same splendid array of closely set windows as the neighbouring churches of Southwold and Blythburgh. Flushwork decoration on the buttresses, the E wall below the four-light window (re-set), and the parapets. – FONT. The stem with four lions, the bowl with four lions and four angels. – PULPIT. Perp, of wood, with tiers of blank quatrefoils. – SCREEN. Only part of the dado remains.

WINDMILL. As the result of a fire in 1960 only the gutted shell remains of what was a brick-built tower-mill with common sails and a tail-pole for winding the boat-shaped cap. She drove a scoop-wheel of about 12 ft diameter with floats 7 in. wide. Her function was drainage.

WALDRINGFIELD

ALL SAINTS. W tower of red brick with blue headers; early C16. – Nave and chancel in one; over-restored 1864. – FONT. Stem with four Wild Men with goats' legs and four seated figures of clerics (or women ?). Bowl supported by demi-figures of angels. On the bowl the Signs of the Four Evangelists and four angels with shields representing the Trinity, the initials of Christ, the Lamb and Cross, and the Cross. – PLATE. Cup *c.* 1567.

BARROWS. One lies on the heath in the SW corner of the parish (*see* Brightwell), a second by the Folly cross-roads (*see* also Martlesham and Foxhall).

WALPOLE

ST MARY. Externally all of 1878, including the tower with its awkward bell-stage and spire. Norman S doorway. The arch has zigzag, the hood-mould a chain of shell motifs. The chancel has broad flat flint buttresses, also probably Norman. – FONT. Octagonal, Perp, moulded only. – PLATE. Elizabethan Cup; Paten 1576.

CONGREGATIONAL CHURCH. Built 1607, adapted as a chapel as early as 1647. Enlarged some time before 1698. Original mullioned windows survive. At the back two tall arched Georgian windows. Three wooden columns run along the middle supporting the roof. The interior has the pulpit (with tester) in the middle of one long side, and pews and galleries on three sides.

THE ELMS, SW of the Congregational Church. House dated 1613 and with pargetting partly of that date (the vine frieze) and partly of 1708 (the very rustic oval cartouche).

WALSHAM-LE-WILLOWS

ST MARY. Perp throughout. W tower with flushwork panelling on the battlements. N porch with a flushwork lozenge pattern all over. Wood panelling inside the porch gives the date 1541 and has Roman lettering. The N aisle has a base of the same flushwork lozenge pattern. The clerestory has doubled windows and flushwork emblems between them. The S aisle is more modest and has no porch. Seven-bay arcades. Concave-sided octagonal piers, double-hollow-chamfered arches. The piers have on each side at the top a small cusped blank ogee arch. Beautiful roof of low pitch with alternating tie-beams and short hammerbeams, both very delicately ornamented. The shafts for the hammerbeams and braces go down between the clerestory windows. – SCREEN. Dated 1441.* Tall one-light divisions with ogee arches. Original coving and cresting. The dado is painted red and dark green with flowers on. – BENCH

---

* A will of 1448 leaves 6s. 8d. to the fabric of the new rood beam and one of 1459 11 marks to the new stonework (ARA).

ENDS. A few. – REREDOS. Last Supper, by *G. Tinworth*, in terracotta. Dated 1883. – DOOR. The inner door to the vestry is leather-covered. – PANELLING. In the aisles. One panel is dated 1620. – STAINED GLASS. Bits in the E window. – PLATE. Elizabethan Cup.

CONGREGATIONAL CHURCH. 1844. White brick with red brick dressings; a pediment on attenuated coupled pilasters at the angles. Three bays. Broad Roman Doric porch.

(THE PRIORY, now Vicarage. The house is supposed to contain pre-Reformation remains.)

(At CRANMER GREEN, 1¼ m. E, is GREEN FARMHOUSE, with a chimneystack of octagonal shafts and a quatrefoil frieze at the base. F. A. Girling)

3030

WALTON

ST MARY. S tower of 1899; S aisle of 1860. The chancel and the nave N side are medieval. A fragment of the old SW corner of the church in the churchyard. The building was of septaria with limestone dressings. – FONT. Octagonal, with two lions and two Wild Men against the stem and four lions and four angels against the bowl. – SCREEN. Only the dado, but of unusual design in its blank tracery. – PLATE. Cup and Paten Elizabethan. – BRASS. William Tabard † 1459 and wife; 1 ft 7 in. figures.

WALTON HALL, opposite the church. A handsome house of c. 1740–50, altered it seems in 1796, the date which appears on a chimney. Red brick, five bays, two and a half storeys. Fine doorcase with Roman Doric pilasters, a metope frieze, and a segmental pediment. The panelling and a good Rococo fireplace on the first floor are also of c. 1740–50. So seems the staircase with three twisted balusters to each step and blank brackets on the tread-ends. The staircase is said to come from Brightwell Hall.

No. 218 HIGH STREET, just E of the church. Early C19, yellow brick, three wide bays with a semicircular porch with attenuated Roman Doric columns. The windows l. and r. are evidently altered.

WALTON CASTLE. About 222 yds offshore, at a point ⅜ m. S along the cliffs from the club house, is the site of the Roman coastal fort first noted in 1613. Like Burgh Castle, it appears to have been rectangular in plan, with bastions and an E entrance. Erosion has led to the collapse of the site into the sea; remains were last seen in 1933. On the present edge of the cliffs is a

Roman cemetery site; coins have also been found ranging from Severus Alexander (222–35) to Honorius (395–423). The castle may be the site of St Felix's see of Dommoc; *see* Dunwich, p. 192n.

WALNUT TREE FARM *see* BENHALL

WANGFORD

7080

3 m. SW of Brandon

ST DENIS. Nave and chancel Norman, W tower Dec. The N and S doorways have one order of shafts with scalloped capitals and altered arches. Handsome E window of *c.* 1300. Three lights, a big circle and in it a finely cusped pointed trefoil and three little circles. In the N wall pretty niche with a nodding ogee arch in the canopy. – PLATE. Silver-gilt Cup and Paten *c.* 1680.

WANGFORD

3 m. NW of Southwold

4070

ST PETER AND ST PAUL. A large, mostly Victorian church, largely due to the munificence of Lord Stradbroke. Of the old church the arcade remains, of two bays, then a short low bay to hold a monument, and then the third bay. Quatrefoil piers and spurs in the diagonals. Arches with two wave mouldings. The arcade connected the old nave with the surviving N aisle. Of the three N windows two are Perp, the third, middle one, still entirely Dec, of a curious design. The three lights have straight-sided arches and the tracery above is a variation on the theme of the four-petalled flower. So the aisle probably dates from the years of transition, say *c.* 1370. Attached to the W end of the aisle is a porch, also original. The nave S wall is original too, though the nave was restored and altered in 1865, when no doubt the flying buttresses were erected. The chancel, NE tower, and vestry were built in 1875. Very ornate reredos, sedilia, piscina, etc. – FONT. Perp, octagonal, simple. – PULPIT and READER'S DESK. Made up of C17 woodwork from Henham Hall, supposedly Flemish. Much fine marquetry. – PLATE. Cup and Paten 1694. – MONUMENTS. Sir John Rous † 1730, a good Rococo piece with three cherubs' heads below and coats of arms in a Rococo cartouche against an obelisk above. – Sir John Rous † 1771, by *John Walsh.* Minor, but elegant. – John, first Earl of Stradbroke, † 1827. By *Behnes.* With a kneeling woman by an urn.

WANTISDEN

St John. Now on the edge of an aerodrome and not easily
accessible. Norman s doorway with one order of colonnettes
and a hood-mould with triangle or flat nutmeg decoration. In
the chancel one Norman window. (Norman chancel arch.) –
FONT. Late C12. Entirely built of small blocks of stone. –
(BENCHES. With poppy-heads and grotesques on the arms.
Cautley)

(WANTISDEN HALL. 1550. Red brick with stepped gables.
Diaper pattern of dark blue headers. DOE)

WASHBROOK

St Mary. In a sheltered position, away from all traffic. Norman
nave with two windows preserved. Surprisingly ornate Dec
chancel. On the s as well as the N six seats in niches with
crocketed ogee gables. Also in the jambs of the windows
blank ogee arches. A bigger such arch for the Easter Sepulchre,
and opposite it PISCINA and SEDILIA. The date is probably
c. 1340–50. Perp w tower, its base with flushwork decoration.
Brick battlements. – FONT. Octagonal, Perp. At the base four
lions, on the bowl four panels with demi-figures of angels and
four with flowers. – (The tester of the former PULPIT, which
was of the C17, is now a table in the vestry. – Fine iron HOUR-
GLASS STAND. LG)

WATER HALL see WIXOE

WATTISFIELD

St Margaret. Unbuttressed w tower, the tower arch of c. 1300
or earlier. Base outside with flushwork panelling. The bell-
openings are Perp, of two lights with tracery. Nave and chancel
Perp with two-light and three-light windows. The s porch
must once have been quite an ambitious piece with flushwork
decoration, but it fell on evil days and was repaired extensively
in brick. Good C14 timber N porch. – FONT. Octagonal, Perp,
with panelled stem and shields on the bowl. – (SCREEN.
Parts in the prayer-desk and lectern. LG) – STAINED GLASS.
E window typical of c. 1850. – PLATE. Two Elizabethan Cups.
Wattisfield Hall. Long C16 range, timber-framed, with a
porch and four fine chimneystacks. The chimneys are polygonal
with star tops. The porch has pretty balustrading in the side

walls. Four gables at the back. One window at the back has kept its original mullions and transom. Walled front garden.

IRON AGE SITE, on the edge of Calke Wood, *c.* 1 m. W of Rickinghall Inferior. Investigations undertaken since 1934 have revealed a series of some twenty-four irregular pits on the clay deposit perhaps for clay extraction. Off the edge of the deposit is a rough rectangular enclosure, some 300 ft square, covering a Roman hearth but with a hut inside containing Early Iron Age pottery.

There are indications of an Iron Age SETTLEMENT and a Roman KILN at PEARTREE FARM, by the source of the Grundle, *c.* ½ m. SE of the village.

Roman KILNS. There are at least twenty-five on a clay belt on Foxledge Common. They are of C1–2 A.D. date, and thus linked with groups in Hinderclay Wood and at Rickinghall. The kiln found just S of the road bounding the S edge of Calke Wood was removed to Wattisfield Pottery for preservation.

WATTISHAM

ST NICHOLAS. Nave and chancel. Unbuttressed W tower with battlements. They are panelled in flushwork. The rest early C14 or Dec, except for the two unexpectedly domestic Victorian chancel dormers with their bargeboarded gables. – BENCH ENDS. With poppy-heads. – SCREEN. Only the dado. The figures are thoroughly re-painted.

(WATTISHAM CASTLE, on the B1078 to Bildeston. A large Gothick farmhouse of *c.* 1770. The S front has two storeys with two rounded towers, the W one roofed and of three storeys. Casement windows with hood-moulds. To the l. of this, facing SW, a wing with a round tower in the centre and an arched four-light window with simple tracery, extending through two floors. All of this is crenellated.)

WELLS HALL *see* BRENT ELEIGH

WENHAM PLACE *see* GREAT WENHAM

WENHASTON

ST PETER. The W tower probably C14. Flushwork panelling on buttresses and parapet. Nave, chancel, and N aisle. The arcade has octagonal piers and double-chamfered arches. The nave has two Norman windows, the chancel two lancet windows. Pretty S doorway with shields in one order of jambs and arch. – PULPIT. Jacobean. – BANNER STAFF LOCKER. W of the S doorway. – PAINTING. Large painting of the Last Judgement, formerly above the chancel arch. The date is *c.* 1520, the quality distressingly rustic. It is done in oil on boards. The main figures are missing – probably because the rood figures originally stood in front of the blank spaces. Above Christ and the Virgin and St John seated, below l. the Resurrection, centre l. the Blessed, centre r. St Michael, below r. Hell. – PLATE. Cup and Paten 1567; Flagon (with fox, dog, and hunter) 1690. – MONUMENT. Philippa Leman † 1757. A handsome work, no longer Rococo. The centre is an urn in a circular niche.

ST MARGARET'S CHAPEL, Mells. *See* Holton, p. 276.

(WENHASTON GRANGE, 2 m. W. C16 with early C18 brick front of eight bays. Doorway with segmental pediment. Pitched roof with dormers. They have alternating triangular and segmental pediments. Group of Early Tudor decorated round chimneys.)

WENTFORD CHAPEL *see* CLARE

1040

WESTERFIELD

ST MARY MAGDALENE. Of a former Norman doorway bits of zigzag re-used in a nave S window. The church has no porches. Most of the windows indicate a date *c.* 1300. W tower with flushwork arcading in the battlements. W doorway with fleurons in jambs and two orders of arch mouldings. Hammer-beam roof in nave and chancel. Upright angels against the hammers, carrying shields. In the chancel the angels have spread-out wings. On the wall-posts also angels, and those in the chancel also have spread-out wings. – FONT. Octagonal. With four lions against the stem, four angels and the Signs of the four Evangelists against the bowl. – STAINED GLASS. E and chancel S by *Powell* (E designed by *Bouvier* 1856, S by *Casolani* 1865). – One-light chancel N by *Morris & Co.* – PLATE. Elizabethan Cup and Paten.

WESTERFIELD HALL. Dated 1656 on an outbuilding. The house has a symmetrical front with slightly projecting wings. These have Dutch gables consisting of a convex quadrant, then a concave quadrant, and then a pediment. The front was refaced about 1700 or so with red and blue chequered brickwork.

St Andrew. An interesting building which is, moreover, aesthetically a pleasure. The present nave and chancel are an addition to a small Norman church. The (later) w tower of this became a sw tower. The Norman nave survives in essence. In its w wall, now covered by the tower, an ambitious portal, with four orders of colonnettes and much ornament in the arches: billet, stylized four-petalled flowers, and beasts' heads touching a roll moulding with their chins, but not biting into it. The w window above is placed in a blank arch and flanked by two blank arches. Zigzag in the arches, and in the middle one more-over a chain of raised circular members. The s doorway is Norman too, but much simpler. One order of colonnettes, the capitals of the block or cushion type. The arch has a scallop or lunette decoration, which is continued incised down the jambs. An outer billet moulding also comprises the jambs and the arch. Of the springing of the Norman apse traces can be seen. The w tower was added about 1300. It has flushwork panelling on the lower parts of the buttresses and on the battlements. Then came the new nave and chancel. Their date must be the mid c14. Arcade of five bays with octagonal piers and double-hollow-chamfered arches. N doorway with hood-mould on two fine heads, chancel s doorway with an ogee arch. Five-light reticulated E window. One N and one s window have two reticulation motifs and cutting into them a circle with an ogee octofoil, a perverse and original idea. Perp s aisle and nave N windows. Good roofs, with arched braces up to the collar-beams. In the old nave and chancel, i.e. the s aisle and s chapel, decorated wall-plates. – FONT. With the Seven Sacra-ments and the Baptism of Christ. Much original colour pre-served. Saints in gesso against the buttresses between the panels. Angels against the underside of the bowl. – PULPIT. Jacobean. The front one large blank Ionic arch. – SCREEN. With sixteen poorly painted panels. – STAINED GLASS. In the E window fragments of the original mid-c14 glass. – PLATE. Cup 1567; Almsdish 1811. – BRASS. Nicholas Bohun † 1602, with a genealogical table going back to Thomas Plantagenet and Eleanor Bohun.

(WESTHALL HALL. 1570 and 1870. Good chimneystacks, windows, and 'Flemish gables'. LG)

PARADISE FARM, on the N side of Cox Common, 1¾ m. NW. c16 with stepped brick gable and beneath it several mullioned brick windows.

WESTHORPE

ST MARGARET. Dec w tower with Perp w window. Dec N aisle
with Perp N windows. Dec chancel with renewed E window and
ogee-arched PISCINA. Dec w window in the s aisle, but Perp s
windows and s porch. Perp clerestory. Attached to the N side
the Barrow Chapel, of brick, with a Jacobean ceiling with
pendant but C18 window surrounds. Dec arcades of four bays
with octagonal piers and double-chamfered arches. Dec tomb
recess in the s aisle. Perp roof of simple hammerbeams alternating with tie-beams on big arched braces. – PARCLOSE SCREEN.
Dec, and quite an important piece, with shafts instead of mullions and three circles with two mouchettes each as tracery.
Much original colour preserved. – PULPIT. Simple, Perp. –
BENCHES. Just a few. – SOUTH DOOR. With tracery. – PAINT-
ING. In the Barrow Chapel black floor slab painted with flower
arrangements. – PLATE. Cup 1631. – MONUMENT. Maurice
Barrow † 1666. Semi-reclining white marble figure, hand on
heart. Two flying putti hold curtains back from a circular
inscription plate with a wreath border. Top entablature with
segmentally raised centre.

WESTHORPE HALL. Georgian, but with a three-arched Tudor
bridge of brick across the moat. The house has an original
pediment and coat of arms above the doorway. It was the
residence of Mary Tudor (1496–1533), daughter of Henry VII,
widow of Louis XII of France, and wife of Charles Brandon,
Duke of Suffolk. She had been married to Louis XII at the age
of seventeen, and he died after two years. Her love had belonged to Charles Brandon, to whom, when widowed, she was
secretly married in France. He had to pay Henry VIII £24,000
to reconcile him.

WESTLETON

ST PETER. The w tower fell in 1776. Nave and chancel thatched.
They seem to be of c. 1300, though no original windows survive.
The chancel is long, and its date can be confirmed by the good
original SEDILIA and PISCINA with shafts carrying cinque-
cusped arches. – FONT. Octagonal, Perp, with four lions
against the stem and four lions and four angels against the
bowl. – (STALLS with good C15 tracery. LG) – PLATE. Cup
and Cover 1570; Flagon 1709.

WESTLEY

Of the medieval church of ST THOMAS A BECKET there remains

in a field, ¼ m. w of the new church, the E wall with the void of the E window.

ST MARY. 1835 by *W. Ranger*. Roman cement, in the lancet style, with a SW tower and a very crude and ignorant spire. – PLATE. Paten 1564; Flagon 1703.

WESTON
4080

ST PETER. Nave and long chancel and w tower. Flint and septaria. Norman N window in the nave, blocked. Norman also the shape of the S doorway as visible from inside. C13 chancel with blocked N lancet windows and other renewed lancets. Tudor brick S doorway with four-centred arch. Nave roof with arched braces meeting at the top. – FONT. The Seven Sacraments and the Baptism of Christ against the bowl. Angels on the underside of the bowl. Panelled stem with buttresses. Three-step base, the top step in the form of a Maltese cross. It has against its sides quatrefoils. – BENCHES. With poppy-heads, also some with animals and figures on the arms. On one in the chancel a post-mill too (LG). Two backs are carved with tracery. – PAINTING. Showing through a later painted text a fragment-ary painting of Christ's Entry into Jerusalem. The date is *c.* 1300. – PLATE. Elizabethan Cup; Paten 1694.

WESTON HALL. Built in the late C16 by John Rede (*see* Beccles). A large part pulled down. What remains has a projecting l. half with polygonal buttresses and a stepped gable, on the ground floor a five-light transomed window, on the first floor one of four lights with transom, and in the gable one of three lights with transom. They are all pedimented. In the recessed r. part a six-light transomed window with pediment on the ground floor.

WESTON COTTAGE, SE of the Hall, on a bluff. The lower part of a former 'standing' or look-out tower. Late C17. Red brick. Ground-floor windows with segmental, dentilled hood-moulds. Round-arched doorway. Brick quoins.

HILL FARM HOUSE, ½ m. SW. Three bays, red brick, Elizabethan. Stepped gable-ends and pediments over altered windows.

WESTON HOUSE *see* MENDHAM
WEST ROW *see* MILDENHALL
WEST STOW
8070

ST MARY. (Norman N doorway into the vestry. With primitive volute capitals and a roll moulding.) Nave and chancel Dec, as is visible in the fine four-light reticulated E window, the PISCINA in the angle of the SE window which is elaborately

crocketed and finialled, and the nave s lancet and s doorway.
Perp nave n windows and w tower. – PLATE. Paten 1710.

48b WEST STOW HALL. Splendid GATEHOUSE, brick of the 1520s.
Built by Sir John Crofts, Master of the Horse to Mary Tudor.
Brick end walls with polygonal turrets. Pretty figural finials.
The centre between has a stepped gable. Three storeys. Above
the archway a panel of lozenge-shaped fields, quatrefoil-
cusped and probably originally holding badges. Below the top
window the coat of arms of Mary Tudor (she died in 1533).*
The turrets have blank panels with double trefoil tops and
brick pinnacles (cf. Giffords Hall and, earlier, Faulkbourne
Essex). The side of the long gatehouse is timber-framed with
brick-nogging. The gatehouse originally crossed the moat. It
stood detached from the house, of which in its original form
not much survives. It is timber-framed with brick-nogging
and had a chimneystack with trefoiled brick decoration. It still
has on the ground floor a room with moulded ceiling beams.
In Elizabethan times the gatehouse was handsomely connected
with the entrance to the house by a colonnade of brick, plastered
and provided with demi-columns and little arches inside. The
same motif was also extended to the inside of the gatehouse
itself. In the room above the gateway interesting and very
naïve Elizabethan WALL PAINTINGS: a hunting scene and the
four Ages of Man represented by a young man out hunting
(inscription: 'Thus do I all the day'), a man embracing a
woman ('Thus do I while I may'), a middle-aged man looking
on ('Thus did I when I might'), and a bent old man leaning on
his stick ('Good Lord, will this world last ever').

Roman KILNS. A group of nine on the n bank of the Lark, on the
edge of sand dunes, c. 1 m. upstream from West Stow church.
They produced imitation *terra sigillata* of early C2 A.D. date, a
sherd of which was found in the 1953 excavations of the Roman
road by Baylham Mill (*see* Coddenham) with a fibula of A.D.
100–20.

PAGAN SAXON VILLAGE. The excavation of an entire pagan
Saxon village in advance of council rubbish tipping was
recently completed. It was about a mile downstream from the
church. There is evidence of small 'halls' with associated huts
(c. 400–650 A.D.), together with considerable quantities of
pottery, objects, and economic data.

The village was established by at least A.D. 400 on an island
in the marsh on the n side of the River Lark and co-existed for

* *See* Westhorpe Hall, p. 480.

more than a generation with the local Romano-British settlement at Icklingham. The structural evidence from the site
indicates a number of small, family 'halls', 30–35 ft long, with
smaller huts grouped around them. These huts, usually
referred to as 'Grubenhäuser', or 'sunken huts', are now
shown from this excavation to have had suspended plank
floors above a hollow storage or air space, and to have had
vertical plank walls and thatched roofs. Some were provided
with internal hearths with a thick clay base to protect the
floor. These huts were clearly used for a number of purposes;
as weaving sheds, for storage, and for sleeping quarters. At
present there are three 'halls', one having a partition at one
end. Some fifty of the smaller huts have been excavated and
show a number of different types, the earlier examples cluster-
ing round the halls. There is the possibility that these represent
family units, each with its 'hall' and 'outhouses'. Apart from
the early boundary ditches on the N side of the settlement
there are no ditches or apparent boundaries between properties
within the village.

The evidence for the very early date for the settlement is the
discovery in a number of the huts of faceted, angled pottery
having close continental parallels of that period. (These notes
were kindly contributed by the County Archaeologist, Mr
Stanley E. West.)

WETHERDEN

ST MARY. Dec w tower and Dec chancel with an E window
which has reticulated tracery and a niche over. Inside it has
niches l. and r. The PISCINA is contemporary too. The rest is
Perp, i.e. the other windows of the chancel, the treasury or
vestry N of the chancel with a curious heavy half-tunnel-
vault with closely set single-chamfered ribs, the tower doorway
and the window above it, the N side of the nave,* and the
spectacular S aisle and S porch. The two latter were built by Sir
John Sulyard c. 1484.‡ The porch is attached to the w end of

* A will of 1470 leaves 6s. 8d. to the nave (ARA).

‡ Mr D. N. J. MacCulloch writes: 'Although Sir John Sulyard certainly
began the S aisle in the 1480s, the difference in appearance of the masonry
between the E part of the S aisle, and the w bay of the aisle and the S porch,
reveals a break in continuity of construction. The heraldry over the entrance
to the porch centres on Bourchier impaling Andrews, the arms of Sir Thomas
Bourchier, who married Sir John Sulyard's widow, Ann Andrews, in 1490.
Work therefore seems to have ceased after Sir John Sulyard's death in 1487
and to have been continued after Dame Ann's remarriage in 1490, finishing
some time before her death in 1520.'

the aisle and forms part of it. Base with a frieze of shields and flushwork panelling. Also a frieze of shields above the entrance. Among the flushwork is a lily in a vase (buttress between porch and aisle). The s arcade inside is Perp too, with capitals only to the shafts towards the arch openings. Double-hammerbeam roof, the lower hammerbeams tenoned into the hammer-posts, arch braces springing from the upper hammerbeams. Three-tier decorated wall-plate. Figures (not original) on the pendants. The aisle roof has cambered tie-beams and figures at the springing of the arched braces. The outer rafters are continuous to the nave wall, the inner rafters are really a ceiling (J. T. Smith). – PULPIT. Perp panels are used. – SCREEN. Fragments of the dado re-used behind the altar. – BENCHES. With poppy-heads and, on the arms, beasts and birds. Carved backs of the seats. – BOX PEWS in the s aisle. – STAINED GLASS. E window by *H. Hughes*, 1863; bad. – PLATE. Cup and Cover *c.* 1680; Set C18. – MONUMENTS. Tomb-chest with three lozenges with shields. Not in a good state. – Sir John Suliarde (Sulyard) † 1574. Tall tomb-chest with fluted pilasters and shields. On it a stone panel with a framed shield with foliage flanked by two columns. Below the panel four small kneeling figures, Sir John and his family. Not a convincing composition. As a rule such monuments as this have no figures at all.

BRICKWALL FARMHOUSE, ½ m. SE. C16. Gabled wing with two carved bressumers.

WETHERINGSETT

ALL SAINTS. A stately church, internally still dominated by the arcades of the late C13. Four wide bays, quatrefoil piers, arches of one hollow chamfer, one roll, and another hollow chamfer. The chancel arch is the same, except that the responds have their diagonal shafts without necking. SEDILIA with pointed trefoiled arches and stiff-leaf decoration. Head corbels to l. and r. To the same period belong the two identical doorways into the aisles: one order of big colonnettes, arches with a keeled roll between a deep chamfer and a slighter continuous chamfer. Dec s aisle w window. Perp the rest, especially the tall w tower, whose E buttresses overlap the arcade inside. It has no normal w doorway, but is on its lowest stage entirely open to the w (cf. Cotton). The entrance has beautiful fine mouldings. There is a niche above it, and there are niches in the buttresses. The buttresses have flushwork chequerboard panelling, the battlements nothing of interest. Perp clerestory with closely set windows. S porch with an entrance decorated on one order of jambs and arch by crowns etc. Arched flushwork panelling in the battlements. Very renewed chancel. N vestry. – FONT. Octagonal, with shields, probably c. 1660–5. – SCREEN. Parts of the dado used for the boiler screen. – STALLS. With two simple MISERICORDS. – PLATE. Two Flagons and Almsdish 1743; Cup and Paten 1745; Cup 1816.

MANOR HOUSE (former Rectory). Large and Gothic; by *Teulon*, of the 1840s.

MALTHOUSE, Brockford Street. A handsome, long, and varied front of plastered, timber-framed cottages with oversailing upper floor. On one part round, decorated chimneys.

WEYBREAD

2080

ST ANDREW. Norman round tower, with trefoil-headed lancet windows round the top. They alternate with blank flushwork windows of the same design. The church is over-restored. The forms are mostly Perp. Four-bay arcades with octagonal piers and double-hollow-chamfered arches. Roof with arched braces meeting at the high-set collar, and alternatingly starting a little higher and lower. – FONT. Panelled stem and damaged bowl. Not in use. – STAINED GLASS. E window by *O'Connor*, 1866; bad. – PLATE. Fine Almsdish of pewter gilt, said to be of the C15.

HOLIDAY HOUSE, SE of the church. With large fragments of C17 pargetting.

WHATFIELD

0040

ST MARGARET. Low broad W tower of the C13, with later pyramid roof. Nave of c. 1300, windows with Y- and intersected tracery, one with pretty little quatrefoils in two of the intersections. The stoup inside belongs to the same date. Dec chancel with reticulated windows. Simple C16 brick S porch. Tie-beam roof with crown-posts in the nave, wagon roof in the chancel. – Plain BENCHES, the date 1589 on one of them, of a pattern different from the others. – COMMUNION RAIL and WEST GALLERY, probably c. 1700, with turned balusters, in effect similar to twisting. – PLATE. Elizabethan Cup; Paten 1691; fine Dutch Paten of 1715 with embossed scenes and arms. – MONUMENT. William Vesey † 1699. Nice, humble black and white marble tablet with shield at the top.

8050
WHEPSTEAD

ST PETRONILLA. A rare dedication. Fragmentary w tower with three niches round the w window. Nave and chancel *c.* 1300 (intersected and Y-tracery). But inside, the imposts of the chancel arch with nook-shafts are Norman. Otherwise only to be noted how the rood-stair climbs up in the window recess (cf. Wingfield). – PULPIT. Made up of Elizabethan panels, including some marquetry work. – STAINED GLASS. Fragment in a chancel s window. – PLATE. Silver-gilt Paten 1725; silver-gilt Cup, said to be Parisian, *c.* 1810.

(DOVEDEN HALL, 1 m. NW. C16 with mid-C19 facing. Octagonal chimneys. Good panelled C17 room with arcading over the fireplace. DOE)

(MANSTON HALL, 1 m. S. Probably late C15. Well restored. Timber-framed with oversailing first floor and thatched roof. Group of polygonal chimneys. NMR)

(PLUMPTON HOUSE, 1¼ m. W. Partly of *c.* 1800, partly after 1911.)

1040
WHERSTEAD

ST MARY. On its own; not in the village. w tower with diagonal buttresses carrying flushwork decoration. Later brick battlements. The rest seems all new, except for the Norman s doorway. One order of colonnettes with zigzags forming lozenges, one zigzag parallel with the wall, the other at r. angles to it. – PLATE. Paten 1735; Almsdish *c.* 1742; Cup 1751. – MONUMENT. Sir Robert Harland † 1848, with a draped urn. By *The Patent Marble Works* of Esher Street, Westminster (Gunnis).

WHERSTEAD PARK. 1792–4. Grey brick, two storeys, seven bays. The ground-floor windows set in blank arches. Inside a very fine large staircase starting in one flight and returning on itself in two. Galleries with pairs of imitation yellow marble columns on the first floor. Shallow vault and glazed dome. Simple iron handrail. The grounds were landscaped by *Repton* (*see* his *Sketches* of 1794).

BOURN HALL. Timber-framed C16 house (one room inside with C17 plasterwork – DOE). Good C16 BARN of five bays. Timber-framed walls with brick-nogging.

WHITE HALL *see* GREAT WALDINGFIELD

WHITTINGHAM HALL see FRESSINGFIELD

WHITTON see IPSWICH, pp. 289n, 293, 296

WICKHAMBROOK

ALL SAINTS. Mostly Dec, and with a fine chancel. In the E
window large circle with figure of six-petalled flower, in the
side windows figures of four-petalled flowers. Finely moulded
chancel arch. N aisle N windows with cusped and uncusped
intersected tracery. Earlier N doorway with two orders of
shafts and dog-tooth decoration in the hood-mould. PISCINA
in the N chapel (vestry) also with dog-tooth. Somewhat later E
window with reticulation. S doorway with two quadrant
mouldings, though the windows here are Perp. Tall two-light
reticulated window in the W tower. Arcades with octagonal
piers but semicircular responds. Double-chamfered arches.
On the N side hood-mould with defaced figures. In the N aisle
an arch was built or planned to the N. There seems to be no
reason for it. The nave roof is of the hammerbeam type, but
Jacobean. – BENCHES. Of an unusual shape, C16 or C17. –
SCULPTURE. A small Saxon figure of a man with a shield, outside in the S wall. – HELM. Above the Heigham Monument, but
not belonging to it. – PLATE. Flagon 1740. – MONUMENTS.
(Good brass to Thomas Burrough † 1597. LG) – Sir Thomas
Heigham † 1630. By *Nicholas Stone*. Good alabaster monument. He is lying on his side, his hand on his sword. Broad
beard. Plain back wall. The inscription is worth reading.
Original grille.

VILLAGE SHOP (Commerce House). With a Gibbs door surround. Probably c. 1740–50.

WINDMILL. Disused post-mill on the hill to the N.

There are three good houses round Wickhambrook, the best-
known being GIFFORD'S HALL, I m. SE. This was built by a
Heigham about 1480 and much restored and enlarged early in
the C20. The SE part is the original house. Hall with five-light
S and seven-light E window. The room above the hall has a
splendid ceiling with moulded beams, and a fireplace with
fleuron decoration. The adjoining smaller room has another
such ceiling.

CLOPTON HALL, ¾ m. NE. C16. Front with three equal gables
and a (modern) one-storeyed gabled central porch. Star-
topped chimneys in three symmetrically arranged stacks.

BADMONDESFIELD HALL, Park Gate, 2 m. N. A moated house
given a drastic mid–C20 beauty treatment. There remain in the

hall,* however, two beautiful doorways, one larger than the other, both with beautiful angels in the spandrels playing musical instruments. In the r. wing an original fireplace, in the l. wing the kitchen fireplace and oven.

At PARK GATE itself, ½ m. S of the above house, COUNCIL HOUSING by *Sir Albert Richardson*.

WICKHAM MARKET

3050

ALL SAINTS. The church has a S tower just E of the W end, and this is octagonal from the ground. It is Perp and has flushwork panelling on the battlements and a recessed lead spire. The W front of the church is Dec too, with a pretty doorway flanked by buttress-shafts with finials and crowned by an ogee gable. Niches l. and r. and a window above with reticulated tracery. Dec N aisle much renewed, Dec chancel with original four-light E window and SEDILIA and PISCINA. The S aisle is of Tudor brick with C19 windows. It was built with the money of Wells Fulburn, who died in 1489. The arcade piers inside, S as well as N, are quatrefoil, the lobes filleted, and with spurs in the diagonals, i.e. C14. – FONT. Octagonal, Dec, with tracery-panelled stem and crocketed gables on the bowl. – SCULPTURE. On the pulpit a small figure of St John. This is said to come from the Savoy Chapel in London. – STAINED GLASS. In the S chapel by *H. Hughes*, 1878; bad. – PLATE. Elizabethan Cup; Paten dated 1567; Paten 1685; Flagon 1737.

PERAMBULATION. The church lies a little to the S of the square, here called THE HILL. To reach it one passes one stately yellow brick house of seven bays with pedimented doorway on Tuscan pilasters. In The Hill the principal building is the WHITE HART HOTEL, with a Late Georgian nine-bay front of red brick, not too regular, and a funny Ionic porch. Opposite is HILL HOUSE, also Late Georgian and of grey brick. On the N side two timber-framed houses. All this is small fry, and so is what else can be mentioned on the road leading down to the mill. There are the occasional orderly Georgian fronts and pedimented doorways, and at the end the picturesque group of MILL and miller's house.

WICKHAM SKEITH

0060

ST ANDREW. Dec W tower with some chequer flushwork panelling. Perp N porch with tall side windows, a front with

* Formerly aisled (P. G. M. Dickinson).

arched flushwork panelling, a niche above the entrance, a flushwork frieze of shields in stars below the battlements, and flushwork-panelled buttresses. Less important Perp s porch,* two-storeyed, with knapped front. Nave and chancel Perp. The chancel arch on big head corbels. To its N three narrow niches, to its s one broad one. Hammerbeam roof. – FONT. Badly preserved. The stem had the Signs of the Evangelists and four Wild Men. The bowl with quatrefoils, blank arches, etc. – BENCHES. A nice set. What might their date be ? – DOORS. W door with tracery, s door with linenfold. – COMMUNION RAIL. With turned balusters, probably mid-C17. – BRASS. Kneeling Lady and her daughters. Fragments, *c.* 1530, the lady 13 in. in length (W of font).

WICKS'S GREEN *see* EARL STONHAM

WILBY   2070

ST MARY. Perp. w tower with flushwork decoration on base, buttresses, and battlements. W doorway with hood-mould. W window flanked by niches. s doorway with hood-mould. s porch faced with panelling in flushwork. Entrance arch with fleurons etc. Nine niches in a row above the entrance, the middle one bigger than the others. s arcade with rather coarsely detailed piers. Polygonal projections to nave and aisles, big shafts to the arch openings. Nave roof with arched braces from below as well as above the wall-plate. Also transverse arched braces from the tops of the others to support the ridge-beam. The aisle roof is original too. – FONT. Eight figures in niches against the stem; against the bowl four seated figures with the Signs of the Evangelists and four standing angels. – PULPIT. A very elaborate Jacobean piece with back panel and tester. – BENCHES. Set with poppy-heads and two animals or groups of figures l. and r. of them and mostly facing the gangway. Among these are the Seven Sacraments, mostly found carved on fonts, and the Works of Mercy, mostly found painted on walls. – STATUE. Stone statue of the Virgin in the SE corner of the chancel; *c.* 1500, not English. – WALL PAINTING. Large St Christopher (N wall). – STAINED GLASS. Canopies in N windows; fragments in the NE window. – PLATE. Cup and Cover Paten (Norwich), Elizabethan; Almsdish 1630; Flagon 1638. – MONUMENTS. Brass to a Civilian (nave floor), *c.* 1530, the figure 2 ft long. – Green Family; an oddly confused affair,

* A will of 1459 leaves money to a new s porch (ARA).

close to the s door. It consists of a Rococo monument (Thoma Green † 1730, George 1739, Jane 1744) with a lively cartouch with two putto heads and foliage, and an oval medallion with portrait, held by two putti. This is very good work, and on would like to know its author. The cartouche is now attache to a very tall and broad tomb-chest with three black ledger stones. Above a large, very bold, if a little coarse cartouche b *Bedford* of London, commemorating later Greens. Asymmet rically composed foliage around the inscription.

(WILBY HALL. 1579; inside a moat. Information from the Rev C. A. Mowbray)

(CHESTNUT LODGE. With a stepped brick end-gable. Tw small windows with steep pediments. Two circular windows i the gable and a stack of polygonal chimneys on its top. NMR)

0050

WILLISHAM

ST MARY. 1878 by *H. J. Green* (GR). Nave, chancel, and bellcote In the Geometrical style. – FONT. Four lions against the stem four angels with shields and four shields against the bowl. PLATE. Cup probably Elizabethan; Paten 1647.

2070

WINGFIELD

ST ANDREW. An impressive sight from the s, with the clerestorie rising above the long tiled roof of College Farm. There ar indeed clerestories, for there is one to the nave and also one with closely set windows, to the chancel – an introduction t the uncommon importance and ambitions of the church. Th date usually quoted in connexion with these ambitions is th foundation of a college of priests by Sir John Wingfield, † 136ı What can be connected with this date? The w tower is Dec, se its bell-openings. The tower arch has the same details as th arcades. Octagonal piers and double-chamfered arches. Th s aisle windows are Dec too. They have tracery with tha pretty figure of a four-petalled flower which is to be found fre quently in Suffolk and also in Norfolk, e.g. at Attleborougł Inside they are shafted. Dec also the N chapel, open to th chancel by a simple arch hung with shields up the jambs an the arch proper. This chapel is indeed connected with th Wingfield benefaction; for inside the chancel is on the N sid the MONUMENT of Sir John Wingfield, † 1361. Effigy on tomb-chest with four quatrefoils enclosing shields. Above it big crocketed ogee gable with buttress-shafts l. and r. and

cusped and subcusped arch. To its r. is a doorway also with a
crocketed ogee gable. This leads into a chamber arranged in a
curious, surprisingly modern, not to say Le-Corbusiesque
manner. The windows are tall, except for one, but the w three-
quarters of the chamber is horizontally divided into two, with
the upper room only accessible by a ladder. On both levels
SCREENS like parclose screens separate the subdivided part
from the high E part. Two squints connect the upper alcove
with the chancel. This upper room was perhaps the dwelling
of a chantry priest. It may be an insertion a little later than the
building of the whole attachment.

But the real glory of Wingfield is not what was paid for by Sir
John Wingfield, but by Michael de la Pole, second Earl of Suffolk, who died in 1415. His monument and that of his wife
stand between the chancel and a S chapel for which he must
have been responsible. This chapel is of three bays and internally quite exceptionally lavish. The first arch is a little wider
and higher than the other two and has, in addition to the shields
which it shares with the N chapel and the two S chapel arches,
a row of fleurons. In the case of the other two arches there is,
either side of the shield-hung hollow, another hollow filled not
with fleurons but with the wings of the Wingfields, the leopard
heads of the de la Poles, and the knots of the Staffords. Above
these two arches a cresting to chancel as well as chapel. Capitals
to the arch openings with demi-figures of angels; all capitals
castellated. Under the E arch stands the MONUMENT. It has
two excellent wooden effigies on a tall tomb-chest. Against its
N side are the SEDILIA: three seats with low stone arms, and
against each back two shields. Niches with crocketed gables on
the W and S sides of the monument. The archaeologically most
curious thing about the chapel is that its windows appear to
have carried on with the tracery of the S aisle with its four-
petalled flowers.* Was this done for uniformity's sake ? The
windows are also shafted inside like those of the S aisle. L. and r.
of the E window are niches.

Now the Perp contributions must be added. Perp is the grand
E window of the chancel which has in its tracery embattled
transoms at two different levels. Perp is the S porch with a
parapet of small quatrefoils and a niche above the entrance.
And Perp is, of course, the clerestory. The nave roof has arched
braces resting on demi-figures of angels holding shields and
meeting at the ridge. One more noteworthy feature of the

* The windows in the S wall are later Perp insertions.

interior is that the rood loft is reached by two stairs, rising in the window reveals of the N and S aisles.

FURNISHINGS. FONT. Four seated lions against the stem. Four lions and four demi-figures of angels against the bowl. – STALLS. Tracery fronts, ends with poppy-heads, on the arms animals and human faces. Simple MISERICORDS. – The W stalls are attached to the ROOD SCREEN, of which only the dado remains. Good. The position of the rood beam appears from the cut-off timbers in the rood-loft stairs. – PARCLOSE SCREENS to the S and N chapels. One-light divisions with four-centred crockets. Also preserved the coving, with pretty lierne ribbing. – STAINED GLASS. Canopies in the E and N windows of the vestry. – PLATE. Elizabethan Cup and Cover. – CURIOSUM. A graveside shelter for the parson; C18. It looks like a sedan chair. – MONUMENTS. For Sir John Wingfield † 1361 and Michael de la Pole † 1415, see above. – John de la Pole, Duke of Suffolk, † 1491 and his wife Elizabeth, sister of Edward IV. Alabaster effigies on a tomb-chest with five shields in quatrefoils. Back arch depressed with a quatrefoil frieze and cresting over.

WINGFIELD CASTLE. Built by Michael de la Pole (see above). Licence to crenellate was given in 1384. Splendid outer front with central three-storeyed gatehouse. Big polygonal turrets with flushwork arcading at the base. Two-storeyed wall l. and r. with angle towers. Brick battlements. The windows still have flowing details. Archway with four-centred arch, with multi-form mouldings dying into the imposts. Original DOOR with blank tracery. Inside the gateway shafts for vaulting and four doorways with two-centred arches. The archway to the inner courtyard is simpler. The house stands at r. angles to the gatehouse. On the outer façade its position and date are indicated by two three-light mullioned and transomed windows. The house is said to date from shortly after 1544. Partly brick, partly timber-framed. Fine circular brick chimneys with three-dimensional decoration.

COLLEGE FARM. Handsome house of c. 1760, rather surprising in its proportions. Nine bays, two storeys, with a pedimented, slightly projecting five-bay centre. The wings have the odd rhythm of a centre with a Venetian window on the ground floor and blank wall above it on the second. Central doorway with segmental pediment on Doric pilasters set against a rusticated ground. (At the back of College Farm is a range of domestic buildings belonging to the C14 priests' college: a long corridor on the ground and first floors, and, projecting to the E, the remains of the great hall (truncated). This has an open truss of raised aisle construction (cf. Church Farm, Fressingfield, p. 223) with a crown-post. J. T. Smith)

WINSTON 1060

ST ANDREW. Unbuttressed W tower with much brick remodelling. Brick S porch. Polygonal buttresses with heavy pinnacles. Many-moulded entrance. Three oblong niches. Stepped gable. In the nave the S doorway and one window early C14. The others Perp. The chancel mostly of 1907. – PULPIT. C18, on slim turned balusters in clusters of five.

WINSTON GRANGE. The former vicarage. By *S. S. Teulon*, 1843–4.

WISSETT 3070

ST ANDREW. Norman round tower with three original windows and the original tower arch towards the nave. This has the plainest imposts and is unmoulded. Norman S doorway with one order of shafts and one roll moulding. Outer frieze of beasts' heads touching the roll moulding with their chins but refraining from biting into it. Norman N doorway with two orders of spiral- and zigzag-decorated shafts. Capitals of the scalloped and the volute types. One arch moulding with zigzag, the next with lunettes. Outer billet moulding up the sides of the jambs and around the arch. Nave Perp, chancel mostly of *c.* 1800. Handsome C14 S porch. In the spandrels of the entrance arch shields with the emblems of the Passion and the Trinity. Nave roof with alternating tie-beams and arched braces. – FONT. Octagonal. Against the stem four lions and four Wild Men. Against the bowl the Signs of the Evangelists and four angels. – (BENCH ENDS. Old poppy-heads on replaced benches.) – STAINED GLASS. Bits in the S nave tracery and one N window. – PLATE. Elizabethan Cup and Paten.

THE GRANGE, *c.* 250 yards NW, on the road to Rumburgh. Timber-framed with a gable on the l. (Inside a small hall open to the roof, with crown-post truss. DOE)

WISSINGTON 9030

ST MARY. A delightful group, with the church above the farm buildings. Nave, chancel, and apse all Norman. The only addition is the pretty weatherboarded bell-turret with its pyramid roof. Unfortunately, however, the Norman church was made more Norman in 1853. The apse was rebuilt on the old foundation and given a rib-vault, and the windows were made grander externally than they had been. But their inner splays are all right. It is possible that the Norman church had a tower over the chancel space, such as still survives in many Norman churches (cf. e.g. Fritton, Ousden). Chancel arch with one order of shafts and zigzag in the arch. Sumptuous tall s doorway. One order of shafts with odd spiral-fluting on the l., horizontal zigzags on the r. Tympanum on a segmental lintel stone, with chip-carving. Zigzag and other decoration in the arch. Simpler N doorway. – FONT. Octagonal, Perp, with panelled stem, and bowl with demi-figures of angels. – WALL PAINTINGS. A comprehensive cycle of c. 1250–75, of which much survives, even if only fragmentarily. The quality can never have been more than provincial. On the s wall of the nave two tiers, the upper with stories from the childhood of Christ, the lower with stories from the lives of St Margaret and St Nicholas. The scenes of the upper tier are framed by arcading with trefoiled arch-heads and roofs and turrets over; the lower panels are simply rectangular. On the upper tier Annunciation (only part of the angel remains), Nativity, Annunciation to the Shepherds (two scenes), Adoration of the Shepherds (two scenes), Adoration of the Magi (two scenes), Dream of the Magi (three men naked in one bed), Flight into Egypt, Murder of the Innocents (two scenes), then a window, then Presentation in the Temple and Christ among the Doctors. Among the scenes below St Nicholas with the three boys in the pickling barrels is recognizable, and the Miracle of the Cup (ship with sail). St Margaret is seen spinning, then part of the body in the scene of the passion, then Beheading, Burial (?), Ascension to Heaven (?). – On the N wall w of the doorway stories of St John Baptist. The Beheading can be recognized. In the tympanum of the doorway two women wearing hats. E of the doorway three tiers. In the upper tier St Francis's Sermon to the Birds. The tree on which the birds are perched has a stylized scrolly shape, as if it were done in metalwork. The Passion of Christ is in the middle tier. Entry into Jerusalem, Last Supper (both much defaced), Christ washing the Apostles' feet, Betrayal (?), Christ carrying the Cross, Crucifixion, Pietà, Resurrection. The stories of the bottom tier have almost completely disappeared. On the w wall the Last Judgement in three tiers. Above the N doorway is a dragon. – STAINED GLASS. The E window by *Wilmhurst & Oliphant* (TK), c. 1853. – PLATE. Elizabethan Chalice; Paten 1697.

WISTON HALL, close to the church. Built in 1791 by *Sir John Soane* for Samuel Beechcroft, a director of the Bank of England. Simple house of three by one bays; red brick. Doorway with Tuscan pilasters and heavy entablature. Windows without any surrounds.

WISTON see WISSINGTON

WITHERMARSH GREEN see STOKE-BY-NAYLAND

WITHERSDALE

2080

ST MARY MAGDALENE. Nave and chancel and weatherboarded bell-turret. In the nave two Norman windows and a plain Norman doorway. The chancel appears to be of *c.* 1300. – FONT. Square, Norman. On three sides arches, intersected arches, a rosette, a tree of life, etc., on the fourth two pointed-trefoiled arches, re-cut *c.* 1300 (?). – PULPIT. Two-decker. – BOX PEWS. – COMMUNION RAIL. Jacobean. – BENCHES. One with linenfold panelling and poppy-heads. Also a very nice, simple, probably Jacobean or mid-C17 pattern. Raised centre with knob, lower sides with knobs. – PLATE. Cup and Paten in leather case 1680.

(MENDHAM PRIORY. Early C19, grey brick, five bays wide, doorway with four Roman Doric columns. DOE)

RED HOUSE. Later Georgian. Red brick. Only three bays, but with two curved walls to connect the façade with the street.

WITHERSFIELD

6040

ST MARY. Perp, except for the S chapel, which is Dec but rebuilt. Chancel rebuilt and S aisle added in 1867. W tower with higher SE stair-turret, S doorway with Perp decoration. The N aisle was built by Robert Wyburgh *c.*1480 (see the brass inscription). But in the roof the mullet of the de Veres also appears (cf. Lavenham). Arcade of four bays, quatrefoil piers, double-hollow-chamfered arches. This is Perp. The former Dec arcade is perhaps represented by the stoup, which seems to be a re-used respond. – FONT. Octagonal, probably C17. Decoration with shields and pointed quatrefoils. – SCREEN. Good; repainted. Two-light divisions with (re-made?) pendants instead of intermediate mullions. Trefoiled ogee arches and tracery above them. – PULPIT. Jacobean. – BENCHES. Some straight-headed with buttresses, others with figured *28a* poppy-heads: St George and the Dragon, St Michael weighing souls, two puppies coming up from the foliage, angel with shield, two birds on a leaf, etc. – (RING HANDLE of the S door, of two Salamanders. LG) – PLATE. Cup and Paten 1701.

RECTORY. Red brick, five bays, two storeys, pitched, not hipped, roof. The doorway is Later Georgian, the building looks *c.* 1690–1700, but must be of *c.* 1720.

(HALL FARM, near Town Green. Timber-framed. The C15 hall is now the barn. P. G. M. Dickinson)

WITNESHAM
1050

ST MARY. Mostly late C13 to early C14. S porch tower with a little flushwork arcading on the battlements. Nave and chancel. The only Perp additions are the S aisle and the clerestory and roof. The roof is of the hammerbeam type, with arched braces up to the collar-beams. These are however hidden by a white ceiling at that height. It has simple oval and lozenge panels in plaster. – FONT. Octagonal, on two high steps. With four squat lions against the stem and four shields and four angels and shields against the bowl. – PULPIT. Jacobean. – BENCHES. With poppy-heads. – STAINED GLASS. E window by *E. Baillie, c.* 1846. – PAINTED TEXTS between the clerestory windows and elsewhere; late C17. – PLATE. Elizabethan Cup. – MONUMENT. R. C. King † 1842. Medallion with portrait in profile. By *Thurlow* of Saxmundham.

WITNESHAM HALL. Elizabethan and much imitation Elizabethan of 1844. Genuine the three-storeyed porch. Red brick with pilasters in three superimposed orders. The first- and second-floor windows with pediments. Big shaped gable (convex and then semicircular). Octagonal chimneys. (Inside two good overmantels and a staircase with slatted balusters. DOE)

REDHOUSE FARMHOUSE, ½ m. SE. On the l. a stepped gable with pedimented windows, probably Elizabethan. Behind this a contemporary ornamental plaster ceiling. The house itself is earlier, as shown by the hall screen of rude boarded work.

HILL FARMHOUSE, ½ m. NE. The gable to the road has two big angle brackets with crenellation and the brackets of former buttress shafts.

WIXOE
7040

ST LEONARD. Nave and chancel with weatherboarded bell-turret. Nave and chancel are Norman, as is seen in the treatment of the flint walling and also the S doorway with one order of shafts with scalloped capitals and a zigzag in the arch,

and the outline of the N doorway.* All windows C19 or C20. –
STAINED GLASS. E window signed by *Cakebread, Robey & Co.*,
c. 1892. – PLATE. Elizabethan Cup and Paten; Cup 1706;
Paten on foot 1728. – MONUMENT. The following inscription
appears in large and dignified letters on a plate in the chancel
floor: 'The Entrance into the Vault of Henry Berkeley Esq.
and Dorothy his wife containing Ten Foot Square.'

(WATER HALL, ½ m. NW, near Sturmer Mere. C17 with Georgian front. Magnificent BARN, dated 1795, exceptionally
large. LG)

At BAYTHORN END, just on the Suffolk side of the bridge, a
pretty early C19 house of three wide bays. It is of flint with
brick trim in vertical as well as horizontal divisions. Wide
porch with Roman Doric columns. Yellow brick parapet.

WOODBRIDGE

2040

ST MARY. The w tower and the N porch are exceptionally lavish
in their display of flushwork decoration. The w tower is 108 ft [12]
high. Bequests of money were made for it in 1444–56. It is
faced with knapped flint all the way through. At the base is a
frieze of initials and quatrefoils. The w doorway has spandrels
with two shields, and above it is another frieze, of quatrefoils
etc. Arched panelling l. and r. Two two-light bell-openings on
each side. Tall parapet and battlements, with arched panels,
and tracery. The side towards the town is the most ornate. The
tower buttresses are interesting too. They start polygonal, but
turn into angle buttresses and higher up into diagonal buttresses.
The N porch, for which there was a bequest in 1455, also has a
base with flushwork tracery panels and initials, arched panelling, another frieze with initials, and battlements with quatrefoils as well as arches. The crenellations are double-stepped,
and there are pinnacles. On the front three niches above the
entrance. The aisle walls are also knapped. Only the s chapel is
quite different. It is built of brick and is now cemented. The
E view displays flushwork parapets on the vestry chapel roofs
and a higher E gable. There is no structural division between
nave and chancel. The arcades run through six bays. The piers
have four shafts and four thinner diagonal shafts. The clerestory has twice as many windows as the bays below. Nave roof
of low pitch with hammerbeams alternating with tie-beams. –
FONT. Panelled stem. The Seven Sacraments and the Cruci-

* The church originally had an apse (P. G. M. Dickinson).

fixion on the bowl. The background of the scenes has rays. Butterfly head-dresses prove a late C15 date. – ROOD SCREEN. The dado with painted figures now in the parclose between s chapel and chancel and in the N aisle. The inscription refers to John Albrede, a twill weaver, whose will is of 1444. – CHANDELIER. Brass, given in 1676. – STAINED GLASS. In the E window Adoration of the Magi, 1929 by *Martin Travers*. The scene is in the style of contemporary English wood engraving and surrounded by much clear glass. – PLATE. Two Cups 1636; Paten 1683; Paten and two Flagons 1752. – MONUMENTS. In the chancel on the N side Thomas Seckford, who built the N chapel. He was Master of the Court of Requests and died in 1587. Tomb-chest with open arcades, not in its original state, as the lower slab has indents for brasses. No effigy left. The arches are depressed-rounded, the type the French call basket arches; the pilasters which separate them are panelled. – Ieoffrey Pitman † 1627, s chapel. Large, and also commemorating his two wives and two sons. Two kneeling pairs, one on top of the other, both pairs facing each other across a prayer-desk. Below are the two sons, above the two wives, and on top of the whole high up Ieoffrey Pitman himself kneeling frontally. All flanking pilasters with ribbon work and bunches of fruit. – Access to the churchyard from Church Street by a pair of handsome C18 wrought-iron GATES.

ST JOHN, St John's Hill. 1844–5 by *John M. Clark* to a design by his friend, a local builder, *Alfred Lockwood*. Yellow brick, in the lancet style, with a W tower that turns higher up into a funny spire. The tower is square below, the spire octagonal, first with long open lancets, and only then steeply pyramidal. The side windows of the church are groups of three stepped lancets. Coved ceiling with ribs and bosses. Penetrations connect the windows with it. Canted-forward W gallery.

FRIENDS MEETING HOUSE (now a storeroom), Turn Lane. 1678. Oblong block of red brick with hipped roof. Large windows on the l., domestic windows on the r. Galleries and a staircase with strong twisted balusters.

CONGREGATIONAL CHURCH, Quay Street. 1805. Red brick, two storeys, six bays by three wide bays. The entrance is not in its original position.

A comparison is recommended between the BAPTIST CHAPEL in Chapel Street and the METHODIST CHURCH in St John's Street, both of yellow brick, the former of 1841, the latter of 1871. Both are round-arched and have pedimented gables, but the former is humbly Gothic, the latter Italianate with some decorated capitals and friezes.

PERAMBULATION. Woodbridge is two separate things: the church with the market place and the streets that radiate from it, and Thoroughfare, about a mile long, with its feelers towards the quay. The two interlock at the junctions of Church Street and New Street with Thoroughfare.

MARKET HILL is dominated by the SHIRE HALL, given by 55a Thomas Seckford and built, it is said, c. 1575. If that is true there must have been many changes. The building stands handsome and modestly proud in the middle of the triangular market space. It is of red brick. It originally had an open ground floor – the arches and windows are clearly C19 – and the main room on the first floor, reached from W and E by open staircases, the former with two straight arms, the latter with two ampler curved ones. Coat of arms over the W doorway. W and E gables, or rather dormers, on a big hipped roof with the kind of strapwork frills characteristic of Vredeman de Vries's engravings and Dutch building of c. 1600. The MARKET HILL PUMP is Gothic and a wheel pump. It dates from 1876. Of the houses surrounding Market Hill the following deserve notice. On the W side the KING'S HEAD INN, timber-framed with an overhanging upper floor to Seckford Street and an oriel sill with five heads. On the N side No. 32, timber-framed with three gables but Georgian shop-fronts on the ground floor. The same applies to the adjoining houses. No. 14 is of grey brick, three-storeyed, and has a specially pretty doorway. The E side is dominated by the BULL HOTEL, nothing special in itself but good as a closure.*

Of the radiating streets we explore first SECKFORD STREET, starting from the SW corner. Here there are Nos. 28–32, with a pretty pargetted oval wreath. Also the SECKFORD HOSPITAL, the design by C. R. Cockerell, 1834, altered in execution (1835–42) by James Noble, who is known to have designed the Porter's Lodge in 1841 and perhaps also the ALMSHOUSES in 1869. All brick with stone dressings. From the NW corner runs THEATRE STREET, where the principal building is the ANGEL INN, timber-framed, with an E gable with two overhangs and two carved bressumers. In No. 11, on the other side, above the present archway four former window heads, four-centred arches. To the r. a little carved angel from the corner post. To

* Between Market Hill and the Churchyard the CHURCH HALL, formerly the stables of an inn. The pointed windows are a churchy insertion.

the N down Angel Lane to No. 30 CHAPEL STREET. Early
Georgian (date 1737 on a pump). Five bays originally, two
storeys, red brick. It deserves special praise how a tongue of
green all along Chapel Street comes into the town nearly as far
as Market Hill. Now down NEW STREET, from the NE corner.
The street was made in the early C16. Here the BELL INN,
with an overhang, buttress-posts, and four-centred arches, and
Nos. 85–87, again with original window arches. Opposite, the
corner of St John's Hill and ST JOHN'S STREET. Building
here started in 1843 and has quite a new urban pretension.
Grey brick, two and a half storeys, with a rounded corner
between St John's Hill and St John's Street and pilasters to
mark the main frontages. Up St John's Hill to the church and
opposite it to THE CASTLE, a very castellated, stuccoed house
with an asymmetrical angle turret. It was designed for William
Lockwood, father of Alfred (*see* above), by *George Thompson*,
and built as a club for officers *c.* 1805 (*Gent. Mag.* 1806).
Opposite the LITTLE CASTLE of *c.* 1812, with a Gothic
GROTTO of 1806 in a neighbouring garden.

Finally to the SE down CHURCH STREET. Here we start with
THE ABBEY. This house, once the manor house of Woodbridge and the seat of Thomas Seckford, stands on part of the
site of the Augustinian Priory, founded *c.* 1190. It has been
altered in most parts, but the three-storeyed porch to the S
remains with a date 1564. It is red brick, as is the rest of the
building, and three storeys in height. It has no buttresses and
instead, slightly distant from the angles, three superimposed
orders of pilasters, Roman Doric, Ionic, and Corinthian. The
windows are mullioned and transomed, the entrance arch is
round. At the top a straight gable and below it a pediment. The
other four S gables have the same motif. The porch is not in the
middle of the front, that is, it implies a hall placed in the medieval way. From the porch one still looks into the open country.
Of other notable houses in Church Street there is No. 23 with a
lovely Georgian façade at the rear and, to the street, a nice
pedimented C18 doorway with decorated frieze, and a house
successfully remodelled in 1946. It has now a recessed front
with two round pillars and a Venetian window over. Opposite
a good double bow-windowed shop. At the foot of Church
Street the other Woodbridge is reached.

The main street is called Thoroughfare in its NE half, Cumberland Street in its SW half. In THOROUGHFARE there are first
of all quite a number of Georgian and Early Victorian façades

which repay attention. Then there is, right at the beginning, the handsome Egyptian lettering of the CROWN HOTEL and the same higher up on the LION INN and the SUN INN. There are also Georgian features such as the Venetian window of No. 18, and Regency features such as the three first-floor balconies of No. 78. Their pattern repeats on No. 85, which is otherwise early C18 (stucco rustication, hipped roof). Nos. 81–83 (1745) and 97 are specially attractive Georgian houses, and No. 40 (Walker's Stores) is an attempt at being metropolitan in the Italian Renaissance of Sir Charles Barry. Probably of the 1840s (earliest date in deeds 1846). A surprise is No. 56, a building of no interest, but which has attached to its façade a broad carved frieze dated 1650, with vine and two demi-figures.

CUMBERLAND STREET has the finest Georgian houses in Woodbridge, but it starts with a neo-Georgian one of interest, the POST OFFICE, in which good Jacobean plaster ceilings and fireplaces are re-set from its predecessor. The staircase has a date 1634. The date looks suspicious but may be true. The balusters are vertically symmetrical. No. 6 opposite has the most charming doorcase in the town, with a decorated frame and frieze, No. 17 opposite a doorway with Roman Doric columns, a metope frieze, and a segmental pediment. Again opposite GORDON HOUSE with a Kentian frieze above the door. Then Nos. 32–34, good Georgian, with a very wide doorway (Corinthian pilasters and pediment). Then BROOK HOUSE, dated on the wind-vane 1674, but structurally earlier. Quoins and hipped roof no doubt of 1674. The dormers also fit that date. No. 44 is the finest of the lot. Early C18. Red brick, five bays, two storeys, a broad brick doorway with Tuscan pilasters and a segmental pediment. Top parapet and segmental pediments on the dormers.

The last expedition ought to be devoted to the QUAY. It is an ²ᵃ object lesson in Victorian callousness. How delightful that part of Woodbridge must have been before the railway and the gas works. There are, is it true, no specially meritorious houses, but the setting is undoubtedly lovely with the TIDE MILL by the river and the quayside cottages. A tide mill in this place is first mentioned in 1170. The present mill, probably C17 in origin, was at work until 1956, when the 22 in. square oak shaft of the water-wheel broke.*

* She drove four pairs of stones, and the 20 ft diameter wheel, 5 ft 10 in. wide, was from breast to undershot according to the height of the water in the pond – the drop being about 6 ft. The timber-framed structure is now clad

BUTTRUM'S MILL, ½ m. W of the church. There is also a windmill at Woodbridge, appearing quite prominently in the skyline from certain points. Buttrum's Mill was built in 1816–17
by *Whitmore & Binyon*, the millwrights of Wickham Market.
She is a typical product of this once famous but now defunct
firm. She stands just over 60 ft high. The red brick tower has
six floors and is surmounted with a Whitmore & Binyon type
ogee cap, with horizontal boarding and a gallery. She has
four patent sails and a fan-tail and drove four pairs of stones
on the third floor. There is also a pulley outside the tower
which enabled the stones to be driven by a portable steam
engine. She last worked in 1928 but was later repaired as
a landmark by the East Suffolk County Council.*

(FARLINGAYE SECONDARY MODERN SCHOOL. 1954–5 by
the County Architect's Department; County Architect *E. J.
Symcox*.)

WOOD HALL *see* SHOTTISHAM

₉₀₆₀

WOOLPIT

ST MARY. The conspicuous spire was built by *R. M. Phipson* in
1854. With its openwork parapet and the double-curved
flying buttresses helping to hold it up, it is Nene Valley rather
than Suffolk, but makes an attractive feature. The tower has a
timber vault of 1854 and a sexfoiled circular window into the
nave. The medieval church of Woolpit is Perp, except for the
modest Dec s aisle and the Dec chancel. This has a five-light E
window with reticulated tracery, niches with ogee heads in the
11a buttresses l. and r., and a shafted doorway. The s porch can be
dated *c.* 1430–55 (money given for it in 1430 and 1452). It is
extremely opulent, much taller than the aisle, with a stone-faced
front panelled all over, an entrance with a big crocketed ogee
gable and five stepped niches above, and the mouldings of the
entrance arch beset with the repeated motif of a beast with a
big leaf coming out of its mouth. The side windows have
crocketed ogee gables too, and so has the doorway inside, whose
arch mouldings are decorated with fleurons. The porch has
openwork cresting and a lierne-vault with many bosses. A will

with corrugated iron and has a tiled mansard roof (Rex Wailes). I have
recently been told that this, the last tide mill to work in the whole of Great
Britain, is to be repaired and preserved.

* This paragraph was kindly sent me by Mr Wailes. – TRICKER'S MILL,
a tower mill, is derelict at the time of writing.

of 1473–4 left £20 for five images for the porch – presumably in the gable niches (Peter Northeast). Excellent flint and stone chequerwork in the E wall (Alec Clifton-Taylor).

Many legacies are recorded for the rest of the church. They run from 1444 to 1462 and refer to 'ye body of ye churche', 'tabernaculum beate Marie de novo faciendo', 'emendacio', 'amendyng', and 'reparacon'. The sums involved range from 1s. 8d. to £14. The sum of 13s. 8d. occurs three times in wills. One of 1500 leaves money to the N aisle, which is not ornate, on condition that it be made within two years (Peter Northeast). Perp arcade inside, of five bays, surprisingly quiet (octagonal piers, arches with one hollow chamfer and one wave moulding). Fine Perp clerestory with doubled windows. The windows are of two lights with panel tracery. The wall has flushwork decoration: panelling, chequerboard pattern, and emblems. When the clerestory was built, the splendid roof 19b was also made, one of the proudest in Suffolk. The roof stands on wall-posts which in their turn rest on angel brackets. Small figures against the wall-posts. The roof has principal rafters, double hammerbeams throughout, with angels against both hammers, and arch-braced collar-beams. The wall-plate is decorated with two tiers of demi-figures of angels. All the spread-out wings make a glorious feathery, spiky pattern. Decorated spandrels and crestings of both hammerbeams and collars. In the aisle roofs also angels on the wall-posts. Large angels in addition against every second pair of principals so that their heads are separated only by big bosses. Against the other pairs wall-posts with demi-figures in niches and angels below them. Does any of the money left in the 1440s and 1450s refer to the clerestory and roof? Of the angels, some are original, but most date from 1875. – SCREEN. On the dado eight repainted figures. One-light divisions with ogee arches and some panel tracery above. High up, below the E window of the nave, is what Cautley calls a ROOD CANOPY. Five bays of finely ribbed coving with lierne patterns. It was erected c. 1875 and came, presumably, from another church. – BENCHES. They have poppy-heads and saints as well as animals on the arms, and traceried ends with a variety of patterns. Carved backs as well. – LECTERN. A fine brass eagle on a substantial base and shaft. It may date from c. 1525. It belongs in a group with Cavendish, Upwell Norfolk, Croft Lincs, Chipping Campden Glos, and Corpus Christi College Oxford. – PLATE. Cup and Paten 1576; Cup 1776.

Facing the little triangular square the SWAN INN, with a lower
part dated 1759, and a higher dated 1826. Both are red brick.
The lower is of two storeys with quoins and a niche in the
centre. From here to the s as well as N the main village street
contains a number of nice minor timber-framed as well as
Georgian houses.

(STEELES ROAD HOUSING SCHEME, a group of thirty-two
houses near the village centre, is by *Peter Barefoot*, 1961–3.)

(THE COTTAGE, The Street. This was probably the hall range
of one building which included the adjoining Tyrells. The
front is brick-faced, with two-headed casements in the upper
storey. Heavy timber-framing is visible inside. DOE)

(DOORWAYS, in Woolpit Street, is a two-storey timber-framed
and plastered building. The N part is an open hall structure of
medieval type (the roof is later); the s part is C17 with a C19
shop built out. DOE)

1030   WOOLVERSTONE

ST MICHAEL. In the grounds of Woolverstone Hall. It looks all
of the restoration of 1889–90. Visibly medieval only the brick
s porch, the s doorway, and the structure of the W tower. –
FONT. Octagonal, Perp. Small lions against the base. Bowl
with panels with lions and angel busts. – PLATE. Paten 1697. –
MONUMENT. Bust to the Ven. Henry Denny Berners, by *R.
Westmacott Jun.*, 1839.

WOOLVERSTONE HALL. Built in 1776 by William Berners (of
London) who built Berners Street. The architect was *John
Johnson* of Leicester, who lived at that time in Berners Street
and later became County Surveyor of Essex. A large, formal
mansion, beautifully situated with wide views along the
estuary of the Orwell. Grey brick and light grey stone. Centre
seven by five bays. To the estuary bow window in the middle
of this centre. To the l. and r. curved wings with Roman Doric
columns. On the entrance side a more complex group. Centre
of two and a half storeys. It is rusticated on the ground floor.
Above this four-column portico of attached Ionic columns
with pediment. First-floor windows with pediments. Then on
either side a one-bay, two-storey attachment. Then one-
storey connecting links to projecting one-and-a-half-storey
wings with attached Roman Doric porticoes in the middle of
the ends. Inside, the three main ground-floor rooms to the s
have fine plaster ceilings and good fireplaces. The centre room
on the first floor also is singled out by decoration. To the SE

STABLES. Quadrangle with handsome front of *c.* 1776 and recent tower over the archway.

The Hall is now a Greater London Council Boarding Grammar School, and in 1958 the Architect's Department (*Sir Leslie Martin** and *B. A. Le Mare*) built two excellent blocks of dormitories to the w. They are two-storeyed with brick walls, of free plan-shapes. E of the house a teaching block, one-storeyed, with a higher assembly hall in the centre.

CAT HOUSE, N of the Hall, by the jetty. Step-gabled Gothic cottage of 1793 (B. Jones). The N wall has a large three-light window with intersected tracery painted on; on its sill is a painted white cat.

(WOOLVERSTONE HOUSE. By *Lutyens*. Courtyard house with one three-storeyed and three one-storeyed wings. Information received from Mr M. J. Slater)

(CLUBHOUSE for the Royal Harwich Yacht Club, overlooking the river, by *Peter Barefoot*, 1968–9.)

WORDWELL   8070

ALL SAINTS. Nave and chancel, restored in 1868. Two Norman doorways survive, both with one order of shafts and primitive volute capitals, and both with carved tympana. That on the S side represents the Tree of Life with two affronted hounds l. and r. The branches and leaves spread and intertwine. The N tympanum is a puzzle. It faces inwards and represents two standing figures so childishly done that an earlier than Norman date seems likely. Perhaps a pagan stone was re-used. Norman also the chancel arch, again with volute capitals. The arch has one big roll moulding and no other mouldings. L. and r. two large Dec niches, no doubt for side altars. – BENCHES. A fine set. The ends have tracery, and poppy-heads with seated animals. The seat backs are carved (not in openwork) with tracery, foliage, and figures (grotesques, a jester, etc.).

(WORDWELL HALL. 'Very interesting'. P. G. M. Dickinson).

WORLINGHAM   4080

ALL SAINTS. W tower with flushwork battlements. Nave and chancel. S chapel of two bays with octagonal piers and double-chamfered arches. – FONT. Perp, octagonal. Against the stem four lions. The bowl is supported by angels' heads. Against the bowl four lions and four angels. – BENCHES. Six. With

* County Architect at the time it was started. Later, *Sir Hubert Bennett*.

poppy-heads. – STAINED GLASS. Seven windows by *Clayton & Bell*, starting *c.* 1885. – PLATE. Cup 1568; Paten 1807. – MONUMENTS. Brass to Nicholas Wrenne † 1511 and wife. – In the churchyard against the S wall of the church a large tomb-chest or sarcophagus to John Felton † 1703. In the wall behind one arched brick niche with arms (cf. Ringsfield). – R. B. Sparrow † 1805 and R. A. B. St J. Sparrow † 1818. Unsigned; of good quality. Grecian man on a Grecian chair hiding his face against a tall pedestal on which two urns with the initials of the deceased.

WORLINGHAM HALL. Remodelled *c.* 1800 by *F. Sandys*. Brick, cemented. Seven bays, two storeys, with a curved Tuscan porch and a tripartite window over. The interior of much more impressive quality. Entrance Hall with a segmental vault. Octagonal Staircase Hall behind in which the staircase rises in one arm and then spreads and returns in two. Charmingly simple iron railing. The same motif in the balcony railings of open arches like opera boxes on the first floor. To the r. of the Entrance Hall the Library, with an apsed end screened by two columns, to the l. Drawing Room. To the l. of the Hall Dining Room with pilasters along the walls. On the first floor also an equally elegantly decorated room. Excellent fireplaces.

WORLINGTON

6070

ALL SAINTS. E.E. chancel, with one N lancet window and an E window with three stepped lancet lights under one arch. Dec W tower with a pretty W window with flowing tracery. Niches l. and r. of it. Finely moulded W doorway. Dec arcade of five bays with concave-sided octagonal piers and double-chamfered arches. The sides of the piers have pointed trefoils applied to the tops. Perp aisles and clerestory. Simple nave roof, although with tie-beams alternating with hammerbeams. – ROOD BEAM. The cambered rood beam is preserved. – BENCH ENDS. Square-headed, with three stepped little arches or big flowers. – PLATE. Cup and Paten 1669.

WORLINGWORTH

2060

ST MARY. Wide chancel of *c.* 1300. Fine four-light E window, the four lights of equal height, and above them two encircled trefoils and a larger crowning encircled sexfoil. The chancel side windows have either two lights and an encircled trefoil or Y-tracery. The rest Perp. W tower with flushwork decoration on the buttresses (chequerboard) and battlements (blank arcading). The SE and NE buttresses also with flushwork: circles etc. W doorway with shields in the spandrels charged with the Symbols of Trinity and Passion. S porch with much flushwork, sacred monograms, etc., at the base and on the battlements and buttresses; arched panelling on the front. In the spandrels of the entrance St George and the Dragon. Fine S doorway with two orders of thin shafts and many continuous mouldings. N doorway with fleurons up the jambs and the arch. Tall Perp nave windows. The nave also has flushwork on base and buttresses. Double-hammerbeam roof with tracery above the first hammers. – FONT. Said to come from Bury St Edmunds Abbey. Octagonal. Four lions against the stem. The Signs of the four Evangelists and four angels with shields (Passion, Trinity, Cross) against the bowl. Inscription at the foot of the stem: 'Orate pro anima Nicholai Moor qui ista fonte fieri fecit.' – FONT COVER. Perp. Nearly 20 ft high. A tall closed lower part and then the crocketed and buttressed canopy. – PULPIT. Jacobean, with a suspended tester. – SCREEN. Parts of the dado. – BENCHES. Two Perp ones with poppy-heads and grotesques in the porch. A whole set of 1630 in the nave. A simple, satisfying, quite unusual form, the most distinguished ones with some carving on the front. The whole block of benches is arranged so that they taper off in length to open out towards the S door and the font. – (DOORS. The S and N doors are carved. LG) – STAINED GLASS. Many fragments in the tops of nave and chancel windows. – In the chancel, E and S windows of c. 1855. – PLATE. Elizabethan Cup; Paten 1699; Flagon 1720. – MONUMENTS. Sir John Major † 1781. Very fine, of white, grey, and pink marbles. No figures. By *Cooper* of Stratford-le-Bow. – Dame Ann Henniker, by *Coade*, 1793, i.e. in Coade stone. Very crisp and dainty; no figures. – Dowager Duchess of Chandos; 1817 by *John Bacon Jun*. A major work; large hanging monument, all white. Obelisk background. Small sarcophagus at its foot. Faith on the l. kneels by the sarcophagus. Hope on the r. stands and points upward. – CURIOSA. FIRE ENGINE dated 1760. – Also a COLLECTING SHOE of 1622.

WINDMILL. A derelict post-mill.

WORTHAM

ST MARY. The largest Norman round tower in England, 29 ft in diameter. About 62 ft high and now open to the sky. The top collapsed in 1780. Cautley regards it as pre-Norman. The church behind it is mostly Perp (but the chancel s doorway, as is so often the case, is Dec). The church has an engaging little weatherboarded bell-turret with an ogee top, peeping out from behind the awe-inspiring rotundity of the medieval tower. The E window is of five lights. There is a two-storeyed NE vestry. The clerestory has double windows, and between them emblems in flushwork with much use of brick. C14 arcades of three bays. Octagonal piers, double-chamfered arches. – FONT. Dec, octagonal. With gables and much decoration with small quatrefoils. At the lower corners of the bowl heads, at the top battlements. – SCREEN. Re-used parts by the altar. – ALTAR SURROUND. 1856. With verses from the Gospels in broad frames with thick vine-leaves and grapes. – STAINED GLASS. Bits in the E window. – PLATE. Cup, Norwich made, 1567–8; Paten 1776.

RECTORY, E of the church. Timber-framed core. Higher addition of 1828, white brick. Inside a small staircase of c. 1700–10 behind a typical arch.

MANOR HOUSE, ¾ m. NW. C17 with C18 front with two gables and a regular two-storeyed centre. In the centre a blank-arched niche or former window. Under the gables canted bays. To the l. round the corner a C17 shaped gable. Square chimneys with blank arches.

GATEWAY, the façade of the former Reading Room; 1870. On the A-road, 1 m. S. Three pedimented bays with three arched entrances, à la Arch of Constantine. Above them the inscriptions Hope, Charity, Faith.

IRON AGE SETTLEMENT on Spears Hill, c. ¾ m. up the road to the NW of the village. Marked by a group of hut circles, bounded by V-section ditches, and a scatter of sherds.

4080

WRENTHAM

ST NICHOLAS. Big C15 W tower. Along the base frieze of shields and lozenges with the Crown of Thorns and hearts. Flushwork panelling on the buttresses and the battlements. Below the bell-openings small square windows with a grille of very close, complex tracery, chiefly consisting of small quatrefoils.* W doorway with niches l. and r. C13 chancel with lancet windows. S aisle Perp, N aisle of 1853. S porch with a front with plain flushwork panelling. Wide nave canted towards the tower. Wide chancel. The S arcade has quatrefoil piers with small raised ridges in the diagonals, Dec no doubt. When the N aisle

* A motif very usual in Norfolk, and there wrongly called sound-holes.

was built the former N windows were re-used, one Dec with
flowing tracery under a two-centred arch, and two Perp under
four-centred arches. It looks as if the wall piers of the same
section as the arcade are medieval material too. But where can
they have been? Were there perhaps remains of a former N
aisle? In 1853 three romantic heads were placed on each wall
pier and arched beams put in to run S as well as E and W from
them. The same was done in the S aisle, only with rude wooden
posts instead of the stone wall piers. At the E end of the N aisle
the wall below the window is treated as a MONUMENT in three
Gothic arched frames, of which the central one refers to Mrs
Clissold, the rector's wife, who died in 1852. So perhaps the
whole aisle is a memorial to her. – FONT. Octagonal, Perp,
bowl only, with six flowers and two shields (disused). –
CANDLESTICKS. Two, with Jacobean carving and little
obelisks. – STAINED GLASS. St Nicholas, N aisle. – Canopy in
the S aisle E window. – Christ carrying the Cross, by *Royal
William Lilly* of Wrentham, 1850. By him perhaps also what
remains of small figures in the tracery heads of several windows.
– PLATE. Cup *c.* 1660. – BRASS. Ele Bowet, *c.* 1400, a 30 in.
figure.

RECTORY. Close to the church, seven bays wide, plastered. C18,
but with a castellated porch, built or remodelled presumably
about 1830.

CONGREGATIONAL CHURCH. Dated 1778. Red brick, three by
two windows. They are arched. On the front there are arched
doorways in the first and third bays. Opposite the doorway the
pulpit. On the other sides galleries. – BOX PEWS. – The ceiling
is coved into the big mansard roof, which is covered with the
local glazed blue tiles.

WYVERSTONE

ST GEORGE. Dec W tower with a tier of small quatrefoil windows.
S porch of timber with carved bargeboards and a hammerbeam
roof. Perp nave and chancel; clerestory, though no aisles. Good
roof with arched braces joining at the high collar-beams. –
FONT. Octagonal, Perp, simple. Panelled stem; bowl with
shields in quatrefoils etc. – BENCHES. Some ends with medieval poppy-heads; also one dated 1616. – SCREEN. Dado with
remains of carved, not simply painted, scenes: Annunciation,
Nativity, Magi, Mass of St Gregory, Visitation. – PULPIT.
Early C16 with linenfold panelling. – COMMUNION RAIL.
Jacobean. – STAINED GLASS. A little in the NW and more in

the NE window of the nave. – PLATE. Paten and Almsdish 1724; Flagon 1729.

YAXLEY

ST MARY. Early C14 W tower with an ogee niche in the W side. Tower arch to the nave with two continuous chamfers. Extremely ornate N porch, one of the most swagger in Suffolk. Two-storeyed front with flushwork panelling and initials. Entrance with spandrels showing a man and a monster and a Wild Man and a lion. Niches l. and r. A frieze of shields l. and r. below them. Two upper two-light windows with three niches. Parapet with shields. Pinnacles. Perp nave with large windows to the N, to the S an aisle and a simple porch, and a clerestory with doubled windows. There is also an E window at clerestory level. The S arcade has octagonal piers and double-chamfered arches. Outside the chancel a flying buttress runs up in front of the priest's door (cf. Blythburgh, Eye, Framlingham, Spexhall). Nave roof with long arched braces up to the castellated collarbeams. Decorated wall-plate. – PULPIT. 1635. With canted back panel and tester, very richly carved. – SCREEN. The dado painted badly with saints. But there is attractive gilding of the ornamental parts. Of the upper part of the screen all the finery has gone except for the extremely richly carved entrance arch, with cusping and subcusping (cf. Eye). Original also the cresting. The position of the rood beam is indicated by its ends remaining in the walls. – WALL PAINTING. Doom above the chancel arch; no longer recognizable. – STAINED GLASS. Made up into a pattern with much use of old fragments from the C13 onwards. Several with C15 figures. – MONUMENT. In the chancel C14 effigy of an Ecclesiastic. – CURIOSUM. Over the S door SEXTON'S WHEEL (cf. Long Stretton, Norfolk), a pair of iron wheels for determining fast days.

(YAXLEY HALL. A composite picture from the gardens. Threebay range, castellated, with little wooden lantern, a pedimented doorway, and two curiously fanciful Gothic windows. Attached on the r. the end of an older range with mullioned and transomed windows and a pedimented gable. NMR)

In the grounds, visible from the Eye–Yaxley road, a FOLLY TOWER, built in imitation of a church tower and said by the DOE to have a genuine C15 doorway.

YOXFORD

ST PETER. The distinguishing feature is the recessed lead spire

on the w tower. The tower is Dec and has battlements with
flushwork panelling. The church is heavily restored and partly
rebuilt. N aisle and N chapel of 1837, altered again later. E window and other renewals 1868. s aisle windows Perp. Arcade of
four bays with octagonal piers and double-hollow-chamfered
arches. Chapel arcade of two bays, with an octagonal pier and
depressed double-hollow-chamfered arches. – FONT. Octagonal. An unusual design. Stem panelled and with eight shafts.
Bowl with cusped quatrefoils alternating with angels on curly
clouds. – PULPIT. Jacobean. – PLATE. Cup and Cover 1580;
Flagon 1720. – MONUMENTS. The tomb-chest mentioned by
Cautley is at the time of writing dissembled under the tower. –
Brass to John Norwiche † 1428 and wife. Good figures of 3 ft
2 in. length. – Brass to Tomesine Tendring, 1485. Young
woman in her shroud, the figure 3 ft 6 in. long. With her a
number of children, five in shrouds. – Sir Charles Blois † 1850.
By *Thomas Thurlow* of Saxmundham. Tablet with two standing
angels.

CHURCH HOUSE, on the s side of the churchyard. Timber-
framed.

SIGNPOST, immediately NW of the church. Very pretty, probably c. 1830, with cast-iron openwork lettering. Three pointing
hands. One points to London.

COCKFIELD HALL. Red brick. The house itself is of less architectural interest than the outbuildings. The house is said to
date from 1613, but the windows were sashed c. 1770, a porch
was added, and then a Victorian upper storey with fancy
gables and some fancy Tudor decorative motifs. However,
behind the house to the E are two original Early Tudor ranges
with stepped gables and decorated chimneys. One is the GATE-
HOUSE, which has a four-centred arch to the gateway* and a
(later ?) mullioned and transomed window above it. The other
contains living quarters, and this has nice square finials to the
stepped gables and a group of polygonal chimneys with star
tops. Outside the gatehouse STABLE YARD with two symmetrically arranged gateways and a polygonal Culver House in
the middle. They seem to be early C19 Tudor, except for the
range on the N side, which is original and of the time of the
parts described above.

  GATEWAY towards Yoxford and range adjoining it. This is
Victorian Tudor in style.

GROVE PARK. 1815. Red brick. Seven-bay garden front of two

* Inside the gateway a terracotta head.

storeys with three-bay pediment. The entrance side round the corner has a recessed three-bay centre with pediment and two wings of two bays projecting by one bay. Porch with two Tuscan columns of cast iron.

(SATIS HOUSE. In the garden an undulating or crinkle-crankle wall. N. Scarfe)

THE VILLAGE. NE of the centre, first a cottage with Gothic details, then, opposite the thatched LODGE of Cockfield Hall, a cottage with some pargetting. The DOE points out that the moulds used are the same as at Hemp Green Sibton (*see* below) and Theberton. W of the centre in THE STREET one Georgian five-bay house of red brick with Roman Doric porch, then at the fork YOXFORD PLACE, also Georgian, also of red brick, also of five bays, and also with a Roman Doric porch. The continuation to Hemp Green, Sibton, is almost without a break.

GLOSSARY

ABACUS: flat slab on the top of a capital (q.v.).

ABUTMENT: solid masonry placed to resist the lateral pressure of a vault.

ACANTHUS: plant with thick fleshy and scalloped leaves used as part of the decoration of a Corinthian capital (q.v.) and in some types of leaf carving.

ACHIEVEMENT OF ARMS: in heraldry, a complete display of armorial bearings.

ACROTERION: foliage-carved block on the end or top of a classical pediment (q.v.).

ADDORSED: two human figures, animals, or birds, etc., placed symmetrically so that they turn their backs to each other.

AEDICULE, AEDICULA: framing of a window or door by columns and a pediment (q.v.).

AFFRONTED: two human figures, animals, or birds, etc., placed symmetrically so that they face each other.

AGGER: Latin term for the built-up foundations of Roman roads; also sometimes applied to the banks of hill-forts or other earthworks.

AMBULATORY: semicircular or polygonal aisle enclosing an apse (q.v.).

ANNULET: *see* Shaft-ring.

ANSE DE PANIER: *see* Arch, Basket.

ANTEPENDIUM: covering of the front of an altar, usually by textiles or metalwork.

ANTIS, IN: *see* Portico.

APSE: vaulted semicircular or polygonal end of a chancel or a chapel.

ARABESQUE: light and fanciful surface decoration using combinations of flowing lines, tendrils, etc., interspersed with vases, animals, etc.

ARCADE: range of arches supported on piers or columns, free-standing: or, BLIND ARCADE, the same attached to a wall.

ARCH: round-headed, i.e. semicircular; pointed, i.e. consisting of two curves, each drawn from one centre, and meeting in a point at the top; segmental, i.e. in the form of a segment;

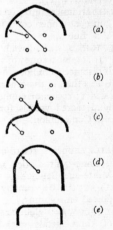

Fig. 1. Arches

pointed; four-centred (a late medieval form), *see* Fig. 1(*a*); Tudor (also a late medieval form), *see* Fig. 1(*b*); Ogee (introduced *c.* 1300 and specially popular in the C14), *see* Fig. 1(*c*); Stilted, *see* Fig. 1(*d*); Basket, with lintel connected to the jambs by concave quadrant curves, *see* Fig. 1(*e*) for one example; Diaphragm, a transverse arch with solid spandrels carrying not a vault but a principal beam of a timber roof. *See also* Strainer Arch.

ARCHITRAVE: lowest of the three main parts of the entablature (q.v.) of an order (q.v.) (*see* Fig. 12).

ARCHIVOLT: under-surface of an arch. Also called Soffit.

ARRIS: sharp edge at the meeting of two surfaces.

ASHLAR: masonry of large blocks wrought to even faces and square edges.

ATLANTES: male counterparts of caryatids (q.v.).

ATRIUM: inner court of a Roman house, also open court in front of a church.

ATTACHED: *see* Engaged.

ATTIC: topmost storey of a house, if distance from floor to ceiling is less than in the others.

AUMBRY: recess or cupboard to hold sacred vessels for Mass and Communion.

BAILEY: open space or court of a stone-built castle; *see also* Motte-and-Bailey.

BALDACCHINO: canopy supported on columns.

BALLFLOWER: globular flower of three petals enclosing a small ball. A decoration used in the first quarter of the C14.

BALUSTER: small pillar or column of fanciful outline.

BALUSTRADE: series of balusters supporting a handrail or coping (q.v.).

BARBICAN: outwork defending the entrance to a castle.

BARGEBOARDS: projecting decorated boards placed against the incline of the gable of a building and hiding the horizontal roof timbers.

BARREL-VAULT: *see* Vault.

BARROW: *see* Bell, Bowl, Disc, Long, *and* Pond Barrow.

BASILICA: in medieval architecture an aisled church with a clerestory.

BASKET ARCH: *see* Arch (Fig. 1*e*).

BASTION: projection at the angle of a fortification.

BATTER: inclined face of a wall.

BATTLEMENT: parapet with a series of indentations or embrasures with raised portions or merlons between. Also called Crenellation.

BAYS: internal compartments of a building; each divided from the other not by solid walls but by divisions only marked in the side walls (columns, pilasters, etc.) or the ceiling (beams, etc.). Also external divisions of a building by fenestration.

BAY-WINDOW: angular or curved projection of a house front with ample fenestration. If curved, also called bowwindow: if on an upper floor only, also called oriel or oriel window.

BEAKER FOLK: Late New Stone Age warrior invaders from the Continent who buried their dead in round barrows and introduced the first metal tools and weapons to Britain.

BEAKHEAD: Norman ornamental motif consisting of a row of bird or beast heads with beaks biting usually into a roll moulding (q.v.)

BELFRY: turret on a roof to hang bells in.

BELGAE: Aristocratic warrior bands who settled in Britain in two main waves in the CI B.C. In Britain their culture is termed Iron Age C.

BELL BARROW: Early Bronze Age round barrow in which the mound is separated from its encircling ditch by a flat platform or berm (q.v.).

BELLCOTE: framework on a roof to hang bells from.

BERM: level area separating ditch from bank on a hill-fort or barrow.

BILLET FRIEZE: Norman ornamental motif made up of short raised rectangles placed at regular intervals.

BIVALLATE: Of a hill-fort: defended by two concentric banks and ditches.

BLIND ARCADE: see Arcade.

BLOCK CAPITAL: Romanesque capital cut from a cube by hav-

Fig. 2. Block capital

ing the lower angles rounded off to the circular shaft below. Also called Cushion Capital (Fig. 2).

BOND, ENGLISH or FLEMISH: see Brickwork.

BOSS: knob or projection usually placed to cover the intersection of ribs in a vault.

BOWL BARROW: round barrow surrounded by a quarry ditch. Introduced in Late Neolithic times, the form continued until the Saxon period.

BOW-WINDOW: see Bay-Window.

BOX: A small country house, e.g. a shooting box. A convenient term to describe a compact minor dwelling, e.g. a rectory.

BOX PEW: pew with a high wooden enclosure.

BRACES: see Roof.

BRACKET: small supporting piece of stone, etc., to carry a projecting horizontal.

BRESSUMER: beam in a timber-framed building to support the, usually projecting, superstructure.

BRICKWORK: *Header:* brick laid so that the end only appears on the face of the wall. *Stretcher:* brick laid so that the side only appears on the face of the wall. *English Bond:* method of laying bricks so that alternate courses or layers on the face of the wall are composed of headers or stretchers only (Fig. 3a). *Flemish Bond:* method of laying bricks so that alternate headers

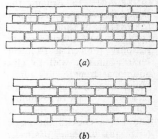

(a)

(b)

Fig. 3. Brickwork

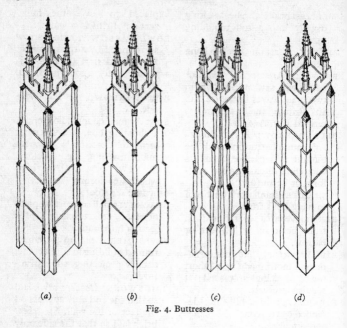

(a)   (b)   (c)   (d)

Fig. 4. Buttresses

and stretchers appear in each course on the face of the wall (Fig. 3b). *See also* Herringbone Work, Oversailing Courses.

BROACH: *see* Spire.

BROKEN PEDIMENT: *see* Pediment.

BRONZE AGE: In Britain, the period from *c.* 1600 to 600 B.C.

BUCRANIUM: ox skull.

BUTTRESS: mass of brickwork or masonry projecting from or built against a wall to give additional strength. *Angle Buttresses:* two meeting at an angle of 90° at the angle of a building (Fig. 4a). *Clasping Buttress:* one which encases the angle (Fig. 4d). *Diagonal Buttress:* one placed against the right angle formed by two walls, and more or less equiangular with both (Fig. 4b). *Flying Buttress:* arch or half arch transmitting the thrust of a vault or roof from the upper part of a wall to an outer support or buttress. *Setback Buttress:* angle buttress set slightly back from the angle (Fig. 4c).

CABLE MOULDING: Norman moulding imitating a twisted cord.

CAIRN: a mound of stones usually covering a burial.

CAMBER: slight rise or upward curve of an otherwise horizontal structure.

CAMPANILE: isolated bell tower.

CANOPY: projection or hood

over an altar, pulpit, niche, statue, etc.

CAP: in a windmill the crowning feature.

CAPITAL: head or top part of a column. *See also* Block Capital, Crocket Capital, Order, Scalloped Capital, Stiff-leaf, *and* Waterleaf.

CARTOUCHE: tablet with an ornate frame, usually enclosing an inscription.

CARYATID: whole female figure supporting an entablature or other similar member. *Termini Caryatids:* female busts or demi-figures or three-quarter figures supporting an entablature or other similar member and placed at the top of termini pilasters (q.v.). Cf. Atlantes.

CASTELLATED: decorated with battlements (q.v.).

CELURE: panelled and adorned part of a wagon roof above the rood or the altar.

CENSER: vessel for the burning of incense.

CENTERING: wooden framework used in arch and vault construction and removed when the mortar has set.

CHALICE: cup used in the Communion service or at Mass. *See also* Recusant Chalice.

CHAMBERED TOMB: burial mound of the New Stone Age having a stone-built chamber and entrance passage covered by an earthen barrow or stone cairn. The form was introduced to Britain from the Mediterranean.

CHAMFER: surface made by cutting across the square angle of a stone block, piece of wood, etc., usually at an angle of 45° to the other two surfaces.

CHANCEL: that part of the E end of a church in which the altar is placed, usually applied to the whole continuation of the nave E of the crossing.

CHANCEL ARCH: arch at the W end of the chancel.

CHANTRY CHAPEL: chapel attached to, or inside, a church, endowed for the saying of Masses for the soul of the founder or some other individual.

CHEVET: French term for the E end of a church (chancel, ambulatory, and radiating chapels).

CHEVRON: Norman moulding forming a zigzag.

CHOIR: that part of the church where divine service is sung.

CIBORIUM: a baldacchino (q.v.).

CINQUEFOIL: *see* Foil.

CIST: stone-lined or slab-built grave. First appears in Late Neolithic times. It continued to be used in the Early Christian period.

CLAPPER BRIDGE: bridge made of large slabs of stone, some built up to make rough piers and other longer ones laid on top to make the roadway.

CLASSIC: here used to mean the moment of highest achievement of a style.

CLASSICAL: here used as the term for Greek and Roman architecture and any subsequent styles inspired by it.

CLERESTORY: upper storey of the nave walls of a church, pierced by windows.

COADE STONE: artificial (cast) stone made in the late C18 and the early C19 by Coade and Sealy in London.

COB: walling material made of mixed clay and straw.

COFFERING: decorating a ceiling

with sunk square or polygonal ornamental panels.

COLLAR-BEAM: *see* Roof.

COLONNADE: range of columns.

COLONNETTE: small column.

COLUMNA ROSTRATA: column decorated with carved prows of ships to celebrate a naval victory.

COMPOSITE: *see* Order.

CONSOLE: bracket (q.v.) with a compound curved outline.

COPING: capping or covering to wall.

CORBEL: block of stone projecting from a wall, supporting some feature on its horizontal top surface.

CORBEL TABLE: series of corbels, occurring just below the roof eaves externally or internally, often seen in Norman buildings.

CORINTHIAN: *see* Order.

CORNICE: in classical architecture the top section of the entablature (q.v.). Also for a projecting decorative feature along the top of a wall, arch, etc.

CORRIDOR VILLA: *see* Villa.

COUNTERSCARP BANK: small bank on the down-hill or outer side of a hill-fort ditch.

COURTYARD VILLA: *see* Villa.

COVE, COVING: concave undersurface in the nature of a hollow moulding but on a larger scale.

COVER PATEN: cover to a Communion cup, suitable for use as a paten or plate for the consecrated bread.

CRADLE ROOF: *see* Wagon roof.

CRENELLATION: *see* Battlement.

CREST, CRESTING: ornamental finish along the top of a screen, etc.

CRINKLE-CRANKLE WALL: undulating wall.

CROCKET, CROCKETING: decorative features placed on the sloping sides of spires, pinnacles, gables, etc., in Gothic architecture, carved in various leaf shapes and placed at regular intervals.

CROCKET CAPITAL: *see* Fig. 5. An Early Gothic form.

Fig. 5. Crocket capital

CROMLECH: word of Celtic origin still occasionally used of single free-standing stone ascribed to the Neolithic or Bronze Age periods.

CROSSING: space at the intersection of nave, chancel, and transepts.

CROSS-VAULT: *see* Vault.

CROSS-WINDOWS: windows with one mullion and one transom.

CROWN-POST: *see* Roof (Fig. 15).

CRUCK: big curved beam supporting both walls and roof of a cottage.

CRYPT: underground room usually below the E end of a church.

CUPOLA: small polygonal or circular domed turret crowning a roof.

CURTAIN WALL: connecting wall between the towers of a castle.

In C20 architecture, a non-load-bearing wall which can be applied in front of a framed structure to keep out the weather; sections may include windows and the spans between.

CUSHION CAPITAL: *see* Block Capital.

CUSP: projecting point between the foils (q.v.) in a foiled Gothic arch.

DADO: decorative covering of the lower part of a wall.

DAGGER: tracery motif of the Dec style. It is a lancet shape rounded or pointed at the head, pointed at the foot, and cusped inside (Fig. 6).

Fig. 6. Dagger

DAIS: raised platform at one end of a room.

DEC ('DECORATED'): historical division of English Gothic architecture covering the period from *c.* 1290 to *c.* 1350.

DEMI-COLUMNS: columns half sunk into a wall.

DIAPER WORK: surface decoration composed of square or lozenge shapes.

DIAPHRAGM ARCH: *see* Arch.

DISC BARROW: Bronze Age round barrow with inconspicuous central mound surrounded by bank and ditch.

DOGTOOTH: typical E.E. ornament consisting of a series of four-cornered stars placed diagonally and raised pyramidally (Fig. 7).

Fig. 7. Dogtooth

DOMICAL VAULT: *see* Vault.

DONJON: *see* Keep.

DORIC: *see* Order.

DORMER (WINDOW): window placed vertically in the sloping plane of a roof.

DRIPSTONE: *see* Hoodmould.

DRUM: circular or polygonal vertical wall of a dome or cupola.

DUTCH GABLE: *see* Gable.

E.E. ('EARLY ENGLISH'): historical division of English Gothic architecture roughly covering the C13.

EASTER SEPULCHRE: recess with tomb-chest (q.v.), usually in the wall of a chancel, the tomb-chest to receive an effigy of Christ for Easter celebrations.

EAVES: underpart of a sloping roof overhanging a wall.

EAVES CORNICE: cornice below the eaves of a roof.

ECHINUS. Convex or projecting moulding supporting the abacus of a Greek Doric capital, sometimes bearing an egg and dart pattern.

EMBATTLED: *see* Battlement.

EMBRASURE: small opening in the wall or parapet of a fortified building, usually splayed on the inside.

ENCAUSTIC TILES: earthenware glazed and decorated tiles used for paving.

ENGAGED COLUMNS: columns attached to, or partly sunk into, a wall.

ENGLISH BOND: *see* Brickwork.

ENTABLATURE: in classical architecture the whole of the horizontal members above a column (that is architrave, frieze, and cornice) (*see* Fig. 12).

ENTASIS: very slight convex deviation from a straight line; used on Greek columns and sometimes on spires to prevent an optical illusion of concavity.

ENTRESOL: *see* Mezzanine.

EPITAPH: hanging wall-monument.

ESCUTCHEON: shield for armorial bearings.

EXEDRA: the apsidal end of a room. *See* Apse.

FAN-VAULT: *see* Vault.

FERETORY: place behind the high altar where the chief shrine of a church is kept.

FESTOON: carved garland of flowers and fruit suspended at both ends. *See also* Swag.

FILLET: narrow flat band running down a shaft or along a roll moulding.

FINIAL: top of a canopy, gable, pinnacle.

FIRRED: *see* Roof.

FLAGON: vessel for the wine used in the Communion service.

FLAMBOYANT: properly the latest phase of French Gothic architecture where the window tracery takes on wavy undulating lines.

FLÈCHE: slender wooden spire on the centre of a roof. Also called Spirelet.

FLEMISH BOND: *see* Brickwork.

FLEURON: decorative carved flower or leaf.

FLUSHWORK: decorative use of flint in conjunction with dressed stone so as to form patterns: tracery, initials, etc.

FLUTING: vertical channelling in the shaft of a column.

FLYING BUTTRESS: *see* Buttress.

FOIL: lobe formed by the cusping (q.v.) of a circle or an arch. Trefoil, quatrefoil, cinquefoil, multifoil, express the number of leaf shapes to be seen.

FOLIATED: carved with leaf shapes.

FOSSE: ditch.

FOUR-CENTRED ARCH: *see* Arch (Fig. 1a).

FRATER: refectory or dining hall of a monastery.

FRESCO: wall painting on wet plaster.

FRIEZE: middle division of a classical entablature (q.v.) (*see* Fig. 12).

FRONTAL: covering for the front of an altar.

GABLE: *Dutch gable:* A gable with curved sides crowned by a pediment, characteristic of c. 1630–50 (Fig. 8a). *Shaped gable:* A gable with multi-curved sides characteristic of c. 1600–50 (Fig. 8b).

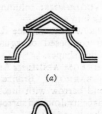

(a)

(b)

Fig. 8. Gables

GADROONED: enriched with a series of convex ridges, the opposite of fluting (q.v.).

GALILEE: chapel or vestibule usually at the w end of a church enclosing the porch. Also called Narthex (q.v.).

GALLERY: in church architecture upper storey above an aisle, opened in arches to the nave. Also called Tribune and often erroneously Triforium (q.v.).

GALLERY GRAVE: chambered tomb (q.v.) in which there is little or no differentiation between the entrance passage and the actual burial chamber(s).

GARDEROBE: lavatory or privy in a medieval building.

GARGOYLE: water spout projecting from the parapet of a wall or tower; carved into a human or animal shape.

GAZEBO: lookout tower or raised summer house in a picturesque garden.

'GEOMETRICAL': see Tracery.

'GIBBS SURROUND': of a doorway or window. An C18 motif consisting of a surround with alternating larger and smaller blocks of stone, quoin-wise, or intermittent large blocks, sometimes with a narrow raised band connecting them up the verticals and along the face of the arch (Fig. 9).

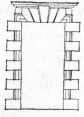

Fig. 9. 'Gibbs surround'

GROIN: sharp edge at the meeting of two cells of a cross-vault.

GROIN-VAULT: see Vault.

GROTESQUE: fanciful ornamental decoration: see also Arabesque.

Hagioscope: see Squint.

HALF-TIMBERING: see Timber-Framing.

HALL CHURCH: church in which nave and aisles are of equal height or approximately so.

HAMMERBEAM: see Roof (Fig. 18).

HANAP: large metal cup, generally made for domestic use, standing on an elaborate base and stem; with a very ornate cover frequently crowned with a little steeple.

HEADER: see Brickwork.

HERRINGBONE WORK: brick, stone, or tile construction where the component blocks are laid diagonally instead of flat. Alternate courses lie in opposing directions to make a zigzag pattern up the face of the wall.

HEXASTYLE: having six detached columns.

HILL-FORT: Iron Age earthwork enclosed by a ditch and bank system; in the later part of the period the defences multiplied in size and complexity. They vary from about an acre to over 30 acres in area, and are usually built with careful regard to natural elevations or promontories.

HIPPED ROOF: see Roof.

HOODMOULD: projecting moulding above an arch or a lintel to throw off water. Also called Dripstone or Label.

ICONOGRAPHY: the science of the subject matter of works of the visual arts.

IMPOST: bracket (q.v.) in a wall, usually formed of mouldings, on which the ends of an arch rest.

INDENT: shape chiselled out in a stone slab to receive a brass.

INGLENOOK: bench or seat built in beside a fireplace, sometimes covered by the chimneybreast, occasionally lit by small windows on each side of the fire.

INTERCOLUMNIATION: the space between columns.

IONIC: see Order (Fig. 12).

IRON AGE: in Britain the period from c.600 B.C. to the coming of the Romans. The term is also used for those un-Romanized native communities which survived until the Saxon incursions.

JAMB: straight side of an archway, doorway, or window.

KEEL MOULDING: moulding whose outline is in section like that of the keel of a ship.

KEEP: massive tower of a Norman castle. Also called Donjon.

KEYSTONE: middle stone in an arch or a rib-vault.

KINGPOST: see Roof (Fig. 14).

KNEELER: horizontal decorative projection at the base of a gable.

KNOP: a knob-like thickening in the stem of a chalice.

LABEL: see Hoodmould.

LABEL STOP: ornamental boss at the end of a hoodmould (q.v.).

LACED WINDOWS: windows pulled visually together by strips, usually in brick of a different colour, which continue vertically the lines of the vertical parts of the window surrounds. The motif is typical of c. 1720.

LANCET WINDOW: slender pointed-arched window.

LANTERN: in architecture, a small circular or polygonal turret with windows all round crowning a roof (see Cupola) or a dome.

LANTERN CROSS: churchyard cross with lantern-shaped top usually with sculptured representations on the sides of the top.

LEAN-TO ROOF: roof with one slope only, built against a higher wall.

LESENE or PILASTER STRIP: pilaster (q.v.) without base or capital.

LIERNE: see Vault (Fig. 23).

LINENFOLD: Tudor panelling ornamented with a conventional representation of a piece of linen laid in vertical folds. The piece is repeated in each panel.

LINTEL: horizontal beam or stone bridging an opening.

LOGGIA: recessed colonnade (q.v.).

LONG AND SHORT WORK: Saxon quoins (q.v.) consisting of stones placed with the long sides alternately upright and horizontal.

LONG BARROW: unchambered Neolithic communal burial mound, wedge-shaped in plan, with the burial and occasional other structures massed at the broader end, from which the mound itself tapers in height; quarry ditches flank the mound.

LOUVRE: opening, often with lantern (q.v.) over, in the roof of a room to let the smoke from a central hearth escape.

LOWER PALAEOLITHIC: *see* Palaeolithic.

LOZENGE: diamond shape.

LUCARNE: small opening to let light in.

LUNETTE: tympanum (q.v.) or semicircular opening.

LYCH GATE: wooden gate structure with a roof and open sides placed at the entrance to a churchyard to provide space for the reception of a coffin. The word *lych* is Saxon and means a corpse.

LYNCHET: long terraced strip of soil accumulating on the downward side of prehistoric and medieval fields due to soil creep from continuous ploughing along the contours.

MACHICOLATION: projecting gallery on brackets (q.v.) constructed on the outside of castle towers or walls. The gallery has holes in the floor to drop missiles through.

MAJOLICA: ornamented glazed earthenware.

MANSARD: *see* Roof.

MATHEMATICAL TILES: Small facing tiles the size of brick headers, applied to timber-framed walls to make them appear brick-built.

MEGALITHIC TOMB: stone-built burial chamber of the New Stone Age covered by an earth or stone mound. The form

was introduced to Britain from the Mediterranean area.

MERLON: *see* Battlement.

MESOLITHIC: 'Middle Stone' Age; the post-glacial period of hunting and fishing communities dating in Britain from *c.* 8000 B.C. to the arrival of Neolithic communities, with which they must have considerably overlapped.

METOPE: in classical architecture of the Doric order (q.v.) the space in the frieze between the triglyphs (Fig. 12).

MEZZANINE: low storey placed between two higher ones. Also called Entresol.

MISERERE: *see* Misericord.

MISERICORD: bracket placed on the underside of a hinged choir stall seat which, when turned up, provided the occupant of the seat with a support during long periods of standing. Also called Miserere.

MODILLION: small bracket of which large numbers (modillion frieze) are often placed below a cornice (q.v.) in classical architecture.

MOTTE: steep mound forming the main feature of C11 and C12 castles.

MOTTE-AND-BAILEY: post-Roman and Norman defence system consisting of an earthen mound (the motte) topped with a wooden tower eccentrically placed within a bailey (q.v.), with enclosure ditch and palisade, and with the rare addition of an internal bank.

MOUCHETTE: tracery motif in curvilinear tracery, a curved dagger (q.v.), specially popular in the early C14 (Fig. 10).

MOURNERS: *see* Weepers.

Fig. 10. Mouchette

MULLIONS: vertical posts or up-rights dividing a window into 'lights'.

MULTIVALLATE: Of a hill-fort: defended by three or more concentric banks and ditches.

MUNTIN: post as a rule moulded and part of a screen.

NAIL-HEAD: E.E. ornamental motif, consisting of small pyramids regularly repeated (Fig. 11).

Fig. 11. Nail-head

NARTHEX: enclosed vestibule or covered porch at the main entrance to a church (see Galilee).

NEOLITHIC: 'New Stone' Age, dating in Britain from the appearance from the Continent of the first settled farming communities c. 3500 B.C. until the introduction of the Bronze Age.

NEWEL: central post in a circular or winding staircase; also the principal post when a flight of stairs meets a landing.

NOOK-SHAFT: shaft set in the angle of a pier or respond or wall, or the angle of the jamb of a window or doorway.

NUTMEG MOULDING: consisting of a chain of tiny triangles placed obliquely.

OBELISK: lofty pillar of square section tapering at the top and ending pyramidally.

OGEE: see Arch (Fig. 1c).

OPEN PEDIMENT: see Pediment.

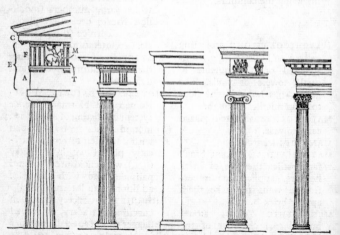

Fig. 12. Orders of columns (Greek Doric, Roman Doric, Tuscan Doric, Ionic, Corinthian) E, Entablature; C, Cornice; F, Frieze; A, Architrave; M, Metope; T, Triglyph.

ORATORY: small private chapel in a house.

ORDER: *see* Fig. 12. (1) *of a doorway or window:* series of concentric steps receding towards the opening; (2) *in classical architecture:* column with base, shaft, capital and entablature (q.v.) according to one of the following styles: Greek Doric, Roman Doric, Tuscan Doric, Ionic, Corinthian, Composite. The established details are very elaborate, and some specialist architectural work should be consulted for further guidance.

ORIEL: *see* Bay-Window.

OVERHANG: projection of the upper storey of a house.

OVERSAILING COURSES: series of stone or brick courses, each one projecting beyond the one below it.

OVOLO: convex moulding.

PALAEOLITHIC: 'Old Stone' Age; the first period of human culture, commencing in the Ice Age and immediately prior to the Mesolithic; the Lower Palaeolithic is the older phase, the Upper Palaeolithic the later.

PALIMPSEST: (1) *of a brass:* where a metal plate has been re-used by turning over and engraving on the back; (2) *of a wall painting:* where one overlaps and partly obscures an earlier one.

PALLADIAN: architecture following the ideas and principles of Andrea Palladio, 1518–80.

PANTILE: tile of curved S-shaped section.

PARAPET: low wall placed to protect any spot where there is a sudden drop, for example on a bridge, quay, hillside, housetop, etc.

PARCLOSE SCREEN: *see* Screen.

PARGETTING: plaster work with patterns and ornaments either in relief or engraved on it.

PARVIS: term wrongly applied to a room over a church porch. These rooms were often used as a schoolroom or as a store room.

PASSING-BRACE: *see* Roof (Fig. 16).

PATEN: plate to hold the bread at Communion or Mass.

PATERA: small flat circular or oval ornament in classical architecture.

PEDIMENT: low-pitched gable used in classical, Renaissance, and neo-classical architecture above a portico and above doors, windows, etc. It may be straight-sided or curved segmentally. *Broken Pediment:* one where the centre portion of the base is left open. *Open Pediment:* one where the centre portion of the sloping sides is left out.

PENDANT: boss (q.v.) elongated so that it seems to hang down.

PENDENTIVE: concave triangular spandrel used to lead from the angle of two walls to the base of a circular dome. It is constructed as part of the hemisphere over a diameter the size of the diagonal of the basic square (Fig. 13).

PERP (PERPENDICULAR): historical division of English Gothic architecture covering the period from *c.*1335–50 to *c.*1530.

PIANO NOBILE: principal storey of a house with the reception rooms; usually the first floor.

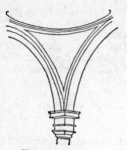

Fig. 13. Pendentive

PIAZZA: open space surrounded by buildings; in C17 and C18 England sometimes used to mean a long colonnade or loggia.

PIER: strong, solid support, frequently square in section or of composite section (compound pier).

PIETRA DURA: ornamental or scenic inlay by means of thin slabs of stone.

PILASTER: shallow pier attached to a wall. *Pilaster Strip: see* Lesene. *Termini Pilasters:* pilasters with sides tapering downwards.

PILLAR PISCINA: free-standing piscina (q.v.) on a pillar.

PINNACLE: ornamental form crowning a spire, tower, buttress, etc., usually of steep pyramidal, conical, or some similar shape.

PISCINA: basin for washing the Communion or Mass vessels, provided with a drain. Generally set in or against the wall of the S of an altar.

PLAISANCE: summer-house, pleasure house near a mansion.

PLATE TRACERY: *see* Tracery.

PLINTH: projecting base of a wall or column, generally chamfered (q.v.) or moulded at the top.

POND BARROW: rare type of Bronze Age barrow consisting of a circular depression, usually paved, and containing a number of cremation burials.

POPPYHEAD: ornament of leaf and flower type used to decorate the tops of bench- or stall-ends.

PORTCULLIS: gate constructed to rise and fall in vertical grooves; used in gateways of castles.

PORTE COCHÈRE: porch large enough to admit wheeled vehicles.

PORTICO: centre-piece of a house or a church with classical detached or attached columns and a pediment. A portico is called *prostyle* or *in antis* according to whether it projects from or recedes into a building. In a portico *in antis* the columns range with the side walls.

POSTERN: small gateway at the back of a building.

PREDELLA: in an altarpiece the horizontal strip below the main representation, often used for a number of subsidiary representations in a row.

PRESBYTERY: the part of the church lying E of the choir. It is the part where the altar is placed.

PRINCIPAL: *see* Roof (Figs. 14, 17).

PRIORY: monastic house whose head is a prior or prioress, not an abbot or abbess.

PROSTYLE: with free-standing columns in a row.

PULPITUM: stone screen in a major church provided to shut

off the choir from the nave and also as a backing for the return choir stalls.

PULVINATED FRIEZE: frieze (q.v.) with a bold convex moulding.

PURLINS: *see* Roof (Figs. 14–17).

PUTHOLE or PUTLOCK HOLE: putlocks are the short horizontal timbers on which during construction the boards of scaffolding rest. Putholes or putlock holes are the holes in the wall for putlocks, which often are not filled in after construction is complete.

PUTTO: small naked boy.

QUADRANGLE: inner courtyard in a large building.

QUARRY: in stained-glass work, a small diamond- or square-shaped piece of glass set diagonally.

QUATREFOIL: *see* Foil.

QUEENPOSTS: *see* Roof (Fig. 16).

QUEEN-STRUTS: *see* Roof (Fig. 17).

QUOINS: dressed stones at the angles of a building. Sometimes all the stones are of the same size; more often they are alternately large and small.

RADIATING CHAPELS: chapels projecting radially from an ambulatory or an apse.

RAFTER: *see* Roof.

RAMPART: stone wall or wall of earth surrounding a castle, fortress, or fortified city.

RAMPART-WALK: path along the inner face of a rampart.

REBATE: continuous rectangular notch cut on an edge.

REBUS: pun, a play on words. The literal translation and illustration of a name for artistic and heraldic purposes (Belton = bell, tun).

RECUSANT CHALICE: chalice made after the Reformation and before Catholic Emancipation for Roman Catholic use.

REEDING: decoration with parallel convex mouldings touching one another.

REFECTORY: dining hall; *see* Frater.

RENDERING: plastering of an outer wall.

REPOUSSÉ: decoration of metal

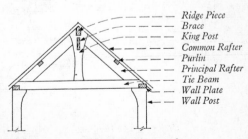

Fig. 14. Kingpost roof

Ridge Piece
Brace
King Post
Common Rafter
Purlin
Principal Rafter
Tie Beam
Wall Plate
Wall Post

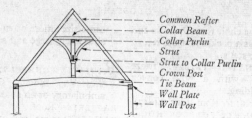

Common Rafter
Collar Beam
Collar Purlin
Strut
Strut to Collar Purlin
Crown Post
Tie Beam
Wall Plate
Wall Post

Fig. 15. Crown-post roof

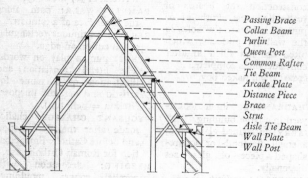

Passing Brace
Collar Beam
Purlin
Queen Post
Common Rafter
Tie Beam
Arcade Plate
Distance Piece
Brace
Strut
Aisle Tie Beam
Wall Plate
Wall Post

Fig. 16. Queenpost roof

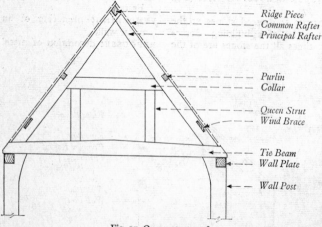

Ridge Piece
Common Rafter
Principal Rafter

Purlin
Collar

Queen Strut
Wind Brace

Tie Beam
Wall Plate

Wall Post

Fig. 17. Queen-strut roof

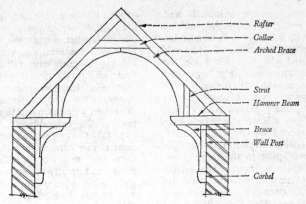

Fig. 18. Hammerbeam roof

work by relief designs, formed by beating the metal from the back.

REREDOS: structure behind and above an altar.

RESPOND: half-pier bonded into a wall and carrying one end of an arch.

RETABLE: altarpiece, a picture or piece of carving, standing behind and attached to an altar.

RETICULATION: see Tracery (Fig. 22e).

REVEAL: that part of a jamb (q.v.) which lies between the glass or door and the outer surface of the wall.

RIB-VAULT: see Vault.

ROCOCO: latest phase of the Baroque style, current in most Continental countries between c. 1720 and c. 1760.

ROLL MOULDING: moulding of semicircular or more than semicircular section.

ROMANESQUE: that style in architecture which was current in the C11 and C12 and preceded the Gothic style (in England often called Norman). (Some scholars extend the use of the term Romanesque back to the C10 or C9.)

ROMANO-BRITISH: A somewhat vague term applied to the period and cultural features of Britain affected by the Roman occupation of the C1-5 A.D.

ROOD: cross or crucifix.

ROOD LOFT: singing gallery on the top of the rood screen, often supported by a coving (q.v.).

ROOD SCREEN: see Screen.

ROOD STAIRS: stairs to give access to the rood loft.

ROOF: see Figs. 14–18. Single-framed: if consisting entirely of transverse members (such as rafters with or without braces, collars, tie-beams, etc.) not tied together longitudinally. Double-framed: if longitudinal members (such as a ridge beam and purlins) are employed. As a rule in such cases the rafters are divided into stronger principals and weaker subsidiary rafters. *Hipped:* roof with sloped instead of vertical ends *Mansard:* roof with a double slope, the lower slope being larger and steeper than the upper. *Saddleback:* tower roof shaped like an ordinary gabled timber roof. The following members have special names: *Rafter:* rooftimber sloping up from the wall-plate to the ridge. *Principal:* principal rafter, usually corresponding to the main bay divisions of the nave or chancel below. *Wall-Plate:* timber laid longitudinally on the top of a wall. *Purlins:* longitudinal members laid parallel with wall-plate and apex some way up the slope of the roof. These are side purlins and may be *tenoned* into the principal rafter, or they may be *through purlins,* i.e. resting in slots cut into the back of the principals. *Clasped purlins:* purlins held between collar-beam and principal rafter. *Collar purlin:* a lengthwise beam supporting the collar-beams, found in the context of crown-post roofs, which do not have a ridgepiece. *Tie-beam:* beam connecting the two slopes of a roof at the height of the wall-plate, to prevent the roof from spreading. *Cambered tie-beam roof:* one in which the ridge and purlins are laid directly on a cambered tie-beam; in a *firred tie-beam roof* a solid blocking piece (firring piece) is interposed between the cambered tie-beam and the purlins. *Collar-beam:* tie-beam applied higher up the slope of the roof. *Strut:* an upright or sloping timber supporting a transverse member, e.g. connecting tie-beam with rafter. *Post:* an upright timber supporting a lengthwise beam. *Kingpost:* an upright timber carried on a tie-beam and supporting the ridge-beam (*see* Fig. 14). *Crown-post:* an upright timber carried on a tie-beam and supporting a collar purlin, and usually braced to it and the collar-beam with fourway struts (*see* Fig. 15). *Queenposts:* two upright timbers placed symmetrically on a tie-beam and supporting purlins (*see* Fig. 16); if such timbers support a collar-beam or rafters they are *queen-struts* (*see* Fig. 17). *Braces:* inclined timbers inserted to strengthen others. Usually braces connect a collar-beam with the rafters below or a tie-beam with the wall below. Braces can be straight or curved (also called arched). *Passing-brace:* a brace, usually of the same scantling as the common rafters and parallel to them, which stiffens a roof laterally by being halved across one or more intermediate timbers within its length (*see* Fig. 16). *Hammerbeam:* beam projecting at right angles, usually from the top of a wall, to carry arched braces or struts and arched braces (*see* Fig. 18). *See also* Wagon Roof.

ROSE WINDOW (or WHEEL WINDOW): circular window with patterned tracery arranged to radiate from the centre.

ROTUNDA: building circular in plan.

RUBBLE: building stones, not square or hewn, nor laid in regular courses.

RUSTICATION: *rock-faced* if the surfaces of large blocks of ashlar stone are left rough like rock; *smooth* if the ashlar blocks are smooth and separated by V-joints; *banded* if the separation by V-joints applies only to the horizontals.

SADDLEBACK: *see* Roof.

SALTIRE CROSS: equal-limbed cross placed diagonally.

SANCTUARY: (1) area around the main altar of a church (*see* Presbytery); (2) sacred site consisting of wood or stone uprights enclosed by a circular bank and ditch. Beginning in the Neolithic, they were elaborated in the succeeding Bronze Age. The best known examples are Stonehenge and Avebury.

SARCOPHAGUS: elaborately carved coffin.

SCAGLIOLA: material composed of cement and colouring matter to imitate marble.

SCALLOPED CAPITAL: development of the block capital (q.v.) in which the single semi-circular surface is elaborated into a series of truncated cones (Fig. 19).

Fig. 19. Scalloped capital

SCARP: artificial cutting away of the ground to form a steep slope.

SCREEN: *Parclose screen:* screen separating a chapel from the rest of a church. *Rood screen:* screen below the rood (q.v.), usually at the W end of a chancel.

SCREENS PASSAGE: passage between the entrances to kitchen, buttery, etc., and the screen behind which lies the hall of a medieval house.

SEDILIA: seats for the priests (usually three) on the S side of the chancel of a church.

SEGMENTAL ARCH: *see* Arch.

SET-OFF: *see* Weathering.

SEXPARTITE: *see* Vault.

SGRAFFITO: pattern incised into plaster so as to expose a dark surface underneath.

SHAFT-RING: motif of the C12 and C13 consisting of a ring round a circular pier or a shaft attached to a pier. Also called Annulet.

SHAPED GABLE: *see* Gable.

SHEILA-NA-GIG: fertility figure, usually with legs wide open.

SILL: lower horizontal part of the frame of a window.

SLATEHANGING: the covering of walls by overlapping rows of slates, on a timber substructure. Tilehanging is similar.

SOFFIT: underside of an arch, lintel, etc. Also called Archivolt.

SOLAR: upper living-room of a medieval house.

SOPRAPORTE: painting above the door of a room, usual in the C17 and C18.

SOUNDING BOARD: horizontal

board or canopy over a pulpit. Also called Tester.

SPANDREL: triangular surface between one side of an arch, the horizontal drawn from its apex, and the vertical drawn from its springer; also the surface between two arches.

SPERE-TRUSS: roof truss on two free-standing posts to mask the division between screens passage and hall. The screen itself, where a spere-truss exists, was originally movable.

SPIRE: tall pyramidal or conical pointed erection often built on top of a tower, turret, etc. *Broach Spire:* a broach is a sloping half-pyramid of masonry or wood introduced at the base of each of the four oblique faces of a tapering octagonal spire with the object of effecting the transition from the square to the octagon. The *splayed foot spire* is a variation of the broach form found principally in the south-eastern counties. In this form the four cardinal faces are splayed out near their base, to cover the corners, while the oblique (or intermediate) faces taper away to a point. *Needle Spire:* thin spire rising from the centre of a tower roof, well inside the parapet.

SPIRELET: *see* Flèche.

SPLAY: chamfer, usually of the jamb of a window.

SPRINGING: level at which an arch rises from its supports.

SQUINCH: arch or system of concentric arches thrown across the angle between two walls to support a superstructure, for example a dome (Fig. 20).

SQUINT: a hole cut in a wall or

through a pier to allow a view of the main altar of a church from places whence it could not otherwise be seen. Also called Hagioscope.

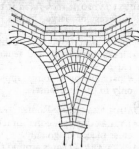

Fig. 20. Squinch

STALL: carved seat, one of a row, made of wood or stone.

STAUNCHION: upright iron or steel member.

STEEPLE: the tower of a church together with a spire, cupola, etc.

STIFF-LEAF: E.E. type of foliage of many-lobed shapes (Fig. 21).

Fig. 21. Stiff-leaf capital

STILTED: *see* Arch (Fig. 1d).

STOREY-POSTS: the principal posts of a timber-framed wall.

STOUP: vessel for the reception of holy water, usually placed near a door.

STRAINER ARCH: arch inserted across a room to prevent the walls from leaning.

STRAPWORK: C16 decoration consisting of interlaced bands, and forms similar to fretwork or cut and bent leather.

STRETCHER: *see* Brickwork.

STRING COURSE: projecting horizontal band or moulding set in the surface of a wall.

STRUT: *see* Roof.

STUCCO: plaster work.

STUDS: the subsidiary vertical timber members of a timber-framed wall.

SWAG: festoon (q.v.) formed by a carved piece of cloth suspended from both ends.

TABERNACLE: richly ornamented niche or free-standing canopy. Usually contains the Holy Sacrament.

TARSIA: inlay in various woods.

TAZZA: shallow bowl on a foot.

TERMINAL FIGURES (TERMS, TERMINI): upper part of a human figure growing out of a pier, pilaster, etc., which tapers towards the base. *See also* Caryatid, Pilaster.

TERRACOTTA: burnt clay, unglazed.

TESSELLATED PAVEMENT: mosaic flooring, particularly Roman, consisting of small 'tesserae' or cubes of glass, stone, or brick.

TESSERAE: *see* Tessellated Pavement.

TESTER: *see* Sounding Board.

TETRASTYLE: having four detached columns.

THREE-DECKER PULPIT: pulpit with Clerk's Stall and Reading Desk below the Clerk's Stall.

TIE-BEAM: *see* Roof (Figs. 14–17).

TIERCERON: *see* Vault (Fig. 23).

TILEHANGING: *see* Slatehanging.

TIMBER-FRAMING: method of construction where walls are built of timber framework with the spaces filled in by plaster or brickwork. Sometimes the timber is covered over with plaster or boarding laid horizontally.

TOMB-CHEST: chest-shaped stone coffin, the most usual medieval form of funeral monument.

TOUCH: soft black marble quarried near Tournai.

TOURELLE: turret corbelled out from the wall.

TRACERY: intersecting ribwork in the upper part of a window, or used decoratively in blank arches, on vaults, etc. *Plate tracery: see* Fig. 22(*a*). Early form of tracery where decoratively shaped openings are cut through the solid stone infilling in a window head. *Bar tracery:* a form introduced into England *c.* 1250. Intersecting ribwork made up of slender shafts, continuing the lines of the mullions of windows up to a decorative mesh in the head of the window. *Geometrical tracery: see* Fig. 22(*b*). Tracery characteristic of *c.* 1250–1310 consisting chiefly of circles or foiled circles. *Y-tracery: see* Fig. 22(*c*). Tracery consisting of a mullion which branches into two forming a Y shape; typical of *c.* 1300. *Intersecting tracery: see* Fig. 22(*d*). Tracery in which each mullion of a window branches out into two curved bars in such a way that every one of them is drawn with the same radius

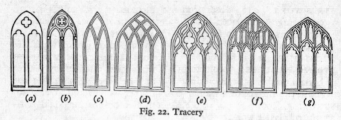

(a)   (b)   (c)   (d)   (e)   (f)   (g)

Fig. 22. Tracery

from a different centre. The result is that every light of the window is a lancet and every two, three, four, etc., lights together form a pointed arch. This treatment also is typical of *c.* 1300. *Reticulated tracery: see* Fig. 22(*e*). Tracery typical of the early C14 consisting entirely of circles drawn at top and bottom into ogee shapes so that a net-like appearance results. *Panel tracery: see* Fig. 22(*f*) and (*g*). Perp tracery, which is formed of upright straight-sided panels above lights of a window.

TRANSEPT: transverse portion of a cross-shaped church.

TRANSOM: horizontal bar across the openings of a window.

TRANSVERSE ARCH: *see* Vault.

TREFOIL: *see* Foil.

TRIBUNE: *see* Gallery.

TRICIPUT, SIGNUM TRICIPUT: sign of the Trinity expressed by three faces belonging to one head.

TRIFORIUM: arcaded wall passage or blank arcading facing the nave at the height of the aisle roof and below the clerestory (q.v.) windows. (*See also* Gallery.)

TRIGLYPHS: blocks with vertical grooves separating the metopes (q.v.) in the Doric frieze (Fig. 12).

TROPHY: sculptured group of arms or armour, used as a memorial of victory.

TRUMEAU: stone mullion (q.v.) supporting the tympanum (q.v.) of a wide doorway.

TUMULUS: *see* Barrow.

TURRET: very small tower, round or polygonal in plan.

TUSCAN: *see* Order.

TYMPANUM: space between the lintel of a doorway and the arch above it.

UNDERCROFT: vaulted room, sometimes underground, below a church or chapel.

UNIVALLATE: of a hill-fort: defended by a single bank and ditch.

UPPER PALAEOLITHIC: *see* Palaeolithic.

VAULT: *see* Fig. 23. *Barrel-vault: see* Tunnel-vault. *Cross-vault: see* Groin-vault. *Domical vault:* square or polygonal dome rising direct on a square or polygonal bay, the curved surfaces separated by groins (q.v.). *Fan-vault:* late medieval vault where all ribs springing from one springer are of the same length, the same distance from the next, and the same curvature. *Groin-vault* or *Cross-vault:* vault of two tunnel-

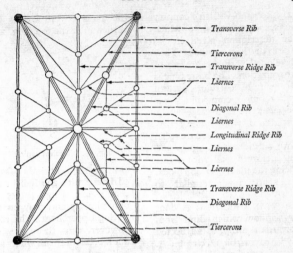

Fig. 23. Vault

Labels (top to bottom): Transverse Rib; Tiercerons; Transverse Ridge Rib; Liernes; Diagonal Rib; Liernes; Longitudinal Ridge Rib; Liernes; Liernes; Transverse Ridge Rib; Diagonal Rib; Tiercerons

vaults of identical shape intersecting each other at r. angles. Chiefly Norman and Renaissance. *Lierne:* tertiary rib, that is, rib which does not spring either from one of the main springers or from the central boss. Introduced in the C14, continues to the C16. *Quadripartite vault:* one wherein one bay of vaulting is divided into four parts. *Rib-vault:* vault with diagonal ribs projecting along the groins. *Ridge-rib:* rib along the longitudinal or transverse ridge of a vault. Introduced in the early C13. *Sexpartite vault:* one wherein one bay of quadripartite vaulting is divided into two parts transversely so that each bay of vaulting has six parts. *Tierceron:* secondary rib, that is, rib which issues from one of the main springers or the central boss and leads to a place

on a ridge-rib. Introduced in the early C13. *Transverse arch:* arch separating one bay of a vault from the next. *Tunnel-vault* or *Barrel-vault:* vault of semicircular or pointed section. Chiefly Norman and Renaissance.

VAULTING SHAFT: vertical member leading to the springer of a vault.

VENETIAN WINDOW: window with three openings, the central one arched and wider than the outside ones. Current in England chiefly in the C17–18.

VERANDA: open gallery or balcony with a roof on light, usually metal, supports.

VESICA: oval with pointed head and foot.

VESTIBULE: anteroom or entrance hall.

VILLA: (1) according to Gwilt (1842) 'a country house for the residence of opulent persons';

(2) Romano-British country houses cum farms, to which the description given in (1) more or less applies. They developed with the growth of urbanization. The basic type is the simple corridor pattern with rooms opening off a single passage; the next stage is the addition of wings. The courtyard villa fills a square plan with subsidiary buildings and an enclosure wall with a gate facing the main corridor block.

VITRIFIED: made similar to glass.

VITRUVIAN OPENING: A door or window which diminishes towards the top, as advocated by Vitruvius, bk. IV, chapter VI.

VOLUTE: spiral scroll, one of the component parts of an Ionic column (see Order).

VOUSSOIR: wedge-shaped stone used in arch construction.

W AGON ROOF: roof in which by closely set rafters with arched braces the appearance of the inside of a canvas tilt over a wagon is achieved. Wagon roofs can be panelled or plastered (ceiled) or left uncovered. Also called Cradle Roof.

WAINSCOT: timber lining to walls.

WALL-PLATE: see Roof.

WATERLEAF: leaf shape used in later C12 capitals. The water-leaf is a broad, unribbed, tapering leaf curving up towards the angle of the abacus and turned in at the top (Fig. 24).

Fig. 24. Waterleaf capital

WEALDEN HOUSE: timber-framed house with the hall in the centre and wings projecting only slightly and only on the jutting upper floor. The roof, however, runs through without a break between wings and hall, and the eaves of the hall part are therefore exceptionally deep. They are supported by diagonal, usually curved, braces starting from the short inner sides of the overhanging wings and rising parallel with the front wall of the hall towards the centre of the eaves.

WEATHERBOARDING: overlapping horizontal boards, covering a timber-framed wall.

WEATHERING: sloped horizontal surface on sills, buttresses, etc., to throw off water. Also called Set-off.

WEEPERS: small figures placed in niches along the sides of some medieval tombs. Also called Mourners.

WHEEL WINDOW: see Rose Window.

INDEX OF PLATES

INDEX OF ARTISTS

INDEX OF PLACES